The Politics of District Elections and Administration in Hong Kong

The Politics of District Elections and Administration in Hong Kong

Sonny Shiu-Hing LO

Steven Chung-Fun HUNG

Jeff Hai-Chi LOO

Cody Wai-Kwok YAU

ISBN: 978-962-937-655-0

Published by
    City University of Hong Kong Press
    Tat Chee Avenue
    Kowloon, Hong Kong
    Website: www.cityu.edu.hk/upress
    E-mail: upress@cityu.edu.hk

Printed in Hong Kong

"All politics is local", thus say many seasoned politicians. This volume, with useful figures and tables, examines the long trajectory of local politics in Hong Kong since British colonial times, covering early municipal, rural and district advisory bodies.

Though Hong Kong lacks real decentralization, district politics have still become a focal point of partisan competition and mobilization between the establishment and opposition. Yet such local politics feature much less prominently in the academic literature when legislative politics and elections as well as high-level constitutional issues are given most attention in the democracy discourse. The authors of this book try to bring them back to the forefront of discussion.

Anthony B. L. Cheung
Research Chair Professor of Public Administration and former President
The Education University of Hong Kong

A systematic, comprehensive and in-depth study of the past and present of the system of District Boards and District Councils in Hong Kong, from their evolution during colonial times all the way up to the 2019 election during the anti-extradition movement and post-National Security Law developments. Essential reading for anyone studying Hong Kong's political system, political culture, district administration and electoral politics.

Albert H. Y. Chen
Cheng Lan Yue Professor and Chair of Constitutional Law
The University of Hong Kong

Professor Lo's new book provides an up-to-date, systematic and authoritative analysis for the study of district council elections and local politics in Hong Kong. It is insightful and has high academic value.

Zhu Guobin
Professor, School of Law
City University of Hong Kong

Table of Contents

Preface

The authors express their gratitude to Mr. Edmund Chan of the City University of Hong Kong Press for supporting this book project. We also thank the reviewer for giving us extensive comments and suggestions. We are also indebted to Chris Chan of the Press for guiding us to complete this book project in the final stage.

The origin of this book could be traced back to not only the work of one of the authors, Sonny Lo, whose doctoral thesis in 1993 on Hong Kong's democratization had a chapter on the evolution of District Boards, but also the experience of another author, Steven Hung, who was a member of the Kwun Tong District Board from 1988 to 1999. Sonny interviewed Steven twice formally in 1989 and 1999 for two separate research projects on District Board elections. After the return of Hong Kong's sovereignty to mainland China, they have been following district elections, administration, and politics closely. In 2013, when they coincidentally became colleagues in the Department of Social Sciences at the Hong Kong Institute of Education, both decided to write a book on district administration, elections, and politics for the sake of describing and analyzing their complexities and transformations. However, they were fully preoccupied with their teaching and administration and did not find the necessary time to write up a solid manuscript on District Councils.

In 2019, the two authors were joined by Jeff Loo and Cody Yau, two young scholars who were interested in the study of political parties in District Council elections. We all decided to write a book on the historical evolution of district administration, party politics, and elections. The reason why we were determined to write this book was that there was a lack of an in-depth and updated study of how politics heavily shaped district administration and elections in Hong Kong. We sincerely hope that this book can and will contribute to our objective and deeper understanding of the very complex politics of district administration and elections in Hong Kong from the British colonial era to the post-1997 period.

The main argument of this book is that district elections and district administration in Hong Kong are closely intertwined from the British colonial era to the post-1997 period. The intertwining relations between electoral politics and district administration run through all the chapters, although some chapters focus more on electoral politics than on district administration.

The division of labor among the four authors was as follows: Sonny was responsible for writing and polishing all the chapters; Steven wrote some draft chapters and dealt with all the statistical data and tables; Jeff handled some tables, bibliography, index, and data collection; and Cody was responsible for the quantitative data collection and analyses in Chapter Six. A lot of preparatory work was done for this book, including an in-depth literature review, comprehensive data collection, data analyses, and the writing process. The project formally began in the summer of 2020 and the first draft was eventually completed in September 2021. The final and revised manuscript was completed in March 2022, incorporating the suggestions from the reviewer and updating our work, especially the addition of Chapter Eight to capture the transformations of District Councils after the promulgation of the national security law in late June 2020.

Finally, we dedicate this book to all the people interested in district elections, politics, and administration in Hong Kong.

Sonny Shiu-Hing Lo
Steven Chung-Fun Hung
Jeff Hai-Chi Loo
Cody Wai-Kwok Yau

December 13, 2022

List of Abbreviations

ACs	Area Committees
ADAS	Annual District Administration Summit
ADPL	Association for Democracy and People's Livelihood
BPA	Business Professional Alliance
CAU	Civic Act-Up
CBE	Commander of the British Empire
CCP	Chinese Communist Party
CDO	City District Office
CDOs	City District Offices
CF	Civil Force
CLDP	Chinese Liberal and Democratic Party
CMA	Chinese Manufacturers' Association
CPPCC	Chinese People's Political Consultative Conference
CRC	Cooperative Resources Center
CUHK	Chinese University of Hong Kong
CVL	City Village Link
CWAU	Chai Wan Act-Up
CWDC	Central and Western District Coalition
DAB	Democratic Alliance for the Betterment and Progress of Hong Kong
DABs	District Advisory Boards
DAS	District Administration Scheme
DB	District Board
DBs	District Boards
DC	District Council
DCs	District Councils
DF	Democratic Foundation
DLAS	District-led Actions Scheme

DFMC	District Facilities Management Committee
DMC	District Management Committee
DMCs	District Management Committees
DMWP	District Minor Works Program
DP	Democratic Party
DVH	Double Village Heads
DWC	District Watch Committee
DWF	District Watch Force
EDC	Eastern District Coalition
FEHD	Food and Environmental Hygiene Department
EKRC	East Kowloon Residents Committee
ERP	Electronic Road Pricing
ExCo	Executive Council
FCCs	Fight Crime Committees
FSCs	Fire Safety Committees
FTU	Federation of Trade Unions
HAB	Home Affairs Bureau
HAD	Home Affairs Department
HKACE	Hong Kong Alliance of Chinese and Expatriates
HKAS	Hong Kong Affairs Society
HKCRA	Hong Kong Chinese Reform Association
HKIF	Hong Kong Island Federation
HKPA	Hong Kong Progressive Alliance
HKPS	Hong Kong Progressive Society
HYK	Heung Yee Kuk
ICAC	Independent Commission Against Corruption
JP	Justice of Peace
KANU	Kenyan National African Union
KFA	Kowloon Federation of Associations
KMT	Kuomintang
KTRA	Kwun Tong Residents Association
KWC	Kickstart Wanchai
LCSD	Leisure and Cultural Services Department
LDF	Liberal Democratic Federation
LegCo	Legislative Council
LP	Liberal Party

MACs	Mutual Aid Committees
MBE	Member of the British Empire
MPP	Mongkok Pedestrian Precinct
MTR	Mass Transit Railway
ND	Neo Democrats
NHKA	New Hong Kong Alliance
NPC	National People's Congress
NPP	New People's Party
NTAS	New Territories Association of Societies
OCs	Owners Corporations
PAC	Public Affairs Council
PLA	People's Liberation Army
PLC	Provisional Legislative Council
PolyU	Hong Kong Polytechnic University
PRC	People's Republic of China
RegCo	Regional Council
SARS	Severe Acute Respiratory Syndrome
SCDA	Steering Committee on District Administration
SCNPC	Standing Committee of the National People's Congress
SHA	Secretary for Home Affairs
SPS	Signature Project Scheme
TAC	Traffic Advisory Committee
TKOPLCG	Tseung Kwan O Livelihood Concern Group
TMTB	Tuen Mun Ten Brothers
UDHK	United Democrats of Hong Kong
UK	United Kingdom
UrbCo	Urban Council

List of Figures and Tables

Tables

A Note on the Authors

Sonny Shiu-Hing LO is Acting Principal and a Professor at HKU SPACE Community College.

Steven Chung-Fun HUNG is an Assistant Professor in the Department of Social Sciences at the Education University of Hong Kong.

Jeff Hai-Chi LOO is a Doctoral Candidate in the Department of Political Science at the University of Waterloo, Canada.

Cody Wai-Kwok YAU is a Post-doctoral Fellow at the Institute of Political Science, Academia Sinica (Taiwan).

Introduction

British Colonial Rule, Administration and Elections

The study of district administration in Hong Kong can be traced back to the practices of the British colonial administration, which had rich experiences in governing its former colonies in Africa and Asia. This Introduction firstly reviews the literature review on the British colonial administration by focusing on its ruling strategy at the territorial and district levels. Then the literature on the functions of elections will be examined, because during the process of decolonization in many former British colonies, elections were introduced to not only improve the delivery of public administration services but also enhance the degree of governmental responsiveness and representative government. In other words, elections were crucial in the process of reforming the governance, democratizing the polity, and improving district administration of former British colonies. While this Introduction focuses on the literature review, the next Chapter will examine in detail the evolution of district administration in Hong Kong under British rule.

British Colonial Rule and Its Characteristics in Administration

Historians and political scientists have utilized two terms, namely direct rule and indirect rule, to study how the former colonies in Africa and Asia were governed by the colonial administration. Direct rule can be defined as "an imperial or central power [that] takes direct control over the legislature, executive and civil administration of an otherwise largely self-governing territory."[1] It can also be seen as the policy of colonial rulers to impose their ideology and cultural values onto the ruled masses, including the implementation of cultural assimilation.[2] Indirect rule refers to a system of colonial governance in which "pre-existing local power structures" were utilized.[3] British colonial rule in their former African and Asian colonies was complex, combining direct with indirect rule and contingent upon the governing context. A recent study of the theory of direct and indirect rule has concluded that the British direct rule tended to be more prominent in former colonies where political institutions were relatively underdeveloped.[4] In other words, indirect rule appeared to be more common in colonies where political institutionalization and centralization had been relatively entrenched. Another argument is that indirect rule had made its inroads in places where "for military or economic reasons, it had been found imperative to rule vast, densely populated areas with a minimal number of European officials and where relatively cohesive and centralized forms of traditional government had been encountered."[5] In addition to political institutionalization, centralization, and size of the colonies concerned, other scholars have identified the reliance on intermediaries in indirect rule. As Adnan Naseemullah and Paul Staniland have argued:

> Indirect rule is understood as a form of political control in which agents of the state delegate day-to-day governance to local powerholders in areas considered beyond the reach of the state's direct authority. Intermediaries — often those holding "traditional" or customary authority — represent and enforce political authority on behalf of titular rulers. Direct rule represents the opposite condition, in which the state maintains and administers a monopoly of law, policy, and administration to the population without intermediaries, through bureaucrats without independent means of actions.[6]

In the case of Hong Kong, the British implemented direct rule in the colony at the beginning but also heavily relied on indirect rule at the district and village levels. Its institutions, ranging from City District Offices (CDOs) to District Boards (later District Councils), from *kaifong* (街坊，neighborhood) associations to Owners Corporations and Mutual Aid Committees, as will be discussed in the next Chapter, could be seen as the "intermediaries" linking the British colonial government and the ordinary people.

The British "direct" rule in Hong Kong at the district level could be seen in how they dealt with two Chinese customary forms of mortgage, *dian* (典) and *diya* (抵押), in a Tang lineage village in the New Territories.[7] The colonial government directly imposed a set of administrative rules and legal measures to regulate these two customary practices. A study of 314 records of mortgages in the Tang lineage community during the 1905–65 period reveals that *diya* was a common form of mortgage bearing the following characteristics: (1) non-kin ties playing a more active and dominant role; (2) Tang mortgagors not receiving special interest rates from kin mortgagees; (3) both grain and cash being used as means of paying interest; (4) one-year loans being the most common in both land and house mortgages; (5) the majority of cases having a one-year redemption period; and (6) monthly interest rates usually being in the range of 1 per cent to 2 per cent of the principal loan.[8]

The British tactically, skillfully, and selectively recognized, protected, redefined, or changed some Chinese customs to meet their needs under different circumstances. For the sake of tighter control, the British colonial rulers could impose new legislative and bureaucratic practices upon land registration and property management, while selectively respecting the customs of patrilineal inheritance, lineage estates, the right of burial, and the dwelling entitlement in the lineage settlement and vicinity. However, other local customs, such as cash inheritance and village guard systems, were left to develop in their own way. The Hong Kong case was the same, meaning that the British colonial rulers had actively normalized and codified Chinese customary mortgage practices into a more standardized and stricter system.[9] Specifically, the British colonial administration did not follow the imperial Chinese government's legal policy that discriminated against the practice of *diya*. Rather, the two practices were treated equally. Among the 314 mortgages of the Tangs recorded during the period 1905–65, *diya* dominated almost all these mortgages. In the early years of their colonial rule in Hong Kong, the British preserved local customary practices in accordance with the principle of indirect rule or non-interference as laid down in the 1905 New Territories Ordinance and the 1910 New Territories Regulation Ordinance.[10] However, the colonial government also introduced a new covenant stipulating that a mortgagor should not be entitled to redeem property unless he or she had given the mortgagee three months' written notice of the intention to do so. In 1965, the British significantly changed the indefinite redemption period of mortgaged property. The legal amendment of limiting the redemption period to 12 years redefined the proprietary rights of the *dian*-holder and the *dian*-maker over the plot of land concerned.[11] Its major objective was to rule out disputes about the legal time limits for redemption in this customary practice of *dian*. Adopting the *dian* custom, the British colonial rulers legalized another form of mortgage, *diya*, which was not legal under the imperial and Republican codes. They also deliberately imposed and enforced the payment of interest on a monthly basis and rejected daily, quarterly, or yearly payments.[12] Overall, the British colonizers imposed some degree of direct rule in Hong Kong's New Territories by standardizing administrative rules and legal measures to regulate Chinese customary mortgage.[13]

Many British colonies in Africa witnessed a mixed mode of direct and indirect rule. In Kenya under the British colonial rule, the chiefs' "tyranny" had its roots in the British administrative style because the colonial government needed strong-handed local leaders to enforce and implement its unpopular laws and regulations.[14] That was why the chiefs acted like tyrannical rulers — because the colonial government tolerated it to some extent. The British colonial rulers saw the local chiefs' position as alien and their duties as interacting with the people at the grassroots level. A kind of indirect rule was therefore adopted by the British colonizers in Kenya.

The first generation of chiefs from Kenya's Kiambu district could be used as an example to illustrate how the British adopted an indirect rule to govern its colony.[15] Although Kenya became a British protectorate in 1895, the British colonial administration was developed at the turn of the 20th century. The completion of the Uganda Railway in 1901 opened the interior part of Africa, leading to an influx of white settlers from 1902 onwards. This gradual metamorphosis led to the establishment of administrative units and centers to facilitate the administration of the Africans and the white settlers. The protectorate of Kenya was administratively divided into provinces and districts and each of them was governed by a white provincial commissioner and a district commissioner, respectively. The districts were sub-divided into locations placed under the colonial government-appointed African chiefs because the protectorate was financially strained and failed to employ all white administrators. As a result, local chiefs became indispensable since they made British colonial rule much cheaper as they were poorly paid. The first generation of colonial chiefs in the Kiambu district were appointed from 1902 to the 1920s.[16]

Kenya's colonial chiefs were, in the past, abused and criticized by some missionaries, regarded with contempt by their superiors, and hated by many of their own people. After Kenya's independence, they were viewed by nationalists as "traitors" who had worked for the colonialists. Negative descriptions, such as tyrants, corrupt officials, self-seekers, and rascals were used to refer to these local chiefs, who were seen by critics as exploiting the local people in land appropriation and tax collection. In short, the chiefs were regarded as the "running dogs" of the colonialists.[17] In reality, the local chiefs were working under difficult circumstances. The period before 1920 was full of turbulence and dislocations because many Africans encountered violent governance under colonialism. The pacification expeditions launched by the British colonialists killed many local people, confiscated their livestock, and destroyed their families and homes. Under these circumstances, the chiefs acted as the local middlemen between the colonizers and the ruled. When the white settlers arrived, the local Africans had to pay tax and work under their exploitation and confiscation of their fertile land. At the same time, Western missionaries arrived to urge them to abandon their cherished culture and religions. During the First World War, many Africans were recruited to help and support their colonizers. The chiefs were naturally utilized by the British colonial rulers to impose on the exploited and suffering local people.[18] Hence, the chiefs and local people were living at a time under colonial exploitation, and as such, their behavior was encouraged, groomed, and condoned by the colonizers. Some of them were loyal to the British colonialists, some were collaborators, but some were resistant fighters opposing European imperialism. The authoritarian or tyrannical behavior of some chiefs were tolerated by the local Africans, because they feared the white colonizers and dared not report the excesses of the chiefs to them. Many locals believed that the chiefs were implementing their colonizers' orders and directives. Once the chiefs became powerful, many of them became corrupt. This was why some critics of colonialism called for the abolition of the chiefs in Kenya. Some called for the reforms of the institution of chiefs to make colonial rule more acceptable to the populace.[19]

When the Kenyan National African Union (KANU) were formed in 1960, it was composed of district-level associations. Many local people were still following their chiefs rather than KANU as a political party. The African political movements in Kenya's Central Nyanza performed one major useful function: they forced the British government to accept the goal of achieving parliamentary democracy and to start the process of democratic reforms. In the transition from decolonization to independence, different political actors played an important role of political modernization, including the missionaries, white settlers, businesspeople, colonial administrators, traditionalists, British Colonial Office, and the relatively "westernized" Africans.[20]

Studies on decolonization have shown that when the British departed from their former colonies in Africa and Asia, they introduced democratic reforms, including the introduction of district councils at the grassroots level, the increased appointment of local people to the legislative and consultative bodies, the injection of direct elections and party politics into the Legislative Council (LegCo), the enhanced representation of the top policy-making Executive Council (ExCo) by appointing more locals, and, finally, the direct elections of the entire legislature while changing the colonial-style ExCo into the British-style cabinet system. Indeed, the case of Hong Kong followed a different path of "decolonization without independence."[21]

In the processes of decolonization and democratization, the local people who could be elected to the political institutions, ranging from district bodies to the legislature, benefited from political liberalization that was unleashed by the British colonial authorities. During decolonization, the "transfer of British parliamentary and electoral institutions to non-Western soil" could be seen.[22] Apart from the introduction of district bodies, the composition of the LegCos in British colonies usually proceeded in the following stages: "elected minority, unofficial majority, elected majority, responsible government."[23] Hong Kong did not follow this pattern of legislative reforms as Britain returned its sovereignty over the colony to China on July 1, 1997.

Yet, the case of Hong Kong showed that when the political system was opened up, the local elites, together with their newly formed political parties and groups, could increasingly bargain with the ruling authorities, exchange information with them, and set the policy agenda in a much wider and diverse manner.[24] Political parties and groups developed their expertise and knowledge in different policy issues, necessitating the ruling elites and policy-makers to interact with and pay attention to them, and resulting in a more diverse content of policy agenda than ever before.[25] Indeed, political parties are not the only political actors which could influence the policy agenda of the ruling elites; other actors such as interest groups, and civil society coalitions composed of different groups and parties could constitute powerful checks and balances against the government administration.[26] The Hong Kong experience fit into these patterns of political change, but British decolonization in Hong Kong did not lead to independence.

Some studies of British colonialism have found that decolonization could have contributed to the making of modern Chinese statecraft in urban form. In the French Concession of Shanghai, for example, the Franco-British conflicts and the Chinese forces both shaped the institutional structure of imperialism.[27] The origins of modern municipal administrations in the relatively westernized Chinese cities, such as Shanghai and Tianjin, in 1905 and 1907 respectively, were regarded as a response to the presence of westerners residing there. These cities were created by Chinese elites who had a working knowledge of western or Japanese urban institutions.[28]

Guilds (會館，*huiguan*) and the native-place associations (同鄉會，*tongxianghui*) in Shanghai played crucial roles in shaping the city life, social order, urban administration, cultural and religious practices, and national identity.[29] In response to the Taiping rebellion from 1853 to 1864, the French and the British authorities in Shanghai established their municipal institutions, including the police force, the tax collection system, the construction of walls, the use of land regulations, and the protection of foreign settlements through fortifications. Hence, the imperial powers used imported institutions to break local resistance and protect their residents. Military conflicts and imperial rivalry shaped the structure of the institutions of imperialism in China.[30]

Other studies of colonial rule in British and French Africa found that Britain and France contributed to the development of fiscal administration of their former colonies.[31] Metropolitan identity could be built up through the establishment of fiscal institutions. Taxes constituted the financial backbone of the colonial state, and they were vital to the state-building efforts of colonial governments. Colonial legacies were shaped by the interactions between the metropolitan imperial policies and institutions on the one hand and the local conditions and responses to these colonial practices on the other. Comparing the fiscal capacity-building efforts in British and French Africa from 1880 to 1940, historians Ewout Frankema and Marlous van Waijenburg found that the utilization of loans and aid from the metropolitan government was temporary. It was crucial to make the French and British colonies to be "fiscally independent as quickly as possible to limit the burden of empire-building on domestic taxpayers."[32] As such, "the pace of colonial state expansion" depended on "the development of a local tax base."[33]

The French colonial rule was "more repressive because of the economic constraints posed by commercially less viable territories; the creation of large federations can be considered as a response to that problem by integrating richer coastal territories with vast hinterland areas through fiscal redistribution."[34] High repression and the federal way of fiscal redistribution explained why French colonies were constrained in their fiscal capacity-building in contrast with the relatively more prosperous and commercial British colonies. The ways in which the French and the British colonizers used forced labor as an alternative to raise trade and customs revenues were also different.[35] The most glaring difference between the French and British colonial rule was the former's tendency of adopting federal governing structures. French colonies such as Niger, Mauritania, Chad, and Oubangui-Chari were heavily supported by federal governance structures where part of the costs of state formation, like defense and administration, were shouldered born collectively. These federations were integrated into the hinterland areas through the construction of roads and railways, but their disadvantage was that some economic centers such as Senegal, Ivory Coast, and Gabon had to surrender part of their control over customs duties and tax revenues. Like the French, the British colonial rulers integrated their colonies through federations which however were relatively loose and ad hoc. The British also adopted the differentiated tax rates at the local level. Hence, colonial governance differed between the French and British and it was an outcome of the varying economic circumstances.[36]

Comparatively speaking, the British colonial rule adopted "indirect" rule in which they tried to maintain the local customs, traditions and practices without direct intervention.[37] The French, however, favored direct rule in that they tried to assimilate the local peoples culturally by using French culture and education. The Belgians, on the other hand, combined the policy of assimilation with paternalism, emphasizing Christian monogamy and the western way of life.[38] In the Belgian Congo, political suppression and integration with the use of Belgian civil servants were prominent. It was argued that the Belgian style of colonial governance was marked by a mixture of cultural and political integration of the colonies into the metropole. The Portuguese adopted a mixture of the French and Belgian rule, merging cultural assimilation with political paternalism. The decline of Portugal as a "poor" colonial empire "forced it into excessive and brutal exploitation of its African colonies."[39] Portuguese colonies had the "highest illiterate populations" in comparison with other colonial empires.[40] Although the Portuguese colony of Macau, prior to its return to the People's Republic of China (PRC) on December 20, 1999, was economically far more prosperous than all the Portuguese colonies in Africa, Macau was characterized by political underdevelopment with very minimal political and inadequate public-sector reforms.[41] During the final years of the Portuguese administration, Macau's government departments underwent frequent merger and reshuffle, but their overall efficiency and effectiveness remained much to be desired. However, the Macau case was much better than other former Portuguese colonies, which were plagued by Portugal's hurried withdrawal, chaotic governance, internal strife and wars, the lack of infrastructure development, and the failure to provide the necessities for the poor and the needy.[42]

While the colonial style of governance differed among the British, French, Belgian, and Portuguese, the transformation of local and district administration could be heavily shaped by the colonialists. The case of British Cyprus was illustrative of this phenomenon. From 1878 to 1882, the municipal council of Nicosia in Cyprus was governed directly by the British, unlike the usual convention that the British adopted "indirect rule" over its colonies. Perhaps the British provided a sort of "trusteeship" until 1882, when a more "indirect" way of governing the city could be seen by having a judiciary independent from the executive and a partially elected legislature.[43] In this process of tutelage, the British district commissioners gradually left the urban affairs to the municipal councils set up in different localities of Cyprus and ran by the local people. From 1895 to 1914, the impetus for reform of the colonial institutions in Cyprus was stimulated by the establishment of newly elected councils, the increase in political space and competitiveness, the rapid growth in literacy, and the emergence of a money economy. Urbanization followed with the birth of a new middle class and its participation in local politics. Political rivalry could be gradually seen in elections held for the legislature and municipal councils. Furthermore, political participation was triggered by the new flourishing newspaper trade and the creation of "Reading Clubs," which were organizations mobilizing citizen participation in middle class politics.[44]

Indirect rule could be seen in British Nyasaland from the 1930s to the early 1950s.[45] Agricultural extension work in Nyasaland depended on the willingness of the native authorities to impose regulations, disseminate information, and propel changes. Colonial rulers believed that the chiefs in Thyolo (known as Cholo by the colonial administration) in southern Nyasaland were fluid, and that the Mzimba chiefs in Mzimba district in the north were politically too strong and hierarchical.[46] The colonial authorities had to ensure that chiefs acted as agents for the government while simultaneously holding powers to control the masses. A chief's willingness to act as a colonial agent was affected by his own economic interests and his role as a representative of the local community. Colonial officials knew that chiefs from time to time opposed colonial policies, but they might act on behalf of their subjects. Colonial rulers believed that "strong" chiefs could act as autocrats and could enforce rules as they liked. The case of Mzimba showed that this was far from certain. The chiefs, known by colonial authorities to be quite powerful, lacked the power to regulate local production processes. They were unwilling to act as agents of the British colonial authorities. This phenomenon showed how indirect rule did not facilitate colonial intervention. In other words, the perception of British colonial authorities on the local chiefs could be inaccurate, leading to difficulties in implementing indirect rule.

Some critics have pointed to the negative legacies of indirect rule of the former British colonies. For example, in Northern Nigeria, Governor Frederick Lugard, who later became the Governor of Hong Kong from 1907 to 1912, introduced cantonments from 1900 to 1906, and these cantonments gradually evolved into townships with committees where appointed members were made by the British colonial government.[47] These cantonments began as a nineteenth-century creation in the British India, where cantonments were accompanied by public health legislation and a whole range of regulations regarding tax, liquor licensing, sanitary control, water supply and drainage, and also buildings management. Lugard had been an army officer in India and brought his experiences of witnessing the development of cantonments to Nigeria. There was even a cantonment magistrate who was usually an army officer but acted as a court judge arbitrating in and dealing with legal affairs. After Lugard left Nigeria for Hong Kong, his successors in Nigeria expanded the cantonments further into townships, where railways and hospitals were built, and where towns took shape quickly. These townships were managed by committees composed of the British expatriates. Gradually, urban local governments took shape, but one main weakness was the exclusion of local Africans from participation.[48] This exclusionary practice was criticized as a negative aspect of the British colonial legacy in their former colonies. Objectively speaking, while the British colonial rule in its early phase did stimulate the development of towns and infrastructure, it might not have done enough to prepare local Africans for their public participation and self-governance especially after independence.

Other critics have pointed to the failure of the British municipal governance in colonial New Delhi from 1863 to 1910.[49] By 1910, the Municipality of Delhi had a large and hierarchical administration that possessed considerable powers of coercion through municipal ordinances, including those on sanitation and registration records.[50] The colonial bureaucracy had extensive powers. In other words, powers were centralized, and the colonial administration conducted extensive policing on the residents of Delhi. Yet, the Delhi municipality was ineffective, failing to tackle drainage and water supply. The colonial state's powers were reproduced and cyclically perpetuated.

Some critics of the indirect rule have pointed to the divide-and-rule tactic of the colonialists, who sowed the seeds of political discontent and struggle in many African states after independence. Nobuhiro Mizuno and Ryosuke Okazawa have concluded in the following way:

> Under indirect rule, the colonial ruler divides the indigenous people into a privileged ruling group and an unprivileged ruled group. The ruling group appropriated the resources of the ruled group both for themselves and for the colonial ruler. Therefore, the ruled group cannot observe how the resources extracted from them are divided between the colonial ruler and the ruling group. Since the ruled group infers the degree of altruism of the ruling group after observing the total quantity of resources lost, large levels of exploitation by the colonial ruler caused the ruled group to distrust the ruling group … [S]uch distrust among indigenous groups could be a source of underdevelopment and political instability in postcolonial Africa.[51]

The colonial legacy of producing distrust and conflicts among indigenous groups was one of the features of the British rule in their African colonies, including Kenya and Nigeria.

Objectively speaking, not all the British efforts at improving their colonial administration failed. In British India, agricultural and market developments laid the foundation of economic and political development at the district level. In the districts of Shahabad and Gaya, which spanned across parts of the current state of Bihar, in northern India during 1800–1920, agricultural trade and markets were largely shaped by the pattern of developing subsistence agriculture, infrastructure projects, and the land rent payment system.[52] There were six striking developments: (1) the construction of all-weather roads and railways as part of the modern public infrastructure; (2) sharp seasonal fluctuations in the market price of food grains persisted; (3) an upsurge in agricultural prices together with the growing trade and the emergence of the land rent payment system led to the rise of new social groups; (4) modern infrastructure that transformed the conduct of long-distance trade; (5) the flourishing market that was integrated into the emerging global system; and (6) the increase in the monetization of the rural economy.[53]

Quite often, the British policy of indirect rule is characterized by not only a gradual transformation of markets and infrastructure development, but also a tolerance of local customs and practices. Yet, in the case of northern Kenya, the British tolerance of local customs and practices did have their limits. In 1931, northern Kenya's Laikipia District witnessed the death of a white ranch manager, Theodore Powys, who was murdered by five Samburu warriors. The warriors were arrested but the trial entailed a struggle between the white settler ranchers, the Samburu pastoralists, and the British colonial administration. The *laibons* (diviners and ritual healers) played a role in the warfare among Samburu pastoralists through their use of divination and sorcery to defeat external enemies, namely the white settler ranchers. Although the warriors eventually were acquitted of murder charge, their *laibon*, Ngaldaiya Leaduma, was arrested before the trial under the Witchcraft Ordinance and he was deported for intimidating witnesses and interfering with the investigation. The Samburu community faced harsh fines and disarmament.[54]

The British rule in India was marked by how the colonial government preserved local monuments and structures through legislation. In 1904, the British Indian government passed the Ancient Monuments Protection Act and enlarged the colonial state's bureaucratic claim to structures defined as monuments. The project of conserving the Hindu temple was punctuated by disagreements.[55] The Ancient Monument Protection Act of 1904 registered temples, but there were tensions between the codes of archaeological conservation and those of popular Hindu rituals.[56] The Act gave officers of the Archaeological Department "complete control over the physical fabric of listed monuments."[57] In 1902, less than 150 buildings in British India were under the protection of the state; many of them were British monuments built in the nineteenth century. In 1915, the number of protected monuments rose to some 700. The Act offered the colonial state the license to impose conservation on monuments, representing direct intervention, but at the same time producing dissensus between the colonizers and the religious activists.

The colonial administration dealt with African ritual leaders like the *laibon* whose power, which was regarded as "sacred and supernatural," could politically influence the community. The British colonial government in Kenya had to create laws, including the Witchcraft and Deportation Ordinances, to deal with these political and spiritual leaders. The colonial administration and settler community believed that Samburu warriors collaborated their *laibon*, Ngaldaiya Leaduma, to murder Powys and many African workers on the white-owned farms. The British colonial rulers viewed the *laibon* as "a powerful and malign figure who used his mystical powers and authority to instigate the warriors to carry out their attacks, protect them from retribution, and frighten other Samburu into silence."[58] This was the reason why Ngaldaiya Leaduma was deported, although he was not charged with any murder. On the other hand, the Samburu community felt threatened by the white settlers, who lobbied and petitioned the colonial government to evict Samburu from Leroki, an important grazing area. For the Samburu and other Africans, their resistance to colonial domination, including the white settlers, had to rely on sacred and secular forces. As such, the *laibon*'s ability to inflict sorcery on their enemies was considered as important as the Samburu arsenal that included both spears and swords. Ngaldaiya Leaduma was an influential *laibon* both feared and respected in his community. The colonial administration and the Laikipia settlers saw the *laibon* as "a dangerous and influential witchdoctor who held sway over murderous spear-carrying Samburu warriors."[59] In short, while the British colonialists usually respected local customs and practices, they were afraid of the local Kenya sorcerers who could galvanize and mobilize the locals to target at the white settlers.

The British colonial policy of indirect rule was accompanied by direct rule, which can be defined as the active intervention on the part of the British colonial administration on how colonial affairs were run and how policies were formulated and implemented. A case in point was British India's state of Bastar where direct rule rather than "indirect" rule could be seen. There was a period of intense rebellion among the indigenous groups, which engaged in tribal conflicts, rural unrests, and violence. In the post-independence period, many colonial-era policies that had triggered revolts were not reformed, resulting in continuous conflicts in the form of the Naxalite insurgency.[60] In fact, Bastar experienced a relatively high degree of British intervention during the colonial period, which ironically constituted the primary cause of tribal violence in the state. During the British colonial era, tribal conflicts began in Bastar precisely because of increasing British influence in the state. This influence took the form of three policies implemented by the British colonialists. First, British colonial officials not only took direct control over the forests and displaced the tribespeople from their land, but also interfered in the politics of succession to the throne, an interventionist style that upset the native population. Second, these policies brought about bloodshed and violent conflicts. Third, the British practice of retaining areas of indirect rule within a colony was taken from India and exported to other colonial territories such as Burma and Malaya. Such practice directly or indirectly led to ethnic separatism in Myanmar.[61]

In the case of India, the British colonial officials regarded tribals as primitive peoples that needed to be brought under the control of a modern and centralized state. They restricted access to forests, dislocating tribals from their land over which they had had privileged access to for a long period of time. When the British officials implemented these policies in the provinces, native princes generally adopted liberal policies towards tribals, thereby reducing the likelihood of tribal rebellions.[62] After independence, the Indian government did not reform the colonial-era policies by retaining their control over the country's forests, leading to the continuation of tribal rebellion in the form of the Naxalite movement. This insurgency was driven mainly by poor *adivasis* (tribes). While British colonialists dismissed several popular rajas from power, the post-colonial Indian government also removed a raja in Bastar from power and brought about widespread political grievances on top of socio-economic discontent.[63] Even worse, the British colonizers implanted a similar pattern of direct intervention into not only the Shan States, Chin Hills, and Kachin State of Burma, but also Malaya where they created the "Unfederated Malay States" under the control of sultans.[64] Critics of British colonialism argued that such governing strategy led to divisiveness and bitter political struggles in their former Asian colonies.

Indirect rule in the former British colony of Nigeria created internal divisions that facilitated colonial governance, sowing the seeds of ethnic rivalries and distrust in the post-independence era. The British colonialists crafted an administrative policy to normalize a combined Hausa–Caliphate socio–cultural and political model to the Middle Belt in colonial Nigeria, and to implement this policy in the non-Hausa speaking part of the Middle Belt.[65] This colonial administrative project of creating politico-cultural uniformity made the Middle Belt more like the Caliphate sector, which was regarded as more suitable for the British indirect rule. Two prerequisites of indirect rule could be seen in Nigeria, namely ethnic differences and a pre-existing and centralized system of governance.[66] The Middle Belt was characterized by ethnic differences and lacked centralized political and cultural institutions of the emirate system that was crucial to the formation of British indirect rule. As a result, the British colonizers utilized those "civilized" ethnic groups to "civilize" those considered not civilized enough for indirect rule.[67] This kind of divide-and-rule governing tactic could be seen in Nigeria, where the British colonial administration artificially promoted the Hausa–Caliphate sector. In the Tiv–Idoma (Benue) axis of the Middle Belt, where Hausa was not spoken or understood to any significant degree and where Caliphate culture had not penetrated much, the colonial governance encountered more difficulties and resistance than the Hausa-speaking areas of the Belt. As such, British colonialism perpetuated cultural differences among the African subject populations, inspiring ethnic jealousies and hatred and laying the foundation of civil war, fierce political struggle, and even genocide in post-independence Africa.[68]

Canada, as the former British colony, institutionally followed the practice of decolonization and democratization, although it had also been affected by colonialism. In Canada, the white settlers disconnected the indigenous Indians from their culture, land, and community.[69] In 1835, the UK Parliament passed the Municipal Corporations Act, which stipulated in detail how municipal governments were formed and elected in Canada. These ideas were raised by Lord Durham to the Governor-General Lord

Sydenham. In response to the rebellions of 1837–38 in the colonies of Upper and Lower Canada, Lord Durham wrote a report in 1939 that called for the creation of municipal governments, the establishment of a supreme court, and the development of a responsible government.[70] Lord Durham was regarded as a liberal reformer who saw autonomous municipalities as the essential components of a modern government.[71] From late 1840 to early 1841, the government of Canada enacted various acts leading to the formation of municipal governments in various provinces of the country. Canadian municipal governments were established primarily as a means of improving the delivery of public services to ordinary citizens rather than as a level of democratic government.[72] As time passed, provincial governments used municipal governments as a means of achieving provincial objectives, changing their structures, roles and boundaries, sometimes "even against the wishes of the affected citizens."[73] In recent years, however, the provincial control over municipal governments has been loosened so that the latter can enjoy more autonomy than ever before. For example, the three Canadian municipalities—the city of Abbotsford (British Columbia), the city of Miramichi (New Brunswick), and the Halifax regional municipality (Nova Scotia) have undergone reforms that have administrative, financial, and political impacts.[74] The objectives of these reforms were mainly improved efficiency and effectiveness in the delivery of public services and municipal governance.[75]

Although decolonization in British colonies usually envisaged the introduction of democratic reforms from the LegCo to ExCo so that responsible government would be established, not all former British colonies followed this path. Apart from Hong Kong, which had decolonization without independence and with very limited democratization, St Helena is another case that lacked the resources to become an independent state. Governor John Field in 1968 established an elected legislature and appointed most members of the new ExCo from the existing LegCo.[76] As early as 1949, a constitutional committee was set up to study various reform options for St Helena, including the possibility of setting up a municipal authority with limited authority. Later, Governor Field democratized St Helena by empowering the LegCo. Yet, "the steps he took owed little to the sustained popular demand for self-government, as was common elsewhere, and much to his determination to make islanders politically more responsible."[77] Public participation was inhibited by a complex local political culture (with a population of mixed European, Asian Chinese, and African origin) and the island's financial dependence on the UK government.[78]

Elections and Impacts on District Administration

In all political systems, including colonial, semi-democratic, and democratic ones, elections are conducive to the regime's legitimacy, responsiveness, and accountability to the public. As Michael Gallagher has pointed out, "The process of election is an essential requirement of any political system that hopes to be regarded as possessing democratic credentials."[79] Elections are politically significant because it is "the main mechanism by which the people are able to express their views about how the country should be governed." In the context of district-level administration, the elected district body can have "democratic credentials" and reflect the opinion of the members of the public. Moreover, "in modern liberal democracies, elections are the central representative institution that forms a link between the people and their representatives."[80] Although Hong Kong under British rule was by no means a democracy, elections at the district level could strengthen the linkage between District Board (DB) members and the voters—also an intention of the British colonial administration in 1982 when DB elections were introduced.

However, the injection of elected elements to district-level bodies like DBs was one thing; it was another matter to decentralize the powers of decision-making from the top to the grassroots level. John Loughlin has emphasized that political decentralization means "the transfer of decision-making power from the central state to any of the sub-national levels of government," and that "political decentralization is not the same as administrative decentralization, or what is called in Latin languages 'deconcentration.'"[81] Loughlin has noted:

> Deconcentration means the transfer of some administrative functions to sub-national levels of the administration. It can take place, however, without political decentralization, in the sense that it is the central organs of the administration which remain in control of policy-making and administrative behavior.[82]

In the context of Hong Kong, as will be elaborated in the next Chapter, the introduction of DBs could be regarded as deconcentration or administrative decentralization because the colonial government delegated the administrative powers of dealing with environmental issues, district transport, and recreational and cultural activities downward to the local level. Nonetheless, the establishment of DBs could not be seen as political decentralization, for the British colonial authorities retained their policy-making power at the top level of both the ExCo and central-level government departments. Although government department officials were required to go down to DBs to understand the views of the elected and appointed representatives at the grassroots level, the bureaucrats at the central level retained their power of formulating policies. As such, DBs represented the British colonial administration's attempt at implementing some degree of administrative decentralization or deconcentration. A recent report on global decentralization and local democracy in the world has made the following observations in Asian states:

> Decentralization is never a smooth process as there are many competing interests at play, some of which resist decentralization. Strong resistance can come from a central ministry that perceives that decentralization erodes its powers and resources. For similar reasons, central civil servants may resist decentralization, especially when it involves their reassignment to a sub-national level of government, as was the case for large numbers of civil servants in Indonesia and Thailand. Party political rivalry can also be a major obstacle, where parties position themselves by opposing proposals for decentralization. By contrast, the recent and quite radical programs of decentralization in the Philippines and Indonesia have been more overly linked to "bottom-up" processes of democratization. This is compounded by political competition at sub-national levels: ruling parties at the national level may get cold feet about decentralization if they perceive that the opposition may gain control of large number of the decentralized units.[83]

If the attitude of central-level civil servants, the rivalries of political parties, and the competition of political elites between "national" and "sub-national" levels are critical to the question of decentralization, this book will later use the case of Hong Kong to study how these actors play out in the politics of decentralization.

According to Gerard Marcou, decentralization is a highly political process in which different actors struggle for power and resources. He concludes that, from the global development of decentralization and local democracy, "decentralization does not exist outside, but it ceases to exist even within where local authorities are no more than executors of policies determined by authorities."[84] He emphasizes that if the classical notion of decentralization accepts the autonomy of local authorities, then the modern concept of decentralization cannot be separated from democracy. In the context of Hong Kong, this book will explore whether district administration has undergone a process of decentralization. If yes, what were factors that could explain the phenomenon? If not, what were the factors hindering decentralization?

Elections are politically significant in terms of their relations with the civil liberties and civil society. In discussing the functions of elections, Azeen Kiani and Hossein Sartipi have asserted that

> What is important here is that free and fair election is an instrument to stabilize and consolidate the democratic system and ensure other instrument and the foundations of democracy itself. This means that freedom is not only an ideal, but a real experience and one of the examples of its realization is freedom of choice.[85]

As early as 1986, prior to the collapse of the former Soviet Union, Guillermo O'Donnell and Philippe Schmitter had long emphasized that elections could contribute to the twin processes of liberalization and democratization, and that any founding election would propel a place to the path of further democratic reforms.[86] They also maintained that elections unleashed the political participation of various social forces and interest groups, leading to an "explosion of a highly re-politicized and angry society."[87] Elections can stimulate not only the growth of political parties but also expand the political space for interest groups, parties, and members of the public to express their grievances through the ballot box, consolidating the existing degree of civil liberties, activating the civil society and laying the foundation of any further democratization.

In the context of public administration, elections are politically significant. Elections can lead to a government that learns how to manage elections fairly, efficiently, and effectively. If complaints from candidates and voters take place, the government concerned needs to deal with them fairly. The question of managing elections is important in many developing countries, which may set up election commission presided over by politically neutral actors so that the electoral processes and governance can enhance the regime's legitimacy. The key elements of organizing elections include (1) voter registration, (2) the choice of electoral system, (3) the establishment of electoral commission, (4) the setting up of a complaint system, (5) and in war-torn places the adoption of confidence-building measures.[88] In Hong Kong, while the electoral system adopted for DBs and currently District Councils (DCs) is the first-past-the-post, or simple plurality, in all constituencies.[89] Under this system, the candidate with most votes is elected and there is no compulsory voting. Voters are expected to vote in designated voting stations in various constituencies. The way in which electoral administration has been handled in the HKSAR will be discussed later in this book.

Although elections were introduced by the British colonial rulers in their settler colonies at the beginning, many of these colonies witnessed a backsliding process of de-democratization after independence.[90] One key feature of this retrogressive move, in either decentralization or democratization, was the presence of the landed classes that opposed further expansion of the electoral franchise and reforms. With the benefit of hindsight, the case of Hong Kong is similar with this pattern; for Hong Kong even before its transfer of sovereignty on July 1, 1997 witnessed the presence of a large capitalist class in collaboration with the PRC to oppose the British-initiated political reforms.[91] After the establishment of the HKSAR, this tendency of having the landlord class in opposition to democratic reforms has become far more prominent than before, for PRC officials have continued the triple alliance with capitalists and the Hong Kong government to stop the local democrats from propelling further democratization, let alone decentralization at the district level.[92] In the case of Hong Kong, this book will later examine why Urban Council (UrbCo) and Regional Councils (RegCo), albeit elected, were eventually abolished by the HKSAR government. The responses of the political elites concerned will also be explored.

The purpose of this book is to use the case study of Hong Kong's district administration and electoral politics to study (1) the historical evolution of district administration, and (2) how electoral politics has been changing district administration. The relationships between district administration and electoral politics are closely intertwined, as this book will show. The introduction of elections to district advisory bodies, like DBs, was expected to improve the public delivery of services. In other words, electoral politics at the district level was expected to improve public administration at the grassroots level. As time passed, electoral politics became far more complex than conventional wisdom assumed, leading to party politics, elite fragmentation, and political struggles. Politicization and hyper-politicization in the HKSAR led to the victory of the pan-democrats in the November 2019 DC elections, which had immediate political impacts. The central government in Beijing introduced and promulgated the National Security Law in late June 2020, leading to a series of steps for the HKSAR government to gradually roll back district-level reforms and culminating in the mass resignations and disqualification of many council members. Due to the paralysis in the operation of many DCs after late 2021, the HKSAR government decided to recentralize the financial management and allocation of minor work projects of all the councils. In short, the British colonial rulers used district-level elections to improve the public delivery of services to ordinary citizens, and the post-1997 administration inherited this practice. However, a drastic change occurred in the post-2019 district elections after which the promulgation of the National Security Law brought about mass resignations and governmental disqualifications of many council members. The hyper-politicization process after the November 2019 elections led to administrative reconcentration and reverse democratization at the district level. Originally, electoral politics was seen by the British colonizers as having positive impacts on district administration, but electoral politics later grew in such a complex and distorted manner that the post-2019 authorities in the HKSAR leadership, under the full support of the central authorities in Beijing, decided to reverse administrative reforms and recentralize district administration. From the colonial era to the post-colonial period, electoral politics and district administration have been closely intertwined, with the former having tremendous impacts on the latter.

Chapter One will focus on the historical evolution of district administration from the British colonial era to the HKSAR period. Chapter Two will discuss electoral politics from the UrbCo to DB elections. Chapter Three will discuss rural politics and factions, followed by Chapter Four that will examine the overall development of the DC elections from 1994 to 2019. Chapter Five will focus on the features of the 2019 DC elections with special reference to the role of candidates, parties, and groups, especially the pro-government and pro-democracy factions. Chapter Six will study the relationships between political violence and the voters' perceptions of the 2019 DC elections. Chapter Seven delineates the evolution of district administration. Chapter Eight examines how the political transformation of DCs after the promulgation of the National Security Law in late June 2020. The Conclusion will sum up our main findings and arguments in this book.

Notes

1 "Direct and Indirect Rule," in https://nigerianscholars.com/tutorials/west-african-colonial-administration/direct-and-indirect-rule/, access date: August 3, 2020.

2 Philip Havik, "'Direct' or 'Indirect' Rule? Reconsidering the roles of appointed chiefs and native employees in Portuguese West Africa," *Africana Studia*, vol. 15 (2010), pp. 29–36.

3 "Direct and Indirect Rule," in https://nigerianscholars.com/tutorials/west-african-colonial-administration/direct-and-indirect-rule/access date: August 3, 2020. Also see D. K. Fieldhouse, *The Colonial Empires: A Comparative Survey from the Eighteen Century* (London: Macmillan, 1966).

4 John Gerring, Daniel Ziblatt, Johan VanGorp and Julian Arevalo, "An Institutional Theory of Direct and Indirect Rule," *World Politics*, vol. 63, no. 2 (July 2011), pp. 377–433.

5 Edouard Bustin, *Lunda Under Belgian Rule: The Politics of Ethnicity* (Cambridge: Harvard University Press, 1975), pp. 88–89.

6 Adnan Naseemullah and Paul Staniland, "Indirect Rule and Varieties of Governance," *Governance*, vol. 29, no. 1 (January 2016), pp. 13–30.

7 Chan Kwok-Shing, "The regulation of customary practices under colonial administration: Kinship and mortgages in a Hong Kong village," *China Information*, Vol. 29, Issue: 3(2015), pp. 377–396.

8 *Ibid.*

9 *Ibid.*, p. 379.

10 *Ibid.*

11 *Ibid.*

12 *Ibid.*, pp. 390–391.

13 *Ibid.*, pp. 391–392.

14 Evanson N. Wamagatta, "British Administration and the Chiefs' Tyranny in Early Colonial Kenya A Case Study of the First Generation of Chiefs from Kiambu District, 1895–1920," Journal of Asian and African Studies, vol. 44, no. 4 (2009), p. 371–388.

15 *Ibid.*

16 *Ibid.* pp. 371–372.

17 *Ibid.*, p. 372.

18 *Ibid.*, pp. 372–373.

19 *Ibid.*, pp. 384–385.

20 Bethwell A. Ogot, "British Administration in the Central Nyanza District of Kenya, 1900–60," *Journal of African History*, vol. 4, no. 2 (1963), pp. 249–273.

21 Lau Siu-kai, "Decolonization without Independence: The Unfinished Political Reforms of the Hong Kong Government," Occasional paper no. 19, Centre for Hong Kong Studies, Institute of Social Studies, the Chinese University of Hong Kong, May 1987.

22 Joel D. Barkan, "Legislators, Elections and Political Linkage," in Joel D. Barkan and John J. Okumu, eds., *Politics and Public Policy in Kenya and Tanzania* (New York: Praeger, 1979), p. 64.

23 Kenneth Robinson, *The Dilemmas of Trusteeship: Aspects of British Colonial Policy Between the Wars* (London: Oxford University Press, 1965), p. 90.

24 Nick H. K. Or, "How policy agendas change when autocracies liberalize: The case of Hong Kong, 1975–2016," *Public Administration*, vol. 97 (2019), pp. 926–941.

25 *Ibid.*, p. 927.

26 *Ibid.*, p. 928.

27 Chong Xu, "Imperialism in the city: war and the making of the municipal administration in the French Concession of Shanghai in the Taiping period, 1853–1862," *Urban History*, vol. 47 (2020), pp. 126–151.

28 *Ibid.*, pp. 126–127.

29 *Ibid.*, pp. 127–128.

30 *Ibid.*, pp. 150–151.

31 Ewout Frankema and Marlous van Waijenburg, "Metropolitan blueprints of colonial taxation? Lessons from fiscal capacity building in British and French Africa," *Journal of African History*, vol. 55 (2014), pp. 371–400.

32 *Ibid.*, pp. 371–372.

33 *Ibid.*, pp. 371–372.

34 *Ibid.*

35 *Ibid.*, pp. 373–374.

36 *Ibid.*, pp.392–394.

37 Ngozi Caleb Kamalu, "British, French, Belgian and Portuguese Models of Colonial Rule and Economic Development in Africa," *Annals of Global History*, vol. 1, no. 1 (2019), pp. 37–47.

38 *Ibid.*, p. 45.

39 *Ibid.*, p. 45.

40 *Ibid.*, p. 46

41 Lo Shiu-Hing, *Political Development in Macau* (Hong Kong: The Chinese University Press, 1996).

42 Walter Rodney, *How Europe Underdeveloped Africa* (London: Bogle-L'Ouverture Publications, 1972); James Duffy, *Portuguese Africa* (Cambridge, Massachusetts: Harvard University Press, 1959); Mai Palmberg, ed., *The Struggle for Africa* (London: Zed Press, 1983); Richard Sandbrook, *The Politics of Basic Needs: Urban Aspects of Assaulting Poverty* (Toronto: University of Toronto Press, 1982); and Richard Sandbrook, *The Politics of Africa's Economic Stagnation* (London: Cambridge University Press, 1985).

43 Diana Markides, "Nicosia and its municipal administration during the very early years of British rule in Cyprus," *Byzantine and Modern Greek Studies* Vol. 37 No. 1 (2013), pp. 92–110.

44 *Ibid.*, p. 109.

45 Erik Green, "Indirect Rule and Colonial Intervention: Chiefs and Agrarian Change in Nyasaland, ca. 1933 to the Early 1950s," *International Journal of African Historical Studies*, vol. 44, no. 2 (2011), pp. 249–274.

46 Ibid., pp. 249–250

47 Robert Home, "From cantonments to townships: Lugard's influence upon British colonial governance in Africa," *Planning Perspectives*, vol. 34, no. 1 (2019), pp. 43–64.

48 *Ibid.*

49 Raghav Kishore, "Urban Failures: 'Municipal Governance, Planning and Power in Colonial Delhi, 1863–1910," *The Indian Economic and Social History Review*, vol. 54, no. 2 (2015), pp. 439–461.

50 *Ibid.*

51 Nobuhiro Mizuno and Ryosuke Okazawa, "Colonial experience and post-colonial underdevelopment in Africa," vol. 141 (2009), p. 147.

52 Alok Sheel, "Agricultural Trade and Markets in British India: Shahabad and Gaya Districts, 1800–1920," *Indian Historical Review*, vol. 42, no. 1 (2015), pp. 90–112.

53 *Ibid.*

54 Elliot Fratkin, "The Samburu laibon's sorcery and the death of Theodore Powys in colonial Kenya," *Journal of Eastern African Studies*, vol. 9, no. 1 (2015), pp. 35–54.

55 Deborah Sutton, "Devotion, Antiquity, and Colonial Custody of the Hindu Temple in British India," *Modern Asian Studies*, vol. 47, no. 1 (2013) pp. 135–166.

56 *Ibid.*, pp. 135–137.

57 *Ibid.*

58 *Ibid.*, pp. 49–50.

59 *Ibid..*

60 Ajay Verghese, "British Rule and Tribal Revolts in India: The curious case of Bastar," *Modern Asian Studies*, vol. 50, no. 5 (2016), pp. 1619–1644.

61 Ibid., pp. 1621–1622.

62 Ibid., p. 1642.

63 *Ibid.*

64 *Ibid.*

65 Moses Ochonu, "Colonialism within Colonialism: The Hausa-Caliphate Imaginary and the British Colonial Administration of the Nigerian Middle Belt," *African Studies Quarterly*, vol. 10, numbers 2 & 3, (2008), pp. 95–127.

66 *Ibid.*

67 *Ibid.*

68 *Ibid.*

69 David Mills, "Durham Report," November 6, 2019, in https://www.thecanadianencyclopedia.ca/en/article/durham-report, access date: August 3, 2020.

70 *Ibid.*

71 Benoit Morissette, "The Foundations of Freedom and Civilization: The Durham Report, Municipal Institutions and Liberalism," *World Political Science*, vol. 15, no. 1 (July 2019), pp. 99–124.

72 Harvey Lazar and Aron Seal, "Local government: Still a junior government? The place of municipalities within the Canadian federation," in Nico Steytler, ed., *The Place and Role of Local Government in Federal Systems* (Johannesburg: Konrad-Adenauer-Stiftung, 2005), p. 27.

73 *Ibid.*, p. 28.

74 Igor Vojnovic, "Municipal consolidation in the 1990s: an analysis of British Columbia, New Brunswick, and Nova Scotia," *Canadian Public Administration*, vol. 40, no. 2 (1998), pp. 239–283.

75 *Ibid.*

76 Stephen Constantine, "Governor Sir John Field in St Helena: Democratic Reform in a Small British Colony, 1962–68," *Journal of Imperial and Commonwealth History*, vol. 44, no. 4 (2016), pp. 672–696.

77 *Ibid.*

78 *Ibid.*

79 Michael Gallagher, "Elections and Referendums," in Daniele Caramani, ed., *Comparative Politics* (New York: Oxford University Press, 2008), p. 242.

80 *Ibid.*, p. 242.

81 John Loughlin, "Federal and local government institutions," in Daniele Caramani, ed., *Comparative Politics* (New York: Oxford University Press, 2008), p. 280.

82 *Ibid.*

83 Andrew Nickson; Alex Brillantes; Wilhelmina Cabo; Alice Calestino; and Nick Devas, "Asia-Pacific," in Elisabeth Gateau, ed., *Decentralization and Local Democracy in the World: First Global Report by United Cities and Local Governments* (Spain, Barcelona: United Cities and Local Government, 2008), pp. 59–60.

84 Gerard Marcou, "Postface: Essay on the clarifications of some key concepts and methodical problems," in Gateau, ed., *Decentralization and Local Democracy in the World: First Global Report by United Cities and Local Governments*, p. 309.

85 Azeen Kiani and Hossein Sartipi, "Functions of Election in a Democratic System," *international Research Journal of Interdisciplinary & Multidisciplinary Studies*, vol. 2, no. 9 (October 2016), p. 23.

86 Guillermo O'Donnell and Philippe C. Schmitter, *Transitions from Authoritarian Rule: Tentative Conclusions about Uncertain Democracies* (Baltimore, Maryland: Johns Hopkins University Press, 1986).

87 *Ibid.*, p. 49.

88 Winrich Kuhne, "The Role of Elections in Emerging Democracies and Post-Conflict Countries: Key Issues, Lessons Learnt and Dilemmas," August 2010, in http://library.fes.de/pdf-files/iez/07416.pdf, access date: August 5, 2020.

89 *White Paper: District Administration in Hong Kong, January 1981* (Hong Kong: Government Printer, 1981), p. 23.

90 Jack Paine, "Democratic Contradictions in European Settler Colonies," *World Politics*, vol. 71, no. 3 (July 2019), pp. 542–585.

91 Shiu-Hing Lo, "Colonial Policy-Makers, Capitalist Class and China: Determinants of Electoral Reform in Hong Kong's and Macau's Legislatures," *Pacific Affairs*, vol. 62, no. 2 (Summer 1989), pp. 204–218.

92 Sonny Shiu-Hing Lo, Steven Chung-Fun Hung and Jeff Hai-Chi Loo, *China's New United Work in Hong Kong: Penetrative Politics and Its Implications* (London: Palgrave Macmillan, 2019).

1

The Historical Evolution of District Administration — From District Watch to the Introduction of District Boards

The District Administration Scheme has been implemented since 1982. The main elements of the Scheme were the District Councils (DCs, formerly known as District Boards, DBs) and the District Management Committees, which were later established in each of the districts in Hong Kong. The aim of the Scheme in 1982 was to "achieve a more effective co-ordination of the provision of services and facilities at the district level, ensure that the government is responsive to district needs and problems and promote public participation in district affairs."[1] As a matter of fact, to understand the district administration of Hong Kong, as well as its local district politics, this Chapter is going to trace the birth and development of DBs and their political and electoral evolution.

District Administration in Hong Kong under Ming and Qing Dynasties

The region of Hong Kong formerly belonged to China's territories during the time when the Imperial Qin dynasty was established. During the Qin dynasty, the region was governed by the Panyu county of the Nanhai region. In the Eastern Jin dynasty (317–420), Baoan county was established. Later, the Tuen Mun town, namely the Castle Peak, was established in 736 during the Tang dynasty in which a local official sent 2,000 soldiers to safeguard its security over Hong Kong, which was at that time incorporated territorially into the Dongguan county. As Hong Kong was relatively far away from the Dongguan county, the Ming dynasty built a new county named Sanon and its headquarters was established in the Nantau town in 1572. The main objective of the Sanon county was to consolidate its governance (*gé gù dǐngxīn qù wēi wéi ān* 革固鼎新去危為安), to create a new phenomenon, to remove danger, and to become stable.[2]

During this long period of dynastic rule of Hong Kong, many clans, great or small, migrated into this enclave. After some communities were established in Hong Kong, many regional markets were formed to exchange their living necessities. Bazaar, whose Chinese name *xu shi* (虛市) refers to the marketplace for the exchange of goods and daily necessities, became an important economic arena for the rural people's interaction and livelihood. The growth of bazaars or markets laid down the foundation of district administration. These markets witnessed the construction of temples and ancestral halls, which were the administrative offices for local officials to manage district areas and affairs. Moreover, the local administrative offices carried the political and economic function of collecting taxes from residents. Indeed, temples were different from ancestral halls, which were established around certain clans or kinship groups. The construction of bazaars and temples were like rituals leading to the rapid emergence of local district administration in Hong Kong. Local gentry and leaders participated in religious rituals, and had a say on how their local districts should be governed.[3] Usually, the establishment of district markets were accompanied by the formation of temples, where local district administration and leaders emerged.

Table 1.1 shows the emergence of old markets and their concomitant temples from 1266 to 1813. In terms of crime control, the Qing dynasty adopted the *baojia* (保甲制) to govern the entire territory of China, including Hong Kong. The *baojia* system was composed of an organized form of district administration in which ten households constituted in *jia* (甲) leader, and ten *jia* leaders (1,000 households) could be administered under a *bao* (保) *chief* (長). As such, residents were tightly and systematically organized into a coherent local district administration with the function of controlling crime and maintaining law and order. Hong Kong under the Qing dynasty was no exception to this rule.

Table 1.1: The Early Markets with their Temples Established in the Hong Kong Region

Old Market	Recordable year	Temple
Joss House Bay	1266	Tin Hau Temple 天后廟
Tuen Mun Hui	1368	Hau Kok Tin Hau Temple 后角天后廟
Yuen Long Hui	1669 1714	Tai Wong Temple 大王古廟 Tuan Kwan Ti Tai Temple 玄關二帝廟
Shek Wu Hui	After 1669	Po Tak Temple 報德祠
Tai Po Hui	1691	Tin Hau Temple 天后廟
Tai O	1699 1722	Yeung Hau Temple 楊侯廟 Tin Hau Temple
Check Chu	1767	Tin Hau Temple
Cheung Chau	1767 1813	Pak She Tin Hau Temple 長洲北社天后廟 Hung Shing Temple
Ap Lei Chau	1773	Hung Shing Temple 洪勝廟

Source: Compiled from the data of the Antiquities and Monuments Office, https://www.amo.gov.hk/en/index.php, access date: August 1, 2020.

The Emergence of District Administration in Colonial Hong Kong

After the British acquired Hong Kong Island in the Treaty of Nanking in 1842, market towns, like the Chinese district administration, continued to operate and thrive. The British grasped the territory of the Kowloon peninsula in 1860 and the New Territories in 1989 for 99 years until 1997. After the British entrenched their sovereignty over Hong Kong, the bazaars and their temples persisted with the continuation of local Chinese customs and tradition. A hallmark of the British colonial rule was to preserve the local customs and tradition. The case of Hong Kong was no exception to this rule. Table 1.2 illustrates the markets and temples that were established in Hong Kong under the British rule.

As early as 1844, the British colonial administration preserved the *baojia* system to maintain local order, collect taxes, and organize construction projects. The British rulers recognized the legality of the *bao* chiefs, who were registered under the colonial government's Registrar General and Protector of Chinese. In all the towns and cities, the Governor appointed a group of Chinese to be law and order officers, who were also called *"dibao"* or land security officials. Since police officers were inadequate in some towns

**Table 1.2: Markets Temples and District Offices
under the British Colonial Administration**

New Market	Year	Related Temple and Office
Shau Kei Wan	1845/1872	Tin Hau Temple
Western Market	About 1847	Man Mo Temple 文武廟
Wan Chai	1847	Hung Shing Temple
Aberdeen	1851	Tin Hau Temple
Yau Ma Tei	1865	Tin Hau Temple
Tai Wo Market	1893	Man Mo Temple
Tuen Mun San Hui	1900	New Town Office
Yuen Long	1915	Lap Ye Tong
Sai Kung	1916	Tin Hau Temple
Luen Wo Market	1948	Luen Wo Office
Sha Tin	1954	Town Office

Source: Compiled from the data of the Antiquities and Monuments Office, https://www.amo.gov.hk/en/index.php, access date: July 15, 2020.

and villages, the local people organized District Watchmen to maintain law and order. These Watchman officers were under the supervision of district police.[4]

In 1853, the power of *dibao* was enhanced by the British colonial authorities, who believed that they could and should mediate in the disputes among the local townspeople and villagers. However, with the passage of time, some *dibao* became corrupt and received bribes from the residents. Some were influenced by the triads, leading to the concerns of the British colonial administration. In 1861, Governor William Robinson announced that the *baojia* system was abolished. The Chinese residents were directly under the administration of the Secretary for Chinese Affairs. Robinson also declared that the Qing dynasty's law would not be applied to Hong Kong; instead, the Hong Kong government promulgated its own statutes and laws.[5]

Early District Administration: From District Watch Force to District Watch Committee

After the abolition of the *baojia* system, the District Watch Force was set up in 1866 under the supervision of the Registrar General. The population of Hong Kong Island increased from 4,000 in 1841 to 70,000 in 1855 and when the *baojia* system was abolished in 1861, the population rose to 120,000. In 1866, some residents requested that the District Watch Force should be established, an idea accepted by the British authorities. The District Watch Force (DWF) became a security organization protecting law and order as well as personal safety. It was built upon the practice of local Chinese merchants who hired local watchmen to supplement the relatively weak regular police force. Later, the DWF helped the government register local population, look for kidnapped girls, rescue the young mainland girls who were smuggled to be prostitutes in Hong Kong, and maintain social stability in the city. The DWF performed other tasks, such as sending officers to be census enumerators, sending runaway girls to Po Leung Kuk for protection and care, and engaging in detective work for the local Chinese communities.[6]

The DWF was later called District Watch Committee (DWC) in 1891.[7] The first meeting of the DWC was held on February 1, 1866, which was a meeting of the *kaifong* leaders, the prosperous shopkeepers and merchants. According to the Registrar General's Report for 1867, after much discussion, the committee agreed to elect a certain number of residents to act as watchmen, "whose pay should be disbursed by themselves and be collected by men especially appointed for the purpose." These residents sent a petition to the government asking for the permission to organize a force of Chinese watchmen. In the petition, they claimed that some people in Canton wanted to sneak into Hong Kong to commit robberies. The government officials in Hong Kong treated this rumor with skepticism; nevertheless, Governor Richard MacDonnell accepted the proposal of setting up the District Watchmen in 1866.[8]

The District Watch became the major means of policing Hong Kong's suburban communities. It proved to be a more effective force than the European and Indian police and became an important tool for the Register General to discharge its responsibilities to the Chinese community. However, later some colonial officials were suspicious of the District Watch's activities, fearing that the existence of an informal Chinese police force could constitute a threat to colonial rule.[9] Another problem of the District Watch was that it created tensions with the regular police and the detective force of the Registrar. Still, in 1868 and 1896, crime fell in the colony of Hong Kong. The District Watch scheme did help to settle family and wage disputes in the Chinese community. In 1872, Charles May, a British police officer, argued that it was problematic to let the local Chinese police themselves, especially as the colonial rulers heavily depended on the Chinese intermediaries for criminal intelligence.[10]

In 1891, Registrar-General Mark Steward reformed the District Watch Force and changed it into District Watch Committee, strengthening the committee's accountability to the colonial administration rather than to the Chinese community.[11] Clearly, the move could be interpreted as a centralization of policing functions so as to consolidate the colonial regime's legitimacy. The establishment of the District Watch Committee was also seen as "an extension of the colonial government's co-optive politics."[12] The committee members were prominent local Chinese leaders who gave advice to the Registrar-General. They assisted the colonial government to manipulate and mobilize local resources to buttress colonial rule. Together with other colonial institutions, such as the Executive Council (ExCo), Legislative Council (LegCo), and Sanitary Board (see Table 1.3), the District Watch Committee played a crucial function of "administrative absorption of politics."[13]

In colonial Hong Kong, there were several ways in which the government understood public opinion. First, there were some appointed unofficial councilors on the LegCo and ExCo and later some elected members on the Urban Council, which were all advisory bodies to the Governor. Secondly, there were appointed unofficial members on statutory committees and ad hoc advisory bodies, whose functions were to give advice to the Governor on various policies. Third, there were a group of "recognized" community leaders who were active in the local community organizations, and whose opinions were listened by the colonial authorities, including their views on social policies affecting the traditional Chinese social and cultural practices. This group of people embraced the leaders of the Tung Wah Hospitals and the Po Leung Kuk, the *kaifongs* and the Justices of the Peace.

In 1880, the Governor appointed Wu Ting-fang (Ng Choy) as the first unofficial Chinese member of the LegCo. The first Chinese member of the ExCo was Sir Chow Shou-son in 1926. Although the Sanitary Board was set up in 1883 to deal with public hygiene and health matters, and although it had elections of some unofficial members starting from 1888, the first Chinese member of the Sanitary Board was Dr. Ho Sai-chuen, who

**Table 1.3: Institutions for Social and Political Participation
of Chinese in Colonial Hong Kong**

Items	Year of Introduction
Executive Council	1926
Legislative Council	1880
Sanitary Board (later Urban Council)	1926
Justice of the Peace	1878
Tung Wah Hospital and Po Leung Kuk	1870 and 1878 respectively
District Watch Committee	1891
District Watchman	1866
Land Security	1844

Source: G. B. Endacott, *Government and People in Hong Kong, 1841–1962: A Constitutional History* (Hong Kong: Hong Kong University Press, 1964).

was nominated by Dr. S.F. Lee and seconded by Robert Kotewall in 1926. Ho was the sixth son of the famous community leader Ho Fook, a young brother of the Eurasian Robert Ho Tung. Sir Lo Man Kam was an ethnic Chinese who was elected as an unofficial member of the Sanitary Board in 1929. The level of socio-political participation of the Chinese was low in the governing boards of Tung Wah Hospital and Po Leung Kuk, which were established in 1870 and 1878, respectively. The system of Justices of the Peace (JP) was established in 1843 and the first Chinese, Wu Ting-fang, was appointed as JP in 1878.

The Land Security System was introduced in 1844. It was reformed later as the District Watch Force (DWF) in 1866. The land security system was composed of Chinese who maintained law and order in the community. The number of District Watchmen in 1878 was small, ranging from three to eight in six districts (see Table 1.4). It became an intermediary between the office of the Registrar-General, who represented the government, and the low strata of the Chinese community. Quite often, the Chinese representatives in the ExCo and LegCo were selected from the District Watch Committee, which evolved from the District Watch Force. The committee became a permanent advisory body comprising the rich, the influential, the prestigious, and the powerful Chinese in Hong Kong. Overall, the colonial political institutions became a means by which the British rulers co-opted the local Chinese elites into the colonial regime effectively.

Table 1.4: Disbursements of Watchmen in October, November and December 1878

District	Wages of the Head District Watchman	Number of Watchmen and their Wages
Number 1	$45	3, $62.50
Number 2	$45	8, $156.00
Number 3	$45	8, $154.50
Number 4	$45	6, $120.86
Number 5	$45	8, $147.00
Number 6	$45	4, $81.00

Source: *The Hongkong Government Gazette*, 12 February 1879, p. 54.

The foundation of Hong Kong's welfare politics was the colonial government's creation of the DWF in 1891, and intermediaries such as the Po Leung Kuk in 1893 and the Tung Wah Hospital in 1896.[14] The DWF's members were appointed from influential members of the Chinese community, most of whom also served on the Tung Wah and the Po Leung Kok advisory boards. The Tung Wah and Po Leung Kuk groups provided the necessary charity and welfare for the poor and the needy, acting as a crucial bridge between the rulers and the ruled. After serving all these organizations, the local Chinese elites could receive government invitations to assume more powerful political positions as being Justices of the Peace, members of the Sanitary Board, and members of the LegCo and ExCo. They played a pivotal role of strengthening the communication between the colonial system and the ordinary people, buttressing the legitimacy of the colonizers.

The District Watch system was brought under the control of the Registrar General. The link established between the Registrar General and the DWF in 1866 was maintained until a change in the District Watch Force Ordinance in 1949, when the Chinese Committee of Management was terminated.[15] According to Henry Lethbridge, the DWF not only maintained law and order but also brought the European administrators, European businessmen, and Chinese community leaders together, thereby harmonizing the society and reducing the possibility of social conflict.[16]

According to the District Watch Force Ordinance in 1930, the Governor could appoint any person to membership of the District Watch Committee. Moreover, such persons would hold office for a period directed by the Governor. The Governor could at any time revoke the appointment of any member of the District Watch Committee. Finally, the Secretary of Chinese Affairs would be the ex-officio chairman of the District Watch Committee. Before 1941, the District Watch Committee was regarded as "the Chinese Executive Council" whose members' views were listened and considered by the British Colonial Office. By 1941, the District Watch Committee's influence gradually decreased. It was revived in 1946 but was later disbanded in 1949. The committee's function of protecting district security was taken over by the police and its consultative role had already been curbed by the members of the ExCo and LegCo.[17]

In the 1960s, John C. McDouall, the Secretary for Chinese Affairs, described the DWF as "an unwelcome anachronism to the Chinese population" and "an imperfectly comprehended mystery" to civil servants.[18] This statement by the official in charge of the DWF between 1957 and 1966 revealed the opposition of some civil servants to the Force, which existed for more than a century between 1866 and 1970. It underwent changes in scope and organization, but one feature that remained unchanged was its racial composition, namely always being a Chinese district policing force. As such, in the colony's history of private security development, the DWF was an important organization at the district level even though its numbers never exceeded 160.[19]

Rural Politics and the Rise of Heung Yee Kuk in the New Territories

Under the Convention signed between Britain and China's Qing dynasty on the lease of the New Territories on 9 June 1898, the New Territories would be governed by Britain for 99 years free of rent. In addition to the population of 240,000 in 1897, the extension of the New Territories in 1898 would witness 100,000 more residents enter Hong Kong. Table 1.5 shows the population and its sub-ethnic composition in the New Territories as of 1898. In April 1899, the Hong Kong government enacted the Hong Kong Extension Exemption Ordinance. It appointed the committees for various sub-districts in the New Territories on 8 July 1899. These committees could be seen as the beginning of district administration in the extended region of the New Territories immediately after the signing of the 1898 Convention. In 1904, the Hong Kong government completed its land surveying of the New Territories, demarcated the land under either private

**Table 1.5: The Population and Sub-ethnic Composition of
Districts in the New Territories, 1898**

Division	Sub-ethnic composition	Number of Villages	Population	Total
Shat'au	*Punti* (local)	4	5,000	5,000
Sham Chun	*Punti*	20	12,900	
	Hakka	6	1,180	14,080
Shat'au Kok	Hakka	54	8,530	
	Punti	1	70	8,600
Un Long	*Punti*	49	20,980	
	Hakka	10	2,040	23,020
Sheung U	*Punti*	60	10,210	
	Hakka	122	10,660	23,020
Kau Lung	*Punti*	22	5,830	
	Hakka	32	9,200	15,030
Islands	*Punti*	5	9,150	
	Hakka	31	4,460	
	Tanka	7	110	13,720
Total		423		100,320

Source: "Report by Mr. Stewart Lockhart on the Extension of the Colony of Hongkong, 8 October 1898, Appendix No. 3: Table showing the distribution of races," in "Extracts from Papers to the Extension of the Colony of Hong Kong, Laid before the LegCo by Command of His Excellency the Governor (Secretary of State to Governor), January 6, 1899," available in Hong Kong Government Reports Outline (1842 -1941), in http://sunzi.lib.hku.hk/hkgrol, access date: July 27, 2020.

possession or governmental control, and facilitated the transfer of land in the New Territories to settle disputes. After the extension of the lease on the New Territories, the British colonial government set up a district office to manage the affairs of the New Territories, where district committees were simultaneously established to enhance the communication between colonial rulers and rural residents.

In May 1925, an anti-Japanese demonstration in Shanghai developed into an anti-foreign and anti-British movement as the British had "the largest stake in China," especially as the Sikh police under the British command opened fire at some Chinese protestors in the Shanghai International Settlement.[20] In June, the strikers in Canton organized a boycott of British and Japanese goods, resulting in street fighting in Shameen between the protestors and the British and French troops. Fifty-two people died and some 170 were injured—an incident triggering the workers' strikes in Hong Kong where 250,000 residents were involved.[21] At the same time, many Hong Kong residents left Hong Kong for the mainland in response to the nationalistic and anti-colonial movement in Canton, where the provincial government organized a boycott of British goods from June to October—a boycott affecting Hong Kong's trade to some extent. The British Hong Kong administration learnt a bitter lesson from the mass strike in 1925, realizing that it was necessary to rebuild the communication and trust between the colonial government and the Hong Kong residents. As such, Governor Cecil Clementi in 1926 swiftly appointed Chow Shouson, a former custom official of the Qing dynasty and the chair of the Bank of East Asia in Hong Kong, to be one of the three unofficial members of the ExCo.[22]

To bridge the communication gap between the rulers and the ruled, the British colonizers also established rural committees in the New Territories. The predecessor of these rural committees was actually the New Territories Association of Agricultural, Industrial and Commercial Research, a body set up by three rural leaders in 1923, including Yeung Kwok-shui from Tsuen Wan, Lee Chung-chong from Fanling, and Tang Wai-tong from Yuen Long.[23] The New Territories Association of Agricultural, Industrial and Commercial Research could be regarded as an interest group lobbying the colonial government for the protection of well-being of rural residents. It was a precursor to the Heung Yee Kuk (HYK), a rural advisory body whose name was given by Governor Cecil Clementi to replace the Research Association in 1926.[24]

At the beginning of its formation, the Heung Yee Kuk had a 40-member Board of Directors, who began to negotiate and discuss with the colonial authorities on a whole range of issues, including land and transportation, with the Hong Kong government. From the perspective of the British colonial authorities, the HYK could help to improve their communication with the rural leaders and residents while establishing a harmonious relationship with the Nationalist or Kuomintang (KMT) government in Nanking. On the other hand, the British colonial administration was apprehensive of the emergence of the Communists in the mainland and their possible infiltration into the colony. As such, establishing good relations with the rural people in the New Territories was a double-edged sword that could not only prevent the penetration of Communists into Hong Kong but also legitimized colonial governance. The Xian incident in China in December 1936, when the Nationalist leader Chiang Kai-shek was kidnapped and then released to form a Nationalist-Communist coalition to fight against the Japanese invaders in northern China, changed how the Chinese Communist Party (CCP) was viewed by the Kuomintang, at least temporarily. Still, the British colonial rulers were worried about the Communist infiltration into Hong Kong. As a matter of fact, after the end of the Second World War in 1945, the British colonial government discovered that many branches of the Rural Committees were pro-CCP; some regional Rural Committees operated separately without much coordination.[25] Given that many rural residents were traditionally politically patriotic, it was not surprising that some Rural Committees were regarded as pro-CCP in the years after 1945, especially in the wake of the Communist takeover in the mainland in 1949.

In 1959, the Hong Kong government reactivated the Rural Committees in Tsuen Wan where the first satellite town emerged in Hong Kong. At the same time, the HYK was given formal status by the Heung Yee Kuk Ordinance (Chapter 1097), which was firstly enacted on 11 December 1959 amid the construction of the first new towns in the New Territories. The HYK, which was established in 1926, became a statutory body in 1960. Its functions were to advise the Secretary for the New Territories on matters affecting the well-being of the people of the New Territories, to promote cooperation and understanding between the colonial government and the people, and to maintain appropriate tradition, customs, and practices.[26] The Full Council of the HYK comprises (1) the chairperson and two vice chairpersons and they are elected by the Council, (2) the chairpersons and vice chairpersons of the 27 Rural Committees, (3) the unofficial New Territories Justices of the Peace, and (4) 21 Special Councilors.[27] The Special Councilors are elected either from among the other village representatives or from other residents of the New Territories.[28] The electoral process commences at the village level with the election by all adult males of one or more Village Representatives, whereas the size of the electorates depends on the size of the village concerned. Villages are grouped under 27 Rural Committees, each of which is composed of an executive committee whose members are chosen by the Village Representatives, normally by secret ballot once every two years. The chairperson and vice-chairpersons of the Rural Committee are chosen by their own members and the Committee has ex-officio members sitting on the HYK. As such, the British colonial administration designed a detailed institutional structure that co-opted the rural elites into the HYK and Rural Committees, thereby enhancing the communication between the colonial rulers and the ruled elites and masses in the New Territories. As of 2020, the HYK had 27 Rural Committees representing 651 villages and it regularly meets with the New Territories Administration to discuss local issues and government policies.[29]

The Heung Yee Kuk Ordinance stipulates that the HYK promotes mutual cooperation in the New Territories on the one hand and between the New Territories and the government on the other, advises the government on socio-economic developments, and fosters traditional customs and culture.[30] Since its formation, the HYK has become a rural interest group actively influencing government policies. For example, the colonial government in 1970 put forward an amendment to the Prevention of Bribery Bill, which allowed officials to accept entertainment from the pubic without being regarded as being guilty of corruption.[31] One of the groups pushing for such amendment was the HYK, whose members threatened to resign if their traditional custom of inviting officials to lavish lunches and dinners would become a criminal offence. Similarly, in 1972, the HYK lobbied the government for a relaxation of building regulations on village houses. The District Commissioner for the New Territories eventually made concessions to their demand. However, the colonial government sometimes rejected the HYK's demands; in 1975, the HYK opposed the government proposal of including agricultural land and buildings to be assessed for rates. Its opposition failed and the government stood firm.[32]

In the past, village representatives were generally appointed through the consensus of village elders. Sometimes, village representatives were elected but they had to be the male heads of households. In 1971, many villagers opposed the Small House Policy, which was eventually approved by the ExCo in November 1972 and has been implemented since December of that year. Under the Small House Policy, an indigenous villager in the New Territories can apply for a small house grant.[33] An indigenous villager refers to a male person who is at least 18 years old, and who is a descendent from the male line of a resident in 1898 of a recognized village in the New Territories. Moreover,

> An indigenous villager may utilize his once-in-a-lifetime right to purchase a whole or portion of a small house from another indigenous villager for his own use without paying an additional premium to government. However, once the assignment has been registered, both the assignor and the assignee will be considered to have utilized their once-in-a-lifetime

right to a small house grant and will not be entitled to any further small house concessionary grants whatsoever.[34]

From the perspective of the colonial government, the Small House Policy helped to reduce the tensions with the indigenous inhabitants, and it facilitated land development in the New Territories. However, once this policy was implemented, it became a vested interest of the indigenous villagers, who have seen land as having economic value and political influence. In other words, the Small House Policy created a huge and direct economic interest for the indigenous inhabitants. The HYK has become a vested interest group that insists on the protection of the interest of the indigenous inhabitants—a protection legally entrenched by Article 40 of the Basic Law that was promulgated in 1990.[35]

One of the architects of the Small House Policy, former New Territories District Commissioner Dennis Bray, admitted that it had strengths and weaknesses. As Bray revealed in his memoir:

> I cannot pretend that the small house policy was without its critics. These were not found among the villagers but among my fellow officials involved in land administration—mainly because the villagers had such freedom from regulation. The definition of a small house was deliberately made simple and precise. I knew perfectly well that it would not be long before some enterprising architect would design pleasant little buildings that fitted the rules but looked nothing like a traditional village house. Sure enough a Spanish-style house began to appear with lovely tiled half-roofs. They were a great improvement. What was less satisfactory was that once some villagers got an Occupation Certificate, they sold the buildings to rich city slickers. This was an abuse that has taken some time to deal with, but I cannot say the result has been seriously damaging to the development of the New Territories. I still maintain that the principal result was a very considerable improvement in the standard of housing that the ordinary villagers have been able to enjoy. The old system stifled building in the interest of rules that were totally unsuitable for the rural environment in which they were meant to operate.[36]

With the benefit of hindsight, Bray identified the possible problem, namely an abuse by the owners of the small houses in the New Territories. He also admitted that there had already been many temporary structures in the rural areas that needed to be regulated by the colonial government.[37] In fact, these temporary structures can be easily seen in many small houses in the New Territories.

In 2016, a court verdict said that a land developer and an indigenous villager were guilty of cheating the Lands Department on the construction and selling of a small house.[38] The court judgment led to the anger of the HYK, which vowed to seek the interpretation of the Basic Law by the Standing Committee of the National People's Congress. Land politics in the New Territories has increasingly involved the indigenous inhabitants and the HYK since the implementation of the Small House Policy. To protect the interest of indigenous inhabitants, the HYK gradually transformed from a socio-economic interest group to a political one, nominating and supporting its candidates to participate in the direct elections held for the Regional Council, District Boards (later District Councils), and LegCo.

The indigenous inhabitants in the New Territories have gradually become the target of political co-optation by the PRC officials. Since the 1980s, especially after July 1, 1997. After the British colonialists occupied Hong Kong in 1842, the residents in Kam Tin, the New Territories, rebelled against the British colonial rulers in April 1899 and defended themselves in Kat Hing Wai—resistance that was regarded as politically patriotic in the mainland. During the Japanese occupation of Hong Kong from December 1941 to 1945, some indigenous inhabitants in the New Territories also joined the Guangdong people's anti-Japanese East River Column guerillas, operating in Sai Kung with about 400 people. Given that the indigenous inhabitants had a track record of resisting the British and Japanese imperialists, the PRC authorities since July 1, 1997 have made tremendous efforts at conducting united front work on them, winning their hearts and minds and wooing them onto the side of the pro-Beijing force against the democratic camp in local elections including the DCs and LegCo direct elections.

Kaifong Associations

Grassroots politics in Hong Kong took place not only at the rural areas but also at the urban areas in the form of establishing and activating *kaifong* (neighborhood) associations. In May 1946, Governor Mark Young believed that the people of Hong Kong should be given more responsibility in managing their own district affairs, suggesting the introduction of an Urban Council (UrbCo) in which two-thirds of its members would be directly elected. The so-called Young Plan became abortive because the British colonial administration was worried about not only the opposition from China, but also the rivalry between the CCP and KMT in Hong Kong.[39] Although the Young Plan was shelved, *kaifong* associations had existed in Hong Kong long ago in the rural areas in the form of village community organizations during the 19th Century. In 1949, the *Kaifong* Welfare Association operated as a voluntary organization providing services to the local community and residents. The Secretary for Chinese Affairs, John Crichton McDouall, encouraged residents to form their *kaifong* associations for the sake of promoting charity work in different districts. These associations also provided medicine and education for the residents, distributed rice to the poor and the needy, and arranged funeral services for the poor.[40] These *kaifong* associations formed a kind of social security system not provided by the colonial government for Hong Kong residents.[41]

From the late 1940s to early 1970s, *kaifong* leaders formally and informally acted as "mediators in civil disputes," helping the Secretariat for Chinese Affairs to handle almost 80% of the family cases.[42] Indeed, many *kaifong* leaders, who became office-bearers in *kaifong* associations, made "the first step towards raising their personal prestige, hoping eventually to gain honors and titles for their contributions to the community, and to be invited into the higher prestige organizations or get appointed to the government councils and committees."[43] On the other hand, the government relied on the *kaifong* leaders "in the absence of a system of popular representation" as non-government elites were appointed to government committees to serve as "indicators of public-opinion."[44] Above all, they acted as the channels of communications between the colonial government and ordinary citizens, promoting government policies to the general public. Finally, the *kaifong* leaders represented "social-cultural" interests in the colonial society.[45] As a result, the colonial administration's legitimacy could be enhanced by the establishment and operation of the *kaifong* associations.

Kaifong associations became a useful vehicle through which District Officers could utilize them to tap public opinions, to solve issues relating to the welfare and well-being of ordinary residents, and to mobilize public support of the government. Dennis Bray, a former Assistant Secretary of

Chinese Affairs due to his fluency in Cantonese in the early 1950s, revealed that when he proposed the idea of some *kaifong* associations forming political parties to participate in the Urban Council election, he was rebuked by his superior for "playing with fire," because if *kaifong* associations "get involved in politics, they will be immediately taken over by the triads or the communists."[46] Bray was advised to maintain the welfare function of *kaifong* associations — a strategy of depoliticization adopted by the British colonial administration. He admitted that in the early 1950s, triads remained active while the communists were "well-organized and hostile."[47] Although the communists penetrated some trade unions, they were checked and balanced by the Nationalist forces.[48] Hence, the British colonial administration preferred to avoid augmenting electoral politics that could provide an arena of political struggle between the underground CCP and KMT.

The functions of *kaifong* associations could be seen in the 1950s, when the 1953 fire accident in the squatters at Shek Kip Mei and the 1956 riot at the Shek Kip Mei public housing estate led to the determination of the Hong Kong government to expand the construction of public housing estates. To organize the residents in a better way, *kaifong* associations mushroomed in Tsim Sha Tsui, Yau Ma Tei, Mong Kok, Sham Shui Po, Cheung Sha Wan, and Kowloon City. The *kaifong* associations in Kwun Tong were also set up, embracing the sub-districts of Yau Tong, Lam Tin, Sau Mau Ping, Chiu Ping, Jordan Valley, and Ngau Tau Kok.[49] The *kaifong* leaders made donations to support district activities, loaned their office space for the work of *kaifong* associations, and lend their secretaries for managerial district work. They gradually became community elites and, most importantly, the "intermediaries" between the government and the public.[50] However, in light of the influx of many refugees from mainland China, *kaifong* associations were under the close supervision of the British colonial government, which was anxious of the likelihood that these associations could become the target of infiltration by the local triads and the undercover political agents from the CCP and the KMT. The *kaifong* associations were expected to be the loyal implementation agents of the colonial rulers, including their assistance of the government in conducting the Road Safety, Keep Our City Clean and anti-epidemic campaigns. During the 1967 riots in Hong Kong, *kaifong* associations were mobilized by the colonial government to denounce the activities of the local Maoists and their terrorist actions of planting bombs on the streets. As such, *kaifong* associations played a crucial role in providing support of and buttressing the legitimacy of the British colonial government in Hong Kong.

The political conservatism of *kaifong* associations in Hong Kong under British rule was understandable. During the 1967 riots, the Heung Yee Kuk office in Tai Po was attacked by left-wing Maoists armed with home-made bombs. The *kaifongs* therefore tended to be resistant to the local Maoists, hoping that the British colonial government could and would restore social and political stability. In the early 1980s, as we will discuss later, the introduction of DB elections provided a channel of political participation of *kaifong* leaders. Yet, the rapid emergence of political groups and parties in the late 1980s, especially after China's Tiananmen incident in June 1989, meant that *kaifong* leaders who had political ambitions and aspirations of climbing up the political ladder had to be better organized. As such, the development of electoral politics in Hong Kong in the 1980s and 1990s was not matched by the self-strengthening movement on the part of *kaifong* associations, which remained largely unorganized, politically marginal, and parochially active in their own district affairs. After July 1, 1997, however, the pro-Beijing political groups, such as the Democratic Alliance for the Betterment and Progress of Hong Kong (DAB), have developed their vested interest in penetrating some *kaifong* associations and acquiring their support in election campaigns.[51] However, the pro-democracy forces, as this book will examine, have remained less interested in the political infiltration into *kaifong* associations because they tend to emphasize the use of liberal democratic ideology in electioneering rather than the cultivation of patron-client networks through the capture of *kaifong* associations. Hence, *kaifong* associations have since the 1990s been declining in their political functions, especially their original role of bridging the communication gap between the colonial rulers and the ruled. Their role has been increasingly usurped by other political actors, including political parties and political interest groups. At present, they are delivering some social services to the residents, including elderly and medical services, but their role has been substantially curbed after the rise of electoral politics.

Area Committees, Owners Corporations, and Mutual Aid Committees

To strengthen the communication between the rulers and the ruled, the British colonial administration introduced the Area Committees (ACs), Owners Corporations (OCs), and Mutual Aid Committees (MACs), which could also be seen as indispensable tools of the Hong Kong government to buttress its colonial regime legitimacy. The ACs were formed in various districts in 1972, primarily to promote citizen participation in the Keep Hong Kong Clean Campaign and the Fight Violent Crime Campaign. These campaigns were part and parcel of the colonial government policy of fostering a sense of Hong Kong belonging among the psyche of the Hong Kong people, especially after the 1966 and 1967 Maoist riots, which were a spillover effect from the Cultural Revolution of the PRC. These ACs could also give advice and provide assistance to the colonial government in the implementation of various initiatives, for Hong Kong underwent a rapid process of urbanization starting from the 1970s. ACs were composed of community leaders appointed by the government, which could groom and encourage them to act as an intermediary between the rulers and the ruled. In a sense, ACs were like *kaifong* associations in being the linkages between the government and ordinary citizens, narrowing the elite-mass gap and enhancing their communication and mutual understandings. Indeed, ACs were pro-government bodies set up by the colonial authorities, while *kaifong* associations were established by ordinary citizens as district-based interest groups that could lobby the government and provide their feedback to government policies.

If urbanization usually leads to the emergence of social groups, as Seymour Martin Lipset and Samuel Huntington had long discussed,[52] the case of Hong Kong under the British rule demonstrated that while interest groups like *kaifong* associations sprung up under the guidance and support of the colonial administration, other pro-government housing groups also emerged, namely OCs and MACs. From 1970 onwards, the colonial government encouraged residents to form their OCs in private buildings and public housing estates. The government justified the formation of OCs in the following way:

> Managing and maintaining a building is no simple task. It involves a myriad of matters, ranging from minor ones like cleansing and refuse clearing in the common parts of the building to major issues such as appointment of property management company and commission of major maintenance works. All these involve a decision-making process. For large residential estates with hundreds or even thousands of owners, it is difficult, if not impossible, to obtain unanimous consent from all the owners on each and every single building management matter. It is therefore necessary to put in place a mechanism to facilitate collective decision-making of owners on building management matters.[53]

When an OC was formed, the rights, powers, privileges, and duties of the owners of a building concerned was exercised and performed by the OC. The owners' liabilities pertinent to the building are enforceable against the OC, which is required to properly manage and maintain the building. As such, the OCs are legal entities that represent the owners of a building and that should manage the building orderly. The Code of Practices of OCs are publicly accessible and available in District Offices, which were set up by the government in 1968 to bridge the communication gap between the colonial rulers and rulers, as will be discussed in detail below. A general meeting of the OC can pass a resolution to control, manage, and administer the common parts of the building, and to renovate, decorate, and improve them.[54] By the end of March 2020, there were 11,043 OCs in the HKSAR in which 8,947 were established with the assistance of District Offices.[55]

On the other hand, MACs were voluntary bodies formed by the residents of buildings in 1973. Originally, they were promoted in private multi-storey buildings, but later they were expanded to embrace public housing estates and industrial buildings.[56] By the end of April 2020, there were 1,679 MACs in the HKSAR. As with the OCs, MACs could promote a sense of community among residents, provide mutual help, strengthen the civic responsibility among members, promote better security in their living and working environment, and achieve better management of the buildings concerned. Together with the ACs which were much larger in the coverage of district issues in their scope, the OCs and MACs constituted the grassroots-level housing organizations through which the colonial authorities could govern an increasingly urbanized and populated Hong Kong in the 1980s in an effective manner. These ACs, OCs, and MACs can be seen as the legacies of the British colonial administration as they have been operating as the essential district-level bodies in the present HKSAR, except for the MACs, which according to the government's plan in early 2022, would be terminated in phases (the plan of dissolving MACs will be discussed in Chapter Eight).

However, as with the *kaifong* associations, OCs and MACs have since July 1, 1997 become the vehicles and targets of infiltration by political groups and parties. The introduction of the direct elections held for the DBs in 1982 and later the LegCo in Hong Kong under British rule led to the victory of many democrats. The pro-government and pro-Beijing camp did well in district-level elections, where the number of candidates and politicians remained relatively insufficient and where the political vacuum allowed them to establish their footholds in some districts. Nevertheless, the pro-Beijing forces suffered heavy defeat in the LegCo direct elections in 1991. Gradually, pro-Beijing forces realized the political significance of penetrating and capturing some of the OCs and MACs. This will allow their candidates to campaign more easily in different kinds of buildings, to consolidate their constituency services to the voters, and to strengthen the PRC's united front work in Hong Kong before and beyond July 1, 1997. Starting from early 2000s, the trends of politicizing MACs have become increasingly prominent, with the pro-Beijing Democratic Alliance for the Betterment and Progress of Hong Kong (DAB) infiltrating and capturing some of them to campaign and grasp votes during elections.[57] Still, the PRC authorities manipulated the electoral system in their 60-member Provisional Legislative Council (PLC), which was set up by the PRC government to counter Governor Chris Patten's political reform in December 1996. The PLC manipulated the electoral method for the LegCo by adopting a proportional representation system in LegCo's direct elections after July 1, 1997. While the proportional representation system tended to favor the smaller and weaker groups, notably the DAB just shortly before and after 1997, the manipulation of electoral system by the PRC-appointed PLC could be easily seen.[58] Objectively speaking, the victory of the democrats in the local legislative elections from 1991 to 1996 was an outcome of the democratization package implemented by the British colonial rulers, especially Patten who sought to maximize the extent of democratic reforms in the final years of the British rule. Patten's ideological affinity with the local democrats actually and unintentionally hurt the latter, who after the sovereignty transfer in July 1997 have increasingly encountered political obstacles in their fight for democratization in the HKSAR.

It is noteworthy that, from the perspective of crime control, the establishment of ACs, OCs and MACs did help the British colonial government maintain law and order in different districts. Similar to the traditional Chinese *baojia* system in which a certain number of households could group together to supervise law and order in their living environment, the networks of ACs, OCs and MACs could provide the British colonial rulers with their eyes and ears in the development of district administration. If the British colonialists tried to prevent the communists from penetrating into various districts in Hong Kong, these district-level bodies constituted the double functions of guarding against communist infiltration and monitoring criminal activities at the grassroots level. In fact, when MACs were formed in the 1970s, many of their members were armed with clubs at nights and they patrolled along their residential buildings, acting like members of the obsolete District Watch Force which were converted into District Watch Committee in 1891 by the British colonial rulers.[59]

The Establishment of the City District Officer Scheme after the 1966–1967 Riots

One of the two most important district-level bodies introduced by the British colonial administration was arguably the City District Officer Scheme in 1968, in addition to the introduction of DBs in 1982 that will be examined later. The 1966 and 1967 riots plunged the Hong Kong government into a crisis of governance. At that time, the local leftists planted home-made bombs to attack citizens and to protest against the British colonial administration. Although the riot was eventually pacified, Governor David Trench decided in October 1967 that the Hong Kong Week should be held to enhance the local sense of belonging of the Hong Kong people. From October 30 to November 5, the Hong Kong Trade Development Council held the Hong Kong week, promoting the Hong Kong-made products to both local citizens and foreign businesspeople.[60] Underlying these activities was an attempt by the colonial government to engender a sense of Hong Kong identity so that the anti-colonial and anti-British sentiment could be diluted and weakened.

Apart from the Hong Kong Week, the colonial government set up the City District Officer scheme in April 1968. For a long period of time, the District Office (理民府) was the key channel of communication between the people and government departments. Originally, the job of interacting with the Chinese during the early years of British rule was headed by the Registrar General, who was also called the "protector of Chinese." In 1913, the department was renamed as the Secretariat for Chinese Affairs. After the 1967 riots, the colonial government introduced the City District Officers (民政主任) as the first sign of outreach to interact with the ordinary people in Hong Kong's society. The idea was to replicate the New Territories District Officer system in the urban areas, where City District Offices (CDOs) were established and where City District Officers interacted with ordinary citizen regularly.

The City District Officer scheme had a similar political objective. It involved what Ambrose King has called "the administrative absorption of politics," utilizing administrative measures to stabilize the political system.[61] According to the government plan, ten CDOs were established in the metropolitan areas. By the end of 1968, five of them were set up in different districts: Eastern, Western, Wan Chai, Mong Kok, and Yau Ma Tei. The other five were opened by the end of 1969, including the Central, Kwun Tong, Sham Shui Po, Kowloon City, and Wong Tai Sin districts. The CDO scheme was under the supervision of the Secretariat of the Home Affairs. Under the Secretary for Home Affairs were two deputies: one responsible for traditional duties such as newspaper registration, trust fund, liquor licensing, and tenancy matters; and the other in charge of the CDO. The Secretary for Home Affairs supervised two City District Commissioners, one responsible for four CDOs on the Hong Kong Island, and the other for the six CDOs in Kowloon.[62] Ambrose King added that,

> "the government's diagnosis of the riots of 1966 and 1967 reflects a belief that the basic problem has not in the colonial system as such but in a metropolitan government structure that is too big to manage and too complex and bureaucratized to be intelligible to the ordinary people. Therefore, what the CDO Scheme tried to accomplish was a decentralization and a de-bureaucratization of the metropolitan government."[63]

Furthermore, King argued that the CDO "as the political agent at the district level, is not aiming at political mobilization of the populace: in fact, it is trying to depoliticize the political process."[64] Hence, CDOs aimed at achieving social stability rather than social change, as well as absorbing and recruiting the most active local leaders and youth into the organization of community-based cultural and recreational activities.[65] Through this "administrative absorption," the "community consciousness or local identification has often been generated; a great deal of energy has been absorbed and channeled into non-political activities; and above all, social solidarity has been enhanced."[66]

The CDO scheme had multiple objectives. According to the government's official report, the aim of the CDO was to "superimpose on the functionally oriented executive departments a geographically based advisory and coordinating organization in order to strengthen the ability of the Government to give everyone a fair hearing and a fair share of the services which the community can afford."[67] In other words, the CDO was the first among equals in various government departments, playing the dual roles of giving advice and coordinating their work at the district level, and bridging the communication gap with the community. As time passed, the CDO scheme, according to Norman Miners, could achieve the following purposes: (1) reporting the opinions and attitudes of the public to the government; (2) explaining government policy; (3) monitoring and coordinating the work of departments in the district; (4) drawing the attention of higher authorities to local needs and articulating the demands of local residents; (5) promoting and supporting community-based organizations; (6) providing public services for individuals; (7) rendering relief in emergency circumstances; and (8) involving and mobilizing the public in community-oriented campaigns and programs sponsored by the government.[68] Hence, the CDO scheme could foster social cohesion, enhance the sense of belonging and community among the people of Hong Kong, and consolidate the colonial regime's legitimacy.

The CDO scheme was later bolstered both administratively and politically by the establishment of the OCs and MACs. Both OCs and MACs were responsible for the better management of buildings in private buildings, public housing estates, and industrial buildings as discussed before. These OCs and MACs could be seen as the auxiliary, administrative, and political arms of the CDO scheme. In other words, the tentacles of the

CDOs could reach out to the residents at the grassroots level through the OCs, MACs and ACs. Nicholas Thomas sharply identified that the MACs could "bolster the reach of the CDOs."[69] Ian Scott believed that the CDO scheme was an obvious attempt by the British colonial administration to strengthen its legitimacy after the outbreak of the 1966–67 riots.[70] To borrow from Ambrose King's term, all these CDOs, ACs, OCs, and MACs were indispensable parts of the British colonial machinery to conduct "administrative absorption of politics" so that its regime legitimacy could be consolidated after the 1966–67 riots launched by the local Maoists severely plunged the colonial administration into a crisis of legitimacy.

In the final analysis, the British colonial administration paid special attention to the role of City District Officers, who could be regarded as their eyes and ears collecting intelligence in different districts, overseeing government policy implementation at the grassroots level, and acting as the necessary glue that could consolidate the elite-mass gap in the colonial political system. Dennis Bray revealed that the quality of the British expatriates who were appointed as City District Officers was high, for they were experienced, senior, and among "the best" in the expatriate circle.[71] These City District Officers went out to contact all social groups in the districts.[72] One Officer, David Li, was contacted by the "non-commissioned police detective" (*taam cheung*) before he called on the *taam cheung*.[73] Li wrote a report on illegal gambling, which was found to be common in Hong Kong during the 1950s and 1960s, but it was "very largely ignored."[74] Illegal gambling persisted because of syndicate corruption involving the police — a phenomenon that began to become a target of elimination by the Independent Commission Against Corruption (ICAC) established in February 1974.

The Introduction of District Boards: From Green Paper to White Paper

In June 1980, the Hong Kong government published a Green Paper titled "A Pattern of District Administration in Hong Kong," inviting public views on the proposed District Administration Scheme (DAS). After consultation with the public, a White Paper on district administrative reform was published in January 1981, emphasizing that DBs would be established in each district "to provide a means of obtaining better local advice and participation."[75] These Boards would be developed from the City District Committees in the urban areas and from District Advisory Boards (DABs) in the New Territories. They would be composed of unofficial members who represented the people in the district and the key official members of the District Management Committee (DMC) of that district. In the New Territories, the DABs that had already existed would be retitled as DBs. In the urban areas, DBs would be established in all districts by March 1982. Specifically, DBs would be of advisory nature with the following terms of reference:

> "(a) to advise on matters affecting the well-being of people living in the district and those working there;
>
> (b) to advise on the prevision and use public facilities and services within the district;
>
> (c) to advise on the adequacy and priorities of government programs for the district;
>
> (d) to advise on the use of public funds allocated to the district for local public works and community activities;
>
> (e) to undertake, where funds are made available for the purpose, minor environmental improvements within the district; and
>
> (f) to undertake, where funds are made available for the purpose, the promotion of recreational and cultural activities within the district."[76]

In terms of the composition of DBs, they would be composed of appointed unofficial members, Urban Council (UrbCo) members or Rural Committee Chairpersons, and official members (civil servants) who would be the key members of the DMC in the district concerned. In the urban areas, the appointed members would include the Chairperson of the ACs in the district and an approximately equivalent number of other members of the public appointed by the government. Moreover, members of the UrbCo, whose origin was the Sanitary Board which established in 1883 and was renamed as a municipal body dealing with arts, culture, recreation, and sports, would have seats provided for them in DBs. This idea was to link the UrbCo with DBs together as they had overlapping functions, but UrbCo was financially autonomous because parts of the property tax known as rates which were levied on the domestic and commercial properties from 1845 went to the UrbCo (the reconstitution of the Urban Council in 1973 and later to the Regional Council or RegCo in 1986 when it was established as the municipal council in the New Territories). The HKSAR government in 1999 proposed to abolish both the UrbCo and RegCo on the grounds of achieving better delivery of public services through administrative centralization after the outbreak of the bird flu in 1997. Hence, from 2000 onwards, the abolition of UrbCo and RegCo meant that the whole amount of rates has returned to the government's treasury. When DBs were established in 1982, UrbCo members were asked to decide among themselves on which DB they should sit.[77] In the New Territories, the appointed members of DBs would be the Chairpersons of Rural Committees who with a commensurate number of members of the public appointed to the DBs would form the official membership.[78] In all DBs, unofficial majority existed until 1982 when constituency-based and directly elected elements would be introduced. Hence, the British colonial administration used elections to change the composition of DBs from unofficial majority to having some directly elected members. The idea was to democratize DBs at the local level in order to achieve better public delivery of services and enhance governmental accountability.

There were District Management Committees (DMCs) in all DBs, both chaired by District Officers, to coordinate the efforts of government departments in their district work. After their establishment in 1982, DBs played an essential advisory role on district matters and sometimes on territory-wide issues. Apart from reflecting public opinions and promoting community-building efforts at the grassroots level, they were expected to play a crucial role in delivering public services at district level effectively, and to act as an additional intermediary between the colonial government and ordinary citizens. These DBs were later renamed as DCs in 2000. Originally, District Officers presided over DBs when there was no elected element. As democratization of DBs proceeded, the role of District Officers was reduced. In 1984, following a review of the structure and composition of DBs, the colonial government decided that, starting from the second term in 1985, government officials would no longer serve on DBs as members. District Officers would cease to be the Chairpersons of DBs; members would elect the Chairpersons from among themselves and the number of elected members was increased simultaneously. As such, the British colonial administration adopted a democratizing approach to coping with district administrative reforms.

In October 1980, after consulting public opinion on the Green Paper, Governor Murry MacLehose said in the LegCo that he was encouraged with the feedback from the members of the public. He said:

> I note that while there is much support for the principle of adding an elected element, there is also support for the retention of appointed membership as well. There appears to be a very large measure of support for elections on a constituency rather than a territory-wide basis, and indeed it does not seem possible to achieve the local focus aimed at by any other means. Some advocate retaining the ten City District Offices rather than amalgamating two districts on each side of the harbor. 21 has generally been supported as the right age for voting rights though some have argued for both higher and lower ages, and some also for educational qualifications. But I note a wide band of opinion which considers three years' residence too little in the present circumstances of Hong Kong. Some have argued that there should be more stringent qualifications for candidates than voters. Honorable Members will also have noted counter proposals for a two-tier electoral system in the Urban Area which would retain the existing territory-wide Urban Council elections by which sitting members have been elected but would be augmented by separate elections for District Boards with the candidates with the most votes having a seat on the Urban Council.[79]

He remarked that the first step would be the establishment of the District Management Committee (DMC) in Wong Tai Sin and a DB in Kwun Tong where there was already a Management Committee, followed by the introduction of all DBs and DMCs in all districts. MacLehose added:

> Hong Kong is now too large, too complex, and geographically too spread out for the old system of centralized Government to continue to be the complete answer; it must be supplemented with more strength at district level. Similarly though there are good arrangements that work well for unofficial advice and participation at central Government level, they are not matched in the most effective way at District level and for this there is now an obvious and growing need.[80]

In the minds of MacLehose, DBs had to be set up not only as a means to respond to the increasing speed and scope of urbanization in Hong Kong, but also as a tool for the colonial government to "close" the communication gap between the administration and the ordinary people.[81]

In January 1981, the colonial government decided to forge ahead with the plan of introducing DB elections. Governor MacLehose said in the LegCo:

> There will be an unofficial majority on the District Boards. The Boards will have a membership of some 25–30 of which approximately one quarter will be officials with the remainder divided more or less equally between elected and nominated or appointed members. They will in due course have a Chairman elected by the Board members. Given the emphasis on district administration and the fact that District Boards may bring matters to the attention of the Director of Home Affairs, the Secretary for Home Affairs, the Secretary for the New Territories, and Heads of Departments, all of whom will no doubt report matters of significance to you and to me, Sir, I have confidence that in the provision of public services and the implementation of Government programs at the district level great weight will be given to the advice from the District Boards.[82]

MacLehose concluded that DBs could create "a partnership between responsive government and responsible citizenship," thereby affirming the intentions of the British colonial administration as not only improving the better delivery of public services through some degree of administrative decentralization on the one hand, but also encouraging citizen participation in district affairs on the other.[83]

While the June 1980 Green Paper suggested that all persons over the age of 21 with at least three years of residence in Hong Kong should be eligible to register to vote, this proposal was "generally supported" according to the 1981 White Paper.[84] The Green Paper's proposal was made on the basis of the existing franchise for the elections held for the UrbCo, which was reconstituted in 1973 with a composition of 12 elected members and 12 members appointed by the Governor. As mentioned before, the UrbCo had control of its own finances with its main revenue being derived from its share of the yield from the rates in the urban areas. The UrbCo had the responsibility of dealing with not only environmental public health, recreation and amenities, and provision of cultural services, but also liquor licensing and the licensing of places of public entertainment.[85] During the public consultation on the voting age for DB elections, some members of the public suggested that the minimum voting age should be lowered to 18 years, or raised to 25 or even 30 years.[86] Such feedback reflected the diverse public opinion, including some conservative views. Yet, the 1981 White Paper said:

> The Government is impressed with the force of these arguments and will propose that a person who has been ordinarily resident in Hong Kong for 7 or more years before the closing date for registration should be eligible to become a registered voter … Government considers that foreign nationals who meet the age and residence requirements should not be excluded from registering and voting. First, this would be a retrograde step in that the existing UrbCo franchise does not exclude them. Secondly, and in Government's view this is a more important consideration, Hong Kong is a very open society and foreign nationals have made and will no doubt continue to make an important contribution to the well-being and development of the community.[87]

Views of Legislative Council Members

In February 1981, some LegCo members expressed different views toward the proposed DBs albeit they all supported the idea of administrative decentralization and the enhancement of government effectiveness in its delivery of public services. Wong Lam believed that if DBs and the central administration held different views on policy issues, then the Chief Secretary who represented the government should make the final decision. Charles Yeung argued that the authority of DBs would not be strong and that they would need the support from the Secretary for the New Territories, the Secretary for Home Affairs, and the Director of Home Affairs. Ho Kam-fai asserted that while citizen participation was a commitment made by the colonial government, citizens would likely perceive a greater sense of belonging in the community because the DBs and DMCs would narrow the elite-mass gap. So Kwong-wing emphasized that prudence should be given in the process of selecting the appointed members into DBs, and that the colonial government did not really reveal the costs of establishing all the DBs. Interestingly, Hu Fa-kuang pointed to the importance of the quality of members appointed by the government, while there would be no guarantee on the quality of elected members. He added that because elected members would sacrifice their time and energy to deal with constituency issues, the government should provide allowances to them. With the benefit

Table 1.6: Remarks of Appointed Legislative Council Members on District Administration

Name	Remarks on District Board and District Administration
Wong Lam	"It is possible that because of different viewpoints or sense of priorities, a District Board and the Central Government may hold divergent views on certain matters. Under such circumstances, the District Board may think it would be more appropriate to bring the matter direct to the attention of the Chief Secretary, who represents the Central Government."
Charles Yeung Siu-cho	"The inherent weakness and danger in the district administrative system set out in the White Paper is found in the missing links in the chain of direct authority. The proposition envisaged in the White Paper is that when local aspirations are not met, the District Board will look to the Secretary for the New Territories, the Secretary for Home Affairs or the Director of Home Affairs to champion their cause."
Dr. Ho Kam-fai	"It confirms the Government's convictions and commitment towards greater participation by the inhabitants of each district and towards better co-ordination of, and responsiveness by, the administration … With the establishment of the District Management Committees and the District Boards, local residents will feel that the distance between them and the Central Government is shortened and they will realize that the Central Government is more comprehensible and accessible on the one hand, and is receptive and responsive to public views and requests on the other. They will gradually come to believe that they are, to a greater extent than ever before, the architects of their environment and lives. In the more distant future, out of pride, sense of achievement and involvement, the residents will develop an identification with, and subsequently a feeling of belonging to, the community in which they live. This civic spirit will give impetus to greater local involvement, leading to the development of a more close-knit, a more mutually caring community."
So Kwok-wing	"Prudence must be exercised in the choice of leaders in the district, be it by election or appointment, because district administration affects the well-being of residents, as well as public facilities and services for them. Prudence in this respect will ensure the proper conduct of affairs and avoid abuses as much as possible. Residents of all districts must play an intelligent and courageous role if they want to make the scheme a success. The ultimate aims of the White Paper are to establish a better society for Hong Kong and to engender a sense of belonging in the people through their participation in local affairs. Hence, implementation of the proposals in the White Paper will inevitably involve a tremendous outlay of both manpower and money. Manpower has indirectly been accounted for in the White Paper; but how much money is required to carry out the scheme is not disclosed by the Government.
Hu Fa-Kuang	"Government has assured us of how genuinely keen it is to involve the public in district affairs and that the District Boards will be successful. The Government has control in selecting and appointing persons of high quality and ability to serve on the District Boards as official and unofficial members, but it has no control over the quality of elected members. The voters can only choose from a list of candidates who seek election to the District Board of his choice. Any member of a District Board has to spend considerable time in attending meetings, discussions, visits and other related activities if the member is to play a useful and valuable role in the function of the District Boards, but time spent would mean financial or career sacrifice on the part of the member as he would have to spend less time on his career or employment and might face objection from his family or employer. These considerations could discourage many suitable potential candidates, especially among the younger generation, from coming forward and the final choice from the list of candidates might be limited. To overcome this possible problem, I would suggest that a reasonable allowance should be made available to the elected member of District Boards so that they would not suffer financially because of their contribution to community involvement. This arrangement might encourage more good candidates to come forward to seek election."

Source: "Official Report of Proceedings, Wednesday, 11 February 1981," Hong Kong Legislative Council, in https://www.legco.gov.hk/yr80-81/english/lc_sitg/hansard/h810211.pdf, access date: June 5, 2020.

of hindsight, these LegCo members were quite far-sighted in anticipating some of the problems encountered by DBs and DB members, especially the limited authority of DBs and the elected members' quality that would be beyond the control of the government.

Some of the views of LegCo members, like Wong Lam and Charles Yeung, were addressed by the colonial government. The 1981 White Paper stated that "should a District Board consider that the response to its advice from the DMC is unsatisfactory the Boards' recourse will be to bring the matter to the attention either of the head of department concerned, or of the Director of Home Affairs, the Secretary for Home Affairs or the Secretary for the New Territories."[88] Trying to ensure that the views of DB members were taken seriously, the colonial administration used the DMC as a tool for the City District Officer and other government officials to interact with elected and appointed DB members. The 1981 White Paper also said:

> As in the case of District Management Committees, the level of departmental representatives serving on the District Boards will be important. Government will therefore ensure that officers with suitable experience and authority are appointed to the District Boards, so that they can speak authoritatively and act effectively in respect of all departmental responsibilities affecting the district.[89]

Administratively, the design of having government officials attending the meetings of both DBs and DMCs was a testimony to the intention of the colonial administration to enhance the communication between bureaucrats and the elected and appointed members of DBs. In a sense, bureaucratic accountability was expected to be enhanced, while public accountability would also be slightly improved by introducing some elected elements to DBs.

Interpretations on Why District Boards were Introduced

An important interpretation of why DBs were introduced in 1982 was that, after Governor MacLehose's trip to Beijing in March 1979, when the PRC leader Deng Xiaoping told them that China would resume its sovereignty over Hong Kong by July 1, 1997 but that they would just bring back the message of putting the hearts of investors at ease to the people of Hong

Kong, the British government started to democratize Hong Kong through the DB scheme.[90] Sir Yuet-keung Kan, who accompanied MacLehose's visit to Beijing in March 1979, was reportedly aware of the PRC government's decision on Hong Kong's future. Kan returned to Hong Kong and later resigned from the top policy-making ExCo as a member in March 1980. He was worried about Hong Kong's future, according to a news report.[91] Kan, however, told one of the authors of this book that "Deng Xiaoping made no such statement [of resuming Chinese sovereignty over Hong Kong] to the former Governor, Sir Murray MacLehose."[92] MacLehose also denied that he was told about the PRC government's decision, saying that,

> Throughout my time as Governor, and for two years afterwards and many years before, the position of the Chinese Government on Hong Kong was that it was Chinese territory and would be recovered but with the time left very vague. I therefore did not know in 1979 that China would recover Hong Kong in 1997. There was therefore absolutely no connection between District Board elections and the possibility of British withdrawal. Their object, as I have said, was improved participation.[93]

MacLehose might not be aware of China's deadline of resuming its sovereignty over Hong Kong, but he was keen to introduce DBs as a means of improving citizen participation and enhancing the communication gap between the British colonial administration and ordinary citizens — a typical governing philosophy of his predecessors in Hong Kong.

The second interpretation was that Sir Jack Cater was a key initiator of DB scheme. According to former ExCo member Sir Roger Lobo, when the idea of forming DBs was raised by Governor MacLehose and Chief Secretary Jack Cater, "there were some doubts as to how they were going to work."[94] Lobo said:

> I feel that members of the Urban Council felt more strongly because districts take a lot of Urban Council's sphere of operation. Some members of Legislative Council's felt that everybody's position was being eroded on changed. They felt that District Boards would take over their positions. But subsequently, District Boards went on very well… Some conservative-minded people have preoccupation that District Boards would get the support of Taiwan and Mainland China and these elected representatives would use District Boards as arenas to fight among themselves.[95]

Lobo remarked that Jack Cater was "a promoter of DBs" and that he worked very hard without worrying about the consequences. Lobo added that the idea of forming DBs had to be approved by the British Foreign Office. According to Lobo, China did not oppose DB elections in 1982 when Hong Kong's future was not yet formally discussed. After all, DBs were of advisory nature and their democratization did not alarm the PRC authorities.

When asked whether DBs were formed by the colonial government to absorb pressure groups, which were viewed by the British-initiated Standing Committee on Pressure Groups (SCOPG) as politically "undesirable," Lobo said:

> From 1979 to 1993, this was the period of having the SCOPG, but Hong Kong wanted to maintain a greater degree of stability. Also, there were a lot of demonstrations during this period. Governor MacLehose allowed these protests and many pressure groups emerged. So the SCOPG was set up to make sure that they were not subversive, that their idea of democratization was logical and justified rather than being troublemakers. After Margaret Thatcher visited China in 1982, Sino-British relations became more nervous over Hong Kong's future. The colonial authorities assessed that it was not necessary for SCOPG to exist. So, it was dissolved in 1983.[96]

In 1978, the British colonial government set up the SCOPG, which according to a British magazine in 1980 was a "new and secret body … coordinating government surveillance of any protest or campaigning group and … mounting counter-attacks."[97] The SCOPG was described negatively as having sinister motives, but it was not surprising for a colonial government to establish a committee to monitor the activities of interest groups, especially if the British colonial rulers in Hong Kong had a track record of worrying about the infiltration of the mainland communists and the contests between the underground CCP and the Nationalist Party in the territory.[98]

During an interview with the former Chief Secretary, Jack Cater, on December 7, 1989, he revealed that "we [the British administrators] had good opportunity to have done more from 1978 onwards."[99] Cater continued:

> We have misread the situation. China had an open-door policy. We developed a new attitude toward China, although there was no intention on the part of mainland Chinese to have democracy in China. The PRC

had no political reformist, but they did have economic reformists. In 1978, I hoped to resurrect the ideas of district elections and to push ahead with an elected body in Hong Kong.[100]

Cater also believed that the Hong Kong people were "mature" enough to enjoy elections at the district level. He remarked:

> I came to Hong Kong in 1945 and had lots of interactions with people at the grassroots level. I set up two vegetables markets and fisherman cooperative system. I was told by old government servants and senior Chinese legislators that Chinese knew nothing about democracy, and that Chinese could not cooperate. That was nonsense. The Hong Kong people are used to having elections in all walks of life. We have village elections to select village representatives. All these go through parts of the Hong Kong society. I cannot accept a story saying that the Hong Kong people cannot have democracy. Even student unions have their leaders elected. Many Africans cannot read and write, but they can vote in elections. I believe that it is a great insult to the Hong Kong people if we say that they are not mature enough. Our living standard is as good as that of the British.[101]

Therefore, Cater and Governor MacLehose put forward the proposal of introducing DB elections into Hong Kong. Cater added that it was "opposed by some Legislative Council and Executive Council members, who said the idea was bad for Hong Kong and who claimed the Hong Kong people were not experienced in elections."

As with MacLehose, Cater asserted that there was "absolutely no connection" between the introduction of DB elections and the question of 1997 for Hong Kong. He said:

> In 1979, some Hong Kong people were concerned about the lease for the New Territories in 1997. I was the Acting Governor in 1979 when Governor MacLehose talked to the PRC leaders in Beijing about the lease for the New Territories. But there was no result and Deng Xiaoping asked the British to tell Hong Kong investors to put their hearts at ease.[102]

When asked whether he was an "instigator" in the plan of introducing DBs, Cater admitted so and he added:

> District Board elections represented a Broad attempt at introducing universal suffrage. We should float the idea of allowing people who reach

> the age of 18 years old to vote. But some members of the public say that the
> eligible voters should be 21 years old. So we settle the eligibility to 21 years
> old. It was always my hope, because of opposition, that this introduction
> of District Board election has to be seen as a part of a long-term strategy
> to introduce democracy in Hong Kong. This was certainly in my mind.[103]

Cater said that he went to the British Foreign Office with the idea of introducing DB elections. The Foreign Office officials were "very positive," including the Minister of Hong Kong Affairs Peter Blaker. Cater's idea also got the "strong support from the Labor government." Cater did not think that DB elections were designed to absorb pressure groups, but the boards would take into consideration their views of expression. Unlike the SCOPG which viewed pressure groups as "subversive," Cater asserted that he was "fond of" them. Defending the SCOPG, Cater said that this committee's objective was "not sinister," and that "there were doubts in the minds of City District Officers on how to deal with these people." As such, the SCOPG "looked at the aspirations of these people." He said that interest groups monitored by the SCOPG, such as the Hong Kong Observers and the Christian Industrial Committee, were "interested in everyday affairs." But the colonial government wanted to "find out more about them."

With the benefit of hindsight, DB elections were attributable more to the British colonial government's incremental step of improving the delivery of public services than to the intention of triggering democratization to prepare for the British withdrawal from Hong Kong. As early as October 1977, Governor MacLehose announced that DABs—the precursor of DBs—would be set up in all districts.[104] Each of these DABs would be chaired by a District Officer and would embrace officials working in the district from various departments, such as the Urban Services Officer, the District Education Officer, the Recreational and Sports Office, the Community and Youth Officer from the Social Welfare Department, and the Public Works Department's Project Manager.[105] The names of the members of these DABs were then published in the Government Gazette in November 1977—almost sixteen months before MacLehose's visit to Beijing in March 1979.[106] At the time when the idea of DABs was floated, the HYK did not welcome it as its members regarded it as lacking consultation and saw DABs as curbing the HYK's power and influence.[107] Hence, judging from the timing of the introduction of DABs—the predecessor of DBs—in October 1977, it was crystal clear that MacLehose and other British colonial officials who raised and supported the idea of setting up DBs had not known about the PRC's plan of taking back the sovereignty of Hong Kong on July 1, 1997.

Evolution of District Administration from 1990 to 1997

A critic of the DB scheme, sociologist Lau Siu-kai, argued in the early 1980s that while local administrative reform aimed at depoliticizing Hong Kong, serving as "mediating institutions" between colonial rulers and ordinary citizens, and filling "the political vacuum resulting from the large-scale internal movements of people and the establishment of new urban areas," it was constrained by the lack of DB's "capacity to cultivate independent sources of revenue and the sole authority to make decisions impacting on a locality."[108] Objectively speaking, when the British colonial administration introduced DBs in 1982, it did not really toy with the idea of elevating the status of DBs to the level of Urban Council. Instead, the institutional design was to connect the DBs with UrbCo, and later with RegCo, so that a three-tiered level of government would be established.

The British colonial government adopted an incremental approach to reforming district administration in Hong Kong. In 1984, the colonial government suggested that the number of elected members on DBs would be increased, and that a new partly elected Regional Council (RegCo) would be established in the New Territories in 1986. As mentioned before, the RegCo was the rural extension of the UrbCo from urban areas to the New Territories. The new RegCo would be composed of 12 directly elected members, nine representatives elected from the New Territories DBs, three ex-officio representatives from the rural advisory Heung Yee Kuk, and 12 appointed members.[109] In 1985, a provisional RegCo would be set up with the same membership as outlined above, except for the 12 directly elected members who would be returned in the 1986 RegCo election. Institutionally, the British planned to use DBs, UrbCo and RegCo as institutions working side by side so that some degree of representative government would be established at the district level. As the 1984 Green Paper alluded,

> The system by which members of the UrbCo and DBs are elected is based
> on an electoral roll on which all residents aged 21 or above who have
> been in Hong Kong for seven or more years are eligible to be registered.
> Out of an estimated total potential electorate of 2.7 million, there are at

present approximately 900,000 registered electors. An intensive campaign to encourage many more eligible persons to register as electors will be conducted in the near future.[110]

In 1984, the Green Paper on the further development of representative government revealed the incremental approach to dealing with democratization of Hong Kong by using the district-level DBs, UrbCo and RegCo to enhance the representativeness of the LegCo. The Green Paper said:

> The main question with regard to the Legislative Council concerns its composition and the methods to be adopted for the selection and appointment of its members … [I]t is considered that the present system whereby all the Unofficial members of the Legislative Council are selected and appointed by the Governor should be developed progressively to provide for a substantial number of the members to be elected indirectly — (a) by an electoral college of Urban Council, new Regional Council and District Board members; and (b) by functional groups, or "constituencies." It is also considered that a number of appointed Unofficial members should be retained on the Council for the time being, in order to ensure continuity and stability; and a number of Official members should also be retained on the Council to maintain a link between the Council and the Administration, although there would be a gradual reduction in the number.[111]

Clearly, the British colonial administration decided to link the LegCo reform with the district-level DBs, UrbCo and the new RegCo. By using a new electoral college, the three tiers of political institutions — LegCo at the territorial level, UrbCo and RegCo at the middle level, and DBs at the grassroots level — would be merged together to enhance the representativeness of LegCo on the one hand and to provide some degree of political mobility upward for the members of UrbCo, RegCo and DBs on the other.

Democratization of Hong Kong from July 1984 to 1988, a period just simultaneously and immediately after the signing of the Sino-British Joint Declaration on the future of Hong Kong in September 1984, became more politically sensitive than ever before. The PRC government criticized the 1984 Green Paper introduced by the British colonial administration in Hong Kong as a move "hurrying to set up a model government system and

Table 1.7: Democratic Reforms and the Composition of Legislative Council, 1984–1988

Legislative Council Members	1984	1985	1988
Elected by electoral college	0	6	12
Elected by functional constituencies	0	6	12
Appointed by Governor	29	23	16
Official members (civil servants)	18	13	10
Total	47	48	50

Source: *Green Paper: The Further Development of Representative Government in Hong Kong* (Hong Kong: Government Printer, July 1984), p. 14.

… demand[ing] to maintain this system under the pretext of 'no change for 50 years.'"[112] As a matter of fact, the 1984 Green Paper outlined a step-by-step process of political reform to be introduced to LegCo (Table 1.7), whose official composition would be reduced from 18 out of 47 in 1984 to 10 out of 50 members in 1988, and where elected members increased from zero out of 47 in 1984 to 24 out of 50 in 1988.

Eventually, the 1984 White Paper pushed forward the British reform proposals but modified them incrementally. In 1985, DB members of the electoral college of LegCo would be grouped into ten geographical constituencies each based on one, two or three districts and representing roughly 500,000 people each, while members of the UrbCo and RegCo would form two special constituencies.[113] Therefore the electoral college would return 12 unofficial members to the LegCo in the 1985 elections rather than having six members originally proposed in the Green Paper (see Table 1.8). Regarding the introduction of directly elected seats to the LegCo, the 1984 White Paper adopted a delaying tactic and said:

> With few exceptions the bulk of public response from all sources suggested a cautious approach with a gradual start by introducing a very small number of directly elected members in 1988 and building up to a significant number of directly elected members by 1997. Proposals that the LegCo's Unofficial members should all be returned by direct elections were in the minority. There was considerable general public concern that too rapid progress towards direct elections could place the future stability and prosperity of Hong Kong in jeopardy. In summary, there was strong public support for the idea of direct elections but little support for such elections in the immediate future.[114]

While the British colonial rulers clearly adopted a cautious approach to coping with democratic reforms to be introduced to LegCo mainly due to China's concerns and opposition, they proceeded quickly in not only the injection of elections to the DBs from 1982 onwards, but also the electoral linkages between DBs, UrbCo and RegCo during the 1980s. The details of the LegCo's electoral college and its constituencies in the September 1985 election could be seen in Table 1.9. Clearly, the British colonial administration utilized the DBs, UrbCo and RegCo as the basis of slightly democratizing the composition of LegCo. Partly because the electoral college of LegCo would comprise members of DBs, UrbCo and RegCo, and partly because it would elect 12 unofficial members to the LegCo in September 1985. Candidates who ran for LegCo elections would naturally need the support of the members of three-district based bodies, namely DBs, UrbCo and RegCo. The political significance of this reform was to enhance the status of members of DBs, UrbCo and RegCo, providing a political ladder for them to climb up in Hong Kong's three-tiered levels of political institutions.

Administratively speaking, the British colonial administration paid considerable attention on how to enhance the linkage between DBs on one hand, and UrbCo and RegCo on the other, and to increase governmental responsiveness to the demands of members of DBs. The 1988 White Paper elaborated in detail the thinking of the British colonial administration in the following way:

> DBs have proved themselves to be a valuable part of the system of representative government in Hong Kong. There is no demand for fundamental changes to their present role or composition. There is however clear support for developing their advisory role. The Government had decided to do this by requiring Government departments to consult the Boards about all district matters. Where the advice of the Boards cannot be accepted, or if proposals on which the Boards have given advice subsequently undergo significant change, the departments concerned will be required to explain their reasons to the Boards. Furthermore, departments will, as far as possible, consult DBs on their annual program of work in the district, rather than piecemeal on individual projects, in order to give the Boards a broad picture within which to advise on priorities.[115]

Table 1.8: Decision on the Composition of the Legislative Council in 1985

Legislative Council Members	1985
Elected by electoral college	12
Elected by functional constituencies	12
Appointed by Governor	22
Official members	10
Total	**56**

Source: *White Paper: The Further Development of Representative Government in Hong Kong, November 1984* (Hong Kong: Government Printer, 1984), p. 8.

Table 1.9: Details of the 12 Constituencies formed from Legislative Council's Electoral College

Constituency	Population	Grouping	Population
East Island	696,000	Eastern district	481,000
West Island	507,000	Wan Chai district	215,000
Kwun Tong	663,000	Kwun Tong district	663,000
Wong Tai Sin	452,000	Wong Tai Sin district	452,000
Kowloon City	441,000	Kowloon City district	441,000
Sham Shui Po	435,000	Sham Shui Po district	435,000
South Kowloon	389,000	Mong Kok and Yau Ma Tei	389,000
East New Territories	524,000	North, Tai Po and Sha Tin	524,000
West New Territories	459,000	Yuen Long and Tuen Mun	459,000
South New Territories	736,000	Tuen Wan, Island, Sai Kung	726,000
UrbCo		Elected by UrbCo members	
RegCo		Elected by RegCo members	

Source: Adapted from *White Paper: The Further Development of Representative Government in Hong Kong, November 1984* (Hong Kong: Government Printer, 1984), p. 16. Appendix A.

In fact, the colonial administration designed the overlapping membership between DBs and UrbCo/RegCo in such a way that the two bodies with elected and appointed members would be able to enhance their communication and understanding so that the delivery of public services would be improved further. The 1988 White Paper concluded in the following way:

> When the next Municipal Council elections take place in March 1989, each of the ten District Boards in the urban area should elect a representative to sit on the UrbCo. Urban Councilors will at the same time cease to be

> ex-officio members of the urban DBs. The Government also believes it is right to amend the legislation concerning cross-membership between the UrbCo and urban DBs, to bring it into line with that presently in force in the RegCo area. Thus, the Government proposes to remove the requirement for a member of the UrbCo to resign from the Council if he is elected to an urban DB, and vice versa. Some of these proposals were announced in December 1987, before the publication of this White Paper, in order to enable Urban Councilors wishing to continue as DB members beyond March 1989 to stand for election in the DB elections on 10 March 1988 … The size of the UrbCo will be increased from 30 to 40 members in 1989, including 15 appointed and 15 directly elected members as at present and ten new members from the DBs … There will be no change in 1989 to the role or composition of the RegCo.[116]

In 1989, the RegCo had one-third (twelve) of its members directly elected, nine indirectly elected with one from each DB in the region, and a chairperson and two vice-chairpersons coming from HYK as ex-officio members. This institutional design was to link the representatives of HYK with the RegCo. The remaining 12 members of RegCo were appointed by the Governor in 1989.

As early as November 1990, a former District Officer of the Eastern District, J. S. Barclay, believed that there were several characteristics of district administration in Hong Kong. First, the scheme of having DB members to meet the members of the public, or the "meet-the-public scheme" as it was called, was not "very high" in its "rate of success."[117] Normally, many citizens contacted government departments to address their grievances first and utilized DBs' meet-the-public scheme as "the last resort." In Eastern District, the majority of cases involved matrimonial arrangements and building management. Most of the citizens tended to find out the details of the law concerned rather than having their problems solved, according to Barclay. As such, the meet-the-public scheme had" mixed results," meaning that citizens usually saw DB members as providing them with "an appeal" alternative. In other words, many citizens tended to contact DB members for further assistance after they failed to resolve their issues with government departments. According to Barclay, in 1990, two DB members in the Eastern District Council were very popular in the meet-the-public scheme. Usually, pre-interviews with the citizens concerned were conducted so that there would be some preliminary research work prior to the formal interviews. Barclay added that the elected DB members had their ward offices and that they were more willing to deal with citizens' affairs in their constituencies, unlike the appointed members who were expected to cope with entire district issues. Overall, the meet-the-public scheme was not only a last resort for many citizens to lodge their complaints against and seek their redress from government departments, but also a relatively rigorous appeal system.

Second, DBs as advisory bodies to the government were functioning "very well," according to Barclay. He emphasized that the government could only solve some problems of the community. Barclay said,

> Some problems cannot be resolved to the satisfaction of all concerned. We solve the resolvable problems. Of course, officials promote government policies. I will not promote anti-government policies. The roles of District Officer are to serve the District Board, to coordinate the activities of government departments at the district level, to act as a two-way communication link between the district and the central government, and to disseminate government views and policies to the public. In return, I monitor the feedback and channels in which the central government has triggered grassroots-level feelings. By promotion, I refer to explanation, answering questions, responding to points, and suggesting ways of doing things. The promotion of government policies is natural.[118]

The regular participants from the government in District Councils included the representatives from the police, housing department, transport, and land department. Barclay added that officials from these departments and District Officers had a "joint purpose in solving the problems" in district administration. These officials attended meetings of DBs on an occasional basis, presenting papers on various issues, including territory-wide ones like the policy of the Hospital Authority, and the 1991 LegCo election guidelines and regulations. They did not make commitments to the views from DBs; instead, they listened to the latter's feedback and comments. Then government officials were expected to "see the general perspectives and study how to amend" their policy suggestions, according to Barclay.

In term of governmental responsiveness, Barclay admitted that it depended on the reactions of government officials from various departments. However, he pinpointed the relative difficulties in lobbying for the police to change policing-related policies, for the police "is a law-enforcement agency that does not have the flexibility as with the Highways Department." Barclay added that "it is dangerous to have political control over the police force which should remain independent of any political body," and that "in the long run, the police force will not respond easily to politicians' views."

Third, DBs dealt with executive works and implemented many projects. As such, DB members, according to Barclay, could influence the timing and priorities of various projects. They could shape the district-level policies and issues, but no single DB "has decisive influence" on the policies of the central government." Still, DBs could "kill the Electronic Road Pricing" policy suggestion in the early 1980s, with only two to three Boards supportive of the idea. Electronic Road Pricing could affect all districts and therefore the opposition from most DBs did have political weight. On the other hand, DBs did not have any significant impact on, say, trade policy, for the government consulted the Trade Advisory Board and the industrial Development Board. Therefore, governmental responsiveness, to Barclay, was shaped by two main factors, namely the types of policy issues and the relevance of the expertise of DBs in relation to the issues concerned.

Fourth, while some members of DBs were appointed by the government, they were" often critical of the government in private." Barclay revealed that "we do not appoint yes-men, but men who gave sensible and reasonable advice," and that "because they are not elected, appointees do not see the necessity of voicing their views publicly." There were indeed some guidelines for the government to appoint members. To ensure the balance of composition of DB members, the colonial government considered, firstly, the individual needs to know or be associated with the district. Secondly, the government expected that the appointees belonged to the representatives of social groups in the community. Thirdly, the appointees should ideally be active and energetic and were equipped with skills and expertise. For instance, some industrialists were appointed to DBs as the views from various industries were useful to the discussions and deliberations in all boards. Barclay unveiled the political criterion of balancing the composition of DBs. If the pro-China forces could get 51% of the seats in a DBs, then the colonial government would appoint more representatives who were defeated in elections but who could represent the views from the districts.[119] Finally, the colonial government liked to balance the gender composition and age groups in DBs so that more women could be appointed while different age groups were generally represented. In short, DBs were expected to play the role of a largely representative body, which could advise the colonial government and served as a safety valve to absorb various demands from the society. If the late Samuel Huntington regarded political institutionalization as a necessary instrument that could absorb social forces and contribute to political stability, DBs in Hong Kong under British rule could function as a legitimizing tool for the colonial administration.

Conclusion

If the concepts of direct and indirect rule are used to study Hong Kong under the British rule, both aspects could be seen in an intertwined manner. The early ExCo and LegCo witnessed the dominance of the British expatriates. The process of gradual decolonization without independence in Hong Kong envisaged a gradual appointment of local Chinese community leaders into both LegCo and ExCo. At the district level, indirect rule was practiced in a more prominent way, for the British colonial administration relied on the Cantonese-speaking British expatriates as District Officers, such as Dennis Bray, who went down to various villages and districts and organized village-level and district-level activities for the local Chinese. As time passed, district-level institutions evolved gradually. The transformations of District Watch Force to District Watch Committee, the alteration from DABs to DBs, the evolution from UrbCo to RegCo, and the proliferation of many district-level bodies, such as DMCs, ACs, OCs, and MACs were a testimony to the development of district administration and institutions in colonial Hong Kong. All these institutions served the old purpose of, as Ambrose King argued persuasively, "administrative absorption of politics." Community elites were absorbed into these district institutions, helping the colonial government to administer various districts, enhancing governmental responsiveness, improving the linkage between the colonial government and ordinary people, and most importantly, legitimizing the colonial regime. Gradually, in the early 1980s, with the onset of the introduction of representative government, and due to the awareness of the British colonial rulers that some degree of political accountability and democratization should be injected into Hong Kong whose sovereignty would be eventually returned to the PRC, the introduction of elected elements to various institutions — DBs, UrbCo and RegCo — had important implications for Hong Kong's political development.

**Figure 1.1: A Framework of Understanding District Administation
and Politics in Hong Kong**

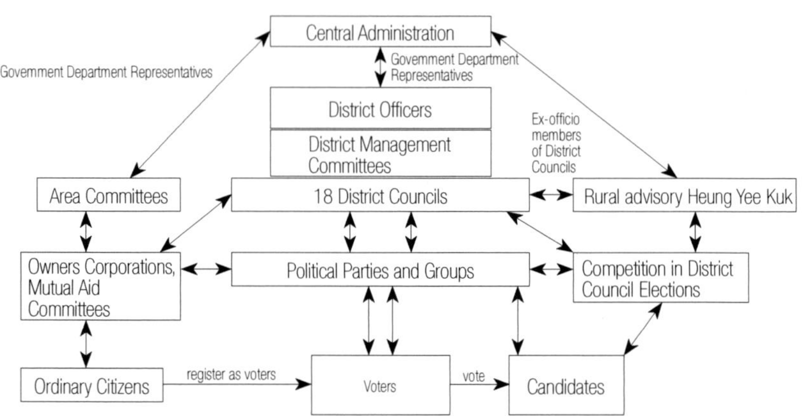

The introduction of DBs was due more to the British colonial administration's determination to improve the delivery of public services and to enhance the communication between the rulers and the ruled than to any British plan of withdrawing from Hong Kong on July 1, 1997. The DABs were planned in October 1977, one and a half year before MacLehose's visit to Beijing in March 1979. The timing of the introduction of DB elections in 1982 coincided with the beginning of the Sino-British negotiations over Hong Kong's future. Understandably, some people speculated that the establishment of DBs aimed at achieving a "glorious" British retreat from Hong Kong in July 1997. Nevertheless, as MacLehose and Cater asserted, there was in fact no connection between the two issues. The introduction of DBs represented an attempt of the British colonial authorities to experiment with some degree of administrative decentralization.

Elections introduced to DBs, as the following chapters will discuss, have become the most important factor shaping the transformations of district politics and administration. Political groups sprung up and competed in DB and later DC elections. Starting from the early 1990s, the growth of political parties became a phenomenon showing how they attached great importance to votes at the grassroots and constituency levels. By grasping more votes at the district level, ambitious politicians who aspired to climb up the political ladder to become LegCo members directly elected by ordinary citizens had to rely on the support of district politicians, who included the elected DB and DC members. At the same time, since the 1990s, the pro-democracy forces have been competing with the pro-government and pro-Beijing forces. The PRC government has seen DB and DC elections as increasingly important after July 1, 1997, launching its united front work to win the hearts and minds of the ordinary people through its supported pro-Beijing district politicians. Gradually, DBs and DCs have become the arena of political bickering, contests, struggles, and targets of capture and control. Figure 1.1 illustrates the complexities of district administration and politics.

Chapters Two to Five will show that, once elections were introduced to DBs (later District Councils) in 1982, the political landscape of Hong Kong changed significantly. Not only did political groups emerge, but the fragmentation of these groups and political elites, both urban and rural, could be gradually seen. This fragmentation of political groups and elites has become so serious that it can be regarded as the hallmark of electoral politics in Hong Kong since the 1980s.

Notes

1 Citied in the Home Affairs Department, in https://www.had.gov.hk/en/public_services/district_administration/admin_main.htm, access date: June 8, 2020.

2 K. C. Fok, *Hong Kong and Modern China* (in Chinese) (Hong Kong: Commercial Press, 1992); K. C. Fok, *Lectures on Hong Kong History: Hong Kong's Role in Modern Chinese History* (in Chinese) (Hong Kong: Commercial Press, 1990). Siu Kwok-kin, *Baoan History: Study and Collections* (Hong Kong: Hin Chiu Books, 1988). Victor Sit Fung-suen and Chi-man Kwong, *The New Territories Heung Yee Kuk* (in Chinese) (Hong Kong: Hong Kong Joint Publishing, 2011) pp. 24–32.

3 Steven Chung-fun Hung, A historical comparative analysis of the community transformation of Tin Hau temples in Sai Kung and Shaukiwan," *Asian Education and Development Studies*, vol. 10, no. 3 (2021), pp. 481–491. Steven Chung-fun Hung, "Historical Comparative Analysis of the Development and Transformation of Lei Yue Mun and Cha Kwo Ling with their Tin Hau Temples," *Social Evolution & History*, Vol. 19, No. 1 (March 2020), pp. 147–169.

4 Liu, Daosheng, "Local Constables in the Basic Level of the Society of the Qing Dynasty," (清代基層社會的地保), in https://www.1xuezhe.exuezhe.com/Qk/art/405096?dbcode=1&flag=2 access date: July 16, 2020.

5 Steve Tsang, *Governing Hong Kong Administrative Officers from the Nineteenth Century to the Handover to China, 1862–1997* (Hong Kong: Hong Kong University Press, 2007).

6 Chan Chak Kwan, Social Security Policy in Hong Kong: From British Colony to China's Special Administrative Region (Maryland: Lexington Books, 2011), pp. 66–67.

7 Henry J. Lethbridge, "The District Watch Committee: 'The Chinese Executive Council of Hong Kong,'" *Journal of the Hong Kong Branch of the Royal Asiatic Society*, vol. 11 (1971), pp. 116–141.

8 J. W. Norton Kyshe, *History of the Laws and Courts of Hong Kong* (Hong Kong, Noronha and Co., 1898), vol.2, p. 86.

9 Chan Chak Kwan, *Social Security Policy in Hong Kong: From British Colony to China's Special Administrative Region* (Maryland: Lexington Books, 2011), pp. 66–67. Carol Jones and Jon Vagg, *Criminal Justice in Hong Kong* (London: Routledge, 2016), p. 42.

10 See Jones and Vagg, *Criminal Justice in Hong Kong*, p. 42.

11 Chan Chak-kwan, *Social Security Policy in Hong Kong: From British Colony to China's Special Administrative Region* (Maryland: Lexington Books, 2011), pp. 66–67.

12 *Ibid.*

13 Ambrose King, "Administrative Absorption of Politics in Hong Kong: Emphasis on the Grass Roots Level." *Asian Survey*, Vol. 15, no. 5 (May 1975), pp. 422–439.

14 Chan, Social Security Policy in Hong Kong: From British Colony to China's Special Administrative *Region*, pp. 75–76.

15 Henry J. Lethbridge, "The District Watch Committee: 'The Chinese Executive Council of Hong Kong,'" *Journal of the Hong Kong Branch of the Royal Asiatic Society*, vol. 11 (1971), pp. 116–141.

16 *Ibid.*

17 Gavin Ure, *Governors, Politics and the Colonial Office: Public Policy in Hong Kong, 1918–58* (Hong Kong: Hong Kong University Press, 2012), pp. 19–20.

18 Sheliah E. Hamilton, *Watching Over Hong Kong: Private Policing 1841–1941* (Hong Kong: Hong Kong University Press), p. 41

19 *Ibid.*

20 G. B. Endacott, *A History of Hong Kong* (Hong Kong: Oxford University Press, 1973), p. 290.

21 Yuen Bong-kin, *A Brief History of Hong Kong* (in Chinese) (Hong Kong: Chung Liu Publisher, 1997), p. 155.

22 Yuen, *A Brief History of Hong Kong*, pp. 157–158.

23 Chan Kwok-shing, *Fanling* (in Chinese) (Hong Kong: Hong Kong Joint Publishing, 2019), pp. 19–37. Also see Victor Sit Fung-suen and Kwong Chi-man, *A History of Heung Yee Kuk in the New Territories* (in Chinese) (Hong Kong: Hong Kong Joint Publishing, 2011), p.7

24 *Apple Daily*, May 30, 2006.

25 Graham E. Johnson (1977). Leaders and Leadership in an Expanding New Territories Town, *The China Quarterly*, Number 69, pp. 109–125.

26 *White Paper: District Administration in Hong Kong, January 1981* (Hong Kong: Government Printer, 1981), p. 35.

27 *Ibid.*

28 Norman Miners, *The Government and Politics of Hong Kong* (Hong Kong: Oxford University Press, 1981), p. 198.

29 The Heung Yee Kuk Ordinance, in https://www.elegislation.gov.hk/hk/cap1097!en-zh-Hant-HK?INDEX_CS=N, assess date, July 27, 2020.

30 Miners, *The Government and Politics of Hong Kong*, p. 198.

31 *Ibid.*, p. 199.

32 *Ibid.*

33 "How to apply for a small house grant," in http://www.landsd.gov.hk/en/images/doc/NTSHP_E_text.pdf, access date: July 28, 2020.

34 *Ibid*

35 "Background brief on processing of small house applications and review of small house policy," Legislative Council, LC Paper No. CB (1)986/05–06(01). Also see "Small House Matters," Lands Department, https://www.landsd.gov.hk/en/small%20house/small%20hse.htm, and "Small house grants in the New Territories," Audit Commission, 15 October 2002. http://www.aud.gov.hk/pdf_e/e39ch08.pdf, access date: July 28, 2020.

36 Dennis Bray, *Hong Kong Metamorphosis* (Hong Kong: Hong Kong University Press, 2001), p. 166.

37 *Ibid.*, p. 165.

38 *Asiaweek*, No. 3, 2016.

39 "Real and Fake District Councils," in https://www.thestandnews.com/politics, access date: July 29, 2020.

40 Aline K. Wong, "Chinese voluntary associations in Southeast Asian cities and the *Kaifongs* in Hong Kong," *Journal of the Hong Kong Branch of the Royal Asiatic Society*, vol. 11 (1971), pp. 62–73.

41 *Ibid.*

42 Aline K. Wong, "Chinese Community Leadership in a Colonial Setting: the Hong Kong Neighborhood Associations." *Asian Survey*, p.593.

43 *Ibid*, p. 600.

44 *Ibid*, p. 600.

45 *Ibid*, p. 600.

46 Dennis Bray, *Hong Kong Metamorphosis* (Hong Kong: Hong Kong University Press, 2001), p. 44.

47 *Ibid.*, p. 45.

48 *Ibid.*

49 See Aline K. Wong, *The Kaifong Associations and the Society of Hong Kong* (Taipei: The Oriental Cultural Service, 1972)

50 *Ibid.*

51 Lo, Shiu Hing Sonny, Hung Chung Fun, Steven & Loo, Hai Chi Jeff, *China's New United Front Work in Hong Kong: Penetrative Politics and Its Implications* (London: Palgrave Macmillan), Chapter 7, pp. 221–253.

52 Seymour Martin Lipset, *Political Man: The Social Bases of Politics* (London: Heinemann, 1960). Samuel P. Huntington, *Political Order in Changing Societies* (New Haven: Yale University Press, 1966).

53 Home Affairs Department, *A Guide on Building Management Ordinance (Cap. 344)* (Hong Kong: Logistics Department, Hong Kong Government, January 2017), p. 5, in https://www.buildingmgt.gov.hk/file_manager/en/documents/bmo_guide/a_guide_on_building_management_ordinance_cap344_en.pdf, access date: August 2, 2020.

54 *Ibid.*, p. 8.

55 "District Administration," Factsheet provided by the Hong Kong government, July 2020, in https://www.gov.hk/en/about/abouthk/factsheets/docs/district_admin.pdf, access date: August 2, 2020.

56 *Ibid.*

57 Sonny Shiu-Hing Lo, "Party Penetration of Society: Political Parties and Mutual Aid Committees in Hong Kong," *Asian Journal of Political Science*, vol. 12, no. 1 (June 2004), pp. 31–64.

58 Sonny Shiu-Hing Lo and Eilo Wing-Yat Yu, "The Politics of Electoral Reform in Hong Kong," *Journal of Commonwealth & Comparative Politics*, vol. 39, no. 1 (July 2001), pp. 98–123.

59 Tsang Tse-yeung, Chung Wai-tak and Lee Chak-tong, "A History of District Administration: The worry of the Colonial Government that it could become grassroots representatives, March 2, 2017, in http://www.hk01.com, access date: August 1, 2020.

60 *Kung Sheung Yat Pao*, October 31, 1967, https://1967riot.wordpress.com/2012/10/31/ksyp-19671031/, access date: May 3, 2020.

61 Ambrose Yeo-Chi King, "Administrative Absorption of Politics in Hong Kong: Emphasis on the Grassroots Level." *Asian Survey,* vol. 15, no. 5 (May 1975), pp. 422–439.

62 *Ibid.,* p. 432.

63 *Ibid.,* p. 431.

64 *Ibid.,* p. 437.

65 *Ibid.,* p. 437.

66 *Ibid.,* p. 437.

67 *The City District Officer Scheme: A Report by the Secretariat of Chinese Affairs* (Hong Kong: Government Printer, 1969), p. 3.

68 Miners, *The Government and Politics of Hong Kong*, pp. 208–210.

69 Nicholas Thomas, *Democracy Denied: Identity, Civil Society and Illiberal Democracy in Hong Kong* (London: Routledge, 2018).

70 Ian Scott, *Political Change and the Crisis of Legitimacy in Hong Kong* (Honolulu: University of Hawaii Press, 1989).

71 Bray, *Hong Kong Metamorphosis*, p. 136.

72 *Ibid.*, p. 136.

73 *Ibid.*

74 *Ibid.*

75 *White Paper: District Administration in Hong Kong* (Hong Kong: Government Printer, 1981), p. 8.

76 *Ibid.*, p.10.

77 *Ibid.*, p. 8.

78 *Ibid.*

79 "The LegCo Debates: Official Report, October 1, 1980," in https://www.legco.gov.hk/yr80-81/english/lc_sitg/hansard/h801001.pdf, pp. 31–32, access date: August 2, 2020.

80 *Ibid.*, p. 32.

81 *Ibid.*

82 "Official Report of Proceedings, January 21, 1981," Hong Kong Legislative Council, in https://www.legco.gov.hk/yr80-81/english/lc_sitg/hansard/h810121.pdf, p. 368, access date: August 2, 2020.

83 *Ibid.*, p. 369.

84 *White Paper: District Administration in Hong Kong*, p. 12.

85 *Ibid.*, p. 32.

86 *Ibid.*, p. 12.

87 *Ibid.*, pp. 12–13.

88 *White Paper: District Administration in Hong Kong* (Hong Kong: Government Printer, January 1981), p. 11.

89 *Ibid.*, p. 11.

90 "Time has passed for officials not to tell lies," *Citizen News*, February 9, 2017, in https:///www.hkcnews.com/article/1622/, access date: July 28, 2020.

91 "The Negotiation Process of Hong Kong's Future in the 1980s," September 30, 2017, in https://medium.com/recall-hk/t-d679f9564ed1, access date: August 2, 2020.

92 Letter from Sir Y. K. Kan to Sonny Lo, February 1991 (no exact date was given), cited in Lo Shiu-Hing, *The Politics of Democratization in Hong Kong* (London: Macmillan, 1997), p. 74.

93 Letter from Lord Murray MacLehose to Sonny Lo, November 27, 1989, also cited in Lo, *The Politics of Democratization in Hong Kong*, p. 74.

94 Sonny Lo's interview with Sir Roger Lobo, December 13, 1989.

95 *Ibid.*

96 *Ibid.*

97 Duncan Campbell, "A Secret Plan for Dictatorship," *New Statesman*, December 12, 1980, p. 8.

98 Governor Alexander Grantham wrote that a "peculiarity affecting Hong Kong 's constitutional situation is the danger that, in a democratically elected legislature, the politics of China—as distinct from those of the Colony—would be a constant issue, which would have a most disturbing effect." Alexander Grantham, *Via Ports: From Hong Kong to Hong Kong* (Hong Kong: Hong Kong University Press, 1965), pp. 111–112.

99 Sonny Lo's interview with Sir Jack Cater, December 7, 1989.

100 *Ibid.*

101 *Ibid.*

102 *Ibid.*

103 *Ibid.*

104 Miners, *The Government and Politics of Hong Kong*, p. 201.

105 *Ibid.*

106 *Ibid.*

107 *Ibid.*, p. 202.

108 Lau Siu-kai, "Local Administrative Reform in Hong Kong: Promises and Limitations," *Asian Survey*, vol. 22, no. 9 (September 1982), pp. 863–868.

109 *Green Paper: The Further Development of Representative Government in Hong Kong* (Hong Kong: Government Printer, July 1984), p. 12.

110 *Ibid.*, p. 6.

111 *Ibid.*, p. 12.

112 *New Evening Post*, July 23, 1984, p. 1.

113 *White Paper: The Further Development of Representative Government in Hong Kong, November 1984* (Hong Kong: Government Printer, 1984), p. 5.

114 *Ibid.*, p. 8.

115 *White Paper: The Development of Representative Government: The Way Forward, February 1988* (Hong Kong: Government Printer, 1988), p. 15.

116 *Ibid.*, pp. 16–17.

117 Interview with Mr. L. S. Barclay, November 27, 1990.

118 *Ibid.*

119 *Ibid.*

2

Electoral Politics from Urban Councils to District Boards

This Chapter aims to show that once elections were introduced to District Boards (DBs), political groups and party politics developed at the district level with the passage of time. Political groups have emerged gradually since the 1982 DB elections, which provided an arena for them to compete among themselves and to learn how to participate in electoral campaigns. In fact, long before the introduction of DB elections, Hong Kong witnessed the emergence of two political groups, namely the Reform Club and the Civic Association. These two political bodies were stimulated by the Young Plan in which Governor Mark Young amended a proposal from the British Colonial Office in 1945 to form a new municipal council with financial autonomy and to reserve half of its seats for the local Hong Kong Chinese.[1] But Young's successor, Governor Alexander Grantham, disliked the idea and shelved his proposal. Grantham remarked that "constitutional changes and development should come from within the community and not from without."[2] Nevertheless, Mark Young's reform plan triggered the desire of the local expatriates to organize themselves in preparation for the 1952 Urban Council (UrbCo) election. The Reform Club was formed by the British expatriates, like Brook Bernacchi, in 1949 to participate in local UrbCo elections. It lobbied the colonial government against the proposal of restricting the franchise to the British subjects in Legislative Council (LegCo) elections.[3] The apex of the Reform Club's development witnessed some 550 members, but it did not function any longer after the retirement of Bernacchi from UrbCo in 1995. In a sense, the Reform Club was like a personalistic political group; once its leader withdrew from politics, the organization faded away gradually.

The Civic Association and the Reform Club: Early Political Groups

The Civic Association was formed by professionals and some businesspeople in 1954, with its chairman Hilton Cheong-leen becoming the first chairman of the UrbCo, and later a LegCo member through LegCo's electoral college. In the late 1980s, the Civic Association formed an alliance with the Hong Kong Progressive Party led by Maria Tam, becoming part of the pro-government and pro-Beijing camp since the 1990s. As Hilton Cheong-leen departed from the political arena in the early 2000s, the Civic Association has no longer been politically active although it occasionally organized seminars and activities. Like the Reform Club, the Civic Association remained a personalistic political group whose longevity is hampered by the lack of political leadership and successors. Another weakness of the Civic Association was the broadness of its platform; it had the objectives of promoting stability and prosperity, improving living standards, and encouraging citizen participation in public affairs.[4]

During the 1980s, the Reform Club and Civic Association participated actively in the early DB elections. In the 1982 DB elections, the Reform Club nominated 35 candidates while the Civic Association nominated 40 candidates.[5] Bernacchi was an influential leader of the Reform Club, but as time passed, some of its members disagreed with him and left, including Elsie Elliott and Alison Bell, who were the first women to be elected to UrbCo in 1956 with some 4,000 votes. Table 2.1 illustrates the core leaders and members of the Reform Club, and all of them could be seen as the elites in the colonial society of Hong Kong.

Table 2.2 shows the core leaders and members of the Civic Association. As with the Reform Club, the founders and core members of the Civic Association were the elites of the colonial society of Hong Kong. Many of them were lawyers, prestigious teachers and successful businesspeople. A few of them were British expatriates who had a strong sense of belonging in Hong Kong. Hence, the two political groups were composed of the elites of the society, and their participation in UrbCo elections could be seen as the early political parties in Hong Kong, especially if political parties are defined as groups that nominate candidates to partake and compete in elections.

However, without grooming young leaders and candidates who ran in local elections, the two increasingly aging political groups encountered a

Table 2.1: Core Leaders and Members of the Reform Club

Core Leaders	Important issues experienced
Charles Edgar Loseby (1881–1970)	He was a captain, lawyer and British Member of Parliament for Bradford East in the 1918 general election and served in the British House of Commons until the 1922 general election. Later he lived in Hong Kong and became the first chairman of the Reform Club of Hong Kong in 1949 and the chairman of the Hong Kong Bar Association in 1953.
Brook Antony Bernacchi (1922–1996)	He was born in London in 1922 and was educated at the Westminster School and the Cambridge University. He arrived in Hong Kong as part of the liberation forces in 1945 and joined the Hong Kong Bar Association in 1946 and became its chairman in 1963. The Reform Club, under Bernacchi's chairmanship, was involved in grassroots politics, calling for the need for building public housing estates and units for all citizens. In 1960 he visited the British Colonial Office officials, arguing that the people of Hong Kong should have more power to manage themselves, and that the unofficial members of the Executive and Legislative Councils should be directly elected by citizens. In 1970, Bernacchi raised the same issue again to the British government. From 1952 onwards, he became the urban councilor several times and was also a member of the Eastern District Board.
Sir Kan Yuet-keung, GBE JP (簡悦強 1913–2012)	He was born in Hong Kong in 1913 to a wealthy family which had its ancestral home in Shunde, Guangdong province. He graduated from the University of Hong Kong in 1934 with a BA degree, then moving to the United Kingdom for legal studies at the London School of Economics. Kan once worked as a senior partner of the famous local law firm, Lo & Lo, and was the chairman of the Law Society and a member of the Society's disciplinary committee. He was also a director of Hong Kong Land and Harbor Centre Development Limited. Kan took over his family banking business and became the chairman of the Bank of East Asia from 1963 to 1983.
George Samuel Zimmern JP (1904–1979)	Born of Eurasian parentage, he attended the Diocesan Boys' School, and then pursued his study at Oxford University. His remarkable positions included a barrister-at-law, a magistrate, a headmaster of Diocesan Boys' School (1955–1961), and an honorary canon of St. John's Cathedral. He was also one of the founders of the Street Sleepers' Shelter Society, the Boys' and Girls' Clubs Association and the Housing Society.
Woo Pak-chuen (胡百全 1910–2008)	He graduated from St. Joseph's College in 1928 and from the University of London in 1937. Woo founded his own law firm P. C. Woo & Co. Solicitor in 1945 and became the President of the Law Society from 1959 to 1960. He was appointed to the LegCo in July 1964 and reappointed in 1972 and was the Senior Unofficial Member for ten years until his retirement in June 1973. He was also appointed to the Executive Council from 1972 to 1976.
Chan Shu-woon (陳樹垣 1921–2003)	Chan was the son of the former Guangdong warlord Chen Ji-tang and he was elected as a member of UrbCo in 1956. He was also a principal of a pro-Taiwan Tak Ming Secondary School.[a] Chan Shu-woon once wanted to run for the chair position of the Reform Club, but his intention aroused Bernacchi's concern. Chan publicly said that if Chiang Kai-shek could recover the PRC, the Nationalist government would appoint him as the governor of Guangdong. Chan's remarks reportedly made the British colonial government displeased because the British feared that, if Chan won the Reform Club chairman election, he would turn the group into a pro-Taiwan political organization. During the election campaign, Chan was found to exceed his campaign expenditure and was forced to withdraw from the election. Eventually, Bernacchi was elected as the Reform Club's chairperson. Still, Chan was elected as a member of the UrbCo from 1956 to 1966.

Table 2.1 Continued

Core Leaders	Important issues experienced
Alison Bell Fok	She was born in Scotland in 1925 and graduated from the University of Edinburgh with a Bachelor's degree in Medicine and Surgery in 1948. She moved to Hong Kong in 1949 and got married with Dr. Fok Hin-tak. She first ran for the Urban Council in the 1956 election as a candidate of the Reform Club and she acquired 4,122 votes, becoming the first woman to be elected to the council. She was a critic of urban hygiene issues, social welfare, poverty, housing policy and bureaucratic corruption. In 1969, she decided not to seek re-election because of the UrbCo's limited executive power..
Elsie Elliott, GBM, CBE (杜葉錫恩 1913–2015)	She was born in England and moved to Hong Kong in 1951. Later she became a spokeswoman for the United Nations Association of Hong Kong, which advocated "self-government" in the colony in the 1960s. She was well-known for her criticisms of colonialism and corruption and her work for the underprivileged people. From 1963 to 1995 she was an elected member of the UrbCo and, from 1988 to 1995, became an elected member of the LegCo. In the transition period from the 1980s to 1997, Tu became a target of the united front work by the PRC government. She was appointed as a member of the Beijing-controlled Provisional LegCo from December 1996 to June 1998 after her defeat in both UrbCo and LegCo elections to democrat Szeto Wah.
Dr Henry Hu Hung-lick (胡鴻烈1920–)	He was born in Zhejiang province in 1920 and later graduated with a Bachelor of Law from the National Chengchi University in 1942. He went to the Soviet Union as a Chinese diplomat and got a doctorate in international law from the University of Paris. In 1955 he became a barrister in Hong Kong. As a vice-chairman of the Reform Club, Hu was also elected as a member of the UrbCo in April 1965. In 1976, he was appointed as a LegCo member. In 1987, he was appointed as a member of the Chinese People's Political Consultative Conference. In 1971, he and his wife Chung Chi-yung found the first private university in Hong Kong, namely the Shu Yan College which later became a university in 2006.

Sources: Compiled from multiple sources, including Lau Yun-wo, *A History of the Municipal Councils of Hong Kong: 1883–1999: From the Sanitary Board to the Urban Council and the Regional Council* (Hong Kong: Leisure and Cultural Service Department, Hong Kong Government, 2002).

a. Tak Ming Secondary School was a pro-Taiwan school established in 1934 and located at Mong Kok district. At the beginning, it was financially supported by Kuomintang members Chen Ji-tang and Wu Han-min. From 1949 onwards, many of the students of Tak Ming Secondary School went to famous universities in Taiwan and other places to pursue their studies. These alumni included, for example, Yam Sin-ling, Joseph Cheng Yu-shek, Chan Yiu-nam, Tik Chi-yuen, and Lam Pak-li. See Fong Foon-li, "Tak Ming Secondary School and Chan Shu-woon," *Ming Pao Monthly* (April 2006).

Table 2.2: Core Leaders and Members of the Civic Association

Core Leaders	Important issues experienced
Brother Brigant Cassian (1889–1957)	He was born in France in 1889 and was educated in the Likes College of the Brothers at Quimper, followed by further education at the Junior Novitiate of the Brothers at Nantes in 1900 and his senior Novitiate and Scholasticate at Vauxbelets, Quernesey by 1907. Brother Cassian began his missionary career in Singapore, teaching there in 1908. He joined the St. Joseph's College in 1921 and taught there for 11 years until in 1932, when he was transferred to the newly opened La Salle College and became the second principal. He also founded the Hong Kong Teachers' Association and became the President for three years; and he was also a co-founder of the Hong Kong Schools Musical Association. In 1954, he helped founding the Hong Kong Civic Association and became the chairman. He was also one of the founders of the United Nations Association of Hong Kong, which later became a political group striving for self-government.
Woo Pak-foo (胡百富 1911–1976)	Woo's father Woo Hei-tong was a rich businessman working for Swire and engaging in shipping and hotel business. Woo Pak-foo's brother was Woo Pak-chuen. Woo Pak-foo was a doctor and an elected UrbCo member from 1956 to 1969. While Woo Pak-chuen joined the Reform Club, Woo Pak-foo participated in the Civic Association.
Hilton Cheong-Leen (張有興 1922–2022)	He was born in 1922 and was educated at the Central High School in Georgetown, British Guyana. He moved to Hong Kong when he was around nine years old and studied at La Salle College. He was a journalist for some years, working for Fox News and BBC. He was a vice-chairman of the United Nations Association of Hong Kong led by Ma Man-fai. From 1957 to 1991, he was an elected UrbCo member and became the first Chinese chairperson of UrbCo from 1981 to 1986. He had been a long-time chairman of the Civic Association. From 1973 to 1979, he was appointed to the LegCo. From1985 to 1988, he was one of the elected LegCo members from the UrbCo constituency in the first LegCo election in 1985.
Li Yiu-bor (李耀波 1909–1976)	He graduated from the Hong Kong Wah Yan College and was the chairman of the Hong Kong Teachers' Association. In 1957, he was elected as a UrbCo member and, from 1963 to 1972, he became a headmaster of the Pui Shing Catholic Secondary School.
Cheung Wing-in (張永賢 1920–2010)	He was born in Canton, China in 1920. He graduated from the Hong Kong Queen's College in 1939 and later studied literature at the University of Hong Kong. In 1953, he obtained the solicitor's qualification in England and opened his own law firm in 1967. In 1962, he and his sister Chow Cheung Wa-bing opened the Cognitio College. In 1963, he was elected as a member of the UrbCo and served there until 1967 when he failed to be re-elected. He had been the chairman of the Civic Association and was the legal adviser of the Hong Kong Chinese Reform Association.
Edmund Chow Wai-hung (鄒偉雄 1925–)	He graduated from King's College and pursued legal studies in England. In 1954, he was one of the founders of the Civic Association and became its vice-chairman. In 1973 he was elected as a member of the UrbCo but withdrew from politics in 1986.
Peter Chan Chi-kwan (陳子鈞 1936–2017)	He was born in Hong Kong in 1936 and graduated from King's College. He studied at the University of Melbourne and later in England for his law degree. In 1954 he was one of the founders of the Civic Association and became its vice-chairman. In 1969 he was elected as a member of the UrbCo and was later re-elected seven times, becoming the most senior and experienced urban councilor. In 1985, he was invited to be a member of the Basic Law Consultative Committee that listened to the people of Hong Kong on their opinion about the mini-constitution for Hong Kong after July 1, 1997.

Table 2.2 Continued

Core Leaders	Important issues experienced
Henry S. L. Wong (王幸利)	He was born in the Mei county of the Guangdong province. Later he ran and managed his mining business in Malaysia and became a leader of the Chinese community in Ipoh. In 1969, he participated in the UrbCo election as a member of the Civic Association. He was supported by the Hong Kong and Kowloon Trade Union Council, which had pro-Taiwan political orientations—a phenomenon showing that Wong was supportive of the Kuomintang in Taiwan.

Note: Compiled from multiple sources, including Lau Yun-wo, *A History of the Municipal Councils of Hong Kong: 1883–1999: From the Sanitary Board to the Urban Council and the Regional Council* (Hong Kong: Leisure and Cultural Service Department, Hong Kong Government, 2002)

lackluster period and witnessed their gradual eclipse. When liberal-minded political groups emerged in the early and mid-1980s and flourished in the 1990s, these two old political groups failed to catch up with the rapidly changing political circumstances and gradually became politically outdated. Although the Civic Association maintains its Facebook as of 2021 and occasionally organizes seminars, its leaders and members appear to be aging without a comprehensive plan of cultivating youngsters.[6] Naturally, these personalistic political groups have gradually become politically insignificant.

Early Electoral and Party Politics in Urban Council Elections, 1949–1981

The origin of Hong Kong's urban elections and politics could be traced back to 1883, when the Sanitary Board, a predecessor of the Urban Council (UrbCo), was established. In 1888, a system of partial elections was adopted, allowing some selected individuals to vote for members of the Board. These voters came from the professionals who were eligible to become jury members. Only 187 of the 669 eligible citizens voted in 1888, when two of the members of Sanitary Board were elected.[7] The number of voters was originally small and the franchise was restricted to expatriates. In 1926, Chinese voters could be seen, but they were mainly civil servants without much influence on the work of the Sanitary Board.

The Sanitary Board was renamed as UrbCo in 1936 when the government enacted the UrbCo Ordinance, which empowered the UrbCo legally to deal with its public services. The UrbCo did not have elected members shortly after the end of the Second World War, but it possessed the

Table 2.3: The Composition of the Urban Council, 1952–1995

Year	Ex-officio Members	Appointed Unofficials	Directly Elected	District Board Elected
1952	5	6	2	–
1953	5	6	4	–
1956	6	8	8	–
1965	6	10	10	–
1973	–	12	12	–
1983	–	15	15	–
1991	–	15	15	10
1995	–	–	32	9

Sources: Lau Yun-wo, *A History of the Municipal Councils of Hong Kong: 1883–1999: From the Sanitary Board to the Urban Council and the Regional Council* (Hong Kong: Leisure and Cultural Service Department, Hong Kong Government, 2002); and Suzanne Pepper, *Keeping Democracy at Bay: Hong Kong and the Challenge of Chinese Political Reform* (Lanham: Rowman & Littlefield, 2008).

powers to carry out its previous duties, such as cleaning the streets, burying the dead, managing bath houses, running public toilets, and controlling hawkers on the streets.

In Hong Kong under British rule, the UrbCo underwent a step-by-step process of democratic reforms (Table 2.3). In May 1952, two out of 13 members of UrbCo were elected. In 1953, the number of directly elected members increased to four in the 15-member UrbCo. In 1956, the number of directly elected members rose to eight (one-third) in the 22-member UrbCo. By April 1956, a voter in UrbCo election had to be at least 21 years of age, to have lived in Hong Kong for at least three years and to be qualified in one of 23 categories, including educational qualifications (such as passing the School Certificate Examination or equivalent), being a juror, a salaried taxpayer, or a member of certain professional organizations.[8] In 1965, for the first time, the number of directly elected members exceeded that of ex-officio members—an indication of the gradual democratization in the composition of UrbCo. In 1973, there was no longer any ex-officio members in UrbCo where half of the 24-member chamber were composed of directly elected ones, and the other half were appointed by the government. The number of UrbCo members expanded to 30 in both 1983 and 1991, but half of them were directly elected and the rest were appointed. Democratization of the UrbCo was in full swing in 1995, when all the 41 members were elected (32 directly elected and 9 members elected by District Boards). The ways in which the British colonial rulers managed the composition of UrbCo showed that they used it as a platform for gradual democratization.

In the 1960s, the jurisdiction and responsibilities of the UrbCo increased. The City Hall in the Central district was opened in 1962, followed by the establishment of the first multi-storey market in Jardine's Bazaar in March 1963.[9] The public library and market fell into the scope of UrbCo management. At the same time, the role of the elected UrbCo members became more important than before. They had to fight for the interests of their constituents, say, by lobbying the government to build more public housing units and to fight against the price increase in public utilities. Elected council members realized that they had to articulate the interests of their voters so that they would be supported by them continuously in elections.

In 1973, the UrbCo was reorganized and given financial autonomy, which meant that the budget could be planned without the LegCo's approval.[10] The percentage of rates paid to the UrbCo remained at 6% until 1977.[11] From 1995 to 1999, the percentage of rates going to the UrbCo amounted to 5.5% of the those levied on properties and premises with ratable value.[12] Of the 5.5% rates levied annually, 3% went to the UrbCo and 2.5% belonged to the government's treasury. Due to the rapid expansion of population and new towns, and accordingly the rising demand for government services in the 1980s, the scope and responsibilities of various government departments increased. As a result, the UrbCo's scope and responsibilities showed a mismatch with the growth of public services delivered by government departments. The UrbCo dealt with mainly urban hygiene issues, hawkers' control, and recreational and cultural activities. It was no longer in charge of housing-related issues due to the establishment of the Housing Authority as a statutory body in April 1973.[13] On the other hand, from 1973 onwards, there were no government officials sitting in UrbCo whereas both the chairperson and vice-chairpersons were elected among the 24 members. At this juncture, UrbCo operated like a board of directors of a statutory body having the powers to decide the policy on urban affairs. In other words, while UrbCo became financially autonomous and could govern urban affairs independently from the government, its scope and responsibilities were simultaneously restricted after the emergence of the Housing Authority in 1973.

Table 2.4: Number of Registered Voters and Voters Who Cast their Ballots in Urban Council Elections, 1952–1995

Year	Number of registered voters	Number of registered voters who voted in elections	Voting rate (%)
1952	9,074	3,368	35.0%
1953	10,798	2,536	23.5%
1954	13,700	4,957	36.2%
1955	Unknown	3,650	*
1956	14,682	6,040	41.1%
1957	19,305	6,916	35.8%
1959	23,584	7,236	30.7%
1961	–	Uncontested	–
1963	25,837	5,320	20.6%
1965	29,529	6,492	22.0%
1967	26,275	10,189	38.8%
1969	34,392	8,175	23.8%
1971	37,788	10,470	26.6%
1973	31,284	8,675	24.4%
1975	34,078	10,903	32.0%
1977	37,174	7,308	19.7%
1979	31,481	12,425	39.5%
1981	34,381	6,195	18.0%
1983	(708,119) 568,537	127,206	22.4%
1986	(998,177) 944,844	218,573	23.1%
1989	(1,045,073) 747,005	105,807	14.2%
1991	(1,124,292) 1,028,541	215,869	21.0%
1995	(1,362,365) 1,180,506	297,988	25.2%

Note: The bracket number denotes all those eligible voters who registered as voters, but due to the fact that some constituencies witnessed automatically elected candidates, the real number of registered voters who could vote was indicated by the number without bracket. * Cannot be counted due to the unclear number of registered voters

Sources: Compiled from multiple sources, including Lau Yun Wo, *A History of the Municipal Councils of Hong Kong: 1883–1999: From the Sanitary Board to the Urban Council and the Regional Council* (Hong Kong: Leisure and Cultural Service Department, Hong Kong Government, 2002); and Suzanne Pepper, *Keeping Democracy at Bay: Hong Kong and the Challenge of Chinese Political Reform* (Lanham: Rowman & Littlefield, 2008).

Since the introduction of DB elections in 1982, the electoral system of UrbCo underwent some reforms, including the adoption of geographical constituencies in direct elections and the expansion of the franchise considerably. Table 2.4 shows the number of registered voters and that of voters who cast their ballots in elections. From 1952 to 1981, the franchise in UrbCo elections was limited. As such, the number of registered voters increased from 9,074 in 1952 to 34,381 in 1981—an increase of almost fourfold in 28 years. The voter turnout was usually around some 20% to 30%, with the highest voter turnout of 39% in 1979 and the lowest turnout of 18% in 1981. The highest number of voters from 1952 to 1981 was 12,425 in 1979. Obviously, not many eligible voters were interested in voting in UrbCo elections.

The expansion of the franchise in UrbCo elections from 1983 to 1995 witnessed an increase in the number of voters. It rose from 127,206 in 1983 to 297,988 in 1995, whereas the voter turnout slightly increased from 22.4 in 1983 to 25.2 in 1995. Many eligible voters were uninterested or unenthusiastic in the electoral participation of UrbCo. Quite a lot of directly elected seats in UrbCo from 1983 to 1995 were uncontested with automatically elected candidates, thereby depriving the opportunity of voters to cast their ballots in elections.

The Hong Kong Chinese Reform Association

Apart from the Reform Club and the Civic Association, the third active political group during the late 1940s and early 1950s was the Hong Kong Chinese Reform Association (HKCRA), which was set up in 1949 by Ma Man-fai and Percy Chen, who advocated political reform in Hong Kong under the British colonial rule.[14] Percy Chan, Ma Man-fai and Mok Ying-kwei were anti-colonialists advocating the establishment of a municipal council with all unofficial members and without any appointed government officials.[15] In July 1949, the HKCRA cooperated with other 142 groups, including the Chinese Manufacturers' Association (CMA) and the Kowloon Chamber of Commerce, to call for political reform and to support the Young Plan. Governor Young, as mentioned before, proposed that Hong Kong should have a new municipal council constituted on a fully representative or elected basis—a bold proposal that met the opposition from some unofficial members of LegCo.[16] He proposed that the new municipal council would have 30 members of which 20 would be directly elected and ten would be returned from groups like business chambers. Young even went so far as to suggest that the LegCo should have some members elected from the UrbCo so that the unofficial members would eventually exceed the number of government officials in the legislature.[17] The HKCRA supported Governor Young's proposal, which however was later shelved due to the Communist victory in China in October 1949, when the British Colonial Office preferred to put it in the backburner.[18] In the 1982 DB elections, the HKCRA nominated candidates to run in Hong Kong Island, especially in the Eastern district, but many of them were defeated.[19] As time passed, many founding members of the HKCRA left the association, which has become more politically pro-PRC (People's Republic of China) especially since July 1, 1997. In the recent years, it has been cooperating with pro-Beijing political party Democratic Alliance for the Betterment and Progress of Hong Kong (DAB) and the Federation of Trade Unions (FTU), as well as other pro-PRC district organizations.[20] After 1997, the PRC's united front work has targeted at the old political groups in Hong Kong, including the HKCRA and the Civic Association.

The story of Percy Chen deserved to be mentioned as his experiences represented how the HKCRA transformed itself gradually. Percy Chen was the son of Eugene Chen Yu-jen, who had been born in Guangdong in Trinidad in 1878 and later became a lawyer. Eugene Chen returned to China in 1911, worked with Sun Yat-sen, the father of the 1911 revolution, and belonged to the left-wing activists of the Kuomintang during the early 1930s, when he went to France for exile. In France, Eugene Chen got married with Agatha Alphosin Ganteaume, a woman of mixed white and black ancestry. One of their sons was Percy Chen, who was born in Trinidad and studied law in England. In 1926, Percy Chen joined the Nationalist Party's foreign ministry and migrated to Hong Kong in 1947 after his father's death. Chen later was one of the founders of the HKCRA, and due to his left-wing political ideology, the British colonial government was reportedly apprehensive of him.[21] In the 1952 UrbCo election, Percy Chen got 461 votes and was defeated by Brook Bernacchi.[22] In 1951, when a fire accident took place in Tung Tau village's squatters area, the Chinese Communist Party (CCP) organized a delegation from Guangdong to bring rice and medicine as logistical supplies to Hong Kong, the HKCRA led by Percy Chen and pro-Beijing *Ta Kung Pao*'s editor Fei Yimin went to receive the delegation.[23] Yet, the British colonial government refused the entry of the CCP delegation and there was a confrontation between the police and the left-wing local supporters. The clash led to a death and ten injuries, while 12 people, including the HKCRA chairman Mok Ying-kwei, were deported out of Hong Kong.[24] Many members of the HKCRA left the group. Percy Chen took over the HKCRA as the chairman, reaching out to acquire the support of local leftists to join the association, including the pro-Beijing FTU and the CMA. At this juncture, the three organizations—HKCRA, FTU, and CMA—formed an alliance that became the pillar of the local left-wing and pro-Beijing forces. In the 1967 riots in Hong Kong, Chen joined the left-wing activists in the Hong Kong and Kowloon Committee for Anti-Hong Kong British Persecution Struggle, demonstrating his anti-colonialist sentiment and action. The gradual metamorphosis of the HKCRA and the associated life experiences of Percy Chen could illustrate the political transformation of this relatively pro-Beijing political group in Hong Kong under British rule.

Table 2.5 illustrates the core leaders and members of the HKCRA. Ma Man-fai, one of the founders of the HKCRA, was born in Hong Kong in 1905, and he was the fourth son of Chinese Australian businessman Ma Ying-biu. Ma Man-fai was regarded as the "father" of Hong Kong's "self-determination" movement in the 1950s, after he had founded the HKCRA and argued for the need for the British colonial administration to democratize Hong Kong. At that time, Governor Grantham succeeded Governor Young and decided to shelve the latter's reform plan due to his fear about the possibility of the infiltration of Chinese communists into Hong Kong's electoral politics. Ma appealed to Governor Grantham to engage in a public debate.[25] But Governor Grantham declined his offer. Ma believed that UrbCo elections were powerless and useless, and as such, he relied on the Hong Kong United Nations Association to call for the promotion of human rights and freedom in Hong Kong.[26] Above all, he organized regular public forms and seminars parallel to the Hyde Park's free discussions on social and political issues in London in the nineteenth century. Even after the death of Ma in 1994, a series of seminars and lectures continued to be held at the Hong Kong City Hall for many years—a testimony to not only the influence of Ma's determination to uphold the freedom of speech and of thought, but also his followers' belief.

Table 2.5: Core Leaders and Members of the Hong Kong Chinese Reform Association

Core Leaders and Members	Important issues experienced
Ma Man-fai (馬文輝 1905–1994)	Ma's father was Ma Ying-biu who set up the first department store, Sincere Company which relied on the local Hong Kong Chinese capital investment. Ma Man-fai worked as a comprador in England and was acquainted with some British politicians. In 1947, when Governor Mark Young proposed his reform plan for Hong Kong, Ma studied the possibilities and options of making Hong Kong people "autonomous" in making their own decisions. When the British Colonial Office abandoned the Young Plan in 1952, Ma cooperated with 500 social groups to oppose the decision of the British government to abandon political reform, and they decided to promote "self-determination and independence" for Hong Kong.
Mok Ying-kwei (莫應溎 1901–1997)	He was the grandson of Mok Si-yeung, the first chairman of the Hong Kong Kwong Wah Hospital. In May 1925, Mok Ying-kwei as a young lawyer rescued the CCP member Ye Jianying (who was trapped in Cheung Chu Island at that time) and some Kuomintang soldiers who were detained by the British colonial government in Hong Kong. In January 1932, when the Japanese military invaded Shanghai, Mok organized a 75-member rescue team composed of Hong Kong medical staff who went to Shanghai to help the injured citizens and soldiers. He also donated money for the Nationalist army to build up its military hospital in Shanghai. In September 1950, Mok was a member of the Board of Directors of the Hong Kong Chinese Chamber of Commerce and he advocated that the chamber should fly the PRC flag — a testimony to his pro-Beijing political orientation. In November 1951, he mobilized the HKCRA members to help the fire victims of the Tung Tau squatter's area. In March 1952, the HKCRA supported the CCP delegation from Guangdong province to provide relief to the fire victims, but the British colonial government sent police to suppress the local leftists. The colonial authorities announced that Mok was unwelcome and deported him back to the mainland, where he later lived in Guangzhou and became a member of the National People's Congress and a vice-chairman of the Guangdong People's Political Consultative Conference. In 1984, Mok was appointed by the PRC government as a member of the Hong Kong Basic Law Drafting Committee — an indication that his pro-Beijing political orientation led to the British colonial administration's persecution but the PRC government's recognition and support.
Zeng Jinghou (曾靖侯 1887–1965)	He was born in Guangdong province's Sanshui in 1887 and became a trainee lawyer in Hong Kong in 1909. In 1911, Zeng became a translator and manager of a shipping company. In 1941, he opened a metallurgical factory. He was later the vice-chairman of the HKCRA. In 1954, Zeng transferred his capital investment from his metallurgical factory back to Guangzhou, where he set up a parallel factory. He was later appointed as a member of the Guangdong People's Political Consultative Conference.

Table 2.5 Continued

Core Leaders and Members	Important issues experienced
Percy Chen (陳丕士 1901–1989)	He was a barrister and a political activist. His father was Eugene Chen who was a foreign minister of the Nationalist government in China. In 1922, Percy Chen graduated with a law degree from London and then practiced law in Trinidad until 1926, when he returned to China and became a secretary in the Chinese Foreign Ministry. In 1927, Eugene Chen asked Percy Chen to escort the Communist International representative, Mikhail Gruzenberg, from China back to the Soviet Union. Percy Chen stayed in the Soviet Union until 1935 when he returned to China and began to conduct united front work. During the Second World War, Percy Chen became the personal secretary of Sun Fo, the chairman of the Legislative Assembly under the Nationalist government in China. In 1947, Percy Chen became a lawyer of the Hong Kong High Court. In 1952 and 1953, Percy Chen participated in the UrbCo elections but was defeated twice. In the 1960s he was one of the founders of the Reform Club, advocating that mainland China should achieve reunification with Taiwan. In the 1967 riots, he was a member of the pro-Beijing Maoist struggle committee in Hong Kong—an indication that he was a dedicated left-wing activist.
Chen Jun-bao (陳君葆 1898–1982)	He was born in Guangdong in 1898 and followed his grandfather to migrate to Hong Kong at the age of eleven. He studied at the Queen's College and later the University of Hong Kong. After graduation from the University of Hong Kong in 1921, he worked in Singapore and Malaya and later at the University of Hong Kong's Fung Ping Shan Library as a librarian. During the Second World War, he preserved many old documents and rare books. In 1946, he succeeded in recovering 111 boxes of books and documents from Japan for the University of Hong Kong's library. He was decorated with an Order of the British Empire by Governor Mark Young in 1947. He was later appointed as a member of the Guangdong People's Political Consultative Conference and a member of the China Federation of Literary and Art Circles.

Note: As of 2020, the HKCRA has become a pro-Beijing social group organizing a variety of activities in support of the PRC's policies toward Hong Kong. Its headquarters is now located at Wan Chai. See its website: http://www. hkcra.com/web/subpage.php?mid=19, access date: August 9, 2020.

Sources: Compiled from multiple sources, including Lau, Yun-wo, *A History of the municipal councils of Hong Kong: 1883–1999: From the Sanitary Board to the Urban Council and the Regional Council* (Hong Kong: Leisure and Cultural Service Department, 2002). For Mok Ying-kwei's history, see "Mok Ying-kwei," in https://www.easyatm. com.tw/wiki/%E8%8E%AB%E6%87%89%E6%BA%8E, access date: August 9, 2020. For the leaders of the HKCRA, see its website, http://www.hkcra.com/web/subpage.php?mid=19, access date: August 9, 2020.

Table 2.6: Urban Council Elections and Success of the Reform Club, 1952–1955

1952: Brook Bernacchi, 1,168 votes; William Louey, 1,068 votes
1953: Brook Bernacchi, 2,100 votes; Woo Pak-chuen, 1,746 votes; Raymond Harry Shoon Lee, 1,304 votes; Philip Au, 1,224 votes
1954: Raymond Harry Shoon Lee, 3,943 votes; Philip Au, 3,830 votes
1955: Brook Bernacchi, 1,624 votes; Woo Pak-chuen, 1,659 votes

Note: These were all the elected Reform Club members.

Sources: Compiled from multiple sources, including Lau, Yun-wo, *A History of the Municipal Councils of Hong Kong: 1883–1999: From the Sanitary Board to the Urban Council and the Regional Council* (Hong Kong: Leisure and Cultural Service Department, Hong Kong Government, 2002)

Urban Council Elections: From Reform Club's Success to Competition from Reform Club

The early years of the UrbCo elections were characterized by the success of the Reform Club. Table 2.6 shows that Brook Bernacccchi's Reform Club tended to grasp elected seats far more easily than the HKCRA until the formation and emergence of the Hong Kong Civic Association in 1954.[27] The Civic Association saw the participation of both local Chinese and non-Chinese residents, including Roger Lobo, Arnaldo de Oliveira Sales, Brother Cassian, and Woo Pak-foo.[28] In 1959, Hilton Cheong-Leen led the Civic Association, and its leaders and members were determined to support political reform in Hong Kong—a stance that directly challenged the Reform Club.[29] Overall, the two political groups—the Reform Club and the Civic Association—played an important role in lobbying the British colonial government and the Colonial Office for political reform in Hong Kong. They could be seen as the progressive political opposition in Hong Kong under British rule.

Table 2.7 shows that the Civic Association began to challenge the dominance of the Reform Club from 1956 to 1991, after which both political groups began to envisage a prominent decline in their activities. Hilton Cheong-Leen represented the Civic Association in the 1956 elections and he was elected. The Civic Association leveled the Reform Club in the 1959 elections with four of its members being elected to the UrbCo. From 1969 to 1972, the Civic Association outperformed the Reform Club in terms of the number of members elected to the UrbCo. Starting from 1986, however, the two groups only managed to grasp one-third of the elected

**Table 2.7: Elected Seats Occupied by Reform Club and Civic Association,
1952–1982 (% Percentage of total elected seats)**

Year	Elected seats	Reform Club	Civic Association
1952	2	1 (50.0%)	Not yet participated
1953	4	4 (100%)	Not yet participated
1954	4	4 (100%)	Not yet participated
1955	4	4 (100%)	Not yet participated
1956	8	6 (75.0%)	2 (25.0%)
1957–1958	8	5 (62.5%)	3 (37.5%)
1959–1960	8	4 (50.0%)	4 (50.0%)
1961–1962	8	4 (50.0%)	4 (50.0%)
1963–1964	8	4 (50.0%)	4 (50.0%)
1965–1966	10	6 (60.0%)	4 (40.0%)
1967–1968	10	4 (40.0%)	4 (40.0%)
1969–1970	10	3 (30.0%)	5 (50.0%)
1971–1972	10	3 (30.0%)	5 (50.0%)
1973–1974	12	5 (41.7%)	4 (33.3%)
1975–1976	12	4 (33.3%)	4 (33.3%)
1977–1978	12	3 (25.0%)	4 (33.3%)
1979–1980	12	3 (25.0%)	4 (33.3%)
1981–1982	12	2 (16.7%)	4 (33.3%)
1983–1985	15	3 (20.0%)	4 (26.7%)
1986–1988	15	2 (13.3%)	3 (20.0%)
1989–1991	15	2 (13.3%)	3 (20.0%)
1991–1994	15	2 (13.3%)	1 (6.7%)
1995–1997	32	0 (0.0%)	1 (3.1%)

Note: From 1953 to 1981, only half of all elected seats were provided for re-election each time.

Sources: Compiled from multiple sources, including Lau Yun-wo, *A History of the Municipal Councils of Hong Kong: 1883–1999: From the Sanitary Board to the Urban Council and the Regional Council* (Hong Kong: Leisure and Cultural Service Department, Hong Kong Government, 2002).

seats in UrbCo—an indication of their gradual decline. Their decline became more prominent in the 1991 elections, in which both groups managed to capture only one-fifth of the elected seats in UrbCo. Hence, without grooming new and young candidates, and without renewing and reforming their political platforms in the mid-1980s and 1990s, both the Reform Club and Civic Association became aging in their membership and increasingly politically outdated.

Table 2.8: Votes Gained by Candidates of Reform Club and Civic Association in Urban Council Elections, 1956–1965

Reform Club (elected persons and votes)		Civic Association (elected and votes)	
Year 1956			
Philip Au	4,465 votes	Li Yiu-bor	2,880 votes
Raymond Harry Shoon Lee	4,293 votes	Woo Pak-foo	2,567 votes
Chan Shu-woon Alison Mary	4,205 votes		
Spencer Bell	4,122 votes		
Year 1957			
Brook Bernacchi	3,923 votes	Li Yiu-bor	4,569 votes
		Woo Pak-foo	3,755 votes
		Hilton Cheong-Leen	3,625 votes
Year 1959			
Chan Shu-woon	5,021 votes	Ernest Charles Wong	3,076 votes
Alison Bell Raymond Harry	3,624 votes		
Shoon Lee	3,385 votes		
Year 1961(uncontested)			
Brook Bernacchi		Li Yiu-bor, Hilton Cheong-Leen, and Woo Pak-foo	
Year 1963			
Chan Shu-woon	4,006 votes	Cheung Wing-in	2,565 votes
Elsie Elliott	2,287 votes		
Raymond Harry Shoon Lee	2,831 votes		
Year 1965			
Brook Bernacchi	4,192 votes	Li Yiu-bor	3,768 votes
Alison Bell	3,913 votes	Woo Pak-foo	3,616 votes
Henry H. L. Hu	3,828 votes	Hilton Cheong-Leen	3,520 votes

Sources: Compiled from multiple sources, including Lau, Yun-wo, *A History of the Municipal Councils of Hong Kong: 1883–1999: From the Sanitary Board to the Urban Council and the Regional Council* (Hong Kong: Leisure and Cultural Service Department, Hong Kong Government, 2002).

Table 2.8 shows that the votes gained by the candidates of the Reform Club and the Civic Association. The results demonstrated that the Reform Club was relatively stronger with more popular candidates, such as Philip Au from the Reform Club in 1956, Bernacchi in 1957 and 1965, and Chan Shu-woon in 1959 in 1963. As a relatively new group, the Civic Association performed well, including Woo Pak-foo in 1956 and 1965, Liu Yiu-bor in 1957 and 1965, Ernest Wong in 1959, and Hilton Cheong-Leen in 1965.

In February 1966, Governor Sir David Trench reopened the question of reforming the local government. He referred to the urban areas of Tsuen Wan, Castle Peak, and Sha Tin, where he thought that some features of the UrbCo could be amended to involve public participation.[30] Then the

UrbCo formed an ad-hoc committee to formulate proposals, involving the alternative of expanding the UrbCo into a greater Hong Kong council with an elected majority taking over the responsibilities of education, fire services, housing, medical services, town planning, public works, social welfare, and transport not only in the urban areas but also in entire Hong Kong. Underneath the UrbCo would be three or more district councils to be set up for the Hong Kong Island, Kowloon, and the New Territories to carry out public health and sanitary functions.[31] It looked as if the UrbCo would expand its jurisdictions and powers in such a way as to usurp the powers of the Colonial Secretariat and other departments. However, a report written by a group of officials under the chairmanship of W. V. Dickinson adopted a more cautious approach, arguing that a mixture of District Councils, Municipal Councils, and Urban District Councils would be necessary to take care of Kowloon, the Hong Kong Island, and the New Territories.[32] It suggested that the number of new councils should be around four to nine, and the functions to be devolved from government departments would be the same functions performed by UrbCo in addition to the management of housing, schools, and social welfare. The effect of the Dickinson report was to abolish the UrbCo and divide it into several councils, including a partition of the New Territories into the scope of these councils. Therefore, while the UrbCo's ad-hoc committee proposed a three-tiered structure in which the central government would be weaker, the middle-level UrbCo more powerful, and district councils more advisory at the bottom, the proposal from the Dickinson report advocated a more powerful central government and a number of councils at the lower level, where UrbCo and the Heung Yee Kuk (HYK) would be dismembered.[33] These two proposals, however, were shelved with the outbreak of the 1967 riots in Hong Kong. Hence, the elected UrbCo members during the mid-1960s did have their ambition of augmenting their powers by grasping the chance of Governor Trench to reopen the discussions on local administrative reforms.

Starting from 1967, there were signs that other candidates without participation in the Reform Club and Civic Association could be elected. Elsie Elliott, a formerly Reform Club member, and Denny Huang Mong-hwa were elected. Their success changed the dominance of these two political organizations (Table 2.9). Since then, UrbCo elections were divided into three groups, namely the Reform Club, Civic Association, and non-affiliated candidates. Those non-affiliated or "independent" candidates

Table 2.9: Urban Council Elections, 1967–1982

Reform Club (elected candidates and votes)		Civic Association (elected candidates and votes)		Others	
Year 1967					
Woo Po-shing	4,254 votes	Hilton Cheong-Leen	4,555 votes	Elsie Elliott	6,924 votes
		Solomon Rafeek	3,459 votes	Denny Huang Mong-hwa	5,197 votes
Year 1969					
Brook Bernacchi	5,455 votes	Raymond Y. K. Kan	4,325 votes	NIL	
Henry H. L. Hu	4,761 votes	Peter C. K. Chan	4,111 votes		
		Henry Won	3,536 votes		
Year 1971					
Cecilia L. Y. Yeung	3,534 votes	Hilton Cheong-Leen,	5,790 votes	Elsie Elliott	7,578 votes
		Charles C.C. Sin	3,898 votes	Denny Huang Mong-hwa	5,550 votes
Year 1973					
Brook Bernacchi	6,124 votes	Peter C. K. Chan	5,274 votes	NIL	
Henry H. L. Hu	5,920 votes	Edmund W. H. Chow	4,533 votes		
Tsin Sai-nin	4,556 votes	Ambrose K. C. Choi	4,482 votes		
Wong Pun-cheuk	4,040 votes				
Year 1975					
Cecilia L. Y. Yeung	3,645 votes	Hilton Cheong-Leen	5,992 votes	Elsie Elliott	8,886 votes
				Denny M. H. Huang	8,346 votes
				Wong Pun-cheuk	4,833 votes
				Henry H. O. Luk	4,245 votes
Year 1977					
Brook Bernacchi	4,363 votes	Edmund W. H. Chow	4,540 votes	Tsin Sai-nin	3,925 votes
Henry H. L. Hu	4,060 votes	Peter C. K. Chan	4,030 votes		
		Ambrose K. C. Cho	3,733 votes		
Year 1979					
Cecilia L. Y. Yeung	4,990 votes	Hilton Cheong-Leen	4,743 votes	Elsie Elliott	8,214 votes
				Denny Huang Mong-hwa	6,348 votes
				Maria Tam Wai-chu	5,488 votes
				Augustine Chung Shai-kit	4,136 votes
Year 1981					
Francis Chaine	3,750 votes	Ambrose K. C. Choi	4,123 votes	Tsin Sai-nin	2,879 votes
		Peter C. K. Chan	3,882 votes	Peter Chan Po-fun	2,781 votes
		Edmund W. H. Chow	3,683 votes		

Sources: Compiled from multiple sources, including Lau, Yun-wo, *A History of the Municipal Councils of Hong Kong: 1883–1999: From the Sanitary Board to the Urban Council and the Regional Council* (Hong Kong: Leisure and Cultural Service Department, Hong Kong Government, 2002).

embraced Elsie Elliott, Denny Huang, Wong Pun-cheuk, Henry Luk, Tsin Sai-nin, Maria Tam, Augustine Chung, and Peter Chan. The rise of non-affiliated or "independent" candidates marked the gradual political metamorphosis of UrbCo elections from the late 1960s to the early 1980s.

At the same time, the British colonial government used political appointments as "administrative absorption of politics," as Ambrose King argued, to co-opt some UrbCo members into the LegCo. For instance, Hilton Cheong-Leen of the Civic Association and Henry Hung-lick Hu and Yuet-keung Kan of the Reform Club were appointed as LegCo's unofficial members. In 1966, Governor David Trench appointed Yuet-keung Kan as the first Chinese member of the Executive Council (ExCo).[34] Before 1973, it was a "constitutional convention" in Hong Kong under British rule that the unofficial Justices of the Peace and the General Chamber of Commerce were entitled to select one of their representatives to sit in LegCo.[35] In 1973, Governor MacLehose grasped the opportunity of the retirement from the LegCo of the Justice of Peace J. C. Browne by appointing Hilton Cheong-Leen, an elected UrbCo member, into the LegCo. According to Norman Miners, "appointed members of the UrbCo had frequently been elevated to the LegCo in the past, but never before had this honor come to a sitting elected member."[36]

Hilton Cheong-Leen became the chairman of the UrbCo in 1980, signaling an apex of the Civic Association's performance. In 1987, the Civic Association had four members in LegCo, another four in UrbCo, one member in Regional Council (RegCo), and 18 members of DBs, with a total of 27 elected representatives of the people.[37] Strictly speaking, the decline of the Civic Association was slower than that of the Reform Club, because the introduction of representative government in the 1980s provided some room for the Civic Association to grow and prosper. Nevertheless, many members of the Civic Association had overlapping memberships with other organizations and their commitment to the association was not strong. During Hong Kong's transition period from the signing of the Sino-British Joint Declaration in September 1984 to the PRC's reassertion of its sovereignty over the territory on July 1, 1997, the Civic Association failed to rejuvenate its members and reform its platform so that it could unite and appeal to the new voters. Instead, with the rise of many other liberal-minded political groups, the Civic Association could not catch up with them ideologically, generationally, and organizationally.

The development of the representative government in the 1980s witnessed the rapid rise of other non-affiliated and liberal-minded candidates, who won increasingly many elected seats in UrbCo's geographical constituencies. Table 2.10 reveals the increasingly weak Civic Association vis-à-vis other candidates in geographical constituency elections. From 1983 to 1989, the Civic Association still outperformed the Reform Club in terms of having more candidates winning the UrbCo's geographical constituency elections. Nevertheless, the other non-affiliated and liberal-minded candidates began to emerge very quickly during the same period and altogether they outperformed the Association. New rising stars like Elsie Elliott, Frederick Fung, Lee Chek-yuet, Man Sai-cheong, and Wong Kwok-tung all succeeded in being elected. Except for Elsie Elliott who tended to be more pro-Beijing later especially in the 1980s and 1990s, all the other four — Fung and Wong from the Sham Shui Po-based Association for Democracy and People's Livelihood (ADPL), and liberal democrats like Lee Chek-yuet and Man Sai-cheong were the rising stars in urban electoral politics. By 1991, UrbCo elections witnessed the rapid decline and defeat of the Civic Association, which managed to have only Joseph Chan being elected. The Reform Club managed to acquire two elected seats, including the uncontested Bernacchi. Overall, the upsurge in the newly rising democrats was simultaneously prominent, pointing to the outdated political platform and declining competitiveness of the Reform Club and Civic Association.

Table 2.11 shows the rapid emergence of many liberal-minded political groups from the 1980s to the early 1990s. The Hong Kong Observers was founded in 1982 by a group of intellectuals, who studied government policies and lobbied the administration. The Hong Kong Prospect Institute was established in 1982 to study public opinion in 1997 and to suggest solutions to deal with Hong Kong's future. The New Hong Kong Society was also formed in 1982 and it discussed and influenced government policies. The Meeting Point was another political group established in 1983; it supported the PRC's reassertion of its sovereignty over Hong Kong and advocated democracy, nationalism, and the people's livelihood. Similarly, the Hong Kong Affairs Society was set up by a group of liberal-minded intellectuals in 1984 to study and analyze government policies. In 1985, a pro-government Hong Kong Progressive Society was formed, supporting the Sino-British Joint Declaration and influencing the government on

Table 2.10: Urban Council's Geographical Constituency Elections
(Elected persons and their votes gained)

Reform Club		Civic Association		Others	
Year 1983					
Kwan Lim-ho	5,873	Hilton Cheong-Leen	uncontested	Maria Tam Wai-chu	9,564
Brook Bernacchi	5,283	Joseph Chan Yuek-sut	6,437	Pao Ping-wing	4,369
Cecilia Yeung Lai-yin,	8,364	Peter Chan Chi-kwan	4,482	Elsie Elliott	uncontested
		Edmund W. H. Chow	5,085	Lam Chak-piu	6,444
				Frederick Fung Kin-kee	7,450
				Lee Chik-yuet	4,268
				Chung Shai-kit	uncontested
				Denny Huang Mong-hwa	4,840
Year 1986					
Cecilia Yeung Lai-yin	10,029	Hilton Cheong-Leen	7,310	Chow Wai-keung	7,554
Kwan Lim-ho	4,114	Joseph Chan Yuek-sut	10,964	Man Sai-cheong	8,688
		Peter Chan Chi-kwan	4,133	Cheung, Wai Bing	4,925
				Pao Ping-wing	uncontested
				Elsie Elliott	21,725
				Lam Chak-piu	13,511
				Chan Kwok-ming	3,923
				Frederick Fung Kin-kee	12,036
				Lee Chik-yuet	10,460
				Fok Pui-yee	7,491
Year 1989					
Brook Bernacchi	5,566	Hilton Cheong-Leen	3,876	Chow Wai-keung	uncontested
Cecilia Yeung Lai-yin	7,838	Joseph Chan Yuek-sut	uncontested	Man Sai-cheong	8,312
		Peter Chan Chi-kwan	5,651	Pao Ping-wing	uncontested
				Lam Chak-piu	7,187
				Elsie Elliott	uncontested
				Chan Kwok-ming	3,564
				Frederick Fung Kin-kee	7,540
				Ma Lee-wo	5,570
				Mok Ying-fan	4,697
				Daniel Wong Kwok-tung	2,877
Year 1991					
Brook Bernacchi	9,045	Joseph Chan Yuek-sut	10,593	Wong Sui-lai	9,327
Cecilia Yeung Lai-yin	uncontested			San Stephen Wong Hon-ching	4,714
				Man Sai-cheong	12,177
				Chiang Sai-cheong	6,686
				Pao Ping-wing	6,372
				Elsie Elliott	14,556
				Li Wah-ming	12,476
				Chan Kwok-ming	4,475
				Frederick Fung Kin-kee	9,944
				Ma Lee-wo	7,931
				Mok Ying-fan	11,089
				Daniel Wong Kwok-tung	3,028

Sources: Compiled from multiple sources, especially Louie Kin-shuen and Shum Kwok-cheung, eds., *A Compilation of Election Materials in Hong Kong, 1982–1994* (Hong Kong: The Hong Kong Institute of Asia-Pacific Studies, The Chinese University of Hong Kong, 1996); Lau Yun-wo, *A History of the Municipal Councils of Hong Kong: 1883–1999: From the Sanitary Board to the Urban Council and the Regional Council*. Hong Kong: Leisure and Cultural Service Department, Hong Kong Government, 2002).

various policies. Finally, the ADPL was formed in 1986 to promote democracy and comment on social policies. Many of these newly emerging political groups nominated candidates to participate in the UrbCo elections, and later DB elections, such as Maria Tam from the Progressive Society and Man Sai-cheong from the Hong Kong Affairs Society. What distinguished these new groups from the Reform Club and Civic Association was their political platform which emphasized how they saw the future of Hong Kong and responded to it. On the contrary, the political platforms of the Reform Club, the Chinese Reform Association, and the Civic Association remained stagnant. As such, the newly emerging political groups quickly replaced the old organizations — Reform Club, Chinese Reform Association, and Civic Association — in the late 1980s and early 1990s.

The emergence of the United Democrats of Hong Kong (UDHK) in 1990, shortly after the Tiananmen tragedy in China on June 4, 1989 when the People's Liberation Army (PLA) was mobilized to suppress mainland student democrats, was a turning point in Hong Kong's political development. The UDHK was a merger of Meeting Point and Hong Kong Affairs Society (HKAS) and included other liberal-minded professionals, such as chairman and barrister Martin Lee. Its two vice-chairmen were Albert Ho, the former chair of the HKAS, and Yeung Sum, the former chairman of Meeting Point. Other founders included medical doctor Ng Sung-man, teacher Lee Wing-tat, social worker Chan Wai-yip, and educator Ng Ming-yum.[38] Ng revealed that the UDHK allowed overlapping memberships among members who joined other political groups, but these groups could not have contradictory political platform and position with the UDHK.[39] Together with the ADPL, a political group led by Frederick Fung and active in the Sham Shui Po district, the UDHK got 8 out of 15 directly elected seats in the 1991 LegCo elections — a shocking result that pointed to the victory of the new Hong Kong democrats. The rise of these new democrats was, however, accompanied by the political eclipse of the old groups such as the Reform Club, Civic Association, and the Chinese Reform Association.

In Table 2.12, during the last elections held for the UrbCo, the results demonstrated the victory of many candidates who belonged to the pro-democracy camp. The March 1995 UrbCo election witnessed 32 elected members in which the Democratic Party (a merger of UDHK and Meeting Point) grasped 12 seats, and the ADPL captured 5 seats. The fact that

Table 2.11 The Emergence of Political Groups in Hong Kong, 1949–1994

Group	Year of Formation	No. of Founding Members	Interests
Reform Club	1949	46,000	Political reform
Chinese Reform Association	1949	Unknown	Freedom and political reform
Hong Kong Observers	1982	30	Influence and supervise the Government
Hong Kong Prospect Institute	1982	9	Understand public views on1997 and look for solutions
New Hong Kong Society	1982	20–30	Discuss and influence policy on education, housing and political reform
Meeting Point	1983	190	Support China's recovery of its sovereignty over Hong Kong and advocate democracy, nationalism and the people's livelihood
Hong Kong Affairs Society	1984	100	Study and analyze policy
Hong Kong Forum	1984	15	Discuss politics
Hong Kong People's Association	1984	50	Discuss politics, organize talks on Hong Kong and promote exchange between Hong Kong and China
Hong Kong Policy Viewers	1984	30	Study and comment on social policy
Hong Kong Progressive Society	1985	150	Support the Sino-British agreement on Hong Kong's future and make suggestions on various policies
Association for Democracy and People's Livelihood	1986	160	Promote democracy and comment on social affairs
New Hong Kong Alliance	1989	36	Support prosperity and stability
United Democrats of Hong Kong	1990	340	Support democratic reform and participate in elections
Liberal Democratic Federation	1990	150	Promote stability and prosperity
Democratic Alliance for the Betterment of Hong Kong	1992	56	Promote stability and prosperity and support gradual political change
Democratic Party (a merger of UDHK and Meeting Point)	1994	300	Support democratic reform and participate in Elections

Sources: Fong Wah, "Hong Kong Political Groups Easy to Emerge but Difficult to Grow," *Ming Pao Monthly* (April 1991), p. 8; and *The Perspective*, no. 184 (September 1985), pp. 4–5.

Table 2.12: The Last Election of Urban Council in 1995

Constituency	Candidates	Affiliation	Votes gained
UC1 Western	Chan Kwok-leung (elected)	Democratic Party	8.084
	Ip Kwok-him	DAB	7,371
UC2 Central	Kam Nai-wai (elected)	Democratic Party	6,164
	Chan Yuk-cheung	Independent	4,186
UC3 Wan Chai West	San Stephen Wong Hon-ching (elected)	Chinese Reform	3,953
	Li Kin-yin	Democratic Party	2,403
UC4 Wan Chai East	Ada Wong Ying-kay (elected)	Liberal Party	3,182
	John Tse Wing-ling	Democratic Party	2,934
	Susanna Yeung Wan king	Independent	1,009
	Thomas Wong Cheung-chi	Independent	143
UC5 North Point West	Jennifer Chow Kit-bing (elected)	Liberal Party	3,370
	Mathias Woo Yan-wai	Independent	2,719
	Chan Tak-wai	DF	1,163
	Yuen King-yuk	Independent	749
UC6 North Point East	Wong Kwok-hing (elected)	DAB	6,718
	Shing Wai-pong	CLDP	1,453
UC7 Quarry Bay	Joseph Lai Chi-keong (elected)	Democratic Party	5,937
	Kong Tze-wing	Independent	3,125
	Yuen Ki-kong	Independent	1,861
UC8 Shau Kei Wan	Daniel To Boon-man (elected)	Independent	2,860
	Alexander Fu Yuen-cheung	Independent	1,716
	Hui Ka-hoo	Independent	1,352
	Chum Ting-pong	Independent	367
UC9 Chai Wan West	Manuel Chan Tim-shing (elected)	Democratic Party	5,047
	Chao Shing-kie	DAB	4,417
UC10 Chai Wan East	Christopher Chung Shu-kun (elected)	DAB	7,477
	Tsang Kin-shing	Democratic Party	4,994
UC11 Aberdeen and Bay Area	Joseph Chan Yuek-sut	Independent	uncontested
UC12 Ap Lei Chau	Ronnie Wong Man-chiu (elected)	New Hong Kong Alliance	4,901
	Andrew Cheng Kar-foo	Democratic Party	4,520
UC13 Pokfulam and Wah Fu	Lai Hok-lim (elected)	Democratic Party	5,696
	Elizabeth Tse Wong Siu-yin	HKACE	2,229
UC14 Yau Tsim	Daniel Wong Kwok-tung (elected)	ADPL	5,775
	Ahuja Gary	Independent	1,721
	Li King-wah	PAC	1,140
	Helen Chung Yee-fong	Independent	785
	Foo Pui-man	Civic Association	189
UC15 Mong Kok	Stanley Ng Wing-fai (elected)	Democratic Party	4,656
	Law Wing-cheung	Independent	3,536
	Chan Kwok-ming	Independent	2,399
	Henry Chan Man-yu	DF	530

Constituency	Candidates	Affiliation	Votes gained
UC16 Sham Shui Po West	Ambrose Cheung Wing-sum (elected)	Independent	6,791
	Ha Ving-vung	Democratic Party	6,734
UC17 Sham Shui Po Central	Eric Wong Chung-ki	ADPL	uncontested
UC18 Sham Shui Po East	Tam Kwok-kiu	ADPL	uncontested
UC19 Kowloon City North	Ronald Leung Ding-bong (elected)	Independent	4,815
	Lee Cheuk-fan	Liberal Party	1,863
UC20 Kowloon City East	Wen Choy-bon (elected)	DAB	3,607
	Lam Ming	Independent	3,114
UC21 Kowloon City South	Pao Ping-wing (elected)	LDF	4,224
	Virginia Fung King-man	Independent	3,447
UC22 Kowloon City West	Chiang Sai-cheong (elected)	Liberal Party	6,275
	Wong Siu-yee	LDF	5,533
UC23 Wang Tung and Lok Tin	Mok Ying-fan	ADPL	uncontested
UC24 Wong Tai Sin and Chuk Yuen	Lam Man-fai (elected)	DAB	9,088
	Andrew To Kwan-hang	Democratic Party	7,120
UC25 Tsz Wan Shan and San Po Kong	Lee Kwok-keung (elected)	Democratic Party	5,171
	Kan Chi-ho	DAB	4,402
	Choi Luk-sing	Independent	3,332
UC26 Choi Hung Wan and Ngau Chi Wan	Wu Chi-wai (elected)	Democratic Party	6,595
	Cecilia Yeung Lai-yin	Independent	2,671
	Chan Chun-fat	HKPA	1,770
UC27 Kwun Tong West	Au Yuk-har (elected)	ADPL	8,047
	Chan Kam-lam	DAB	7,204
UC28 Kwun Tong North	Sze To Wah (elected)	Democratic Party	9,175
	Elsie Tu	Independent	6,778
UC29 Shun Sau	Kwok Bit-chun (elected)	DAB	8,725
	Law Chun-ngai	Democratic Party	6,030
UC30 Kwun Tong Central	Hung Chung-fun (elected)	Democratic Party	5,884
	Kan Wing-kay	DAB	3,462
UC31 Kwun Tong South	Li Wah-ming (elected)	Democratic Party	6,798
	Ng Siu-wah	DAB	4,161
UC32 Lam Tin	Francis Tang Chi-ho (elected)	Democratic Party	4,237
	Yiu Cheuk-hung	DAB	4,058
	Li Ting-kit	123 Democratic	1,556

Note: DAB—Democratic Alliance for the Betterment of Hong Kong; DF—Democratic Foundation; CLDP—Chinese Liberal and Democratic Party; HKPA—Hong Kong Progressive Alliance; LDF—Liberal Democratic Federation; 123 Democratic—One Two Three Democratic Alliance; ADPL—Association for Democracy and People's Livelihood; PAC—Public Affairs Council; HKACE—Hong Kong Alliance of Chinese and Expatriates; Chinese Reform—Hong Kong Chinese Reform Club; NHKA—New Hong Kong Alliance

Sources: Compiled from multiple sources, including Louie Kin-shuen and Shum Kwok-cheung, *A Compilation of Election Materials in Hong Kong, 1995* (Hong Kong: The Hong Kong Institute of Asia-Pacific Studies, The Chinese University of Hong Kong, 1996); Lau Yun-wo (2002). *A History of the Municipal Councils of Hong Kong: 1883–1999: From the Sanitary Board to the Urban Council and the Regional Council* (Hong Kong: Leisure and Cultural Service Department, Hong Kong Government, 2002).

Table 2.13: Major Political Parties' Election Performance in Urban and Regional Councils' Direct Elections in 1995

Political Parties	Council	Number of candidates	Number elected	Votes gained	% popular votes	Successful Rate (%)
Democratic Party	Urban	19	12	108.182	36.3%	63.2%
	Regional	17	11	97,641	37.0%	64.7%
ADPL	Urban	5	5 (3)	13,822	4.6%	100%
	Regional	4	3	25,096	9.5%	75.0%
DAB	Urban	12	5	70,690	23.7%	41.7%
	Regional	5	3 (1)	19,858	7.5%	60.0%
LDF	Urban	2	1	9,757	3.3%	50.0%
	Regional	4	3 (1)	15,641	5.9%	75.0%
Liberal Party	Urban	4	3	14,690	4.9%	75.0%
	Regional	2	0	3,828	1.5%	0.0%

Note: The RegCo in 1995 was composed of 27 directly elected members, 9 elected from New Territories District Boards, and three representatives from HYK.

ADPL—Association for Democracy and People's Livelihood; DAB—Democratic Alliance for the Betterment of Hong Kong; LDF—Liberal Democratic Federation

The brackets denote the uncontested seats.

Sources: Louie Kin-shuen and Shum Kwok-cheung, *A Compilation of Election Materials in Hong Kong, 1995* (Hong Kong: The Hong Kong Institute of Asia-Pacific Studies, The Chinese University of Hong Kong, 1996).

the ADPL did not join the Democratic Party (DP) in 1994 illustrated the beginning of the fragmentation of the pro-democracy camp. Still, in total the ADPL and DP captured 17 out of 32 seats. There were nine constituencies in which a candidate of the DP faced a counterpart from the pro-Beijing DAB, and six of them witnessed the victory of DP candidates while three envisaged the victory from the DAB. The pro-Beijing groups did not perform well; the DAB grasped five seats, the New Hong Kong Alliance (NHKA) one, the Chinese Reform Association one, and Liberal Party two seats.

In Table 2.13, the democrats as represented by the DP and the ADPL were much stronger than the pro-government and pro-Beijing forces in the performance of UrbCo and RegCo elections in 1995. The DP gained 11 out of the 27 directly elected seats, followed by the ADPL (3 seats), DAB (3 seats), and the Liberal Democratic Federation (3 seats) in the RegCo election. Overall, the success rate of candidates running in UrbCo and RegCo election was 60% for DP members—a performance better than the pro-Beijing DAB. The ADPL remained a relatively strong pro-democracy group, achieving the success rate of 100% in UrbCo elections and 75% in RegCo ones. The other two pro-business groups, the Liberal Democratic Federation (LDF) and Liberal Party (LP) were much weaker than the DAB, but they represented a moderate attempt by businesspeople to participate in electoral politics.

District Boards Elections and the Emergence of Political Parties, 1982–1997

Since 1982, District Boards (DBs) emerged as "quasi-political institutions with a democratic component" by introducing directly elected members and by listening to the views of the people's representatives on government policies outside the LegCo.[40] The first DBs elections were held in 1982 with 132 directly elected members, 134 appointed members, and 167 officially appointed ones. District Officers chaired all the district boards officially. Democratic representations were limited to less than one-third of all the DBs members, showing a limited pace and scope of democratization in Hong Kong under British rule. Although Governor MacLehose and Jack Cater, as mentioned in the last Chapter, aimed at making DBs an arena where elected representatives could and would hold government officials and departments accountable, and where the communication gap between the rulers and the ruled could be narrowed, the reality was that some elected DBs members were unhappy with the governmental responses to their demands. For instance, an appointed member of the first Wong Tai Sin district Board Mak Hoi-wah maintained that DBs could not really influence the government departments, especially the handling of cultural and recreational facilities, not to mention the government's night-time and part-time schools.[41] Moreover, although the funds distributed by DBs gradually replaced the donations from community leaders and activists, many people at district level perceived DBs as relatively inactive and they did not feel the interest in or necessity of voting in DB elections.[42]

Regardless of how elected DBs members viewed their influence, the British colonial administration in 1983 set up a working group to collect the opinions on local administrative reforms. The views were collected through the City District Offices. In December 1983, the government held six meetings to allow 267 unofficial members of 18 DBs to voice their views.[43] Although the British colonial administration's working group conducted internal discussions on the progress of local administrative reform, it did show the serious attitude of the colonial rulers. In February 1984, Chief Secretary Philip Haddon-Cave remarked that the government had its determination to develop the functions of DBs, including the options of (1) expanding the number of directly elected members from 132 in 1982 to 235 in late 1984 (thereby increasing the proportion of elected members from one-third to two-thirds); (2) electing the DB chairperson from among the DB members so as to reduce official involvement in district administration; (3) withdrawing the appointed members from DBs; (4) changing the role of government officials to attend DBs to explain government policies and answer questions from DBs members; and (5) setting up RegCo to deal with the work of UrbCo in rural areas where a body controlling hawkers, licensing, and cultural and recreational activities was absent.[44] In other words, the British colonial administration was keen to develop district administration further regardless of how DBs were received by the community. The plans discussed by Haddon-Cave were spelt out in the 1984 Green Paper on the development of representative government. In the 1985 DBs elections, the number of elected seats increased to 237; all government officials ceased to be members of DBs; and the chairperson of each District Board would be elected among its members.[45] Further, DBs were grouped into 10 electoral college constituencies in which each of them returned a member to LegCo.

Before the RegCo was formally established in 1986, the British colonial administration set up a provisional RegCo from 1985 to 1986. The provisional RegCo was composed of 12 members appointed by the Governor, nine members elected by the New Territories District Boards, and three members from the chair and two vice chairs of the HYK.[46] From 1986, these 24 members would be joined by 12 members who would be elected from 12 constituencies in the New Territories at the same time as the next elections for the UrbCo took place.

As mentioned in the last Chapter, the 1988 White Paper decided that each of the ten DBs in the urban area would select a representative in the UrbCo. At the same time UrbCo members would cease to be the ex-officio members of the urban District Boards. However, UrbCo members who were elected to urban District Boards would not need to resign their positions from the Council, and vice versa.

Table 2.14 illustrates the evolutions of democratization of DBs or later DCs. From 1982 to 1985, the 134 members appointed by the government

Table 2.14: The Democratization of the Composition of District Boards and District Councils (seats)

Term of office	Elected	Appointed	Ex Officio
Apr 1982–Mar 1985	132	134 (+167)	27(+30)
Apr 1985–Mar 1988	237	132	27(+30)
Apr 1988–Mar 1991	264	141	27(+30)
Apr 1991–Sept 1994	274	140	27
Oct 1994–Jun 1997	346	0	27
Jul 1997–Dec 1999	346	96	27
Jan 2000–Dec 2003	390	102	27
Jan 2004–Dec 2007	400	102	27
Jan 2008–Dec 2011	405	102	27
Jan 2012–Dec 2015	412	68	27
Jan 2016–Dec 2019	431	0	27
Jan 2020–Dec 2013	452	0	27

Note: Initially, District Board chairs were also the District Officers. After 1985, the chairs have been elected among members. The 27 ex-officio members from 1985 to 1991 came from the chairpersons of the Rural Committees.

Sources: Compiled from multiple sources, including Louie Kin-shuen and Shum Kwok-cheung, *A Compilation of Election Materials in Hong Kong, 1995* (Hong Kong: The Hong Kong Institute of Asia-Pacific Studies, The Chinese University of Hong Kong, 1996).

and 167 official members (civil servants) altogether outnumbered the 132 elected members, while there were 57 ex-officio members of which 30 came from the UrbCo. Gradual democratization could be seen in the 1985–88 DBs where elected members began to outnumber appointed members and ex-officio members. The situation changed further in 1994 when there were 346 elected members and no more appointed members. Hence, the British colonial administration democratized the composition of DBs before the retrocession of Hong Kong's sovereignty to the PRC. The Chinese government, however, did not accept the British model of gradual democratization of DBs. The PRC authorities reorganized all the provisional DBs, which were made up of all original members shortly before July 1, 1997 and 96 appointed members. From 1997 to 2011, the HKSAR government maintained the appointed members in DBs until 2012 when all of the appointees were abolished. As such, the fluctuations in the number of appointed members from 1982 to 2016 reflected the political tug-of-war between the British and the PRC government. The final abolition of all

Table 2.15: The Classification of Careers of Elected District Board Members, 1982–1997 (number and percentage)

Careers	1982		1985		1988		1991		1994	
Businessmen	70	53.0%	82	34.6%	54	20.5%	63	23.2%	61	17.6%
Managers or officers	10	7.6%	28	11.8%	57	21.6%	70	25.7%	113	32.7%
Professionals	8	6.1%	38	16.0%	42	15.9%	32	11.8%	37	10.7%
Educators	24	18.2%	43	18.1%	41	15.5%	47	17.3%	47	13.6%
Social workers	3	2.3%	18	7.6%	34	12.9%	15	5.5%	20	5.8%
Community organizers	4	3.0%	6	2.5%	15	5.7%	23	8.5%	47	13.6%
Technicians/workers	9	6.8%	14	5.9%	15	5.7%	14	5.1%	18	5.2%
Retirees or housewife	3	2.3%	8	3.4%	6	2.3%	6	2.2%	0	0.0%
Others	1	0.8%	0	0.0%	0	0.0%	2	0.7%	3	0.9%
Total	132	100%	237	100%	264	100%	272	100%	346	100%

Note: Businessmen — Business owners, board of directors, directors, merchants and traders; Managers — General managers, managers, assistant managers, secretaries, administrative officers; Professionals — Barristers, solicitors, medical doctors, accountants, engineers, designers, news reporters and nurses; Educators — principals, lecturers, teachers and school officers; Community organizers — directors of organizations, trade unionists, district community officers, executive secretary of organizations, and full-time DB members; Technicians/workers — technicians, mechanics, skilled workers, laborers and drivers.

Sources: Louie Kin-shuen and Shum Kwok-cheung, *A Compilation of Election Materials in Hong Kong, 1982–1994* (Hong Kong: The Hong Kong Institute of Asia-Pacific Studies, The Chinese University of Hong Kong, 1996); and Louie Kin-shuen and Shum Kwok-cheung, *A Compilation of Election Materials in Hong Kong, 1995* (Hong Kong: The Hong Kong Institute of Asia-Pacific Studies, The Chinese University of Hong Kong, 1996).

appointed members in DCs in 2012 could be hailed as a small step toward democratization.

Table 2.15 analyzes the careers of the elected members of DBs, showing that district politicians were basically of middle-class background. The percentage of businesspeople declined in DBs from 53% in 1982 to 17.6% in 1994. If the middle class is occupationally composed of managers, professionals and educators, its members increased from about one-third of all Board members in 1982 to almost 55% of all members in 1994. If social workers and community workers were regarded as socio-political activists in the society, they increased from 5% of all Board members in 1982 to almost 19% in 1994. Nevertheless, lower-class citizens, such as technicians, workers

**Figure 2.1: Percentage Shares of the Electoral Participation
of District Board Members, 1982–1994**

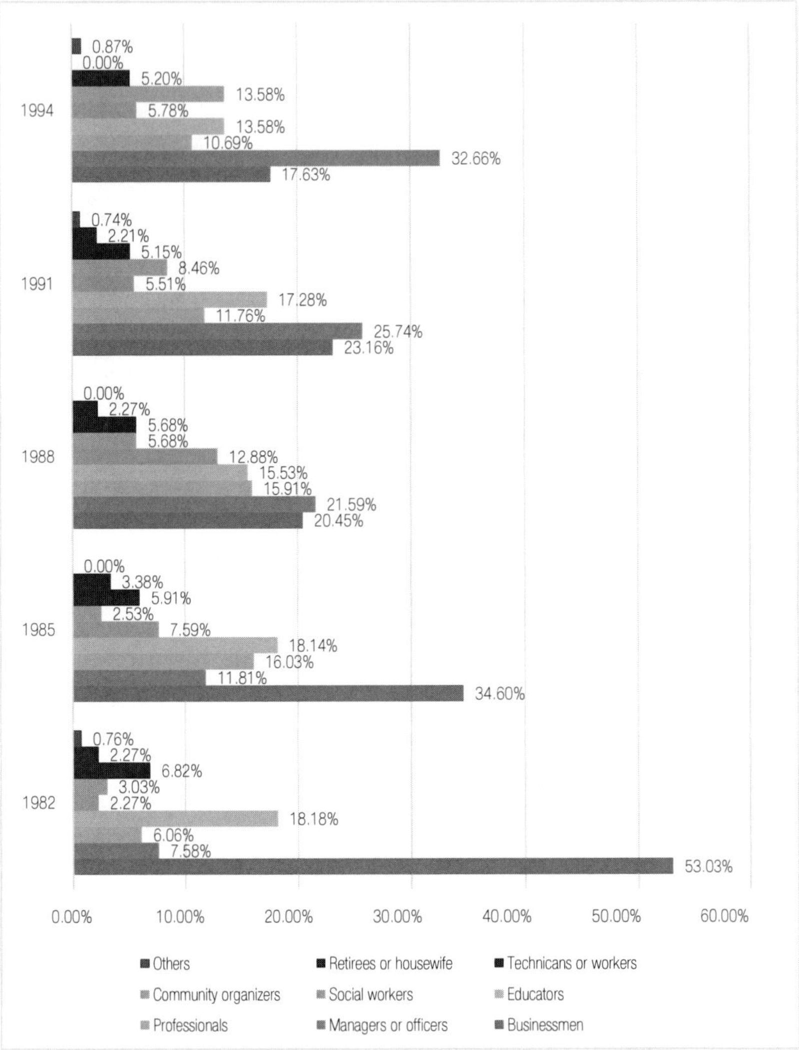

Source: The authors' tabulation from the data of electoral participation.

and retirees, were of the minority in DBs, ranging from 9% in 1982 to only 5% in 1994. Apart from the elected members who were of middle-class background, all the appointed members in DBs from 1982 to 1994 came professionals and managers. Their withdrawal from DBs in did not change the middle-class feature of all DBs, because many elected members also came from professional and managerial background.

Figure 2.1 captures the percentages of all the occupational groups. At the beginning, the participation of businesspeople and managers in district elections was commonplace; in 1982, 70 of them ran in DBs elections. The decline in business participation was, however, compensated by an increase in professional participation, especially in 1994 when professionals occupied one-third of the participants. Professionals, who included many lawyers and school principals, were not prominent in their participation in 1982 with only 6% of the total participants. Nevertheless, the share of professionals increased over time, thanks to the active participation from more lawyers and school principals. Social workers' participation in DBs elections was at one time controversial, for many of their affiliated social groups and agencies received the government's funding support. However, through electoral participation, social workers could help their affiliated organizations to acquire more funding support from DBs at the district level, thereby explaining the unprecedented 13% of participants in 1988. However, there was no study on how many social workers who were affiliated with the government-supported social organizations ran in the same districts. After 1988, the percentage of social workers in electoral participation decreased, but the participation of managers increased sharply.

The electoral system for the 1985 LegCo elections was complex (Table 2.16). There were 24 elected seats out of 56 members. Two kinds of elected seats existed: the first belonged to 12 functional constituencies or occupational sectors (like accountancy, law, teachers, commerce, labor, medicine, engineering, etc.); and the second type comprised functional constituencies in the electoral college. The electoral college was composed of ten constituencies based on the areas served by 19 DBs, and two special constituencies for the UrbCo and the new RegCo.[47] Each of the ten constituencies contained about 500,000 people. Four of these ten constituencies were in the densely populated Kowloon with each area covered by one DB. Four other constituencies covered the areas belonging to two DBs, and the remaining two constituencies was composed of the

Table 2.16: Composition of the Legislative Council from 1984 to 1995

Year	1984	1985	1988	1991	1995
Officials	16	10	10	3	–
Appointed members	30	22	20	18	–
Elected by functional constituencies	–	12	14	21	30
Elected by direct elections	–	–	–	18	20
Elected by electoral college	–	12	12	–	–
Elected by election committee	–	–	–	–	10
Total	46	56	56	60	60

Note: The Governor was the President of the LegCo from 1984 until February 1993 when he was replaced by an elected President. The total number of seats in the above table did not include the Governor.

Sources: Compiled from multiple sources including Louie Kin-shuen and Shum Kwok-cheung, *A Compilation of Election Materials in Hong Kong, 1982–1994* (Hong Kong: The Hong Kong Institute of Asia-Pacific Studies, The Chinese University of Hong Kong, 1996); and Louie Kin-shuen and Shum Kwok-cheung, *Election Information Compilation of Hong Kong, 1995* (Hong Kong: The Hong Kong Institute of Asia-Pacific Studies, The Chinese University of Hong Kong, 1996).

districts covered by three to four DBs. In each of the ten constituencies, the voters were composed of the elected and appointed members of DB, including the chairpersons of the Rural Committees, who were the ex-officio members of the New Territories DBs.[48] For the seat allocated to UrbCo, all the elected and appointed members of UrbCo could vote, as with the seat allocated to RegCo. All UrbCo members were DB members—a situation similar to some of the RegCo members. But these RegCo and UrbCo members were not allowed to vote in DB constituencies for the sake of avoiding them to have two votes in elections. While 12 members of the LegCo members in 1985 and 1988 elections came from the electoral college, this arrangement was abolished in the 1991 and 1995 LegCo elections. In the 1995 LegCo elections, however, ten legislators were returned from an Election Committee.

It is noteworthy that the electoral system of LegCo provided a political ladder for some members of DBs to climb up gradually. For example, Desmond Lee Yu-tai, Conrad Lam Kui-shing, Jackie Chan Chai-keung, and Richard Lai Sung-lung won in the electoral college through DBs. They also became the democrats supportive of the introduction of direct elections to the 1988 LegCo. In 1987, the PRC government opposed the British colonial government to introduce direct elections to the LegCo in 1988. Eventually, the British government made concessions to PRC authorities and postponed the introduction of direct elections to LegCo from 1988 to 1991. When the last Governor Christopher Patten came to Hong Kong, he proposed political reforms in his 1992 policy address, including the controversial proposals of reinvigorating DBs which would be given more powers and funds to manage environmental projects, public works, and community-building activities.[49] Moreover, he proposed that the appointment system for DBs would be scrapped, retaining some ex-officio members in the New Territories DBs. Most importantly, in the 1995 LegCo elections, all elected DBs members could form an Election Committee to elect ten members of the LegCo. Although his proposals met the PRC government's opposition, the reform package illustrated the importance of DBs in the British plan of democratization in Hong Kong. Eventually, Governor Patten decided to abolish all appointed seats in DBs in 1994 and retained the ex-officio seats from the 27 Rural Committees in the New Territories DBs—a small breakthrough in the process of democratizing DBs in Hong Kong during the twilight of the British colonial rule.

Table 2.17, Table 2.18, and Table 2.19 show the importance of the members of DBs in the Electoral College or Committee of the LegCo elections in 1985, 1988, and 1995 respectively. In 1985, the LegCo's electoral college returned 12 members from the UrbCo, Provisional RegCo, and other DBs. Except for Andrew Wong Wang-fat who was elected automatically without any contenders, all other constituencies envisaged competition. In the 1988 electoral college elections, three candidates were elected automatically without any contestant, including Elsie Tu, Daniel Tse, and Chung Wai-lam. It is noteworthy that the British colonial administration's proposal of injecting ten directly elected seats to LegCo in 1991, from the perspective of some DB members, curbed the power and influence of District Boards. To appease the anger of some DBs members, the government decided to increase the monthly stipend of each DB member from HK$3,200 to HK$6,400.

In Table 2.19, the democrats managed to get four out of ten seats from the LegCo's election committee, which was composed of the members of DBs in 1995. They included Cheung Bing-leung and John Tse of the Democratic Party, Yim Sin-ling from the pro-Taiwan One Two Three

Table 2.17: Electoral College Elections of the Legislative Council in 1985

Constituency	Candidates	Votes
Urban Council	Hilton Cheong-Leen	16
	Elsie Tu	13
Provisional Regional Council	Lau Wong-fat	Uncontested
Hong Kong Island (East)	Desmond Lee Yu-tai	24
	Kwan Lim-ho	16
	Albert Cheung Chi-piu	0
	Lee Kam-kee	0
	Peggy Lam Pei	0
	Chum Ting-pong	0
Hong Kong Island (West)	Liu Lit-for	18
	Anthony Ng Sung man	16
	Keith Lam Hon-keung	0
Kwun Tong	Poon Chi-fai	18
	Cheng Kwan-suen	11
	Li Wah-ming	0
Wong Tai Sin	Conrad Lam Kui-shing	16
	Liu Koon-sing	15
Kowloon City	Daniel Tse Chi-wai	13
	Pao Ping-wing	11
	Peter Chan Chi-kwan	0
Sham Shui Po	Chung Pui-lam	19
	Ambrose Cheung Wing-sum	8
South Kowloon	Jackie Chan Chai-keung	12
	Ena Yuen Yin-hung	7
	Jacob Chan Lai-sang	6
	Ip Kwok-chung	0
New Territories (East)	Andrew Wong Wang-fat	29
	Pang Hang-yin	25
	Liu Ching-leung	0
	Wong Yuen-cheung	0
	Wai Hon-leung	0
New Territories (West)	Tai Chin-wah	22
	Man For-tai	18
	Alfred Tso Shiu-wai	0
	Kingsley Sit Ho-yin	0
	Tang Siu-tong	0
New Territories (South)	Richard Lai Sung lung	34
	Lam Wai-keung	28
	John Ho Tung-ching	0

Note: The first candidate who got most votes was elected.

Source: Louie Kin-shuen and Shum Kwok-cheung, *A Compilation of Election Materials in Hong Kong, 1982–1994* (Hong Kong: The Hong Kong Institute of Asia-Pacific Studies, The Chinese University of Hong Kong, 1996).

Table 2.18: Electoral College Elections of the Legislative Council in 1988

Constituency	Candidates	Votes
Urban Council	Elsie Tu	Uncontested
Regional Council	Cheung Yan-lung	19
	Tang Kwok-yung	13
	Choy Kan-pui	8
Hong Kong Island (East)	Chan Ying-lun	21
	Desmond Lee Yu-tai	20
Hong Kong Island (West)	So Chau Yim-ping	18
	Liu Lit-for	16
	Joseph Chan Yuek-sut	11
Kwun Tong	Poon Chi-fai	21
	Li Wah-ming	12
Wong Tai Sin	Michael Cheng Tak-kin	16
	Conrad Lam Kui-shing	13
Kowloon City	Daniel Tse Chi-wai	Uncontested
Sham Shui Po	Chung Pui-lam	Uncontested
South Kowloon	Kingsley Sit Ho-yin	12
	Ng Kin-sun	10
	Clement Tao Kwok-lau	5
New Territories (East)	Andrew Wong Wang-fat	30
	Michael Lai Kam-cheung	25
New Territories (West)	Tai Chin-wah	27
	Man For-tai	18
New Territories (South)	Lam Wai-keung	38
	Yeung Fuk-kwong	31
	Richard Lai Sung-lung	20
	William Wan Hon-cheung	9

Source: Louie Kin-shuen and Shum Kwok-cheung, *A Compilation of Election Materials in Hong Kong, 1982–1994* (Hong Kong: The Hong Kong Institute of Asia-Pacific Studies, The Chinese University of Hong Kong, 1996).

Alliance, and Law Cheung-kwok from ADPL. The pro-government and pro-Beijing forces remained quite strong in the Election Committee results with six candidates being elected. They included Lo Suk-ching from the pro-Beijing New Territories Association of Societies, Choy Kan-pui from the pro-government Civic Force, Lau Hon-chuen from the politically conservative Progressive Alliance, David Chu from the pro-business Liberal Democratic Federation, and Chan Kam-lam and Ip Kwok-him from the pro-Beijing DAB.

Table 2.19: Election Committee Constituency of Legislative Council in 1995

Candidates	Affiliation	Value of votes
1. Yeung Fuk-kwong	Independent	0
2. Lee York-fai	Independent	0
3. Fung Kwong-chung	Independent	0
4. Lo Suk-ching	Independent (New Territories Association of Societies)	26 (elected)
5. Choy Kan-pui	Independent (Civic Force)	26 (elected)
6. Cheung Bing-leung	Democratic Party	26 (elected)
7. Lau Hon-chuen	Progressive Alliance	26 (elected)
8. Chan Kam-lam	DAB	26 (elected)
9. Leung Kwong-cheong	ADPL	0
10. Law Cheung-kwok	ADPL	26 (elected)
11. Ip Kwok-him	DAB	26 (elected)
12. John Tse Wing-ling	Democratic Party	26 (elected)
13. David Chu Yu-lin	Liberal Democratic Federation	26 (elected)
14. Yuen Bun-keung	Democratic Party	0
15. Mark Lin	Liberal Party	0
16. Louis Leung Wing-on	Independent	0
17. Yum Sin-ling	123 Democratic Alliance	26 (elected)
18. Paul Chan Sing-kong	Independent	0

Source: Louie Kin-shuen and Shum Kwok-cheung, *A Compilation of Election Materials in Hong Kong, 1995* (Hong Kong: The Hong Kong Institute of Asia-Pacific Studies, The Chinese University of Hong Kong, 1996).

Politicization and Party Politics Since 1990s: Pro-Beijing versus Pro-Democracy Camps

If the LegCo's Election Committee results showed the dominance of two main political camps, namely the pro-democracy on the one hand and pro-Beijing and pro-government on the other, then the politicization of Hong Kong's elections could be seen in not only the legislative level but also the district level. The rivalries among political parties since the 1990s has become the hallmark of Hong Kong's territorial and district politics. The emergence of party politics originated from the evolution of political groups, which as mentioned before sprung up in the late 1980s and 1990s as a response to the development of representative government and the Sino-British negotiations over Hong Kong's future. By 1990s, all these embryonic political parties were well-positioned to compete in the elected seats in DBs, UrbCo, RegCo, and LegCo. Although there was and is no political party law in Hong Kong, these self-proclaimed parties have been registered under the Company Ordinance and actively participated in local elections.

The pro-government and pro-Beijing forces gradually have emerged as an indispensable political camp in Hong Kong's district politics for several reasons. First and foremost, the pro-government forces originally were composed of a loose coalition of community activists and leaders coopted by the colonial administration. They included *kaifong* leaders and activists from the Owners Corporations (OCs) and the Mutual Aid Committees (MACs). Some of them helped the colonial government in various Area Committees (ACs). Once the democratization of DBs began in the early 1980s, some of them were encouraged to participate in politics. Gradually they became a pro-establishment force to be reckoned with and become a target of co-optation by the pro-Beijing camp that remained relatively weak electorally in the 1980s. Secondly, the businesspeople were actively involved in district elections during the early 1980s and, once the Sino-British negotiations over Hong Kong's future began in 1982–84, they sensed the political necessity of organizing themselves in a much better way for the sake of protecting their interests. As such, they also became a target of political support from the pro-Beijing and pro-government camp. After all, many businesspeople have remained traditionally pro-establishment and politically conservative—political orientations that protected their business interests and networks and made their coalition with pro-Beijing forces much easier. Thirdly, the rural political forces, like HYK, have risen since the early 1980s to protect the interests of the indigenous peoples in the New Territories. The introduction of DB elections provided a golden opportunity for the rural elites to participate in electoral politics and gain more experiences in electioneering, apart from the village elections in which many of them had rich experiences. Since the 1980s, the rural elites have become an economic and a political interest group, protecting their land interests that could straddle over July 1, 1997. They lobbied the PRC government over the content of the Basic Law, where Article 40 says that "the lawful traditional rights and interests of the indigenous inhabitants of the New Territories shall be protected by the HKSAR."[50] The rural elites, including the HYK leaders, have remained traditionally politically conservative and supportive of the *status quo*. Ideologically, the *kaifong* leaders and activists, the businesspeople, and the HYK elites could form a loose coalition with pro-Beijing forces, such as the DAB, to become a more organized and powerful pro-PRC camp in Hong Kong's territorial and district politics.

However, as this book will discuss, the formation of loose political coalitions in district elections was simultaneously marked by bitter struggle and fragmentation among the pro-government and pro-Beijing camp. The rural elites are by no means homogeneous, as with the pro-Beijing and pro-business forces as well as the *kaifong* leaders and activists. As a result, Hong Kong's territorial and district politics have been characterized by temporary coalitions but simultaneously tense relations and political struggles. In short, the fragmentation of district and rural politics has become the hallmark of district-level political development, having tremendous impacts on district administration, as we will discuss later.

Table 2.20 shows the core leaders of pro-business and pro-Beijing political groups, which include the Hong Kong Progressive Society (HKPS), the Liberal Democratic Federation, and the Hong Kong Progressive Alliance (HKPA). In February 1985, the HKPS was set up and its involved political heavyweight Maria Tam and other businesspeople, such as Philip Kwok and Po Ping-wing. Some other businessmen joined the HKPS, including James Tien and Vincent Lo.[51] The Society held its first general meeting in June 1985, when Maria Tam was elected as the first chairman, Philip Kwok as the vice chairman, Lester Kwok as treasurer, and Pao Ping-wing as the secretary. Other executive committee members included Veronica Wu, Kan

Table 2.20: Core Leaders of Pro-Business and Pro-Beijing Political Groups

Core Leaders	Experiences
Maria Tam Wai-chu	She was born in 1945 in Hong Kong and later graduated from the St. Paul's Co-educational College. She obtained a Bachelor of Laws from the University of London and was then admitted as a barrister at the Gray's Inn. She first participated in politics when she ran in the 1979 Urban Council election as an advocate for women's rights. She was elected. In 1981, Tam was appointed to the LegCo. Two years later, she was appointed to the Executive Council in 1983. She was at one time a member of the four different levels of representative institutions, namely, ExCo, LegCo, UrbCo, and Central and Western District Board in the 1980s. In 1985, she was appointed by the PRC government to be a member of the Hong Kong Basic Law Drafting Committee. Tam founded the HKPS in 1985 to nominate candidates to participate in the elections. The HKPS became the backbone of the Liberal Democratic Federation (LDF), which was established by a group of conservative business and professional elites in 1990 for preparation of the LegCo's direct election in 1991. She later became the vice-chair of the LDF.
Philip Kwok Chi-kuen	He was born in Guangdong's Zhongshan and graduated from the St. Paul's Co-educational College. He studied physics at the Massachusetts Institute of Technology and later obtained master and doctoral degrees in Physics in Harvard University. Kwok worked as a researcher at the IBM after his studies. His grandfather, Kwok Chuen, was the founder of the Wing On Company, a famous Chinese department stores. Philip Kwok returned to Hong Kong to help his family business at Wing On in 1970 and became its chairman in 1983. In 1984, Kwok became the vice chairman of the Progressive Society. In 1990, he was one of the co-founders of the LDF. He was appointed by the PRC government to be a deputy director of the Hong Kong Basic Law Drafting Committee. In 1993, he was appointed as a Hong Kong Affairs Adviser.
Hu Fa-kuang	He was born in Jiangsu's Wushi city and later became a teacher in Shanghai. He worked in the China Merchant Shipping Company before he went to work in UK in 1949. Hu returned to Hong Kong to develop the Mitsubishi Electric Company in 1969. In 1983 he became the director of Ryoden (Holdings) Ltd. In 1979 he was appointed as an unofficial member of the LegCo and served there until 1991. He became the chairman of the LDF in 1991.
Ambrose Lau Hon-chuen	He was the chairman of the Hong Kong Progressive Alliance from 1997 to 2005. As a solicitor, Lau also served as the chairman of the Central and Western District Board from 1988 to 1994, and he was the President of the Law Society from 1992 to 1993. Lau was a member of LegCo elected from the Election Committee in 1995.

Sources: Compiled from multiple sources, including "Hu Fa-kuang: staying in Hong Kong to develop his foundation business," *Wen Wei Po*, October 3, 2007, in http://paper.wenweipo.com/2007/10/03/MR0710030001.htm, access date: August 6, 2020.

Fook-yee, Tung Chee-ping, Lee Kai-ming, and Raymond Wu.[52] At that time, the HKPS had 131 members, including 41 members of DBs, eight UrbCo and Provisional RegCo members, two LegCo members, four HYK members, three members from Rural Committees, and 17 trade unionists.[53] In terms of the background of leaders and members, the HKPS stood out as an influential political group in Hong Kong.

In the DB elections in March 1988, nine out of 11 nominated candidates from the HKPS were elected. During the HKPA's general meeting held in April 1988, Tam was re-elected as chairman; Lester Kwok, Chung Pui-lam and Yeung Fuk-kwong were elected vice-chairmen; and George Pang Chun-sing elected as a treasurer.[54] Other new executive committee members included Leung Chun-ying, Edward Ho, Lee Yiu-kwong, Kwan Yiu-wing, and Peter Wong Man-kong.[55] In the September 1988 LegCo elections, the HKPS had eight candidates elected to LegCo, an unprecedented result for a pro-business political group. In 1991, Maria Tam was not reappointed to the ExCo and LegCo; rumors were rife that this was due to media reports in 1990 that she had been involved in the ownership of some taxi licenses, and that she might have potential conflict of role.[56] The incident, however, had a short and temporary impact on Tam's political career. She continued to be a political elite in Hong Kong straddling July 1, 1997.

In 1994, the HKPA was formed in 1994 by a group of businesspeople, like Lau Hon-chuen, but the political group suffered from internal opinion differences among some of its core members. It was rumored that the HKPA's chief executive director, Ng Kun-chit, was sent from Guangzhou to work in Hong Kong.[57] In September 1994, the HKPA nominated seven candidates to run in DB elections, but only one of them won. The LegCo had one of its members, Lau Hon-chuen. Due to its weakness, in 1997, the HKPA was merged into the Liberal Democratic Federation (LDF), trying to become a stronger pro-business party. Yet, the other pro-business Liberal Party viewed the HKPA-LDF as a merged political group orchestrated and backed up by the New China News Agency in Hong Kong.[58] Mutual distrust and jealousies prevented the LP from merging with the alliance between the HKPA and LDF. In 2005, the HKPA and the LDF merged with pro-Beijing Democratic Alliance for the Betterment of Hong Kong to become a new political party, namely Democratic Alliance for the Betterment and Progress of Hong Kong (DAB). The word progress was added into the "old" DAB, a move that incorporated the business elites into the traditionally pro-Beijing party. The new DAB became an umbrella absorbing not only pro-Beijing middle-class citizens but also some upper-class businesspeople from the HKPA and LDF.

The LDF was set up in 1990 by some conservative business elites, who worried about the possibility that Hong Kong would turn into a welfare state and an "adversarial" society. Its formation was a business response to the emergence of the United Democrats of Hong Kong (UDHK) in 1990. Due to the lack of political experiences, the LDF invited Maria Tam to join the group, together with four members of the Civic Association. The LDF won 27 seats in the 1991 DB elections, three seats in the 1991 UrbCo and RegCo elections, and three functional constituency seats in the 1991 LegCo elections. However, the LDF encountered competition from the Liberal Party, which was formed in 1993 and which attracted three LDF members to defect, namely Ngai Shiu-kit, Howard Young, and Peter Wong. In 1997, the LDF merged with the HKPA, and both were integrated into the DAB in 2005.

The Liberal Party (LP) was formed in 1993 and its predecessor was the Cooperative Resources Center (CRC), a legislative "clique" in the LegCo under the British rule.[59] The LP was founded by a group of conservative politicians, business elites, and professionals who were either appointed by the Governor or elected through LegCo's functional constituencies to balance the rise of the increasingly popular pro-democracy camp. The CRC had been formed by the politically conservative legislators, including Allen Lee, Steven Poon, Selina Chow, Rita Fan, Edward Ho, and Stephen Cheong. The CRC was composed of 12 legislators appointed by the government and eight legislators indirectly elected through LegCo's functional constituencies. The CRC was influential as four of its members — Selina Chow, Allen Lee, Rita Fan, and Edward Ho — were appointed to the ExCo. When Governor Christopher Patten arrived Hong Kong in 1992, Allen Lee and other ExCo members resigned from ExCo to give a free hand to the Governor to appoint new members. The CRC sensed the urgent need to form a new political party in view of not only the arrival of a more liberal-minded Governor but also the rapidly emerging pro-democracy UDHK. However, the LP was different from either the HKPA or the LDP, which had a narrower business base and less political weight than the LP. Led by chairman Allen Lee and vice-chairman Ronald Arculli, the LP opposed Patten's political reform blueprint, arguing that it "violated" the Sino-British Joint Declaration over

Hong Kong's future.[60] Because of the LP's ideology of political conservatism, it became the target of cooptation by the PRC government. In the 1994 DB elections, the LP fielded 89 candidates, and 18 of them were elected. In the 1995 LegCo election, its chairman Allen Lee succeeded in gaining a directly elected seat, together with nine other seats acquired through the LegCo's functional constituencies. The LP's success in direct elections and mostly importantly functional constituency elections has become a hallmark of business participation in LegCo's electoral politics.

The most influential pro-Beijing political party is the Democratic Alliance for the Betterment and Progress of Hong Kong (DAB), which was founded in July 1992 by a group of 56 pro-PRC loyalists. They had a track record of supporting the PRC policies toward Hong Kong. Six months before the DAB's formation, the director of the Hong Kong and Macau Affairs Office, Lu Ping, openly encouraged the Hong Kong people to organize a pro-Beijing party for the 1995 LegCo elections. When the DAB was founded in July 1992, Jasper Tsang Yok-shing was chosen as its chairman. He openly debated with Governor Patten over the political reform blueprint and criticized Pattern for ignoring the Sino-British Joint Declaration. The DAB's founding members had many political heavyweights, including left-wing members of the FTU such as Chan Yuen-han, Tam Yiu-chung, and Chan Kam-lam, and other middle-class members, like Cheng Kai-nam and Ip Kwok-him. In the 1994 DB elections, the DAB nominated 83 candidates and 37 of them were elected—a satisfactory result for a new political party.[61] In the 1995 UrbCo and RegCo elections, the DAB nominated 17 candidates and eight of them were elected. During the 1995 LegCo direct elections, the DAB grasped two directly elected seats—not a bad performance given the strong showing of the pro-democracy camp.

The pro-democracy camp has since the late 1980s undergone a period of political adaptation and realignment. It adapted quickly to Hong Kong's transfer of sovereignty from Britain to the PRC on July 1, 1997. The elected DP legislators stepped down from the LegCo and prepared to re-enter the post-1997 LegCo through elections. It has also experienced a process of political realignment, including merger and cooperation, coordination, and competition in the process of nominating candidates to run in the elections held at the legislative, urban, rural, and district levels. During the 1970s, some democrats had already organized various activities to articulate the people's interest in housing and social welfare and they formed groups such as the Christian Industrial Committee and the Council of Public Housing Policy. These liberal-minded groups absorbed a lot of members of the MACs to participate in their social movement. As such, the 1980s and 1990s witnessed the continuous rise in the political influence of the democrats in Hong Kong.

Throughout the 1980s, the rise of many pro-democracy and liberal-minded political groups, which discussed and analyzed politics, gradually transformed themselves into electoral machines and replaced the relatively old groups like Reform Club and Civic Association. One of these political discussion groups was Meeting Point, which was set up in January 1983. It supported the PRC's reassertion of the Chinese sovereignty over Hong Kong, and advocated a free, democratic, and autonomous Hong Kong.[62] The Meeting Point was founded by Lau Nai-keung and Yeung Sum, both graduates from the University of Hong Kong. Its support of Hong Kong's reunification with China attracted Beijing's attention and its leader Lau Nai-keung later became a target of the PRC's united front work. In 1987, he was appointed by the PRC government to be a member of the Chinese People's Political Consultative Conference (CPPCC).

The ADPL was set up in October 1986 and it has been very active electorally in the Sham Shui Po district.[63] Its platform was to "realize a democratic and strong China and 'a high degree of autonomy' for Hong Kong."[64] Moreover, the mission of the ADPL was to promote democracy, improve the people's livelihood, and to protect the interests of the citizens from middle-lower classes through "reasonable distribution of social resources."[65] Ideologically, it was supportive of the PRC while striving to achieve an autonomous Hong Kong with a "fair" distribution of social resources and welfare. As such, the ADPL ideology was and is compatible with the PRC government's policy toward Hong Kong. The ADPL later joined the Hong Kong Affairs Society (HKAS), which was formed in 1984 by 100 liberals, and other like-minded groups in 1986 to call for the introduction of direct elections for LegCo in 1988. All these liberal political groups participated in the Joint Committee on the Promotion of Democratic Reform (JCPDR) to call for direct elections in the 1988 LegCo.

In April 1990, some members of the Meeting Point and the HKAS merged their organization to become a bigger UDHK, which was led by liberal barrister Martin Lee and which became the flagship of the pro-democracy camp in Hong Kong. In the first direct elections held for the LegCo in 1991, the UDHK grasped 12 directly elected seats and two functional constituency seats—an unprecedented victory for the pro-democracy camp in Hong Kong under British rule. Eventually, in 1994, the UDHK merged with Meeting Point and formed the Democratic Party (DP). The Meeting Point's merger with the UDHK was partly due to its internal split; some members supported Patten's reform proposal, but others opposed it. Some conservatives within the Meeting Point, such as Lau Nai-keung, Tsang Shu-ki, and Wong Chack-kie, quit the group after it voted in a general meeting supportive of Patten's reform package. When Meeting Point merged with the UDHK to become the DP, the former's vice-chairman Anthony Cheung Bing-leung became the vice-chairman of the DP until 2004, when he resigned from the party due to opinion differences with some Young Turks within the DP.

It is noteworthy that a pro-Taiwan political group, namely, the One Two Three Democratic Alliance, was established in March 1994. Its chairman Yam Sin-ling was a vice-chairman of the Federation of Taiwan Graduates in Hong Kong, while vice-chairman Ng Wai-cho was a DB member in Tuen Mun. The Alliance had about ten UDHK members when it was formed. Due to the merger between UDHK and Meeting Point into DP, those UDHK members who joined the Alliance could continue their membership in the pro-Taiwan group, because the formation of the new DP meant that overlapping membership was no longer a contentious issue among the former UDHK members. In the 1994 DB elections, the Alliance nominated 20 candidates but only six of them were elected. Yam managed to become a LegCo member through the LegCo Election Committee in 1995. In 1998, Yam participated in the LegCo direct elections and was defeated. One year later, he migrated to the United States.

The evolution of political groups and parties could be easily seen in the DB elections from 1982 to 1994. Table 2.21 showed the dominance of the Civic Association in 1982, followed by the Reform Club and other non-affiliated candidates. This situation changed quickly in the 1985 elections during which the Professional Teachers' Union acted like a political group not only grasping 24 elected seats but also achieving an impressive success rate of 80%. As shown in Table 2.22, other new political groups emerging in the 1985 elections included the Central and Western District Coalition (CWDC) and the Eastern District Coalition (EDC). The

Table 2.21: The Performance of Political Groups in the 1982 District Board Elections

Political Affiliation	Candidates	Elected	Successful rate
Civic Association	25	14	56.0%
Reform Club	14	2	14.3%
Individuals and others	362	116	32.0%
Total	**401**	**132**	**32.9%**

Sources: Compiled from multiple sources including Louie Kin-shuen and Shum Kwok-cheung, eds., *A Compilation of Election Materials in Hong Kong, 1982–1994* (Hong Kong: The Hong Kong Institute of Asia-Pacific Studies, The Chinese University of Hong Kong, 1996).

Table 2.22: The Performance of Political Groups in the 1985 District Board Elections

Political Groups	Number of Candidates	Number Elected	Success Rate (percentage)
Hong Kong Professional Teachers' Union	30	24	80.0%
Hong Kong Civic Association	25	19	76.0%
Hong Kong Reform Club	29	17	58.6%
Eastern District Coalition	11	11	100%
People's Council on Public Housing Policy	11	9	81.8%
Central and Western District Coalition	12	9	75.0%
Hong Kong People's Association	8	8	100%
Meeting Point	4	4	100%
Hong Kong Affairs Society	3	3	100%
Total	**501**	**237**	**47.3%**

Note: Some candidates had overlapping memberships.

Sources: Compiled from multiple sources, including Louie Kin-shuen and Shum Kwok-cheung, eds., *A Compilation of Election Materials in Hong Kong, 1982–1994* (Hong Kong: The Hong Kong Institute of Asia-Pacific Studies, The Chinese University of Hong Kong, 1996).

CWDC nominated 12 candidates and nine of them were elected, while the EDC had all 11 candidates winning the elections. Another interest group, namely the People's Council on Public Housing Policy, witnessed 11 candidates being elected. The Meeting Point and the Hong Kong Affairs Society nominated seven candidates and all of them were elected. Clearly, a new generation of political groups emerged and replaced the aging Civic Association and Reform Club.

Table 2.23 shows that in the 1988 DBs elections, 71 candidates were nominated by the three pro-democracy groups, namely the ADPL, HKAS and Meeting Point. Above all, 56 of the 71 candidates were elected, a success rate of almost 80%. In total, the democrats had almost 100 members of DBs because there were other liberal-minded groups, like Hong Kong Democratic Foundation (DF), and individuals who won the elections. Their presence in DBs could promote governmental responsiveness and accountability, raising suggestions and views that could improve government policies.

In the 1988 DB elections, the democrats performed very well in Kwai Tsing district, where they captured 15 out of 16 elected seats. In the Tsing Yi constituency where there were two candidates elected to the Kwai Tsing District Board, democrat Ting Hin-wah managed to get 3,331 votes, and he was elected together with a rural activist Chan Kar-mun who got 1,872 votes and came from the Rural Committee. Under the circumstances in which the democrats captured 15 of the 16 elected seats in Kwai Tsing DB, the government relied on the support of Chan, eight appointed members, and an ex-officio member from the Rural Committee. Still, the pro-government force became a minority dominated by the democratic majority—an unprecedented situation in district politics in Hong Kong under the British rule. The democrats in the Kwai Tsing DB promoted a lot of activities, including civic education and cultural and recreational activities. It was the first time that the British colonial administration had to form a working partnership with the democratic majority in the Kwai Tsing DB.

The 1991 DB elections showed that the UDHK became a large and an influential political force (Table 2.24). It nominated 83 candidates and 60% of them were elected—a success rate of 72.3%. The ADPL captured 15 seats while Meeting Point grasped 11 seats. These three pro-democracy groups altogether acquired 109 seats out of 272 elected seats—a very impressive result. However, the 1991 DB elections revealed that many constituencies had uncontested candidates. Of the 272 elected seats, there

Table 2.23: The Performance of Political Groups in the 1988 District Board Elections

Political Groups	Number of Candidates	Number Elected	Success Rate (percentage)
Association for Democracy and People's Livelihood	31	27 (1)	87.1%
Civic Association	34	17 (1)	50.0%
Meeting Point	23	16 (1)	69.6%
Hong Kong Affairs Society	17	13	76.4%
Progressive Hong Kong Society	11	9 (1)	81.8%
Reform Club	13	6 (1)	46.2%
Federation of Trade Unions	2	2	100%
Total	**493**	**264 (34)**	

Note: Some memberships were overlapping as the democrats joined two groups.

The brackets referred to the number of uncontested seats in DBs.

Sources: Compiled from multiple sources, including Louie Kin-shuen and Shum Kwok-cheung, *A Compilation of Election Materials in Hong Kong, 1982–1994* (Hong Kong: The Hong Kong Institute of Asia-Pacific Studies, The Chinese University of Hong Kong, 1996).

Table 2.24: The Performance of Various Political Groups in the 1991 District Board Elections

Political Groups	Number of Candidates	Number Elected	Success Rate (percentage)
Hong Kong United Democrats	83	60 (15)	72.3%
Liberal Democratic Federation	59	27 (12)	45.8%
Hong Kong Civic Association	28	17 (2)	60.7%
Association for Democracy and People's Livelihood	19	15 (3)	78.8%
Meeting Point	12	11 (3)	91.7%
Kwun Tong Residents Association	13	10 (3)	76.9%
New Territories Association of Societies	6	5 (1)	83.3%
East Kowloon Residents Committee	6	4 (3)	66.7%
Tuen Mun Prospect Society	4	3	75.0%
Hong Kong Democratic Foundation	6	2	33.3%
Reform Club of Hong Kong	3	2	66.7%
Federation of Trade Unions	2	2 (1)	100%
Total	**467**	**272 (81)**	**58.2%**

Note: Some group members joined two groups at the same time — double membership was commonplace.

Sources: Compiled from multiple sources, including Louie Kin-shuen and Shum Kwok-cheung, *Election Information Compilation of Hong Kong, 1982–1994* (Hong Kong: The Hong Kong Institute of Asia-Pacific Studies, The Chinese University of Hong Kong, 1996)

were 81 uncontested candidates who won automatically without any opponent—over one-third of the seats did not envisage any contender. This phenomenon illustrated the relative immaturity of political groups in Hong Kong, regardless of whether they were pro-democracy, pro-government, or pro-Beijing. The pro-government force was relatively weak in 1991. The LDF nominated 59 candidates and only got 27 seats—a success rate of 46%. In some districts, the pro-government and pro-Beijing forces had to pool their manpower and resources to prevent the pro-democracy camp from capturing more elected seats. A good example was Kwun Tong, where the pro-Beijing Kwun Tong Residents Association grasped ten seats. In Wong Tai Sin district, the East Kowloon Residents Committee got four seats. Other pro-Beijing groups remained weak, such as the New Territories Association of Societies that acquired only five seats, and the FTU got merely two seats.

In the 1991 DB elections, the democrats captured the Kwai Tsing DB again. They won all 17 elected seats in Kwai Tsing DB. In the Sham Shui Po DB, the ADPL grasped nine elected seats; the UDHK four seats and the pro-government force got five elected seats. However, there were nine appointed seats in the Sham Shui Po DB, leading to a slight majority of the pro-government force. Since appointed seats remained the instrument by which the colonial government could curb the influence of the democrats, the democrats could not easily influence the operation of DBs after the 1991 DB elections.

Seeing that the democrats performed quite well in the 1988 and 1991 DB elections, the pro-Beijing forces began to reorganize themselves to check the influence of the democrats after 1991. The DAB was formed in 1992, while district-level forces supportive of Beijing were reorganized. For instance, after the defeat of former UDHK member Lau Kong-wah in the 1991 DB elections, PRC authorities began to co-opt him, and he eventually formed a district-based Civil Force (CF) in Sha Tin in December 1993. The CF was composed of pro-government and pro-Beijing DB members so that it could challenge the democrats in local elections.

The result of the 1994 District Boards elections showed that the pro-democracy camp could dominate five DBs: Kwai Tsing, Tuen Mun, Kwun Tong, Sham Shui Po, and Central and Western (Table 2.25). Even though pro-government elites and appointed members, including ex-officio members from the Rural Committees, could constitute the instruments through which the colonial government could check the democrats, these five DBs fell into the hands of the democrats—another testimony to the rapidly rising influence of the pro-democracy force in Hong Kong's district politics. However, the democratic force's control of the five DBs was arguing not challenging the legitimacy of the colonial administration. First and foremost, DBs were of advisory nature and its jurisdictions were limited to environmental affairs and cultural and recreational activities. Second, the democrats still listened to the views of the pro-government and pro-Beijing elites in DBs. For example, while the democratic majority led to the selection of DP member Sin Chung-kai as the Kwai Tsing DB chairman, some democrats in Tuen Mun voted for HYK chairman Lau Wong-fat to continue as the DB chairman. Due to Lau's respectable status and reputation, he gained the support of some democrats in the Tuen Mun DB even though they occupied most of the seats. The ability of Lau to hold the chairman position in Tuen Mun DB from 1985 to 2015 showed that there was a constitutional convention of accepting a highly respectable rural leader as the chairman. As such, some degree of consensual politics could be seen between the democrats and pro-government elites. Third, the democratic presence in DBs could bring about better checks and balances on the local government officials, who were held more accountable for their policies and actions than before. Fourth, the democrats focused on how the resources in DBs were spent, leading to some pro-Beijing local district forces to resist them. For instance, in Kwun Tong DB, the Kwun Tong Residents Association mobilized some members of the public to criticize the democrats' position in the DB, including their support of the government's proposal of building an Integrated Treatment Center of HIV-related services, the Mass Transit Railway Corporation's Development Plan, and the relocation of the Kwun Tong District Branch Office.[66] Factional rivalries between the democrats and pro-Beijing forces could be seen after the 1991 DBs elections, which demonstrated the strength of the democrats in electoral politics at the district level. Overall, the dominance of democrats in some DBs led to stronger governmental accountability, but the rivalries with pro-government forces did increase.

Table 2.26 shows the pro-democracy force became so influential that the rising pro-Beijing DAB played a major role in checking its inroads in the 1994 DB elections. While the DP nominated 133 candidates and 75 of them won (success rate of 56.4%), the DAB nominated 83 candidates and

Table 2.25: Comparing the Pro-Beijing Force with Pro-democracy Camp: Political Parties in District Boards, 1994

District	DP	ADPL	123	DAB	LP	LDF	Civil	Demo	Cons
Central & Western	8			2	1			9	5
Wan Chai	3			3	1			3	7
Eastern	4			9	3			10	22
Southern	4				2			4	12
Yau Tsim Mong	1	2	1	1		1		6	8
Sham Shui Po	3	11			1			14	6
Kowloon City	2		1	2	2	6		4	16
Wong Tai Sin	4	3		4	1			8	14
Kwun Tong	7	1	2	4	1			17	16
Tsuen Wan	2			1				6	9+2
Tuen Mun	9	4	2	2		1		15	10+1
Yuen Long	3			1				3	16+6
North	2			4				3	8+4
Tai Po	4			2	4	3		4	13+2
Sai Kung	2	2						5	6+2
Sha Tin	8				2		10	12	19+1
Kwai Tsing	9	6						21	5+1
Islands				2				0	6+8
Total	75	29	6	37	18	11	10	144	225

Note: DP—Democratic Party; ADPL—Association for Democracy and People's Livelihood; 123—One Two Three Democratic Alliance; DAB—Democratic Alliance for the Betterment of Hong Kong; LP—Liberal Party; LDF—Liberal Democratic Federation; Civil—Civil Force; Demo—Democratic Camp; Cons—Conservative and Pro-establishment camp.

+ Ex-officio members of District Boards from 27 chairs of the Rural Committees

Sources: Compiled from multiple sources, including Louie Kin-shuen and Shum Kwok-cheung, eds., *A Compilation of Election Materials in Hong Kong, 1982–1994* (Hong Kong: The Hong Kong Institute of Asia-Pacific Studies, The Chinese University of Hong Kong, 1996).

37 of them were elected (success rate of 44.6%). Factional rivalry between the pro-democracy and pro-government/pro-Beijing camps became far more fierce and prominent than before. The democratic force composed of the DP, ADPL, One Two Three Alliance, the Kowloon City Observers, and the Hong Kong Democratic Foundation (DF) captured 115 seats out of 346 seats. The pro-government and pro-Beijing force that comprised Liberal Party, LDF, DAB, CF, HKPA, and other district groups acquired

Table 2.26: The Performance of Political Groups in the 1994 District Board Elections

Political Groups	Number of Candidates	Number Elected	Success Rate (percentage)
Democratic Party	133	75(4)	56.4%
Democratic Alliance for the Betterment	83	37(3)	44.6%
Association for Democracy and People's Livelihood	40	29(2)	72.5%
Liberal Party	89	18(8)	20.2%
Liberal Democratic Federation	28	11(2)	39.2%
Civil Force	10	10(2)	100%
East Kowloon Residents Committee	11	8(5)	72.7%
Kwun Tong Residents Association	12	7(3)	58.3%
123 Democratic Alliance	20	6	30.0%
United Front for the Service of the People	8	4	50.0%
New Territories West Residents' Service Association	7	3(2)	42.8%
Hong Kong Democratic Foundation	5	3	60.0%
Public Affairs Council (with members from the Reform Club)	15	2(1)	13.3%
Kowloon City Observers	6	2	33.3%
Hong Kong Progressive Alliance	7	1	14.3%
Total	**757**	**346(50)**	

Sources: Compiled from multiple sources, including Louie Kin-shuen and Shum Kwok-cheung, eds., *A Compilation of Election Materials in Hong Kong, 1982–1994* (Hong Kong: The Hong Kong Institute of Asia-Pacific Studies, The Chinese University of Hong Kong, 1996).

at least 101 seats. Hence, both camps performed quite strongly. In a sense, the pro-government and pro-Beijing forces caught up the democrats quite quickly in the 1994 elections compared with the situation in 1988.

Overall, the number of candidates increased significantly from the 1982 to 1994 DBs elections (Table 2.27). Moreover, the success rate improved over time, ranging from only 32.9% in 1982 to 45.7% in 1994. The highest success rate was in 1991 when the figure was 58.2%. In general, incumbents tended to have an upper hand over challengers, but this was not the norm because the election results also depended on whether the incumbents worked hard in their constituency services. Other factors shaping the candidate's success included whether he or she was backed up by a political group with the ability of mobilizing voters to cast their ballots, and how the voters perceived different candidates and political groups and parties.

**Table 2.27: The Number of Nominated and Elected Candidates
in District Boards Elections, 1982–1994**

Year	No. of Nominated Candidates	No. of Elected Candidates	Success Rate (percentage)
1982	401	132(4)	32.9%
1985	501	237(24)	47.3%
1988	493	264(34)	53.5%
1991	467	272(81)	58.2%
1994	757	346(50)	45.7%

Note: In 1994, the Hong Kong government adopted a new election system for DBs, namely one seat for one constituency with the first-past-the-post system. From 1982 to 1991, a mixed system was implemented with (1) two seats coexisting in constituency and (2) one single-seat for one constituency simultaneously.

Source: Louie Kin-shuen and Shum Kwok-cheung, eds., *A Compilation of Election Materials in Hong Kong, 1982–1994* (Hong Kong: The Hong Kong Institute of Asia-Pacific Studies, The Chinese University of Hong Kong, 1996).

Due to the Sino-British row over Patten's political reform, the PRC government decided not to allow the British-initiated political institutions to straddle July 1, 1997. All political institutions witnessed their provisional bodies, including the LegCo, UrbCo, RegCo, and DBs. For DBs, the new HKSAR government reappointed more members to each DB, leading to the phenomenon that one-third of the members of DBs after 1997 were appointed until 2015, when all appointed seats were abolished.

Table 2.28 shows the chairpersons of DBs from 1985 to 1999. In Wan Chai, Yau Tsim Mong, Tuen Mun, Yuen Long, and Islands, there was only one chairperson who could serve for a sustained period from 1985 to 1999. This was partly due to the respected status of the chairperson concerned, and partly because the pro-government forces tended to dominate that DB. Sometimes, the democrats respected the continuation of the previous chair, such as the case of Tuen Mun.

Some of the chairpersons of DBs were experienced and politically significant. Table 2.29 sums up the experiences of the chairs of some DBs, including Shum Choi Sang, Peggy Lam, Chow Chun-fai, Lau Wong Fat and Tai Kuen. Shum Choi Sang and Peggy Lam were the pro-government DB chairs for more than ten years. The other prominent chairs were Lau Wong-fat, and Tai Kuen. While Lau played a crucial role in being the rural leader communicating with the government on rural affairs, Tai Kuen stood out as the rural leader who had many followers. Both of them could be regarded as the influential patron in the politics of the New Territories. Chow Chun-fai

Table 2.28: Chairpersons of District Boards, 1985–1999

District	1985–1988	1988–1991	1991–1994	1994–1997	1997–1999
Central & Western	Vincent Ko Hon-chiu	Ambrose Lau Hon-chuen		Yuen Pun-keung	Stephen Chan Chit-kwai
Wan Chai	Peggy Lam Pei Yu-dja				
Eastern	Shum Choi-sang			Chan Ping-woon	
Southern	Lam Kwok-kwong		Hui Yung-chung	Ko Tan-kan	Ma Yuet-har
Yau Tsim Mong*	Chow Chun-fai				
Yau Ma Tei	Yip Wah			–	–
Sham Shui Po	Stephen Cheng Po-hong		Raymond Choi Wai-shek	Eric Wong Chung-ki	Tam Kwok-kiu
Kowloon City	Wong Sik-kong			Tang Po-hong	
Wong Tai Sin	Michael Cheng Tak-kin	Michael Lee Yuk-kwan	Chan Kam-man		
Kwun Tong	Lam Hang-fai			Winnie Poon Yam Wai-chun	Hau Shui-pui
Tsuen Wan	Chow How-chen			Chan Lau-fong	
Tuen Mun	Lau Wong-fat				
Yuen Long	Tai Kuen				
Northern	Raymond Pang Hang-yin			Tang Kwok-yung	
Tai Po	Wong Yuen-cheung	Ho Yung-sang	Cheung Hok-ming		
Sai Kung	William Wan Hon-cheung			George Ng Sze-fuk	
Sha Tin	Ng Chan-lam		Choy Kan-pui		
Kwai Ching	John Ho Tung-ching	Lee Wing-tat	Leung Kwong-cheong	Sin Chung-kai	
Islands	Daniel Lam Wai-keung				

Note: *Between 1982 to 1994, there were two separate districts boards, namely Mong Kok and Yau Ma Tei, which later were merged to form the Yau Tsim Mong district in 1994.

Table 2.29 Influential Chairpersons of District Boards

District Board Chairperson	Experiences
Shum Choi-sang (Eastern District Board)	His father, Shum Wai Yau, founded the *Wah Kiu Yat Po* in 1925 and he later became the publisher. Shum was appointed as Justice of the Peace in 1967; and awarded with an MBE in 1968, an OBE in 1986, the Silver Bauhinia Star in 2002 and an Honorary Fellowship from the Chinese University of Hong Kong in 2003. He was a chair of the Eastern DB for ten years from 1985 to 1994.
Peggy Lam Pei Yu-dja (Wan Chai District Board)	She is the youngest cousin of the famous architect, Pei Ieoh-ming, who designed the Bank of China Tower in Hong Kong. Peggy Lam graduated from the University of Shanghai with a Bachelor of Arts. She received a certificate in family planning from the University of Chicago and a certificate in Public Health Administration from the University of Michigan. In 1961 she was the chief executive officer of the Family Planning Association of Hong Kong. In 1993, she was the chairlady of the Hong Kong Federation of Women, an organization formed under the support of the PRC government. Lam was the chairlady of the Wan Chai DB from 1985 to 2003.
Chow Chun-fai (Mong Kok District Board)	He was born in Hong Kong's Mong Kok district and was an influential community leader. In 1982, he was appointed as a DB member in Mong Kok. From 1985 to 2019, he was the chairperson of the Mong Kok (and later Yau Tsim Mong) DB. Chow was originally pro-Taiwan and was a politician acceptable to many DB members from different political forces.
Chow How-chen (Tsuen Wan)	Chow was appointed as a Tsuen Wan DB member and Provisional RegCo member in the early 1980s. In 1985, he was elected as a chairman of the Tsuen Wan DB and continued to be the chair for 21 years. Chow was a chairman of the New Territories Chiu Chow Federation. In 2006 he was appointed as a member of the Shenzhen People's Political Consultative Conference.
Lau Wong-fat	He participated in New Territories rural politics as a village representative in the Tuen Mun Rural Committee and became the chairman of Heung Yee Kuk from 1980 to 2015, a position he kept for 35 years. Lau was also the chairman of the Tuen Mun District Board (later Council) from 1985 to 2011 and the chairman of the RegCo from 1995 to 1999. He was a LegCo member from 1985 to 2016. From 2009 to 2012, he was a non-official member of the ExCo. He served as the member of the Chinese People's Political Consultative Conference.
Tai Kuen	He was born in Yuen Long's Nam Bin Wai district with his ancestors living there for a long period of time. In the 1980s, Tai managed his family business. Tai was a chairman of the Rural Committee for 35 years and became the chair of DB for five times. In 2000, he was defeated by Tang Siu-tong in the election of the Yuen Long DB chair position. Since then, Tai gradually withdrew from politics.
Choy Kan-pui	As a Sha Tin villager, Choy ran in the 1982 DB elections and was elected to office until 2003. He was a member of the Hong Kong Affairs Society, a pro-democratic group in the 1980s. Choy was also a founding member of the UDHK, but later he and Lau Kong-wah quitted the party and formed Civil Force. He was elected as member of the LegCo in 1995 through the Election Committee which was composed of DBs members. He later joined the pro-Beijing and pro-business Hong Kong Progressive Alliance (HKPA) and was appointed to the Provisional LegCo in 1996.

Sources: Compiled from multiple sources, including, "In memory of Mr. Shum Choi-sang (1922–2016)," https://jmsc.hku.hk/in-memory-of-mr-shum-choi-sang/, access date: August 2, 2020; "The passing away of 'Tsuen Wan' mayor Chow How-chen," *Oriental Daily*, August 7, 2017, in https://hk.on.cc/hk/bkn/cnt/news/20170807/bkn-20170807112546334-0807_00822_001.html, access date: August 2, 2020; "Tai Kuen," in https://baike.baidu.com/item/%E6%88%B4%E6%9D%83/1717966, access date: August 2, 2020.

was an urban leader who was respected by many members of the Mong Kok DB and later Yau Tsim Mong District Council (DC).

Conclusion

The introduction of DB elections in the early 1980s provided a golden opportunity and an indispensable political platform for old and new political groups to participate in electoral politics, to groom their members and leaders, and to transform themselves into political parties. The Sino-British negotiations over Hong Kong's future from 1982 to 1984 triggered the emergence of many new political groups, which were later stimulated by the June 1989 Tiananmen incident in the PRC to turn into political parties. The rapid emergence of the liberal-minded and pro-democracy political groups and parties brought about the immediate reaction from pro-government and pro-Beijing forces, which also organized themselves in a better way to check and curb the democratic movement. Gradually, these two camps in Hong Kong's district politics, namely the pro-democracy force on the one hand and the pro-government and pro-Beijing front on the other, have become more prominent, visible, and assertive in the district politics of Hong Kong than ever before. However, there was a diversity of groups within the pro-democracy camp, as with the pro-government and pro-Beijing forces. As such, the fragmentation of political forces from both sides of the ideological spectrum, namely pro-democracy and pro-Beijing sides, was looming. This characteristic of political fragmentation, as will be discussed in the following chapters, became prominent in the district politics of the HKSAR after July 1, 1997.

Notes

1 Norman Miners, "Constitutional Reform in Hong Kong, 1945–1952," *Asian Journal of Public Administration*, vol. 11, no. 1 (June 1989), p. 96.

2 Despatch of Governor Grantham to the Secretary of State, September 1, 1949, Colonial Office file 54145/4/49, no. 58.

3 *Ibid.*

4 Civic Association's newsletter, February 1990.

5 *The Nineties*, no. 182 (March 1985), p. 54.

6 See its Facebook, https://www.facebook.com/pages/category/Nonprofit-Organiza tion/%E9%A6%99%E6%B8%AF%E5%85%AC%E6%B0%91%E5%8D%94 %E6%9C%83-Hong-Kong-Civic-Association-160495437320180/, access date: August 6, 2020.

7 Norman Miners, *Government and Politics of Hong Kong* (1981), p. 219. Also see G. B. Endacott, *Government and Politics in Hong Kong 1841–1962* (Hong Kong: Hong Kong University Press, 1964), pp. 148–162.Lau Yun-wo, *A History of the Municipal Councils of Hong Kong: 1883–1999: From the Sanitary Board to the Urban Council and the Regional Council* (Hong Kong: Leisure and Cultural Service Department, Hong Kong Government, 2002).

8 Y. W. Lau, *A History of the Municipal Councils of Hong Kong: From the Sanitary Board to the Urban Council and the Regional Council* (Hong Kong: Leisure and Cultural Service Department, Hong Kong Government, 2002).

9 *Ibid.*

10 Miners, *Government and Politics of Hong Kong*, p. 227.

11 *Ibid.*, p. 228.

12 Miners wrote: "The rateable value of a building is the annual rent that could be charged for it in a free market (*Ibid.*, p. 228)."

13 "Public Housing Development," in https://www.housingauthority.gov.hk/en/ about-us/public-housing-heritage/public-housing-development/index.html, access date: August 9, 2020.

14 Discussion with Hilton Cheong-Leen, November 2011. Also see the website of the Hong Kong Chinese Reform Association, in http://www.hkcra.com/web/subpage. php?mid=15, access date: August 9, 2020.

15 Pui Ka-yee, "China calls me: Percy Chen's revolutionary path," in https://sparkpost. wordpress.com/2014/02/06/percy-chen/, access date: August 9, 2020.

16 Miners, *Government and Politics of Hong Kong*, p. 236.

17 Steve Yu-sang Tsang, ed., *Government and Politics* (Hong Kong: Hong Kong University Press, 1995), p. 122. Also see Pui Ka-yee, "The Abortive Democratic Promises: The Young Plan," in https://sparkpost.wordpress.com/2014/07/16/ young-plan/, access date: August 9, 2020.

18 *Ibid.*, p. 237.

19 Steve Yui-sang Tsang, ed., *Government and Politics*, pp. 122–127; and Suzanne Pepper, *Keeping Democracy at Bay: Hong Kong and the Challenge of Chinese Political Reform* (Lanham: Rowman & Littlefield, 2008), pp. 95–97.

20 For details, see the Association's activities, in http://www.hkcra.com/web/subpage. php?mid=9, access date: August 9, 2020.

21 Pui Ka-yee, "China calls me: Percy Chen's revolutionary path," in https://sparkpost. wordpress.com/2014/02/06/percy-chen/, access date: August 9, 2020.

22 *Ibid.*

23 *Ibid.*

24 *Ibid.*

25 Pui Ka-yee, "The Father of 'Hong Kong independence:' The Democratic Movement in the 1960s," in https://sparkpost.wordpress.com/2012/12/04/ma-man-fai-1/, access date: August 9, 2020.

26 *Ibid.*

27 *Ibid.*

28 Lau Yun-wo, *A History of the Municipal Councils of Hong Kong: 1883–1999: From the Sanitary Board to the Urban Council and the Regional Council* (Hong Kong: Leisure and Cultural Service Department, Hong Kong Government, 2002).

29 Edmond Tsang, *The Earliest Political Parties and Fighter for Democracies: Reform Club and the Hong Kong Civic Association* (in Chinese) (Hong Kong: Chung Hwa, 2019), pp. 63–70.

30 Norman Miners, *Government and Politics of Hong Kong*, p. 239.

31 *Ibid.*, p. 239.

32 *Ibid.*, p. 239.

33 *Ibid.*, p. 240.

34 *Miners, Government and Politics of Hong Kong*, p. 406.

35 *Ibid.*, p. 71.

36 *Ibid.*

37 See Edmond Yik-man Tsang, *The Earliest Political Parties and Fighter for Democracies: Reform Club and the Hong Kong Civic Association* (in Chinese) (Hong Kong: Chung Hwa, 2019).

38 Lo Shiu-hing, *The Politics of Democratization in Hong Kong*, pp. 155–156.

39 Interview with Ng Ming-yum, June 19, 1990.

40 See Benjamin K. P. Leung, *Perspectives on Hong Kong Society* (London: Oxford University Press, 1992).

41 *Wide Angle,* no. 118, (July 16, 1982), p. 31.

42 *Wide Angle,* no. 118, (April 16, 1982), pp 18–20.

43 *Ibid.*, pp. 58–59.

44 *Ibid.*, pp. 64–65.

45 *Green Paper: The Further Development of Representative Government in Hong Kong, July 1984* (Hong Kong: Government Printer, 1984); and *White Paper: The Development of Representative Government—The Way Forward, February 1988* (Hong Kong: Government Printer, 1988), pp. 15–17.

46 Norman Miners, *The Government and Politics of Hong Kong* (Fourth Edition) (Hong Kong: Oxford University Press, 1989), p. 180.

47 Miners, *The Government and Politics of Hong Kong* (1989), p. 119.

48 *Ibid.*

49 Chris Patten, "Policy Address (1992 Excerpt)," in Jiang Shigong, ed., *A Compilation of Information on Hong Kong's Political Development (1): From Colonial Period to the Drafting of Basic Law* (Hong Kong: Joint Publishing, 2015), p. 424. Lo Shiu-hing, "An Analysis of Sino-British Negotiations Over Hong Kong's Political Reform," *Contemporary Southeast Asia*, vol. 16, no. 2 (September 1994), pp. 178–209.

50 "The Basic Law of the Hong Kong Special Administrative Region of the People's Republic of China," promulgated in April 1990, in https://www.basiclaw.gov.hk/en/basiclawtext/chapter_3.html, access date: August 12, 2020.

51 Chow Kin-wah, "An Analysis of Political Party Development in Hong Kong before and after 1997," *Journal of Guangdong Institute of Public Administration*, vol. 17, no. 2 (April 2005), pp. 90–93. Also see Chow Chin-wah, *The Development of Hong Kong Political Parties and Elections, 1949–1997* (in Chinese) (Hong Kong: Misi Dalei Technology and Art, 2003), pp. 82–192; and Mainland Affairs Council (Taiwan), *A Comparative Study of Hong Kong Political Parties* (Taipei: Mainland Affairs Council, 1995).

52 *Ibid.*

53 *Ibid.*

54 Mainland Affairs Council (Taiwan), *A Comparative Study of Hong Kong Political Parties* (Taipei: Mainland Affairs Council, 1995).

55 *Ibid.*

56 *Ibid.*

57 *Ibid.*

58 Lo Shiu-Hing, "Political Parties, Elite-Mass Gap and Political Instability in Hong Kong," *Contemporary Southeast Asia*, vol. 20, no. 1 (April 1998), pp. 67–87.

59 Sonny Shiu-hing Lo, "Legislative Cliques, Political Parties, Political Groupings and Electoral System," in Joseph Cheng and Sonny Lo, eds., *From Colony to SAR: Hong Kong's Challenges Ahead* (Hong Kong: The Chinese University Press, 1995).

60 Mainland Affairs Council (Taiwan), *A Comparative Study of Hong Kong Political Parties* (Taipei: Mainland Affairs Council, 1995).

61 *Ibid.*

62 For its first meeting in January 1983, see the Meeting Point's archival documents, in https://web.archive.org/web/20120425045705/http://meetingpoint.hk/PDF/doc02.pdf, access date: August 12, 2020.

63 See its website, http://www.adpl.org.hk/?page_id=50, access date: August 12, 2020.

64 *Ibid.*

65 *Ibid.*

66 Observations from Steven Hung when he was a DB member in Kwun Tong.

3

Rural Elites, Political Participation, and Factional Struggle

The British colonial rule in the New Territories was characterized by indirect rule, respecting and preserving local customary practices, and utilizing village elders as a bridge between the colonial administration and the rural residents. Some people in the New Territories, on the other hand, were politically and traditionally "patriotic", and the British military decided on April 7, 1899 that the UK flag would be hoisted in Tai Po on April 17, 1899.[1] The rural residents in Tai Po destroyed a police station which was established by the British, and they believed that the British move violated their *feng shui* (風水，geomancy). In response, the British navy and army were mobilized to occupy Tai Po on April 14, 1899. The British soldiers proceeded to Yuen Long, where rural residents in Kam Tin's Kut Hing Wai resisted them by defending a village wall.[2] The British soldiers used cannon to attack the rural defenders and eventually captured Kut Hing Wai, but the fierce resistance from the rural dwellers marked the anti-colonial struggle in Hong Kong.

The historical tradition of the resistance of rural residents in the New Territories to colonialists could also be seen from December 25, 1941 to September 2, 1945, when the Japanese invaded and occupied Hong Kong. The Guangdong communist guerillas, namely the East River Column, got the intelligence that the Japanese army invaded Hong Kong through Guangdong in December 1941, and they informed the British Hong Kong government.[3] Originally, the British colonial administration toyed with the idea of providing weapons, including machine guns and ammunition, to 2,000 to 3,000 Chinese communist guerillas to resist the Japanese; nevertheless, Governor Mark Young hesitated and did not sign the proposed agreement.[4] After the Japanese military occupied Hong Kong, the communist guerillas penetrated various districts in the New Territories and collected the weapons left by the British and Canadian soldiers. The communist guerrillas led by Tsang Hung-man pacified the gangsters and thugs who were active in the New Territories, gradually becoming active and organizing "friends" of the Chinese Communist Party (CCP) in Yuen Long, Tai Po, Tai O, and Sai Kung, and eliminating some local collaborators of the Japanese force.[5] The CCP guerillas not only resisted the Japanese military and its collaborators, but also assisted many intellectuals, artists and American and British soldiers to escape from Hong Kong to the mainland through the routes of Sai Kung and Macau.[6] From the perspective of Chinese nationalism, the rural residents in the New Territories put up their heroic and glorious fight against the colonialists, firstly the British and later the Japanese.

Colonial Administration, Elite Conflicts, and Fragmentation in the New Territories

After the British occupied the New Territories in 1898, Governor Sir Henry Blake issued a proclamation in 1900 saying that the rural people's "interests will be safeguarded and your usages and good customs will not in any way be interfered with."[7] All laws and ordinances in force in Hong Kong were applicable to the New Territories; nevertheless, the leased area of the New Territories was governed by newly appointed District Officers who had the first duty of carrying out a land survey. Through the New Territories Land Court Ordinance of 1900, all land in the New Territories belonged to the property of the Crown for 99 years under the Convention of Peking. After the land survey, Block Crown Leases were issued in 1906 and the "former landowners were converted into leaseholders of land granted by the Crown and confirmed in the possession of their land for 75 years on payment of a fixed annual rental to the government."[8] Two District Officers, one in the North and the other in the South, were magistrates for criminal and civil matters. They also collected Crown rents and controlled the allocation of land while cooperating with the police and agricultural department. After the end of the Second World War in 1945, and with the gradual expansion of population and the inception of urbanization in the New Territories, the workload of District Officers increased over time and covered other areas such as public health, licensing, squatter control, and labor disputes. In 1961, civil disputes were taken over by District Courts, while the Social Welfare department tackled welfare-related issues in 1959. In 1960, the Urban Services department took over the responsibilities of refuse removal, sanitation, and public health.[9] Later, in 1982, the control of land was transferred from District Officers to the Lands department. As urbanization proceeded quickly, the New Territories were divided into five districts prior to 1974, with each district under the supervision of a District Officer. All the five officers were coordinated by a District Commissioner. Administratively speaking, the functions of District Officers changed over time, delegating their responsibilities to central-level departments while playing a major coordinating and communicating function. Their responsibilities included (1) gathering political intelligence, especially the communist movement and rural infighting; (2) representing rural interests to the higher governmental authorities; (3) coordinating the activities of government departments; (4) explaining and supporting government programs and policies; (5) negotiating with rural people an amount of compensation for terminating or exchanging land lease; (6) controlling squatters; (7) encouraging rural infrastructure development and improvement; (8) arbitrating disputes among villagers; (9) providing assistance to villagers and schools in educational administration; (10) organizing relief work in emergencies; (11) managing social welfare activities; (12) liaising with the British army especially if military exercises caused any damage to villages and necessitated compensation; (13) organizing recreational and youth camps; and (14) consulting rural people on town planning.[10]

As mentioned in Chapter One, the British colonial rule relied on indirect rule, tolerating the existing customs and practices and setting up institutions as a form of, to borrow from King, "administrative absorption of politics." In 1926, Governor Cecil Clementi established the Heung Yee Kuk (HYK) and allowed a group of appointed village elders to advise the colonial government.[11] However, in 1957, this cooptation mechanism broke down due to factional struggles within the HYK. A majority faction claimed that the HYK was the only body of representing the rural people and that the government had no right to interfere with its constitution.[12] Fanling's village elder Lee Chung-chong led the villagers to oppose the government's policy of compensating their land for development purpose.[13] But the villagers' position was rejected by the government, which refused to recognize the New Territories Agricultural, Industrial and Commercial Study Federation led by Lee. Governor Cecil Clementi decided to cope with the villager's opposition by passing a new ordinance to make the HYK a statutory body with a new composition. Nevertheless, the colonial government coopted Lee Chung-chong as the HYK leader, stipulating that the HYK would maintain local charity work, carry out reforms, protect rural interests, improve local malpractices, and allow locals to address their grievances.[14] Hence, the British colonial administration intervened in rural politics directly by using the establishment of the HYK, but it also adopted indirect rule by co-opting local villagers to tip the political balance in favor of its own legitimacy and a smooth process of rural policy implementation.[15]

When the Japanese military occupied Hong Kong by the end of 1941, they also combined direct rule with indirect rule. Directly speaking, the Japanese divided the entire Hong Kong into 28 districts, utilizing the local Chinese to govern the Chinese residents.[16] In Fanling, there were 13,330 rural residents, but only 12 Japanese.[17] As such, the Japanese created district chiefs, deputy chiefs, supervisors, and members in each of the districts, but all of them were led by the Japanese directors and the Imperial Army. Furthermore, the Japanese army used the village staff members, local police, defense teams, and *Kempeitai* (secret police) to monitor the Chinese district-level staff.[18]

After the end of the Second World War, rural politics in Hong Kong underwent rapid political metamorphosis. Originally, in the Song dynasty, the New Territories were inhabited by four great clans, namely the Tang, Liu, Hau, and Pang clans.[19] Later, the Hakkas migrated to Hong Kong and resided in various villages, some becoming the tenants and some organizing themselves in either local defenses or *yuek* to resist the abuses of the rent collection teams. Before the nineteenth century, Yuen Long and Tai Po markets were occupied by two large Tang clans. These large clans, including the Tangs, Lius, Haus, Pangs, and Mans, became the local gentry class and some of them monopolized the official positions and rent collection. The poor Hakka people were discriminated against and were outnumbered in the list of local officials.[20] The expansion of trade led to the increasing prosperity of some Hakka villages and villagers, who then groomed their own community leaders to resist the encroachment and influences of the other relatively large clans. The increasing population and settlement curbed the influence of the Tang clans, which gradually sold out their bottom-soil rights.[21] When the British arrived in the New Territories in April 1899, the Tangs and the Hakkas resisted the British soldiers but eventually failed in the Ping Shan and Kam Tin areas. The British colonial rulers then conducted land surveys in the New Territories, required villagers to submit their land deeds in return for a Block Crown Lease, and abolished the white deeds (top-soil rights) by tenant farmers in Hakka villages and also the red deeds (bottom-soil rights) owned by the Tangs.[22] In a sense, the tenant Hakka farmers were "liberated" while the influence of the Tangs was curbed. Hence, the elite conflicts between the Tangs and the Hakkas were gradually maneuvered by the British colonial rulers to create a level-playing field for them. The imposition of District Officers into the New Territories meant that these colonial officials acted as the arbitrators among the rural factional elites; some villagers even found District Officers as having less bias in favor of the Tangs than the Qing dynasty's magistrates.[23]

In the 1950s, with the influx of mainland immigrants and the process of urbanization, rural politics became more fragmented than ever before. The HYK was divided into two factions, one led by Ho Chuen-yiu, Chan Yat-sun, and Cheung Yan-lung of the Tsuen Wan faction, and the other by Pang Fu-wah of the Yuen Long faction. The Yuen Long faction was complex as it involved not only the Pangs but also some Tangs, notably Tang Tak-yuk and Tang Hoi-yip.[24] The Tsuen Wan faction supported development and was pro-government, while the Yuen Long faction was anti-development.[25] The politics of development became more complex than before, because when the government tried to demolish some temporary buildings in the Tang's Tong land in 1957, it met rural opposition.[26] Similarly, the construction of the Tai Lam Reservoir and the resettlement plan encountered rural resistance and therefore delays in construction and implementation, respectively. The Yuen Long faction controlled the HYK, but the colonial government in 1955 decided to change the HYK's constitution by changing the composition of executive councilors from each of the seven electoral districts and by adding the chairs of Rural Committees as ex-officio members.[27] As a result, the pro-government Tsuen Wan faction leader, Ho Chuen-yiu, was eventually elected as the HYK chair, thereby tipping the political balance in favor of the colonial regime. Ho played the role of a power broker for the colonial government, demobilizing the rural people from a petition in May 1956 against the policy of restricting private conversions of land use.[28]

However, rural elite conflicts flared up again in February 1957 when the anti-development Yuen Long faction launched a *coup d'état* by changing the HYK constitution in such a way that the pro-development and pro-government faction would be ousted in the mid-1957 election. The pro-government Tsuen Wan faction lobbied some representatives of Rural Committees for political support, while the colonial government decided to issue an ultimatum to the HYK and urged its leaders to register the HYK under the new Societies Ordinance (Amendment) 1957. When the HYK remained to be dominated by the anti-government faction, the colonial administration decided to declare the HYK as illegal on the eve of the August 1957 election.[29] The Yuen Long faction then launched a "HYK Protection Committee" against the government. In November 1957, the Colonial Secretary moved a bill on the HYK, which was eventually passed by the Legislative Council (LegCo), and which stipulated that the government had to be satisfied with the composition of the HYK before it could be recognized as representative of rural opinions.[30] Obviously, the power struggle between the Yuen Long faction on the one hand, and the government and Tsuen Wan faction on the other, boiled down to the question of whether the colonial administration should recognize the HYK without interfering with the HYK's constitution. The Yuen Long faction believed that the HYK should elect its members autonomously from the colonial government, which however maintained that it had a say on its constitution and on whether the HYK was "truly representative."[31] Eventually, the LegCo bill restored the 1955 HYK constitution, and in 1959 the Tsuen Wan faction registered the HYK under the HYK ordinance passed by the colonial legislature. The entire sage illustrated the triangular relations between the colonial government, the pro-administration Tsuen Wan faction, and the anti-government Yuen Long faction. Again, the colonial authorities utilized direct rule to forestall the attempt by the Yuen Long faction to change the constitution and dominate the HYK. In other words, rural elite conflicts were enmeshed with the colonial administration, which favored a scenario in which the HKY was controlled by the pro-establishment camp.

In the early 1960s, the HYK had some members critical of the colonial government, including Tang Tak-yuk from the old Yuen Long faction and

Kan Chung-hing from the left-wing agricultural groups. But they failed to dominate the HYK which was controlled by the Tsuen Wan faction. During the 1970s, Chan Yat-san from the Tsuen Wan faction became the HYK chairman and he appealed to HYK members to maintain their "constructive" criticisms of the government.[32] In the 1980s, Lau Wong-fat, who was supported by Chan Yat-san, became the HYK chairman. The dominance of the Tsuen Wan faction in HYK opened the green light to many government policies, especially land development, the small house policy, and the policy of compensating rural landowners for development. The HYK was allowed to participate in the government's land development plans during the 1970s and 1980s, giving its views and inputs and "benefiting its members in a profitable way."[33] During the drafting process of the Basic Law, the HYK under Lau Wong-fat succeeded in protecting the rights of the indigenous inhabitants in the New Territories by incorporating it under Article 40 of the HKSAR's mini-constitution. Moreover, in 1986, the HYK succeeded in lobbying the colonial government to include the HYK as a functional constituency in LegCo elections in 1991.[34] At the same time, in order to match the four years' term of office of LegCo members, the HYK members' term of office from 1991 onwards was changed from three years to four years. Overall, it became a pro-government rural interest group which has also become a target of co-optation by the authority of the People's Republic of China (PRC). From the perspective of patron-client politics, the HYK under the control of the Tsuen Wan faction was a client of its political patron, the Hong Kong government under the British colonial rule. While the colonialists tolerated and allowed the pro-government elites to dominate the HYK, these elites in return could gain easy access to the details and developmental trends of the government's land policy. A win-win situation was therefore created between the HYK elites and the colonial regime.

From a political perspective, the British colonial government manipulated the HYK in such a way as to support its policies. On the other hand, the rural elites in the HYK protected and advanced their self-interests through the protective umbrella provided by the British colonialists. Under these circumstances, the rural elites in the HYK became increasingly influential, penetrating into the colonial government's advisory committees on land development, helping it to acquire land for infrastructure projects, facilitating the governmental compensation for rural residents in the process of land requisition, and most importantly collaborating with land

Figure 3.1: Organizational Structure of Heung Yee Kuk

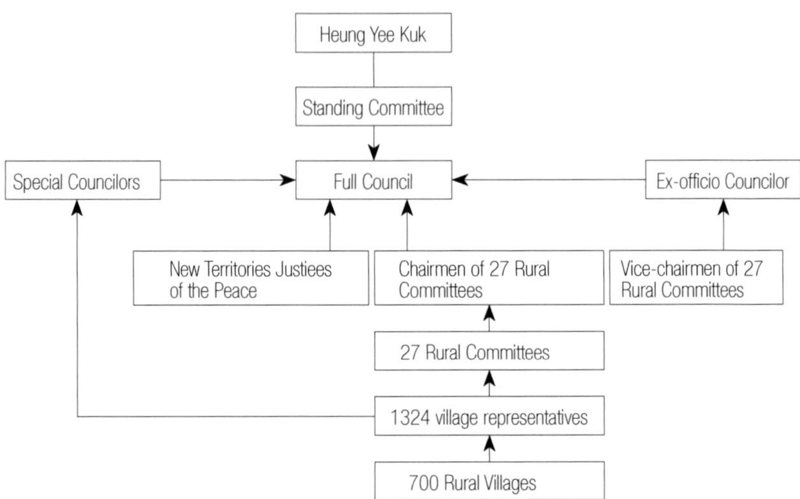

Table 3.1: The Political Role of Heung Yee Kuk Members During the Transition Period

Political Role	Name of HYK members
Hong Kong Affairs Advisors	Lau Wong-fat Chan Yat-san Tang Siu-tong
Preliminary Working Committee members	Lau Wong-fat Chan Yat-san
Members of the Selection Committee (an Electoral College set up by the Preparatory Committee in 1996 for electing the first Chief Executive and Provisional LegCo after the establishment of the HKSAR)	Wan Yuet-kau Chan Yat-san Lau Wong-fat Choy Kan-pui Tang Siu-tong Cheung Yan-lung Cheung Hok-ming
Hong Kong Basic Law Drafting Committee member	Lau Wong-fat

Source: *New Territories Heung Yee Kuk 70th Anniversary's Special Collection* (Hong Kong: New Territories Heung Yee Kuk, 1996).

developers so as to maximize the land interests and profits of the rural landowners. The rural elites in HYK bought land from some rural residents and then resold them to the colonial administration, thereby profiting themselves substantially.[35] The small house policy was regarded as a political exchange between the colonial government and the rural elites for the latter's acceptance of the rapid development of new satellite towns in the New Territories.[36] By the time the PRC authorities prepared Hong Kong for its transition to July 1, 1997, the HYK became a powerful rural interest group succeeded in lobbying the PRC government to protect the interests of rural residents. The role of HYK as an influential player in rural politics has become more prominent in the HKSAR after July 1, 1997, because different political forces, especially the pro-government and pro-Beijing camps, have been trying to secure their support in elections. If the British colonizers were the old political patron of the HYK elites, then PRC authorities became the new political patron after July 1, 1997. Figure 3.1 below illustrates the organizational structure of the HYK.

During the transition period in Hong Kong from the final years of the British rule to the PRC's reassertion of its sovereignty on July 1, 1997, the HYK members were politically recognized and influential (Table 3.1). Many of them were appointed by the PRC government as the members of the Hong Kong Affairs Advisors, Preliminary Working Committee, Selection Committee, and the Basic Law Drafting Committee. Seven HYK members, including Chan Yat-sun and Lau Wong-fat, were appointed as the members of the Selection Committee, which was an Electoral College set up by the Preparatory Committee in 1996 for the election of the first Chief Executive and the Provisional LegCo after the establishment of the HKSAR. As such, the core members HYK became politically influential in the political development of Hong Kong after 1997. Clearly, PRC authorities were keen to co-opt them into the political institutions of the HKSAR.

Rural Elites: Chan Yat-san, Lau Wong-fat, Benton Cheung Yan-lung, and Tai Kuen

The study of rural politics in Hong Kong has to understand the changing political roles of four main HYK elites, namely Chan Yat-san, Lau Wong-fat, Benton Cheung Yan-lung, and Tai Kuen. This section discusses their role and political significance in district politics.

Chan Yat-san belonged to the first generation of the influential landlords in the New Territories after the end of the Japanese occupation of Hong Kong in 1945. He assisted the colonial government to implement the policy of land resumption and acquisition in many villages, receiving monetary rewards through his land and property investments. He succeeded a pro-government elite, Ho Chuen-yiu, to become the HYK's chairman from 1962 to 1964.[37] Chan was regarded as an influential leader in the New Territories for 60 years. His father was an intellectual managing a pharmacy and a restaurant in Tuen Mun, while his mother possessed a huge farmland. At the age of 19, Chan's father passed away and he took up his family business, arousing the attention of the British colonial rulers. Chan told the media that, in 1940, the British agents asked him to store sufficient food in Tuen Mun and the outlying islands for the sake of resisting the Japanese Imperial Army.[38] During the Japanese military occupation of Hong Kong, Chan kept a low profile in managing his father's pharmacy while distributing rice to rural residents. He helped the British convey messages to the Chinese communist guerrillas in Tuen Mun. By the end of the Second World War, Chan became a "dragonhead" of Yuen Long and eight villages in Tuen Mun.[39] He was reportedly cultivating close connections with the Kuomintang (KMT), whose generals and soldiers retreated from the mainland to Hong Kong before the CCP takeover of mainland China in October 1949. Chan assisted many KMT officials and even went to Taiwan's Academia Sinica to study politics in 1952—an unusual but significant move at that time.[40] In the 1960s, he became acquainted with Heung Chin, who had been a KMT general and who founded a triad named Sun Yee On in Hong Kong.[41] Because Chan went to study in Taiwan in the early 1950s, the British colonial government once blacklisted him and did not allow him to return to Hong Kong.[42] In short, Chan's historical experiences were unique, working for the British, conveying messages to the CCP, and retaining close connections with the KMT.

Later Chan was allowed to return to Hong Kong and then he climbed up the political ladder by becoming a chairman of the Tuen Mun Rural Committee in 1966. Since then, the colonial government had to rely on his influence and personal network (*guanxi*) to acquire land from the rural landowners and residents, such as the land requisition for the construction of the Tuen Mun highway in 1974—an accomplishment after Chan had represented the government to buy the ownership of the farmland in two key villages, namely Sau Gwun Mat village and Tai Lam village.[43] It was a common practice for Chan to buy the farmland, knowing that the government would develop the pieces of land concerned and acquiring profits by reselling land to the colonial administration at a higher price.[44] In the 1967 riots in Hong Kong, Chan contacted the rural elites and residents to set up pro-government interest groups, mobilizing other rural leaders such as Cheung Yan-lung, Pang Fu-wah, and Tang Nai-man. They were labelled by the leftwing Maoists as the "four Hong Kong British running dogs."[45] The colonial government even sent several agents as bodyguards to protect Chan's personal safety and allowed him to guard himself by having a defensive pistol. In 1968, Chan was rewarded with a Member of the British Empire (MBE) by the colonial government. In June 1971, Chan mobilized 700 rural elites to hold a meeting to call for the protection of the rights of indigenous inhabitants to build their small houses. In response, the Commissioner of the New Territories, Dennis Bray, wrote to the HYK in November 1972, announcing that the small house policy was formally supported by the Governor in Executive Council (ExCo). The experiences of Chan demonstrated how a rural elite emerged successfully from the end of the Second World War to the early 1970s.

Benton Cheung Yan-lung was another rural elite rising up politically in Sheung Shui, where he was a chairperson of the Rural Committee and where he organized relief and relocation for the victims of fire accidents in the 1950s.[46] He won the hearts and minds of rural residents by lobbying the government to reestablish a new market in Sheung Shui after two fire accidents. After the market was re-established, many streets used the word "Sun" (new) as the starting name and one street was even named in accordance with the surname of Cheung and his wife. Cheung made a lot of friends in rural areas and his father had been a Chinese medicine practitioner who later opened a miscellaneous store that sold all kinds of food products. His father became rich and Cheung later enrolled in Kowloon's La Salle College, therefore establishing his firm English language foundation. During the Japanese invasion of China, Cheung originally wanted to enroll in the KMT army in Guangzhou, but later he went to study economics at the Sun Yat Sen University and worked for many KMT officials.[47] Cheung was reportedly involved in smuggling of kerosene and food products to

China during the early 1950s when the United Nation imposed an embargo on the mainland. He earned a lot of money and later profited himself by buying old buildings in Sheung Shui and then by reselling them. In 1967, he supported the British colonial government and was targeted by the leftists. The government allowed him to arm himself with a pistol. After the riots, the colonial government arranged Cheung to visit the Chinatown in London to persuade Hong Kong's rural people, who migrated to live in the UK, not to fall under China's united front work easily.[48] During the 1980s, the colonial government also relied on his personal networks and influence to develop the New Territories. His role was to accurately buy considerable farmland in Sheung Shui, Fanling, Sha Tau Kok, and Ta Ku Ling, and then resold it to the government. He became affluent not only through the process of land development, but also through his investment in stocks, securities, land development and construction. After Cheung became rich, he returned some of his proceeds to the society by donating to schools, organizing clan associations, and opening columbarium where urns were placed to store the ashes of the dead. Cheung got famous for his assistance to many refugees from the mainland, who arrived Hong Kong and who received his monetary support and exchange. He was later rewarded with the Justice of Peace and Commander of the British Empire (CBE).

Both Chan Yat-san and Cheung Yan-lung had some features in common. Both of their historical experiences had encounters with the CCP and KMT. They also acted as middlemen between the colonial government and other rural landowners. Their role as the intermediaries between the colonial rulers and the ruled was politically and socially significant. The personal protection allowed by the British to both during the left riots in 1967 was significant, illustrating their contribution to the British colonial governance in Hong Kong. Unsurprisingly, Chan and Cheung were rewarded with a MBE and CBE respectively.

Tai Kuen was regarded as a "godfather of Yuen Long" as his rural influence was tremendous.[49] He and his brothers opened and managed a transport company. Later he got affluent and began to buy a lot of farmland, which was turned into residential areas. From 1993 and 1996, his company amassed considerable profits in land development, transport, and restaurants, especially in the Yuen Long district. Although Tai's company later invested in the buying of a lot of commercial and industrial buildings, it suffered financial losses during the financial crisis in 2002.[50] He was a member of the Shap Pat Heung (Eighteen Villages) Rural Committee for 35 years and became a chairman of the Yuen Long District Board (DB). In March 1999, Tai was accused of committing fraud in village elections and he was also allegedly involved in three violent incidents, including an event during which 300 people reportedly attacked the Yuen Long District Office, a violent attack on a village elder, and a firebomb attack on another village head.[51] In response, the Independent Commission Against Corruption (ICAC) in May 1999 sent 200 staff members to detain 27 people, including Tai himself.[52] He and his friends were also suspected of arranging 31 village representatives to join a tour to Singapore for four days, inviting some of them to visit Macau for two days, and mobilizing all of them to vote on the village election day.[53] However, the charges against six accused rural residents were dropped and they were acquitted. Tai continued to be chairman of the Shap Pat Heung Rural Committee. The incident showed that village elections were affected by the accusations and suspicions of involving "fraud," "violence," and "bribery." Regardless of the accusations against Tai, he remained a crucial and respected middleman between the colonial rulers and the rural landowners.

Another influential rural elite was Lau Wong-fat, who was born in 1936 in Tuen Mun's Lung Ku Tan, which was a remote place with access to Castle Bay only by a small ferry.[54] Lau's mother was strict as he was the only son in the family. His parent raised livestock animals, like pigs, and grew vegetables. Lau worked in a Kowloon-Canton railway for some years and his father later got the franchise of running a ferry, thereby improving his family's livelihood. Lau opened a grocery store in Yuen Long and became a village head in a volunteering capacity. In 1960, Lau was groomed by his patron Chan Yat-san, who asked him to participate in the village election as a village representative in the early 1960s.[55] In 1966, Lau Wong-fat was elected as a vice-chairman of the Tuen Mun Rural Committee. In the same year, the Hong Kong government planned to make Tuen Mun a satellite town in the future. Grasping this golden opportunity for land development, Lau used five cents per square feet to buy a considerable amount of farmland in Tuen Mun's Lung Ku Tan, laying the foundation of his economic profits. His move, however, was criticized by some villagers as profiting himself at the expense of their interest.[56] Four years later, he became the chairperson of the Rural Committee. In 1973, Lau was appointed as a Justice of Peace, and in 1978, he became the vice-chairman of the HYK.

His meteoric rise was attributable partly to the patronage of Chan Yat-san and partly to the support of the colonial government. In the early 1980s, the China Electricity Company Limited built an electricity station in Lung Ku Tan and Lau supported its move by acting as a negotiating representative to acquire land from landowners and villagers, who then got monetary compensation.[57] At the same time, Lau acquired more farmland and then resold them to the government, thereby profiting himself quickly.[58] Moreover, Lau helped the government relocate the affected villagers by selecting the relocated land for them and building roads to facilitate their transport. Some villagers appreciated and greatly respected Lau for his work. In 1980, Lau was elected as the HYK chairman, succeeding Wong Yuen-cheung. One year later, Lau was awarded with the MBE. At this juncture, many land developers who invested in the New Territories had to cultivate good networks with Lau, including the Hutchinson company under the leadership of business tycoon Li Ka-shing.[59] In the late 1970s, Hutchison succeeded in building the Green Island Cement Factory in Tuen Mun through the support of Lau Wong-fat, whose friendships and personal connections minimized the rural residents' opposition to the construction and completion of the project in 1983.[60] In the 1980s, Lau rose up the political ladder quickly, becoming a legislator through the Electoral College of the Urban Council (UrbCo) and Regional Council (RegCo) in 1985. In 1987, the colonial government revised a legislation governing the control of animal and industrial waste and this move sparked the opposition of many rural people, who went to protest at the LegCo and who surrounded the limousine of Governor David Wilson. Lau intervened in the crisis, appeased the anger of the rural residents, and let Governor Wilson leave the LegCo premises smoothly. In 1990, Lau was politically rewarded with the OBE. Three years later, he was appointed by the PRC government as a member of the Chinese People's Political Consultative Conference (CPPCC). In 1997, he became the chairperson of the Provisional UrbCo and RegCo. In 1998 Lau was awarded with the Golden Bauhinia by the HKSAR government, reaching an apex of his political career and public service for Hong Kong.

A significant development in the meteoric rise of Lau Wong-fat was how the British colonial government utilized his personal networks and connections to achieve the objective of land acquisition in the New Territories. In 1978, Lau and Chan Yat-san were appointed as members in a Work Committee to Study the Requisition of Land in Towns and Land of the New Territories.[61] Because Lau and Chan were aware of the government's land development plans, they could easily play the role of being middlemen in the process of land requisition. As such, under the tutelage and support of the British colonial government, rural elites such as Chan Yat-san, Benton Cheung, and Lau Wong-fat became the co-opted rural leaders who acted as the effective intermediaries between the colonial rulers and rural residents. Their political rise was clearly due to the patronage of the British colonial authorities. Later, Lau Wong-fat was spotted by PRC authorities as a crucial target of political co-optation. After the Sino-British agreement over Hong Kong's future was reached in September 1984, Lau Wong-fat and some rural elites were invited to Beijing, whose authorities agreed to protect the interests of the indigenous inhabitants by stipulating their interest protection in Article 40 of the Basic Law. Lau's insistence that the Basic Law should protect the rights and interests of indigenous inhabitants was a hallmark of his lobbying efforts in Beijing.[62] From the perspective of patron-client politics, the British patron of Lau gradually shifted to the PRC patron after the mid-1980s. From 1998 to 2016, Lau continued to be a LegCo member; nevertheless, due to his very busy schedule and hectic work, his frequent absence in LegCo meetings was criticized by a Catholic group that monitored the performance and work of legislators.[63] Overall, Lau Wong-fat's contributions to rural politics were tremendous; he acted as the traditional Chinese rural elites mediating between the colonial rulers and the rural elites and masses — an action same as Chan Yat-san, Cheung Yan-lung, and Tai Kuen.

The rural elites are by no means homogenous. Their heterogenous and fragmented nature could be seen in the HKSAR government's attempt at introducing the double village heads elections after a court case concerning the village election in Po Toi Au village and Shek Wu Tong village, where two residents argued that the election violated not only the International Covenant on Civic and Political Rights, but also the Sexual Discrimination Ordinance. The Court of Final Appeal ruled in favor of the two litigants, and in response to the court judgement, the government decided to introduce the double village heads elections, one for the indigenous inhabitants and the other for non-indigenous residents.[64] Lau Wong-fat supported the government's proposed electoral reform, which however was opposed by Kan Ping-chee's Yuen Long rural faction.[65] Kan set up the New Territories Residents Council to oppose the government, while Hau Chi-keung of the Sheung Shui Rural Committee threatened to form a political party in opposition to the double village heads elections.[66] Lau's political influence was diluted by the HKSAR government, which attempted to play down the role of the HYK.[67] Before Carrie Lam became the Chief Executive in 2017, she had handled the illegal structures of the small houses in the New Territories, leading to the anger of many rural elites and residents. The pro-Beijing *Ta Kung Pao* described Lau Wong-fat as deliberately distancing from the HKSAR government as he was appointed to the ExCo under the leadership of Chief Executive Donald Tsang.[68] In fact, Lau's political influence gradually declined in 2011, when the Liaison Office reportedly supported Junius Ho to unseat Lau as the new chairman of the Tuen Mun Rural Committee.[69] Ultimately, the rural elites did not have shared interests; they often electorally competed with each other, with or without the support of either the British colonial government or the HKSAR administration. Still, Lau was a highly respected rural leader as pro-government legislators waited for his arrival at LegCo on the day when the government's constitutional reform blueprint was voted in the LegCo on June 18, 2015.[70] Lau passed away at the age of 80 in July 2017, but his political legacy continued. His son Lau Ip-keung was appointed to the ExCo during the Carrie Lam administration.[71] As early as September 2008, Lau Wong-fat openly argued that the ExCo should have its representative from the rural people.[72] Compared with his late father, it takes some time for Lau Ip-keung to build up his political networks and influence in the New Territories. In particular, rural politics have already been evolving in such a fragmented way that many other rural elites are now increasingly active and politically influential.

Heung Yee Kuk's Participation in Political Institutions

Table 3.2 shows that the HYK members have been traditionally influential in the local political institutions, being members of LegCo and ExCo. From 1988 to 1991, there were six rural elites elected to LegCo through the Electoral College and functional constituencies. However, these rural elites had different affiliations with political parties, showing the fragmented nature of the rural faction. On the other hand, it demonstrated the penetration of political parties into various rural areas, where elites formed alliances with them. From 1991 to 1995, the rural faction was divided into

Table 3.2: Heung Yee Kuk Members as Members of the Legislative Council and Executive Council, 1977–2020

Year	Legislative Council (LegCo, Political Party Affiliation)	Executive Council (ExCo, Political Party Affiliation)
1977–1981	Yeung Siu-cho (Independent)	No member of the Heung Yee Kuk was appointed to ExCo.
1981–1985	Cheung Yan-lung (Independent) Yeung Siu-cho (Independent)	
1985–1988	Cheung Yan-lung (Independent) Lau Wong-fat (Independent) Andrew Wong Wang-fat (Independent)	
1988–1991	Cheung Yan-lung (Progressive Hong Kong Society) Lau Wong-fat (Independent) Daniel Lam Wai-keung (Independent) Kingsley Sit Ho-yin (Progressive Hong Kong Society) Tai Chin-wah (Independent) Andrew Wong Wang-fat (Independent)	
1991–1995	Lau Wong-fat (Co-operative Resources Centre) Andrew Wong Wang-fat (Independent) Tai Chin-wah* (Federation for the Stability of Hong Kong) Tang Siu-tong** (Independent) Gilbert Leung Kam-ho*(Federation for the Stability of Hong Kong) Tso Shiu-wai** (Liberal Democratic Federation)	
1995–1997	Lau Wong-fat (Liberal Party) Tang Siu-tong (Independent) Choy Kan-pui (Independent) Andrew Wong Wang-fat (Independent)	
1996–1998 Provincial Legislative Council	Lau Wong-fat (Liberal Party) Tang Siu-tong (Independent) Choy Kan-pui (Hong Kong Progressive Alliance) Andrew Wong Wang-fat (Independent)	
1998–2000	Lau Wong-fat (Liberal Party) Tang Siu-tong (Independent) Andrew Wong Wang-fat (Independent)	
2000–2004	Lau Wong-fat (Liberal Party) Tang Siu-tong (Hong Kong Progressive Alliance) Andrew Wong Wang-fat (Independent)	
2004–2008	Lau Wong-fat (Liberal Party) Daniel Lam Wai-keung (Independent) Cheung Hok-ming (DAB) Li Kwok-ying (DAB)	
2008–2012	Lau Wong-fat (Economic Synergy) Cheung Hok-ming (DAB)	Lau Wong-fat (Economic Synergy from 2009 to 2017)

Table 3.2 Continued

Year	Legislative Council (LegCo, Political Party Affiliation)	Executive Council (ExCo, Political Party Affiliation)
2012–2016	Lau Wong-fat (Business and Professional Alliance)	Cheung Hok-ming (DAB from 2012 to 2017)
2016–2021	Lau Ip-keung (Business and Professional Alliance) Junius Ho Kwan-yiu (Independent)	Kenneth Lau Ip-keung (ExCo from 2017 to 2021)

Sources: This table is compiled from multiple sources, including Louie Kin-shuen and Shum Kwok-cheung, *A Compilation of Election Materials in Hong Kong, 1982–1994* (Hong Kong: The Hong Kong Institute of Asia-Pacific Studies, The Chinese University of Hong Kong, 1996); Yip Tin-sang, *A Compilation of Election Materials in Hong Kong, 2001–2004* (Hong Kong: The Hong Kong Institute of Asia-Pacific Studies, The Chinese University of Hong Kong, 2005); Yip Tin-sang, *A Compilation of Election Materials in Hong Kong, 2005–2012* (Hong Kong: The Hong Kong Institute of Asia-Pacific Studies, The Chinese University of Hong Kong, 2015). Also see "The Database of Legislative Councilors," in https://www.legco.gov.hk/general/english/library/initiatives_legco_collections.html#a, access date: August 9, 2020.

Note: *In March 1992 it was discovered that Tai had not passed his professional examination in England and that he had forged credentials to enable him to practice as a solicitor since 1983. He resigned from his elected seat in LegCo the next day. In 1993, Gilbert Leung was found guilty of trying to bribe two regional councilors to vote for him in the 1991 LegCo election and he was removed from the seat.

** Tang was elected in the by-election after an incumbent LegCo member Ng Ming-yam of New Territories West died of cancer on June 22, 1992. Tso won an by-election and was elected to the RegCo in 1991 and replaced the unseated Gilbert Leung.

two groups, one pro-business group led by Lau Wong-fat and the other more pro-Beijing and politically conservative side led by Tai Chin-wah and Gilbert Leung Kam-ho. Tai, whose uncle was Tai Kuen, was a LegCo member from 1985 to 1991, but he was later barred from practicing law in Hong Kong due to his falsified qualifications. With the decline of the Tai Chin-wah faction, Lau Wong-fat's political influence grew in the HKSAR; in 2009 he was appointed to the ExCo. From 1995 to 2008, Lau was also a member of the pro-business Liberal Party. Later he joined the Economic Synergy and then the Business and Professional Alliance. Other rural elites like Cheung Yan-lung and Sit Ho-yin joined the Progressive Hong Kong Society in 1988. After 2004, some rural elites, such as Cheung Hok-ming, joined the DAB. Different political parties began to compete for the support for rural elites, who could utilize their personal connections to strengthen the voting power base of different parties. Furthermore, by joining political parties, the rural elites could consolidate their power base and find it easier in their election campaign which was supported by the party machinery. A kind of political symbiosis emerged between the rural elites and political parties in the HKSAR.

**Table 3.3: Participation of Members from Political Parties
in the Full Council of Heung Yee Kuk, 2020**

Political Party	Key Members in HYK
Business Professional Alliance	Kenneth Lau Ip-keung Mok Kam-kwai
Civic Force	Wai Kwok-hung
Democratic Alliance for the Betterment and Progress of Hong Kong (DAB)	George Ng Sze-fuk William Wan Hon-cheung Wan Yuet-kau Wong Mo-tai Li Kwok-ying Cheung Hok-ming
The Federation of Hong Kong and Kowloon Labor Unions	Li Fung-ying

Source: "Full Council of the 35th Term of the Heung Yee Kuk," in https://www.had.gov.hk/rre/eng/other/35th_rural_assembly_list.html, access date: August 9, 2020.

Heung Yee Kuk and Political Parties

The intertwined relationships between political parties and HYK can be seen in Table 3.3. As of 2020, the HYK witnessed the infiltration of some members of political parties, which included the Business Professional Alliance (BPA), the DAB, and the Federation of the Hong Kong and Kowloon Labor Unions. Lau Wong-fat's son, Kenneth Lau, joined the BPA, while six members of HYK participated in the DAB. Clearly, the pro-Beijing DAB infiltrated the HYK for the sake of consolidating its voters' base in the rural areas. Overall, the HYK remains a loosely organized institution where members have their different interests; their participation in political groups and parties are allowed with individual autonomy.

Table 3.4 corroborates the phenomenon that political parties and groups have already targeted at the rural elites. From 2019 to 2023, a minority of elected village representatives in the 1,700 villages has affiliation with political parties and groups, notably the BPA, the DAB, and the New Territories Association of Societies (NTAS). The NTAS can be regarded as a united front group cooperating with the DAB to enhance the chances of electoral success of pro-Beijing and pro-government candidates in elections at the LegCo and District Council (DC)levels. Given the minority of village representatives having party affiliation, it can be argued that political parties

Table 3.4: Village Representatives and their Political Party Affiliation, 2019–2023

Political Parties	Name of Village Representative
Business Professional Alliance (BPA)	Kwong Koon-wan Kenneth Lau Ip-keung
DAB	Lee Kwai-chun Mealoha Kwok Wai-man Tony Tang Kun-nin Wan Wo-fai Liu Hing-hung
New Territories Association of Societies (NTAS)	Peter Lau Wai-cheung Kwu Hon-keung To Sheck-yuen Lai Wing-tim Cheung Muk-lam Chan Siu-kuen

Source: "List of Village Representatives, 2019–2023," in https://www.had.gov.hk/rre/eng/elections/map19-23.html, access date: August 9, 2020.

in the HKSAR are by no means strong among the rural elites. Still, the pro-Beijing and pro-government groups aspire to strengthen their power base in electoral campaigns in the New Territories.

Table 3.5 delineates those candidates of the rural faction participating in the LegCo's direct elections. There were some rural candidates who won the elections, including former LegCo President Andrew Wong Wang-fat and Junius Ho Kwan-yiu. Andrew Wong could be seen as a candidate belonging to the rural faction, for he gained the support of the HYK and many rural residents. However, his power base was consistently much stronger than any other members of the rural faction. First and foremost, Wong was a former lecturer at the Chinese University of Hong Kong (CUHK) with an academic and educational background appealing to intellectuals and middle-class voters. Second, Wong projected an image of being an independent candidate without being coopted by any political force. Third, his harmonious relations with the rural elites and residents meant that his popular support was strong. Hence, from 1998 to 2000, he could be directly elected while other members of the rural faction, including Kan Ping-chee, remained relatively weak. In 2016, Junius Ho Kwan-yiu also projected an image of being a politically non-affiliated candidate, but he was reportedly

Table 3.5: Candidates of the Rural Faction Participating in LegCo's Geographical Constituency Elections, 1998–2016

Year	Constituency	Candidate* (Political Party Affiliation)	Number of votes (%)
1998	New Territories West	Lam Wai-keung (Independent)	25,905 (6.91%)
	New Territories East	Brian Kan Ping-chee (Independent)	6,637 (2.01%)
		Andrew Wong Wang-fat (Independent)	44,386 (13.43%)*
2000	New Territories East	Brian Kan Ping-chee (Independent)	7,945 (2.58%)
		Choy Kan-pui (Hong Kong Progressive Alliance)	8,835 (2.87%)
		Andrew Wong Wang-fat (Independent)	44,899 (14.59%)*
2004	New Territories West	Chow Ping-tim (Independent)	1,725 (0.37%)
	New Territories East	Andrew Wong Wang-fat (Independent)	23,081 (5.36%)
2012	New Territories West	Junius Ho Kwan-yiu (Independent)	10,805 (2.17%)
		Chan Keung (The Third Force)	16,737 (3.36%)
	New Territories East	Yau Wing-kwong (Economic Synergy)	5,717 (1.23%)
2016	New Territories East	Gary Hau Chi-keung (Independent)	6,720 (1.16%)
	New Territories West	Junius Ho Kwan-yiu (Independent)	35,657 (5.91%)*

Sources: This table is compiled from multiple sources, including Yip Tin-sang, *A Compilation of Election Materials in Hong Kong, 2001–2004* (Hong Kong: The Hong Kong Institute of Asia-Pacific Studies, The Chinese University of Hong Kong, 2005); and Yip Tin-sang, *A Compilation of the Election Materials in Hong Kong, 2005–2012* (Hong Kong: The Hong Kong Institute of Asia-Pacific Studies, The Chinese University of Hong Kong, 2015); and the website of the Registration and Electoral Office, in https://www.eac.hk/ch/legco/lce.htm, access date, August 9, 2020.

* Elected

groomed and supported by the pro-Beijing forces. Ho was eventually elected to the LegCo, like Wong's image of being an independent candidate well connected with the rural faction.

The rural faction participated in LegCo's direct election for the first time in 1998, when HYK vice-chairman Law Wai-keung teamed up with Tai Kuen and other rural elites to run in New Territories West. Although Lam's votes were comparatively far more than another rural elite Kan Ping-chee, his overall votes failed to get him elected. Kan Ping-chee ran in another constituency, the New Territories East, but he got only 6,637 votes. It was reported that Kan was unhappy with the reluctance of the HYK to nominate any candidate to participate in the New Territories East.[73] In any case, the total votes obtained by Lam and Kan reflected the relatively weak appeal of the HYK alone—an electoral pattern repeated in 2004, 2012, and 2016. While independent Andrew Wong got only 23,081 votes in 2004 and got defeated, other rural candidates like Chan Keung and Junius Ho competed and failed to be elected in 2012. With the strong support of the pro-Beijing district forces, Junius Ho eventually got elected in 2016. As a lawyer, Ho could attract the support of voters from the middle-class professionals. Clearly, while the HYK alone lost its attractiveness to voters, candidates who come from the rural faction and who want to win the direct election must either project themselves as politically independent or a professional to secure the support of more middle-class voters.

It is noteworthy that many political parties acquire the support of rural elites to widen their political base in the New Territories. For instance, in the 2000 LegCo direct elections, Lau Hon-chuen of the Hong Kong Progressive Alliance secured the support of Lau Wong-fat and helped its member Tang Siu-tong to compete in the elections.[74] Tang got more voters in the September 1998 election than his performance in the by-election held in May 1998, a phenomenon attributable to the fact that his rural faction improved its relations with the DAB.[75] In May 1998, Tam Yiu-chung of the DAB went to compete for a directly elected seat in the New Territories West, leading to the displeasure of some members of the rural faction. Tam's participation was regarded by the rural elites as politically pre-emptive as they had not been consulted beforehand. Moreover, another DAB member, Ngan Kam-chuen, also competed with Tang Siu-tong in the LegCo functional constituency seat which was returned from the UrbCo and RegCo. The electoral assertiveness of the DAB in 1998 raised the eyebrows of the HYK.

Table 3.6 shows the members of the rural faction who joined the DAB lists in their participation in LegCo's direct elections. The higher the ranking of the rural faction's candidates in the DAB list, the higher their chances of being directly elected to the LegCo. Tang Siu-tong was ranked second and was directly elected in the 2000 LegCo election. Similarly, Cheung Hok-ming was elected in 2004, so as Li Kwok-ying although both ran in different geographical constituencies. Cheung was again elected in the 2008 LegCo elections. Hence, a symbiosis could be seen in the temporary coalition composed of the rural faction and the DAB in their participation in the LegCo direct elections. While the rural faction can mobilize their rural residents to vote for its candidates due to their strong personal, clans and family networks, the DAB could mobilize its manpower and resources effectively to enhance the chance of its candidates, including those from the rural faction, to be directly elected. A marriage of political convenience

**Table 3.6: Rural Faction Members Who Participated in
the DAB Lists in LegCo's Elections**

Year and Constituency	Rural Faction's Candidate (E—elected)	Ranking of the Rural Faction's Candidate in DAB list	Number of Votes for the list	Number of seat(s) obtained from the DAB List
1998 New Territories East	Wan Yuet-kau	6	56,731 (17.17%)	1
2000 New Territories West	Tang Siu-tong [E]	2	101,629 (29.58%)	2
2000 New Territories East	Wan Yuet-kau Li Kwok-ying	2 5	66,943 (21.75%)	1
2004 New Territories West	Cheung Hok-ming [E]	2	115,251 (24.87%)	2
2004 New Territories East	Li Kwok-ying [E] Mok Kam-kwai	2 3	95,434 (22.15%)	2
2008 New Territories West	Cheung Hok-ming [E]	2	92,037 (23.11%)	2
2008 New Territories East	Mok Kam-kwai	3	102,434 (28.38%)	2

Sources: This table is compiled from multiple sources, including Yip Tin-sang, *A Compilation of Election Materials in Hong Kong, 2001–2004* (Hong Kong: The Hong Kong Institute of Asia-Pacific Studies, The Chinese University of Hong Kong, 2005); and Yip Tin-sang, *A Compilation of Election Materials in Hong Kong, 2005–2012* (Hong Kong: The Hong Kong Institute of Asia-Pacific Studies, The Chinese University of Hong Kong, 2015); and the website of the Registration and Electoral Office, in https://www.eac.hk/ch/legco/lce.htm, access date, August 9, 2020.

between the DAB and the rural faction contributed to their success in LegCo's direct elections.

In Yuen Long, however, the rural faction was at loggerheads with the DAB for some years. In 2000, the ranking of Tang Siu-tong as the second one in the DAB list was reportedly a move to repair the relations between the two groups. Yet, on the other hand, Tang had strained relations with the rural faction.[76] In this regard, the DAB tried to be a middleman, avoiding the contest between Tang and other members of the rural faction. In return, Tang promised that he would not nominate candidates from the Progressive Alliance to compete with the DAB in DC elections.[77] In short, the triangular relations between Tang's Progressive Alliance, the DAB, and the rural faction were messy and complex. Tang also competed with Tai Kuen to be the chair of the Yuen Long DC, leading to Tai's eventual decision of withdrawing from the election. Learning from this experience of mutual competition, the DAB later nominated Cheung Hok-ming, who had rural faction's background, to run in New Territories West in 2004 and

2008—a strategy that worked well because Cheung was more influential than Tang and he was not a member of the Progressive Alliance. Under these circumstances, the collaboration between the DAB and the rural faction tended to be more simple and smoother in 2004 and 2008 LegCo elections. Tang's collaboration with DAB's Tam Yiu-chung, who was ranked number one, in the 2000 election led to their victory. This model of collaboration set an example for Cheung Hok-ming to follow suit in 2004 and 2008,[78] but Cheung was simply coopted into DAB and thereby making the collaboration like an alliance between the rural faction and the DAB. The 2000 model of collaboration was politically significant as the rural faction's alliance with the DAB defeated Lee Wing-tat of the Democratic Party in the New Territories West.[79] If the objective of the PRC's united front work in the HKSAR was to form alliances between the DAB and other pro-Beijing forces, like the rural faction, then the cooperation between Tang Siu-tong and Tam Yiu-chung represented a breakthrough in the prevention of the democrats from getting more directly elected seats in the LegCo.

In the 2004 LegCo elections, it was reported that the HYK's Lau Wong-fat supported DAB's Lau Kong-wah, who was an advisor of the HYK.[80] Lau was ranked number one in the DAB list, the second one being Li Kwok-ying, and the third one being Mok Kam-kwei. Li and Mok were the indigenous inhabitants in Tai Po and Sha Tin, respectively. Li joined the DAB in 1993. Hence, the alliance between the rural faction and the DAB was forged. Li was eventually elected, together with Lau Kong-wah. Again, the coalition between the rural faction and the DAB worked well in the 2004 LegCo elections. According to Lau Wong-fat, other candidates of the New Territories East, such as Andrew Wong and James Tien, also sought his support. To be diplomatic and polite to Andrew Wong and James Tien, Lau Wong-fat decided to write a letter to all villages, saying that Li Kwok-ying, Mok Kam-kwei, Andrew Wong, and James Tien were all HYK's friends, meaning that the HYK members felt free to vote for their preferred candidates.[81] Of course, since Li and Mok were nominated by the HYK, they tended to be the more preferred candidates than Andrew Wong and James Tien, if the HYK members and village representatives saw HYK and Lau Wong-fat as their institutional and rural leader, respectively. In fact, the 2004 LegCo elections witnessed an unprecedented success of the HYK, which got four members entering the legislature, namely Lau Wong-fat, Cheung Hok-ming, Lam Wai-keung, and Li Kwok-ying.[82] On the other hand, the alliance between the DAB and HYK got a total of four directly elected seats in both New Territories East and West—a huge success from the DAB's strategic perspective.[83] After the HYK's success in the 2004 LegCo elections, Lau Wong-fat vowed to form a rural alliance by acquiring the additional support from DAB's Wong Yung-kan (elected from agricultural and fisheries functional constituency) and the Federation of Labor's Lee Fung-ying.[84] Lau Wong-fat told his friends that his way of practicing politics was "to help others who also help you."[85] His political finesse undoubtedly contributed to the electoral success of the HYK. After the 2004 LegCo election, Lau revealed that he had asked James Tien whether the latter had enough votes to win, and that after Tien said he should have sufficient votes, Lau decided to mobilize HYK members and supports to vote for the HYK candidates. A win-win situation was therefore created after the formation and success of the alliance between the HYK and DAB.

After the 2008 LegCo elections, Lau Wong-fat decided to quit the Liberal Party. Lau remarked that because he helped and supported Cheung Hok-ming of both the DAB and HYK to win, he owed something to the Liberal Party.[86] In fact, Cheung got the strong support of the HYK members and supporters. Although Lau decided to withdraw from the Liberal Party, he politely commented that they would still cooperate as friends for the sake of protecting the interests of Hong Kong.[87] Yet, Lau was criticized by Selina Chow Liang Suk-yee of the Liberal Party for his staunch support of Cheung Hok-ming.[88] Selina Chow was defeated in the LegCo election and her Liberal Party colleague Miriam Lau Kin-yee questioned whether Lau, by supporting another party's candidate, violated the Liberal Party's regulations for members. Lau responded by saying that he accepted the criticism, and that since Cheung was nominated by the HYK, he had to support Cheung.[89] Hence, the ways in which Lau handled his withdrawal and criticism from the Liberal Party showed that he was a skillful rural politician who cultivated personal networks with all like-minded parties, groups, and individuals.

The 2008 LegCo elections also showed how Lau Wong-fat handled the HYK's relations with the DAB, apart from forming an alliance with the pro-Beijing party to nominate candidates in the New Territories. In late July 2008, Lau announced that he changed the route of running in LegCo's functional constituency elections from the DCs constituency to the HYK constituency.[90] In other words, Lau gave way to DAB member Ip Kwok-him who would run in the DC constituency. Lau's decision provoked the anger of some members of the rural faction. One elderly member said angrily that "the DAB often sits on the heads of the HYK to have pee pee and poo poo," and that "if we tolerate like this, it would humiliate our ancestors."[91] In response, Lau lobbied for support from the HYK elders, while allowing DAB chair Tam Yiu-ching and vice-chair Ip Kwok-him to pay a visit to HYK and seek political support from its members. Many HYK members argued that the HYK should nominate candidates to participate in direct elections, while Kan Ping-chee said that the HYK members should be united. Some HYK members criticized political parties for utilizing the votes from the HYK and they argued that the HYK should run in direct elections as a separate electoral list. Some HYK elders appealed to HYK members to withdraw from the DAB. Eventually, Lau Wong-fat held a closed-door meeting among HYK members, reaching a consensus on the need to avoid affecting the chance of Cheung Hok-ming, who joined the DAB, from being directly elected. Again, Lau utilized his personal influence and connections to settle the internal disputes within the HYK regarding the nomination of candidates in functional constituency and geographical constituency elections for the LegCo.

However, the 2012 LegCo elections could be regarded as a watershed for the relations between the rural faction and the DAB. The rural faction had a tense relationship with the DAB. To demonstrate the rural faction's dissatisfaction with the DAB, its members formed a new organization, namely the City Village Link (CVL) to garner the support of rural residents in the 2012 direct elections. The CVL was established in January 2012 with the objectives of promoting the integration of cities and villages, advocating the preservation of the local culture of the New Territories, building up a harmonious society, organizing social services to help the needy, paying attention on public policies and governance, reflecting the opinions of residents to the government, and improving the people's livelihood.[92] The CVL emphasized that the development of the New Territories was not just about "blind urbanization," but it was also concerned about the conservation work of rural areas and the harmonious integration of urban and rural areas.[93] At the same time, it supported the development of local economy by setting up a social service fund to subsidize the local communities, charity work, and residents' organizations.[94] As a matter of fact, 161 villages, 150 village representatives, 12 District Councilors, and 20 district organizations joined the CVL.[95] Some rural elites became the CVL leaders (see Table 3.7).

Table 3.7: City Village Link (CVL) Leaders and Relations with Rural Committee

Name	Affiliated Rural Committee
Man Chi-sheung (vice-chair of CVL)	San Tin Rural Committee
Tang Ho-nin (vice-chair of CVL)	Kam Tin Rural Committee
Tang Lai-tung (vice-chair of CVL)	Ha Tsuen Rural Committee
Ching Chan-ming (vice-chair of CVL)	Shap Pat Heung Rural Committee
To Sheck-yuen (chairman of CVL)	Tuen Mun Rural Committee
Tsang Chin-hung (vice-chairman of CVL)	Tuen Mun Rural Committee

Source: *Hong Kong Economic Journal,* March 13, 2012, p. A12.

The establishment of CVL can be seen as an attempt by the rural faction to contain the DAB's electoral influence and inroads in rural areas. It also illustrates the contradictions between the rural faction and the DAB.

The CVL's president was Chan Keung, who was a member of the Guangdong Chinese People's Political Consultative Conference and who was very active in Tsuen Wan.[96] He started his business by operating a mahjong parlor.[97] After Chan gained his fortune, he became involved in the development of real estates in the mainland. He was regarded as a middleman to help land developers acquire land in Yuen Long and Tuen Mun.[98] His political participation was seen as an attempt at challenging the position of Lau Wong-fat, but Chan encountered the rivalry from some rural elites, such as Leung Che-cheung.[99] Chan also obtained the support from many village elders, especially in Ha Tsuen. The CVL leaders were affiliated with different rural committees (see Table 3.7). The rapid rise of Chan Keung and his CVL group represented a new challenge to the mainstream rural faction led by Lau Wong-fat.

There were two main reasons for the rural factions to participate in the 2012 LegCo elections. Firstly, disputes over land interests in the New Territories became increasingly fierce and lucrative in view of the rapid infrastructure development.[100] From the perspective of some rural elites, the construction of new roads and railways were expected to directly affect the distributions of their land interests and economic benefits. Secondly, from 2009 to 2010, the emergence of the anti-Hong Kong Express Rail Link movement, as exemplified in the opposition of some villagers in the Choi Yuen village to the Guangzhou-Shenzhen-Hong Kong Express Rail, witnessed the rise of the political consciousness of many rural residents in the New Territories.[101] Some indigenous inhabitants began to realize that their interests could be easily sacrificed by some rural elites and undermined by the intervention from external forces. Nor did the political groups and HYK could protect their interests, except for their own collective action to protect themselves.[102]

The DAB calculated that it had to nominate candidates to run in LegCo direct elections and that some degree of competition with the increasingly divided rural faction would become inevitable. In the 2004 and 2008 LegCo elections, the alliance between the DAB and rural faction provided a strong support for their candidates, paving the way for their smooth victory.[103] However, in 2012, the DAB was ambitious and decided to run three lists in New Territories—the lists led by Leung Che-cheung, Tam Yiu-chung, and Chan Han-pan—apart from the list led by Alice Mak Mei-kuen of the pro-Beijing Federation of Trade Unions (FTU). All four of them—Leung, Tam, Chan, and Mak—were directly elected, with the rest of the five directly elected seats being grasped by businessman Michael Tien and democrats Lee Cheuk-yan, Leung Yiu-chung, Kwok Ka-ki, and Albert Chan Wai-yip. Clearly, the DAB decided to win as many directly elected seats as possible. Under these circumstances, the 2012 LegCo elections in New Territories West witnessed a loose alliance between the DAB and the rural faction led by Leung Che-cheung, but the DAB competed with Chan Keung, who was seen as a challenger to the mainstream rural faction. Table 3.8 shows the background of the members under the lists led by Chan Keung and Leung Che-cheung, illustrating the fragmented nature of the rural elites in the New Territories.

The competition between the rural faction led by Chan Keung and the DAB led by rural elite Leung Che-cheung can be seen in the 2012 LegCo elections. The number of votes of Chan Keung from the Third Force was 16,767 and that of Leung Che-cheung amounted to 33,777 votes. But if we focus on the rural areas (Table 3.9), Chan Keung's votes ranked the second highest and Leung's votes were the first highest among seven pro-Beijing candidates. Both obtained more than 8,000 rural votes, showing that their competition was very fierce. Their votes illustrated that the mobilization of the supporters of rural factions remained significant in LegCo elections. A similar situation could be seen in the 2016 LegCo election as the number of rural votes obtained by Michael Tien increased from 5,002 in 2012 to 11,007 in 2016, while Leung Che-cheung only acquired 10,402 rural votes. It appeared that many of the rural votes grasped by Chan Keung in 2012

Table 3.8: Background of Chan Keung's List and Leung Chee Cheung's List in the 2012 LegCo Elections

Chan Keung's List	Background
Chan Keung	Standing Committee Member of the Guangdong Province's Chinese People's Political Consultative Conference (CPPCC)
Ting Hin-wah	Former District Councilor in Kwai Tsing district
So Ka-man	District Councilor in Tuen Mun district
Chow Ping-tim	District Councilor in Tsuen Wan district
Tang Pa-leung	District Councilor in Yuen Long district
Nancy Poon Siu-ping	Former District Councilor in Kwai Tsing district
Gurung Raju	Hong Kong-born Nepalese
Leung Che-cheung's List	**Background**
Leung Che-cheung	President of New Territories Associations of Societies District Councilor in Yuen Long district
Tsang Hin-keung	Chairman of Pat Heung Rural Committee Ex-officio member of Yuen Long District Council
Lui Kin	District Councilor in Yuen Long District
Christina Maisenne Lee	Businesswoman
Wong Wai-lin	District Councilor in Yuen Long District
Chui Kwan-siu	Social Worker

Sources: This table is compiled from multiple sources, including Yip Tin-sang, *A Collection of Election Materials in Hong Kong, 2005–2012*, (Hong Kong: The Hong Kong Institute of Asia-Pacific Studies, The Chinese University of Hong Kong, 2015); and the Website of the Registration and Electoral Office, in https://www.eac.hk/ch/legco/lce.htm, access date: August 9, 2020. Also see *Hong Kong Economic Journal*, March 13, 2012, p. A12.

were later shifted to Michael Tien and that some rural votes also moved to support Junius Ho Kwan-yiu. Indeed, the rise of rural votes for Michael Tien and Junius Ho Kwan-yiu illustrated the fragmented nature of the rural faction. Table 3.9 shows that while Chan Keung was the strongest rural elite grasping 8,122 votes in rural districts in the 2012 LegCo elections, Junius Ho turned out to be the strongest rural elite acquiring 8,429 votes in rural districts in the 2016 elections.

Table 3.10 demonstrates that the power base of both Chan Keung in 2012 and Junius Ho in 2016 was located at more rural districts than non-rural ones. Junius Ho appeared to successfully penetrate into the electoral base of Chan Keung in the 2016 LegCo elections, increasing his rural support substantially from two rural districts in 2012 to seven rural districts in 2016. Compared with Leung Che-cheung's five rural districts and his

Table 3.9: Performance of Pro-Beijing Candidates in the Rural Areas of the New Territories West in 2012 and 2016 LegCo Elections

Pro-Beijing Candidates	Vote In Tsuen Wan Rural Area	Vote In Tuen Mun Rural Area	Vote In Yuen Long Rural Area	Vote in Island Rural Area	Total Number of Rural Votes
2012 LegCo Election					
Michael Tien (New People's Party)	1,970	892	1,958	182	5,002
Junius Ho Kwan-yiu (Independent)	312	764	1,229	322	2,627
Leung Chi Cheung (DAB)	256	294	6,422	1,734	8,706
Alice Mak Mei-kuen (FTU)	313	410	727	253	1,703
Chan Han-pan (DAB)	1,294	174	297	1,809	3,574
Tam Yiu-chung (DAB)	726	1,381	1,445	470	4,022
Chan Keung (The Third Force)	57	1,344	5,823	958	8,122
2016 LegCo Election					
Michael Tien (New People's Party)	1,592	2,664	6,004	747	11,007
Junius Ho Kwan-yiu (Independent)	470	1,671	5,875	413	8,429
Leung Che-cheung (DAB)	156	965	7,033	2,248	10,402
Alice Mak Mei-kuen (FTU)	310	717	2,334	650	4,011
Chan Han-pan (DAB)	1,035	454	949	1,867	4,305

Source: See the website of the Registration and Electoral Office, in https://www.eac.hk/ch/legco/lce.htm, access date, August 9, 2020.

total 10,402 votes, Ho got more two more rural districts than Leung but less rural votes (8,429). In other words, Ho's power base lied in rural districts, unlike Leung whose electoral base appeared to be more evenly distributed in rural and non-rural areas. This phenomenon also illustrated that Leung, who joined the DAB, could have the party machinery's support and whose votes were spreading out in both rural and non-rural areas. Still, given that rural votes in rural areas could shape the chance of candidates to be directly elected, it was understandable why the Liaison Office's officials had to conduct extensive and intensive united front work targeted at the rural elites and residents in the New Territories.

Before the September 2012 LegCo elections, the police arrested some rural elites for suspected electoral bribery.[104] Moreover, in August, the police arrested 130 rural elites and residents for suspected money-laundering activities.[105] The timing of the police arrests suddenly coincided with the election campaign. Rural candidate Chan Keung, who was not among those arrested by the police, said that the police action might be related to the

Table 3.10: Ten Electoral Districts Where Pro-Beijing Candidates Acquired More Votes

	Number of Rural Districts	Number of Non-rural Districts	Ten Electoral Districts Where Pro-Beijing Candidates Acquired More Votes
Year 2012			
Chan Keung (The Third Force)	7	3	Ha Tsuen* Shap Pat Heung North* Shap Pat Heung South* Tuen Mun Rural* Kam Tin* Cheung Hong Sam Shing Ping Shan North* Peng Chau & Hei Ling Chau*
Leung Che-cheung (DAB)	3	7	Tin Yiu Pat Heung South* Fung Nin Tin Shing Shui Oi Kingswood North Shui Pin Yuen Long Centre Lantau* Ping Shan North*
Michael Tien (New People's Party)	2	8	Discovery Park Greenfield Chung Pak Lai To Tsuen Wan Rural East* Lai Hing Hoi Bun Allway* Kingswood North Chung Wah
Junius Ho Kwan-yiu (Independent)	2	8	On Ho Wah Lai Kwai Shing East Estate San Hui* Cheung Hang Cheung Ching Ping Shan North* Tung Chung North Cho Yiu Shek Yam

Table 3.10 Continued

	Number of Rural Districts	Number of Non-rural Districts	Ten Electoral Districts Where Pro-Beijing Candidates Acquired More Votes
Alice Mak Mei-kuen (FTU)	0	10	Tin Heng Fu Tai Yat Tung Estate North Fuk Loi On Yam Hing Tsak Kwai Shing West Estate Wai Ying Tin King Ching King
Chan Han-pan (DAB)	1	9	Yeung Uk Road Tsing Yi South Kwai Shing East Estate Shing Hong Lai To Cheung On Shek Wai Kok* Tung Chung South Tsuen Wan Centre
Tam Yiu-chung (DAB)	0	10	Lung Mun Leung King Kin Sang Yau Oi South Siu Hong Siu Chi Siu Hei On Ting Fu Sun Butterfly
Year 2016			
Michael Tien (New People's Party)	3	7	Discovery Park Ting Sham* Fu Sun Shek Lei South Po Tin* Tsui Hing Tin Shing Ha Tsuen* Sam Shing Hoi Bun

Table 3.10 Continued

	Number of Rural Districts	Number of Non-rural Districts	Ten Electoral Districts Where Pro-Beijing Candidates Acquired More Votes
Junius Ho Kwan-yiu (Independent)	5	5	Pat Heung South* Lok Tsui San-Tin* Luk Yeung Pat Heung North* San Hui* Yuet Wu Siu Hei Yat Chak Shap Pat Heung Central*
Leung Che-cheung (DAB)	1	9	Tin Yiu Shui Oi Tin Shing Kingswood North Fung Nin Pek Long Yuen Long Pin Shan South* Nam Ping Yiu Yau
Alice Mak Mei-kuen (FTU)	0	10	Kwai Shing West Estate Yat Tung Estate North Fuk Loi Fu Tai On Yam Tin Heng Hing Tsak Wai Ying Ching King Yat Tung Estate South
Chan Han-pan (DAB)	0	10	Kwai Shing East Estate Tai Pak Tin Jo Yiu Shek Yam Cheung Hang Shek Lei North Cheung On Hoi Bun Shing Hong Lai To

Source: Tabulated from the website of the Registration and Electoral Office.

* Rural constituencies.

DAB's need to get 30,000 votes, which according to a news report had been grasped by another rural elite Leung Fook-yuen but which became the target of the DAB in the 2012 LegCo elections.[106] In view of the fact that two office-bearers of the CVL were arrested by the police, Leung stressed that he was not among those rural people who were arrested, that some people made "lots of small gestures" and that he preferred to mobilize the rural residents to support a democratic candidate Albert Chan Wai-yip.[107] Leung's reactions showed that the rural faction was divided into two groups, one led by Chan Keung and the other co-opted by the DAB. Leung added that in the past the rural elites and residents voted for the DAB, and that in 2012 they would not be "so foolish."[108] There were reports saying that officials of the Liaison Office tried to persuade Chan Keung to withdraw from the elections.[109] If so, PRC officials in the New Territories appeared to side with the DAB and hoped that ideally Chan should not divide and weaken the pro-Beijing votes. Rumors were rife that a DAB candidate complained to the police and Independent Commission Against Corruption (ICAC) about the infiltration of "black gold politics" in the 2012 LegCo elections, thereby arousing the anger of some rural elites.[110] On the other hand, it was reported that because Cheung Hok-ming, a rural elite, was co-opted by the DAB and that even Lau Wong-fat did not like to envisage this phenomenon. As a result, Lau tacitly agreed that another rural elite, Yau Wing-kwong, could participate in the LegCo direct elections in New Territories East.[111] Officials from the Liaison Office were reportedly surprised by Yau's move and tried to contact Lau, who however did not receive their phone calls.[112] The entire dispute illustrated the fragmentation and complexity of the rural elites and politics. Once there were elections, the rural elites competed among themselves fiercely; those who joined pro-Beijing political parties were seen as being politically coopted; and those who came out to participate in elections were regarded as challenging the mainstream rural faction. Factional rivalries were serious in rural elections and politics.

The Complexities of Rural Politics and Opposition to Double Village Heads Elections

Although some rural elites give the public the impression that they are politically active, many other rural residents are politically apathetic. In Table 3.11, there were many vacant village representatives and rural

Table 3.11: Total Number of Village Representatives and Vacant Village Representatives and Rural Representatives in 27 Rural Committees, 2011–2019

RC	Total Number of VR	No. of Vacant VR in 2019 VR Election	No. of Vacant RR in 2019 RR Election	No. of Vacant VR in 2015 VR Election	No. of Vacant RR in 2015 RR Election	No. of Vacant VR in 2011 VR Election	No. of Vacant RR in 2011 RR Election	Total Vacant Representatives in six election from 2011 to 2019
Tung Chung	14	0	1	1	0	1	1	4
Tai O	23	2	3	3	3	2	4	17
Lantau South	14	1	3	0	4	1	3	12
Ping Chau	12	0	0	0	0	0	0	0
Mui Wo	18	1	2	1	2	1	2	9
Lamma South	10	2	4	2	4	2	4	18
Lamma North	19	1	0	0	0	0	0	1
Cheung Chau	38	0	0	0	1	0	0	1
Tsing Yi	15	0	0	0	0	1	0	1
Tsuen Wan	60	0	2	0	4	0	2	8
Ma Wan	20	0	3	0	3	0	4	10
Sha Tin	54	0	8	1	10	1	8	28
Sai Kung North	47	1	20	0	15	0	20	56
Tai Po	118	2	11	0	15	0	20	48
Hang Hou	26	1	1	0	1	0	1	4
Sai Kung	23	3	18	3	20	2	23	69
Ta Kwu Ling	24	1	0	0	1	0	0	2
Sha Tou Kok	55	0	15	2	14	0	15	46
Fan Ling	37	2	2	0	0	0	2	6
Sheng Shui	27	0	0	1	2	0	0	3
Ha Tsuen	24	0	0	0	0	1	0	1
Kam Tin	17	0	0	1	0	0	0	1
Pat Heung	34	0	1	0	0	0	1	2
Ping Shan	54	0	0	0	0	0	0	0
San Tin	31	0	0	1	0	0	1	2
Shap Pat Heung	45	0	1	1	0	0	0	2
Tuen Mun	42	0	1	0	4	0	2	7
Total	**971**	**17**	**96**	**17**	**103**	**12**	**113**	**358**

Source: Compiled by the website of the Registration and Electoral Office on village elections, 2011–2019.

Notes: RC stands for Rural Committees. VR stands for village representatives. RR stands for rural representatives.

Table 3.12: Proportion of Non-indigenous Villagers in the Village

Proportion of Non-indigenous Villagers	%
0–19%	40
20–39%	19
40–59%	12
60–79%	15
80–100%	14
Total	100

Source: Sonny Shiu-hing Lo and Cheung Yat-fung, "The Political Attitude of Village Representatives in the New Territories," paper presented at the Foreign Correspondents Club, Hong Kong, December 12, 2001.

representatives in the village elections held for the 27 rural committees from 2011 to 2019. Those Rural Committees that witnessed relatively stronger political apathy included Sai Kung, Sai Kung North, Sha Tau Kok, Tai Po, Sha Tin, Lama South, and Tai O. The reasons for such apathy might include factors such as the reluctance of any rural resident to run for elections, the satisfaction with the *status quo*, the absence of infiltration by political parties or groups, and the sense of political uselessness of voting in elections. While some rural elites have been traditionally active, others remain relatively politically quiescent.

Nevertheless, on issues affecting the self-interests of the rural elites and residents, they tended to be far more participatory. From August 16 to October 19, 2001, 971 questionnaires were sent out to 971 village representatives in about 650 villages and 236 answered questionnaires (24.3% of respondents) were returned.[113] Table 3.12 shows that 40% of the respondents said there were less than 20% of non-indigenous villages in their villages. Table 3.13 shows that 84% of the respondents said that there were no non-indigenous village representatives in their villages. Table 3.14 illustrates that 78% of the respondents believed that there was harmony between indigenous and non-indigenous villagers in their villages. Table 3.15 shows that while 51% of the respondents agreed that women should not have the right of ownership possession in their villages, 41% disagreed—a result showing a split in their opinion. Table 3.16 shows that while 32% supported the proposed double village heads elections, 53% opposed the idea, again demonstrating a divided opinion in the New Territories. Table 3.17 reveals that 80% of the respondents were satisfied with the old electoral arrangements.

Table 3.13: Having Non-indigenous Village Representatives in the Villages

Non-indigenous Village Representatives	%
Yes	16
No	84
Total	100

Source: Lo and Cheung.

Table 3.14: Harmony between Indigenous and Non-indigenous Villagers in the Village

Harmony	%
Agree	78
Neutral	19
Disagree	3
Total	100

Source: Lo and Cheung.

Table 3.15: Women cannot have the right for the ownership possession

Women Right	%
Agree	51
Neutral	8
Disagree	41
Total	100

Source: Lo and Cheung.

Table 3.16: Support of the Double Village Heads System

Double Village Heads System	%
Support	32
Neutral	15
Not support	53
Total	100

Source: Lo and Cheung.

Table 3.17: Satisfaction with the Old Rural Electoral Arrangements

Old Rural Electoral Arrangements	%
Satisfactory, and do not need to have any amendments	80
So far so good, but need minor amendments	17
Not satisfactory, and need major amendments	3
Total	100

Source: Lo and Cheung.

Table 3.18 shows that when respondents were asked about the elections of their village representatives, a majority of them replied that double village heads elections would accelerate the penetration of political parties, that the elections would speed up the disunity between indigenous and non-indigenous villagers, that the elections had no violence, and that the elections were incorrupt. A minority of the respondents remarked that elections were monopolized by interest groups, and that the act of voting was based on *renching* (human emotions and sentiments).

On the role of HYK in rural politics, 49% of the respondents said the HYK had much responsiveness to their demands, while 22% thought that its responsiveness was average (Table 3.19). A slight majority (51%) believed that the HYK was a middleman between the government and villagers, whereas 31% remained neutral and 18% disagreed that HYK was an intermediary (Table 3.20). This showed that quite a lot of village representatives had reservations about the HYK's role. Table 3.21 shows that most respondents believed that the chair and vice-chairpersons of the HYK should be directly elected by all indigenous villagers rather than by a combination of indigenous and non-indigenous villagers. This result illustrates that most rural representatives appeared to be politically conservative.

When asked about the role of the government branches in dealing with rural affairs, Table 3.22 shows that a majority of respondents believed that the Home Affairs Department could not act as a paternalistic and an authoritative body compared with the colonial government's District Offices, that the government could not protect the right of indigenous villagers, that the government was complicated and bureaucratic without solving the disputes of villagers, that the double village elections aimed at reducing the right of indigenous villagers, and that the court judges in Chan Wah case did not understand village traditions. Clearly, there were gaps between the village representatives and the government on the one hand and village representatives and the court decision on the other.

On whether district organizations and political parties contacted village representatives, most of the respondents said that they did not do so (Table 3.23). About 38% of the respondents revealed that patriotic political groups and organizations contacted village representatives, showing the inroads of pro-Beijing groups in penetrating the rural areas (Table 3.24). Most respondents replied that they were not affiliated with district organizations

Table 3.18: Elections of Village Representatives

Opinion	Agree %	Neutral %	Disagree %	Total %
Elections of Village Representatives are incorrupt	68	23	9	100
Elections of Village Representatives have no violence	76	11	13	100
Elections of Village Representatives are monopolized by interest groups	19	10	71	100
The act of voting for the specific Village Representative candidate is based on *renching* (human emotions and sentiments)	15	17	68	100
'Double Village Head' system will accelerate the disunity between indigenous villagers and non-indigenous villagers	70	9	21	100
'Double Village Head' system will accelerate political parties' penetration.	79	7	14	100

Source: Lo and Cheung.

Table 3.19: The Extent of Responsiveness of the Heung Yee Kuk

Extent of Responsiveness	%
Much	49
Average	29
Limited	22
Total	100

Source: Lo and Cheung.

Table 3.20: Heung Yee Kuk as a middleman between the Government and Villagers

Heung Yee Kuk as a middleman	%
Agree	51
Neutral	31
Disagree	18
Total	100

Source: Lo and Cheung.

**Table 3.21: Electoral Arrangements of
Heung Yee Kuk Chairperson and Vice-chairpersons**

Electoral Arrangements	Agree %	Neutral %	Disagree %	Total %
Heung Yee Kuk chairperson and vice-chairpersons should be directly elected by all indigenous villagers and non-indigenous villagers.	24	5	71	100
Heung Yee Kuk chairperson and vice-chairpersons should be directly elected by all indigenous villagers.	63	4	33	100

Source: Lo and Cheung.

Table 3.22: The Role of Government Branches in Dealing with Rural Affairs

Role of Government Branches	Agree %	Neutral %	Disagree %	Total %
HKSAR Government's Home Affairs Department cannot act as a paternalistic and authoritative body compared with the colonial government's District Offices	57	24	19	100
Government can protect the right of indigenous villagers	15	27	58	100
The branches of government are complicated and bureaucratic, and they cannot solve village disputes	83	10	7	100
The government intends to use "Double Village Heads" systems to reduce the rights of indigenous villagers	71	7	22	100
The Court of Final Appeal's judgement (namely, Chan Wah and Tse Kwan-san's case about indigenous villagers' rights to participate in village election) reflects that court judges do not understand village traditions.	84	4	12	100

Source: Lo and Cheung.

Table 3.23: District Organizations and Political Parties Contacting Village Representatives

Contacting Village Representatives	%
Yes	43
No	57
Total	100

Source: Lo and Cheung.

Table 3.24: Types of Political Groups Contacting Village Representatives

Political Groups Contacting Village	%
Independent district organizations	14
Patriotic organizations	22
Patriotic political parties	16
Political Parties in the democratic camp	4
Others	6

Source: Lo and Cheung.

and political groups (Table 3.25). Table 3.26 shows that while 10% of the respondents were affiliated with independent organizations, 21% of them were affiliated with patriotic organizations and political parties. Moreover, only one percent of the respondents admitted that they joined pro-democracy groups and parties. Table 3.27 shows that most respondents believed that village representatives would be increasingly respected by

Table 3.25: The Affiliations of Village Representatives with District Organizations and/or Political Parties

Affiliations	%
Yes	28
No	72
Total	100

Source: Shiu-hing Lo and Cheung Yat-fung, "The Political Attitude of Village Representatives in the New Territories," Paper presented at the Foreign Correspondents Club, December 12, 2001.

Table 3.26: The Affiliations of Village Representatives with District Organizations and/or Political Parties

Affiliations of Village Representatives	%
Independent District Organizations	10
Patriotic Organizations	16
Patriotic Political Parties	5
Political Parties in Democratic Camp	1
Others	5

Source: Lo and Cheung.

Table 3.27: Village Representatives and Parties Penetration

Parties Penetration	Agree %	Neutral %	Disagree %	Total %
Village Representatives will be increasingly respected by political parties' expansion in rural areas.	78	12	10	100
Political Parties' penetration will reduce harmony in the village life.	67	14	19	100

Source: Lo and Cheung.

political parties, whose expansion however would likely reduce the harmony in village life. The results show that at the time of the survey was undertaken in 2001, the penetration of political and district groups into the rural elites was relatively light.

Response of Rural Elites to the Court Judgement on the Rights of Indigenous Villagers

In 2000, two non-indigenous villagers—Chan Wah and Tse Kwan-san—challenged the validity of the 1999 electoral arrangements for the position of village representative at their respective villages by judicial review.

In respect of the challenge, the Court of Final Appeal held that (1) the exclusion of non-indigenous villagers from voting or standing for election at village representative elections was unreasonable and contrary to the right to participate in public affairs; and (2) the electoral arrangement under which non-indigenous women married to indigenous men had the right to vote but non-indigenous men married to indigenous women were excluded from voting contravened the Sex Discrimination Ordinance.[114] In response to the Court of Final Appeal's judgement, the HKSAR government proposed the double village elections, which could address the court's ruling relating to the right of the non-indigenous villagers to vote and stand for election at village representative elections by establishing a resident representative for each existing village. This resident representative would not deal with any matter relating to the traditional rights and interests of indigenous inhabitants. Moreover, a person would not be eligible to be registered as an elector for an existing village unless he has been a resident of the village concerned for three years before electoral registration. Furthermore, a person would be eligible to be nominated as a candidate for the election of the resident representative if he has been a resident in the village concerned for six years preceding the nomination.[115] At the same time, the government proposed to establish the office of indigenous inhabitant representative in each indigenous village with effect from July 1, 2003 onwards. Furthermore, there would be up to five indigenous inhabitant representatives for a "composite indigenous village" which was composed of two or more indigenous villages.[116]

Table 3.28 reveals the reactions of the rural elites to the judgement of the Court of Final Appeal. They included Sing Hon-keung, Tony Kan, and Lam Wai-keung, who all expressed some degree of disappointment. However, Kan was politically optimistic while Lam embraced the court's decision and a new system of electing village representatives. Hence, the rural elites in HYK adapted quickly to the court decision and the HKSAR government's proposed reform.

Table 3.29 sums up the response of the rural elites to the Double Village Heads (DVH) system. Except for Tang Sik-hung and Brian Kan who opposed the DVH system, other rural elites, especially Lau Wong-fat, supported it. Lau argued that since LegCo elections witnessed two votes acquired by some voters, who could cast their ballots in both geographical constituencies and functional constituency elections, the DVH election proposal was acceptable and in conformity with the existing HKSAR's

Table 3.28: Response of Rural Elites to the Court Judgement

Rural Elites	Response
Sing Hon-keung (Chairman of Hang Hou Rural Committee)	He was disappointed with the judgement, believing that the verdict had far-reaching impact, especially the gradual deprivation of the traditional rights and interests of the indigenous residents.
Tony Kan Chung-nin (Member of HYK)	The cultural flavor of the rural communities in the New Territories would be affected, and the HYK's political would also be impacted. He said that allowing non-indigenous residents to participate in the election of village representatives would have little impact on the rural structure in the short term, but in the long run, the political influence of indigenous inhabitants would be curbed. However, he believed that the circumstances changed, and the rural elites should not fear political competition. As long as the indigenous inhabitants tried their best, the HYK could represent the New Territories villages and increase its influence.
Daniel Lam Wai-keung (Vice-chairman of HYK)	Disappointed with the judgement and HYK respected the court's decision. However, the villagers were worried that the decision would have impacts. He believed that in addition to the two villages that had controversies, village representatives from other New Territories villages were elected in a fair, open, and fair way. They should be allowed to complete the current term of office before adopting any new system to produce village representatives.

Sources: *Wen Wei Po*, December 23, 2000, p. A14.

electoral system. Lau's argument represented the mainstream view of the rural elites. As Lai Kwok-yiu also contended, 21 of the 27 Rural Committees supported the DVH proposal. Hence, the government's proposed reform secured the support of most rural elites.

Some LegCo members criticized the arbitrary provisions in the DVH electoral arrangements, such as the requirement that voters for the post of Rural Representatives must be a resident living in the specific village for at least three years, whereas the requirement of being the candidate for the post of Rural Representative must be a resident living in the specific village for at least six years required by the government.[117] Opponents argued that such arbitrary provisions in the Bill would likely increase the possibilities of triggering legal dispute and court cases. Overall, with the onset of modernization, rural politics in the New Territories became more complicated, more diversified, and more conflict-ridden than ever before.[118] The decision of the Court of Final Appeal in response to the issues of human rights and sexual equality propelled the HKSAR government to propose electoral reform in the New Territories by adopting the double village election method, which however led to the disagreement between the pro-government rural elites and the anti-reform ones. Still, the pro-government rural elites led by Lau Wong-fat succeeded in supporting the

Table 3.29: Response of Rural Elites to the Double Village Heads System

Rural Elites	Response
Lau Wong-fat (Chairman of HYK)	He believed that the proposal of DVH was applying the Hong Kong election model and that it reflected the spirit of Article 40 of the Basic Law concerning the protection of the legitimate traditional rights and interests of the indigenous inhabitants. He pointed out that under the current LegCo election system, some voters had only one vote for geographical constituencies, and some voters had one vote for LegCo's functional constituency elections. Therefore, he did not think the proposed DVH system would be unfair to non-indigenous residents.
Tang Siu-tong (Member of HYK)	The DVH system would affect the interests of the indigenous inhabitants because indigenous inhabitants and non-indigenous inhabitants had different opinions. He said he adopted an open attitude toward reform.
Daniel Lam Wai-keung (Vice-chairman of HYK)	At present, some of the 600 villages already had the DVH system. He believed that the DVH system could take care of the interests of the indigenous inhabitants on the one hand, and that it could protect the livelihood and the demands of non-indigenous residents on the other hand. The DVH system had more space and could achieve balance more easily.
Tang Sik-hung (Chairman of Ping Shan Rural Committee)	He opposed the DVH system. The DVH system planned by the government was vague and it changed the original intention of the HYK to represent the rights and interests of the indigenous inhabitants. It undermined the long-term harmonious relationship between the rural associations and the old and new residents, causing chaos and difficulties in the future operation of rural organizations.
Lai Kwok-yiu (Chairman of Pat Heung Rural Committee)	He supported the DVH system. Indigenous residents, according to Lai, had to respect the rule of law and the spirit of democracy, to accept the Court of Final Appeal's ruling that non-indigenous residents had the right to participate in the elections of indigenous village representatives, and to accept the DVH system. The government consulted the 27 Rural Committees in the New Territories regarding the DVH arrangement. Twenty-one of them supported it. Lai believed that the opposition to the DVH system was a minority.
Brian Kan (Chairman of Sheng Shui Rural Committee)	He opposed the DVH system. The Heung Yee Kuk's handling of the issue of village representative elections was like an "ostrich." He felt very sad about this. Kan argued that "external people" were not allowed to "bully" the indigenous residents of the New Territories. He pointed out that the HYK had many executive committee members appointed by the government as Justices of the Peace. Kan suggested that the HYK's executive committee should be reformed to represent only the indigenous inhabitants and that this solution could solve the problems.

Sources: *Ming Pao,* February 27, 2001 p. K7; *Hong Kong Commercial Daily,* March 28, 2001, p. B2.; *Ming Pao,* July 2, 2000, p. A4. and *Ming Pao,* July 10, 2001 p. K9.

HKSAR government to get the double village heads proposal approved by the LegCo in February 2003 for implementation in July. Overall, while the British colonial state refrained from intervening in the village election methods, the post-colonial government in the HKSAR reversed the policy of non-intervention to direct intervention, responding to the decision of the Court of Final Appeal but triggering the debates among rural elites over the double village election system.

The intra-elite disagreement in the New Territories over the double village election in the early 2000s had several political implications.[119] Firstly, the Hone Affairs Bureau (HAB) and the Home Affairs Department (HAD) underestimated the internal disagreement inside the HYK, and they failed to act as a middleman. Of course, it can also be argued that the government was uninterested in mediating the disagreement within the HYK. So long as the HYK leaders and LegCo members could secure the passage of the bill on DVH, the government regarded the DVH proposal as a necessary response to the court judgment. The HAD was formerly known as the New Territories District Offices that enjoyed the *de facto* power to coordinate amongst different government departments. The British colonial government used District Offices to communicate with the rural elites and indigenous inhabitants. Arguably, the colonial state acted like an impartial referee identifying and mediating the conflicts between pro-development elites and anti-development elites.[120] However, the HAB and HAD after the handover failed to monitor and manage rural affairs, and their status declined compared with the role of District Offices in the colonial era. Furthermore, District Officers after July 1, 1997 adopted a relatively non-interventionist approach to dealing with intra-elite disagreement and conflicts in the New Territories.[121] Unlike some District Officers who acted as fatherly officials mediating in rural disputes in Hong Kong under the British colonial era, they have changed to policy implementation actors rather than socio-political mediators, although the role of District Officers as coordinators among government departments at the district level persists.

Secondly, the HYK's privileged status was questioned in the debate over the double village election system, and many Village Representatives and villagers were challenging its representativeness.[122] The indigenous inhabitants rapidly became a minority in the process of urbanization. According to the 2001 census, the total population in the New Territories was 3,343,046, but only 240,000 people were indigenous inhabitants, and there were 224,000 non-indigenous villagers.[123] In the same year, 2.8 million out of 3.3 million rural residents in the New Territories lived in high-rise buildings in new towns instead of village houses. Therefore, the interests of indigenous inhabitants and non-indigenous people were different. The HYK no longer could claim to represent all the rural residents. Instead, it articulated the interests of a minority of the rural residents. At the same time, within the HYK, rural elites were deeply divided over the double village election system, as could be seen in the divergent views between the pro-government faction led by Lau Wong-fat and the anti-reform faction led by Brian Kan. Moreover, some indigenous inhabitants viewed the HYK as too pro-government, questioning its legitimacy.[124] Some indigenous inhabitants, including the HYK's oppositionists, thought that the dispute over the double village election provided a golden opportunity to push for HYK reforms, as Brian Kan openly argued.

Thirdly, the HKSAR government had the intention of recentralizing its powers and diluting the uniqueness of the New Territories—a policy quite different from the British colonial rulers. The post-colonial government dissolved the two municipal councils, including the UrbCo in the urban areas and the RegCo in the rural areas in December 1999 in the name of centralizing the powers of administering public health and environmental hygiene. Such policy eroded the influence of the HYK and of the rural elites, depriving them of a channel of political participation. In addition, the HKSAR government eliminated the distinction between DCs in the New Territories and that in urban areas.[125] For example, the Electoral Affairs Commission did not produce any statistical data on the differences between the voter turnout in the urban areas and that in the New Territories during the 1999 DB elections. Arguably, the post-colonial government's centralization of powers and its dilution of rural uniqueness could be seen as a silent revolution in the rural politics of the HKSAR shortly after 1997. However, it proceeded without the sharp notice from most rural elites, who were pro-government and who had the vested interests to support the policies of the HKSAR government. In a sense, the small minority of rural opposition led by Brian Kan was sharp in identifying the post-colonial government's attempts at diluting the influence of the rural elites in general. While the success of the British colonial government was to adopt a relatively laissez-faire policy towards rural elites and politics, the HKSAR government's centralization of powers not only exacerbated intra-elite conflicts in the New Territories but also paved the way for party penetration into rural politics—an inevitable process of the politicization of rural elites and an irresistible trend toward their fragmentation.[126]

In November 2012, the HYK witnessed intra-elite conflicts again due to a dispute over the government's attempts at removing illegal structures of the small houses in the New Territories. Angry villagers gatecrashed the HYK meeting, accusing its leaders of failing to defend the interests of the

Table 3.30: The Response of Rural Elites to then Unauthorized Construction on Village Houses in the New Territories

Name	Remarks
Tsang Hin-keung	He argued against the idea that village houses had "illegal" construction. Tsang added that many outsiders, including members of the LegCo, did not understand the problems left over from the history of village houses in the New Territories. These legislators were "talking nonsense." He also criticized the government of taking advantage of the Heung Yee Kuk to insist on a strict enforcement of the law, and that there might be ulterior motives behind it.
Leung Fook-yuen	He said that safety was the primary consideration for village houses' construction, and that the authorities would have to consider the historical factors left over in the rural areas for many years.
Lau Wong-fat	The most important thing, to Lau, was to consider the security issues of village houses, and he hoped that the government's policy of dealing with unauthorized construction in a more socially harmonious way. He added that the "illegal" construction on village houses in the New Territories had a unique historical background, and that it was "unrealistic to use a one-size-fits-all approach."
Tsang Shu-wo	He disagreed with the idea that the unauthorized construction on village houses was "illegal" and that these structures should not be demolished. Tsang added that the rural people in the New Territories dared to fight against Britain and Japan in the past, and that today they dared to fight against the government, even threatening to "fight with force."
Man Chi-sheung	"When the government deals with the illegal construction on village houses in the New Territories, it insists to treat the people equally. But now it is obviously unfair to the people in the New Territories."
Gary Hau Chi-keung	"The government should allow the villagers to continue to retain some 'illegal' structures on village houses that are structurally safe and beautiful and that do not hinder others." He added that most of the village houses currently had migrants living in the New Territories, and that the indigenous inhabitants only constituted 30% of the total residents. Hau said that all households would be affected by the enforcement of the law against unauthorized construction. He stressed that the problem of "illegal" construction was not unique to village houses in the New Territories, because they also existed in the urban areas. He said the government should treat the rural residents fairly.

Sources: *Sing Tao*, April 29, 2011, p. A14; *Sing Pao*, April 29, 2011, p. A12; *Ta Kung Pao*, May 15, 2011, p. A02; *Ming Pao*, May 17, 2011, *Oriental Daily*, May 18, 2011 and *The Sun*, May 22, 2011, p. A18.

rural residents.[127] The protests initiated by about 100 rural residents took place when the HYK held a closed-door meeting in Sha Tin. The protestors were unhappy with the weakness of the HYK vis-à-vis the government, which decided to crack down on "illegal" structures on village houses. However, most village houses had "illegal" structures. As such, many rural residents and indigenous inhabitants were angry with both the government and HYK. The government planned to demolish extra storeys on top of the standard three-storey village houses. Junius Ho, a spokesman for an alliance of rural residents opposing the government policy, argued that the move was "unfair" to villagers and urged the administration to drop the policy.[128]

Later, the HKSAR government did abandon the policy for the sake of the harmony with the rural residents and indigenous inhabitants.

Table 3.30 sums up the response of the rural elites to the "unauthorized" construction on village houses in the New Territories in 2011, a year prior to the government's serious consideration to push ahead the plan of demolishing the "illegal" structures on village houses. Most rural elites opposed the government policy, arguing that "illegal" structures on village houses were a product of historical legacy, that the HKSAR administration was unfair to rural residents, that "illegal" structures also existed in urban areas, and that safety should be the most important issue. Even pro-government Lau Wong-fat criticized the government for adopting a simplistic policy toward "illegal" structures on the village houses. Due to the fierce opposition from the rural elites, the government later abandoned the enforcement of demolishing "illegal" structures on village houses in the New Territories.

The Politics of the Concessionary Rights of the Small House

The small house policy was introduced in 1972 in Hong Kong with the objective of improving the rural housing situation in the New Territories. Since 1972, this policy has allowed an indigenous male villager who reaches the age of 18 years old, who is a descendent of the male line from an indigenous resident in 1898 of a recognized village in the New Territories, to be entitled to one concessionary grant to build one small house during his lifetime.[129] According to the policy, an indigenous villager refers to "a male person at least 18 years old who is descended through the male line from a resident in 1898 of a recognized village."[130] In 2012, the HKSAR government started to review the small house policy. During CY Leung's election campaign in 2012 and in a meeting with the senior members of the HYK in November of the same year after winning the election, Chief Executive Leung said that the problems associated with small houses and small house concessionary rights could be resolved by the method of "drawing a line," i.e. stipulating that New Territories male indigenous villagers born after a specified year would no longer be entitled to small house concessionary rights.[131] Carrie Lam, during her tenure as the former Secretary for Development, remarked that the small house concessionary rights could not be granted to New Territories male indigenous villagers indefinitely. She suggested setting a deadline for such rights would be in conformity with the Basic Law's principle of guaranteeing Hong Kong's way of life to remain unchanged for 50 years. The government toyed with the idea that the New Territories male indigenous villagers born after 2029 (i.e. reaching the age of 18 after 2047) would no longer be entitled to small house concessionary rights.[132] The HKSAR administration thought that it would be necessary to review the small house policy on the premise of optimal utilization of land resources.[133] The Secretary for Development, Paul Chan, revealed the government's intention of delaying the issue of reviewing small house policy on the grounds of complexities. He said:

> The policy has been implemented for more than 40 years. The government recognizes the need to review the Policy in the context of prevailing land use planning as well as optimal utilization of land resources. Such review will inevitably involve complicated issues in various aspects such as legal, environment, land use planning, and demand on land, all of which require careful examination. The government will continue to handle this review carefully and judiciously, engaging stakeholders as well as the wider community in dialogue over the relevant issues as and when necessary … The work priorities of the Development Bureau are to increase land supply in the short to medium term and to implement and control costs of various public works projects, the review or consideration of suggestions to amend the policy would not be a priority task in the remainder of the current term of the Government. It is neither realistic nor practicable as far as time is concerned. The demand for small houses may change with factors such as birth and growth of indigenous villagers. Whether or not an indigenous villager would apply for a small house grant is dependent on his own circumstances and wishes, and not all eligible indigenous villagers aged 18 years or above will submit an application. It is thus impossible for the Lands Department to project the number of small house applications in the next ten years. As a matter of fact, it is not the Government's policy objective to provide adequate land to cater for applications by the estimated number of eligible indigenous villagers.[134]

Because of a court case involving the small house policy, the HKSAR government in 2016 delayed the review of this policy and looked for other alternatives to provide more land for building housing units for the ordinary people, including the Lantau Vision Tomorrow that proposed 1,700 hectares of reclaimed land for housing units off the Lantau Island.

In 2015 and 2016, some rural elites engaged in a debate over the concessionary rights of the small house policy. Table 3.30 sums up the views of some rural elites, who emphasized that the concessionary rights of small house were granted by the Basic Law rather than a privilege enjoyed by indigenous villagers. Moreover, the indigenous villagers who invested in building the houses had the right to reside in or sell them. In view of public criticisms of the small house policy and due to the demand for more land for housing units in the rapidly changing society of Hong Kong, some rural elites felt that the small house policy was "unfairly" targeted. Overall, the controversy over the small house policy after 2012 has illustrated that the changing circumstances of the HKSAR made the government review it and propelled the society to assess the policy in a far more critical way than ever before.

In 2015, some rural elites argued that, to defend the right of villagers to monetize their small houses, they would be prepared to seek judicial review. They also asserted that they reserved the right to go to the Standing Committee of the National People's Congress (SCNPC) for a resolution of the dispute over their concessionary right, which was and is protected by the Basic Law as they maintained.[135] In fact, the dispute originated from the conviction of 11 villagers in November 2015, when they were found by the court for "conspiracy to defraud."[136] Some indigenous residents in Sha Tin were discovered for falsely claiming their ownership of plots in Tai Che village and transferring the possession right to a land developer. However, the HYK and some rural elites insisted that the indigenous residents had "lawful" traditional rights and interests as protected by Article 40 of the Basic Law. Since 1972, the small houses have been subject to less zoning control than others and it has been a common practice for villagers to sell their once-in-a-lifetime concessionary right to land developers. Between 2003 and 2007, applicants for small house construction were required to "declare that their inherent right had not been sold to any other parties."[137] The HYK insisted that the government should clarify the legal interests and entitlement of indigenous villagers, and that they would seek interpretation from the SCNPC on Article 40 of the Basic Law. Nevertheless, some lawyers doubted whether the HYK might invoke Article 40, because the villagers were convicted because of fraud and false claims they had made in the signed documents.[138] The conviction of the villagers in 2015 sparked a debate

**Table 3.31: The Remarks of Rural Elites on the Acquisition
of the Concessionary Rights of the Small House**

Name	Remarks
Lam Kwok-cheong	The small house's concessionary rights are rights and interests granted by the Basic Law, not privileges. Although the government gives indigenous residents the small house concessionary rights, the idea behind it is "self-occupation," but "self-occupation" is not a prerequisite. Lam thought that indigenous residents are free to dispose of or sell their properties. As such, there was nothing wrong with the idea of turning the small house concessionary rights into money, just like ordinary citizens selling houses to make money.
Gary Hau Chi-keung	He thought that small houses could be bought and sold freely, not just for "self-occupation," which meant that the government should not "block people from doing business."
Kenneth Lau Yip-keung	Lau believed that most of the land on which small houses were built were privately owned or purchased by the indigenous residents. The construction costs of the small houses were also paid by the indigenous residents. As such, he felt that it was unfair to say the land premium was "low." To Lau, the original small house policy did not require land premiums. He also said that the concessionary right of small house is a right granted to the indigenous residents by the Basic Law, but not a privilege enjoyed by them. Lau added that the indigenous residents had the right to build houses, but whether they would live in or sell them after completion would be up to them. Lau stressed that the small house policy did not stipulate that indigenous residents had to live in the houses themselves, and that the outside world would not view the "problem" of small houses lopsidedly.

Sources: *Ming Pao*, January 3, 2016, p. A08; January 18, 2016, p. A03 and January 24, 2016, p. A08.

over the technicality, legality, and transfer of the concessionary rights of the indigenous villagers.

Conclusion

This chapter traces the development of rural politics in Hong Kong from the colonial era to post-colonial period. Under the British colonial administration, the rural elites were politically divided. However, the colonialists co-opted the pro-government rural elites to smoothen the process of land acquisition and infrastructure development. Those rural elites who sided with the colonial government tended to benefit politically, economically, and socially, while those who resisted the colonial administration were politically marginalized and defeated. This phenomenon has persisted in the HKSAR since July 1, 1997, but the China factor has come into the picture of rural politics. The PRC authorities have seen some rural elites as the target of united front and political cooptation. As such, once elections were held, the pro-Beijing and pro-government forces have creeped into rural areas, seeking for and wooing the support from rural elites. Yet, this politicization has been exacerbating the fragmentation among rural elites. The fragmentation could be seen easily among the rural elites, some siding with the HYK while others joined the DAB. At the same time, PRC authorities in the HKSAR have groomed some rural elites, thereby complicating the landscape of rural politics. The fragmentation of rural elites could also be seen in a whole range of policy issues, including some of their opposition to the double village elections, the controversy over "illegal" structures in the New Territories, and their bitter feelings about the court case concerning some villagers who were convicted of fraud in the transfer of their concessionary rights of small houses. Given the fragmented nature of the rural elites, and considering the rapid socio-political development of the HKSAR, the divided nature of rural politics is likely to persist.

Notes

1 Yuen Kin-bong, ed. *A Brief History of Hong Kong* (in Chinese) (Hong Kong: Chong Liu, 1997), p. 71.

2 Peter Wesley-Smith, *Unequal Treaty, 1898–1997: China, Great Britain and Hong Kong's New Territories (Revised Edition)*, (Hong Kong: Oxford University Press, 1998), pp. 64–94.

3 Yue, *A Brief History of Hong Kong*, p. 177.

4 *Ibid.*, p. 177.

5 *Ibid.*, pp. 179–180.

6 *Ibid.*, pp. 180–184. Peter, Wesley-Smith, *Unequal Treaty, 1898–1997: China, Great Britain and Hong Kong's New Territories (Revised Edition)*, (Hong Kong: Oxford University Press, 1998), pp. 64–94

7 *Supplement to the Hong Kong Government Gazette 1900* (after p. 635), p. xxx, Appendix IX, cited in Miners, *Government and Politics of Hong Kong* (1981), p. 192.

8 Miners, *Government and Politics of Hong Kong* (1981), p. 192.

9 Miners, *Government and Politics of Hong Kong* (1981), p. 193.

10 *Ibid.*, pp. 194–196.

11 Kwong Chi-man, "From the "New Territories People" to 'Indigenous Inhabitants' Identity Construction of the Rural Population in Colonial Hong Kong," *Hong Kong Journal of Social Science,* vol. 52 (2018), pp. 39–72.

12 Miners, *Government and Politics of Hong Kong* (1981), pp. 197–198.

13 Chan Kwok-shing, ed., *Fanling* (in Chinese) (Hong Kong: Joint Publishing, 2019), p. 29.

14 *Ibid.*, p. 33.

15 Chan Kwok-shing argued that the HYK creation represented the British "indirect rule," but actually the passing of the ordinance by the colonial administration could arguably be seen as "direct rule" although the leadership of the HYK was filled by the rural people (indirect rule). See *Ibid.*, p. 33.

16 *Ibid.*, p. 33.

17 *Ibid.*, p. 33.

18 *Ibid.*, p. 33.

19 *Ibid.*, pp. 23–24. Also see Stephen W. K. Chiu and Ho-fung Hung, "The Colonial State and Rural Protests in Hong Kong," occasional paper no. 59 (Hong Kong: Hong Kong Institute of Asia-Pacific Studies, The Chinese University of Hong Kong, April 1997), pp. 12–14.

20 *Ibid.*, p. 14.

21 *Ibid.*, pp. 14–15.

22 *Ibid.*, p. 18.

23 *Ibid.*, p. 19.

24 *Ibid.*, p. 24.

25 Kwong Chi-man, "From the "New Territories People" to 'Indigenous Inhabitants' Identity Construction of the Rural Population in Colonial Hong Kong," pp. 39–72.

26 *Ibid.*, p. 25.

27 *Ibid.*, p. 25.

28 *Ibid.*, p. 26.

29 *Ibid.*, p. 27.

30 *Ibid.*

31 *Ibid.*

32 *Ibid.*, p. 29. Also see Fung Wai-chung, "The Influence of Land Policy on the New Territories Heung Yee Kuk under the British Hong Kong Government from 1968 to 1984," MPhil Thesis (in Chinese), National Cheng Kung University, Taiwan, 2019.

33 Kwong Chi-man, "From the "New Territories People" to 'Indigenous Inhabitants' Identity Construction of the Rural Population in Colonial Hong Kong," pp. 39–72.

34 "The History of Heung Yee Kuk," *Wen Wei Po*, October 24, 2006.

35 Fung Wai-chung, "The Influence of Land Policy on the New Territories Heung Yee Kuk under the British Hong Kong Government from 1968 to 1984," MPhil Thesis (in Chinese), National Cheng Kung University, Taiwan, 2019.

36 *Ibid.*

37 Cheung Yat-fung, "Modernization and Rural Politics in Hong Kong," MPhil Thesis, University of Hong Kong, 2004, pp. 149–150.

38 *Next Magazine*, October 3, 2002, pp. 94–99.

39 *Ibid.*

40 *Ibid.*

41 *Ibid.*

42 *Ibid.*

43 *Ibid.*

44 *Ibid.*

45 *Ibid.*

46 *Next Magazine*, August 8, 2013, pp. 42–46.

47 *Ibid.*

48 *Ibid.*

49 *Sing Tao Daily*, May 22, 2003, p. A01.

50 *Ibid.*

51 *Ibid.*

52 *Ibid.*

53 *Ibid.*

54 *Next Magazine*, September 12, 2002, pp. 46–54.

55 *Hong Kong Economic Journal*, July 24, 2017, p. A13.

56 *Ibid.*

57 *Next Magazine*, September 12, 2002, pp. 46–54.

58 *Ibid.*

59 *Ibid.*

60 *Ibid.*

61 *Hong Kong Economic Journal*, July 24, 2017, p. A13.

62 *Ta Kung Pao*, July 24, 2017, p. A2.

63 *Ibid.*

64 LegCo's Home Affairs Committee, "Village Elections," CB(2)928/00-01(01), February 26, 2001, in https://www.legco.gov.hk/yr00-01/chinese/panels/ha/papers/928c01.pdf, access date: September 4, 2020.

65 *Ta Kung Pao*, July 24, 2017, p. A2.

66 *Ibid.*

67 *Ibid.*

68 *Ibid.*

69 *Ibid.*

70 "Hong Kong reform package rejected as pro-Beijing camp walk out in 'miscommunication,'" *South China Morning Post*, June 18, 2015, in https://www.scmp.com/news/hong-kong/politics/article/1823398/hong-kong-political-reform-package-voted-down-legco-leaving, access date: September 4, 2020.

71 "Lau Wong-fat and the Traditional Political Force in New Territories," *HK01,* July 28, 2017, in https://www.hk01.com, access date: August 9, 2020.

72 *Hong Kong Daily News*, September 20, 2008, p. A7.

73 *Wen Wei Po*, April 3, 1998.

74 *Ming Pao*, December 18, 1998.

75 *Ming Pao*, October 30, 1998, p. A12.

76 *Sing Tao Daily*, July 28, 2020, p. A17.

77 *Ibid.*

78 *Ibid.*

79 *Ta Kung Pao*, September 9, 2004, p. A11.

80 *Ibid.*

81 *Ibid.*

82 *Wen Wei Po*, September 26, 2004, p. A13.

83 *Oriental Daily*, September 14, 2004, p. A7.

84 *Hong Kong Economic Times*, October 30, 2004, p. A19.

85 *Ibid.*

86 *Ta Kung Pao*, September 17, 2008, p. A10.

87 *Ibid.*

88 *Ibid.*

89 *Ibid.* Also see *Ming Pao*, September 11, 2008, p. A6.

90 *Ming Pao*, July 23, 2008, p. A4.

91 *Ibid.*

92 *Ta Kung Pao*, January 13, 2012, p. B16.

93 *Ibid.*

94 *Ibid.*

95 *Apple Daily*, August 13, 2012, p. A02.

96 *Ibid.*

97 *Ibid.*

98 *Ibid.*

99 *Ibid.*

100 *Eastweek,* August 8, 2012, pp. 26–30.

101 For details, see Hong Kong Institute of Land Administration, "A Review of the Approach in Land Acquisition of Choi Yuen Tsuen for the Guangzhou-Shenzhen-Hong Kong Express Rail Link Project, and Recommendations for a Possible and Reasonable Approach in Land Acquisition in Future Government Projects," 2012, in https://www.fig.net/resources/proceedings/2012/Hungary_2012_comm7/6.5_paper_fung.pdf, access date: September 8, 2020.

102 *Eastweek,* August 8, 2012, pp. 26–30.

103 Ibid.

104 *Apple Daily*, August 5, 2012, p. A8.

105 *Eastweek*, August 8, 2012, pp. 20–30.

106 *Apple Daily*, August 5, 2012, p. A8.

107 *Apple Daily*, August 5, 2012, p. A8.

108 *Ibid.*

109 *Ibid.*

110 *Eastweek*, August 8, 2012, pp. 26–30.

111 *Ibid.*

112 *Ibid.*

113 Sonny Shiu-hing Lo and Cheung Yat-fung, "The Political Attitude of Village Representatives in the New Territories," paper presented at the Foreign Correspondents Club, December 12, 2001.

114 See "Paper for the Bills Committee of the LegCo on Village Representative Election Bill," LC Paper No. LS 15/02-03, in https://www.legco.gov.hk/yr02-03/english/bc/bc51/papers/bc511122cb2-ls15-e.pdf, access date: September 13, 2020.

115 *Ibid.*

116 *Ibid.*

117 See Cheung Yat-fung, "Modernization and Rural Politics in Hong Kong." Unpublished MPhil Thesis, University of Hong Kong, 2004, pp. 113–114.

118 *Ibid.*

119 *Ibid.*, p.135.

120 *Ibid.*

121 *Ibid.*, pp. 135–136.

122 *Ibid.*, p. 136.

123 *Ibid.*

124 *Ibid.*

125 *Ibid.*

126 Ibid.

127 Lai Ying-kit, "Rural leaders slammed over illegal structures U-turn," *South China Morning Post*, November 20, 2012, in https://www.scmp.com/news/hong-kong/article/1086807/rural-leaders-slammed-over-illegal-structures-u-turn, access date: September 13, 2020.

128 *Ibid.*

129 "The New Territories Small House Policy," in https://www.landsd.gov.hk/en/images/doc/NTSHP_E_text.pdf, access date: September 17, 2020.

130 *Ibid.*

131 *Ibid.*

132 *Ibid.*

133 "Issues relating to New Territories small house policy and small house concessionary rights," The Hong Kong government's press release, December 14, 2016, in https://www.info.gov.hk/gia/general/201612/14/P2016121400461.htm, access date: September 17, 2020.

134 *Ibid.*

135 Kabon Chan, "Rural leaders vow to defend sale of small house right," *China Daily*, December 25, 2015.

136 *Ibid.*

137 *Ibid.*

138 *Ibid.*

4

Electoral Politics of District Councils, 1997–2019

After the previous chapter has discussed the evolution of rural politics after the introduction of District Boards (DBs) and the emergence of political groups and parties in Hong Kong under colonial rule, this chapter is going to focus on the electoral politics of District Councils (DCs) from 1997 to 2019. It will show that with the expansion of elections in the DCs, electoral politics have become increasingly fierce and divided between the pro-government and pro-Beijing camp on the one hand and the pro-democracy forces on the other.

Analysis of District Council Elections

Table 4.1 shows that while ex-officio members of DCs in the New Territories has been persisting since 1997, the appointed members no longer existed in 2016 and 2020. The implication of the abolition of appointed seats since 2016 has been the inability of the HKSAR government to use appointments to balance the composition of various DCs. In the past, both the colonial administration and the HKSAR government before the 2016 DB (later DC) elections appointed pro-establishment elites to balance the influence of the pro-democracy district councilors. Since 2016, appointed seats as the tool of the government to curb the influence of the democrats in DCs were abolished.

Table 4.2 illustrates the results of DCs elections from 1999 to 2019. First and foremost, because of the long anti-extradition bill protests from May to November 2019, the November 2019 DCs elections witnessed an

Table 4.1: Number of Various (Ex-officio, Elected and Appointed) Members of District Councils

District	Ex	1997	2000	2004	2008	2012	2016	2020
Central & Western	–	14+4	15+4	15+4	15+4	15+3	15	15
Wan Chai	–	10+3	11+3	11+3	11+3	11+2	13	13
Eastern	–	34+9	37+9	37+9	37+9	37+6	35	35
Southern	–	16+4	17+4	17+4	17+4	17+3	17	17
Yau Tsim Mong	–	15+4	16+4	16+4	16+4	17+3	19	20
Sham Shui Po	–	20+5	21+5	21+5	21+5	21+3	23	25
Kowloon City	–	21+5	22+5	22+5	22+5	22+3	24	25
Wong Tai Sin	–	22+6	25+6	25+6	25+6	25+4	25	25
Kwun Tong	–	33+8	34+8	34+8	34+8	35+5	37	40
Tsuen Wan	2	15+4	17+5	17+5	17+5	17+3	18	19
Tuen Mun	1	25+7	29+7	29+7	29+7	29+5	29	31
Yuen Long	6	19+6	23+7	29+7	29+7	31+5	35	39
North	4	11+4	16+5	16+5	16+5	17+3	18	18
Tai Po	2	17+5	19+5	19+5	19+5	19+3	19	19
Sai Kung	2	11+3	17+5	20+5	23+5	24+3	27	29
Sha Tin	1	31+8	36+9	36+9	36+9	36+6	38	41
Kwai Tsing	1	26+7	28+7	28+7	28+7	29+5	29	31
Islands	8	6+4	7+4	8+4	10+4	10+3	10	10
Direct elected	–	346	390	400	405	412	425	452
Appointed total	–	96	102	102	102	68	–	–
Overall Total	27	469	516	529	534	507	452	479

Note: Ex: Ex denotes the ex-officio members of District Boards (later Councils) who are the Chairpersons of the 27 Rural Committees. Moreover, the numbers shown in the Table are the result of elected seats plus (+) appointed seats.

unprecedented voting turnout of 71.2%. In fact, the voter turnout increased over time from 33.13% in 1994 to 35.82% in 1999, and from 38.83% in 2007 to 47.01% in 2015. The 44.1% high voter turnout in 2003 was, like the situation in 2019, due to the half a million people's protests against the Tung Chee-hwa government on July 1, 2003. Second, the number of candidates participating in elections increased over time; it rose from 744 in 1994 to 837 in 2003, and from 907 in 2007 to 1,095 in 2019. Hence, a rising number of candidates participated in district direct elections from 1994 to 2019, reflecting the increase in competition. Third, because of the

Table 4.2: The Results of the District Councils Elections, 1999–2019

	1994	1999	2003	2007	2011	2015	2019
Total No. of Eligible Voters	2,450,372	2,832,524	2,973,612	3,295,826	3,560,535	3,693,942	4,132,977
Voters registered to vote	2.093,603	2,279,504	2,418,078	2,958,953	2,898,180	3,121,238	4,132,977
Total votes casted	693,215	816,503	1,066,373	1,148,815	1,202,544	1,467,229	2,943,842
Voting turnout	33.13%	35.82%	44.10%	38.83%	41.49%	47.01%	71.2%
No. of Candidates	747	798	837	907	915	935	1,090
No. of Seats	346	390	400	405	412	431	452
No. of Uncontested Seats	50	76	76	41	76	66	0

Democratic Alliance for the Betterment and Progress of Hong Kong (DAB)

	1994	1999	2003	2007	2011	2015	2019
No. of Candidates *	83(7)	184(8)	200(3)	177(24)	182(24)	171(3)	181(19)
Elected Candidates	37	83	62	115	136	119	21(0)
No. of Votes	81,126	192,115	241,202	292,916	282,119	309,262	492,042
Percentages of the Votes	11.82%	23.5%	22.9%	25.7%	23.5%	21.1%	16.8%

Pro-Beijing forces (including DAB)

	1994	1999	2003	2007	2011	2015	2019
No. of Candidates **	442	435	417	430	436	486	498
Elected Candidates	196	233	201	298	299	298	62
Percentage of Seats	56.65%	59.74%	50.25%	73.58%	72.57%	69.14%	13.72%
No. of Votes	371,455	442,286	491,067	614,621	652,840	788,389	1,233,030
Percentages of the Votes	54.12%	54.5%	46.7%	54.0%	54.3%	53.7%	42.1%

Democratic Party

	1994	1999	2003	2007	2011	2015	2019
No. of Candidates	133	173	120	110	132	95	99
Elected Candidates	75	86	95	59	47	43	91
No. of Votes	157,929	201,461	223,675	175,054	205,716	196,068	362,275
Percentages of the Votes	23.01%	24.85%	21.27%	15.38%	17.42%	13.56%	12.4%

Pan-Democrats (including Democratic Party)

	1994	1999	2003	2007	2011	2015	2019
No. of Candidates	249(9)	283	288	335	369	335	515
Elected Candidates	146	157	198	127	103	126	388
No. of Votes	280,707	325,829	477,596	445,781	464,512	581,058	1,674,083
Percentages of the Votes	40.89%	40.18%	45.54%	39.15%	39.34%	40.20%	57.1%

* Brackets denote the double membership of pro-Beijing Federation of Trade Unions (FTU) and DAB. The FTU members who ran in the elections independently were excluded from the number of DAB candidates.

**The pro-establishment camp's candidates included those from the DAB, the FTU, Liberal Party (LP), the Liberal Democratic Federation of Hong Kong (LDF), Hong Kong Progressive Alliance (HKPA that merged with the DAB in 2005), the New People's Party, the Business and Professional Alliance for Hong Kong and other related districts' residential groups, such as Hong Kong Island Federation (HKIF, established in 1999 with 130,000 members), the Kowloon Federation of Associations (KFA, established in 1997 with 220,000 members), and the New Territories Association of Societies (NTAS established 1985 with 250,000 members).

Sources: *Reports on the District Councils Election* in 1999, 2003, 2007, 2011, 2015 and 2019; *A Compilation of Election Materials in Hong Kong* (Hong Kong: Hong Kong Institute of Asia-Pacific Studies, the Chinese University of Hong Kong, 1996, 2001, 2005 and 2015).

**Table 4.3: Percentages of Re-Elected Pro-Democracy and
Pro-Establishment Incumbents**

Year	DI	DIE	DIE%	EI	EIE	EIE%	Percentage of establishment seats
1994	71	61(7)	86%	114	91(39)	79.82%	56.65%
1999	79	56(10)	81.16%	110	57(28)	69.51%	59.74%
2003	118	109(6)	97.32%	135	59(29)	55.66%	50.25%
2007	134	80	59.70%	98	65(17)	80.25%	73.58%
2011	92	64(1)	70.33%	136	89(33)	86.41%	72.57%
2015	80	59	73.75%	189	126(26)	77.30%	69.14%
2019	99	99	100%	162	23	14.20%	13.72%

Note:

(1) DI—Democratic Incumbents; DIE—Democratic Incumbents who were re-elected; DIE%—percentage of Democratic Incumbents re-elected; EI—Establishment Incumbents; EIE—Establishment Incumbents re-elected; EIE%—percentage of Establishment Incumbents re-elected. The numbers inside the brackets are the uncontested seats.

(2) Those who ran in the elections as "independents" in the past, especially before 2003, could not be easily categorized as pro-establishment because many of them maintained their relative autonomy vis-à-vis political parties and groups. As time passed, we can categorize these "independents" into either pro-democracy or pro-establishment camp as their political orientations have become much clear since 2003.

increase in competition, the number of uncontested seats reduced from 50 in 1994 to 41 in 2007, and from 76 in 2011 to zero in 2019. The 2019 elections were the most competitive one in the history of DC elections. Fourth, the pro-Beijing DAB performance fluctuated over time; its votes increased from 81,126 in 1994 to 492,042 in 2019. But in terms of the percentage of votes, the DAB oscillated from 11.82% in 1994 to 25.7% in 2007, and then from 23.5% in 2011 to 16.8% in 2019. Overall, the pro-Beijing forces, including not only the DAB but other like-minded groups and candidates, also fluctuated from 56.65% of the seats in 1994 to a high level of 73.58% in 2007, but then they declined from 72.57% in 2011 to 13.72% in 2019. Fifth, the pro-democracy flagship, the Democratic Party (DP), has shown signs of gradual decline from 23% of the votes in 1994 to 12.4% in 2019. The other pro-democracy parties, groups, and individuals enhanced their performance by increasing from 41% of the votes in 1999 to 57% in 2019. Overall, citizen participation in voting in DC elections increased, including candidates. On the other hand, while the pro-Beijing DAB signs of electoral oscillations, the pro-democracy DP has shown signs of decline from 1994 to 2019. But other pro-democracy groups and candidates emerged and tended to improve their strength and performance over time.

Table 4.3 shows the percentages of pro-democracy and pro-establishment incumbents who ran in the elections again and who were re-elected. The percentages of pro-democracy incumbents who were re-elected were the highest in 2003 with 97.32 and 2019 with 100. Pro-Beijing incumbents envisaged the lowest figure of 14.2% in 2019 and a relatively low figure of 55.66% in 2003. In 1994, 2007 and 2011, pro-establishment incumbents performed well, but they showed a sign of decline in 2015. Again, the two political turning points were 2003 and 2019, with the former witnessing half a million protestors on July 1 against the maladministration of the Tung Chee-hwa government and the latter in 2019, when protests engulfed the HKSAR from May to December as many citizens were rising up against the extradition bill, showing unhappiness with not only the performance of the police in handling the protests but also the tendency of Hong Kong to drift toward "mainlandization."[1] It can be inferred from the election results that when territory-wide controversial issues were involved, like the mass protests against the Tung Chee-hwa government on July 1, 2003 and the mass protests against the extradition bill in the latter half of 2019, the pro-Beijing and pro-government forces suffered prominently in DC elections, although DCs were supposed to be district-based advisory bodies dealing with district rather than territory-wide matters. Figure 4.1 highlights the different performance between pro-democracy and pro-establishment incumbents. Obviously, the pro-democracy candidates who were elected stood out in 2003 and 2019, while the pro-establishment candidates who were defeated tremendously suffered in these two years. As such, although DCs are advisory bodies focusing on district matters, the voters who went to the polls appeared to be deeply affected by territory-wide controversies in 2003 and 2019. The maladministration of the Tung Chee-hwa government in 2003, including the public discontent with the proposed legislation on Article 23 of the Basic Law, the management of the Severe Acute Respiratory Syndrome (SARS), civil service reform, and the chaos in housing policy, appeared to affect the voters' decisions in the 2003 DC elections. Similarly, the anti-extradition bill movement in the latter half of 2019 impacted the voters' decisions in the November 2019 DC elections.

Table 4.4 analyzes the performance of the pro-Beijing DAB in district elections from 1994 to 2019. Its performance was the worst in 2003, when

Figure 4.1: Comparing the Proportion of Pro-Democracy and Pro-Establishment Candidates Being Re-elected, 1994–2019

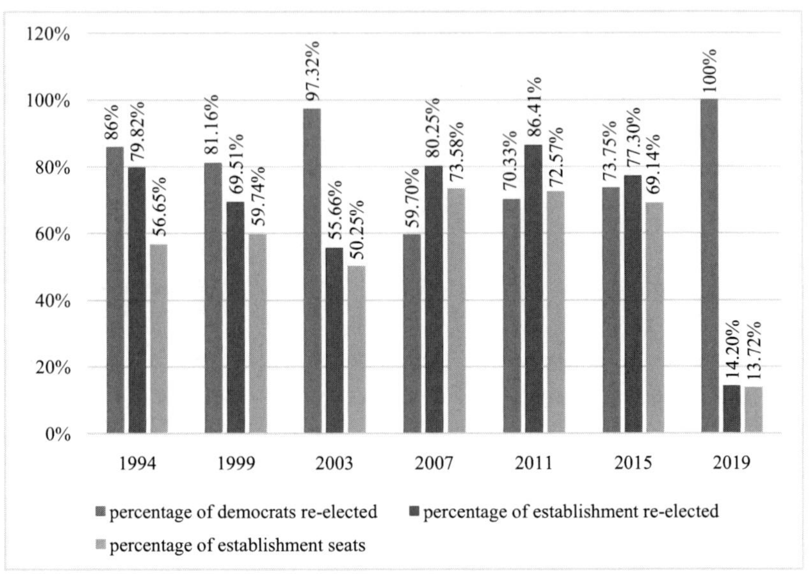

the party showed only 31% of the success rate of candidates who were nominated to run in elections, and in 2019, as the DAB got only 11.6% of the success rate. The 2003 and 2019 DC elections witnessed the worst results of DAB in district elections, showing its liability of supporting unpopular government policies (Article 23 legislation in 2003 and the extradition bill in 2019). Hence, whenever major political events against the government took place, like the half a million people's protests on July 1, 2003 and the May-November 2019 protests against the extradition bill, the pro-Beijing and pro-establishment DAB suffered immensely in direct elections held for DCs. The crux of the problem is that the DAB was and is too close to both the government and the policy line of the central government in Beijing. When the members of the public were afraid of the Article 23 legislation in 2003 and the extradition bill in the latter half of 2019, most of the voters tended to vote against pro-government forces and for the pro-democracy or anti-government camps. The 2019 election result was the poorest for the DAB, whose strongholds were totally wiped out in many districts except for Kwun Tong, Kowloon City, and Kwai Tsing.

Table 4.4: The Performance of DAB in District Elections, 1994–2019

District	1994	1999	2003	2007	2011	2015	2019
Central/Western	2	3	1	3	5	6	0
Wan Chai	3(1)	3(2)	1	2	3(1)	4(1)	0
Eastern	9(1)	13(3)	12(3)	14(2)	16(22)	10(4)	1
Southern	0	2(2)	1	1	2	2(1)	0
Yau Tsim Mong	1	2(2)	2	7	8	9(1)	1
Sham Shui Po	0	3	1	3	4	5	2
Kowloon City	2	3	2	6	7	8	4
Wong Tai Sin	4	5(2)	5	8(1)	9(3)	8(1)	0
Kwun Tong	4(1)	6	4(1)	9(3)	12(5)	10(5)	6
Tsuen Wan	1	1	1	3	4	4	0
Tuen Mun	2	7(2)	9(2)	11(1)	12(2)	8(1)	0
Yuen Long	1	7(3)	4(2)	7	7(3)	6	0
North	4(1)	6	5(2)	9	14	8(4)	0
Tai Po	2	4(1)	3	7	8(3)	5	0
Sai Kung	0	5(1)	4(3)	9(4)	74()	8(1)	0
Sha Tin	0	9(2)	2	8	9(1)	7	1
Kwai Tsing	0	2	1	4	5(2)	8(1)	3
Islands	2	2(1)	4(1)	4(1)	4(1)	3(1)	1
All around	37(4)	83(21)	62(14)	115(13)	136(36)	119(21)	21
Candidates	83	176	200	178	182	171	181
Success Rate (%)	44.6%	47.2%	31.0%	64.6%	74.7%	69.6%	11.6%

Note: The numbers inside backets represent the uncontested seats.

Table 4.5 focuses on the Federation of Trade Unions (FTU), which is an auxiliary political organization of the DAB to grasp more votes from the working-class citizens. The number of elected FTU candidates increased from only 6 in 1994 to 24 in 2007 and 35 in 2011, but again as with the DAB, the FTU suffered from the political protests in 2003 and 2019, when the union obtained only six and five directly elected seats respectively. The success rate of the FTU candidates was the lowest in 2019 as it had only 8%, whereas the July 2003 turmoil witnessed a success rate of 66.7%. The FTU's liability, like the DAB, remains its pro-government and pro-Beijing orientation. If the performance of the government was satisfactory to most citizens, both DAB and FTU performed well in DC elections. However, if

Table 4.5: FTU District Councils Members, 1999–2019

Year	1994	1999	2003	2007	2011	2015	2019
Candidates	7	8	9	30*	51	51	62
FTU alone	0	1	1	4	23	48	43
DAB alone	7	7	6	3	0	0	0
DAB/FTU alliance	0	0	2	22	28	3	19
Uncontested	0	2	0	0	6	7	0
Elected	6	8	6	24	35	29	5
Unelected	1	0	3	6	16	22	57
Successful rate	83.3%	100%	66.7%	80%	68.6%	56.8%	8.06%
Votes Gained	8,148	10,860	15,248	49,153	82,290	95,583	128,796
Average votes obtained	1,164	1,810	1,694	1,638	1,829	2,172	2,077

* One candidate Kwok Wai-keung declared himself as an independent candidate.

Sources: *Reports on the District Councils Election* in 1999, 2003, 2007, 2011, 2015 and 2019; *A Compilation of Election Materials in Hong Kong* (Hong Kong: Hong Kong Institute of Asia-Pacific Studies, The Chinese University of Hong Kong, 2001, 2005 and 2015).

the performance of the government was unsatisfactory in the minds of most voters, the DAB and FTU suffered electorally.

Table 4.6 focuses on the performance of the Democratic Party (DP) in district elections. Contrary to the performance of the DAB and FTU, the DP performed very well in the 2003 and 2019 elections. The success rate of DP candidates was 79.2 in 2003 and 91.9 in 2019, while their performance ranged from 36% to 56% in 2011 and 1994 respectively. Comparatively speaking, the DP remains the strongest political party in the pro-democracy camp, for its electoral performance was relatively stable and could threaten the pro-Beijing and pro-government camps seriously. The 2019 election envisaged the party's breakthrough in many districts, such as the Southern, Kowloon City, Kwun Tong, Tuen Mun, Sha Tin, and Kwai Tsing districts.

Table 4.7 demonstrates the success rate of the DP against the DAB. In 2003 and 2019, the DP had 84% success rate against the DAB and 95% success rate against it respectively. These results showed the strong performance of the DP against the DAB whenever there were political events unfavorable to the government of the HKSAR. Except for 2011 when the DP had only 30% success rate against the DAB, other district elections witnessed the relatively strong showing of the DP against the DAB.

Table 4.6: The Performance of the Democratic Party in District Elections

District	1994	1999	2003	2007	2011	2015	2019
Central & Western	8(1)	5	6	6	4	4	7
Wan Chai	3	2	2	0	0	0	0
Eastern	4	6	6	3	2	2	4
Southern	4	2	2	3	5	4	7
Yau Tsim Mong	1	4(1)	4	1	1	1	4
Sham Shui Po	3	3	2	2	0	1	2
Kowloon City	2	4	7	2	1	0	10
Wong Tai Sin	4	7(1)	4(1)	3	3	2	6
Kwun Tong	7	9(1)	9	3	2	3	9
Tsuen Wan	2	6	5	3(1)	1	1	3
Tuen Mun	9(2)	9(1)	9(1)	7	7	4	8
Yuen Long	3	1	2	2	3	2	7
North	2	7	8	4	1	3	5
Tai Po	4	5	7	4	1	1	0
Sai Kung	2	3	4	4	2	2	0
Sha Tin	8(1)	3	7	3	5	7	6
Kwai Tsing	9	10(2)	11(1)	9	9(1)	4	12
Islands	0	0	0	0	0	1	1
All around	75(4)	86(6)	95(3)	59(1)	47(1)	43	91
Candidates	133	173	120	110	132	95	99
Success Rate (%)	56.4%	49.7%	79.2%	53.6%	35.6%	45.3%	91.9%

Note: The numbers inside backets were the uncontested seats.

Therefore, it is not surprising that the pro-Beijing camp still sees the DP as the most significant threat to its electoral contests.

Table 4.8 shows the one-to-one contest between the DP and the DAB in some districts. In the Central, Yuen Bun-keung of the DP performed strongly compared with the candidates from the DAB and FTU from 1999 to 2007. Similarly, Joseph Lai of the DP defeated the DAB/FTU candidates comfortably from 1999 to 2007. Other strongholds of the DP included Wah Fu North, Kai Yip, Jordan Valley, Tak Tin/Hong Tin, San King, Siu Hong, Nam Ping, and Tai Pak Tin. Other districts saw DP candidates and DAB/FTU counterparts fighting fiercely, changing hands from time to time. These hotly contested districts included Shun Tin West, Yan Do/

Table 4.7: Election Performance of Democratic Party against DAB

Year	1994	1999	2003	2007	2011	2015	2019
Seats	346	390	400	405	412	431	452
DP nomination	133	173	120	110	132	95	99
DP elected	75	86	95	59	47	43	91
DAB nomination	83	177	203	181	202	219	224
DAB elected	37	84	62	116	147	146	26
DP and DAB Contested	**44**	**96**	**85**	**59**	**73**	**57**	**57**
DP won in HK Island	11	14	14	7	3	3	12
DP won in Kowloon	2	16	17	6	3	5	16
DP won in NT	10	26	40	22	16	17	26
DP won total	**23**	**56**	**71**	**35**	**22**	**25**	**54**
DAB won in HK Island	9	13	1	5	8	6	0
DAB won in Kowloon	8	10	5	3	12	9	1
DAB won in NT	3	12	6	14	31	17	2
DAB won total	**20**	**35**	**12**	**22**	**51**	**32**	**3**
Others won	1	5	2	2	0	0	0
DP success rate	56.39%	49.71%	79.17%	53.64%	35.61%	45.26%	91.92%
Against DAB success	52.27%	58.33%	83.53%	59.32%	30.14%	43.86%	94.74%
Seats of Democrats	146	157	198	127	103	126	389

Source: The authors' tabulation from the open and accessible election results.

Shing, and Kam Fung To. In Kam Fung To, for example, Shirley Ho of the DP was defeated in 1999, won in 2003 but defeated again in 2007. Cheung Kwok-cheung of DP in Sau Mau Ping was defeated again and again, whereas Shun Tin West witnessed the defeat of political heavyweight Li Wah-ming in 1999 and then the victory of Ho Wai-to in 2003 and Ho's eventual defeat in 2007. Hence, in some districts, the DP and DAB competed fiercely on a one-to-one basis and changed hands from year to year.

The picture of electoral contests between the DP and DAB became more complex when there were other candidates involved. Table 4.9 shows four patterns in the electoral competition between DP and DAB when a third party or an independent candidate was involved. The first pattern was that the independent candidate was weak and could not change the electoral results between the DP and DAB. This phenomenon could be seen

Table 4.8: The One-to-One Contests between Democratic Party and DAB in 1999, 2003 and 2007

District	Democratic Party candidate/votes		DAB/FTU candidate/votes	
Central				
1999	Yuen Bun-keung	1,179	Li Man-kuen	546
2003	Yuen Bun-keung	1,481	Lee Wai-keung	650
2007	Yuen Bun-keung	1,107	Lee Wai-keung	689
Fei Tsui				
1999	Joseph Lai Chi-keong	1,636	Ma Tak-sing	1,446
2003	Joseph Lai Chi-keong	1,650	Ma Tak-sing	1,129
2007	Joseph Lai Chi-keong	1,932	Ma Tak-sing	1,080
Wah Fu North				
1999	Huang Chen-ya	1,618	Mak Chi-yan	1,003
2003	Henry Chai Man Hon	2,112	Mak Chi-yan	1,550
2007	Henry Chai Man Hon	2,450	Marina Tsang Tze-kwan	1,046
Kai Yip				
1999	Grace Au Yuk-har	2,060	Tam Wai-leung	958
2003	Grace Au Yuk-har	2,030	Sze Lun-hung	1,596
2007	–	–	Sze Lun-hung	uncontested
Jordan Valley				
1999	Alice Lee Ling	1,783	Chan Mei-kuen	1,476
2003	Alice Lee Ling	2,759	Chan Kam-bor	1,404
2007	Wong Wai-tag	1,697	Wat Chi-wah	1,499
Shun Tin West				
1999	Li Wah-ming	1,650	Kwok Bit-chun	1,846
2003	Ho Wai-to	3,052	Kwok Bit-chun	2,524
2007	Ho Wai-to	2,715	Kwok Bit-chun	3,357
Sau Mau Ping North				
1999	Cheung Kwok-cheung	1,242	Mak Fu-ling	2,107
2003	Cheung Kwok-cheung	1,804	Mak Fu-ling	2,159
2007	Cheung Kwok-cheung	1,613	Mak Fu-ling	2,330
Tak Tin/Hong Tin				
1999	Chan Man-kin	1,949	Chin Kwan-ming	1,009
2003	Chan Man-kin	2,314	Chan Ping-yee	948
2007	Chan Man-kin	2,096	Sun Hung-wa	1,822
San King				
1999	Catherine Wong Lai-sheung	2,930	Lam Kwan-yui	954
2003	Catherine Wong Lai-sheung	2,621	Wong Man-ho	793
2007	Catherine Wong Lai-sheung	2,185	Sze Cheng-chong	1,164
Siu Hong				
1999	Josephine Chan Shu-ying	2,249	Tong Sek-ping	773
2003	Josephine Chan Shu-ying	2,543	Dennis Leung Tsz-wing	916
2007	Josephine Chan Shu-ying	1,994	Hon Yat-yung	1,175

District	Democratic Party candidate/votes		DAB/FTU candidate/votes	
Nam Ping				
1999	Zachary Wong Wai-yin	2,129	Raymond Ng Wai-tak	853
2003	Zachary Wong Wai-yin	2,085	Raymond Ng Wai-tak	489
2007	Zachary Wong Wai-yin	2,298	Yau Ka Keung	909
Yan Do/Shing				
1999	Adrian Lau Tak-cheong	1,196	Stephen Li Tung-fong	1,155
2003	Adrian Lau Tak-cheong	1,930	Lau Kwok-fun	1,930
2007	Adrian Lau Tak-cheong	1,239	Lau Kwok-fun	4,159
Choi Yuen				
1999	Wong Ching Han	1,471	So Sai-chi	1,580
2003	Wong Sing-chi	1,886	So Sai-chi	1,986
2007	Hung Ming-lun	2,086	So Sai-chi	2,309
Kam Fung To				
1999	Shirley Ho Suk-ping	1,648	Chan Hak-kan	1,875
2003	Shirley Ho Suk-ping	2,163	Lau Kong-wah	1,885
2007	Shirley Ho Suk-ping	1,680	Yeung Man-yui	2,030
Tai Pak Tin				
1999	Sammy Tsui Sang-hung	uncontested	–	–
2003	Sammy Tsui Sang-hung	1,872	Tang Chi-chiu	1,298
2007	Sammy Tsui Sang-hung	1,429	Tso Lap-ho	1,151

Source: Tabulated from various open sources in Hong Kong's elections results.

in most constituencies, such as Central and Western, Siu Sai Wan, Lower Yiu Tung, Charming, Ka Wai in 2003, Mei Foo South, Wong Tai Sin, Tsuen Wan, Tuen Mun, Yuen Long, and Northern (except for Ka Shing/Fuk and Tin Ping East). The second pattern was that the entry of the independent candidate benefited the DP candidates — a phenomenon that could be seen in Nam Fung and Hing Tung in 1999, To Kwa Wan North in 1999, Wah Kwai in 2003, Ka Shing/Fuk in 2003, Tin Ping East in 2007, Wan Hang in 1999, King Lam in 1999 and 2003, Kwai Tsing Estate in 1999, and Tsing Yi South in 2003. The third pattern was that the participation of the independent candidate favored the DAB candidate, a situation that could be found in Mount Parker in 1999, Wai Kwai in 2007, Po Nga in 2003, Shek Lei in 1999. The fourth pattern was that the independent was so strong that both the candidates of DP and DAB were defeated, such as Wah Kwai in 1999 and Kwai Tsing Estate in 2007.

Table 4.10 compares the performance of various political groups in the 1999 DC elections. District-based political groups, such as the Civil Force (CF) in Sha Tin, the One Two Three Democratic Alliance in Kowloon

Table 4.9: The Contests between DP and DAB with Other Candidates in 1999, 2003 and 2007

Central and Western						
Belcher	Democratic Party		DAB		Other/independent	
1999	Lam Kee-shing	1,157	Wong Chit-man	1,262	–	
2003*	Victor Yeung Sui-yin	1,937	Wong Chit-man	1,497	Lam Kee-shing	841
2007	Victor Yeung Sui-yin	2,135	Wong Wang-hong	1,835	Peter Fong Siu-wah	79
Sheung Wan	Democratic Party		DAB		Independent	
1999	Kam Nai-wai	1,468	Yuen Chiu-hing	688		
2003	Kam Nai-wai	1,756	Chiu Wah-kuen	729		
2007	Kam Nai-wai	1,783			Leung Yuen yee	791
Eastern						
Siu Sai Wan	Democratic Party		DAB		Other/ independent	
1999	Wiggo Lee Wai-chiu	910	Chan Oi-kwan	1,824		
2003	–		Chan Oi-kwan	1,997	Leung Suet-fong	874
2007	Susan Yan Shun-kwan	555	Chan Oi-kwan	2,308		
Mount Parker	Democratic Party		DAB		Other/independent	
1999	Alexander Yan Wing-lok	488	Wong Kin-pan	1,065	Yuen Ki-kong (HKPA)	622
2003	Chris Wong Shing-fai	1,222	Wong Kin-pan	1,549		
2007			Wong Kin-pan	2,120	Alan Leung Koon-lun	475
Lower Yiu Tung	Democratic Party		DAB		Independent	
1999	Stephen Ho Wai-ming	807	Hui Ka-hoo	1,281		
2003	–		Hui Ka-hoo	1,305	Wong Sang-kam	1,301
2007	Wong Sang-kam	1,071	Hui Ka-hoo	1,491		
Nam Fung	Democratic Party		DAB		Independent	
1999	Leung Suk-ching	1,404	Sze Tin-chee	1,075	Kwan Lok-ping	671
2003	Leung Suk-ching	2,672	Hung Lin-cham	1,167	–	
2007	Leung Suk-ching	1,874	Wong Kit-hin	1,409	–	
Hing Tung	Democratic Party		DAB		Independent	
1999	Wong Yuet-mui	1,521	Lai Wing-wah	1,323	Wong Kwok-yau	733
2003	Wong Yuet-mui	2,775	Siu Lao-na	1,870		
2007	Wong Yuet-mui	1,828			Chan Chun-fuk	1,197

Table 4.9 Continued

Southern

Wah Kwai	Democratic Party		DAB		Independent	
1999	Yeung Siu-pik	1,087	Ada Mak Tse How-ling	1,483	Hung Tenny	2,204
2003	Yeung Siu-pik	1,763	Ada Mak Tse How-ling	1,309	Hung Tenny Lam Chun Kwong	1,720 707
2007	Yeung Siu-pik	2,077	Ada Mak Tse How-ling	2,161	Hung Tenny	1,337

Yau Tsim Mong

Charming	Democratic Party		DAB		Independent	
1999	James To Kun-sun	1,670	Chung Kong-mo	934	Chan Wai	316
2003	James To Kun-sun	2,565	Chung Kong-mo	1,961		
2007	Lai Lai Ha	1,402	Chung Kong-mo	2,851		

Kowloon City

To Kwa Wan South	Democratic Party		DAB		Other/independent	
1999	Mak Tak Chuen	592	Or Wing-ki	341	Chu Yung (HKPA)	409
2003	Mak Tak Chuen	1,296	Siu Pui-yau	684		
2007	Poon Chi-man	980	Ng Yuen-tat	826		

Ka Wai	Democratic Party		DAB		Other/independent	
1999	Lau Ting-pong	1,501			Chan Noi-yue (Liberal Party)	1,383
2003	Lau Ting-pong	2,112	Chan Ho-wing	1,054	Lau Kai-shing Mo Tze-man	698 60
2007	Lau Ting-pong	1,305			Lo Chiu-kit	2,086

Oi Cook/Man	Democratic Party		DAB		Other/independent	
1999			Lau Tat-chor	1,515	Chan Sing-kwong (Liberal Party)	1384
2003	Chan Lai-kwan	2,110	Lau Tat-chor	1,728		
2007	Chan Lai-kwan	2,320	Ng Fan-kam	1,817	Herdy So Wai-yin (Liberal Party)	189

Table 4.9 Continued

Sham Shui Po

Mei Foo South	Democratic Party		DAB		Independent	
1999	Joe Wong Tak-chuen	1,017	Tanny Tsang Yau-fat	1,048		
2003	Joe Wong Tak-chuen	1,936	Yeung Yiu-chung	1,324		
2007	Joe Wong Tak-chuen	1,493	Wallace Yeung Hon-sing	1,487	Se Kwok-hung	244

Wong Tai Sin

Tsz Wan West	Democratic Party		DAB		Independent	
1999	Tam Yuet Ping	1,282	–		Yeung Lai-yin Fan Wai-keung	1,065 461
2003	Tam Yuet Ping	3,034	Lo Yee-hang	1,290	Fan Wai-keung	425
2007	Tam Yuet Ping	2,646	Yuen Kwok-keung	2,165		

King Fu	Democratic Party		DAB		Independent	
1999	Wu Chi-wai	2,605	Chan Chow-fan	1,419		
2003	Wu Chi-wai	4,480	Li Tak-hong	1,466		
2007	Wu Chi-wai	4,370			Wong Shui-wan	1,344

Tsuen Wan

Tak Wah	Democratic Party		DAB		Independent	
1999	Kwong Kwok-chuen	1,094	Ng Kung-fong	555		
2003	Kwong Kwok-chuen	1,248	Lau Wing-ning	628		
2007	Kwong Kwok-chuen	1,024			Lo Siu-kit	1,048

Fuk Loi	Democratic Party		DAB		Other/independent	
1999	Chiu Ka-po	1,680	Luk Wai-sing	927	Lok Cheong-hon (HKPA)	223
2003	Chiu Ka-po	2,182	Luk Wai-sing	1,088		
2007	Chiu Ka-po	1,777	Sham Cheuk-lam	1,444		

Cheung Shek	Democratic Party		DAB		Independent	
1999	Choy Tsz-man	1,847	Hui Chui-fai	1,350		
2003	Choy Tsz-man	1,749	Hui Chui-fai	1,350		
2007	Choy Tsz-man	1,565	Chan Chn-chung	1,463	Liu Chi-keng	164

Table 4.9 Continued

Tuen Mun					
Siu Lun/Tsui	**Democratic Party**		**DAB**		**Independent**
1999	Chan Kan-kam	2,188	Yu Sau-king	896	
2003	Lo Man-hon	2,696	Yu Sau-king	1,105	
2007	Lo Man-hon	2,226			Li Wing-hang 896 Tong Man-pui 251
Lok Tsui	**Democratic Party**		**DAB**		**Independent**
1999	Ho Chun-yan	1,255			She Chi-keung 879
2003	Ho Chun-yan	2,187	Kong Chi-hung	469	
2007	Ho Chun-yan	1,606	Li Kam-man	1,007	
Yuen Long					
Wang Yat/King	**Democratic Party**		**DAB**		**Independent**
1999	Not yet established				
2003	Cheung Yin-tung	715	Lo Man	579	Wong Lai-sheung 183
2007	Cheung Yin-tung	1,321	Yau Kwok Wai	1,684	
Northern					
Wah Sum/Do	**Democratic Party**		**DAB**		**Other/independent**
1999	Poon Chung-yuen	1,562	Chu Oi-ping	641	Chow Kam-wah 473 (Liberal Party)
2003	Poon Chung-yuen	3,059			Lai Sum 629
2007	Poon Chung-yuen	2,547	Yiu Ming	1,739	
Wah Ming	**Democratic Party**		**DAB**		**Independent**
1999	Wong Leung-hi	1,952	Wan Chung-ping	1,757	
2003	Wong Leung-hi	2,594	Wan Chung-ping	1,427	
2007	Wong Leung-hi	1,776	Lai Sum	1,882	Ho Chi-wing 123 Chu Yee-wan 111 Cheung Chin-ming 30
Ka/Shing Fuk	**Democratic Party**		**DAB**		**Independent**
1999	Sham Wing-kan	1,762	Wong Loi-tai	1,105	
2003	Sham Wing-kan	2,342	Wan Wo-tat	1,176	Cheung Kwan-ho 1,192
2007	Sham Wing-kan	1,980	Wan Wo-tat	2,801	

Table 4.9 Continued

Choi Fuk/Yu Tai	Democratic Party		DAB		Other/independent	
1999	Chow Kam-siu	1,840	Chan Wai-chun	767	Lee Mo-kan	500
2003	Chow Kam-siu	2,656	Yau May-kwong	1,023		
2007	Chow Kam-siu	1,040	Larm Wai-leung	1,269	Peggy Tong Kei Hiu (Civic Association)	25
Shek Wu Hui	**Democratic Party**		**DAB**		**Other/independent**	
1999	Chan Hing-fok	1,006	Wong Chi-wah	993		
2003	Chan Hing-fok	1,361			Cheung Yuk-shu (Liberal Party)	704
					Wong Luen Fat	307
2007	Wong Sing-chi	1,543	Wong Yun-keung	1081	Liu Kam-cheong	525
					Wong Luen Fat	115
Tin Ping East	**Democratic Party**		**DAB**		**Other/independent**	
1999	Wong Sing-chi	1,281	Yong Sheung-ying	608	Yung Ip Siu-mui	167
2003	Paul Yu Chi Shing	1,538	Wong Hoi-hung	865		
2007	Paul Yu Chi Shing	813	Windy Or Sin-yi	531	Wong Hoi-hung	597
					Lin Shui-lin	357
					Nip Ching-keung (Liberal Party)	154
Tai Po						
Po Nga	**Democratic Party**		**DAB**		**Other**	
1999	Lee Wai-man	1,408	Wong Yung-kan	1,886		
2003	Cheung Wai-yip	1,272	Wong Yung-kan	2,054	Lam Wai-yin (Liberal Party)	842
2007			Wong Yung-kan	2,516	Wong Yeung-tak (Liberal Party)	563
Old Market	**Democratic Party**		**DAB**		**Other**	
1999	Wong Chun-wai	1,158	Wong Sai-ping	409	Irene Luk Ngai-ling (Liberal Party)	577
2003	Wong Chun-wai	2,103	Tsui Kwai-fong	729		
2007	Wong Chun-wai	1,444	Yau Sze-sang	984	Cheung Kam-tak (Liberal Party)	139
Sai Kung						
Wan Hang	**Democratic Party**		**DAB**		**Independent**	
1999	Fan Kwok-wai	924	Leung Chi-kong	679	Liu Kwong-sang	654
2003	Fan Kwok-wai	3,070	Chan Wing-hung	604		
2007	Fan Kwok-wai	2,567	Lin Chor-keung	988		

Table 4.9 Continued

King Lam	Democratic Party		DAB		Other	
1999	Lam Wing-yin	1,201	Ki Lai-mei	1,055	Ko Wing-luen (ADPL)	1,081
2003	Lam Wing-yin	1,956	Ki Lai-mei	1,224	Ko Wing-luen (ADPL)	1,480
2007	Lam Wing-yin	1,997	Ki Lai-mei	2,593		
Sheung Tak	**Democratic Party**		**DAB**		**Independent**	
1999	Lam Lok-yin	300	Luk Wai-man	570		
2003	Ho Wai-yee	758	Luk Wai-man	1782	Lin Leung-ying	437
2007			Luk Wai-man	2,201	Yip Chun-keung	1,257

Kwai Tsing

Upper Tai Wo Hau	Democratic Party		DAB		Independent	
1999	Hui Kei-cheung	1,694	Ho Leung	1,170		
2003	Hui Kei-cheung	2,134	Ho Leung	1,104		
2007	Hui Kei-cheung	2,221			Kong Wan-ching	392
Lower Tai Wo Hau	**Democratic Party**		**DAB**		**Independent**	
1999	Wing Bing-kuen	1,917	Wong Kam-fai	1,662		
2003	Wing Bing-kuen	3,043	Suen Moon-kan	594	Mak Wai-yin	217
2007	Wing Bing-kuen	2,464			Kong Chi-wah	449
Kwai Chung Estate	**Democratic Party**		**DAB**		**Other/independent**	
1999	Chow Lap-yan	944	Kam Ho-kai	763	Chung Hou-ping (NWSC)	410
					Lam Yuk-kui	76
2003	Chow Lap-yan	1,314	Chan Chi-kwong	809	Mak Hon-ching	205
					Ng Hai-ming	149
2007	Lam Lap-chi	734	Au-Yeung Po Chun	821	Wong Yun-tat (NWSC)	1,410
Shek Lei	**Democratic Party**		**DAB**		**Independent**	
1999	Lam Siu Fai1	422	Lee Sun-ho	566	Leung Kwok-on	483
2003	Lam Siu Fai	2,511	Tam Tsuen	425		
2007	Lam Siu Fai	1,776			Liu Ming-kin (Liberal Party)	765
Lai Wah	**Democratic Party**		**DAB/FTU**		**Independent**	
1999	Not yet established					
2003	Lee Wing-tat	2,310	Chan Chun-chung	772	Poon Shu-kee	615
2007	Lee Wing-tat	1,349	Yeung Man-tat	885		

Table 4.9 Continued

Hing Fong	Democratic Party		DAB		Independent	
1999	Ng Kim-sing	762	Peter Cheung	634		
2003	Ng Kim-sing	1,350	Peter Cheung	913		
2007	Ng Kim-sing	1,716	Leung Kai-ming	1,451	Luk King-shing	106
Greenfield	**Democratic Party**		**DAB**		**Other/independent**	
1999			Law King-shing	611	So Tak-wah	391
2003	Wong Suet-ying	1,516	Law King-shing	979	Lee Moses	676
					Tang Yuk-choi	377
2007	Wong Suet-ying	1,893			Cheung Wai-ching (Liberal Party)	1,563
					Leung Kam-wah	191
Tsing Yi South	**Democratic Party**		**DAB**		**Independent**	
1999	–		–		Au Cheong-wa	uncontested
2003	Wong Kwong-mo	1,650	Poon Chi-shing	1,269	Au Cheong-wa (ADPL)	1,149
2007	Wong Kwong-mo	1,115	Poon Chi-shing	1,771		

Source: Tabulated and compiled from the election results that are publicly accessible.

City, and the Association for Democracy and People's Livelihood (ADPL) in Sham Shui Po, tended to have relatively higher percentages of candidates being directly elected. The pro-democracy Neighborhood and Workers Center emerged quickly in the Kwai Tsing district, performing well with other like-minded groups such as the One Two Three Democratic Alliance and the Frontier. The DP and DAB, which nominated candidates to run in various districts, had a success rate of nearly 50%. Both the DP and DAB had the highest number of candidates being nominated and elected, becoming the two largest flagships of political parties in Hong Kong shortly after July 1, 1997. Pro-business Liberal Party and the Hong Kong Progressive Alliance had 31 candidates being elected, an ordinary but unimpressive performance.

This pattern of having better performance among the district-based political groups could also be seen in the 2003 DC elections (Table 4.11). District-based ADPL, CF, and the Neighborhood and Workers Center in Kwai Tsing performed quite well in terms of the percentages of their candidates being elected. While the DAB suffered from a low success rate of 31% of its candidates being elected, the DP and the ADPL benefited from

Table 4.10: The Performance of Various Political Groups
in the 1999 District Council Elections

Political Groups	Number of Candidates	Number Elected	Success Rate (percentage)
Democratic Party	173	86(6)	49.71%
Democratic Alliance for the Betterment of Hong Kong	176	83(18)	47.16%
Association for Democracy and People's Livelihood (ADPL)	32	19(4)	59.38%
Hong Kong Progressive Alliance	25	16(6)	64.00%
Liberal Party	34	15(3)	44.12%
Civil Force	14	11(3)	78.57%
123 Democratic Alliance	10	6	60.00%
Frontier	9	4	44.44%
East Kowloon Residence's Committee	5	2	40.00%
Neighborhood and Workers Centre	3	2	66.67%
Total	**798**	**390(76)**	**48.87%**

Note: The numbers in brackets represented uncontested candidates.

Table 4.11: The Performance of Various Political Groups
in the2003 District Councils' Elections

Political Groups	Number of Candidates	Number Elected	Success Rate (percentage)
Democratic Party	120	95(3)	79.17%
Democratic Alliance for the Betterment of Hong Kong	200	62(14)	31.00%
Association for Democracy and People's Livelihood (ADPL)	37	25(3)	67.57%
Civil Force	21	17(8)	80.95%
Liberal Party	27	14(1)	51.85%
Hong Kong Progressive Alliance	23	13(4)	56.52%
Frontier	14	6	42.86%
One Two Three Democratic Alliance	10	6	60.00%
Neighborhood and Workers Centre	5	4	80.00%
East Kowloon Residents Committee	6	2	33.33%
Total	**837**	**400(76)**	**47.79%**

Note: The numbers in the brackets represented uncontested candidates.

the political unpopularity of the HKSAR government. The pro-business Liberal Party and the Hong Kong Progressive Alliance maintained their performance in 2003 as with the situation in 1999. The Shatin-based and pro-Beijing CF maintained arguably the best performance among pro-establishment groups, garneting 80.95% of the success rate of its candidates. Compared with other district-based pro-democracy groups, like One Two Three Democratic Alliance and the Frontier, the CF was the strongest district-based pro-government political organization in 2003, when other pro-Beijing forces like DAB suffered tremendously.

The 2007 DCs elections witnessed the political comeback of the DAB with 64.61% of its success rate of candidates being elected. On the contrary, the DP trailed behind the DAB with only 53.64% success rate, showing a considerable decline in the performance of the pro-democracy flagship compared with its 79% success rate in 2003. The election result showed that the pro-Beijing DAB could bounce back resiliently four years after the political earthquake on July 1, 2003. In constituencies where DAB candidates were defeated in 2003, the DAB groomed new activists for the preparation of the 2007 elections. The pro-Beijing CF performed strongly with 90% of its success rate of candidates. Except for the Neighborhood and Workers Center, the pro-democracy groups like the Frontier and the ADPL showed signs of electoral decline. However, the pro-welfare and pro-democracy League of Social Democrats rose up with 20% of its success rate, signaling the gradual rise in popularity of the democratic left in the HKSAR. The League projected an image of fighting for the interests of the lower-class citizens while being critical of the HKSAR government—a position that earned the support of many voters. The pro-business Liberal Party showed signs of electoral decline after its rapid increase in popularity in 2003, when its leader James Tien quit the Executive Council (ExCo) in defiance of the legislation on Article 23 of the Basic Law. The relatively underdeveloped business sector in electoral participation meant that, given the gradual rise in the popularity of the pro-Beijing flagship DAB, more business elites would be increasingly recruited by and co-opted into this electoral battleship. Traditionally, the business elites in Hong Kong under the colonial era were politically co-opted into various political institutions and advisory bodies without the need to run in elections. This politically spoiled tendency has been perpetuated in the HKSAR since July 1, 1997.

**Table 4.12: The Performance of Various Political Groups
in the 2007 District Councils' Elections**

Political Groups	Number of Candidates	Number Elected	Success Rate (percentage)
Democratic Alliance for the Betterment and Progress of Hong Kong	178	115(13)	64.61%
Democratic Party	110	59(1)	53.64%
Civil Force	20	18(5)	90.00%
Association for Democracy and People's Livelihood	37	17	45.95%
Liberal Party	55	14(1)	25.45%
Civic Party	41	8	19.51%
League of Social Democrats	29	6	20.69%
East Kowloon Residents Committee	7	4(2)	57.14%
Neighborhood and Workers Centre	5	4	80.00%
Frontier	15	3	20.00%
Total	**907**	**405(41)**	**44.65%**

Note: The numbers in the brackets represented uncontested candidates.

Business elites have tended to side with the government and pro-Beijing forces, protecting their vested interests and enjoying political influence more easily. This underdevelopment of business participation in electoral politics is arguably not conducive to the democratization of the HKSAR, where a truly politically autonomous business sector remains relatively weak and where politics have been increasingly polarized between the pro-democracy on the one hand and the pro-government and pro-Beijing camp on the other.

Table 4.13 illustrates the performance of various political groups, including old and new, in the 2011 DCs elections. The DAB maintained its relatively good performance as with the 2007 elections, retaining a high success rate of 74.73%. The DP still trailed behind the DAB with 53.64%. Many new political groups sprung up, ranging from the pro-Beijing Kowloon West New Dynamic to the pro-democracy Neo Democrats, and from the pro-government New People's Party to the pro-Beijing Kowloon Federation of Associations (KFA). The Neo Democrats performed well with 80% of its success rate of candidates being elected, showing its rapid rise under the leadership of Gary Fan Kwok-wai, a former member of the DP.

**Table 4.13: The Performance of Various Political Groups
in the 2011 District Councils Elections**

Political Groups	Number of Candidates	Number Elected	Success Rate (percentage)
Democratic Alliance for the Betterment and Progress of Hong Kong	182	136(36)	74.73%
Democratic Party	110	59(1)	53.64%
Kowloon West New Dynamic	20	17(4)	85.00%
Association for Democracy and People's Livelihood	26	15	57.69%
Civil Force	20	15(3)	75.00%
Liberal Party	55	14(3)	25.45%
Hong Kong Federation of Trade Unions*	23	12(2)	52.17%
Neo Democrats	10	8	80.00%
Civic Party	41	7	17.07%
Kowloon Federation of Associations	8	7(1)	87.50%
League of Social Democrats	29	6	20.69%
Neighborhood and Workers Centre	6	5	83.33%
New People's Party	12	4	33.33%
Professional Power	11	4	36.36%
East Kowloon Residents Committee	6	3(2)	50.00%
Total	**915**	**412(76)**	**45.03%**

Notes: *There were other 28 FTU members participating in elections as the DAB/FTU alliance was formed; they were not counted in the FTU's electoral participation.

Fan projected an image of a new democrat and succeeded in attracting some young pro-democracy followers. However, some pro-democracy groups, such as the Civic Party and the League of Social Democrats, did not appear to improve significantly in their electoral performance. This phenomenon was due to the fact that both the Civic Party and the League of Social Democrats tended to rely far more on ideological appeals than on district-based constituency work and services. Unlike the pro-Beijing FTU and KFA which offered extensive constituency services, like elderly services, legal aid, and local tours, the pro-democracy groups usually played down upon the utilization of concrete material incentives to lure the support of voters. Like the previous district elections, the pro-business Liberal Party tended to have a low percentage of success rate of its candidates, a situation again showing the underdevelopment of business participation in electoral politics.

**Table 4.14: The Performance of Various Political Groups
in the 2015 District Councils Elections**

Political Groups	Number of Candidates	Number Elected	Success Rate (percentage)
Democratic Alliance for the Betterment and Progress of Hong Kong	171	119(21)	69.59%
Democratic Party	95	43	45.26%
Hong Kong Federation of Trade Unions	48	27(7)	56.25%
New People's Party	42	26(7)	61.90%
Civil Force/New People's Party	22	11(4)	50.00%
Association for Democracy and People's Livelihood	26	18	69.23%
Kowloon West New Dynamic	24	18(3)	75.00%
Positive Synergy	21	16(5)	76.19%
Neo Democrats	16	15	93.75%
Business and Professionals Alliance	16	10	62.50%
Civic Party	25	10	40.00%
Liberal Party	20	9(2)	45.00%
Neighborhood and Worker's Centre	6	5	83.33%
Labor Party	12	3	25.00%
Total	**935**	**431(66)**	**46.10%**

Note: The numbers in brackets represented uncontested candidates.

Table 4.14 shows a fragmented scenario of Hong Kong's electoral development in 2015, when the DC elections witnessed a slight decline in the electoral performance of both the DAB and DP but a variety of competitiveness among other smaller political groups. Both the DAB and DP saw their success rates of candidates declining slightly. The slight decline of DAB performance was, however, matched by an increased level of competitiveness among other pro-Beijing groups, notably the FTU and the New People's Party (NPP). Similarly, other smaller pro-democracy groups showed relatively improved performance, including the ADPL, Civic Party, and the Neo Democrats. The pro-democracy and pro-welfare Labor Party emerged, but it only got 25% of the success of its candidates being elected. Even the pro-business Liberal Party and the Hong Kong Business and Professional Alliance performed relatively well. The entire electoral landscape pointed to the fragmented nature of political forces.

Politics Within District Councils

While political groups have been competing among themselves for directly elected seats in DCs since the early 1980s, particularly after July 1997, the administration of DCs has become politicized after the establishment of the HKSAR. A good case was the selection of chairpersons of DCs. Table 4.15 shows how political groups managed to get their members to become chairpersons and vice-chairpersons of various DCs. The watershed of selecting DC chairpersons was the 2019 election, after which an overwhelming majority of chairpersons of DCs was captured by the members of the pro-democracy camp, except for the Islands DC with the chair and vice-chair remain pro-government. Before 2019, because the democrats failed to grasp a majority of directly elected seats in DCs, the chairpersons and vice-chairpersons were usually given to the members of the pro-government camp. From the perspective of the District Officers, who are the representatives of the government, chairpersons and vice-chairpersons are ideally supportive of the government. A harmonious relationship between District Officers on the one hand and Council chairs and vice-chairs has been consistently the preferred scenario from the government's perspective. This preferred scenario could be easily achieved in the HKSAR before the 2019 DC elections, for many chairs and vice-chairs could work with the government, particularly District Officers, relatively easily. However, after the 2019 elections, because most democrats grasped the position of the chairs, some of them had tense relations with District Officers. A good example was Cheng Lai-king of the DP, whose relations with the government became tense. She was criticized by the police for being "hostile" to the police representatives who attended a DC meeting.[2] After the 2019 elections, some pro-democracy DC members initiated a move to set up a sub-committee to look into how police dealt with protestors in 2019, a move that from the government's perspective exceeded the powers of DCs which are of consultative nature. Hence, the government issued a guideline to District Officers, saying that they could be absent from those meetings that "violated" the District Council Ordinance. However, from the perspective of the elected democrats, they were elected by the voters in the 2019 elections and were "empowered" to initiate motions and committee action that, to them, could protect "public interest." As such, the 2019 elections represented a turning point in the development of DCs, for the

Table 4.15: Chairpersons and Vice Chairpersons of District Councils 2000–2019

District	2000–03	2004–07	2008–11	2012–15	2016–19	2020–23
Central & Western Chair	Wu Chor-nam (A)	Kam Nai-wai (DP)	Chan Tak-chor	Yip Wing-shing (HKIF)		Cheng Lai-king (DP)
Vice-chair	Chan Tak-chor	Wu Chor-nam (A)	Stephen Chan Chit-kwai		Chan Hok-fung (DAB)	Yeung Sui-yin (DP)
Wan Chai Chair	Peggy Lam Pei Yu-dja		Suen Kai-cheong (DAB)		Stephen Ng Kam-chun (HKIF)	Clarisse Yeung Suet-ying
Vice-chair	Suen Kai-cheong	John Tse Wing-ling	Stephen Ng Kam-chun (HKIF)		Jennifer Chow Kit-bing (DAB)	Mak King-sing
Eastern chair	Christina Ting Yuk-chee			Christopher Chung Shu-kun (DAB)	Wong Kin-pun (DAB)	Joseph Lai Chi-keong (CP)
Vice-chair	Christopher Chung Shu-kun (DAB)	Wong Kwok-hing (FTU)	Christopher Chung Shu-kun (DAB)	Kung Pat-cheung (FTU)	Chiu Chi-keung (FTU)	Chiu Ka-yin (DP)
Southern Chair	Joseph Chan Yuek-sut	Ma Yuet-har		Chu Ching-hung (HKIF)		Lo Kin-hei (DP)
Vice-chair	Wong King-keung	Chu Ching-hung (HKIF)		Chan Fu-ming (HKIF)		Paul Johannes Zimmerman
Yau Tsim Mong chair	Chow Chun-fai	Henry Chan Man-yu	Chung Kong-mo (DAB)		Chris Ip Ngo-tung (DAB)	Lam Kin-man
Vice-chair	Ip Kwok-chung (DAB)	Leung Wai-kuen		Ko Po-ling (A)	Wong Shu-ming (KFA)	Yu Tak-po (CP)
Sham Shui Po chair	Tam Kwok-kiu (ADPL)		Chan Tung (A)	Kwok Chun-wah	Ambrose Cheung Wing-sum (KWND)	Yeung Yuk (ADPL)
Vice-chair	Chan Tung (A)	Leung Lai (ADPL)	Tam Kwok-kiu (ADPL)	Wong Tat-tung (DAB)	Chan Wai-ming (DAB)	Ng Yuet-lan (CP)
Kowloon City chair	Leung Tin (A)	Peter Wong Kwok-keung (A)		Lau Wai-wing	Poon Kwok-wah	Siu Leong-sing (DP)
Vice-chair	Chan Ka-wai (DP)		Lau Wai-wing	Poon Kwok-wah (DAB)	Cho Wui-hung (KWND)	Kwong Po-yin
Wong Tai Sin chair	Lam Man-fai (DAB)	Wong Kam-chi (EKRC)	Li Tak-hong (DAB)			Hui Kam-shing (ADPL)
Vice-chair	Wong Kam-chi (EKRC)	Kan Chi-ho (DAB)	Wong Kam-chi (EKRC)	Wong Kam-chiu	Joe Lai Wing-ho (DAB)	Wong Yat-yuk
Kwun Tong chair	Hau Shui-pui (KTRA)	Bunny Chan Chung-bun (KFA)				Choy Chak-hung
Vice-chair	Wu Kwok-cheung	Leung Fu-wing (KTRA)	Ann So Lai-chun (KFA)		Hung Kam-in (DAB)	Mok Kin-shing

Table 4.15 Continued

District	2000–03	2004–07	2008–11	2012–15	2016–19	2020–23
Tuen Wan chair	Chow How-chen (A)			Star Chan lu-sng (A)	Chung Wai-ping (HYK)	Sumly Chan Yuen-sum (CP)
Vice-chair	Chan Wai-ming (HYK)	Chung Wai-ping (HYK)			Wong Wai-kit (NTAS)	Li Hung-bor
Tuen Mun chair	Lau Wong-fat (HYK)				Leung Kin-man (DAB)	Josephine Chan Shu-ying
Vice-chair	Leung Kin-man (DAB)				Lee Hung-sham (FTU)	Wong Tan-ching
Yuen Long chair	Tang Siu-tong (HKPA)		Leung Che-cheung (DAB)		Shum Ho-kit	Zachary Wong Wai-ying
Vice-chair	Leung Che-cheung (DAB)		Tang Yun-chor (HYK)	Leung Fuk-yuen (HYK)	Wong Wai-shun	Johnny Mak Ip-sing
Northern Chair	Raymond Pang Hang-yin (HYK)	Li Kwok-fung (HYK)	So Sai-chi (DAB)			Law Ting-tak
Vice-chair	Cheung Fu-tai (A)	Chow Kam-siu (DP)	Hau Chi-keung (HYK)	Hau Kam-lam (DAB)	Lee Kwok-fung (HYK)	Chan Yuk-ming (DP)
Tai Po chair	Cheung Hok-ming (HYK and DAB)	Cheng Chun-ping (HKPA)	Cheung Hok-ming (HYK & DAB)			Kwan Wing-yip (ND)
Vice-chair	Cheng Chun-ping (HKPA)	Wan Kwok-lim (HYK)	Man Chen-fai	Wong Pik-kiu (DAB)		Lau Yung-wai
Sai Kung chair	George Ng Sze Fuk (DAB)					Ben Chung Kam Lun (ND)
Vice-chair	Francis Chau Yin-ming		Wan Yuet-kau (DAB)	Chan Kwok-kei (DAB)	Shing Hon-keung (HYK)	Francis Chau Yin-ming
Sha Tin chair	Wai Kwok-hung (CF)			Ho Hau-cheung (CF)		Ching Cheung-ying (DP)
Vice-chair	Thomas Pang Cheung-wai (DAB)					Wong Hok-lai
Kwai Ching chair	Chow Yick Hay (DP)		Tang Kwok Kwong (A)	Fing Pong (A)	Law King Sing (DAB)	Sin Chung Kai (DP)
Vice-chair	Edinson So Hoi-pan (A)	Leung Wing-kuen	Alice Mak Mei-kuen	Law King-sing (DAB)	Chow Yick-hay	Cheung Man-lung
Islands chair	Daniel Lam Wai-keung (HYK)			Chow Yuk-tong (HYK)		Randy Yu Hon-kwan
Vice-chair	Chau Chuen-heung (DAB)				Randy Yu Hon-kwan	Wong Man-hon (HYK)

Sources: Websites of District Councils and one of the authors was a former District Council member who had extensive contacts with and information from District Councilors in various districts.

Note: A—Appointed Member; DAB—Democratic Alliance for the Betterment and Progress of Hong Kong; DP—Democratic Party; CP—Civic Party; ND—Neo Democrats; ADPL—Association for Democracy and People's Livelihood; HYK—Heung Yee Kuk; HKIF—Hong Kong Island Federation; KFA—Kowloon Federation of Associations; NTAS—New Territories Association of Societies; EKRC—East Kowloon Residents Committee; KTRA—Kwun Tong Residents Association; CF—Civil Force.

capture of most DCs, including the chairpersons, by the pan-democrats constituted a "threat" to the legitimacy and operation of the HJSAR government.

Unethical Politics and By-Elections

Since July 1, 1997, DCs have witnessed quite a lot of by-elections that were held because of the unethical and problematic behavior of a minority of council members. Table 4.16 shows the patterns of the reasons why by-elections were held from 1999 to 2019. There were four main reasons for such by-elections, namely legal issues, the sickness or death of a council member, criminal matters, and personal bankruptcy. Naturally, unethical politics seeped into DCs as a minority of elected council members were involved in various criminal and legal issues.

Table 4.17 sums up the main court cases that eventually led to by-elections held for DCs. Some of the cases involved malpractices, like false declaration in the case of Miu Wa-chun and illegal pretension as a government official in the case of Wong Chung-kei. Other cases embraced fraudulent practices, such as the cases of Tai Yuen-ming, Lam Yuet, and Man Kwong-ming; and deception of government subsidies, such as the cases of Ng Chung-tak, Fung King-man, Leung Kwong-cheong, and Lam Shun-chuen. The unethical and problematic practices of some DC members reflected that a minority of elected representatives might forget the importance of retaining their ethical behavior to win the hearts and minds of their supporters and voters. The politics of personal greed and egoism usually came into play whenever by-elections had to be held for some constituencies of DCs. Some of these cases unfortunately involved the democrats, such as Wong Chung-kei, Leung Kwong-cheong, and Fung King-man, whose political careers and futures were undermined by their own scandals. Other democrats, such as Ho Wai-to of the Shun Tin constituency, was arrested by the mainland Chinese public security for soliciting prostitute in August 2004, a scandal that eventually led to his defeat by rival Kwok Bit-chun of the DAB in the 2007 DC elections.[3] Although Ho helped his assistant Mok Kin-shing to defeat Kwok in the 2015 DC elections, he died of cancer in May 2016. A balanced assessment of Ho Wai-to was that he worked very hard for his constituents in his district, but he might not be aware that he

Table 4.16: Reasons for By-Elections, 1999–2019

Reasons	1999–2003	2003–2007	2007–2011	2011–2015	2015–2019
By-election related to legal issues	2	3	1	1	0
By-election related to sickness or death	2	3	3	2	2
By-election related to criminal issues	1	3	2	2	1
By-election related to personal bankruptcy	0	1	0	1	0
By-election related to other issues	0	1	2	3	3
Total	5	11	8	9	6

Sources: Compiled for news reports from wisenews search, 1999–2019.

Table 4.17: Selected Court Cases leading to District Councils By-Elections

District Councilor Involved	Details for the Court Cases
Wong Chung-kei	Wong was a former District Council member and a DP member. From 1995 to 1997, he was a chairperson of the Sham Shui Po District Council. In 2003, Wong was an assistant editor of *Eastweek* and he pretended to be a housing official to sneak into the home of an assistant of DAB council member Kwok Bit-chun to take photos. He was found guilty of acting as a civil servant illegally and was imprisoned for four months. Wong lost his position in District Council and a by-election would have to be held.
Miu Wah-chun	Former DAB council member Miu Wah-chun, after being elected as a councilor in 2003, was found by his opponent for not reporting his leave from Hong Kong for 279 days, an act that was allegedly violating the electoral regulations of District Council elections. Miu was penalized by the court for a fine of HK$500 and he lost his elected seat. A by-election had to be held.
Tai Yuen-ming	Tai was a former District Council member, who was found to "conspire" with a contractor and an engineer to pretend as eligible pipe repair experts for a qualification interview by the Fire Department, and who tried to assist two engineering companies to get registration from the Fire Department as qualified contractors. The fraudulent practice was discovered, and he was imprisoned for two years. A by-election had to be held.
Ng Chung-tak	He was a former District Council member who was found to falsify the salary of his assistant to deceive HK$110,000 subsidy from the government. He was found guilty and imprisoned for 18 months. Because Ng could not perform his duty as District Council member consecutively for four months, he lost his elected position. A by-election had to be held.
Wong Kwok-hung	Wong was a former District Council member and a former member of the Frontier. He was found guilty of seeking bribes of HK$100,000 from a bus company and of collecting HK$30,000 to help the company's board of directors to acquire a mini-bus license in a public housing estate. He was imprisoned for 12 months and lost his elected position in December 2006.
Fung King-man	Fung was a former District Council member in Kowloon City, and she was found guilty of exaggerating the amount of her office rent receipt to deceive HK$600,000 subsidy from the government. She allegedly provided 4 items of fake documents. She was imprisoned for 18 months and lost her elected position in May 2007.

Table 4.17 Continued

District Councilor Involved	Details for the Court Cases
Leung Kwong-cheong	Leung was a former chairperson of the Kwai Tsing District Council from 1991 to 1994. He was found guilty of deceiving HK$69,000 from the government in March 2009 by utilizing fake receipts. He was imprisoned for 16 months and fined for HK$130,000. Due to his sickness, he received suspended sentence and lost his elected position in 2008.
Leung Wai-kuen	In 2011, Leung defeated his opponent Lam Kin-man of ADPL by 2 votes in the elections. But Lam sought judicial review to reverse the election result on the grounds that Leung's publicity materials had not gained the formal and written consent of some supporters. In March 2013, the High Court ruled that the election result in the constituency of King's Park, where Leung and Lam competed, was invalid. A re-election would be held. Leung then appealed to the Court of Final Appeal, which in July 2013 ruled against Leung's appeal. Leung eventually was fined by the Kowloon City court for HK$15,000 for violating the election law.
Lam Yuet	Lam was a former District Council member in Tung Chung. He was imprisoned for 21 months due to his illegal action of falsifying income statement to apply for bank loans.
Law Shun-chuen	Law was a former District Council member in Tai Po and a member of the Business and Professional Alliance. He was found guilty of deceiving HK$500,000 from the government and was imprisoned for 5 months.
Man Kwong-ming	Man was a council member in San Tin and was found guilty of falsifying the employment of a person as part-time assistant. He was imprisoned for 8 months.

Sources: *Apple Daily*, June 14, 2003, p. A25; *Sing Tao Daily*, June 14, 2003, p. A15; *Ming Pao*, May 17, 2003, p. A14; *Ming Pao*, November 24, 2004, p. B12; *The Sun*, December 5, 2004, p. A6; *Sing Pao*, December 5, 2004, p. A5; *Sing Pao*, October 13, 2004, p. A13; *Sing Tao Daily*, May 20, 2005, p. A12; *Hong Kong Economic Times*, December 21, 2005, p. A31; *Wen Wei Po*, March 10, 2007, p. A22; *Sing Tao Daily*, March 12, 2007, p. A14; *Wen Wei Po*, December 23, 2006, p. A15; *Ta Kung Pao*, January 25, 2006, p. A27; *Hong Kong Daily News*, January 18, 2006, p. A9; *Sing Pao*, August 23, 2007, p. A4; *The Sun*, November 9, 2006, p. A15; *Ming Pao*, October 26, 2006, p. A17; *Hong Kong Daily News*, October 17, 2006, p. A7; *Hong Kong Commercial Daily*, March 29, 2009, p. A2; *Sing Tao Daily*, March 29, 2009, p. A5; *Sing Pao*, March 29, 2009, p. A6; *Wen Wei Po*, July 12, 2013, p. A22; *Oriental Daily*, July 5, 2013, p. A28; *Wen Wei Po*, December 7, 2013, p. A20; *Headline News*, December 7, 2013, p. 28; *Sing Tao Daily*, April 15, 2015, p. A16; *Ta Kung Pao*, April 15, 2015, p. A8; *Oriental Daily*, April 1, 2015, p. A10; *Ming Pao*, March 21, 2019; *Sing Tao Daily*, March 22, 2019, p. A13; *Hong Kong Commercial Daily*, March 9, 2019, p. A14.

could become a target of arrest when he entered the mainland—an incident that turned into a campaign issue unfavorable to the democrats just before the 2007 DC elections. Suffering from a huge defeat in the 2003 DC elections, the pro-Beijing electoral machinery skillfully utilized the Ho Wai-to scandal as a chance to launch an electoral comeback. Overall, regardless of whether the elected council members came from the pro-government or pro-democracy camp, the temptation of being lured by personal greed and unethical and impetuous actions entailed huge political costs.

Table 4.18: The 2019 District Council Election's Performance of District Council Members who were Members of the 2017 Chief Executive Election Committee's Hong Kong and Kowloon District Councils Subsector

Groups	Number of District Councilors from the 2017 Chief Executive Election Committee's Hong Kong and Kowloon District Councils Subsector (%)	Number of District Councilors who were successful re-elected in the 2019 District Council election (%)	Number of District Councilors who failed to be re-elected in the 2019 District Council elections (%)	Number of District Councilors who did not run for re-election in the 2019 District Council election (%)
DAB	29 (51%)	3 (10%)	23 (80%)	3 (10%)
Hong Kong Island Federation (pro-Beijing group)	7 (12%)	2 (29%)	4 (57%)	1 (14%)
Business and Professional Alliance	5 (9%)	1 (20%)	2 (40%)	2 (40%)
Federation of Trade Union	4 (7%)	1 (25%)	2 (50%)	1 (25%)
Positive Synergy	4 (7%)	1 (25%)	3 (75%)	0 (0%)
West Kowloon Dynamics	2 (3.5%)	1 (50%)	1 (50%)	0 (0%)
New Century Forum	2 (3.5%)	0 (0%)	2 (100%)	0 (0%)
Kowloon Federation of Associations	1 (1.5%)	0 (0%)	0 (0%)	1 (100%)
Liberal Party	1 (1.5%)	0 (0%)	1 (100%)	0 (0%)
Federation of Hong Kong Kowloon Labor Unions (FLU)	1 (1.5%)	0 (0%)	1 (100%)	0 (0%)
New People's Party	1 (1.5%)	0 (0%)	1 (100%)	0 (0%)
Total	57	9 (16%)	40 (70%)	8 (14%)

District Council Seats as a Channel for Local Politicians to Climb Up Politically

The emergence and persistence of scandals and unethical behavior involving DC members reflected a reality in Hong Kong's local politics, namely DCs remaining to be a useful channel of attracting some local politicians who aspire to climb up the political ladder. This political ladder embraces their possibility of being nominated as the five candidates running for the Legislative Council's (LegCo) DC subsector since 2012 and as candidates for the Chief Executive Election members. Table 4.18 shows the performance of DC members in the 2019 DC elections. There were four categories of DC members who ran in the 2019 DC elections: 57 members were also the members of the 2017 Chief Executive Election Committee, nine were successfully re-elected in 2019, 40 failed to be re-elected, and eight did not run for re-election in 2019. Of the 57 DC members who were also members of the 2017 Chief Executive Election Committee, all of them came from the pro-Beijing camp, especially the DAB, Hong Kong Island Federation, and the Business Professional Alliance (BPA).

Table 4.19 shows the electoral performance of DC members who came from the 2017 Chief Executive Election's New Territories DC subsector. Of the four categories of DC members, the pro-Beijing forces occupied an overwhelming majority of elected positions, with the DAB taking the lead and followed by the pro-Beijing New Territories Associations of Societies. Table 4.20 demonstrates the evolution of the number of DC members who were also the members of the Chief Executive Election Committee from 1998 to 2017. Overall, the numbers increased from 42 in 1998 to 119 in 2011 and to 117 in 2017. The transformations were a testimony to the increase in the status of DC members, some of whom naturally aspired to become more influential players in the higher level of Hong Kong's political landscape.

Conclusion

Once DCs entered the HKSAR era, party politics have become far more fierce, serious, and competitive than ever before. The pro-Beijing DAB and the pro-democracy DP remained the two largest political parties occupying directly elected seats in DCs until November 2019, when the democrats

Table 4.19: The 2019 District Council Electoral Performance of District Council Members Who also came from the 2017 Chief Executive Election's New Territories District Councils Subsector

Group	Number of District Councilors from the 2017 Chief Executive Election Committee's Hong Kong and Kowloon District Councils Subsector (%)	Number of District Councilors who were successful re-elected in the 2019 District Council election (%)	Number of District Councilors who failed to be re-elected in the 2019 District Council elections (%)	Number of District Councilors who did not run for re-election in the 2019 District Council election (%)
DAB	20 (30%)	0 (0%)	16 (80%)	4 (20%)
New Territories Association of Societies (NTFS)	12 (20%)	2 (17%)	10 (83%)	0 (0%)
Independent	10 (17%)	3 (30%)	6 (60%)	1 (10%)
FTU	7 (12%)	1 (14%)	6 (86%)	0 (0%)
NPP	6 (10%)	0 (0%)	6 (100%)	0 (0%)
BPA	3 (5%)	0 (0%)	3 (100%)	0 (0%)
Professional Power	1 (2%)	0 (0%)	1 (100%)	0 (0%)
Roundtable	1 (2%)	1 (100%)	0 (0%)	0 (0%)
Total	60	7 (12%)	48 (80%)	5 (8%)

Table 4.20 Number of District Councilors as Members of the Chief Executive Election Committee, 1998–2017

	Hong Kong and Kowloon District Councils		New Territories District Councils		
	Number of Seats	Special Member(s)	Number of Seats	Special Member(s)	Total
1998	21	0	21	0	42
2000	21	0	21	0	42
2006	21	0	21	0	42
2011	57	2	60	2	119
2017	57	0	60	0	117

swept through 17 of the 18 DCs and captured a majority of the seats, including eventually the chairpersons of various councils. The pro-Beijing and pro-government DAB suffered most in two critical moments, the first in November 2003 after the July 1 protests against the maladministration of the Tung Chee-hwa government, and the second in November 2019 after several months of anti-extradition bill protests. These phenomena showed that whenever the HKSAR government became unpopular, the pro-Beijing and pro-establishment DAB suffered electorally. On the contrary, the pro-democracy groups, especially the DP, gained much from the unpopularity of the HKSAR administration. This political seesaw reflected the landscape of Hong Kong politics, namely a spectrum occupied by the democrats and anti-government force on one side and the pro-Beijing and pro-establishment front on the other side. In the middle are smaller pro-democracy and pro-Beijing groups, whose performance varied from time to time. The persistence of these smaller groups, including both pro-democracy and pro-Beijing forces, is a testimony to the fragmentation of electoral politics in the HKSAR. The pro-business groups, notably the Liberal Party, remain electorally weak in district elections, showing that they were politically spoiled in the colonial era when business elites were appointed to various political institutions and advisory bodies. This colonial legacy has continued in the HKSAR, meaning that pro-business groups and parties remained relatively weak in district elections. The options for the business groups are twofold, either staying independently or joining the pro-Beijing front. The latter is the most pragmatic option for most business elites, many of whom have joined the pro-Beijing DAB or formed their own business groups participating in district elections. In short, the electoral politics of DCs are characterized by the tug-of-war between the democrats and the pro-Beijing camp on the one hand, and by the fragmentation of all political groups on the other hand.

Notes

1 Sonny Shiu-Hing Lo, Steven Chung-fun Hung, and Jeff Hai-chi Loo, *The Dynamics of Peaceful and Violent Protests in Hong Kong: The Anti-Extradition Movement* (London: Palgrave, 2020).

2 *Oriental Daily*, October 1, 2020, p. A19.

3 *Ta Kung Pao*, January 4, 2005, p. A8.

5

Candidates, Voters, Parties and Groups in the 2019 District Council Elections

While the previous chapter has examined the evolution of electoral politics of District Councils (DCs) from the 1990s to 2019, this chapter focuses on the characteristics of candidates, voters, political groups, and political parties in the 2019 DC elections, which stood out as a political watershed in the history of the HKSAR—not only because of the overwhelming victory of the pan-democrats but also because of the candidates' strategies and voters' orientations.

The 2019 District Council Elections as a Watershed

The 2019 DC elections were a political turning point in several aspects. First, an unprecedented number of 1,090 candidates competed for 452 seats without any uncontested seat, unlike the previous elections during which uncontested seats were the highest in the years 1999 and 2003. Even the 2003 DC elections saw the active participation of 837 candidates, the average candidate per seat in 2003 was only 2.093, a figure less than the competitive situation in 2007, 2011, and 2015. With an average of 2.412 candidates competing for each seat in 2019, the DC elections in 2019 stood out as the most fiercely competitive district elections in the history of Hong Kong.

If the 2019 DC elections were the most competitive in Hong Kong's political history, a closer analysis in Table 5.2 shows that among the 452 seats, 305 of them witnessed two candidates competing against one another for each seat. For the rest of the 147 seats, 116 seats envisaged three

Table 5.1: Candidates Participating in the District Elections, 1994–2019

Year	1994	1999	2003	2007	2011	2015	2019
No. of Candidates	757	798	837	907	915	935	1090
No. of Seats	346	390	400	405	412	431	452
Average candidates per seat	2.188	2.046	2.093	2.240	2.221	2.169	2.412
No. of Uncontested Seats	50	76	76	41	76	66	0
No. of constituencies needing contests	296	314	324	364	336	365	452
No. of candidates needing contests	707	722	761	833	839	869	1090
Average candidates contesting after excluding uncontested seats	2.389	2.299	2.348	2.228	2.497	2.380	2.412

Source: Authors' compilation of open sources on election outcomes, 1994–2019.

candidates competing for each elected position. Under these circumstances, there were some candidates who were intentionally sent to these hotly contested constituencies to affect the chances of the other two candidates in the same constituency. Some candidates might be mobilized by the pro-Beijing front to portray as having a profile and platform similar to the pro-democracy candidate so as to confuse the voters, to minimize the chance of the targeted pro-democracy candidate to be elected, and to allow the pro-Beijing candidate to win. In Chinese, these candidates, who were usually sent or encouraged by the pro-Beijing front to reduce the votes gained by the target candidates, could be seen as those responsible for "cutting the votes" (鎅票, *kai piu* in Cantonese). Sending a candidate to "cut the votes" of an opponent needed a systematic strategy, such as analyzing the features of the targeted candidate, including the same gender, the same class background, and similar political orientation, and then portraying the candidate who can "cut the votes" of the opponent to grasp the support of voters. Quite often the third candidate who "descended" or sent into the constituency to "cut the votes" of the targeted democrat tended to be an independent, whose image had an advantage of confusing the voters, many of whom did not really realize that one of the three candidates did not have much chance to win but carried a "mission" of "stealing" the votes of a targeted candidate. Usually, the independent candidate who was encouraged to "cut the votes" of the target had lower chance of being directly elected. As a result, the pro-democracy candidates who were strong in their public appeal could still compete strongly with the pro-Beijing candidate, even if the so-called "independent" candidate came to compete and to reduce the votes gained by the pro-democracy candidate.

Table 5.2 illustrates that in the 2019 DC elections, there were 47 "independent" candidates without party affiliation competing in constituencies with three candidates. Indeed, not all 47 were candidates aiming at "cutting the votes" of the targeted candidates. Moreover, 42 constituencies saw two pro-democracy candidates competing among themselves, while only 27 constituencies witnessed the competition among pro-government candidates. Eight constituencies saw the competition of five candidates in each constituency—a testimony to the fierce contests. Moreover, 305 constituencies had two candidates competing against each other; 116 constituencies had three candidates in each constituency; and 23 constituencies saw four candidates competing among themselves. Hence, the degree of electoral competition among candidates was the highest in the 2019 DC elections.

Although there were some candidates being sent to "cut the votes" of targeted candidates, the impacts were minimal due to several reasons. First, some voters familiar with their own constituencies could guess which candidates were suddenly "descending downward" to compete with other candidates. Second, the pro-democracy camp itself was not homogeneous and witnessed internal competition even though independent candidates trying to cut into their votes suddenly appeared. In fact, the number of competitions among pan-democrats was minimized by having coordination prior to the elections. Such coordination was made traditionally by a political group named Power for Democracy. Still, compromises among all pro-democracy candidates could not be easily achieved. Eventually, some 20 constituencies saw the competition only among two democrats in each constituency. Third, sometimes the pro-democracy front also sent independents to compete with the pro-government candidates for the sake of making the pro-establishment candidates to encounter difficulties of being directly elected. Quite often, if a pro-government and/or pro-Beijing incumbent was strong in a constituency, the pan-democrats still sent a pro-democracy candidate or encouraged an independent to compete with the targeted candidate, thereby making him or her difficult to be directly elected. The purpose of sending an opponent to prevent the targeted candidate, either from pro-Beijing or pro-democracy side, from being automatically

Table 5.2: The Number of Competing Candidates in the 2019 District Council Elections with a Comparison of Constituencies Having Three Candidates

District/Seats/Ex-officio/ Number of Candidates			Number of Constituencies with 2, 3, 4 or 5 Competing Candidates					Competition Among Dominantly Pro-Democracy (PD), Pro-Government (PG), and Independent (I) Candidates		
Areas	Seats	Ex-officio	No.	2	3	4	5	2 PD	2 PG	I
A	15		35	10	5			2		3
B	13		29	10	3			3		
C	35		81	25	9	1			4	5
D	17		37	14	3				1	2
E	20		46	16	3		1			3
F	25		61	16	7	2		3	2	2
G	25		64	11	14			6	1	7
H	25		53	23	1	1		1		
J	40		87	35	3	2		2	1	
K	19	2	47	12	5	2		1	2	2
L	31	1	70	24	6	1		1	2	3
M	39	6	107	18	14	6	1	5	6	3
N	18	4	47	8	9	1		5	2	2
P	19	2	42	16	2	1				2
Q	29	2	73	19	7	1	2	5	1	1
R	41	1	107	23	13	3	2	5	2	6
S	31	1	80	18	10	1	2	2	2	6
T	10	8	24	7	2	1		1	1	
	452	27	1,090	305	116	23	8	42	27	47

Note: The categories of three candidates competing among themselves were 2 PD: two pro-democracy candidates and one pro-government candidate running in the constituency; 2 PG: two pro-government candidates and one pro-democracy candidate running; I: the constituency has one pro-democracy candidate, one pro-government candidate, and one independent candidate running.

Abbreviations: A: Central and Western; B: Wan Chai; C: Eastern; D: Southern; E: Yau Tsim Mong; F: Sham Shui Po; G: Kowloon City: H: Wong Tai Sin; J: Kwun Tong; K: Tsuen Wan; L: Tuen Mun; M: Yuen Long; N: Northern; P: Tai Po; Q: Sai Kung; R: Sha Tin; S: Kwai Tsing; T: Islands.

Source: "District Council Election 2019," Registration and Electoral Office, in website https://www.elections.gov.hk/dc2019/eng/intro_to_can.html, access date: October 1, 2020.

elected without any opposition was prominent in DC elections—a strategic move that became a commonplace when Hong Kong's political development was politicized, polarized, and ideologized. The ideologies between pro-government and pro-Beijing and pro-government on the one hand and pro-democracy and anti-extradition bill on the other hand were prominent in the 2019 DC elections, leading to sharp contests among the candidates for the support of voters.

Figure 5.1 shows that, compared with all the voter turnouts from 8:30 am to 10:30 pm in 1994, 1999, 2003, 2007, 2011, and 2015, the 2019 DC elections stood out as the most participatory in every hour. Voters went to cast their ballots actively in every hour from 7:30 am to 10:30 pm either voluntarily or being mobilized. Traditionally, Hong Kong voters were described by some commentators and analysts as relatively "apathetic," but such apathy was a myth in the 2019 DC elections. The total voter turnout of 71.23% was unprecedented in the history of Hong Kong's DC elections. For a district-level election that could achieve such a high voter turnout, it meant that many voters were determined to express their political preferences at the ballot boxes, especially in view of the ongoing protests in the HKSAR over the extradition bill. Although the government decided to withdraw the extradition bill in September 2019, the combination and peaceful and violent protests continued. Just days before the 2019 DC elections, the siege at the Polytechnic University witnessed the surrender and arrests of some 1,100 people—an event that perhaps stimulated many voters to come out to express their views over the entire protest movement, including how the government managed the extradition bill. In a sense, the 2019 DC elections provided voters a chance to vent their grievances and voice their views regardless of whether they were pro-government, pro-Beijing, pro-democracy, or pro-Hong Kong.

For a local-level election that reached 71.23% of the voter turnout, it was significant in many aspects. First, as mentioned above, the 2019 election provided a safety valve for the political system of Hong Kong, which underwent turmoil because of the government's introduction of the extradition bill. While some voters who voted for the democrats saw the bill as unacceptable and as endangering the human rights of Hong Kong people, who according to the pro-democracy propaganda could be sent to the mainland for trial under the extradition bill, other voters who supported the bill and the government believed that the bill had the good intention of

Figure 5.1: Comparing Voting Rate with Different Time Period, 1994–2019

Time	1994	1999	2003	2019
22:30	33.10%	44.10%	41.49%	71.23%
21:30	29.50%	40.68%	38.54%	69.04%
20:30	26.50%	37.33%	35.57%	66.50%
19:30	24.10%	34.36%	32.88%	63.65%
18:30	21.90%	31.35%	30.20%	60.36%
17:30	19.70%	28.30%	27.08%	56.42%
16:30	17.60%	25.27%	24.33%	52.14%
15:30	15.50%	22.27%	21.48%	47.26%
14:30	13.50%	19.38%	18.73%	42.26%
13:30	11.40%	16.27%	15.85%	36.89%
12:30	9.40%	13.44%	13.20%	30.98%
11:30	7.10%	10.12%	10.10%	24.37%
10:30	4.60%	6.59%	6.73%	17.43%
9:30	2.30%	3.30%	3.59%	10.41%
8:30	0.80%	1.06%	1.19%	3.82%

Legend: ■1994 ■1999 ■2003 ■2007 ■2011 ■2015 ■2019

Source: For the detailed and hourly voter turnout, see "Voter Turnout Rate," in https://www.elections.gov.hk/dc2019/eng/turnout.html, access date: October 11, 2020.

maintaining law and order in the HKSAR. Ironically, the bill's origin could be traced back to Chan Tong-kai, a young man who killed a Hong Kong girl in Taiwan, but he could stay in the HKSAR without being extradited to Taiwan as there was no extradition agreement between Hong Kong and Taiwan. The voters who voted against the pro-government and pro-Beijing candidates believed that the crux of the problem was not necessarily the Chan case, but that there was a lack of extradition arrangement between Hong Kong and Taiwan. These voters also believed that the extradition bill would endanger the rights of many Hong Kong people, because the bill's content was so broad that those Hongkongers who violated mainland law and who stayed in the HKSAR might be even sent to the mainland. Objectively speaking, the pro-democracy protestors exaggerated the detrimental impacts of the extradition bill on Hong Kong, while the government failed to explain the bill's content clearly to ordinary citizens.

As many Hong Kong people identified themselves as culturally Chinese but not with the ruling regime in the PRC, the extradition bill created huge public fear. Even though the government withdrew the bill in September, the controversy led to numerous protests. The police arrests of protestors at the Polytechnic University just days before the November 2019 DC election unintentionally politicized the voters, who were determined to voice their views over a whole range of issues, including the extradition bill, the violent protests, the arrests of demonstrators, the performance of the police, and the way in which the government handled the entire controversy. In short, the 2019 DC elections were abnormal because the voters cast their ballots based on their perception of territory-wide events instead of narrowly district-based issues.

Second, if the democrats could get 389 seats out of 452 directly elected seats (85% of the seats), it meant that the voters' verdict was clear.[1] In the 2015 DC election, the democrats grasped 104 seats or 24.1% of the total elected seats. The huge increase in the pan-democratic camp's elected seats showed that most voters believed that the HKSAR government performed a poor job in handling the extradition bill, and that most voters saw the pro-government and pro-Beijing candidates as representing the HKSAR government. Moreover, some voters questioned the police's performance in the entire protests, including how they dealt with the July 21 triad attacks at some passengers at the Yuen Long Mass Transit Railway (MTR). The HKSAR government led by Chief Executive Carrie Lam naturally sided with the police in handling the protests, including the tragedy of the July 21 attacks. Nonetheless, it was clear from the voters' verdict that many voters expressed their deep dissatisfaction with the HKSAR government.

Third, many pro-government heavyweight politicians were defeated—a testimony to the unpopularity of the HKSAR government. Except for the DAB chairlady Starry Lee, many pro-government candidates were soundly defeated, including Michael Tien, Alice Mak Mei-kuen, and Holden Chow. The poor result of the pro-government forces led to the central government's decision in January 2020 to remove the Liaison Office director, Wang Zhimin, who reportedly failed to assess and report accurately the situation of the HKSAR to Beijing. Even the director of the Hong Kong Macau Affairs Office (HKMAO), Zhang Xiaoming, had to be demoted to be the deputy director of the HKMAO in February 2020.[2] The significance of the 2019 DC election was clear: even the top PRC officials responsible for HKSAR affairs had to be removed or demoted. Perhaps in the minds of the top PRC authorities, Wang and Zhang mishandled the extradition controversy and must shoulder the responsibility for the unprecedentedly poor election results of the pro-Beijing and pro-government front in the 2019 DC election.

Fourth, due to the victory of the pan-democrats, they would likely grasp the 117 seats allocated to DC members in the 1,200-member Chief Executive Election Committee in 2022. This meant that the PRC authorities would likely encounter difficulties to reduce the influence of the pan-democrats in the 2022 Chief Executive election. Moreover, in the September 2021 Legislative Council (LegCo) elections, which were postponed due to the continuous outbreak of COVID-19, the pan-democratic DC members would be able to nominate candidates to run for the five LegCo superseats for DC candidates, who would be nominated by DC members and directly elected by the Hong Kong voters. Even though the 2021 LegCo elections were delayed, the victory of the pan-democrats was posing a serious threat to not only the PRC authorities in controlling the selection of candidates in the 2022 Chief Executive election but also the pro-Beijing forces in nominating candidates to run for the five LegCo superseats in the 2021 LegCo direct elections. This political threat explained why the central government in Beijing decided to turn the political situation in the HKSAR upside down by promulgating the National Security Law through the SCNPC in late June 2020. As will be discussed in Chapter Eight, the National Security Law and its implementation had immediate impacts on the operation of DCs.

Table 5.3 shows the comparisons and contrasts between the elected candidates and the defeated ones. The average age of democrats who were nominated to run in the election was 35.24 years old, while the average age of being elected was 33.76 years old. On the other hand, the average age of pro-establishment candidates who were nominated to run in the election was 42.14 years old, whereas the average age of the pro-establishment candidates being elected was 40.95 years old. Hence, the pro-government and pro-Beijing candidates were on average much older than the democrats. The relative youthfulness of the pro-democracy candidates was understandable, for many candidates were unhappy with the extradition bill and the HKSAR government's performance and they decided to participate in the 2019 DC election. Moreover, 68 pro-democracy female candidates were elected, while only 15 pro-establishment female candidates were elected. Only 16

Table 5.3: Comparing the Ages of the Elected Candidates with Defeated Candidates

Age	D Elected	D Defeated	E Elected	E Defeated	Female D Elected	Female D defeated	Female E Elected	Female E Defeated
21	7				1			
22	7	8		1		2		
23	12	3		5	4			2
24	13	4		4	4			1
25	16	4		5	2	1		2
26	20	6		5	1	1		3
27	21	3	1	10	4	1	1	5
28	27	7	1	16	1	2		1
29	12	2	1	9	1		1	4
30	12	6		16	1	1		2
31	19	2	2	11	2			3
32	15	4	2	13	4	2	1	1
33	12	3	3	12	2	2	1	1
34	12	2	2	18	2			4
35	11	1	2	14				1
36	9	2	4	19	3			3
37	12	2	3	14				2
38	11	1		7	2			1
39	13	2	2	16	2		2	4
40	6		3	14	3		2	3
41	5	1	4	13	1		1	
42	2	1	1	9				1
43	7	3	1	14				4
44	7	3		11				2
45	4	2	2	11	2	1	1	4
46	1	1	3	5				1
47	6	3		7	1			2
48	3	2	1	1			1	1
49	2	1		4				1
50	2	1	1	4			1	1
51	4	1	1	5				
52	4	1	4	6				1
53	4	2	1	5	3	1	1	1
54	3	1		7				2

Table 5.3 Continued

Age	D Elected	D Defeated	E Elected	E Defeated	Female D Elected	Female D defeated	Female E Elected	Female E Defeated
55	3		2	4	1			
56	3	2		5	1			
57	3		1	13	1			2
58	3			5	1			1
59	7		2	6	1		1	
60	5	1	2	5	1			
61	6		2	6			1	
62	4	1	1	5	4			
63	2	2	2	4				
64	1			1	1			1
65	1	1	1	4				
66	1	1	1	6				
67		1	1	1				
68		1		3				
69				4				
70	1							
71	1			1				
72				2				
73								
74								
75								
76								
77	1							
78								
79				1				
Not available	26	9	2	51	11	2	0	20
total count	389	104	62	438	68	16	15	88

Note: D denotes democrats; E denotes pro-establishment.

Average age of democrats nominated = 35.24; average age of establishment nominated = 42.14; average age of democrats elected = 33.76; average age of establishment elected = 40.95.

Table 5.4: Participation of Female and Male Candidates in District Elections, 1982–2019

Area	Hong Kong Island				Kowloon				New Territories				Overall			
year	FP	FE	MP	ME	FP	FE	MP	ME	FP	FE	MP	ME	FP	FE	MP	ME
1982	8	3	72	23	7	1	140	49	4	1	170	55	19	5	382	127
1985	14	8	94	45	12	5	160	89	6	3	217	90	32	16	471	224
1988	19	10	85	47	17	10	150	86	15	6	186	103	51	26	421	236
1991	14	7	86	52	18	7	125	84	15	7	208	116	47	21	419	252
1994	25	11	139	62	23	10	217	101	47	14	303	146	95	35	659	309
1999	28	15	124	65	37	16	207	103	64	25	338	168	129	56	669	336
2003	30	16	127	64	40	22	224	99	75	30	343	173	145	68	694	336
2007	38	19	133	61	47	20	214	98	79	37	392	169	164	76	739	328
2011	34	20	133	61	37	20	220	100	91	39	375	174	162	79	728	335
2015	42	17	129	62	48	20	224	98	85	38	404	185	175	75	757	345
2019	55	27	127	53	55	25	256	110	104	33	493	204	214	85	876	367

Note: FP = Number of females participating in elections; FE = Number of females who were directly elected; MP = Number of males participating in elections; ME = Number of males who were directly elected.

pro-democracy female candidates were defeated, but 88 pro-establishment female counterparts were defeated.

Table 5.4 demonstrates the political participation of female and male candidates in DC elections from 1982 to 2019. It shows that the trend pointed to an increase in both female and male candidates participating in elections and getting directly elected. In all the three big constituencies in Hong Kong Island, Kowloon, and the New Territories, female candidates increased in the number of participants and of being elected. While 19 female candidates were nominated and five of them were elected in 1982, the number increased drastically to 129 and 56 respectively in 1999, and then to 214 and 85 respectively in 2019. Similarly, the same pattern could be seen in the male candidates. The number of male candidates being nominated and elected were 382 and 127 respectively, but the number rose to 876 and 367 respectively. Overall, district boards and later councils could stimulate the political participation of many females and males as candidates in elections.

In terms of the success rate of female candidates who won DC elections from 1982 to 2019, Table 5.4 shows that their success rate did increase from only 3.8% in 1982 to 14.3% in 1999, and from 16.8% in 2003 to 18.8% in

Table 5.4: Success Rate of Female Candidates in District Council Elections, 1982–2019

Area	Hong Kong Island			Kowloon			New Territories			Total Average		
Year	SR	PR	%seats	SR	PR	%seats	SR	PR	%seats	SR	PR	%seats
1982	0.375	0.1	**11.5%**	0.1429	0.0476	**0.7%**	0.25	0.023	**1.8%**	0.2632	0.0474	**3.8%**
1985	0.5714	0.1296	**15.1%**	0.4167	0.0698	**3.0%**	0.5	0.0269	**3.2%**	0.5	0.0636	**6.7%**
1988	0.5263	0.1827	**17.5%**	0.5882	0.1018	**6.3%**	0.4	0.0746	**5.5%**	0.5098	0.1081	**9.9%**
1991	0.5	0.14	**11.9%**	0.3889	0.1259	**5.3%**	0.4667	0.0673	**5.7%**	0.4468	0.1009	**7.7%**
1994	0.44	0.1524	**15.1%**	0.4348	0.0958	**4.4%**	0.2979	0.1343	**8.8%**	0.3684	0.126	**10.2%**
1999	0.5357	0.1842	**18.8%**	0.4324	0.1516	**7.2%**	0.3906	0.1592	**13.0%**	0.4341	0.1617	**14.3%**
2003	0.5333	0.1911	**20.0%**	0.55	0.1515	**8.9%**	0.4	0.1794	**14.8%**	0.469	0.1728	**16.8%**
2007	0.5	0.2222	**23.8%**	0.4255	0.1801	**8.6%**	0.4684	0.1677	**18.0%**	0.4634	0.1816	**18.8%**
2011	0.5882	0.2036	**24.7%**	0.5405	0.144	**8.3%**	0.4286	0.1953	**18.3%**	0.4877	0.182	**19.1%**
2015	0.4048	0.2456	**21.5%**	0.4167	0.1765	**8.2%**	0.4471	0.1738	**17.0%**	0.4286	0.1878	**17.9%**
2019	0.4909	0.3022	**33.8%**	0.4545	0.1768	**8.9%**	0.3173	0.1742	**13.9%**	0.3972	0.1963	**18.8%**

Note: SR refers to success rate = number of women elected/number of women nominated; PR denotes participation rate = number of women nominated/number of persons nomination; % of seats refers to the percentage of seats occupied = number of women elected/number of persons elected.

Sources: Reports on the District Councils elections in 1999, 2003, 2007, 2011 and 2015; *A Compilation of the Information on Hong Kong Elections* (Hong Kong: Hong Kong Institute of Asia-Pacific Studies, the Chinese University of Hong Kong, 1996, 2001, 2005 and 2015). Also see District Council Elections 2015, https://www.elections.gov.hk/dc2015/chi/intro_to_can.html, and https://www.elections.gov.hk/dc2015/chi/results_hk.html?1527837316296, District Council Elections 2019, https://www.elections.gov.hk/dc2019/eng/intro_to_can.html, and https://www.elections.gov.hk/dc2019/eng/results.html, access date: October 1, 2020.

2019. It can be said that their success rate increased steadily within 37 years, but not drastically. The increase in success rate had regional differences; the New Territories envisaged over an eightfold increase; Kowloon also witnessed a similar eightfold increase; and the Hong Kong Island showed a twofold increase. But traditionally, the Hong Kong Island has seen a larger success rate of female candidates than the New Territories and Kowloon. Perhaps the middle-class voters and the composition of voters in the Hong Kong Island have traditionally been more receptive to female candidates. Moreover, pro-Beijing, pro-government, and pro-democracy groups and parties usually fielded female candidates to appeal for the support of voters on the Hong Kong Island.

Table 5.5 compares the age range of pro-democracy and pro-establishment candidates in the 2019 DC elections. Clearly, there were far more pro-democracy candidates than pro-establishment ones who belonged to the age groups of 21 to 25 and 26 to 30. The pro-establishment

Table 5.5: Comparing the Age Range of Pro-Democracy and Pro-Establishment Candidates in the 2019 District Council Elections

Age range	Democrats	Establishment	Democrats %	Establishment %
21–25	74	15	16.16%	3.36%
26–30	116	59	25.33%	13.20%
31–35	81	98	17.69%	21.92%
36–40	58	82	12.66%	18.34%
41–45	35	66	7.64%	14.77%
46–50	22	26	4.80%	5.82%
51–55	23	40	5.02%	8.95%
56–60	24	39	5.24%	8.72%
61–65	10	26	2.18%	5.82%
>65	7	20	1.53%	4.47%
Total	450	471	100%	100%

Note: The ages of some candidates were not available online and therefore the number of candidates counted does not equal to the total number of candidates in this Table.

Figure 5.2: Comparing the Age Range of Pro-Democracy and Pro-Establishment Candidates in the 2019 District Council Elections

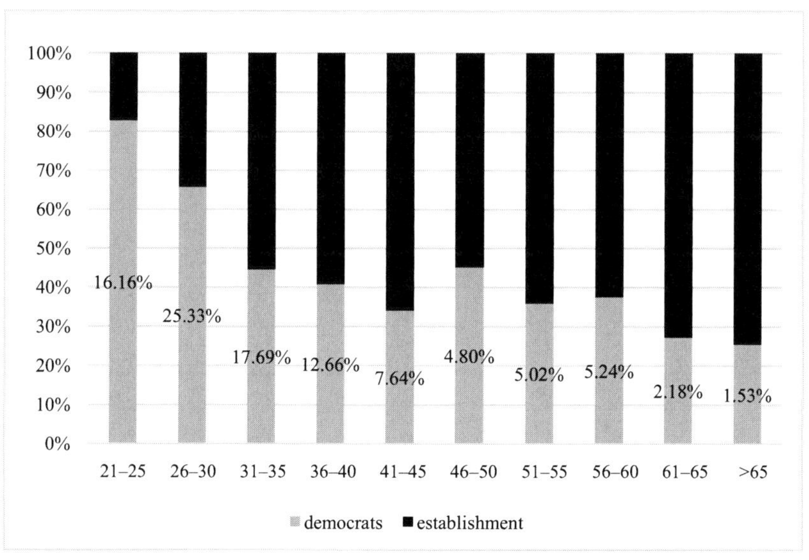

Table 5.6: Age Range of the Nominated and Elected Pro-Democracy and Pro-Establishment Candidates in the 2019 District Council Elections

Age Group	Democrats Nominated	Pro-Establishment Nominated	Pro-Democracy Elected	Pro-Establishment Elected
21–30	190	74	147	3
31–40	139	161	120	23
41–50	57	92	39	13
51–60	47	74	39	13
60 above	25	46	18	8
Not Available	35	53	26	2
Total	493	500	389	62

Figure 5.3: Age Range of the Nominated and Elected Pro-Democracy and Pro-Establishment Candidates

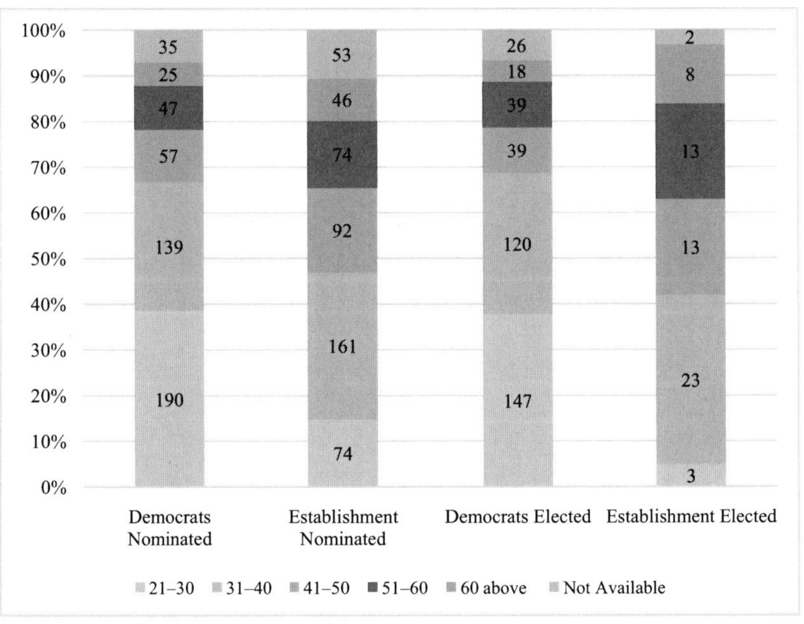

candidates were mostly from the age groups of 31 to 35, 36 to 40, and 41 to 45. In general, as shown in Figure 5.2, pro-establishment candidates were much older than pro-democracy ones, leading to a problem that they tended to be less appealing and attractive to many young voters in the 2019 DC elections. The phenomenon also showed that the pro-establishment camp failed to groom enough young candidates to compete with the pro-democracy front in the 2019 DC elections.

Table 5.6 shows the age range of the nominated and elected pro-democracy and pro-establishment candidates in the 2019 DC elections. Again, since the pro-democracy candidates were much younger than the pro-establishment counterparts, the former got more young candidates aged between 21 to 40 being nominated and elected. Quite alarmingly, although the pro-democracy camp nominated less candidates than the pro-establishment counterpart in the age groups between 41 and 60 and above, the democrats managed to get more candidates in these groups directly elected (Figure 5.3). The result demonstrated a resounding failure of the pro-establishment camp in winning the hearts and minds of most young and old voters.

The Pro-Establishment Strongholds

If we analyze the strongholds maintained by the pro-establishment forces, Table 5.7 shows that they could perform better in the constituencies with high income households, such as the Peak and Jardine Hill, where many rich voters tended to be pro-*status quo*. Moreover, the pro-establishment candidates did better in the new public housing estates, the reconstructed public housing units, the Fujianese community and areas where the police dormitories were located. In those "purely" rural areas, the pro-establishment candidates were expected to perform better than the pro-democracy counterparts. However, Table 5.8 shows that the pro-democracy forces could outperform the pro-establishment camp in seven out of the latter's eleven expected strongholds. Hence, the pro-establishment camp suffered a severe setback in the 2019 DC election.

Even in constituencies where police dormitories were located, and where voters were expected to support the police rather than the protesters in the latter half of 2019, the election results were more complex than conventional wisdom assumed. Table 5.9 shows that in the nineteen

Table 5.7: Constituencies that belonged to the Strongholds of Pro-Establishment Camp

Category	Number of constituencies	Name of Constituencies
Rural areas	11	Shap Pat Heung North, Ha Village, Ping Shan North, San Tin, Pat Heung North, Pat Heung South, Sheung Shui Village Suburb, Sha Ta, Lantau Island, Ping Chau and Hei Ling Chau, Lamma Island and Po Toi Island
High income	8	Peak, Jardine Hill, Lok Wood, Stubbs Road, Braemar Hill, Hoi Wan, Kowloon Station, Kowloon Tong
New Public Housing and Reconstructed Public Housing	6+2	Kai Tak North, Kai Tak East, Kai Tak Central and South, Kwun Tong Tai On, On Tat, Yan Tin, So Uk, Ngau Tau Kok Upper Estate
Constituencies that clashed with pro-democracy forces	6	Ai Chun, Shing Fook, Do Shin, Wan Po North, Tai Yee and Tai Pak Tin West
Fujianese community	2	Mount Parker, Wo Fu
Police Dormitories	2	Sheung Shun, Yau Chiu
Other constituencies with great differences in the strengths between pro-establishment and pro-democracy forces	24	Ying Tao, Nam Cheong Central, To Kwa Wan North, Jordan Valley, Sau Mau Ping South, Lam Tin, Shing Hong, Choi Tak, Sau Mau Ping Central, Kwong Tak, Yau Tong West, King Hing, Cheung Hong, Mong Kok West, Fook Loi, Aberdeen Estate, Lok Man, Shek Wai Kok, Po Tin, Southern, Loong Shing, Hoi Sum, Tsuen Wan Suburb, Wan Po South
Others	2	Cheung Heng and Hung Hom
Total	**63**	

Source: Choi Chi-keung and Chan Chun-man, "Which districts were defended by the pro-establishment forces?," *Ming Pao*, December 6, 2019, in https://news.mingpao.com/, access date: November 1, 2020.

Table 5.8: Rural Areas where Pro-Establishment Forces maintained their Strongholds

Constituencies	Pro-establishment camp	Pro-democracy force
Ping Shan Central	48.06%	51.94%
Queen's Hill	36.86%	53.28%
Sai Kung North	41.84%	58.16%
Pak Sha Wan	42.92%	57.08%
Sai Kung Islands	42.19%	57.81%
Hang Hau East	41.77%	49.57%
Hang Hau West	40.22%	59.78%
Pat Heung North	66.09%	33.91%
Sheung Shui Suburb	56.56%	43.44%
Ping Chau and Hei Ling Chau	57.83%	42.17%
Lamma Island and Po Toi Island	50.78%	49.22%
Average percentage of votes gained	**47.57%**	**50.63%**

Source: Choi Chi-keung and Chan Chun-man, "Which districts were defended by the pro-establishment forces?," *Ming Pao*, December 6, 2019, in https://news.mingpao.com/, access date: November 1, 2020.

Table 5.9: Performance of Pro-Establishment and Pro-Democracy Camps in Constituencies at where Police Dormitories were located

Constituencies	Pro-establishment	Pro-democracy	Police and Disciplinary Forces Dormitories concerned
Central district	44.91%	55.09%	Married police dormitory
Chui Wan	44.37%	55.63%	Married police dormitory in Chai Wan
Wong Chuk Hang	42.07%	57.93%	Married police dormitory in Aberdeen
Tai Kok Tsui North	47.84%	52.16%	West Kowloon Disciplinary Forces Dormitory
Loong Tsui	47.66%	52.34%	Wong Tai Sin Disciplinary Forces Dormitory
Choi Wan East	48.23%	51.77%	Fung Shing Street Disciplinary Forces Dormitory
Sheung Shun	63.14%	36.86%	Shun Lee Disciplinary Forces Dormitory
Chun Cheung	37.79%	62.21%	Police Dormitory
Yau Chui	46.82%	42.15%	Police Dormitory
Lok Wah South	49.27%	50.73%	Sau Mau Ping Disciplinary Forces Dormitory
San Shing	43.68%	56.32%	Naval Police Sergeants Dormitory in Tai Lam
Yuet Woo	36.65%	63.35%	Tuen Mun Police Dormitory
Siu Hong	43.72%	56.28%	Castle Peak Government Employees Dormitory
Fung Nian	46.35%	53.65%	Married Police Dormitory in Yuen Long
Yue Tai	46.88%	53.12%	Sheung Shui Disciplinary Force Dormitory
Upper Tai Wo Hau	42.79%	57.21%	Police Dormitory
Kwai Chung Estate South	43.06%	55.60%	Police Dormitory
Cho Yiu	48.52%	51.48%	Lai King Disciplinary Forces Dormitory
Chui Yee	18.44%	52.52%	Tsing Yi Married Police Dormitory
Average votes gained	**44.04%**	**53.35%**	

Source: Choi Chi-keung and Chan Chun-man, "Which districts were defended by the pro-establishment forces?," *Ming Pao*, December 6, 2019, in https://news.mingpao.com/, access date: November 1, 2020.

constituencies where police and disciplinary forces dormitories were located, only two of them — Sheung Shun and Yau Chui — witnessed the victory of pro-establishment candidates. All other 17 constituencies saw the victory of pro-democracy candidates — a phenomenon showing that the voters in all these constituencies were not necessarily pro-government, pro-police, and pro-Beijing. Many voters cast their ballots for the pro-democracy candidates for a variety of reasons, including the likelihood of putting the blame of the violent protests on the government, expressing their anger at the unbalanced use of force by the police toward the protestors, and venting their grievances on the pro-establishment candidates. Because police and disciplinary dormitories occupied only parts of the residential areas in each of the constituency, which was complex in class background and composed of a mixture of private buildings, public housing estates, and civil servants' dormitories, the presence of police and disciplinary forces dormitories alone could not adequately mobilize their members and relatives to vote for pro-government candidate to defeat the pro-democracy opponents.

The Performance of Political Groups and Parties in the 2019 Elections

Table 5.10 shows the elected DC members of political groups and parties in 2015 and 2019. For the pro-government forces, except for two groups, namely the Business Professional Alliance (BPA) and the Kowloon Federation of Associations (KFA), all other groups and parties, including the DAB, suffered a drastic decline in the percentage of votes share. The drastic decline of the DAB from having 119 elected candidates in 2015 to only 21 elected ones in 2019 was shocking, like the Federation of Trade Unions (FTU) whose elected candidates dropped from 27 to 5. On the contrary, the pro-democracy forces gained tremendously in the 2019 elections. The Democratic Party envisaged a gain from 43 elected candidates to 91 elected ones; the Civic Party increased the number from 10 to 32; the Neo-Democrats rose from 15 to 19; Team Chu Hoi-dick rose from zero to 7; the Labor Party increased the number from 3 to 7; the Shatin Community from zero to 15; the Tai Po Alliance from 6 to 16; and the Tuen Mun Ten Brothers from zero to 8. Many new pro-democracy and district-based groups emerged in the 2019 DC elections, defeating pro-government and pro-Beijing candidates prominently.

Table 5.11 shows the success rate of the pro-establishment camp in the 2019 DC elections. It shows that while the DAB and FTU performed poorly, the higher successful rates went to the Liberal Party and the Federation of Public Housing Estates. The New People Party led by Regina Ip was wiped out in DC election, same as the Shatin-based Civil Force (CF). It was noteworthy that the CF, as one of the united front groups groomed by the PRC officials in the HKSAR and as one of the auxiliary groups assisting the DAB, failed to grasp any seat in the 2019 DC elections. Interestingly, the district federations formed by the pro-Beijing forces and backed up by the Liaison Office, notably the Hong Kong Island Federation and the

Table 5.10: Elected Members of Political Groups and Parties in 2015 and 2019

Political Groups	Nominated Candidates in 2015	Elected	Votes gained	% of votes share	Seats before election	Nominated Candidates in 2019	Elected	Votes gained	% of votes share
Pro-Establishment									
DAB	171	119	309,262	21.39%	116	181	21	492,042	16.78%
FTU	48	27	88,292	6.11%	27	43	5	128,796	4.39%
Liberal Party	20	9	25,157	1.74%	8	11	5	27,684	0.94%
BPA	16	10	27,452	1.90%	21	25	3	66,504	2.27%
FPHE	1	1	3,457	0.24%	1	7	3	19,495	0.66%
Roundtable	8	8	16,761	1.16%	8	13	2	26,655	0.19%
New People Party	42	26	75,793	5.24%	13	28	0	79,975	2.73%
Civil Force	21	11	33,298	2.03%	11	18	0	53,438	1.82%
NCF	8	6	15,482	1.07%	6	5	0	12,962	0.44%
HKIF	25	18	32,109	7.21%	18	15	3	38,459	1.31%
KFA	8	5	10,135	0.70%	5	18	2	44,872	1.53%
KWND	27	18	47,747	3.30%	18	7	1	18,933	0.64%
Positive Synergy	24	20	45,640	3.16%	20	19	3	61,630	1.92%
NTAS	20	14	29,123	2.01%	14	20	0	50,125	1.72%
Professional Power	10	4	32,663	2.26%	4	7	3	16,531	0.56%
Pro-Democracy									
Democratic Party	95	43	196,068	13.56%	37	99	91	362,275	12.36%
Civic Party	25	10	52,346	3.62%	12	36	32	141,713	4.83%
Neo-Democrats	16	15	42,148	2.92%	13	20	19	87,923	3.00%
ADPL	26	18	55,275	3.82%	12	21	19	77,099	2.63%
Team Chu Hoi-dick	1	0	1,482	0.10%	0	9	7	31,369	1.07%
Labor Party	12	3	23,029	1.59%	3	7	7	28,036	0.96%
NWSC	6	5	16,105	1.11%	2	4	4	16,176	0.55%
Civic Passion	6	0	3,006	0.21%	0	5	2	14,326	0.49%
LSD	5	0	6,526	0.45%	0	3	2	8,384	0.29%
People Power	9	0	11,503	0.80%	0	2	1	8,149	0.28%
TKO Livelihood	8	3	15,223	1.05%	3	10	5	26,352	0.90%

Table 5.10 Continued

Political Groups	Nominated Candidates in 2015	Elected	Votes gained	% of votes share	Seats before election	Nominated Candidates in 2019	Elected	Votes gained	% of votes share
Shatin Community*	–	–	26,734	1.85%	11	17	15	70,640	2.41%
Tai Po Alliance	7	6	19,064	1.32%	6	17	16	69,600	2.37%
TM Ten Brothers	–	–	–	–	–	10	8	37,977	1.30%

Source: Authors' tabulation from open sources on the election results in 2015 and 2019.

Note: DAB—Democratic Alliance for the Betterment and Progress of Hong Kong; FTU—Hong Kong Federation of Trade Unions; BPA—Business and Professional Alliance for Hong Kong; FPHE—Federation of Public Housing Estates; NCF—New Century Forum; HKIF—Hong Kong Island Federation; KFA—Kowloon Federation of Associations; KWND—Kowloon West New Dynamic; NTAS - New Territories Association of Societies; APPL—Hong Kong Association for Democracy and People's Livelihood; NWSC—Neighborhood and Worker's Service Centre; LSD - League of Social Democrats; TKO Livelihood—Concern Group For Tseung Kwan O People's Livelihood; Tai Po Alliance—Tai Po Democratic Alliance; TM ten brothers—Tuen Mun Ten Brothers. *Shatin Community was formed after the 2015 District Council election.

Table 5.11: Performance of the Pro-Establishment Camp in the 2019 District Councils Elections

Political Groups	Nominated Candidates in 2019	Elected	Votes gained	Votes percent share	Successful Rate
DAB	181	21	492,042	16.78%	11.60%
FTU	43	5	128,796	4.39%	11.63%
Liberal Party	11	5	27,684	0.94%	45.45%
BPA	25	3	66,504	2.27%	12.00%
FPHE	7	3	19,495	0.66%	42.86%
Roundtable	13	2	26,655	0. 19%	15.38%
New People Party	28	0	79,975	2.73%	0.00%
Civil Force	18	0	53,438	1.82%	0.00%
NCF	5	0	12,962	0.44%	0.00%
HKIF	15	3	38,459	1.31%	20.00%
KFA	18	2	44,872	1.53%	11.11%
KWND	7	1	18,933	0.64%	14.29%
Positive Synergy	19	3	61,630	1.92%	15.79%
NTAS	20	0	50,125	1.72%	0.00%
Professional Power	7	3	16,531	0.56%	42.86%

Source: Authors' tabulation of the open sources on the election results.

Table 5.12: Electoral Performance of Pro-government Chairs and Vice-Chairs of the 2015–2018 Councils in the 2019 District Councils Elections

District	Position	Name	Affiliate	Result in 2019
Central and Western	Chairman	Yip Wing-shing	HKIF	Defeated
	Vice-chairman	Chan Hok-fung	DAB	Defeated
Wan Chai	Chairman	Ng Kam-chun	HKIF	Withdrawal
	Vice-chairman	Jennifer Chow	Dab	Defeated
Eastern	Chairman	Wong Kin-bun	DAB	Withdrawal
	Vice-chairman	Chiu Chi-keung	FTU	Defeated
Southern	Chairman	Chu Hing-hung	HKIF	Defeated
	Vice-chairman	Chan Fu-ming	HKIF	Defeated
Yau Tsim Mong	Chairman	Yip Ao-tung	DAB	Defeated
	Vice-chairman	Wong Shu-ming	BPA/ KWND	Defeated
Sham Shui Po	Chairman	Cheung Wing-sum	KWND	Withdrawal
	Vice-chairman	Chan Wai-ming	DAB	Defeated
Kowloon City	Chairman	Poon Kwok-wah	DAB	Re-elected
	Vice-chairman	Jaw Hui-hung	BPA/ KWND	Re-elected
Wong Tai Sin	Chairman	Lee Tak-hong	DAB	Defeated
	Vice-chairman	Lai Wing-ho	DAB	Defeated
Kwun Tong	Chairman	Chan Chun-bun	KFA	Defeated
	Vice-chairman	Hung Kam-yin	DAB	Defeated
Tsuen Wan	Chairman	Wong Wai-kit	NTAS	Defeated
	Vice-chairman	Chan Sung-yip	HYK	Re-elected*
Tuen Man	Chairman	Leung Kin-man	DAB	Defeated
	Vice-chairman	Lee Hong-sum	FTU	Re-elected
Yuen Long	Chairman	Shum Ho-kit	HYK	Re-elected
	Vice-chairman	Wong Wai-shun	DAB	Defeated
Northern	Chairman	So Sai-chi	DAB	Defeated
	Vice-chairman	Lee Kwok-fung	NKAS/HYK	Re-elected*
Tai Po	Chairman	Wong Pik-kiu	DAB	Defeated
	Vice-chairman	Cheng Chun-ping	DAB	Defeated
Sai Kung	Chairman	Ng Si-fook	DAB	Defeated
	Vice-chairman	Ling Man-hoi	DAB	Withdrawal
Sha Tin	Chairman	Ho Hau-cheung	NPP/CF	Withdrawal
	Vice-chairman	Thomas Pang	DAB	Withdrawal
Kwai Shing	Chairman	Law King-shing	DAB	Defeated
	Vice-chairman	Chow Yik-hei	Independent	Defeated
Islands	Chairman	Chow Yuk-tong	HYK	Re-elected*
	Vice-chairman	Yu Hon-kwan	HYK	Re-elected

Notes: DAB — Democratic Alliance for the Betterment and Progress of Hong Kong, HKIF — Hong Kong Island Federation, KWND - Kowloon West New Dynamic, BPA — Business and Professionals Alliance for Hong Kong, KFA — Kowloon Federation of Associations, PS — Positive Synergy, NTAS — New Territories Association of Societies, HYK — Heung Yee Kuk,

Remark: * Ex-official member of the Rural Committee

**Table 5.13: Electoral Performance of DAB Legislators
in the 2019 District Council Elections**

Constituency	DAB Legislators' votes gained		Competitors' votes gained and their political affiliation	
Sai Wan	Cheung Kwok-kwan	2,494	Pang Kai-ho (Victoria Coordination)	3,289
Nam Cheong North	Cheng Wing-shun	1,747	Lao Ka-hang (CP)	2,193
			Wong Hiu-shing	55
To Kwa Wan North	Starry Lee Wai-king	1,881	Leung Kwok-hung (LSD)	1,538
Kwong Tak	Or Chong-shing	4,514	Tam Tak-chi (PP)	4,327
Yan Shing	Lau Kwok-fun	4,329	Lam Yuk-ching (ND)	5,939
Tung Chung South	Holden Chow Ho-ding	3,619	Wong Chun-yeung	5,049
			Lai Wing-on	183
			Lau Wing-yin	87

Source: "Election Results of 2019 District Council Elections," Registration and Electoral Office, in https://www.elections.gov.hk/dc2019/eng/results_hk.html, access date: November 15, 2020.

Kowloon Federation of Associations, managed to get a few elected seats. The results showed that in a political tsunami like the 2019 DC elections, which were held shortly after the police siege at the Polytechnic University of Hong Kong where protesters fought against the police fiercely, violently and illegally, most of the voters appeared to believe that the government did a poor job in handling the extradition bill. As such, most voters did not even vote for the pro-government candidates in the DC elections.

Table 5.12 demonstrates the poor performance of the pro-government elites, who were elected as the chairpersons and vice-chairpersons of DCs after the 2015 DC elections, and who were mostly defeated. Six withdrew from participation in the 2019 DC elections. Most incumbents were defeated, while a minority were elected in 2019. The phenomenon of having pro-government and pro-Beijing elites occupying an overwhelming majority of chairpersons and vice-chairpersons of DCs in 2015 was a thing of the past. The landslide victory of the pan-democrats in the 2019 DC elections led to a reverse phenomenon.

Table 5.13 shows the unsatisfactory performance of DAB legislators in the 2019 DC elections, during which only chairlady Starry Lee and Or Chong-shing managed to get re-elected. Starry Lee narrowly defeated leftwing democrat Leung Kwok-hung, who did little work in the constituency but who got 1,538 votes easily. All others, including vice-chairperson Cheung Kwok-kwan, rising stars Cheng Wing-shun and Holden Chow, and Lau Kwok-fun were all defeated. Table 5.14 illustrates

Table 5.14: Elected Members of the Democratic Alliance for Betterment and Progress of Hong Kong and their Competitors in the 2019 District Council Elections

Constituency	Elected members of DAB and votes gained		Competitors' votes gained and their political affiliation	
Mount Parker	Lee Ching-har	2,664	Lai Yik-ming	2,491
Kowloon Station	Hung Chiu-wah	1,928	Lo Wing-yin (DP)	1,821
			Yung Hei-chi	82
Nam Cheong Central	Lau Pui-yuk	1,640	Lam Sin Tung (Sha Shui Po Concern Group)	1,538
So Uk	Ho Kwan-chau	2,650	Chan Ming-kei (ADPL)	2,522
			Lam Pui-man	51
Lung Shing	Ng Po-keung*	1,983	Fung Tat-chun	1,884
			Fong Ngai-yin	101
Hoi Sham	Pun Kwok-wah*	2,916	Tung Kai-man	2,890
To Kwa Wan North	Starry Lee Wai-king*	1,881	Leung Kwok-hung (LSD)	1,538
Hung Hom	Lam Tak-shing	1,779	Kwan Siu-lun	1,524
Choi Tak	Tam Siu-cheuk	2,882	Lam Tsz-kuen	2,156
Jordan Valley	Ngan Man-yu	3,694	Lam Ka-lok	3,560
Sau Mau Ping Central	Cheung Pui-kong	4,176	So Wai-yeung	3,872
On Tat	Hsu Yau-wai	3,499	Siu Ho-yin	2,393
			Lau Pak-yuen	43
			Lee Seng-chang	38
Kwong Tak	Or Chong-shing*	4,514	Tam Tak-chi	4,327
Upper Ngau Tau Kok Estate	Leung Tang-fung	3,247	Cheng Chun-wah	3,093
Yan Tin	Lai Ka-man	2,203	Lo Wai-ming (DP)	1,865
			Wong Chi-chun (Round Table)	611
Sha Ta	Ko Wai-kei	3,143	Choy Yuk-wai (Northern Coalition Line)	2,242
Di Yee	Lam Kong-kwan	1,923	Tse Kit-wing (Sha Tin Community)	1,666
			Liu Qing (DP)	830
Tai Pak Tin West	Kwok Fu-yung	2,449	Szeto Kong-sun	2,106
			Ho Cheuk-wai	544
Shing Hong	Leung Kar-ming	3,531	Chiu Po-kam	3,417
Cheung Hang	Lo Yuen-ting	3,759	Yim Ho-yuen (Civic Passion)	3,270
Lamma & Po Toi	Lau Shun-ting	1,003	Chui Caan-jing	972

Source: "Election Results of 2019 District Council Elections," Registration and Electoral Office, in https://www.elections.gov.hk/dc2019/eng/results_hk.html, access date: November 15, 2020.

the performance of those elected DAB candidates in the 2019 DC elections and their opponents' votes gained. It shows that all these successful DAB candidates just narrowly defeated their opponents—a result reflecting the strong performance of their political foes and pointing to the political liability of the DAB as a pro-government and pro-Beijing political party.

A detailed breakdown of the DAB performance in the 18 districts can be seen in Table 5.15. The DAB was eliminated in districts like the Central and Western, Wan Chai, Southern, Wong Tai Sin, Tsuen Wan, Yuen Long, Tai Po, and Sai Kung, which all had seen DAB presence in the past. The DAB managed to defend their bases at Eastern, Yau Tsim Mong, Sham Shui Po, Kowloon City, Kwun Tong, Tuen Mun, Northern, Sha Tin, Kwai Tsing and Island. The two strongest bases of the DAB remained Kwun Tong and Kowloon City. The 2019 DC election results represented the poorest performance of the DAB in its political history. As mentioned before, the crux of its problem was the pro-government and pro-Beijing stance, which if not adjusted would mean that the pro-PRC flagship will remain oscillating between good and bad performance—a phenomenon contingent upon how voters see the government's popularity and Beijing's policy toward the HKSAR. The legislation on Article 23 of the Basic Law was like an issue haunting the voters in the 2003 DC elections even though the government in July postponed it. The extradition bill was highly unpopular in the minds of the voters in the November 2019 DC elections even though the government had already postponed it. Still, the anti-extradition movement in 2019 provided a powerful ammunition for the old and new pan-democratic forces to uproot the bases of the DAB in many districts.

Table 5.16 shows that the FTU performed poorly in the 2019 DC elections, with a success rate of only 8% compared to 80% in 2007, 68.6% in 2011, and 56.8% in 2015. In the past, the FTU teamed up with the DAB candidates, as the DC elections in 2007 and 2011 saw 22 and 29 of them respectively running as joint tickets. However, in 2015, the FTU tried to make itself a full-fledged political party and nominated 48 candidates. It also nominated 43 candidates in the 2019 DC elections, but due to the changing political tide, only 5 FTU members were elected. Having said that, the FTU gained more votes in 2019 than ever before and the 128,796 supporters for the FTU candidates showed that the quasi-political party would likely have huge potential for a political comeback in the future elections.

Table 5.15: The Success Rate of the DAB Candidates in Various Districts, 2019

(Success rate = the number of elected candidates divided by the number of nominated candidates)

District	1994	1999	2003	2007	2011	2015	2019
Central	2/6 33.3%	3/10 30%	1/8 12.5%	3/6 50%	5/6 83.3%	6/6 100%	0/7 0%
Wan Chai	3/5 60%	3/5 60%	1/8 12.5%	2/3 66.7%	3/3 100%	4/4 100%	0/4 0%
Eastern	9/15 60%	13/22 59.1%	12/22 54.1%	14/20 70%	14/15 94.1%	10/14 76.9%	1/15 6.7%
South	0/5 0%	2/4 50%	1/6 16.7%	1/2 50%	2/3 66.7%	2/5 40%	0/8 0%
Yau Tsim Mong	1/3 33.3%	2/5 40%	2/8 25%	7/7 100%	8/8 100%	9/9 100%	1/9 11.1%
Sham Shui Po	0/1 0%	3/13 23.1%	1/14 7.1%	3/7 42.9%	4/8 50%	5/8 62.5%	1/10 10%
Kowloon City	2/4 25.0%	3/8 37.5%	2/8 22.2%	6/10 60%	7/10 70%	8/9 88.9%	4/8 50%
Wong Tai Sin	4/6 66.7%	5/11 45.5%	5/11 45.5%	8/11 72.7%	9/13 69.2%	7/9 72.7%	0/10 0%
Kwun Tong	4/7 57.1%	6/15 40%	4/13 28.6%	7/13 69.2%	12/14 85.7%	10/13 76.9%	6/13 46.2%
Tsuen Wan	1/2 50%	1/5 20%	1/6 16.7%	3/5 60%	4/6 66.7%	4/6 66.7%	0/7 0%
Tuen Mun	2/3 66.7%	7/16 43.8%	9/19 47.3%	11/17 61.1%	12/18 66.7%	8/13 61.5%	2/14 14.3%
Yuen Long	1/4 25%	7/10 70%	4/10 40%	7/11 63.6%	7/10 70%	6/11 54.6%	0/12 0%
North	4/6 66.7%	6/13 46.2%	5/13 38.5%	9/14 64.3%	14/15 93.3%	9/13 66.7%	1/10 10%
Tai Po	2/5 40%	4/8 50%	3/13 23.1%	7/10 70%	8/10 80%	5/10 50%	0/8 0%
Sai Kung	0/4 0%	5/8 62.5%	4/10 40%	9/13 69.2%	7/10 70%	8/11 72.7%	0/10 0%
Sha Tin	0/3 0%	9/12 69.2%	2/13 15.4%	8/12 66.7%	9/14 64.3%	7/13 53.9%	1/15 6.7%

Table 5.15 Continued

District	1994	1999	2003	2007	2011	2015	2019
Kwai Tsing	0/1	2/9	1/18	4/10	5/12	8/13	3/15
	0%	22.2%	5.6%	40%	41.7%	61.5%	20%
Island	2/3	2/2	4/4	4/5	4/4	3/4	1/6
	66.7%	100%	100%	80%	100%	75%	16.7%
Total	37/83	83/176	62/203	113/175	134/179	119/171	21/181
	44.6%	47.2%	30.5%	64.6%	74.9%	69.6%	11.6%

Sources: Louie Kin-shuen and Shum Kwok-cheung, eds., *A Compilation of Election Materials in Hong Kong, 1982–1994* (Hong Kong: The Hong Kong Institute of Asia-Pacific Studies, The Chinese University of Hong Kong, 1996); Yip Tin-sang, ed., *A Compilation of Election Materials in Hong Kong, 1996–2000* (Hong Kong: The Hong Kong Institute of Asia-Pacific Studies, The Chinese University of Hong Kong, 2001; Yip Tin-sang, ed., *A Compilation of Election Materials in Hong Kong, 2001–2004* (Hong Kong: The Hong Kong Institute of Asia-Pacific Studies, The Chinese University of Hong Kong, 2005); Yip Tin-sang, ed., *A Compilation of Election Materials in Hong Kong, 2005–2012* (Hong Kong: The Hong Kong Institute of Asia-Pacific Studies, The Chinese University of Hong Kong, 2015); and Democratic Alliance for the Betterment and Progress of Hong Kong, *The 25th Anniversary Commemoration of the Democratic Alliance for the Betterment and Progress of Hong Kong: Choices and Promises* (Hong Kong: Democratic Alliance for the Betterment and Progress of Hong Kong, 2017), pp. 105–107, p. 109 and p. 111. Also see "Election Results, District Council 2019," Electoral Affairs Commission, https://www.elections.gov.hk/dc2019/eng/results.html, access date: November 15, 2020.

Table 5.16: District Councils Members who were also Members of Federation of Trade Unions, 1999–2019

Year	1994	1999	2003	2007	2011	2015	2019
Candidates	7	8	9	30*	51	51	62
FTU alone	0	1	1	4	22	48	43
DAB alone	7	7	6	3	0	0	0
DAB/FTU alliance	0	0	2	22	29	3	19
Uncontested	0	2	0	0	6	7	0
Elected	6	8	6	24	35	29	5
Unelected	1	0	3	6	16	22	57
Successful rate	83.3	100%	66.7%	80%	68.6%	56.8%	8.1%
Votes Gained	8148	10,860	15,248	49,153	82,290	95,583	128,796
Average votes obtained	1,164	1,810	1,694	1,638	1,829	2,172	2,077

* One candidate Kwok Wai-keung declared himself as an independent candidate.

Sources: *Reports on the District Councils Election* in 1999, 2003, 2007, 2011 and 2015; *A Compilation of Election Materials in Hong Kong* (Hong Kong: Hong Kong Institute of Asia-Pacific Studies, The Chinese University of Hong Kong, 2001, 2005 and 2015); "Election Results, District Council 2019," Electoral Affairs Commission, https://www.elections.gov.hk/dc2019/eng/results.html, access date: November 15, 2020.

Table 5.17: The 2019 Electoral Performance of
Members of the Federation of Trade Unions

Constituency	FTU members who won and votes		Competitors and their votes	
Woo Fu	Kwok Wai-keung,	3,229 (49.68%)	Chan Ka-yeung Lam Sze-nam	3,181 90
Lam Tin	Kan Ming-tung	4,080 (50%)	Fung Tak-sum	4,030
Fok Loi	Kot Siu-yuen	2,871 (53%)	Wong Cham-luen (DP) Ng Ka-yee (Non-affiliated)	2,351 226
King Hing	Chan Yau-hoi	2,893 (50%)	Law Cheuk-yung (Tuen Mun Ten Brothers) Lau Hang-yee (Non-affiliated)	2,756 105
Shing Fook	Wan Wo-tat	3,181 (42%)	Lui Chi-hang (Independent democrat and North Coalition Line) Wong Leung-hei (Neo-Democrats)	2,656 1,754
Constituency	FTU members who were defeated and votes		Competitors and their votes	
Pak Ngar	Ho Kai-ming	3,066	Chan Man-kin (elected) (DP) Chan Yu-ming (Non-affiliated)	3,825 (54%) 138
Tin Hang	Luk Chung-hung	3,731	Wong Pak-yu (elected) (Tin Shui Wai Livelihood Concern Platform) Chan Chi-shing Chan Ka-chun	6,004 (64%) 37 37
Wai Ying	Alice Mak Mei-kuen	3,480	Sin Ho-fai (elected) (Civic Party)	5,194 (59.88%)

Source: The authors' tabulation from open sources on the election results.

Table 5.17 shows the electoral performance of the FTU members. It is noteworthy that three FTU members were defeated, including Ho Kai-ming, Luk Chung-hung, and Alice Mak Mei-Kuen. Alice Mak's outspoken and critical approach to dealing with the democrats failed to help her acquire sufficient support to be re-elected. Still, those elected FTU members defeated their opponents with a relatively narrow margin, especially Kam Ming-tung who defeated his opponent by only 50 votes in the constituency of Lam Tin. Hence, the battles were extremely hard fought for the FTU in the 2019 DC elections.

The most astounding defeat of the pro-government and pro-Beijing force was the CF formed by the former Secretary for Home Affairs Lau Kong-wah, who left an opportunistic impression on many pan-democrats

Table 5.18: Electoral Performance of Civil Force, 1994–2019

Year	No. of Candidates	Number Elected	Success Rate (%)
1994	10	10(2)	100.00%
1999	14	11(3)	78.57%
2003	21	17(8)	80.95%
2007	20	18(5)	90.00%
2011	20	15(3)	75.00%
2015	22	11(4)	50.00%
2019	18	0	0.00%

Note: Bracket numbers denote those who were automatically elected.

Source: Tabulated from open data on the election results, 1994–2019.

for turning from originally a pro-democracy activist to a pro-establishment elite and later a government official. In the 2015 DC election, the CF still maintained a success rate of 50%, but in fact its success rate declined steadily from 2007 onwards. The 2019 DC elections saw the CF being wiped out electorally—again a testimony to how the voters perceived the pro-government district group. Although the CF in 2019 teamed up with Regina Ip's New People's Party (NPP), this effort failed to win the hearts and minds of the voters.

Table 5.19 shows the performance of the Round Table, which is a pro-government group led by Michael Tien since May 2017 and could be seen as a faction divided from the NPP led by Regina Ip. Tien was originally a core member of the NPP in 2011. Tien and 6 DC members withdrew from the NPP in April 2017 apparently due to opinion differences. In October 2019, a list of all the pro-government and pro-Beijing candidates to be supported and voted by FTU members was leaked out, showing the names of 449 candidates, among which 13 of them came from the Round Table.[3] Table 5.19 shows the electoral performance of the Round Table in the 2019 DC elections. The Round Table nominated 13 candidates to run in the elections, and seven of them faced pro-democracy candidates in a one-to-one battle. Only two of the six, namely So Ka-man and Tsui Hiu-kit, were elected. The other six candidates of the Round Table encountered more than one opponent and all of them were defeated, showing the relatively weak performance of the pro-government and pro-Beijing group.

**Table 5.19: Electoral Performance of Round Table
in the 2019 District Council Elections**

Constituency	Political Affiliation	Votes Gained (%)
Tsuen Wan South		
Chan Kit	DAB	1,860
Luk Ling-chung	Civic Party	3,621 (elected, 54.34%)
Ma Ting-hei	Round Table	880
Yu King		
Lau Cheuk-yu	Tsuen Wan Residents Discussing Political Affairs	4,498 (elected, 54.18%)
Michael Tien	Round Table	3,804
Ting Shum		
Wan Chuen-lun	Abandoned to participate in elections eventually	18
Lau Chi-hing	Pro-Democracy Faction DC Election Alliance	3,489 (elected, 52.97%)
Cheng Chit-bun	Round Table	2,931
Lam King-fang	Residents' Alliance, Hong Kong Political Study Association (pro-government and pro-Beijing)	149
Chui Hing		
Poon Chi-kin	Tuen Mun Ten Brothers, Pro-Democracy Faction DC Election Alliance	4,662 (elected, 60.62%)
Chu Yiu-wah	Round Table	2,653
So Kun Fat		
Chan Kar-ching	New People's Party	982
Lau Kai-man	Round Table	466
Ma Kay	Democratic Party	1,648 (elected, 53.32%)
Po Tin		
So Ka-man	Round Table	2,562 (elected, 57.61%)
Cheung Tsan-wah	Tuen Mun Ten Brothers, Pro-Democracy Faction DC Alliance	1,885
Yan Tin		
Wong Tze-chun	Round Table	611
Lai Ka-mun	DAB	2,203 (elected, 47.08%)
Lo Wai-ming	Democratic Party, Professional Teachers' Union	1,865

Table 5.19 Continued

Constituency	Political Affiliation	Votes Gained (%)
Shing Yan		
Chong Ho-fung	Round Table	1,195
Lam Wai-ming	New Territories Federation of Associations	1,495
Ng Ka-chun	Substitute of Ao Kwok-kuen	61
Wong Kwok-hung	Non-affiliated	60
Ao Kwok-kuen	Team Eddie Chu Hoi-dick, Pro-Democracy Faction DC Alliance	3,530 (elected, 55.67%)
Tin Shing		
Chan Sze-ching	Round Table	2,830
Wong Ping-hung	Tin Shui Wai Joint Line, Pro-Democracy Faction DC Alliance	3,347 (elected, 54.18%)
Yat Chat		
Wong Wing-sze	Civic Passion	4,454 (elected, 58.14%)
Fan Shun-yu	Round Table	434
Kwok Hing-ping*	Non-affiliated	2,607
Shek Lei South		
Leung Kwok-wah	Democratic Party	4,780 (elected, 58.93%)
Ng Ka-chiu	Round Table	3,331
Cheung Hong		
Wong Chun-lam	Kwai Tsing Heritage	2,949
Tsui Hiu-kit	Round Table	3,427 (elected, 53.75%)
Tung Chung North		
Tsui Sheng-hung	Democratic Party	1,332 (elected)(39.56%)
Poon Chun-yan	Round Table	990
Yip Pui-kei	DAB	1,045

Source: Tabulated from open sources on the 2019 District Council elections.

*   Note: Kwok Hing-ping participated as a DP member in 2007 and 2011, and his opponent was Wong Yu-ping. Kwok was elected in 2011 and withdrew from the DP, becoming a non-affiliated pro-government candidate who was later re-elected in 2015.

Table 5.20 shows the electoral performance of the pro-government and pro-business Liberal Party, which performed quite well from 1994 to 2007. But the party suffered a decline in its performance from 2011 to 2019 in terms of the number of nominated and elected candidates. Although the average votes obtained by the Liberal Party candidates increased in the 2015

Table 5.20: Electoral Performance of Liberal Party and Performance in the 2019 District Council Elections

Year	Total votes	LP's Popular vote	Vote share %	Standing	Elected	Average votes of candidates
1994	686,417	50,755	7.39%	89	18	570
1999	816,503	27,718	3.39%	34	15	815
2003	1,066,373	29,108	2.73%	27	14	1,078
2007	1,148,815	50,026	4.35%	55	14	910
2011	1,202,544	23,408	1.95%	24	9	975
2015	1,467,729	25,151	1.71%	20	9	1,258
2019	2,943,842	28,547	0.97%	12	6	2,379

Constituency in 2019	Liberal Party members and votes gained		Competitors and their votes gained	
Wai Shing	Fung Ka-leung	2,559	Cheng Lai-king (DP)	2,669 (elected)
Peak	Yeung Chit-on	2,422 (elected)	Thomas Uruma (The 2047 Hong Kong Monitor)	1,106
Jardine Hill	Lam Wai-man	2,570 (elected)	Cheung Chiu-dun (Kickstart Wan Chai)	1,355
			Tse Wing-ling	464
Braemar Hill	Yuen Kin-chung	3,111 (elected)	Lai Hok-him	2,522
Chui Tak	Lee Chun-keung	2,612	Choi Chi-keung	2,994 (elected)
Hoi Wan	Leung Chun	1,882 (elected)	Ting Wai-leung	807
Kowloon Tong	Ho Hin-ming	2,952 (elected)	Wan Chung-yin	2,567
Yau Yat Chuen	Lee Chi-king	2,391	Lau Wai-chung (Non-affiliated democrat)	2,487 (elected)
Kai Tak Central and South	Cheung King-fun	1,547 (elected)	Leung Wing-yan (Civic Party)	1,367
Tin Keung	Chan On-tai	3,075	Cheng Man-kit (Civic Party)	4,608 (elected)
Wong Uk	Leung Chi-wai	2,215	Lai Chi-yan (Shatin Community)	4,440 (elected)
Chun Ma	Ho Wai-lok	1,211	Chow Hiu-nam (Democratic Party)	2,611 (elected)
			Siu Hin-hong (Non-affiliated)	1,355

Source: Tabulated from open sources on the election results.

and 2019 elections, the party failed to nominate more candidates to compete with other candidates from either pro-Beijing or pro-democracy camps. As such, the Liberal Party needs to reflect on its strategy of nominating candidates and to groom more candidates from now onwards. Otherwise, it remains a fringe party failing to compete with either the pro-Beijing or pro-

Table 5.21: Performance of the Pan-Democrats and Pro-Establishment Camp in the 2019 District Council Elections

Political nature	No. of participants	No. of failed candidates	No. of elected	Success rate (%)
Pan-democratic faction	516	227	389	75.39%
Pro-democracy Faction District Council Alliance	397	54	343	86.40%
Democratic Party	99	8	91	91.92%
Pro-establishment Camp	498	436	62	12.45%
DAB plus FTU	224	198	26	11.61%

Source: Tabulated from the election results, 2019.

democracy forces. However, in the 2019 DC elections, those Liberal Party candidates who were elected were mostly running in constituencies where a sizable number of upper-class votes resided, such as the Peak, Jardine Hill, Braemar Hill, and Kowloon Tong. This result showed that the party remained upper-class in its image and power base. Therefore, a challenge of the Liberal Party is to reach out to other classes, especially the middle and middle-lower classes if it needs to achieve a breakthrough in its political and electoral development.

Electoral Performance of the Pro-Democracy Forces

Although the pro-democracy camp scored a very impressive victory in the 2019 DC elections, its factions were complicated. In general, these factions performed quite well, and as such, the pro-Beijing and pro-government forces suffered an unprecedented defeat. Table 5.21 illustrates the performance of pan-democrats in the 2019 DC elections. The pan-democratic faction nominated 516 candidates and 389 of them were elected with a success rate of 75.3%. Among the 516 candidates, the pan-democrats nominated 397 candidates of them through the coordination and compromise of the Pro-democracy Faction DC Alliance. Of the 397 coordinated candidates, only 54 of them were eventually defeated, with a high success rate of 86.4%. On the contrary, the pro-establishment camp nominated 498 candidates and only 62 of them were elected with a poor success rate of only 12.45%. The pro-Beijing DAB and the FTU nominated altogether 224 candidates, but only 26 of them were elected with a low success rate of 11.61%. Undoubtedly, the 2019 DC elections constituted a political earthquake sweeping the pan-democratic candidates into victory.

Table 5.22 analyzes the results of the defeated democrats in the 2019 DC elections. The defeated democrats, who joined the mainstream pan-democratic camp and accepted the coordination work among themselves, were characterized by six features. First, there might be a third candidate, who claimed to be an independent democrat, coming out and he or she grasped votes that reduced the chance of the mainstream pro-democracy candidate. This situation occurred in constituencies such as So Uk, Oi Chun, Shing Fok and Tai Pak Tin West. Second, the mainstream pro-democracy candidates were defeated partly because an independent ran for the election and affected their chance to some extent, such as Kowloon Station, Loong Shing, Kai Tak North, Tsuen Wan Suburb, King Hing, Sun Tin, and Dou Shin. Third, the phenomenon of independent democrats competing in these constituencies was due to the failure of coordination work led by Chiu Ka-yin's Pro-democracy Faction DC Alliance. The Alliance succeeded in coordinating only 397 out of 516 pro-democracy candidates. Fourth, some pan-democratic candidates were too weak in the 2019 DC elections and their defeat was inevitable, such as King Lam, Tai Yee, and Tai Pak Tin West. Fifth, the opponent of the mainstream pan-democratic candidate was so strong that defeat was unavoidable, such as Jardine Hill, Kai Tak North, Sheung Shun, An Tat, Fuk Loi, Pat Heung North, Pat Heung South, Shing Fok, Fu Hang, and Lantau Island. Sixth, there were some cases in which the mainstream democrats were concerned about the possibility of being disqualified to run in elections, and therefore they nominated substitutes, like the constituencies of Pat Heung South and Lantau Island. For the first two characteristics mentioned above, it was unclear whether the self-proclaimed independent democrats and the independents were tacitly or hiddenly encouraged by the pro-government and pro-Beijing forces to compete in the elections, trying their best to minimize the votes gained by the mainstream pan-democratic candidates. In Cantonese, the strategy of nominating a third candidate, no matter whether he or she was an "independent" or "independent democrat", was called "dividing the votes (*kai piu*)." In the past, according to rumors, the Liaison Office might be behind the scenes in encouraging third candidates to run and compete with the mainstream democrats, curbing the chance of the latter to be directly elected. It was difficult to verify any possible behind-the-scenes support of

Table 5.22: Defeated Democrats in the 2019 District Council Elections

Constituency	Defeated candidates and votes		Competitors and votes	
Jardine Hill	Cheung Chiu-tun (Wanchai Act-Up)	1,355	Lam Wai-man (Liberal Party)	2,570 (58.56%, elected)
			John Tse Wing-ling	464
Wo Fu	Chan Ka-yeung (North Cannon Alliance)	3,181	Kwok Wai-keung (FTU)	3,229 (49.68%, re-elected incumbent)
			Lam Si-nam	90
Kowloon Station	Lee Wing-yin (Democratic Party)	1,821	Hung Chiu-wah (DAB)	1,928 (50.33%, re-elected incumbent)
			Hung Hei-chi (independent)	82
So Uk	Chan Ming-kei (ADPL)	2,522	Ho Sun-chau (DAB)	2,650 (50.74%, elected)
			Lam Pui-man (independent democrat and incumbent)	51
Loong Shing	Fung Tat-chun	1,884	Ng Po-keung (DAB)	1,983 (49.97%, re-elected incumbent)
			Fong Ngai-yin (independent)	101
Kai Tak North	Tsang Chun-tat	2,043	Leung Yuen-ting (Business and Professional Alliance or BPA)	2,480 (54.48%, re-elected)
			Wong Tze-chun	29
Oi Chun	Chan Lai-kwan	3,237	Tso Wui-hung (BPA and West Kowloon New Dynamic)	3,268 (46.96%, re-elected incumbent)
			Leung Kar-lei (independent democrat)	454
Sheung Shun	Leung Hon-kei (ADPL)	3,006	Fu Pik-chun (Positive Synergy—a pro-government group in Wong Tai Sin district)	4,200 (51.50%, re-elected incumbent)
			Chan Cho-kwong (former chairman of the Police Rank-and-File Association)	949
An Tat	Siu Ho-yin	2,393	Hui Yau-wai (DAB)	3,499 (58.58%, elected)
			Lee Shing-cheung	38
			Lau Pak-yuen	41
Yau Chiu	Chung Chut-kwan	2,572	Pong Chi-sang (Federation of Public Housing Estates)	2,857 (46.82%, elected)
			Chan Fu-king (chairman of Police Residents Association)	605
			Leung Kar-sing (People's Power)	68 (abandoned to run in the election)
Fuk Loi	Wong Cham-luen (Democratic Party)	2,351	Kot Siu-yuen (FTU)	2,871 (52.70%, elected)
			Ng Kar-yee	226
Tsuen Wan Suburb	Tam Pui-yan (Tsuen Wan Residents Discussing Politics)	3,054	Ng Hin-loong	3,409 (43.37%, re-elected incumbent)
			Kwan Sun-wai (Hong Kong Political Affairs Study Association)	1,221

Table 5.22 Continued

Constituency	Defeated candidates and votes		Competitors and votes	
King Hing	Law Cheuk-yung	2,756	Chan Yau-hoi (FTU)	2,893 (50.28%, re-elected incumbent)
			Lau Heng-yee (independent)	105
Yan Tin	Lo Wai-ming (Professional Teachers' Union)	1,865	Lai Kar-man (DAB)	2,203 (47.08%, elected)
			Wong Tze-chun (Round Table)	611
Sun Tin	Tsui Kai-loong	2,032	Man Fu-yan	2,257 (48.91%, elected)
			Chow Chun-kuen	161
			Man Kwei-kay	160
Pat Heung North	Lee Kan-ming	1,833	Tang Yung-yiu	1,948 (34.19%, elected)
			Tang Chi-kwong (New Territories Federation of Associations or NTFA)	1,724
Pat Heung South	Eddie Chu Hoi-dick	3,435	Lai Wing-tim (NTFA)	3,799 (52.21%, elected)
			Chui Cheuk-yin (Eddie Chu's substitute)	41
Shing Fok	Wong Leung-hei (Neo-Democrats)	1,754	Wan Wo-tat (FTU)	3,181 (41.90%, re-elected incumbent)
			Lui Chi-hang (independent democrat)	2,656
Fu Hang	Yam Wan-chuen (incumbent)	2,161	Ho Wai-lum (independent democrat)	3,435 (41.41%, elected)
			Wu Cheuk-him (DAB)	
Dou Shin	Chong Wing-fai (Democratic Party)	1,741	Cheung Chin-pang (Professional Synergy)	2,568 (49.05%, re-elected incumbent)
			Lee Pak-tong (Tseung Kwan O Residents Concern Group)	927
King Lam	Lam Wing-yin	788	Cheung Wai-chiu (Tseung Kwan O Youth Power)	4,265 (51.47%, elected)
			Wun Kai-ming (DAB)	3,233
Tai Yee	Lau Ching	830	Lam Kong-sun (DAB)	1,923 (43.52%, elected)
			Tse Kit-bing (Shatin Community)	1,666
Tai Pak Tin West	Ho King-shing	544	Kwok Fu-yung (DAB)	2,449 (48.03%, elected)
			Szeto Kong Sun (independent democrat)	2,106
Lantau Island	Fung Siu-yin	2,633	Yu Hon-kwan	2,873 (51.98%, elected)
			Ho Yan-ching (Fung Siu-yin's substitute)	21

Source: Tabulated from 2019 election results.

Note: Defeated democrats refer to those members of the pan-democratic camp and those who accepted the coordination among the camp to run for the 2019 election, but who lost the election. This coordination was led by Chiu Ka-yin's Pro-Democracy Faction DC Alliance. The table selected those constituencies in which there were three candidates or more competing against each other.

* Independent democrats refer to those candidates who claimed themselves as democrats but who did not join the coordination work among the pan-democratic camp.

Table 5.23: Democrats and Independents Elected in Constituencies which were affected by Police-Protesters Conflicts

Constituency	2019 election result		2015 election result		Areas affected by the police-protesters' conflicts and confrontations
East Tsim Sha Tsui	Chan Ka-long (independent)	1,003 (48%, elected)	Hung Chiu-wah (DAB)	1,213 (59%, elected)	1. Tsim Sha Tsui East
	Poon King-wo (DAB)	783 (38%)	Lau Chi-hing (independent)	828 (41%)	2. Nathan Road (Park Lane Shoppers' Boulevard)
	Fung Kin-kei (independent)	153 (7%)			3. Austin Road
	Leung Hang-fai (independent)	124 (5%)			
	Kan Ho-ming (independent)	35 (2%)			
Yau Ma Tei South	Wu Shui-shan (Community March)	2,984 (55%, elected)	Yeung Tze-hei (DAB)	2,124 (62%)	1. Nathan Road
	Yeung Tze-hei (DAB)	2,432 (45%)	Au Yeung Tung (ADPL)	1,298 (38%)	2. Yau Ma Tei Fruit Market
Mong Kok West	Hui Tak-leung (Kowloon Federation of Associations)	2,102 (54%, elected)	Hui Tak-leung (West Kowloon New Dynamic)	automatically elected	1. Nathan Road
	Chan Yuen-bun (independent)	1,787 (46%)			2. Argyle Street
					3. Shan Tung Street
					4. Nelson Street
Mong Kok North	Siu Tak-kin (independent)	2,161 (51%, elected)	Wong Shu-ming (West Kowloon New Dynamic)	1,712 (66%, elected)	1. Mong Kok Police Station
	Wong Shu-ming (BPA)	2,076 (49%)	Wong Ka-chun (Youngspiration)	869 (34%)	2. Nathan Road
					3. Lai Chi Kok Road
					4. Prince Edward Road West
Mong Kok East	Lam Siu-bun (Community March)	2,663 (59%, elected)	Wong Kin-sun (West Kowloon New Dynamic)	1,442 (53%, elected)	1. Mong Kok Police Station
	Wong Kin-sun (BPA)	1,821 (41%)	Lau Chun-yip (DP)	1,172 (43%)	2. Nathan Road
			Tze Cheuk-nam (independent)	112 (4%)	
Tai Nan	Lee Kwok-kuen (Community March)	2,943 (58%, elected)	Chong Wing-chan (BPA)	1,424 (48%)	1. Mong Kok Police Station
	Lee Si-man (BPA)	2,046 (41%)	Fung Man-to (DP)	962 (32%)	2. Prince Edward Road West
	Choi Kay-loong (independent)	57 (1%)	Chiu Yuk-kwong (Youngspiration)	606 (20%)	3. Portland Street
Mong Kok South	Chu Kong-wai (Community March)	1,977 (53%, elected)	Shou Chun-fai (West Kowloon New Dynamic)	automatically elected	1. Nathan Road
	Shou Chun-fai (West Kowloon New Dynamic)	1,747 (47%)			2. Shan Tung Street
					3. Sai Yeung Choi Street South
					4. Argyle Street
					5. Soy Street
					6. Nelson Street

Table 5.23 Continued

Constituency	2019 election result		2015 election result		Areas affected by the police-protesters' conflicts and confrontations
Yau Ma Tei North	Lam Kin-man (Pro-democracy Faction DC Alliance)	2,573 (67%)	Lam Kin-man(ADPL) Man Yun-wah (FTU)	1,682 (71%, elected) 689 (29%)	1. Nathan Road 2. Pitt Street 3. Dundas Street 4. Soy Street 5. Waterloo Road
	Lee Man-kit	1,243 (33%)			
East Tsim Sha Tsui and King's Park	Chu Tze-lok (DP) Tang Ming-sum (independent)	1,745 (53%) 1,567 (47%)	Tang Ming-sum (independent) Chan Man-yau (Professional Commons)	852 (56%) 681 (44%)	1. Tsimshatstui East 2. Nathan Road 3. Waterloo Road
Jordan North	Ho Fu-wing (independent) Yeung Chun-wah (DAB)	1,423 (56%) 1,117 (44%)	Yeung Chun-wah (DAB) Chik Chi-leung	941 (71%) 386 (29%)	1. Nathan Road 2. Gascoigne Road
Tsim Sha Tsui Central	Ho Cheuk-hin (Community March) Kwan Sau-ling (DAB)	1,533 (57%) 1,167 (43%)	Kwan Sau-ling (DAB) Liu Siu-fai (independent)	1,099 (69%) 486 (31%)	1. Nathan Road 2. Austin Road 3. Hillwood Road

Source: Tabulated from the 2015 and 2019 election results.

some third or "independent" candidates even though many of them were really non-affiliated and ran in the elections autonomously.

Table 5.23 shows that for those districts and constituencies mostly affected by serious police-protesters' confrontations and conflicts from June to November 2019, democrats and independents were elected. Except for Mong Kok West where a pro-Beijing candidate won, the results showed the unpopularity of pro-government candidates in all other constituencies affected by police-protesters conflicts, which might lead to the inconvenience and anger of many residents. Although some residents were pro-police and pro-government, others were sympathetic with the protesters and felt that the police might use teargas in their constituencies excessively. The election results appeared to show that many residents who held the view sympathetic with the protesters tended to vote for pro-democracy candidates, who in fact won in many constituencies plagued by serious police-protesters' conflicts. One pro-Beijing independent won in Mong Kok West, where residents were perhaps angry with the protesters. But in Mong Kok North, East, and South constituencies, an independent and two democrats won. In other constituencies, pro-government candidates from DAB and BPA were all defeated, such as East Tsim Sha Tsui, Yau Ma Tei South, Tai Nan, Jordan North and Tsim Sha Tsui Central. Hence, a hypothesis advanced by some pro-government elites that the more violent the constituency was during the 2019 protests, the more likely the defeat of pro-democracy candidates was disapproved.

The Emergence of New Pro-Democracy Groups in the 2019 Elections

The rapid emergence of new pro-democracy groups was a hallmark of the 2019 DC elections. Table 5.24 illustrates that in Wan Chai, the new Kickstart Wan Chai (KWC) emerged rapidly, for it was non-existent in the 2015 DC elections but gained six seats in the 2019 elections. The 2003 mass protests against the legislation on Article 23 of the Basic Law witnessed the rise of Civic Act-Up (CAU) in the DC elections in the same year, with three members being elected to the Wan Chai DC. However, the pro-government and pro-Beijing DAB and the Hong Kong Island Federation came back forcefully from 2007 to 2011 DC elections. Hence, a case study of Wan Chai shows that while the largest political groups in 1994 included both the DAB and DP, the development oscillated from the sudden rise of CAU in 2003 to the return of pro-Beijing forces from 2007 to 2011, and then to the abrupt emergence of the KWC in 2019. While the mainstream pro-DAB and DP performed as relatively stable political forces in DC elections, the rise of locally based pro-democracy groups took place from time to time, especially when the government was unpopular during the election year.

A closer look at the electoral performance of KWC showed that it was formed in 2019 and led by Yeung Shuet-ying. It nominated ten members to run in the 2019 DC elections and six of them were elected. Among the six elected candidates, three defeated the pro-Beijing DAB and HKIF, and the rest defeated other independents (Table 5.25). Those KWC members who were defeated were relatively inexperienced and weak in comparison with the pro-Beijing candidates in the constituencies of Jardine Hill, Lok Wood, Stubbs Road, and Southorn. With a success rate of 60% of its nominated candidates being elected, the KWC performance could be seen as relatively satisfactory—a result also—illustrating that the pan-democratic camp decentralized the electioneering strategy to locally based like-minded

Table 5.24: The Evolution of New Groups in Wan Chai District Councils Elections, 1994–2019

Year	Number of Seats	Elected Seats	Appointed Seats	Pro-Beijing Seats	Democratic Seats	Largest Parties (Seats)
1994	10	10	0	7 (70%)	3 (30%)	DAB/DP (3 each)
1999	14	11	3	11 (79%)	3 (21%)	DAB (4)
2003	14	11	3	6 (43%)	8 (57%)	CAU (3)
2007	14	11	3	11 (79%)	3 (21%)	DAB (3)
2011	13	11	2	11 (85%)	2 (15%)	DAB (4)
2015	13	13	0	11 (85%)	2 (15%)	DAB/HKIF (4)
2019	13	13	0	4 (31%)	9 (69%)	KWC (6)

Note: One of the appointed members belonged to DAB member in each term. HKIF: Hong Kong Island Federation. CAU: Civic Act-Up. DAB: Democratic Alliance for Betterment and Progress of Hong Kong. DP: Democratic Party. KWC: Kickstart Wan Chai.

Table 5.25: The Electoral Performance of Kickstart Wan Chai in the 2019 District Council Elections

Constituency	Member of Kickstart Wan Chai		Competitors and their background	
Hennessy	Ku Kwok-wai	1,373 (elected)	Wong Shuo-tung	1,033
			Ha Hei-nok	845
Oi Kwan	Law Wai-shan	2,363 (elected)	Muk Ka-chun (DAB)	1,750
Ngor Keng	Mak King-sing	1,891 (elected)	Chung Ka-mun (DAB)	1,383
Causeway Bay	Yau Man-shan	1,918 (elected)	Ng Yuen-ting (Hong Kong Island Federation or HKIF)	1,572
Tin Hau	Chan Kwok-lam	2,899 (elected)	Lee Man-loong	2,623
Tai Hang	Yeung Shuet-ying	2,340 (elected)	Liu Tim-shing	1,433
Jardine Hill	Cheung Chiu-tun	1,355	Lam Wai-man (Liberal Party)	2,570
			John Tse	464
Lok Wood	Yeung Tze-chun	1,887	Tze Wai-chun	2,121
Stubbs Road	Chow Kam-kei	1,591	Wong Wang-tai (HKIF)	1,908
Southorn	Chan Kam-shing	1,652	Lee Pik-yee (HKIF)	1,790

Source: Tabulated from the 2019 District Council elections results.

Table 5.26: The Electoral Performance of Tuen Mun Ten Brothers in 2019

Constituency	Members and Votes		Competitors and their votes	
Chui Hing	Poon Chi-kin	4,662 (elected)	Chu Yiu-wah (Round Table)	3,028
Shan King	Wong Dan-ching	4,780 (elected)	Ng Dip-pui	2,653
King Hing	Law Cheuk-yung	2,756	Chan Yau-hoi (FTU)	2,893
			Lau Yeung-yee	105
Hing Chak	Tsang Chun-hing	3,815 (elected)	Tsui Fan (FTU)	3,390
Sun Hui	Cheung Ho-sum	3,276 (elected)	Ku Hon-keung (New Territories Federation of Associations)	2,140
San Shing	Mo Fong-tai	2,834 (elected)	So Siu-shing (New People's Party)	2,198
Fu Sun	Lee Ka-wai	5,486 (elected)	Kam Man-fung (New People's Party)	3,599
Loong Mun	Tsang Kam-wing	4,410 (elected)	Lung Shui-hing (DAB)	2,931
Leung King	Wong Tak-yuen	4,073 (elected)	Ching Chi-hung	2,697
			Tang Man-kit (Civic Passion)	303
Tin King	Leung Ho-man	4,254 (elected)	Lee Hung-sum (FTU)	3,038
			Leung Yat-long (Civic Passion)	758
			Lui Mei-yuk	37
Po Tin	Cheung Tsan-wah	1,885	So Ka-man (Round Table)	2,562

groups after coordination. This pro-democracy strategy of coordination and decentralization worked well in the case of Wan Chai district.

Similarly, pro-democracy coordination and decentralization could work successfully in the Tuen Mun district, where the Tuen Mun Ten Brothers (TMTB) was formed in 2019 by a group of people without previous experiences in electoral participation. In fact, the TMTB was composed of eleven members. It was led by Cheung Ho-sum and the group was concerned about various district matters, ranging from the territory-wide extradition bill to the Tuen Mun Park's noise produced by some mainland-born singers and dancers. The TMTB was deeply concerned about a mysterious odor that was suspected as a gas leaked from somewhere affecting the entire district in October 2019. Its members were also critical of the "excessive" way in which the police used teargas in Tuen Mun during the anti-extradition protests. The eleven members ran in the 2019 DC elections and nine of them were elected—a very impressive election result for a new pro-democracy district group. Except for the constituencies in King Hing and Po Tin, where two members of the TMTB failed to compete with the pro-establishment candidates, all other nine constituencies witnessed the strong showing of the

**Table 5.27: The Electoral Performance of Chai Wan Act-Up
in the 2019 District Council Elections**

Constituency	Members and Votes		Competitors and their votes	
Heng Fa Chuen	Wong Yee	5,323 (elected)	Ho Ngai-kam (FTU)	4,114
Chui Wan	Ku Kwei-yiu (incumbent)	3,569 (elected)	Lau Shuk-yin (DAB and FTU)	2,847
Yan Lam	Lee Fung-king	3,982 (elected)	Wong Kin-hing (HKIF)	3,543
			Chan Yee-chun (Chai Wan Kaifong Association or CWKA)	106
Siu Sai Wan	Chan Wing-tai	3,212 (elected)	Lee Lok-kan (DAB and FTU)	2,485
			Chu Yat-on (CWKA)	288
King Yee	Tsang Yan-ying	4,936 (elected)	Leung Kwok-hung (FTU)	3,079
Wan Chui	Ng Cheuk-wah	3,412 (elected)	Kung Pak-cheung (FTU)	2,866
			Wong Kam-yin (Chai Wan Federation of Sports Associations)	39
Fei Chui	Lai Chi-keung (incumbent, also Civic Party)	3,591 (elected)	Chan Hoi-wing (DAB and FTU)	2,742
Hing Man	Tse Miu-yee	3,297 (elected)	Lau Hing-yeung (DAB)	3,113
Lok Hong	Tsang Kin-shing (also League of Social Democrats)	3,563 (elected)	Lee Chun-chau (HKIF)	2,800
Chui Tak	Choi Chi-keung	2,944 (elected)	Lee Chun-keung (Liberal Party)	2,612
Yue Wan	Tsui Chi-kin (incumbent)	3,814 (elected)	Lau Kin (DAB and FTU)	2,374
			Wu Kin-nam (Chai Wan Federation of Sports Association)	30
			Choi Chui-wan	196
Kai Hiu	Lai Chi-yan	3,200 (elected)	Chik Kit-ling (DAB and FTU)	2,712
			Chan Chun-chun (CWKA)	581

Source: Tabulated from the 2019 election results.

TMTB. Their sharp political platform with diligent work in the district won the hearts and minds of many voters.

Another pro-democracy group parallel to KWC and TMTB in the 2019 DC elections was the Chai Wan Act-Up (CWAU), which was also formed by a group of democrats in the Chai Wan district to support the demands of the anti-extradition movement and to work for the district interests. The CWAU was very strong, nominating 12 candidates and all of them were elected with 100% of the success rate (Table 5.27). Three of them were incumbents and two were affiliated with the Civic Party and the League of Social Democrats. The strong showing of the CWAU could be seen in how they defeated many candidates affiliated with the DAB and FTU in constituencies such as Heng Fa Chuen, Chui Wan, Siu Sai Wan, King Yee, Wan Chui, Fei Chui, Hing Man, Yue Wan, and Kai Hiu. Traditionally, Chai Wan district was a stronghold of the pro-Beijing DAB and FTU. The 2019 DC elections were a turning point as most DAB and FTU members running in Chai Wan were bitterly defeated.

The successful coordination and district-based decentralization of the pro-democracy election strategy led to the fragmentation of like-minded groups in many districts, including not just Wan Chai, Tuen Mun, and Chai Wan but also Tseung Kwan O and Sha Tin. Table 5.28 shows the electoral performance of the Tseung Kwan O Livelihood Concern Group (TKOPLCG). The TKOPLCG was formed by four democrats, including former DP member Gary Fan Kwok-wai, in 2000 to care about Sai Kung's district affairs, such as environment, transport, housing, and leisure activities. The group evolved into a larger electoral organization in 2019, which witnessed seven of its 12 candidates being elected. Interestingly, fragmentation began in September 2020 when its convenor Yip Ka-wing and three DC members Lee Yin-ho, Lee Ka-yui, and Wong Cheuk-nga withdrew from the group. The group was then led by Or Yiu-lam and had four members only. Their split illustrated the complexities of pro-democracy groups, which had internal personality and opinion differences, and which raised a serious question whether district-based pro-democracy groups would have their sustainability and longevity. The rise and decline of the TKOPLCG demonstrated not simply the internal personal differences among the pro-democracy camp but also the relatively strong showing of a district-based professional group, namely the Professional Synergy led by Fong Kwok-shan. The Professional Synergy captured three seats in the constituencies of Dou Sin, Huan Po North, and Huan Po South, for it projected an image of being relatively independent from the government, although rumors were rife that the pro-Beijing forces were interested in grooming Fong as a potential elite running for LegCo direct elections in the long run. In 2021, Fong supported her assistant Connie Lam So-wai, who was defeated in the 2019 DC elections, to run in the December 2021 LegCo election. Lam was eventually directly elected, demonstrating the importance of political mentorship under Fong's tutelage of Lam.

Unlike the TKOPLCG which encountered an internal split but like the WCAU and CWAU which displayed more unity, the Shatin Community

Table 5.28: The Electoral Performance of
Tseung Kwan O People's Livelihood Concern Group, 2019

Constituency	Members and Votes		Competitors and votes	
Hang Hau East	Lee Yin-ho	1,850 (elected but withdrew from the group in September 2020)	Lau Wai-chang (New Territories Federation of Associations)	1,559
			Lau Man-choi	323
Choi Kin	Wong Ping-hung	434	Ho Man-kit	1,989
			Wong Yan-kay (Professional Synergy)	88
			Chan Wai-lit (Tseung Kwan O Youth Power)	4,724
			Tai Ka-chu (DAB)	1,306
Dou Shin	Lee Pak-tong	927	Cheung Chin-pang (Professional Synergy)	2,568
			Chong Wing-fai (DP)	1,741
Hoi Chun	Chiu Chi-man	240	Lai Wai-tong (Neo-Democrats)	2,099
			Lam Lok-yee (Professional Synergy)	1,350
			Ho Kam-wing	234
			Lau Wai-cheuk	17
Po Yee	Tse Ching-nam	4,121 (elected)	Chu Lam (FTU)	2,480
			Wong Heung-yin (Professional Synergy)	255
Fu Kwan	Luk Ping-choi	4,948 (elected)	Wong Yuen-hong (FTU)	3,123
Sheung Tak	Lee Ka-yui	5,585 (elected but withdrew in 2020)	Kan Siu-kay (FTU)	3,527
Kwong Ming	Or Yiu-lam	5,240 (elected and chair of the group)	Chong Yuen-tung	3,985
Hau Tak	Wong Cheuk-ngar	5,244 (elected but withdrew in 2020)	Mok Siu-on (DAB)	3,579
Fu Lam	Chan Chor-yiu	4,743 (elected)	Chan Pok-chi (DAB)	3,606
Huan Po North	Chan Chin-chun	943	Fong Kwok-shan (Professional Synergy)	2,998
			Ho Chi-chung	2,828
Huan Po South	Keung Sun-wah	2,063	Cheung Mei-wai (Professional Synergy)	3,577
			Ng Ho-kay	1,139

Source: Tabulated from the open data on the 2019 DC elections.

formed by a group of democrats in Sha Tin district in December 2017 tended to be politically successful and stable. The Shatin Community nominated 17 members and 15 of them were elected—an impressive result (Table 5.29). Its members defeated many candidates from the pro-government and pro-Beijing coalition, namely the New People's Party led by legislator Regina Ip and the CF formed by the former Secretary for Home Affairs Lau Kong-wah. The CF was once an influential pro-government group in the Sha Tin district. In 2019, it teamed up with the New People's

Table 5.29: The Electoral Performance of Shatin Community in 2019

Constituency	Members and Votes		Competitors and their votes	
Yu Shing	Shek Wai-lim	4,406 (62.88%, elected)	Leung Ka-fai (New People's Party and Civil Force)	2,668
Wong Uk	Lai Chi-yan	4,440 (66.72%, elected)	Leung Chi-wai (Liberal Party)	2,215
Sha Kok	Chan Siu-yeung	4,321 (59.25%, elected)	Ha Kim-kwan (New People's Party and Civil Force)	2,930
Pok Hong	Chiu Chu-bong	6,421 (73.61%, elected)	Kwok Suen-tung	2,302
Shui Chuen O	Lo Tak-ming	3,101 (50.15%, elected)	Tang Ka-biu (FTU and DAB)	3,069
Yuet Chuen	Yau Man-chun	5,280 (66.39%, elected)	Leung Ming-kai (New People's Party and Civil Force)	2,673
Chun Fung	Chan Nok-hang	4,732 (68.10%, elected)	Ngai Chi-wai (Civil Force)	2,174
Chui Tin	Hui Yuet-yu	4,552 (64.97%, elected)	Lam Yuk-wah (Shatin Women's Association and Federation of Public Housing Estates)	2,454
Hin Ka	Cheung Yu-tim	1,246 (17.38%)	Chan Wun-tung (independent democrat)	3,101
			Lam Chung-yan (Civil Force)	2,547
Ha Shing Mun	Wong Ho-fung	3,894 (55.49%, elected)	Hong Hok-leung (New People's Party and Civil Force)	3,124
King Hau	Ng Kam-hung	5,453 (60.11%, elected)	Cheung Pak-yuen (New People's Party and Civil Force)	3,443
Chung Tin	Wong Hok-lai	4,313 (60.51%, elected)	Yiu Ho-yee (DAB)	2,815
Hoi Nam	Chan Pui-ming	3,019 (65.15%, elected)	Yu Cheuk-kwan	1,615
Chung On	Yip Wing (Labor Party)	4,665 (60.92%, elected,	Kung Mei-chi (DAB)	2,993
Wu Kai Sha	Lee Wing-shing	4,167 (60.51%, elected)	Ng Cheuk-king (DAB)	2,469
Kam Ying	Ting Shi-yuen	4,775 (53.46%, elected)	Choi Wai-shing (DAB)	3,401
Tai Yee	Tse Kit-bing	1,666 (37.70%)	Lam Kong-sun (DAB)	1,923
			Lau Ching (DAB)	830

Source: Tabulated from the open data on the 2019 DC elections.

Table 5.30: The Electoral Performance of Civic Party, 2007–2019

Year	Number of nominated candidates	Number of elected candidates	Success rate	Total number of votes gained	Total percentage of votes gained
2007	42	8	19%	48,837	4.29%
2011	41	7	17%	47,603	4.03%
2015	25	10	40%	52,346	3.62%
2019	36	32	89%	141,713	4.85%

Source: Tabulated from the election results from 2007 to 2019.

**Table 5.31: The Electoral Performance of the League
of Social Democrats, 2007–2019 and Performance in 2019**

Year	Total Votes cast in the election	Popular vote	Vote share %	Number of candidates	Elected	Average votes of candidates
2007	1,148,815	28,601	2.49%	29	6	986
2011	1,202,544	21,883	1.81%	28	0	782
2015	1,467,729	6,526	0.44%	5	0	1,305
2019	2,943,842	8,384	0.28%	3	2	2,794
Constituency	**Candidates**			**Competitors**		
Lok Hong	Tsang Kin-shing (also joining Chai Wan Act-Up)	3,563 (56.00%, elected	Lee Chun-chau (HKIF)			2,800
To Kwa Wan North	Leung Kwok-hung	1,538	Starry Lee Wai-king (DAB)			1,881 (55.02%)
Lek Yuen	Sham Tsz-kit	3,283 (57.33%, elected)	Wong Yu-hon (Civil Force)			2,443

Party to consolidate their power base, but many of the coalition members were defeated. This result showed the widespread anger of many voters who were dissatisfied with the performance of the government. As the supportive agents of the HKSAR government, all the pro-establishment candidates encountered great difficulties to be elected in the 2019 DC elections.

While the new pro-democracy and district-based groups performed impressively, the same situation could be found in some relatively old pro-democracy parties. The Civic Party, which did not perform well in previous DC elections in 2007, 2011, and 2015, managed to get 32 candidates to be elected with a success rate of 89% of its nominated candidates (Table 5.30). The votes gained by the Civic Party candidates jumped from 52,346 in 2015 to 141,713 in 2019—again a phenomenon of the landslide victory of pro-democracy forces.

Compared with the Civic Party, the left-wing and pro-welfare League of Social Democrats nominated very few candidates to run in the 2019 DC elections. With only three candidates running, two of them were elected and on average its candidate got 2,794 votes, a much better result than the past (Table 5.31). The problem of the League of Social Democrats was that it tended to rely on ideological appeals to gain votes in elections, regardless of whether they were LegCo direct elections or DC ones. However, it

Table 5.32: The Electoral Performance of the Civic Passion, 2015–2019

Constituency	Members of the Civic Passion		Competitors and their votes	
2015 election				
Lei Tung One	Wong Yun-kei	177	Au Nok-hin (DP)	3,068 (60.69%, elected)
			Lee Ka-ying (DAB)	1,810
Lei Tung Two	Choi Man-lung	119	Law Kin-hei (DP)	2,564 (56.25%)
			Pang Siu-kei (DAB)	1,854
			Tang Ka-lok	21
Ying Tao	Hitsujiko Nakade (also a member of the now-defunct group advocating Hong Kong as a "nation")	172	Chung Chak-fai (West Kowloon New Dynamic)	1,611 (61.00%)
			Lam Ho-yeung (DP)	858
Yuen Chau and So Uk	Fong Chi-lung	1,160	Chan Wai-ming (DAB)	3,491 (75.06%)
Nam Shan, Tai Hang East and West	Fu Wai-lok	54	Tam Kwok-kiu	2,563 (57.25%)
			Wai Hoi-ying	1,991
Hung Hom Bay	Fung King-man	162	Cheung Yan-hong (West Kowloon New Dynamic)	1,811 (48.16%)
			Chiu Shi-shun (Labor Party)	1,740
			Lee Kam-cheung	47
Chi Wan West	Leung Yau-king	362	Yuen Kwok-keung (DAB)	3,285 (54.28%)
			Yung Shing-kwong (DP)	2,405
Lok Chui	Cheng Chung-tai	391	Junius Ho	2,013 (46.19%)
			Albert Ho (DP)	1,736
			Yuen Wai-chung	99
			Shum Kam-tim	94
			Cheung Wing-wai	25
Tin Ping West	Lee Ching-hei	797	Wong Wang-to (FTU)	2,219 (49.74%)
			Poon Tak-wing (DP)	1,445
2019 election				
Pik Hui	Ma Yu-sheng (Proletariat Political Academy, a training school of the Civic Passion)	120	Chow Wing-hang (DP)	1,462 (53.51%)
			Wong Wing-wai (BPA)	1,150
Po Lai	Fu Wai-lok	122	Mak Wai-ming	3,517
			Tam Chun-yu	1,860
Ha Pak Tin	Fong Chi-lung	436	Yan Kai-wing	3,206 (56.89%)
			Chan Chak-shing	41
			Lam Wai-man (DAB and FTU)	1,952

Table 5.32 Continued

Constituency	Members of the Civic Passion		Competitors and their votes	
Leung King	Tang Man-kit	303	Wong Tak-yuen (Tuen Mun Ten Brothers)	4,073 (58%)
			Ching Chi-hong (DAB)	2,697
Tin King	Leung Yat-long	758	Leung Ho-man (Tuen Mun Ten Brothers)	4,254 (53%)
			Lee Hong-sum (FTU)	3,038
			Lui Mei-yuk	37
Yat Chak	Wong Wing-sze	4,454 (58.14%, elected)	Kwok Hing-ping	2,607
			Fan Shun-yu (Round Table)	600
Wun Tau Tong	Wong Siu-kin	5,541 (60.61%, elected)	Yu Chi-wing (New Territories Federation of Associations)	3,603
Wu Kai Sha	Choi Kai-hang (a member of the group supporting Hong Kong as a nation)	250	Lee Wing-shing (Shatin Community)	4,167 (60.51%)
			Ng Cheuk-king (DAB)	2,469
Cheung Hang	Yim Ho-yuen	3,270	Lo Yuen-ting (DAB)	3,759 (53.48%),

Source: Tabulated from 2015 and 2019 election results.

benefited from the drastic change of public opinion against the government in the November 2019 DC elections. While Leung Kwok-hung did little constituency work in To Kwa Wan and failed to unseat DAB chairlady Starry Lee, Jimmy Sham Tsz-kit was one of the high-profile leaders of the anti-extradition movement in the latter half of 2019. Sham was attacked mysteriously by some gangsters in the protests, perhaps helping him gain more supportive and sympathetic votes from voters and leading to his electoral victory. Unlike Leung, Tsang Kin-shing did constituency work and he managed to be elected in Chai Wan. What was impressive about Tsang was that although he was sometimes defeated, he ran in the district elections again and again—a phenomenon demonstrating his political perseverance and tenacity. Overall, the relatively strong showing of the three members of the League of Social Democrats proved that ideology played a pivotal role in shaping the 2019 DC election results.

One left-wing pro-democracy group that performed relatively poorly was the Civic Passion. Formed by Wong Yeung-tat in February 2012, the Civic Passion advocated the use of local culture to resist Chinese communism. In a sense, the Civic Passion was quite localist, pro-minorities

Table 5.33: The Battle Between Democrats and Pro-Beijing/Pro-Government Forces in Rural Districts

Constituency	Democrats and their votes		Pro-government and pro-Beijing candidates	
Constituency where democrats were defeated				
Tsuen Wan suburb	Tam Pui-yan (Pro-democracy Faction DC Alliance)	3,054	Ng Hin-lung Kwan Sun-wai (Hong Kong Political Study Association)	3,409 (44.37%) 1,221
Shap Pat Heung North	Lau Chun-yu (Pro-democracy Faction DC Alliance)	1,602	Shum Ho-kit	1,896 (54.20%)
Ha Village	Tung Ching-cheuk (Pro-democracy Faction DC Alliance)	2,091	Tang Ka-leung	2,937 (58.41%)
Sun Tin	Tsui Kai-lung (Pro-democracy Faction DC Alliance)	2,032	Man Fu-yan Chow Chun-kan Man Kwei-kay	2,257 (50.04%) 61 160
Pat Heung North	Lee Kan-ming (Pro-democracy Faction DC Alliance)	1,833	Tang Yung-yiu Tang Chi-kwong (New Territories Federation of Associations, or NTFA)	1,849 (34.20%) 1,724
Pat Heung South	Eddie Chu Hoi-dick (Pro-democracy Faction DC Alliance)	3,435	Lai Wing-tim (NTFA)	3,799 (52.52%)
Sheung Shui suburb	Hau Hiu-tung (Pro-democracy Faction DC Alliance)	2,589	Hau Fok-tat	3,371 (56.56%)
Sha Ta	Choi Yuk-wai (Pro-democracy Faction DC Alliance)	2,242	Ko Wai-kei (DAB)	3,143 (58.37%)
Lantau Island	Fung Siu-yin (Pro-democracy Faction DC Alliance)	2,633	Yu Hon-kwan	2,873 (52.18%)
Ping Chau and Hei Ling Chau	Tsui Yat-long (Pro-democracy Faction DC Alliance)	1,093	Tsang Sau-hao	1,499 (57.83%)
Lamma and Po Toi	Chun Ching-ching (Pro-democracy Faction DC Alliance)	972	Lau Shun-ting (DAB)	1,003 (50.78%)
Constituency where democrats won				
Tuen Mun suburb	Cheung Kam-hung (Pro-democracy Faction DC Alliance)	3,797 (60.17%)	To Shek-yuen (NTFA)	2,513
Shap Pat Heung Central	Fong Ho-hin (Pro-democracy Faction DC Alliance)	4,013 (60.57%)	Leung Ming-kin Chow Yip-ming	2,473 139
Shap Pat Heung East	Lee Chun-wai (Pro-democracy Faction DC Alliance)	1,838 (48.04%)	Lam Tim-fook Wong Pak-yan	1,500 488
Shap Pat Heung West	Szeto Pok-man (Pro-democracy Faction DC Alliance)	3,391 (49.76%)	Leung Fook-yuen Chan Yau-hung	3,080 344

Table 5.33 Continued

Constituency	Democrats and their votes		Pro-government and pro-Beijing candidates	
Ping Shan South	Leung Tak-ming (Pro-democracy Faction DC Alliance)	3,172 (53.12%)	Cheung Wai-shum (NTFA) Tang Lung-wai	2,270 529
Ping Shan Central	Cheung Chi-yeung (Pro-democracy Faction DC Alliance)	2,479 (51.93%)	Tang Tat-sin	2,294
Kam Tin	Lee Chung-chi (Pro-democracy Faction DC Alliance)	2,569 (52.84%)	Tang Cheuk-yin	2,293
Sun Fu	Wu Yiu-cheong (Neo-Democrats and Pro-democracy Faction DC Alliance)	4,435 (56.43%)	Law Hiu-fung (BPA)	3,424
Lam Chuen Valley	Chan Chun-chit (Pro-democracy Faction DC Alliance)	3,605 (52.05%)	Chan Cho-leung (BPA)	3,321
Shuen Wan	So Tat-leung (Pro-democracy Faction DC Alliance)	3,583 (50.99%)	Lau Chi-shing (NTFA)	3,444
Sai Kung North	Tam Yee-pui (Pro-democracy Faction DC Alliance)	2,730 (58.16%)	Lee Wah-kwong	1,964
Sai Kung City Central	Leung Hin-kan (Pro-democracy Faction DC Alliance)	2,550 (54.41%)	Ng Si-fook	2,137
Pak Sha Wan	Ho Wai-hong (Labor Party and Pro-democracy Faction DC Alliance)	2,805 (57.08%)	Chan Kuen-kwan (DAB)	2,109
Sai Kung Islands	Chan Ka-lum (Pro-democracy Faction DC Alliance)	2,127 (57.81%)	Lee Ka-leung	1,552
Cheung Chau	Leung Kwok-ho (Pro-democracy Faction DC Alliance)	5,142 (61%)	Kwok Wai-man (DAB)	3,233

Source: Tabulated from 2019 election results.

and it was advocating constitutional reforms in the HKSAR. Wong participated in the 2012 LegCo election in Kowloon East and was narrowly defeated by pro-government candidate Tse Wai-chun. Nevertheless, a younger member of the Civic Passion, Cheng Chung-tai, got directly elected to LegCo in 2016. This election result was a watershed for the Civic Passion in which Wong Yeung-tat let Cheng to take the leadership while Wong himself focused on his political commentaries on the HKSAR through the Internet. The Civic Passion, however, did poorly in the 2015 DC elections, for all its nine candidates got relatively few votes. The reason was that they did not pay attention to local constituency work and relied heavily on ideological appeals on the streets to campaign for electoral support. In 2015,

Cheng Chung-tai participated in a constituency named Lok Chui where a heavyweight politician of the Democratic Party, Albert Ho, was targeted by pro-Beijing candidate Junius Ho. Cheng got 391 votes which could ideally be transferred to Albert Ho for the sake of competing with Junius Ho. The Lok Chui battle was significant because there were other unknown candidates intentionally or unintentionally coming out to divide the votes gained by Albert Ho, who eventually lost to Junius Ho. The Civic Passion appeared to learn from its mistake of lacking constituency work in the 2015 DC elections. The 2019 DC elections witnessed the victory of at least two members of the Civic Passion, namely Wong Wing-sze and Wong Siu-kin. The two performed very well and could beat the pro-government and pro-Beijing candidates.

Democratic Victory in Rural Areas in the 2019 District Council Elections

The 2019 DC elections also witnessed the victory of many democrats over the pro-Beijing and pro-government candidates in many rural areas. There were at least 26 constituencies that could be seen as located in rural districts (Table 5.33). Among the 26 constituencies, 11 of them envisaged the defeat of democrats and 15 witnessed their victory. For the fifteen democrats who could defeat rural elites in rural constituencies, they outperformed the candidates from the DAB, BPA, and NTFA as well as from some clans, like the Tang clan. This phenomenon broke the political tradition that rural areas were usually occupied by the rural factions and their elites.

Conclusion

This chapter uses the rich data to analyze the features of the 2019 DC elections. In many ways, the 2019 DC elections constituted a watershed in the development of Hong Kong's electoral and district politics. Not only did the pan-democratic camp score an unprecedented victory, but it also made significant breakthroughs in the emergence of new pro-democracy and district-based groups and in the massive victory over pro-government candidates in rural areas. The degree of political participation of the voters and candidates, including female candidates, was also unprecedentedly high. None of the seats in the 2019 DC elections was automatically elected—a special feature different from the past. The victory of the pan-democrats was characterized by their better coordination among themselves, a strategy of decentralization that allowed district-based like-minded groups to emerge and compete with their opponents, and the coexistence of a fragmented pro-democracy camp in various districts. On the other hand, the pro-government and pro-Beijing candidates suffered an unprecedented defeat, showing their unpopularity after the long struggles between the anti-extradition protesters and the government. It can be said that the landslide victory of the democrats in the 2019 DC elections was a testimony to the discontent of most voters with the performance of the government in handling the extradition bill. Even in constituencies where the police dormitories were located, pro-democracy candidates performed strongly and defeated many pro-government and pro-Beijing candidates. This meant that most voters cast their ballots against not only the government but also arguably the police performance. In a sense, the 2019 DC elections constitute a referendum for the voters to express their grievances against the government, whose unpopularity became a huge political liability and burden to the candidates of the pro-establishment and pro-Beijing forces.

Notes

1 Chiu Kwan-sok, "The Meaning of District Council Elections," Voice of Tang, November 25, 2019, in https://www.voicettank.org/single-post/2019/11/25/112501, access date: October 25, 2020.

2 "HKMAO chief Zhang Xiaoming demoted," February 23, 2020, in https://news.rthk.hk/rthk/en/component/k2/1508301-20200213.htm, access date: October 25, 2020.

3 One of authors got a list of the full names of all the 449 candidates, October 2019. Rumors were rife that the list was prepared by officials of the Liaison Office, but such a rumor could not be verified.

6

Violence and Elections — A Text-mining Analysis Based on Twitter Feeds[1]

The 2019 District Council (DC) election was the most politicalized one in Hong Kong's history. Two main factors explained such politicization. One was the cumulative effect of the post-1997 reforms to the DC: (1) DC members held 117 out of 1,200 votes in the Chief Executive election before 2020; (2) an increase in the number of DC seats allocated in the functional constituencies of Legislative Council (LegCo) from one seat to five seats; and (3) direct elections for all DC seats. These reforms increased the importance of DC elections for both pro-establishment and pan-democracy politicians engaging in the competition for seats in the LegCo and in the Election Committee for the Chief Executive. Arguably, DC members obtained a stronger mandate from voters in monitoring the government's performance, selecting legislators, and having the chance of electing the Chief Executive. Another factor was the anti-extradition movement that took place in the summer of 2019. This unprecedent large-scale social movement intensively politicized the entire DC elections, as mentioned in the last Chapter. During the six months of protests from June to November that preceded the 2019 DC elections, both camps — the pro-establishment camp and the anti-extradition camp, including firstly the localists (本土派，*ben tu pai*), pan-democrats (泛民，*fanmin*), and the "bold and militant" or "resolute" (勇武，*yongwu*) faction — became political antagonists and lost political trust in each other.[2]

Following a Beijing-directed strategy that called for an end to violence and disorder and a strong support from the pro-establishment camp, the HKSAR government took a hardline stance, responding to the protesters' "five demands" by escalating the use of force, rather than through political dialogue.[3] This approach triggered numerous police–civilian conflicts, including violent clashes at the Chinese University of Hong Kong (CUHK) and the Hong Kong Polytechnic University (PolyU) and conflicts between supporters of the two camps. These conflicts and clashes turned the focus of the DC elections from candidates' approaches to district affairs to an outlet for their dissatisfaction with the government, such as "punishing the establishment faction at the ballot-box" (血債票償，*xie zhai piao chang*) as proposed by the pro-democracy *Apple Daily* special issue, namely *freedom summer* (自由之夏，*zi you zhi xia*), which framed the elections as a *de facto* referendum. Also, nearly one-third (298 of 1,090) of the candidates' echoed with the political trends, such as calling for either "five demands" or "resuming social order" in the election platforms.

The results of the DC elections affirmed an observation made by *Foreign Policy* that "the more teargas had been used by the increasingly brutal Hong Kong police, the bigger the movement toward the democrats."[4] They also affirmed the success of the pan-democracy faction's strategy of creating a quasi-referendum and showing Hong Kong's opposition to the extradition bill and the police's use of force.[5] As a result, the pro-democracy parties and groups won a landslide victory in the election, grasping 389 out of a total of 452 seats and leaving pro-establishment camp with merely 61 seats. The turnout of the election was an unprecedented 71.2%, compared with a 47% turnout in the previous DC election. The 2019 DC elections gave the pro-democracy camp control of 17 of 18 local district councils, as discussed in the previous Chapter.

While the hardline police response was an important factor in the election result, regarding it as the sole or even primary reason for the election outcome is over-simplified and lacks an in-depth analysis of the outcome. After all, the police possessed the legitimate use of force in dealing with those protesters who violated the law, and who plunged the HKSAR society into chaos. In any event, a deeper exploration of the DC election results is needed, including the views of residents on the protests, the public, and emotional reactions to the events rather than simply offering an explanation based on the ballot figures. As such, this Chapter examines a relatively under-explored source of public emotions and sentiment during the DC elections. Unlike a closed-question static survey poll, this Chapter uses text messages from the social networking service (SNS) Twitter as textual data (soft data). There was evidence that Hong Kong residents increasingly turned to SNSs such as Facebook and Twitter to express their views on the DC elections. As of January 2020, there were about 5.8 million active SNS users, making up 78% of Hong Kong's population.[6] The majority of these were users of Facebook (4.8 million), Instagram (2.3 million), and Twitter (750,000).[7] Messages circulated via SNS platforms illustrated public opinion and represented a largely untapped text-mining source.

To explore public opinions expressed through SNS messaging, namely the "tweets" from Twitter, this Chapter employs a text-mining technique: structural topic modelling (hereafter STM).[8] Another text-mining method, namely sentiment analysis, is also adopted to explore public sentiments expressed in Twitter users' tweets of the election results. The remainder of this Chapter proceeds as follows: Section 2 presents our data, which include tweets related to the election. Section 3 presents the STM and an analysis of its results, including STM-identified topics and trends. The effect of the violent police–civilian clashes at the CUHK and PolyU on topical trends will also be analyzed. Section 4 presents the results of the sentimental analysis, showing Twitter users' sentimental trends were related to police clashes for the members of both pro-establishment and the pan-democracy factions. Section 5 offers our conclusion and the broader implications for violence and strategic coalitions between the pan-democratic and the "resolute" or "militant" camps.

Twitter Feeds as Textual Data

We use Twitter feeds as data. Through Twitter, users can openly post their microblogs, and textual messages (in Chinese) up to 140 characters are called tweets. Moreover, the "like" and "share" functions on Facebook are available on Twitter; these are called "favorite" and "retweet." We chose Twitter as the data source for two reasons. First, Twitter is currently a mainstream SNS used all over the world. Although the number of Facebook users in Hong Kong is still higher than the number of Twitter users, this gap has been narrowing. The number of Twitter users in Hong Kong increased by nearly 270,000 between 2019 and 2020.[9] The second reason is the accessibility of data collection. Facebook currently only allows posts to be obtained from pages that are open to the public; Twitter has no such limitation.

Figure 6.1: Distribution of Tweets in Our Final Dataset for the 2019 DC Election (n=8,471)

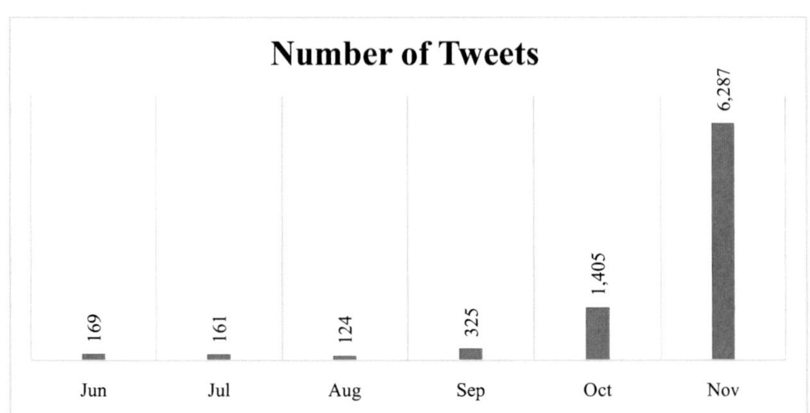

For the tweets collection, we search for tweets on the topic of the 2019 DC election. The search inquiry is consisted of the following phrases in traditional Chinese characters: "the 2019 District Council elections" (*2019 qu xuan*); "District Council elections" (區議會選舉 *qu yi hui xuan ju*); "District Council elections" (區選 *qu xuan*); "establishment" (建制 *jianzhi*); "pan-democrats" (泛民 *fanmin*); and "constructive force" (建設力量 *jian she li liang*).[10] The search range was set from June 1, 2019 to November 24, 2019. This range covered the nearly six months that preceded the date of the November 2019 DC election. After deleting duplicates, non-traditional Chinese characters, and irrelevant tweets, we had 8,471 tweets, including 23,345 retweets and 63,405 favorites. Figure 6.1 depicts the monthly number of tweets over the period, reflecting the fact that Twitter users began voicing concerns from the beginning of the nomination of candidates for the DC election in October. The number of tweets soared to 1,453 in October before skyrocketing to 6,287 in November 2019.

Structural Topic Modelling

We first use STM, a frequency-based automated content analysis, to identify the meaningful semantic clusters related to "District Council elections." We employed STM because it can process a very large amount of messy textual data. More importantly, STM can identify both the latent topics and topical trends over time. Topics can be understood here as particular views of

Twitter users toward the events associated with DC elections. Furthermore, STM allows us to measure the effect of covariates on topic prevalence, namely, the proportion of a document and tweets devoted to a topic. We use this function to estimate the effects of the CUHK and PolyU clashes on the topic proportion.[11]

Previewing the Twitter Content: Tearful or Protest Votes

The STM generated a 13-topic model (see the Specification of Topic Model Selection). We selected 12 interpretable topics for elaboration, cataloguing them into three major themes: Theme 1: Views on the election; Theme 2: Violence; and Theme 3: Voting. Topic prevalence indicated that the following topics were of the most central concerns to Twitter users: Topic 11: "Infringing on human rights" (topic prevalence, 0.077) in Theme 1: Views on the election; Topic 8: "A candidate who was disqualified" (0.114) in Theme 2: Violence, and Topic 7: Opposed to casting null or void ballots (0.112) in Theme 3: Voting.

Most Twitter users believed that violence stimulated the users' desire to vote; this was particularly felt by pro-democracy candidates and the finding echoes *Foreign Policy*'s observation. But more than that, conflicts between the pan-democratic faction and the resolute faction were surging among tweets. These conflicts embodied the debate within the resolute faction over casting either a "tearful vote" (so-called 含淚投票 *han lei tou piao*) for pan-democratic candidates or a "protest vote" (that is, a void or blank ballot 投廢票/白票). The term "tearful vote" is used directly for our translation. Some users expressed their view that the moderate line of democrats failed, but they had little choice except for supporting the democrats, who they thought were much better than the pro-government and pro-Beijing forces.

Theme 1: Views of the Elections

The first theme of the topic model focuses on Twitter users' views of the DC elections. This theme reflects the fact that most users believed that radical protest actions (e.g., road blockage and even throwing petrol bombs) were more powerful than the pan-democracy faction's moderate line. However, users became more and more reluctant to engage in confrontations with the increasingly "brutal" police crackdown. Some users accepted a parallel strategy, connecting the anti-extradition protest with the DC elections.

Figure 6.2: Trendlines in Theme 1 topics

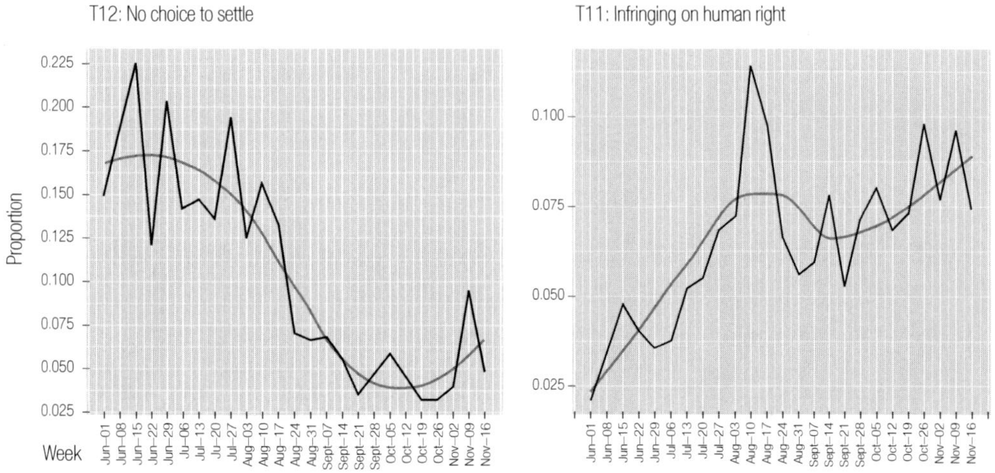

T12: No choice to settle

T11: Infringing on human right

Note 1: The black line in the plot represents the topic's annual prevalence. The topic prevalence's grey line is plotted by using a smooth function (to decrease noise). We set 0.075 topic prevalence as a threshold, indicating that something happened at that time was worth noting.

Figure 6.2 shows a rise in Topic 12: "No chance to settle" and Topic 11: "Infringing on human rights." Topic 12 reveals users' views that the anti-extradition movement could not end peacefully and that it was unstoppable. They decried the pan-democracy faction's "outdated" moderate line as fighting democracy in the "comfort zone." For example, a user said: "Facing the suppression of the authority, the youngers responded to it in an alternative tactic. But it is making things escalating or going bad, and unstoppable … In a word, that is, 'the moderate faction returns to the old way or comfort zone (that is, parliamentary politics impacting on electoral campaign)."[面對當權者的打壓，小朋友變陣回應，令事件升溫或變質，更加難以收拾……一句話：溫和派回到老路或舒適區……]." This view was prevalent before the week of August 24, as Figure 6.2 illustrates (the plot on the left). As noted by numerous tweets, Chief Executive Carrie Lam gave "pitiless feedback" to the initial peaceful demonstrations and the subsequent police crackdown on street protests was conducted in the name of "upholding the rule of law." To the members of the "resolute" faction, Carrie Lam's hardline approach was equivalent to repudiating the moderate line which was advocated by the pan-democratic camp. Although some old hands in the pro-establishment faction, such as Jasper Tsang Yok-sing, attempted to break the political deadlock, the HKSAR government's view was further hardened during the PolyU conflicts, as indicated by the new upsurge in the trendline for Topic 12 in the week beginning November 9. Objectively speaking, the PolyU confrontation with the police was unacceptable to the government and the police, which had to restore social order as soon as possible. On Twitter, the users liked to quote Jasper Tsang's statement that "the Chief Executive obeyed the hard-liners' words." Tsang's remarks implied that it was impossible for the HKSAR government to consider and offer an amnesty to the convicted offenders and violent lawbreakers of the anti-extradition movement, which was in fact one the five demands made by protesters.

The second topic is Topic 11: "Infringing on human rights." For instance, during the three strikes (*san ba,* namely labor strikes, merchants' strikes, and student strikes), a female protestor was allegedly shot by the police, which caused her to become injured in her right eye. However, there were reports saying that she was actually shot and injured by the protesters. The woman's injured eye incident became a skyrocketing prevalence in Topic 11 during the week starting from August 10, as shown on the right plot of Figure 7.2. Other concerns were escalating again after October that corresponded to the incidents mentioned by Twitter users. These incidents included the following:

(1) The HKSAR government's consideration of introducing the provisions of the Emergency Regulations Ordinance, which had been legislated during the British Hong Kong colonial era, and of imposing a Prohibition on Face Covering Regulation in early October. These measures were aimed at deterring demonstrators, who wore face masks or cover, from staging protests and was deemed to be an infringement of the freedom of assembly.[12]

(2) The interpretation of the Hong Kong Basic Law by the Standing Committee of the National People Congress. This possible move was seen as reversing the previous Hong Kong High Court's "unconstitutional" decision over the controversial Face Covering Regulation.

(3) The alleged "torture" of Cheng Man-kit, a former officer of the UK Consulate in Hong Kong, in the mainland when he travelled there. Cheng was allegedly interrogated by PRC authorities on the UK's role in Hong Kong's anti-extradition protests during his custody in mainland China.[13]

(4) US President Donald Trump's statement that "Hong Kong [would be] obliterated in 14 minutes" and the report saying that he asked the PRC to "stop any military crackdown" on the anti-extradition protest.[14] Of course, Trump's statement was regarded by the PRC authorities as intervening in the affairs of the HKSAR. But his remarks triggered the discussion among the Tweeter users.

We also found that tweets calling for street protests and protests in LegCo (including the action of filibustering) were going together. Thus, users regarded the DC elections as providing a golden opportunity for them to express their demand for "true universal suffrage", not only to the HKSAR government but also to the international community. For example, a user remarked: "Street protests and LegCo protests are compatible with the fight for democracy…The DC elections on November 24 will be a big chance for the Hong Kong people … The Hong Kong people should make an appeal for 'genuine universal suffrage' so that we can make our voice heard to the international community." [「街頭‧議會」雙腿爭民主⋯⋯11月24日區議會選舉，是港人大好機會⋯⋯港人都要鎖定「真普選」訴求⋯⋯向國際發聲]. However, a small number of tweets with opposing views highlighted the precondition that if the Hong Kong people were behaving lawfully, they could enjoy human rights. As it turned out, the radical users' argument could be seen as "inviting" foreign intervention in Hong Kong's democratic reform—an argument that could be regarded as violating the National Security Law, which was eventually promulgated in late June 2020.

Theme 2: Violence

The second theme illustrates the persistence of extensive electoral violence (Figure 6.3).

The first topic (Topic 8: "A candidate who was disqualified") is composed of tweets on Joshua Wong Chi-fung's invalid nomination for the candidacy of DC elections.[15] Some Twitter users expressed their resentful emotions in response to the requirement for a "confirmation letter," namely "the one-person-one-letter campaign against the usage of the confirmation letter to disqualify the candidate [namely Joshua Wong]." ["一人一信反對區議會選舉確認書DQ參選人"] This requirement for candidates acquiring confirmation letters to run in elections was viewed as a political screening system, a kind of "structural violence."[16] Thus, some tweets showed an upsurge in users' hostile

Figure 6.3: Trendlines in Theme 2 topics

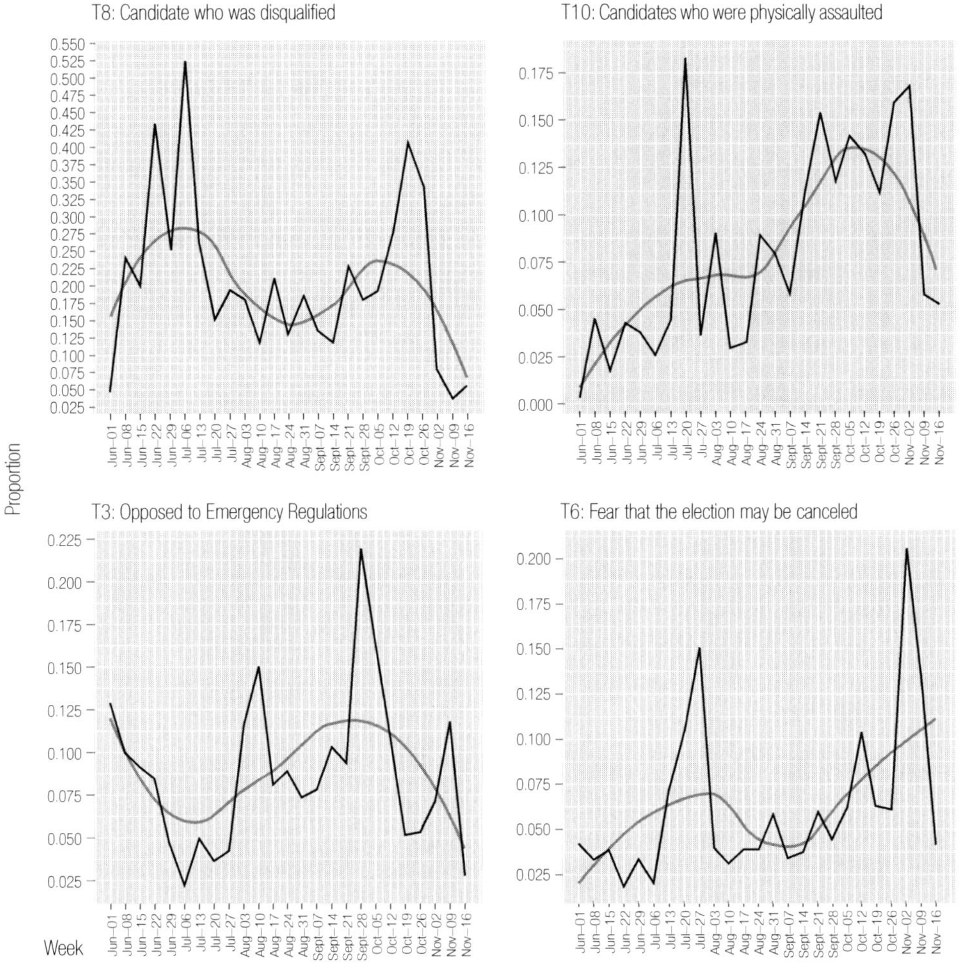

T8: Candidate who was disqualified

T10: Candidates who were physically assaulted

T3: Opposed to Emergency Regulations

T6: Fear that the election may be canceled

Proportion

Week

attitude towards and distrust of the HKSAR government due to the Joshua Wong case. These feelings were reflected in users' posts related to Joshua Wong's criticisms of the Electoral Office, such as "a violation of administrative neutrality" (e.g., "administrative neutrality ceases to exist except in name" ["公務員政治中立「名存實亡」"]. In Figure 7.3, T8 highlights that this topic's trendline soared between June 22 and July 6, corresponding to the Election Affairs Commission's formal announcement of the confirmation letter system. The other peak of the trendline occurred in the week beginning from October 19, when Joshua Wong's candidacy nomination was officially declared as "void." Certainly, some pro-establishment users offered their counterarguments, stating that this was a "political price" that should be paid by Joshua Wong and his "anti-China" activist partners (i.e., "Wong and his associates have to pay for their opposition to China and destabilization of Hong Kong") ["黃之鋒們 反中亂港 必有代價"]. Another articulation of the radical argument for "structural violence" is Topic 3: "Opposed to Emergency Regulations" which manifests users' fear that the HKSAR government would postpone or even cancel the DC elections by using the Emergency Regulations Ordinance, a view reflected in the upward trend of this hot topic in August when, apparently, Chief Executive Carrie Lam and her Executive Council (ExCo) advisors were reportedly considering to use the Emergency Regulations Ordinance after the PRC State Council's Hong Kong and Macau Affairs Office had called for "an end to violence and a cessation of disorder." On October 4, 2019, the promulgation of the Prohibition on Face Covering Regulation took place in the HKSAR.

In contrast to the surging perception on "structural violence," the second topic (Topic 10: "Candidates who were physically assaulted") conveys public suspicions of the intimidation cases affecting some pro-democracy members. These suspicions were reflected in the sharp upward trends in the week that began from July 20 and then from late September onwards (see Figure 7.3, T10). The first tide covered the July 21 Yuen Long violent incident in which gang members dressed in white T-shirts allegedly and prominently attacked some anti-extradition activists at the Yuen Long MTR station—a tragedy immediately shown on the television and Internet news programs in the HKSAR. The second tide matched the occurrence of several other incidents, including the intimidation of pro-democracy candidates running for office that appeared to threaten them to withdraw from the elections. For example, a Labor Party member, Stanley Ho Wai-hong, and a leading convener of the Civil Human Rights Front, Jimmy Sham Tsz-kit, were mysteriously assaulted. A member of the Democracy Party, Cary Lo Chun-yu, who competed in the DC elections 2019, reportedly received a death call. Indeed, violence was commonplace in the anti-extradition protests and even in the election campaign of the 2019 DC elections.

The above-mentioned violent incidents triggered users' fear that the elections would be halted (Topic 6: "Fear that the election may be canceled"). Tweets in this topic repeated a conspiracy theory that the elections would be called off. Specifically, some users believed that someone would perhaps create an excuse for the government to call off the election, like the creation of disturbances in voting stations, because the electoral situation was unfavorable to pro-establishment candidates. The territory-wide hottest topic of such conspiracy theory included an incident in which a citizen used a knife to attack Junius Ho, but some users queried the incident as being suspected of being a "self-directed act" in their tweets. Conspiracy theories were abound in the users' discussion.

Users' fear that the elections would be cancelled triggered some protesters' concessions, as shown by the last topic in Topic 9 of Theme 2: "Force the government to hold elections as scheduled." In this topic, tweets expressed the opinion that the confrontational or the resolute faction's hardline position, such as the "three strikes" in September, had not worked out at all. Conversely, protesters changed their strategy, bargaining with the HKSAR government through concessions made as the date of the November DC elections approached, as the Twitter feeds demonstrated. Interestingly, some protesters reopened the blocked Tolo highway outside the CUHK in exchange for the HKSAR government's promise that it would hold the DC elections. However, this move also reflected the protesters' ambivalent and oscillating attitude towards the hardline and moderate tactics when they were confronting the HKSAR government's superior police force and the increasingly effective crackdown.

Theme 3: Voting

Theme 3 illustrates the debates and opinions within the resolute faction over the voting issue (Figure 6.4).

Topic 2, namely "Pro-democracy faction has betrayed Hong Kong," exemplifies the entire debate. For instance, most users were hostile towards the pro-democracy faction's preeminent concern about its number of DC seats, rather than about the protesters' lives. For examples, a user wrote, "Is the DC election more important than the chivalrous persons' lives? Why is the pan-democracy faction trying hard to campaign for votes? Is there a person going to rescue the 100 heroes who are still staying and defending at the Polytechnic University?" ["區選重要還是義士性命重要？為甚麼有泛民努力拉票？死守理大的一百人誰去拯救？"] However, some users believed that the spirit of solidarity was critical to any confrontation with the government, recalling a million-strong peaceful demonstration at the beginning of the

Figure 6.4: Trendlines in Theme 3 topics

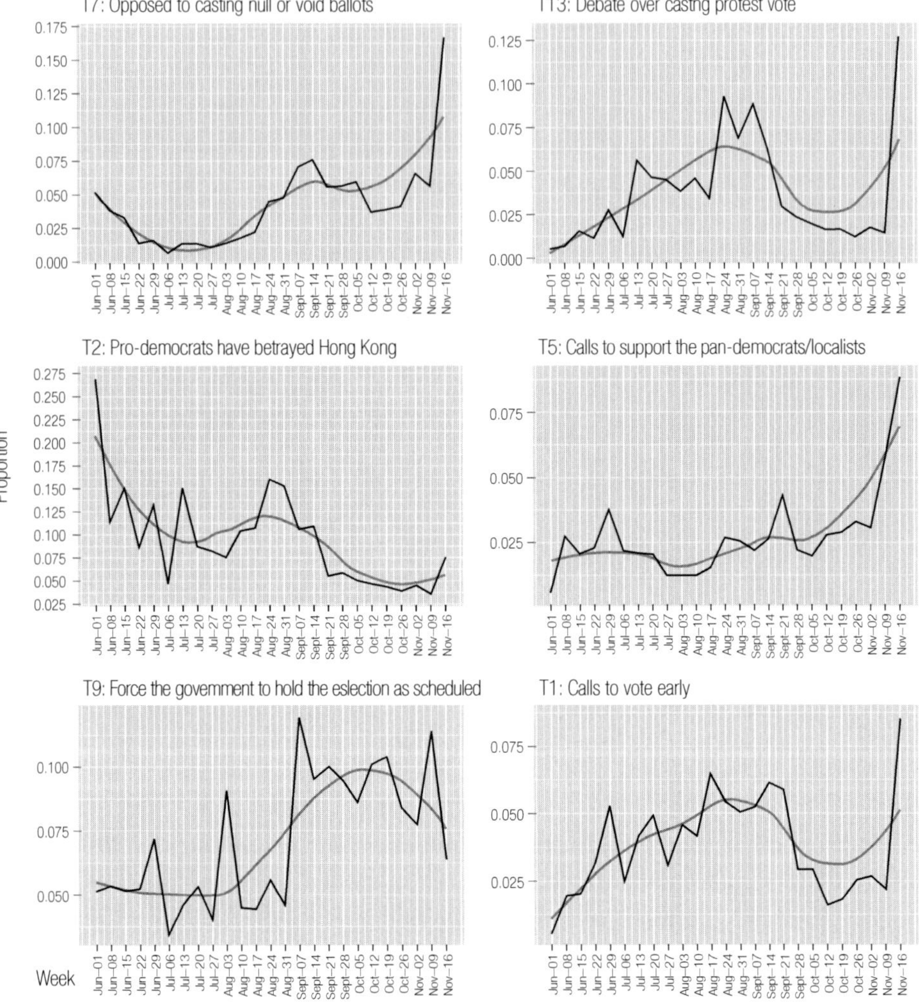

anti-extradition movement and reiterating their belief that such a soft approach could be replicated in the DC elections (i.e., hashtags #the first homework #2019 DC election) (i.e., hashtag #第一份功課 #2019區選).

Similar argument can be found in Topic 13: "Debate over casting void ballots." Some users criticized the pan-democrats, who thought themselves to be "the only voice against the government." They urged that the pan-democracy faction should revise its election platforms in order to attract voters, rather than resorting to a "moral blackmail." They contended that the pan-democrats were using the anti-extradition movement to enhance the possibility of winning the DC elections. Another side disagreed with idea of giving the "void votes" to pan-democratic candidates, because both the pro-democracy faction and the resolute faction could not afford to be divided in the face of "unprecedented suppressive tactics." For example, one user wrote: "People who don't vote, or cast void/invalid votes: we thank you for supporting the institutional violence on behalf of the pro-establishment faction!" ["唔投票/投白票/投廢票嘅人： 代親中建制多謝你支持制度暴力！"].

Experiencing numerous points of contention, some users called for a consensus for the "void ballot" issue—a position adopted in Topic 7: "Opposed to casting null or void ballots." This trendline soared from the week beginning from November 9, two weeks before the DC elections. A mainstream assertion in this topic among users was that the pro-democracy faction was "the lesser of two evils" compared with the pro-establishment faction. For instance, a user remarked: "Even though the pan-democracy faction did not do it well enough, at least it did not work against you as what the pro-establishment faction did. Kicking the pro-establishment faction away may not be useful. But retaining the pro-establishment faction in LegCo must be harmful." ["泛民做得唔夠做得唔好，但係起碼佢哋唔會好似建制咁同你對著幹。踢走建制可能無咩用，但係留佢哋喺度就一定有害"] However, a consensus supportive of pro-democracy candidates could not completely calm down the users because of their entrenched and profound distrust of the HKSAR government. One of the reasons for their deep distrust of the pro-government forces was vote-cheating (presented in Topic 5: "Calls to support pro-democrats"). Almost all the tweets in this topic reminded voters that they should avoid any possible information leakage to the pro-establishment camp for the sake of conducting tactical voting. For example, a user said: "Don't dress in black and wear a face mask. Be patient and the whole situation is important. Avoiding the pro-establishment faction from seeing our votes! Tactical voting! If someone ask you who you vote for, you must answer in a standard way that you vote for the pro-establishment camp." ["*唔好穿黑衫戴口罩* 忍一忍　大局為重。避免被建制派睇通票數！配票！如果有人問你投左邊個，一律答建制派"] Moreover, as seen in Topic 1: "Call to vote early," Barnabas Fung, Chairman of the Electoral Affairs Commission, said that the DC elections would be terminated in case of being disrupted. In response to his remarks, some users believed there was a plan of terminating the elections once the pro-establishment candidates received enough votes. For example, a user said: "Barnabas Fung claimed that he would halt the elections once the voting stations get into chaos that last for three hours. As long as the pro-establishment candidates get enough ballots, they would dispatch those men dressed in black T-shirt [like gangsters] to cause troubles in polling stations, thereby helping to generate an excuse to terminate the elections." ["馮驊說，只要有票站持續三小時有混亂，即停止選舉……只要建制早上一夠票，即刻派人扮黑衣人在選舉站前搗亂，然後大有藉口把選舉煞停"]. Therefore, some users were very keen to urge voters to cast their ballots early, a view corresponding with the sharp upward trend in the week beginning from November 16, the week before voting would take place.

The Effect of Conflicts on Topic Patterns

As tweets often mentioned police–civilian conflicts when they discussed the void ballots, we therefore select the CUHK and PolyU police-protestors clashes as covariates to examine whether the violent conflicts affected the topical patterns. We chose these clashes for two reasons: First, the clashes at the CUHK and PolyU were the two most severe police–civilian conflicts that occurred during the anti-extradition protests. In both cases, the police fired over 2,000 tear gas cannisters. Second, the incidents were regarded as having the unintended consequence of "assisting" the pro-democracy faction's electoral situation, stimulating the voting rate to a high level.[17]

The "CUHK" Effect

Figure 6.5 shows the proportion estimated for all the selected topics in the "cuhk" covariate. Comparing the left plot with the right plot, it is apparent that Topic 7 — "Opposed to casting ballots"/"Say no to blank vote" (topic prevalence: 0.046) — takes the first place after conflicts and is far ahead of the topic in second place (i.e., Topic 13: "the debate over casting void ballots" [0.016]), whereas the first place in the left plot is taken by Topic 8: "A candidate who was disqualified" (0.075) and the second place by Topic 10: "Candidates who were physically assaulted" (0.068). It must be said that, since the CUHK conflicts, the focus of mainstream tweets had shifted from Joshua Wong's candidature in elections to the issue of void ballots.

Figure 6.5: The Effect of the CUHK Conflict on Topic Proportions

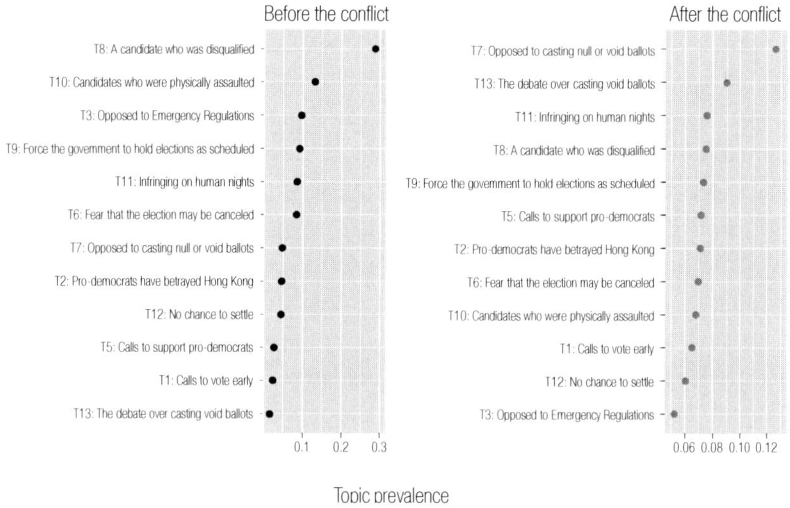

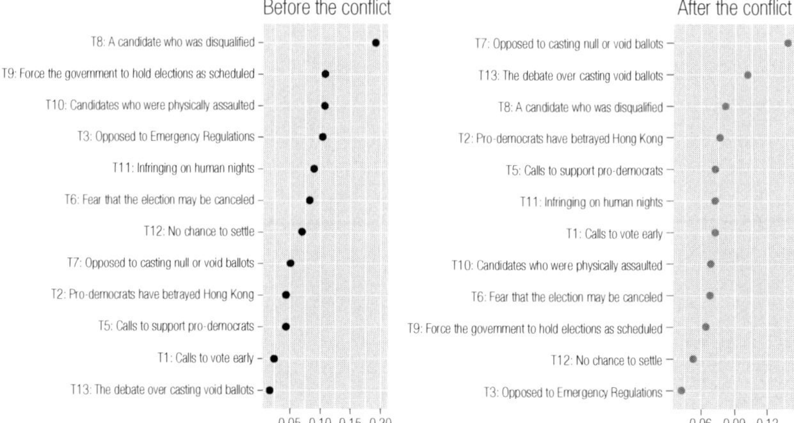

Note: the number below the plot is the mean score of topic prevalence. Here, the total of the topic prevalence is 1. The character "T" refers to the "topic" case as the plot space is limited.

Figure 6.6: The Effect of the PolyU Conflicts on Topic Proportions

The "PolyU" Effect

Figure 6.6 illustrates a similar pattern with the "PolyU clashes" as the CUHK conflicts. Both Topic 7 (0.138) and Topic 13 (0.102) also occupy the first two ranks following the PolyU conflicts. The only difference between the PolyU and CUHK patterns is Topic 9: "Force the government to hold the elections as scheduled" ([0.064]), as the left plot demonstrates. Thus, we believe that Twitter users were overwhelmingly worried that the DC elections would be canceled before the inception of the PolyU conflicts.

This section provides a response to the commentary about why the clashes "assisted" the pan-democracy camp in a high-voting-rate situation. The result concludes that severe clashes strongly pushed the users to cast their ballots for the pan-democratic candidates. Certainly, it does not mean that all Twitter users sincerely and really supported the pro-democracy candidates. Overall, the users eagerly waited for the pro-establishment camp's crushing defeat in the elections, a type of retaliation of the pro-establishment faction's pro-police stance. A tweet from Topic 7 exemplified this position: "The pro-establishment and royalist camp supports the 'black' (referring to those people violating Hong Kong's law) police beating "brothers" (the protesters), and opposes the 'Five Demands.' If you cast a null vote against the pan-democratic faction, it is equivalent to supporting the pro-establishment faction whose candidates hold iron votes. If you are finally against the pan-democratic faction, you cast blank votes." Objectively speaking, the term "black police" was a sentimental one without any evidence, for the police tried their best to maintain law and order. However, the tweet's content illustrated a profound sense of some users' distrust toward the police, which had the duty of maintaining law and order in a highly chaotic society of Hong Kong in the latter half of 2019.

Sentiment Analysis

This section attempts to investigate the relationships between Twitter users' feelings and the DC elections by probing their sentiments. We employ sentiment analysis, a dictionary-based text-mining technique. This technique uses a sentiment dictionary to count the words in the documents (i.e., the tweets) that match those in the dictionary. The calculation is straightforward: where one word (e.g., "chivalrous person" [*yi shi* 義士])

matches a positive word in the dictionary, count 1; where one word (e.g., "rioter," [*bao tu* 暴徒]) matches a negative word in the dictionary, count -1. Where the sum of positive/negative words in one document is a positive number (i.e., 1 or above), the document is deemed as containing positive sentiments. A negative sum (i.e., -1 or below) means it would be regarded as containing negative sentiments. "0" is classified as neutral. The technique has indeed been increasingly used in electoral studies that aim at predicting election outcomes.[18]

According to the algorithm of sentiment analysis, we can assume that the more positive the sentiment directed towards the pro-democracy (including the pan-democratic and localist faction) and the pro-establishment camps, the more ballots that a particular camp would obtain, and vice versa. We keep using the same processed data as it contains all the tweets about the DC elections. We also choose the police, the pan-democracy faction, and the pro-establishment faction as research subjects. It is because the Hong Kong police's use of force embodied the hardline stance of Beijing and the HKSAR government. The pan-democracy faction and the pro-establishment faction as the main political camps participating in the DC election reflected the Twitter users' attitude toward the government's policy on the anti-extradition bill movement.

To conduct sentiment analysis, we first subset the data by using the following Traditional Chinese search words: "police" (*jing cha* 警察), "the pan-democrats" (*fanmin* 泛民), and "the establishment" (*jian zhi* 建制). By so doing, we returned 869, 1,544, and 3,976 hits respectively. We then counted "favorite" and "retweet" from the tweets to get an overview of *the share of the voice* in Twitter before proceeding with the sentiment analysis to probe and illustrate the positive, negative, and neutral sentiments directed at the pan-democracy and establishment camps, which were the two major participants in the DC elections.

Results

Figure 6.7 clearly illustrates the number of tweets stemming from each of the three groups. It shows that the number of tweets increased in November, the month during which the DC elections were held. Tweets containing "the pro-establishment camp" (3,653 tweets) almost tripled those that mentioned "the democracy camp" (1,216 tweets), and were five times more

Figure 6.7: Number of Tweets Containing the "police," "pro-democracy camp," and "pro-establishment camp" for 6 months

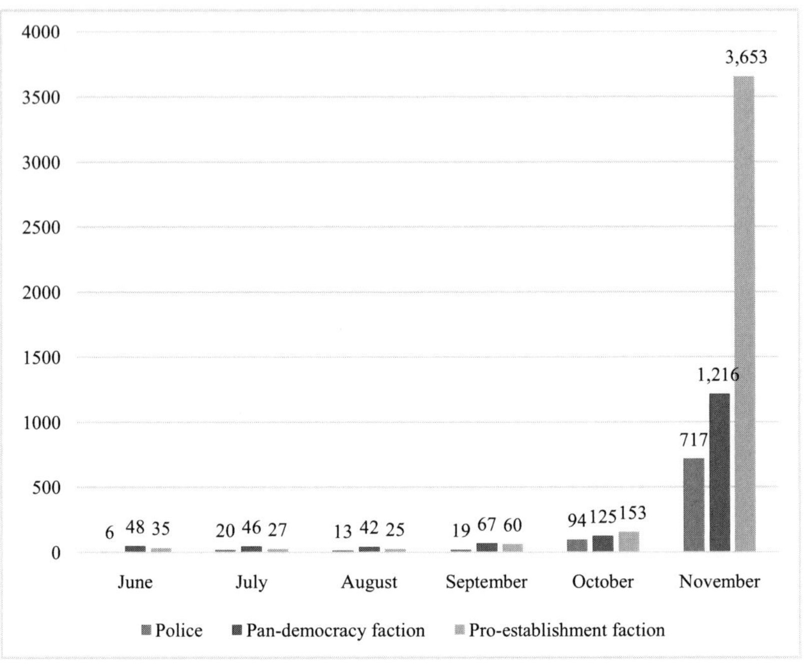

Figure 6.8: Number of the Favorites and Retweets for the "police," "pro-democracy camp" and "pro-establishment camp"

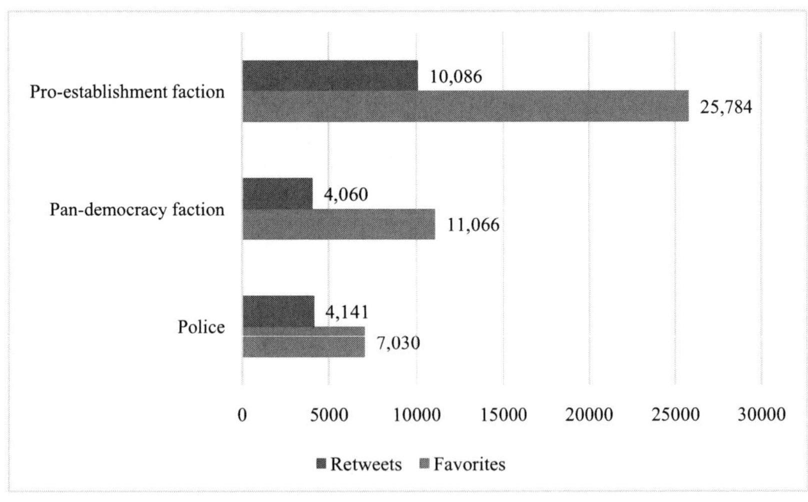

than those that mentioned the "Hong Kong police" (717 tweets). The number of tweets reflected Twitter users' far more intensive discussion on "the pro-establishment camp" than others.

Figure 6.8 demonstrates the number of favorites and retweets. "The pro-establishment camp" had a total of 4,060 retweets and 25,784 favorites, a number far beyond "the pan-democratic camp" (4060 retweets, 11,066 favorites) and the "police" (4,141 retweets, 7,030 favorites).

The number of favorites for the pro-establishment camp was far more than that for the pan-democratic camp (Figure 6.8). This pattern is at odds with the STM results. We thus further examined the content of the tweets with the most retweets and favorites. We found that a tweet posted on 23 November 2019 (i.e., one day before the DC voting date) had the most users' interest (819 favorites and 494 retweets), both in the pro-democracy camp and the pro-establishment camp. This post attacked those people "who were calling for votes and who prefer to cast a void ballot than to support the pan-democratic candidates" and it said: "Please look back at why the amendment to the Fugitive Offenders Ordinance was passed in the second reading? The reason for its passage was that the pro-establishment faction occupied most of the seats in LegCo." ["話叫人唔好投泛民 寧願投白票……麻煩大家回憶下點解會修訂逃犯條例會通過二讀？因為多建制派囉!"] The mainstream opinion was that the principal "enemy" of Hong Kong was the pro-establishment faction, rather than the pan-democratic front.

For the "police" group, the most shared tweet (407 retweets) slammed the police's "brutal crackdown" on the freedom of speech and of assembly. It was posted on November 4 and said that the police "bullied the people under the disguise of 'maintaining law and order,' which was reduced to become a political tool of suppressing Hong Kong's freedom of speech and freedom of assembly with violence, and of intervening in the DC elections." ["假借「維護法紀」之名欺壓市民……淪為政治工具……以暴力打壓香港言論及集會自由，干預區議會選舉"]. The date of this tweet coincidentally matched the court appearance of some pan-democratic candidates who were charged with illegal assembly in an anti-extradition rally.[19] The most favorite tweet (773 favorites) which was posted in November discussed a story of a former constable, Yau Man-shan, who resigned from the police and participated in the DC elections because "she disapproved of how the police handled protests." ["她(邱汶珊)不認同同事處理當地示威浪潮的手

Figure 6.9: Sentiment Analysis of the Pan-democracy/Pro-establishment camps

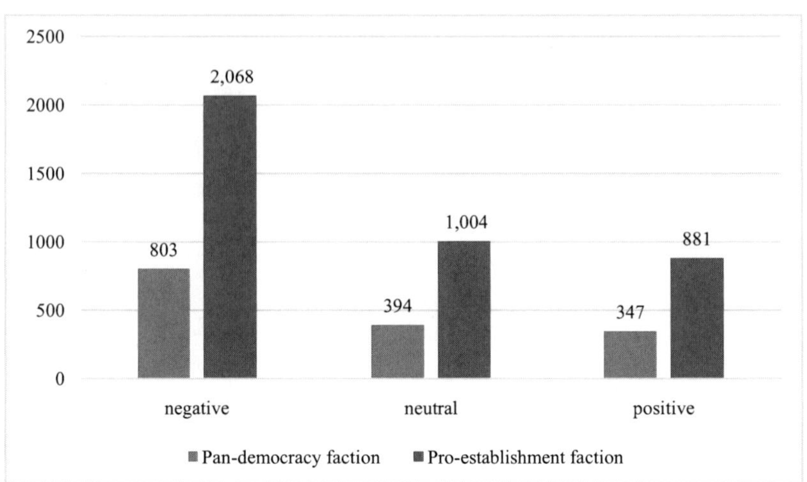

法"]. The content of the two tweets showed that the police were regarded as not only being a "suppressive machine" during the DC elections but also providing a legitimate argument for many users to support the pro-democracy candidates.

Finally, Figure 6.9 shows the result of our sentiment analysis of the pro-establishment and pro-democracy factions. The number of tweets (2,068 tweets, 66%) expressing negative sentiments on the pro-establishment faction doubled compared with the figure of negative pan-democracy faction tweets (803 tweets, 57%). However, by ratio, the negative sentiment on pro-establishment faction was moderately higher than the pan-democracy faction one. This phenomenon shows that both factions' images to Twitter users were negative. But the degree of users' antagonism toward the pro-establishment faction mildly exceeded their negative feelings of the pro-democracy faction, illustrating the users' mindset that the pan-democratic faction was perhaps "the lesser of two evils." It was especially true in the political atmosphere of "referendum" or two camps stood against each other. Moreover, the mindset of "the lesser of two evils" was a key factor that help explain why there were many freshman or independent pro-democracy candidates successfully elected in the 2019 DC elections.[20]

Conclusion

This Chapter contributes to our deeper understanding of the most politicalized DC elections in Hong Kong history through an in-depth study of Twitter feeds. Specifically, we explore why the elections favored the pro-democracy camp. With the help of STM, we portrayed the context of the six months of violent and peaceful protests that preceded the DC elections. To the pro-democracy voters, voting in the DC elections became a mirror and even a "referendum" of the government's performance in handling the extradition bill and the protests,[21] but the voting was less about district governance. On the other hand, to the supporters of the resolute or militant faction, the elections became a battlefield since the street protests met the police crackdown. This situation fostered the strategic cooperation between the moderate democrats and the radical/militant/resolute faction. The reason, as we found out from the tweets, was that the support for users who argued for the need for a protest vote against the pro-democracy candidates was waning alongside with the escalation of police crackdown on protests and the increasing number of police assaults on protesters. At the same time, the voice of the "tearful vote" for the democrats was increasing. We can conclude that the escalation of police crackdown on protests had an unintended consequence of shifting the contentions between the pan-democratic faction and the radical/resolute/militant faction to a deliberately strategic cooperation of casting ballots in the DC elections. If so, the "tearful vote" phenomenon, i.e., supportive of the pro-democracy candidates based on their resistance to the pro-government and pro-Beijing camp, was a hallmark of the 2019 DC elections. The phenomenon was unique and abnormal in the 2019 DC elections, whose results would not be easily repeated in future district elections, especially if the factor of physical violence under the enacted National Security Law would likely fade away over time.

Indeed, this Chapter's methodology is not without any limitation. Tweets associated with the DC elections might have been missed, even though we employed the most searched keywords. Additionally, there is currently no in-depth Cantonese dictionary, which would considerably improve the word-segment accuracy. Furthermore, our critics may question the over-representation issue of tweets because of the users' extreme

Figure 6.10: Diagnostic Values by Number of Topics in the Candidate Models

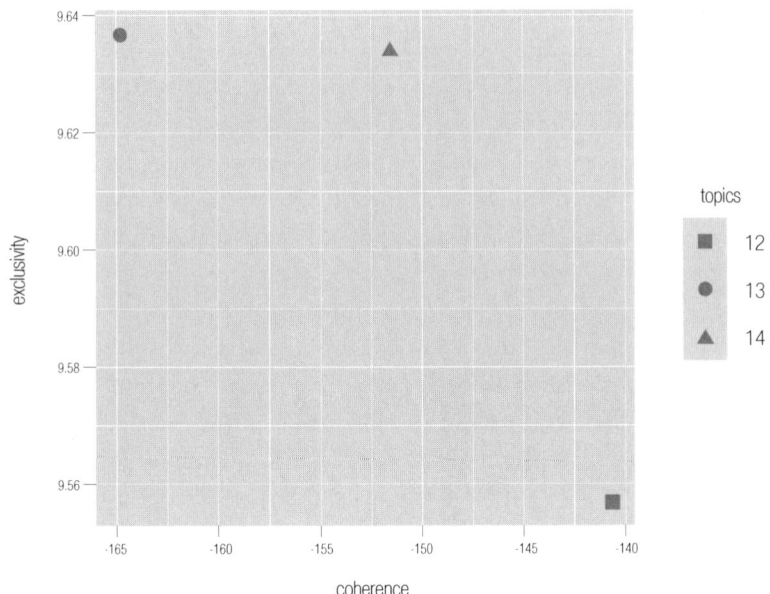

ideological preferences, but in turn, such ideological bias illustrated a high degree of political polarization,[22] as our study showed happened in the 2019 DC elections. Still, our study of the content and context of Tweets during the period from June to November 2019 provided the in-depth understanding of the views of users and their transformation in the DC elections, especially when public opinion poll could not be easily conducted at that time.

A Note on Methodology:
Specification of Topic Model Selection

STM is a statistical modelling technique used in the process of extracting meaningful topics from natural language text (such as news articles). We used the R package stm (version 1.3.5) to estimate the topic model we adopted in this chapter, operating in R (version 3.6.1) on the RStudio platform (version 1.2.1335). After processing the data, we had to determine a "correct" number of topics (number of clusters, K) because there is no overarching gold standard (Grimmer and Stewart 2013, 19–20). To find the most substantive, "fittest" model, we referred to Quinn's method, first narrowing down the searching scope by using the stm built-in function search. We set the number of topics, ranging from five topics to 40 topics in five-topic increments, then repeated this step with five-topic to 15-topic.

Initially, we chose three candidate models (12-topic, 13-topic, 14-topic) by referencing the model's diagnostic scores: "exclusivity" (the top words in a topic that significantly differ from others) and "semantic coherence" (the top words in a topic that are most likely to co-occur in a passage. See Figure 6.10).

After examining the scores, we validated the candidate models by conducting an independent and closed reading of the top ranked news articles in each candidate's topic model. We thus selected the 13-topic model because it was the best and most intuitive model for our research task. To avoid overwriting the selected model, in the topic selection step we needed to select the relevant topics and to discard those topics unrelated to our research. Therefore, we discarded the "American politics" topic because it focused on the two-party politics in the United States that was not closely related to our research tasks. We further assigned corresponding labels in accord with the core meaning of the tweets for each topic.

Notes

1 We thank Professor Robert Reynolds for his useful opinion and are grateful to Bocheung Liu for his assistance in data collection.

2 "Localist" is a complicated term that refers to different democratic factions. In this chapter, the terms include (1) "liberal localists," namely the mainstream moderate pro-democracy faction, which adopts a peaceful, rational, non-violent approach; and (2) "confrontational localists," namely the faction that uses protests and/or violence to call for political reform. In this chapter, we also refer the confrontational localists to the resolute faction. For consistency, the term resolute faction is adopted in this chapter. For the "liberal" and "confrontational" factions of localists, see Sonny Shiu-Hing Lo, "Ideologies and Factionalism in Beijing–Hong Kong Relations," *Asian Survey*, vol. 58, no. 3 (2019), pp. 395–415.

3 The five demands were as follows: (1) the withdrawal of the Fugitive Offenders amendment bill, (2) an investigation into alleged police brutality and misconduct, (3) the release of all the arrested individuals, (4) a retraction of the official characterization of the protests as "riots," and (5) the introduction of universal suffrage in the territory.

4 According to HKSAR official figures, police fired around 10,000 rounds of tear gas in the territory-wide region during the six-month-long anti-extradition protest. Hillary Leung, "Tear Gas Sparks Public Health Anxiety in Hong Kong," December 4, 2019, in https://time.com/5743663/tear-gas-hong-kong/, access date: August 19, 2020.

5 Choi Chi-keung said that the pan-democracy faction believed that the politicization of the DC election (such as framing the election as a *de facto* referendum) could push keen-on-politics young voters to come out to vote, thereby elevating the voting rate, which would benefit the pan-democracy candidates. See Choi Chi-keung, "the DC election was converted to be a referendum—why the pan-democracy faction got a landslide victory" *Apple Daily*, November 27, 2019, in https://tw.appledaily.com, access date: August 1, 2020. Francis Lee Lap-fung also refers to an Internet survey stating that 71.2% of respondents who voted for pan-democracy candidates regarded the DC elections as a *de facto* referendum, compared to only 28.8% of voters for pro-establishment candidates. Francis Lee Lap-fung, "The figures of the ballot and the survey in the District Council election, and the current state of the public opinion." *Ming Pao*, December 5, 2019, in https://news.mingpao.com, access date: August 19, 2020.

6 Simon Kemp, "Digital 2020: Hong Kong. DataReportal — Global Digital Insights," February 13, 2020, in https://datareportal.com/reports/digital-2-2--hong-kong, access date: August 15, 2020.

7 *Ibid.*

8 Margaret E. Roberts, Brandon M. Stewart and Dustin Tingley, "Stm: R Package for Structural Topic Models." *Journal of Statistical Software*, vol. 20, no. 2 (2016), pp. 1–40.

9 Kemp, "Digital 2020: Hong Kong."

10 We add "constructive force" because the word "establishment" may have a political meaning with negative connotation in Hong Kong.

11 To measure the effects of the two cases, we manually coded two covariates: "cuhk" (i.e., representing before [coded "0"] and after [coded "1"] the police–civilian CUHK conflict); and "PolyU" (i.e., representing before [coded "0"] and after [coded "1"] the police–civilian PolyU conflicts).

12 The HKSAR Government, "Prohibition on Face Covering Regulation Gazetted." *HKSAR Press Release*, October 1, 2019, in https://www.info.gov.hk/gia/general/201910/04/P2019100400613.htm, access date: August 5, 2020.

13 John Sudworth, "Simon Cheng: Former UK Consulate Worker Says He Was Tortured in China." *BBC News*, November 20, 2019, in https://www.bbc.com/news/world-asia-china-50457262, access date: August 25, 2020.

14 *RTHK*, "Trump 'HK Obliterated in 14 Minutes without Me,'" November 22, 2019, in https://news.rthk.hk/rthk/en/component/k2/1493927-20191122.html, access date: August 19, 2020.

15 Joshua Wong was the former General Secretary of the pro-Hong Kong political group named *Demosisto*, which was supportive of "self-determination" and which was abolished shortly before the enactment of the Hong Kong National Security Law on June 30, 2020. His party member, Agnes Chou Ting, had been disqualified in her candidacy nomination in the 2018 LegCo by-election for the same reason; that was, the party's assertion of "self-determination, including the option of Hong Kong independence." The News Lens, "Joshua Wong is disqualified for the District Council Elections: Is there a plan of depriving my right to be elected for life?," *The News Lens*, October 29, 2019, in https://www.thenewslens.com/article/126680, access date: August 25, 2020.

16 The "confirmation letter" system imposed in recent years requires those who are running for election to prove that they support Hong Kong Basic Law and HKSAR. Also, the system mandates that electoral officers have to affirm a nominee, whether *sincere* or not, in his or her attitude toward the Basic Law. As such, the electoral officers have considerable discretion to make their decisions on the eligibility of candidates in DC elections.

17 Lee Hong-yan, "Unveiling the big data for the District Council election; the police to 'assist' the pro-democracy faction at the last moment," *CitizenNews*, December 16, 2019, in https://www.hkcnews.com/, access date: August 25, 2020. Lo Chi-kin, "'Making violence' failed to drum up votes, the regime [should be] tuned to couple hardness with softness," *CitizenNews*, December 18, 2019, in https://www.hkcnews.com/, access date: August 19, 2020.

18 Widodo Budiharto and Meiliana Meiliana, "Prediction and Analysis of Indonesia Presidential Election from Twitter Using Sentiment Analysis," *Journal of Big Data*, vol. 5, no. 1 (2018), pp. 1–10; Bae Jung-Hwan, Ji-Eun Son and Min Song, "Analysis of Twitter for 2012 South Korea Presidential Election by Text Mining Techniques," *Journal of Intelligence and Information Systems*, vol. 19, no. 3 (2013), pp. 141–56; Ibrahim Mochamad, Omar Abdillah, Alfan F. Wicaksono and Mirna Adriani, "Buzzer Detection and Sentiment Analysis for Predicting Presidential

Election Results in a Twitter Nation, IEEE (2015), pp. 1348–1353; Murphy Choy, Michelle L. F. Cheong, Ma Nang Laik and Koo Ping Shung, "A Sentiment Analysis of Singapore Presidential Election 2011 Using Twitter Data with Census Correction," 2011, in http://arxiv.org/abs/1108.5520, access date: August 5, 2020; Sameki Mehrnoosh, Mattia Gentil, Kate K. Mays, Lei Guo, and Margrit Betke, "Dynamic Allocation of Crowd Contributions for Sentiment Analysis during the 2016 U.S. Presidential Election," 2016, in http://arxiv.org/abs/1608.08953, access date: August 6, 2020.

19 Fung Chia-chi, "November 2 Rally: Three candidates running for the DC elections arrested in the rally of Victoria Park are go to the court with the charge of holding illegal assembly," November 4, 2019, in https://www.hk01.com/, access date: August 1, 2020.

20 We are grateful of the anonymous reviewers' opinion at this point.

21 According to the survey result from Hong Kong Public Opinion Research Institute, there was 87.8% of respondents who voted the democrat faction's candidates having a referendum mindset for the DC elections. Francis Lee: The current state of public opinion reflected in the votes and polls of the District Council election. Litenews.hk. December 5 2019. https://bit.ly/3rt2Gcp (access date: January 17, 2022).

22 Barberá, Pablo, & Rivero, Gonzalo, "Understanding the political representativeness of Twitter users," *Social Science Computer Review*, vol. 33, no. 6 (2015), pp. 712–729.

7

The Politics of District Administrative Reforms, 1999–2019

District administrative reforms in the Hong Kong Special Administrative Region (HKSAR) could be traced back to the Tung Chee-hwa era (1997–2005), when the Urban Council (UrbCo) and Regional Council (RegCo) were abolished in December 1999. As early as October 1998, the Tung administration proposed to abolish the two councils on the grounds that streamlining the governance of the HKSAR was necessary, and that centralization of the municipal services would be desirable. Table 7.1 sums up the main arguments of the HKSAR government's proposal of abolishing the UrbCo and RegCo. The proposed repeal of the Provisional UrbCo and RegCo Ordinance, the formation of a new Liquor Licensing Board, and the proposed establishment of a Municipal Services Appeals Board were clearly moves to centralize the delivery of municipal services to the hands of the government rather than empowering two elected bodies to cope with them. Financially, the new fee-setting mechanism for various fees and charges related to municipal services would go back to the HKSAR government—an amount that would be substantial and lucrative from the perspective of increasing the income revenue of the administration. The main objective of the abolition of the two councils was to implement the plan proposed by the HKSAR government to reorganize the provision of municipal services.[1] Specifically, it aimed to transfer the existing property, functions, rights, and obligations of the two Municipal Councils to the government and other statutory bodies; to eliminate the inconsistencies between the by-laws of the two Municipal Councils; and to repeal a number of outdated legislative provisions.[2]

Table 7.1: Main Objectives of the Abolition of Urban Council and Regional Council

The objectives of the government proposal to abolish the two councils included the following:

(1) "The transfer of all existing property, rights, liabilities, functions and powers of the PMCs to the Government or designated public officers."

(2) "The repeal of the Provisional Urban Council Ordinance and the Provisional Regional Council Ordinance."

(3) "The formation of a new Liquor Licensing Board and a Licensing Appeals Board in place of existing boards and committees under the PMCs performing similar licensing and review functions."

(4) "the formation of a Municipal Services Appeals Board in place of the existing Urban Services Appeals Board and Regional Services Appeals Board."

(5) "A new fee-setting mechanism for various fees and charges related to municipal services."

(6) "The deletion of certain obsolete provisions in the Public Health and Municipal Services Ordinance (Chapter 132) and its subsidiary legislation and the repeal of duplicate subsidiary legislation."

(7) "Various transitional provisions and savings to maintain legal and administrative continuity."

(8) "Consequential amendments in related ordinances and subsidiary legislation".

Sources: "Legislative Council Brief: Provision of Municipal Services (Reorganization) Bill," available in: https://www.legco.gov.hk/yr98-99/english/bc/bc73/general/73_brf.pdf (access date: August 16, 2020).

At the same time, the HKSAR claims that it "definitely recognizes the past achievements of the two Municipal Councils in promoting people's participation in public affairs and in the provision of services relating to food hygiene, environmental sanitation, culture and recreation."[3] It added that "we have never bad-mouthed the two Municipal Councils, nor have we ever even attempted to do so, for we definitely recognize their achievements."[4] However, with the development of representative government, the HKSAR administration contended that the "political functions of the two Municipal Councils have very much faded, because, with their elected elements, the Legislative Council (LegCo) and the District Councils (DCs) are now much better able to monitor the government."[5] In addition, some political commentators and members of the two Councils, according to the government's explanation, had expressed the view that in such a tiny but densely populated place like Hong Kong, a three-tier representative government would "inevitably result in duplicated functions and therefore low efficiency."[6] Therefore, the HKSAR government advocated that that the three-tier structure should be "rationalized to become a two-tier arrangement."[7]

The HKSAR government asserted that it had triggered a review on the structure of district organizations in late 1997. Most importantly, the outbreak of the avian flu in late 1997 and a series of food hygiene incidents "had highlighted many problems brought about by the fragmented responsibilities and poor co-ordination for food safety and environmental sanitation among several organizations."[8] From the HKSAR administration's perspective, the bird flu and food hygiene issues were "not just the problem of the two Municipal Councils; but it is related to the problem of internal co-ordination within the government."[9] Hence, to address the concerns of the public, the HKSAR government were determined to reassert its direct responsibility for food safety, public health, and environmental sanitation. This reform entailed the need to enhance co-ordination between the different government department, to improve public service delivery and to strengthen the ability of the government to deal with food safety incidents.[10]

The government claimed that after the abolition of UrbCo and RegCo, the role of DCs would be enhanced, including their functions and the allocation of more resources for them.[11] First and foremost, the chairman and vice-chairman of each DC would become the members of their respective District Management Committee (DMC), and they would take part in coordinating community services and prioritizing facility planning within their districts.[12] Second, there would be an increase in the accountable allowance for each DC or to rent offices and employ personal assistants, thereby enhancing councilor's services to residents.[13] Third, the Food and Environmental Hygiene Department (FEHD) and the Leisure and Cultural Services Department (LCSD) would consult the 18 DCs on the issues pertinent to environmental hygiene services, and the planning and facilities of leisure and cultural services.[14] Moreover, the government claimed that regular briefings would be given to DCs with a view to raising the level of their participation in and monitoring of public affairs.[15] Fourth, the government asserted that it would suitably increase the funding for DCs to improve the environment of districts and to organize more district-based cultural and leisure activities.[16] Fifth, the Home Affairs Department (HAD) would deploy more manpower to assist DCs in their work.[17] In short, the HKSAR government gave lots of promises to enhance the role of DCs in exchange for the abolition of the two Municipal Councils.

Table 7.2 shows the remarks of some LegCo members on the proposed abolition of the two councils. While James To, Ambrose Cheung, and Cyd Ho opposed the government's proposal, other pro-government legislators like Leong Che-hung, Lui Ming-wah, Chan Wing-chan, and Tam Yiu-chung supported it. Those who were against the idea raised the issues of the government's lack of accountability to the public after the abolition of the two councils and the absence of public opinion polls in support of the idea.

Table 7.2: The Remarks of Legislative Councilors on the Abolition of Urban Council and Regional Council

Legislative Councilor	Remarks
Leong Che-hung	"Following the reconstitution of the Urban Council in 1973, the Municipal Councils had been devoid of input from professional team with medical knowledge and experience in public health. Regrettably, the standard of food safety, especially in food premises, and environmental hygiene has fallen considerably…There is a lack of a central body responsible for policy formulation of food safety and environmental hygiene. This shameful and deplorable management of the avian flu, the cholera, and subsequently the red tide highlighted the embarrassment that Hong Kong has witnessed a lack of coordination at its best."
James To	"The streamlining is obviously related to the 'scrapping' of the two Municipal Councils. The government wants to retrieve the power of members directly elected by the people… Of course, the government would argue that powers are distributed among the two Municipal Councils, the district boards, and the Legislative Council. In fact, the degree of democracy in the Legislative Council insofar as election is concerned is lower than that in the two Municipal Councils. The government thinks if a certain structure is politically translucent or over which it has insufficient mobilization power, the only solution is to retrieve powers from it. The government is thus using this opportunity of 'streamlining' to retrieve the powers and develop in this direction."
Lui Ming-wah	"A district administrative structure is set up in consideration of the administrative environment, efficiency and cost-effectiveness. Owing to historical reasons, Hong Kong was separated many years ago into two parts to facilitate administration. Thus, we had the two Municipal Councils. At that time, the separation did have merits. But with the development of the New Territories, the differences between urban areas and the New Territories have become increasingly small. As we have seen, in the past few years, there are overlapping and deficiencies in the administrative structure of the two Municipal Councils. So, a proposal for restructuring by the government fits the principles and theories of modern management, for the benefit of better management and service delivery."
Ambrose Cheung	"Its underlining political motive is crystal clear — the Administration prefers an executive-led administration but is worried that the executive-led government will gradually come under threat when the local authority amasses resources and becomes financially autonomous… The two Municipal Councils are the only bodies through which Hong Kong people can directly and indirectly participate in the formulation and implementation of municipal policies. The fact that the Administration does not trust the municipal authorities and the judgement of the people and fails to give them more opportunities to take part in the formulation and implementation of policies and shoulder responsibilities does reflect that the Administration has cast a vote of no confidence in the public!"
Chan Wing-chan	"The FTU has always been of the view that the structural overlapping of the three-tier representative government should be reviewed when appropriate. With regard to the future development of the structure of municipal services, someone has proposed the 'two Municipal Councils, one department' and the 'one Municipal Council, one department' models. However, no matter which model is adopted, it still does not solve the existing problem of structural overlapping, such as the overlapping of the Urban Council and the district boards and the overlapping of the Urban Council and the Legislative Council… Hong Kong is a small and densely populated place. In the FTU's view, it is appropriate to have a two-tier structure comprising the Legislative Council and District Councils. We fail to see the need for a third tier to supervise or monitor the provision of municipal services. Instead, this monitoring role can be played by the District Councils and the Legislative Council by having their functions strengthened."

Table 7.2 Continued

Legislative Councilor	Remarks
Tam Yiu-chung	"From the point of view of serving the public, I think that we should reconsider how these structures can provide us with services more effectively, and such a reconsideration does merit our support… I do not think such retrogression is the aim and effect of the dissolution of the Municipal Councils… I do not think a reorganization will deprive public opinion representatives of the chance to take part in municipal services or lead to a retrogression in democracy…I do not think that the abolition of the Municipal Councils will contravene Articles 97 and 98 of the Basic Law… We hope that all the new arrangements will meet the needs of social development so that the services provided will meet the public's expectations."
Cyd Ho	"The government has not given us room and time to conduct a detailed review, and it is going to 'scrap' the Municipal Councils in a hurry. It also turns a blind eye to the public opinion expressed over the years. The government often says that public opinion supports the 'scrapping' of the Municipal Councils. The government often says that public opinion supports the 'scrapping' of the Municipal Councils… I do not know what public opinion polls the government has conducted but it is not willing to conduct a referendum to obtain the most scientific and objective proof. Therefore, each of them sticks to its own views. This is most disappointing. It is a great pity that Hong Kong will miss a chance to review the structure of district organizations. The government wants to abolish the two Municipal Councils in a hurry to centralize power… The government is biased when releasing the relevant information and making preparation for the consultation document. The government affixes the responsibility for the 'avian flu' incident on the Municipal Councils. When the government put forward this argument, some people really supported it but the subsequent development of the issue later clarified the situation…Yet, the government has been making publicity and creating the false impression of popular support, turning a deaf ear to dissident voices.

Sources: "Official Record of Legislative Council Proceedings, December 1, 1999," in https://www.legco.gov.hk/yr99-00/chinese/counmtg/floor/991201cd.pdf, access date: August 16, 2020. Also see "Official Record of Legislative Council Proceedings, December 2, 1999," in https://www.legco.gov.hk/yr99-00/chinese/counmtg/floor/991202ca.pdf, access date: August 16, 2020.

They criticized the government of seizing the chance of using the bird flu as an excuse to abolish the two councils and to centralize municipal services in the hands of the administration. A representative from the UrbCo, Ambrose Cheung, believed that the government proposal had the political motives of reasserting its executive-led power, withdrawing the resources from the elected local authorities, and of emasculating the financial autonomy of UrbCo and RegCo. Those who supported the idea argued that the three-tier structure was unnecessary, that the bird flu issue reflected the lack of government coordination, and that streamlining the municipal services and structures was the way forward. The government's proposal was politically controversial and divisive. Nevertheless, abolishing the two councils would deprive many pro-democracy and pro-government UrbCo and RegCo members of their elected positions and the related stipends. Most importantly, the government would be able to grasp more revenues from the charges of various municipal services. Politically and financially, the HKSAR government gained much from the abolition of the UrbCo and RegCo.

Table 7.3 shows the voting result of Legislative Councilors on the Provision of Municipal Services (Reorganization) Bill. There were 35 pro-government legislators and one pro-democracy legislator supporting the bill. For pro-government side, only the Heung Yee Kuk (HYK) Chairman Lau Wong-fat, RegCo representative Tang Siu Tong, and UrbCo representative Ambrose Cheung opposed the bill. Except for moderate democrat Andrew Wong Wang-fat, all the democrats opposed the bill. Hence, the government bill was eventually passed by LegCo.

Table 7.4 shows the public attitudes towards the structure and consultation of district organizations in Hong Kong. Only 5% of the respondents were familiar and very familiar with the structure of district organizations, while 67.1% of them were quite unfamiliar and very unfamiliar with the structure. It showed that most ordinary people were not familiar with the structure of district organizations in Hong Kong. For the government proposal, only 1.8% of the respondents were familiar with the document on the evaluation of district organizations and 80.4% of them were quite unfamiliar and very unfamiliar with the government's consultation document. The results proved that many Hong Kong citizens did not really understand the government's proposal on district organization reform, a phenomenon contrary to what the government claimed, namely public opinion supporting the district organization reform. Strictly speaking, the government interpreted public opinion in such a way as to legitimize its determination of abolishing the two councils. In fact, political scientist Michael DeGolyer argued that the abolition of the two councils was "a clear step backward in the development of representative government in Hong Kong," and that the government did not rely on any scientifically selected sample to prove that public opinion supported the proposal.[18]

Table 7.5 illustrates the public attitudes towards the work of the Legislative Councilors, Urban Councilors, and District Board (DB) members. It shows only 10.2%, 6.9%, and 13.4% of the respondents were familiar with the work of legislative councilors, urban councilors, and DB members respectively. More people were familiar with the work of DB members compared with the urban councilors and legislative councilors. This finding shows that DB members were much closer to the public than Urban Councilors and Legislative Councilors. The survey result also

Table 7.3: Position of Legislative Councilors on the Provision of Municipal Services (Reorganization) Bill

Camp	Number of Support the Bill	Number of Oppose the Bill
Pro-government	35	3 (Lau Wong-fat, Tang Siu Tong, and Ambrose Cheung)
Pro-democracy	1 (Andrew Wong Wang-fat)	18
Total	36	21

Sources: "Official Record of Legislative Council Proceedings, December 2, 1999," in https://www.legco.gov.hk/yr99-00/chinese/counmtg/floor/991202ca.pdf, access date: August 16, 2020.

Table 7.4: Public Attitude towards the Structure and Consultation of District Organizations in Hong Kong

Attitude	The structure of district organizations in Hong Kong	The evaluation of district organizations in Hong Kong
Very familiar	0.4%	0.5%
Quite familiar	4.6%	1.3%
Half-half	25.2%	12.3%
Quite unfamiliar	54.5%	52.9%
Very unfamiliar	12.6%	27.5%
Hard to Say	2.7%	5.5%

Source: "Survey conducted by the Social Sciences Research Centre of the University of Hong Kong [CB(2)343/98-99(01)]," in https://www.legco.gov.hk/yr98-99/chinese/panels/ca/papers/p343c01.pdf, access date: August 16, 2020.

Table 7.5: Public Attitudes towards the work of the Legislative Councilors, Urban Councilors, and District Board Members

Attitudes	Legislative Councilors	Urban Councilors	District Board Members
Very familiar	1.10%	0.40%	0.70%
Quite familiar	9.10%	6.50%	12.70%
Half-half	30.70%	24.80%	29.60%
Quite unfamiliar	46.50%	50.00%	41.30%
Very unfamiliar	10.90%	16.00%	13.60%
Hard to Say	1.60%	2.20%	2.10%

Source: "Survey conducted by the Social Sciences Research Centre of the University of Hong Kong [CB(2)343/98-99(01)]," in https://www.legco.gov.hk/yr98-99/chinese/panels/ca/papers/p343c01.pdf, access date: August 16, 2020.

demonstrated that 77.2%, 74.8%, and 70.9% of the respondents were not familiar with the work of Legislative Councilors, Urban Councilors, and DB members. Clearly, the work of Legislative Councilors, Urban Councilors, and DB members was not fully understood by the public. If many ordinary citizens were confused with the duties, responsibilities and work of their elected representatives in DBs, UrbCo, and RegCo, it also meant that these elected bodies and representatives failed to reach out sufficiently to the citizens at the grassroots level.

Table 7.6 demonstrates the public perception of the differences between the functions of DB members and UrbCo members. While 42.9% of the respondents believed that there were many differences, 42.3% of the respondents said there were not many differences, showing a split in public opinion.

Table 7.7 shows the public attitudes towards whether the UrbCo and RegCo should be merged or dissolved. 60.7% of the respondents would like to see a merger between the two councils while only 16.2% agreed with the idea of dissolving the two councils. 68.4% of the respondents openly disagreed with the option of dissolving the two councils. Clearly, public opinion favored their merger rather than dissolution. The result also illustrated that a majority of the respondents saw the UrbCo as an important district organization.

Table 7.8 reveals how the members of the public viewed the principles that should be adopted in the process of reforming district organizations. 27% of the overall respondents believed that improving the efficiency and quality of services was of ultimate importance in district organizations reforms; 18.5% highlighted the need of encouraging people to participate in community affairs; 14.8% saw the balance of different parties' interests as significant; 12.7% pointed to the necessity of promoting democratic development; 10.3% said the accountability of the organizations should be improved; and 8.7% perceived the development of district characteristics as important. Only 4.4% said that strengthening the power of the central government was significant. As such, the HKSAR government's decision of abolishing the two councils and centralizing the municipal services to its own hands was actually a move contrary to the opinions of the members of the public. Although the HKSAR government interpreted public opinion in a way that favored its decision to abolish the two councils, the disbandment of the two councils was clearly ignoring public opinion.

Table 7.6: Public Perception of the Differences between the Functions of District Board Members and Urban Councilors

Perception of the Differences	%
Many Differences	42.9%
Not Many Differences	42.3%
Don't Know/Hard to Say	14.7%

Source: "Survey conducted by the Social Sciences Research Centre of the University of Hong Kong [CB(2)343/98-99(01)]," in https://www.legco.gov.hk/yr98-99/chinese/panels/ca/papers/p343c01.pdf, access date: August 16, 2020.

Table 7.7: Public Views Toward the Merger or Dissolution of the Urban Council

Public Views	Merging with RegCo	Dissolving
Agree	60.70%	16.20%
Neutral/ Doesn't Matter	12.30%	6.80%
Disagree	16.20%	68.40%
Don't Know/Hard to Say	10.80%	8.50%

Source: "Survey conducted by the Social Sciences Research Centre of the University of Hong Kong [CB(2)343/98-99(01)]," in https://www.legco.gov.hk/yr98-99/chinese/panels/ca/papers/p343c01.pdf, access date: August 16, 2020.

Table 7.8: Principles that Should be Adopted in District Organization Reforms

Opinion	Percentage of overall responses
Improve the efficiency and quality of services	27.00%
Encourage people to participate in community affairs	18.50%
Balance different parties' interests	14.80%
Promote democratic development	12.70%
Improve the accountability of the organizations	10.30%
Develop district characteristics	8.70%
Strengthen the power of the central government	4.40%
Don't Know/Hard to Say	3.70%

Source: "Survey conducted by the Social Sciences Research Centre at the University of Hong Kong [CB(2)343/98-99(01)]," in https://www.legco.gov.hk/yr98-99/chinese/panels/ca/papers/p343c01.pdf, access date: August 16, 2020.

District Administrative Reform in the Donald Tsang Era, 2005–2012

After Donald Tsang was elected as the Chief Executive in 2005, the HKSAR government decided to enhance district administrative reforms. As a former District Officer in Sha Tin from 1982 to 1984, Tsang was familiar with the work of DCs, thereby explaining why later he was supportive of some district administrative reforms. In the 2005–2006 policy address, Chief Executive Donald Tsang stressed that "the government will allow each DC to assume responsibility for the management of some district facilities, such as libraries, community halls, leisure grounds, sports venues and swimming pools," and that "executive departments will follow the decisions of the DC in managing such facilities, within the limits of their existing statutory powers and resources available."[19] Tsang outlined his proposal of enhancing the responsibilities of DCs and of the related supportive measures from the government. In a sense, he delegated more authority from the government to DCs. According to the government's consultative document, entitled *Review the Role, Functions and Composition of District Councils*, the main objectives of district administrative reform were to understand public views on (1) the enhancement of the role of DCs in district management, (2) the composition of DCs, and (3) DCs election-related matters.[20]

To enhance the role of DCs in district management, the government proposed to set up a District Facilities Management Committee (DFMC) under each DC to steer and oversee the work involved.[21] The reforms would be characterized by the following operations: (1) the DFMCs would operate in a way similar to other committees under DCs; (2) district representatives of the departments concerned would attend DFMC meetings to present their departmental plans and proposals for DC's endorsement; (3) issues discussed at DFMCs that required inter-departmental co-ordination by the District Officers could be put forward to the respective DMC for discussion and resolution; and (4) if a DFMC was dissatisfied with the department's response, it could forward the case to the Steering Committee on District Administration.[22] In short, the establishment of the DFMC could enhance the autonomy of DCs in district affairs as all DC members would join the respective DFMC and elect a chairperson and a vice-chairperson for the committee. Also, the DC and different government departments would

Table 7.9: Three Major Types of District Council Funding

Funds	Functions
DC Funds	Carry out community involvement and minor environmental improvement projects.
Minor Building Works Block Vote under the Architectural Services Department	Carry out upgrading work and enhancement of building facilities under the management of Architectural Services Department, including all district facilities that would come under the purview of DFMCs.
Urban Minor Works Program	Improving local facilities, the living environment and hygiene black spots, the provision of recreational and leisure facilities, amenity planting, and the construction of rain shelters in urbanized areas. These projects would be undertaken with the advice of a district working group comprising the DC chairpersons, members, and some local people.

Source: "Review the Role, Functions and Composition of District Councils," available in https://www.legco.gov.hk/yr05-06/english/panels/ca/papers/ca0427cb2-consultation-e.pdf, access date: August 17, 2020, pp. 15–17.

coordinate with each other and DC members would be able to express the demands of their districts.

Table 7.9 indicated three major types of DC funding as proposed by the Donald Tsang administration. The first type was the DC fund which would be used for carrying out major community involvement projects and some minor environmental enhancement projects in the district. The second one would be the Minor Building Works Block Vote under the management of the Architectural Services Department. The main objective for this fund would be to upgrade district facilities, not only under the supervision of the Architectural Services Department but also under the purview of the DFMC. The third one was the Urban Minor Works Program, whose objective was to improve local facilities, the living environment, hygiene conditions, and the provision of recreational and leisure facilities. These projects would need the consensus from a district working in consultation with DC members and the local people. In fact, DC funding was tremendously important for the district to improve its facilities as it could be linked up with livelihood issue. Donald Tsang's reforms aimed at increasing the involvement of DC members in deliberating and deciding these funding through the creation of a dedicated capital works block vote for the concerned departments to implement the decisions of the DFMCs. The new block vote would have an ambit to cover building works relating to the district facilities under DFMCs' purview, including community halls, district libraries, leisure grounds, sports venues, swimming pools, and public beaches as well as minor works in all districts.[23] To ensure efficient delivery, the government devised a hierarchy to differentiate projects of different scale so that very minor improvement items (for example, those costing less than HK$1 million) would be carried out more promptly. The cost ceiling of each project initiated or endorsed by DCs would remain at HK$15 million.[24]

In order to improve the district administration, the Tsang administration also proposed to strengthen the role of districts by introducing the Steering Committee on District Administration (SCDA) and the Annual District Administration Summit (ADAS). The SCDA would be chaired by the Secretary for Home Affairs (SHA) or the Principal Secretary for Home Affairs and attended by the Heads of Departments.[25] Regular members would comprise those core departments with a major role in district management while other department heads could be invited to attend to address the problems falling under their respective purview on an ad hoc basis.[26] The main objective for setting up the SCDA was to provide a forum for top management in various departments to exchange views on issues of mutual concern and resolve inter-departmental district management issues.[27] As such, some controversial and complex district problems would be expected to be easily solved by the coordination between the government and district councilors. More importantly, the SCDA would formulate strategies and provide a direction to District Officers and DMCs on the enhancement of district work.[28] Another way of enhancing the role of District Officers in district affairs was to introduce the ADAS, whose objective was to "(1) provide a steer to District Officers and DMCs by formulating strategies and measures to enhance district work; (2) to oversee the implementation of the strategies and measures in district affairs; (3) to refer district management issues that cannot be resolved among bureau and departments to the Policy Committee; (4) to advise on the allocation of resources to DCs; and (5) to consider and decide on cases from DMCs."[29] More significantly, the establishment of the ADAS would be able to reduce the communication gap between DCs and the government so that district affairs and problems would be easily resolved.

Because Donald Tsang perceived that the importance of district management in Hong Kong's future social and political development would grow, it would be necessary for the HKSAR government to nurture local talents in DCs to participate and manage in regional and political affairs.[30]

Table 7.10: Remarks and Position of District Council Chairpersons on District Administrative Reforms Proposed by the Donald Tsang Administration

Name of Chairs (District)	Remarks and Position
Wai Kwok-hung (Sha Tin)	The government is nominally decentralizing its administration to District Councils, which in fact remain within the advisory framework, but the difference is that they become more direct in expressing their views than ever before. Moreover, the government's management structure in the future must be improved.
Wu Chor-nam (Central and Western)	The government cannot fully decentralize its administration. Different representatives should be elected in the District Councils to join the DFMCs, which would be managed in cooperation with government departments responsible for the implementation of management decisions.
Christina Ting Yuk-chee (Eastern)	The government should gradually devolve its powers to the District Councils and the pace should not be rushed.
Mar Yuet-har (Southern)	Eighteen Districts Councils cannot use their own approaches to handle district affairs, rather a unified system should be formulated to manage regional facilities.

Sources: *Ming Pao Daily News*, October 29, 2005, p. K6 and *Hong Kong Economic Journal*, November 12, 2005, p. P4.

His reform proposal sought to empower DCs and DC members within the existing advisory functions and framework. Donald Tsang described district affairs as "not always on the front pages of newspapers" but as "closely related to the interests of the public."[31] He highlighted that seemingly minor matters, such as the opening hours of community facilities, booking procedures, types of books, and small park facilities were actually matters of great concern to the public in their lives.[32] In fact, he saw district affairs as important issues and concerns. Tsang also believed that the expansion of the functions of DCs could be made through empowering DC members to manage more district facilities that were closely related to people's livelihood, such as libraries, community halls, recreation areas, sports venues, and swimming pools. After all, all these livelihood issues could be managed better according to local conditions, thereby benefiting the local people and the community.[33] At the same time, his administrative reform proposals could bridge the communication gap between the government and DCs through the establishment of the SCDA and the ADAS, directly or indirectly strengthening local governance at the 18 districts.[34]

In response to the proposals for empowering DCs and decentralizing government administration, some chairpersons of DCs supported these ideas. Table 7.10 illustrates the responses from some chairpersons. Wai Kwok-hung from Sha Tin realized the limitation of the government's

**Table 7.11: Pilot Scheme in Four Districts on the Enhanced Functions
of District Councils During Donald Tsang's Era**

District	Major Content of the Pilot Scheme	Events Organized during Pilot Scheme
Wan Chai	Setting up a District Facilities Management Committee (DFMC). Setting up a Park Facilities Management Working Group under the Community Building Committee. Setting up a Regional Cultural, Arts and Public Library Activities Planning Working Group under the Cultural and Leisure Services Committee. Setting up a working group on beautification of the overpass project under the Cultural and Leisure Services Committee.	Improving Wan Chai Waterfront Promenade. Introducing Outdoor Culture Festival program to promote community art and culture in new forms. Introducing Park Vitality Program as to absorb public opinion. Improving Library activities and facilities through public consultation. Organizing more leisure activities. Introducing more Greening plan in district facilities. Beautifying the overpass in the district.
Wong Tai Sin	Setting up a District Facilities Management Committee (DFMC). Dissolving the Cultural and Leisure Services Committee. Setting up a working group to review funding for community engagement programs. Setting up a working group to manage the Code of Practice for the Rental of Community Halls and Facilities. Setting up a working group to review the implementation of pilot scheme.	Renovation of the vacant Creative Workshop venue as a leisure facility. Organizing the Wong Tai Sin Martial Arts Festival.
Sai Kung	Introducing the District Partnership Program. Setting up a District Facilities Management Committee (DFMC). Setting up a working group on manage District Minor Works Program. Setting up a working group on manage District Facilities and community engagement.	Completing 28 District Minor Works. Finishing 16 District Partnership projects.
Tuen Mun	Setting up a District Facilities Management Committee (DFMC). Setting up a working group on District Minor Works and Community Engagement.	Completing 5 District Minor Works. Finishing 9 Community Participation projects.

Sources: "Wan Chai District Council Pilot Scheme," in https://www.had.gov.hk/file_manager/tc/documents/home/wan_chai_district.pdf, access date: August 30, 2020; "Wong Tai Sin District Council Pilot Scheme," in https://www.had.gov.hk/file_manager/tc/documents/home/wong_tai_sin_district.pdf, access date: August 30, 2020; "Sai Kung District Council Pilot Scheme," in https://www.had.gov.hk/file_manager/tc/documents/home/sai_kung_district.pdf, access date: August 30, 2020; and "Tuen Mun District Council Pilot Scheme," in https://www.had.gov.hk/file_manager/tc/documents/home/tuen_mun_district.pdf, access date: August 30, 2020.

administrative reform, because DCs had to remain operational within the advisory framework, but the proposals did make DCs more direct in expressing their views than ever before. Similarly, Wu Chor-nam from Central and Western district admitted that the government could not fully decentralize its administration. Christina Ting saw the reform proposals as a step from the government to devolve its powers downward. As such, district administrative reform proposals could be seen as a progressive step forward within the confines of the advisory nature of DCs.

Table 7.11 demonstrates four districts—Wan Chai, Wong Tai Sin, Sai Kung, and Tuen Mun—that experimented with the DC pilot scheme. All four districts witnessed the establishment of the DFMC and the setting up of one or more working groups to implement the scheme. Table 7.12 shows the results of the evaluation of the pilot scheme in four districts. The advantages of the pilot scheme were to empower DCs to manage more new district facilities, reduce the communication gap with residents, establish a partnership between DCs and the government departments, and to involve more district groups in district affairs. However, the disadvantages were the short time span of the pilot scheme, the heavy workload of government departments, and the need for more clarity in district management projects. Overall, it seemed that the pros outweighed the cons of the pilot scheme.

District Administration in the CY Leung Era, 2012–2017: Fluctuations from Expansion of the Pilot Scheme to Tapering Off

The HKSAR government under the leadership of Chief Executive CY Leung from 2012 to 2017 was marked by an enhancement of district administrative reforms through the utilization of the DMCs. In his policy address in 2013, the Leung administration injected an additional HK$100 million to each district to allow DCs to promote community projects. Meanwhile, a summit on district administration would be held to explore the ways of improving district administration. In 2014, his administration proposed to enhance the role of District Officers through their coordination with government departments. However, this proposal appeared to be a stagnant one, because the Tsang administration had already proposed to elevate the role of District Officers by having the ADAS. Moreover, under the Donald Tsang proposal, the SCDA would be created and chaired by the

Table 7.12: Evaluation of Pilot Scheme in 4 Districts

District	Pros of the Pilot Scheme	Cons of the Pilot Scheme
Wan Chai	The pilot scheme can balance the interests of different parties. It is purposely oriented and can help understand some key issues in district affairs. It provides more opportunities for DC to have more new district facilities. It absorbs public opinions that reduce the communication gap between residents and the government.	Lack of centralized department that worked with the District Council.
Wong Tai Sin	The participation of District Council in managing district facilities can better meet the needs of the district. With the increase in funding, the commitment in the project has increased and its flexibility has been increased. Encouraging cross-sector cooperation in district affairs.	The time for pilot scheme is short. As such, DC can only choose fast-impact projects to implement. As departments face heavy workload, there is no time to discuss in detail the management of district facilities. Insufficient resources to complete all district minor works.
Sai Kung	Working with government departments and district organizations can enhance the communication with residents.	There is a need for more clarity on the scope of community collaboration program. The pilot scheme is too short, and District Council needs longer timespan to establish a co-operative model with the government departments. There is room for greater involvement and better advice on facility management.
Tuen Mun	Encouraging the involvement of district partner groups and other professional groups.	All district management projects must set clear ideas and goals before planning. The project should win the support of most district councilors.

Sources: "Wan Chai District Council Pilot Scheme," in https://www.had.gov.hk/file_manager/tc/documents/home/wan_chai_district.pdf, access date: August 30, 2020; "Wong Tai Sin District Council Pilot Scheme," in https://www.had.gov.hk/file_manager/tc/documents/home/wong_tai_sin_district.pdf, access date: August 30, 2020; "Sai Kung District Council Pilot Scheme," in https://www.had.gov.hk/file_manager/tc/documents/home/sai_kung_district.pdf, access date: August 30, 2020; and "Tuen Mun District Council Pilot Scheme," in https://www.had.gov.hk/file_manager/tc/documents/home/tuen_mun_district.pdf, access date: August 30, 2020.

SHA or the Principal Secretary for Home Affairs and it would be attended by the Heads of Departments. Theoretically and practically speaking, the Leung administration in 2013 and 2014 should have implemented these proposals. The Secretary for Home Affairs, Tsang Tak-shing, did little from 2007 to 2015, especially during his last two years as the secretary, on district administrative reforms. If Donald Tsang as the former Chief Executive laid out the concrete plan for district administrative reforms, Tsang Tak-shing as the Secretary for Home Affairs should have enforced and implemented them during the early period of the Leung government. In the 2015 policy address (Table 7.13), CY Leung mentioned the need to increase funding support for DCs and the push for implementation of the pilot scheme established by the Tsang administration. However, the HKSAR government had no concrete timeline for the full implementation of the pilot scheme. Tsang Tak-shing retired from politics in July 2015, but there was little evidence to show that his successor Lau Kong-wah really implemented fully the pilot scheme in district administrative reforms. From a critical perspective, the Donald Tsang proposals for district administration reforms became stalled toward the end of the tenure of office of Tsang Tak-shing, whose successor Lau Kong-wah did not really push for a full-scale and speedier implementation of the pilot scheme. District administrative reforms were put on the backburner in the priorities of policy agenda of the Leung administration.

There were perhaps two main reasons explaining why district administrative reforms fluctuated from an expansion in the early stage of the CY Leung era to a process of tapering off from 2015 to 2017. First and foremost, there were rumors that Leung and Jasper Tsang, the brother of the Secretary for Home Affairs Tsang Tak-shing, were at loggerheads. Such sour relations might affect Leung's relations with Tsang Tak-shing, who was eventually removed in 2015.[35] As such, Tsang Tak-shing toward the end of his office in 2014 and 2015 did not appear to have any incentive to propel the administrative reform scheme forward to a full implementation of the pilot scheme before his departure in July 2015. Second, Tsang's successor Lau Kong-wah came from the DAB, although Lau had originally been a founding member of the United Democrats of Hong Kong. Developing an increasingly pro-government and pro-Beijing background, Lau did not seem to be keen to witness a scenario in which the pilot scheme would be implemented fully so as to give more financial resources to DCs, thereby benefiting the pan-democrats in various districts. After all, Lau was

**Table 7.13: CY Leung's Remarks on District Administrative Reform
in his Policy Address**

Year	Remarks on District Administrative Reform in His Policy Address
2013	Signature Project Scheme: An additional HK$100 million was allocated to each district to enable District Councils to promote community-focused projects during the current term of office. A summit on district administration would be held to explore ways to improve district administration. It was planned to increase the resources of district councils and increase the level of funding for district small-scale projects.
2014	Proposed to strengthen the role of the District Officers and work with the District Councils to coordinate the work of different departments to respond positively to the public's demands.
2015	Increased support for District Councils and District Councilors to make the work of district councils smoother and more effective. The 18 districts would fully implement the pilot scheme, and further implement the regional problems of regional solutions, regional opportunities to grasp the concept. An additional $20.8 million would be allocated annually to the Community Participation Scheme in the next five financial years to enhance support for district councils in promoting arts and cultural activities.

Sources: "Review of CY Leung Policy Address," in https://www.hk01.com/, access date, August 30, 2020.

removed by Chief Executive Carrie Lam in April 2020 and his position was replaced by DAB member Caspar Tsui Ying-wai. However, there were reports saying that Carrie Lam was dissatisfied with the performance of Lau Kong-wah, according to former DAB chairman Jasper Tsang.[36] Perhaps the most important reason why Lau Kong-wah's tenure as the Secretary for Home Affairs saw a process of the district administration reform's tapering-off phenomenon was the political tsunami in the November 2019 DC elections, during which the DAB and the pro-Beijing front suffered a heavy defeat in the hands of the pan-democrats. In view of the democrats capturing an overwhelming majority of the directly elected seats, the HKSAR government, including Lau Kong-wah and even Chief Executive Carrie Lam, became reluctant to push ahead the implementation of the pilot scheme. Doing so would continue to politically benefit the pro-democracy DC members. Hence, when Caspar Tsui Ying-wai from the DAB took over as the Secretary for Home Affairs in April 2020, he continued to adopt this go-slow approach in the full implementation of the district administrative reform until October 2020 when he reportedly met the pro-democracy DC members for the first time after the November 2019 elections. In other words, district administrative reforms showed signs of oscillations, witnessing an inception of gradual expansion of the pilot scheme in the

CY Leung era to the suddenly stalled process during the Carrie Lam administration, including a prominently tapering-off phenomenon at the end of Lau Kong-wah's tenure of office as the Secretary for Home Affairs in early 2020.

Although the administrative reform scheme showed signs of tapering off, a bit of progress could be seen in the early phase of the Leung administration, especially the Signature Project Scheme (SPS), whose objective was to provide more resources to DCs for implementing large-scale and sustainable projects to address the needs of the districts.[37] The SPS projects included works and/or non-works components which were expected to bring about "a visible and lasting impact" on the districts.[38] The projects were expected to be commenced and accomplished within the current DC term as far as practicable.[39] If the SPS projects involve both works and non-works components, consideration was given to community involvement activities during the process of implementation.[40] For non-works projects, consideration would be given to organizing trial and/or pilot services to meet district needs.[41] DCs were expected to undertake the initiation, planning, and the selection of partner organizations as well as the delivery, promotion, publicity, and monitoring of all SPS projects.[42] All SPS projects required the funding approval from the Finance Committee of the LegCo.[43] The SPS projects had to be of a considerable scale. Each project would be subject to an upper limit of $100 million and a lower limit of $30 million.[44] Capital costs, consultants' fees, works contingency, expenses for community involvement activities, as well as expenditure on manpower, promotion, and publicity for project delivery were all included. Each district could use the allocation to implement one to two SPS projects.[45] In addition, HK$200 million would be reserved for the HAD for conducting the necessary preliminary studies and employing non-civil service contract staff to undertake preparatory and supporting work for DCs prior to the move of seeking funding approval from LegCo.[46] Table 7.14 delineates the details of the projects in 18 districts under the SPS.

Table 7.15 shows the remarks of several DC members on the SPS. The sharpest remark came from Raymond Ho of Momentum 107. He pointed to the fact that an increase in project costs over time could be "bottomless and profound." Most importantly, DC members might see a change of blood, including their party and group affiliations, after the direct elections.

Table 7.14: List of Projects from 18 Districts Under the Signature Project Scheme

District	Details of the project	Approved by LegCo
Central and Western	Harbor front enhancement and revitalization at the Western Wholesale Food Market	Approved by LegCo on July 14, 2015
Wan Chai	Construction of the Moreton Terrace Activities Centre	Approved by LegCo on November 30, 2018
Eastern	Eastern District Cultural Square	Approved by LegCo on May 13, 2016
Southern	Provision of Ophthalmic Examination Services	Approved by LegCo on June 1, 2018
	Provision of Shuttle Bus and Rehabilitation Bus Services	
Kowloon City	Revitalization of the Rear Portion of the Cattle Depot	Approved by LegCo on May 13, 2016
Sham Shui Po	Shek Kip Mei Community Services Centre	Approved by LegCo on April 15, 2015
	Mei Foo Neighborhood Activity Centre	Approved by LegCo on July 14, 2015
Sha Tin	Revitalization of Shing Mun River Promenade near New Town Plaza	Approved by LegCo on July 14, 2015
	Decking of Tai Wai Nullah in Sha Tin	Approved by LegCo on April 22, 2016
Tai Po	Establishment of an Arts Centre by retrofitting Tai Po Government Secondary School	Approved by LegCo on May 13, 2016
Yuen Long	Construction of a Yuen Long District Community Services Building	Approved by LegCo on May 13, 2016
Islands	Improvement Works at Silvermine Bay Beach, Mui Wo, Lantau Island	Approved by LegCo on July 14, 2015
	Yung Shue Wan Library and Heritage and Cultural Showroom, Lamma Island	
North	Improvement of Trails and Provision of Ancillary Facilities at Wu Tip Shan and Wa Mei Shan in Fanling	Approved by LegCo on July 14, 2015
	Improvement of Trails and Provision of Facilities in Sha Tau Kok	
Sai Kung	Reconstruction of the Sharp Island Pier	Approved by LegCo on June 28, 2016
	Construction of the Tseung Kwan O Heritage Hiking Trail and the Heritage Information Centre	
Kwai Tsing	Enhancement of Community Healthcare	Approved by LegCo on July 12, 2014
Tsuen Wan	Redevelopment of Sai Lau Kok Garden	Approved by LegCo on April 22, 2016
Tuen Mun	Revitalization of Tuen Mun River and Surrounding Areas	Approved by LegCo on May 13, 2016
	Promotion of Youth Development in Tuen Mun	Approved by LegCo on June 10, 2016 and the service were provided to the youth in Tuen Mun

Table 7.14 Continued

District	Details of the project	Approved by LegCo
Yau Tsim Mong	Yau Tsim Mong Multicultural Activity Centre	Approved by LegCo on May 13, 2016
Kwun Tong	Construction of Music Fountains at Kwun Tong Promenade	Approved by LegCo on November 30, 2018
	Construction of Lift Tower at Shung Yan Street in Kwun Tong	Approved by LegCo on May 13, 2016
Wong Tai Sin	Expansion and improvement of Wong Tai Sin Square	Approved by LegCo on April 17, 2015 and Completed
	Enhancement of leisure facilities at Morse Park	Approved by LegCo on July 14, 2015

Sources: "List of Projects from 18 Districts Under Signature Project Scheme," in https://www.had.gov.hk/file_manager/en/documents/home/SPS_Project_list_en.pdf, access date: August 30, 2020.

Table 7.15: Remarks of District Councilors on the Signature Project Scheme

Name (Political Party/ Group Affiliation)	Remarks
Raymond Ho (Momentum 107)	Apart from the fact that the project may encounter different views on environmental assessment and land use rights prior to the project implementation, an increase in project costs over time is bottomless and profound. With the immediate changing terms of District Councils, DC members may change their blood after elections. As a result, new DCs may have different ideas and the projects established out in the previous district councils would be pushed back.
Wong Kwok-hing (FTU)	The progress of the Signature Project Scheme reflects that Hong Kong's claim to be the most advanced city is lagging behind and showing gaps.
Au Nok-hin (DP)	There is a lack of communication between government departments on the Signature Project Scheme.
Christopher Chung Shu-kun (DAB)	The main challenge for the Signature Project Scheme is the filibustering efforts from the democrats in LegCo.

Sources: *Oriental Daily*, March 17, 2015, p. A17 and January 3, 2016, p. A19.

As such, new DCs might have different views on the previously projects established by DCs. The implication here was that elections could change the political composition and profile of different DCs, and therefore, from the government's perspective, giving more funding to DCs would perhaps be beneficial to the pan-democrats.

Assessment of the Signature Pilot Scheme

Some media assessed the SPS by following how the monies allocated to DCs were approved and spent. One program director, Lam Chi-kit, visited 18 districts and found that, in the case of the Kwun Tong music fountain, DC members did consult the members of the public, but as with other districts, the methods of public consultation were traditional, such as mailing letters to citizens, and consulting the views of the public at the town halls.[47] Nevertheless, this kind of consultation was outdated, because many residents began to use the social media through which public consultation over the SPS was virtually non-existent. The Kowloon City DC bypassed consultation procedures by having discussions and a resolution within an hour to approve HK$100 million for the use of cultural heritage preservation.[48] In Wong Tai Sin, no public consultation was held in the improvement of Morse Park. Moreover, some DC members wanted the SPS to benefit their own constituencies, leading to attempts made by them to balance their interests. A good example was Sha Tin Shing Mun River where the SPS cut across a few constituencies. As such, when resources were allocated to DCs, they were politically divided among and between various districts where local politicians had the vested interest to ensure that the financial allocation would be beneficial to their voters, constituents, and their re-election chances. In the case of Lam Tsuen in Tai Po, a platform with a rooftop was built by using HK$50 million, but netizens criticized it as a structure akin to the Tiananmen in Beijing. Critics said that the contractor which got the tender of constructing the platform had two directors who were allegedly also members of the Tai Po DC.[49] Even worse, the two members were criticized for voting for various projects without declaring their interest.[50] Having said that, some SPS had some elements of creativity, such as Kwai Tsing's mobile dental clinic that could benefit residents in different constituencies.[51] In Central and Western district, the DC used the SPS to beautify the artistic images of the pillars of highway bridges. Hence, there were creative usages of the SPS, but their implementation lacked public consultation in some districts. Table 7.16 illustrates the controversies over the SPS, including the potential conflicts of interests among some DC members, its cost effectiveness, the lack of public consultation, and the alternative of using the resources to care for the poor and the needy.

Table 7.16: Controversies over the Signature Project Scheme

District	Controversies over the project
Tai Po	Some of the district councilors who approved the project had "conflicts of interests."
Tsuen Wan	The project was not cost effective and the decision-making process was hasty without hearing the views of the residents.
Sha Tin	The project could not provide sufficient facilities for the public and the design wasted public money.
Kwun Tong	The government funding was misused in the construction of a music fountain and the public money should have been utilized to help the poor and the needy in the district.

Sources: *Apple Daily*, July 16, 2015, p. A20 and September 6, 2015, p. A04; *Ming Pao*, May 12, 2015, p. A12.

Table 7.17: Details of Sham Shui Po Pilot Scheme and Yuen Long Pilot Scheme

District	Details of the Pilot Scheme
Sham Shui Po Pilot Scheme	Helping Non-Governmental Organizations (NGOs) to strengthen support services for street sleepers. As of 31 October 2014, the NGOs conducted a total of 31 outreaching service sessions and successfully made 1,982 contacts with street sleepers. These NGOs followed up intensively with 22 more complicated cases by arranging referrals to relevant departments for assistance. Eventually, 13 street sleepers agreed to leave the streets, with three of them being allocated with public housing units, seven renting private places and three being admitted to singleton hostels and elderly homes. Improving environmental hygiene conditions of the locations where street sleepers gathered. Six large-scale cleansing exercises were planned under the service contract with NGOs. Promoting environmental hygiene, fire safety and building management through assistance under the pilot scheme so as to encourage some residents to play a more active role in building management by serving as Resident Liaison Ambassadors or by forming Owners' Corporations.
Yuen Long Pilot Scheme	Curbing the extensions of shops front through Joint Publicity Campaigns against black spots and enhancing enforcement and cleansing operations. Clearing illegally parked bicycles. Enhancing anti-mosquitoes and grass cutting efforts.

Sources: "Progress Report of Pilot Scheme on Enhancement of District Administration Through District Management Committees in Sham Shui Po and Yuen Long," in https://www.legco.gov.hk/yr14-15/english/panels/ha/papers/ha20141212cb2-407-6-e.pdf, access date: August 30, 2020.

A progress report issued by the HKSAR government asserted that SPS was successful and useful. CY Leung in his 2014 policy address introduced the SSP in Yuen Long and Sham Shui Po DCs, where the DMCs were expected to have the "decision-making power to tackle the management and environmental hygiene problems of some public areas."[52] The two DCs were invited to advise on the work priorities of the respective districts. The pilot scheme, which was expected to be completed in August 2015, provided "useful experience for and shed light on practical and effective ways to tackle specific district issues, so as to progressively take forward the concept of addressing district issues at the local level and capitalizing on local opportunities."[53] The HKSAR government provided a one-off allocation of HK$5 million, including a provision for the employment of non-civil service contract staff, to each of the Yuen Long and Sham Shui Po districts to implement the pilot scheme.[54] The pilot scheme was described as empowering DMCs chaired by the District Officers to tackle some problems relating to environmental hygiene and district management. The scheme, to the government, "responded proactively to community needs and was well received and supported by the local communities."[55] Table 7.17 delineates the detailed content of the pilot scheme in Sham Shui Po and Yuen Long. Activities included the assistance provided to street sleepers, the promotion of hygiene and safe environment, the mobilization of residents to be resident liaison ambassadors, the formation of Owners' Corporation, the reduction of front shops' extensions through publicity work, the clearing of illegally parked bicycles, and the enhancement of anti-mosquitoes campaign and grass-cutting efforts. These were all issues related to the improvement of the people's livelihood, a main purpose of the district administrative reform planned by the Tsang administration.

Table 7.18 shows the reactions of some DC members to the Sham Shui Po and Yuen Long pilot schemes. Politicians from the pro-government and pro-Beijing camp, such as Leung Che-cheung of the DAB and Chan Yuen-han of the FTU, praised the scheme. Leung added that the scheme could increase efficiency whereas Chan felt that CY Leung fulfilled his commitment to decentralize district administration to DCs. Ip Kwok-him of the DAB believed that some District Officers could not coordinate different departments in the past and that the scheme could empower them to some extent. Albert Ho of the DP was lukewarm, saying that it was difficult for the people to oppose decentralization. Hence, the pilot scheme was embraced by local politicians at the district level.

Although the pilot scheme in both Sham Shui Po and Yuen Long was regarded as a success in helping street sleepers and improving the environment,[56] the occurrence of the Occupy Central Movement from September to December 2014, when some democrats and young people pushed for the democratization of the HKSAR by occupying some streets in the HKSAR, led to the government's idea of expanding the pilot scheme to

Table 7.18: Response of District Councilors to the Sham Shui Po and Yuen Long Pilot Schemes

Name (Political Parties Affiliation)	Remarks
Leung Che-cheung (DAB)	The new pilot scheme is a good thing. In the past, when major events were encountered, different departments could push the responsibility to each other in district council meetings, and the problems could drag on for half a year, and the new measures can help to enhance efficiency. The decentralization of powers to district councils does not involve any political considerations.
Chan Yuen-han (FTU)	When the two Municipal Councils were abolished, the government promised to devolve their powers to the DCs, and CY Leung used the pilot scheme to fulfill his commitment.
Albert Ho (DP)	District Councils are dominated by the pro-establishment force, and CY Leung's move is clearly not only a sign of the political potential of the District Councils but also a reward for the pro-establishment camp. Decentralization is always a good thing and it is hard for people to oppose.
Ip Kwok-him (DAB)	The District Officers may not be able to direct or co-ordinate different departments at the various levels, and the new reporting mechanism can help to resolve this situation.

Sources: *Hong Kong Daily News*, January 16, 2014, p. A06 and *Hong Kong Economic Journal*, January 16, 2014, p. A12.

all 18 districts to "repair the political wounds."[57] It was reported in December 2014 that the Leung administration would announce the expansion of the pilot scheme to all 18 districts in his policy address in January 2015.[58] The crux of the problem was coordination among different departments, NGOs, and DCs, which required considerable manpower.

Politically speaking, some local elites who aspire to be politicians climbing up the political ladder, from districts to LegCo at the territorial level, naturally see DCs as having their political value. As Chong Chun-shun, a member of the now defunct Youngspiration, a political group formed by former legislators-elect Baggio Leung and Yau Wai-ching in January 2015, said openly that after the 2010 electoral reform in the HKSAR, 15 members of DCs could initiate nomination of a candidate running for the LegCo's DC constituency elections in 2012.[59] Hence, to those local people who aspire to become legislators in the future, their electoral participation in DC elections is the first step for them to climb up the political ladder. Additionally, the pilot scheme of district administrative reform aimed at decentralizing administration to the local DCs, giving them more resources which can easily become the target of contests among the local politicians. In other words, the Donald Tsang reform plan of district administration reform did arouse the interest of more local politicians to run in DC elections, for they could seize the opportunities of being elected to perpetuate their influence in the district and advancing their political career to the LegCo level. This perhaps explained why the 2019 DC elections attracted a lot of participation from the democrats, especially the young ones who participated in the anti-extradition bill and anti-government movement from May to November 2019.

In spite of the district administrative reform and its related pilot scheme, the status of District Officers has been regarded as relatively low, failing to achieve Donald Tsang's idea of elevating their status by having the Annual DCs Summit. Some experienced DC members in Sham Shui Po and Yuen Long said that, although the pilot scheme was implemented, the ranking of District Officers remained relatively low and many government departments adopted "parochialism" or "mountainism," thereby leading to the scenario that departments shifted their responsibilities without an influential official to direct them.[60] To make the pilot scheme successful, some DC members in the two pilot districts said that higher level officials would have to be involved. They referred to Donald Tsang's plan of district administrative reform as "a loud thunder with small raindrops."[61] Ho Hau-cheung, a chairperson of the Sha Tin DC, remarked that the HKSAR government had to enhance the status of District Officers, empower the DMCs, and provide even more resources to DCs.[62] Otherwise the pilot scheme could not really achieve breakthrough in the reform of district administration.

As mentioned before, Chief Executive CY Leung announced in his policy address in January 2015 to expand the scheme to 18 districts, which was known as the District-led Actions Scheme (DLAS), with a view to tackle district problems which were long-standing, of large magnitude, and complex.[63] The DLAS followed the concept of "addressing district issues at the local level and capitalizing on local opportunities".[64] On the one hand, the HKSAR government sought to tackle issues on management of public area and district problems through the DMCs chaired by District Officers, with the active participation of DCs and the collaboration of relevant government departments.[65] On the other hand, the DMCs identified actively local opportunities in the districts with a view to providing appropriate services and enhancing the living quality of the community.[66] To implement DAS in all 18 districts, the HKSAR government vowed to provide, from the 2016–17 financial year onwards, an additional annual funding of HK$63 million, and created 38 new civil service posts and

33 contract staff posts.[67] All these posts had already been created under the HAD, the FEHD, 18 District Offices and the Lands Department.[68] As of April 2016, 18 District Offices, had already implemented a total of 39 projects, including 34 projects relating to management of local issues, such as improving environmental hygiene conditions, enhancing anti-mosquito work, curbing shop front extension, and clearing illegally parked bicycles.[69] Besides, five projects aimed at capitalizing on local opportunities for enhancing the living quality of residents and community facilities in response to the unique circumstances and needs of respective districts (see Table 7.19).[70] Out of the 18 districts, six, namely, Kwun Tong, North District, Sai Kung, Tsuen Wan, Tuen Mun, and Yuen Long, selected the control over shops front extension as a major initiative under the DLAS.[71] The relevant District Offices tapped the inter-departmental efforts in curbing these shops front extension through public education and publicity in the districts.[72] On the whole, the shops front situation improved, thereby allowing smoother pedestrian flow.[73]

Furthermore, to target the problem of illegally-parked bicycles that caused obstruction to passenger walkways, five districts, namely Islands, North District, Sha Tin, Tuen Mun and Yuen Long, made joint efforts with relevant government departments, such as the Land Department and FEHD, to enforce actions against illegally-parked bicycles at black spots.[74] The situation of illegally parked bicycles was reportedly improving.[75] Finally, seven out of 18 districts (Central and Western, Eastern, Southern, Wan Chai, Kowloon City, Islands, and Tai Po) selected the improvement of environmental hygiene conditions as one of their DAS projects. For example, the Southern District Office and the Marine Department conducted a special cleansing operation to improve the marine hygiene conditions in the vicinity of Aberdeen Typhoon Shelter.[76] The Tai Po District Office also conducted a large-scale coastal cleanup in Tap Mun, while the Central and Western District Office collaborated with government departments to clean up the vicinity of Lan Kwai Fong before and after Halloween.[77] District Offices also worked with the FEHD, the Lands Department, the Drainage Services Department (DSD), and the LCSD to step up anti-mosquito work in the districts, including the promotion of anti-mosquito messages and the enhancement of anti-mosquito efforts at more than 300 territory-wide black spots.[78] Hence, district environmental work was conducted by using the expanded pilot scheme.

Table 7.19: Expanded Projects to Address District Issues in 18 Districts

District	Details of the Project
Central &Western	Enhancing local environmental hygiene
Eastern	Enhancing anti-mosquito efforts Enhancing local environmental hygiene
Southern	Improving the overall traffic conditions of Aberdeen Strengthening action against illegal parking and pick-up/drop-off of passengers in the Southern district Stepping up efforts to address the environmental hygiene problems in the Centre of Aberdeen and Aberdeen Typhoon Shelter
Wan Chai	Enhancing local environmental hygiene
Islands	Efforts against illegally parked bicycles Enhancing local environmental hygiene Enhancing anti-mosquito and grass-cutting Efforts
Kowloon City	Enhancing local environmental hygiene Handling tourism-related issues
Kwun Tong	Enhancing anti-mosquito and grass-cutting efforts Curbing shop front extensions
Yau Tsim Mong	Cleansing common areas of buildings Mosquito, rodent and pest Control
Sham Shui Po	Strengthening support for "three-nil" buildings Strengthening support for street sleepers
Sai Kung	Curbing shop front extensions Tackling problems caused by illegal recycling activities
Tai Po	Enhancing local environmental hygiene Enhancing anti-mosquito efforts
Tsuen Wan	Curbing shop front extensions Enhancing anti-mosquito efforts
Yuen Long	Curbing shop front extensions Tackling problems caused by illegal recycling activities Enhancing anti-mosquito efforts
Sha Tin	Enhancing anti-mosquito and grass-cutting efforts Stepping up efforts against illegally parked bicycles
Tuen Mun	Enhancing anti-mosquito efforts Curbing shop front extensions Stepping up efforts against illegally parked bicycles
North	Curbing shop front extensions Stepping up efforts against illegally parked bicycles

Sources: "Legislative Council Panel on Home Affairs District-led Actions Scheme: Progress Report," in https://www.legco.gov.hk/yr16-17/english/panels/ha/papers/ha20161221cb2-401-6-e.pdf, access date: August 30, 2020.

Table 7.20: Projects to Capitalize on Local Opportunities

District	Details of the Project
Yau Tsim Mong	Hearing Care Action was made to enhance the community's understanding and concerns about aural protection through educational programs and the provision of free mobile hearing test service.
Sha Tin	The creation of space to address district needs to develop the land underneath the Sha Lek Highway in three stages.
Wong Tai Sin	The establishment of Community Resource Centre
Sai Kung	The introduction of electric carts at Pak Tam Chung
Kwai Tsing	Help prepare the community to tackle an upsurge in dementia population

Source: "Legislative Council Panel on Home Affairs District-led Actions Scheme: Progress Report," in https://www.legco.gov.hk/yr16-17/english/panels/ha/papers/ha20161221cb2-401-6-e.pdf, access date: August 30, 2020.

On the capitalization of local opportunities, Yau Tsim Mong District Office launched the Hearing Care Action plan to enhance the community's understanding and awareness of aural protection through public education and the provision of free aural testing for local residents (Table 7.20).[79] The services were launched in September 2016 with about 540 local residents being provided with free aural testing.[80] The Sha Tin District Office introduced a project, "Creation of Space to Address District Needs," which aimed at developing the land underneath the Sha Lek Highway through three stages.[81] Other projects capitalizing on local opportunities embraced the establishment of a community resource center in Wong Tai Sin and the introduction of electric carts at Pak Tam Chung in Sai Kung.[82] These projects involved alteration works and tendering procedures which required relatively longer lead time for implementation.[83] Hence, the district administrative reform introduced by the Tsang government in 2005–2006 took almost ten years to witness some minimal progress—a reflection of the relatively slow and piecemeal nature of the reform process straddling the Tsang and Leung government.

From a critical perspective, when the former Secretary for Home Affairs Lau Kong-wah went to LegCo to discuss the role of enhanced reforms of DCs in November 2016, his ideas of district administrative reform were by no means new compared with the Donald Tsang reform blueprint. Lau said that the government encouraged citizen participation in district affairs, and that DCs were the "important partners" of the government in district administrative work.[84] Lau outlined three areas of reforms: (1)

consolidating the functions of DCs where DMCs managed and supervised district facilities, such as libraries, sports facilities, community halls, and other street-level projects; (2) providing more financial support for DC members, raising their stipends for 15% from 2016 onwards; and (3) the need for government departments to coordinate and communicate with DCs. However, all these three aspects were nothing special compared with the Tsang administration's reform proposals. The challenge for Lau was to fully implement the DLAS, which unfortunately remained in the pilot stage. Moreover, Lau as the former Secretary for Home Affairs failed to put forward any concrete policy on sports development, as with his predecessor Tsang Tak-shing. Critically speaking, while Tsang Tak-sing did not accelerate Donald Tsang's district administrative reform proposals, Lau also could not do so but talked about piecemeal reforms. In short, Chief Executive Donald Tsang set out an ambitious blueprint of administrative reforms, but disappointingly the two Secretaries of Home Affairs did not appear to accelerate them at the district level.

The Influence of District Councils: From the Opposition to Electronic Road Pricing to the Approval of Abolishing Pedestrian Precinct in Mong Kok

District Councils (DCs) on the whole played not only a crucial role to influence territory-wide government policy but also a critical function of deciding the fate of district-based initiative. A good example was the opposition to the Electronic Road Pricing (ERP) initiative proposed by the Hong Kong government in the 1980s. Another example of district-based policy that was controversial and yet decided by the Mong Kok DC was the abolition of the pedestrian precinct in 2018.

Table 7.21 shows the historical evolution of the ERP scheme, which was proposed by the British colonial administration in the early 1980s to tackle road congestion problems in the urban areas. The pilot scheme, if approved, would be implemented in the Central district. The ERP scheme was first discussed in general terms by DBs in December 1984 and January 1985.[85]

The government commissioned a study which concluded the feasibility of the ERP scheme, however, it was supported by none of the 19 DBs. This was the outcome of a serious round of government consultation with DBs in early June 1985.[86] Of the 19 Boards, 11 initiated a voting decision, nine

Table 7.21 The Development of the Electronic Road Pricing Scheme

Date	Event
Early 1980s	The government announced its intention to introduce an ERP system in the territory to tackle road congestion problems in the urban areas and it commissioned a study to design and conduct a pilot scheme in Central district. The study concluded that the ERP scheme for tackling road traffic congestion was feasible on technical, administrative, and legal grounds.
December 1984–January 1985	The ERP scheme was first discussed in general terms by District Boards. The consensus of the Boards was to oppose the ERP, and only 2 of 19 supported the scheme.
1990s	There was a sharp increase in the number of private vehicles in the early 1990s, prompting the community's discussion on how to control car growth and to address traffic congestion. The government commissioned a feasibility study with the objectives of examining the practicability of implementing an ERP system in Hong Kong and assessing the need for such a system to meet transport objectives.
2000s	ERP scheme was preferred to be implemented in the commercial areas on the Hong Kong Island after the provision of a free-of-charge alternative route for motorists to bypass the charging area.
2014	The Traffic Advisory Committee (TAC) recommended that planning for ERP pilot scheme in Central District should begin to alleviate the localized road traffic congestion and to maximize the efficiency of the available road space.
2015	The government took the TAC recommendation by launching a three-month public engagement exercise for the planning of the pilot scheme in Central district and its adjacent areas to enhance the public understanding of the basic elements, pertinent issues and overseas experiences of ERP. The exercise aimed at encouraging public discussions and building consensus in the community.
2017	The government commenced an in-depth feasibility study on the pilot scheme in Central district and its adjacent areas. The feasibility study includes a detailed analysis of the views collected during the public engagement activities in 2015, of the latest traffic data, and of the overseas experiences.
2019	The government proposed to adopt a multi-pronged approach, with the use of technology, including a Pilot Scheme, to enhance traffic management for tackling the traffic congestion in Central district. The preliminary concept of the Pilot Scheme was framed for consultation with stakeholders in mid-2019. Various views were received on the effectiveness of the Pilot Scheme.
2020	An International Expert Panel comprising members from the UK, US, Singapore, Sweden and Hong Kong was set up to help the HKSAR government to implement the ERP Pilot Scheme in Central district.

Sources: "ERP in Hong Kong," available in: https://www.td.gov.hk/mini_site/erpgovhk/erp_in_hk.html (access date: October 12, 2020).

were opposed to the scheme, and the other two thought that it should be delayed. Eight boards did not vote, but six of them opposed the scheme or felt that it should be shelved. Finally, two boards were neutral to the scheme. Therefore, not one single DB really came out in favor of it.[87] In the 1990s, the government refloated the idea of ERP, but it slowed down the process of implementing a Pilot Scheme until 2019. Hence, the opposition of DBs in the 1980s and bureaucratic delay in the early 2000s have made the implementation of the Pilot Scheme very slow. Yet, with the reclamation work finished in the Central and Wan Chai districts in the 2018, traffic congestion in the Central district has appeared to ease to some extent. It remains to be seen how the government deals with the ERP scheme in the coming years, but the role of DBs' opposition to it in the early 1980s was a watershed postponing the entire scheme up to the present.

In January 2017, the Transport and Housing Bureau published a public engagement report on ERP pilot scheme, saying that the Central district was the most suitable location for launching the scheme because: (1) the Central district "is strategically important to Hong Kong, yet its traffic conditions are far from satisfactory."[88] Traffic speeds on some road sections during the morning peak hours on weekdays were only about 10 km/hour, which was not much faster than an adult's average walking speed of 4 to 5 km/hour. A DC forum was held at which views of 15 DC members from ten DCs on the Pilot Scheme were gathered.[89] Among the DC members who spoke at the forum, more were in support of the Pilot Scheme. Some supporters pointed out that Hong Kong was a small place, but the vehicle fleet was growing, resulting in serious traffic congestion in some parts of Hong Kong. They argued that, sooner or later, the HKSAR government inevitably needed to implement ERP in congested areas.[90] However, some DC members expressed reservation about the scheme, asserting that there was no pressing need to introduce the scheme as the traffic congestion in the Central District would ease off after the completion of the Wan Chai Bypass. Other DC members pointed out that the traffic congestion problem at the Cross Harbor Tunnel was far more serious than that in the Central District and they requested the government should first tackle the congestion near and at the tunnel. The divergent views among the members of the public, including DC members, made it easy for the government to adopt a wait-and-see attitude toward the implementation of the ERP, not to mention its Pilot Scheme.

Another example showing the importance of DC in dealing with district-based issues was the abolition of the Mong Kok Pedestrian Precinct (MPP) in August 2018. The MPP operated in 2000 and many artists, singers, and performers liked to use the precinct to attract residents and earn their living. However, the noise pollution stood out as a serious

**Table 7.22 Remarks of District Councilors on the Abolition
of Mong Kok Pedestrian Precinct**

District Councilor (Political Party Affiliation)	Remarks
Andy Yu (Civic Party)	"Street performances has not disappeared after the abolition of the Mong Kok Pedestrian Precinct. Most performers in Mong Kok have moved to the vicinity of the ferry pier in Tsim Sha Tsui to stage their performances. The noise and street obstruction problems in the precinct has only been transferred to other places without being resolved at all." Therefore, Yu submitted a paper with the hope that the government would set out a policy on street performances, introduce a regulatory system and consider licensing in the long run so that performers could stage street performances legitimately. Yu also said, "The government thought that the abolition of the precinct could address the noise and street obstruction caused by street performances, but this treated only the symptoms but not the root cause of the problems."
Chan Siu-tong (Business Professional Alliance or BPA)	"The residents of Mong Kok can enjoy peace after the abolition of the precinct." Chan thanked councilors for their support of abolishing it and the DC for its follow-up work so that the case had been satisfactorily concluded without any conflicts. But a few sporadic problems remained at the location, such as the street obstruction problems caused by easy-mounted frames and the promotional stands for telecommunication services. Chan hoped that the police and the Food and Environmental Hygiene Department would improve their law enforcement. Moreover, the nuisance problem caused by street performances was transferred to other places, such as Causeway Bay and Tsim Sha Tsui. Chan added that blaming government departments and the police for the nuisance problem would be unfair, but he and the BPA requested the government reconsider establishing a Culture Bureau to regulate street performances with a view to exploring ways to enable members of the public to appreciate street culture, arts performers to exhibit their talents, to allow residents to enjoy peace.
Derek Hung (DAB)	Hung claimed that when the abolition of the precinct was discussed, he had already foreseen that the performers in Mong Kok would move to other places. For the first two weeks after the abolition of the precinct, the vicinity of the Tsim Sha Tsui Star Ferry Pier was in chaos. Hung expressed his gratitude to the police for deploying many officers to maintain law and order during the transition period. During the first two weeks of the transition, Hung said he received 30 complaints from members of the public, residents and shop operators in the area, reporting the seriousness of the problem. Hung requested the DC chair to convene a special meeting to discuss this issue.
Lam Kin-man (Independent democrat)	"The government should not think that it has accomplished its mission as there is no complaint from the residents of Mong Kok after the abolition of the precinct. Although the responses of the departments showed that the number of complaints and that of performance groups in the vicinity of Star Ferry Pier have declined recently, it might be due to temporary factors such as the typhoon attack. Performance groups may return or perform in other places. The government should not turn a blind eye to the issue, but it should face the problems to resolve them. Therefore, more regulatory efforts and the implementation of a licensing system will be necessary."

Sources: "Minutes of the 18th Meeting of Yau Tsim Mong District Council (2016–2019)," in https://www.districtcouncils.gov.hk/ytm/doc/2016_2019/en/dc_meetings_minutes/YTM_DC_18th_Minutes_EN.pdf, access date: October 13, 2020; "Suggestions of Introducing Regulatory System for the Promotion of Street Performance Culture," in https://www.districtcouncils.gov.hk/ytm/english/records/dc_meetings_doc.php?year=2018&meeting_id=14748, access date: October 13, 2020.

problem, especially after the individual visit scheme from the mainland was introduced to the HKSAR in late July 2003. The influx of many mainland tourists into the HKSAR from 2004 to 2018 made the MPP an attractive tourist spot, where foreigners, mainland tourists, and residents enjoyed the performance of many artists and singers. Nevertheless, the noise problem necessitated the Mong Kok DC to control and eventually abolish it. Table 7.22 illustrates the remarks made by some DC members on the abolition of the MPP. Some saw the noise problem as being transferred to other places like Tsim Sha Tsui. Others believed that the government should implement a licensing system to regulate the artists and singers while exploring ways for them to perform in places for the benefit of ordinary citizens. Some also suggested that the government should set up a Culture Bureau to not only regulate the artists and street performers but also develop a long-term and coherent policy on culture and creative arts.[91] From a critical perspective, the HAD of the HKSAR government has been weak in not only the development of any coherent and long-term sports policy but also the establishment of cultural and creative arts policy.

Conclusion

This Chapter examines the origins of the abolition of the UrbCo and RegCo, the evolution of the Donald Tsang government's district administrative reform proposals, and the recent politicization of DC administration. Originally, when DBs were set up in the early 1980s, it was a move made by the British colonial administration to decentralize the management and delivery of public services to locally elected councils. Nevertheless, the abolition of the UrbCo and RegCo could be seen as a retrogressive move made by the HKSAR government to recentralize district administration into the hands of government departments, believing that the government could and would do a better job in managing environmental issues, hygiene, and crises. Moreover, the dismantling of the UrbCo and RegCo had financial and hidden political grounds, centralizing the financial resources to the government headquarters while depriving the chances of more democrats to grasp directly elected seats and to enjoy receiving their regular stipends from the administration. Yet, the abolition of UrbCo and RegCo was a short-sighted step that cannot really bring about the better delivery of public services. Prior to and during the outbreak of COVID-19 in early 2020, the mass media had already severely criticized the HKSAR government for failing to deal with environmental hygiene, ranging from the failure to control the rapidly growing number of rats to the absence of any effective measures to maintain the hygiene of district-based markets. The role of District Officers was curbed in their status after July 1, 1997, for they are only one of the players coordinating with other central-level government departments. Chief Executive Donald Tsang's plan of administrative reforms sought to empower District Officers, but unfortunately his reform blueprint was implemented by the Secretaries of Home Affairs in a half-hearted, piecemeal, and relatively slow manner,

In short, the metamorphosis of district administration in Hong Kong has been characterized by political oscillations, fluctuating from decentralization in the early 1980s to recentralization in December 1999. Such oscillations have become prominent after the 2019 DC elections that envisaged the landslide victory of the pan-democratic forces. Still, since DC members could climb up the political ladder to become LegCo members and members of the Chief Executive Election Committee, DC elections remained a precious and significant channel of political participation for politicians at the grassroots and district levels, at least until the promulgation of the National Security Law in June 2020.

Notes

1 "Official Record of Legislative Council Proceedings, December 2, 1999," available in: https://www.legco.gov.hk/yr99-00/chinese/counmtg/floor/991202ca.pdf (access date: August 16, 2020), p. 1911.

2 *Ibid.*

3 *Ibid.*, p. 1912.

4 *Ibid.*

5 *Ibid.*

6 *Ibid.*

7 *Ibid.*, pp. 1912–1913.

8 *Ibid.*, p. 1912.

9 *Ibid.*

10 *Ibid.*

11 *Ibid*, p. 1914.

12 *Ibid.*

13 *Ibid.*

14 Ibid.

15 Ibid.

16 Ibid.

17 Ibid., pp. 1914–1915.

18 See the views of academics, including Michael DeGolyer, in "Submissions to LegCo Panel on Constitutional Affairs," November 2, 1998, LC Paper No. CB(2)570/98-99/01, in https://www.legco.gov.hk/yr98-99/english/panels/ca/papers/p_submis.pdf, access date: October 4, 2020.

19 "Chief Executive Policy Address, 2005–2006," in https://www.policyaddress.gov.hk/2005/eng/index.htm, access date: August 17, 2020.

20 "Review the Role, Functions and Composition of District Councils," in https://www.legco.gov.hk/yr05-06/english/panels/ca/papers/ca0427cb2-consultation-e.pdf, access date: August 17, 2020.

21 *Ibid.*, p.8.

22 *Ibid.*, pp. 8–9.

23 *Ibid.*, pp.18–19.

24 *Ibid.*

25 *Ibid.*, p.20.

26 *Ibid.*

27 *Ibid.*

28 *Ibid.*, p.21.

29 *Ibid.*

30　*Wen Wei Po,* October 15, 2020, p. A19.

31　*Ibid.*

32　*Ibid.*

33　*Ibid.*

34　*Ibid.*

35　"Tsang Tak-shing's departure raises rumours and C. Y. Leung and traditional pro-Beijing force were at loggerheads," in https://www.thestandnews.com, July 21, 2015.

36　"Jasper Tsang says Carrie Lam wanted to fire two DAB secretaries," in https://www.singtao.ca, October 10, 2020.

37　'District Council Paper Implementation of Signature Project Scheme," available in: https://www.had.gov.hk/file_manager/en/documents/home/DC_paper_on_SPS_20130225_BIND_eng.pdf (access date: August 30, 2020), p.1

38　Ibid.

39　ibid.

40　*Ibid.*

41　*Ibid.*

42　*Ibid.,* pp. 1–2.

43　*Ibid.*

44　*Ibid.,* p.2.

45　*Ibid.*

46　*Ibid.*

47　*Ibid.*

48　*Ibid.*

49　*Apple Daily,* September 6, 2015, p. A4.

50　*Ibid.*

51　*Ibid.*

52　"Progress Report of Pilot Scheme on Enhancement of District Administration Through District Management Committees in Sham Shui Po and Yuen Long," in https://www.legco.gov.hk/yr14-15/english/panels/ha/papers/ha20141212cb2-407-6-e.pdf, access date: August 30, 2020, p. 1.

53　*Ibid.,* pp. 1–2.

54　*Ibid.,* p.2.

55　"Legislative Council Panel on Home Affairs District-led Actions Scheme: Progress Report," available in: https://www.legco.gov.hk/yr16-17/english/panels/ha/papers/ha20161221cb2-401-6-e.pdf (access date: August 30, 2020), p.1.

56　*Headline News,* September 26, 2015, p. 35.

57　*Wen Wei Po,* December 12, 2014, p. A16.

58　*Ibid.*

59 *Ming Pao*, July 29, 2015, p. A23.

60 *Oriental Daily*, March 10, 2014, p. A23.

61 *Ibid.*

62 *Ibid.*

63 "Legislative Council Panel on Home Affairs District-led Actions Scheme: Progress Report," available in: https://www.legco.gov.hk/yr16-17/english/panels/ha/papers/ha20161221cb2-401-6-e.pdf (access date: August 30, 2020), p.1.

64 *Ibid.*

65 *Ibid.*

66 *Ibid.*

67 *Ibid.*, p.2.

68 *Ibid.*

69 *Ibid.*

70 *Ibid.*

71 *Ibid.*

72 *Ibid.*

73 *Ibid.*

74 *Ibid.*

75 *Ibid.*

76 *Ibid.*, p.3.

77 *Ibid.*

78 *Ibid.*

79 Ibid.

80 Ibid.

81 Ibid.

82 *Ibid.*

83 *Ibid.*

84 "LegCo: The Secretary for Home Affairs made remarks on how to strengthen the role of DCs and their functions," Hong Kong Government News, November 24, 2016.

85 Sandford F. Borins. "Electronic road pricing: An idea whose time may never come," *Transportation Research Part A: General,* Volume 22, Issue 1, (January 1988), pp. 37–44.

86 *Ibid.*

87 "Democratic dilemma: Government caught at the cross-roads," *South China Morning Post*, June 15, 1985.

88 Ibid.

89 "A summary of views of various stakeholder groups on the Pilot Scheme," available in: https://www.td.gov.hk/filemanager/en/content_4838/eng_td_pe1report_annex_2.pdf (access date: October 12, 2020).

90 Ibid., p. A2–6.

91 "The Issue of Street Performance Needs to be Addressed, Calling for Improved Cultural Policy and Re-consideration of Establishment of a Culture Bureau," in https://www.districtcouncils.gov.hk/ytm/doc/2016_2019/en/dc_meetings_doc/14748/YTM_DC_102_2018_TC.pdf, access date: October 20, 2020. Also see "Request for the Government to Enact Legislation for the Effective Management of Street Performances," in https://www.districtcouncils.gov.hk/ytm/doc/2016_2019/en/dc_meetings_doc/14748/YTM_DC_103_2018_TC.pdf, access date: October 13,2020.

8

Hong Kong Post-National Security Law — Changing District Council Politics and Administrative Recentralization

The outbreak of the anti-extradition, anti-police, and anti-government protests from May to November 2019 led to the landslide victory of pan-democrats and the poor performance of pro-Beijing forces in the November 2019 District Council (DC) elections. This Chapter argues that with the promulgation of the National Security Law in late June 2020, the mass resignations and disqualification of many DC members eventually led to the government's decision to recentralize district administration. As such, political change at the territorial and district level since late June 2020 brought about the administrative recentralization of district administration.

Deteriorating Relations between District Councils and the Government

After the November 2019 DC elections, the relationships between the directly elected and pro-democracy DC members and the government remained tense and poor. Table 8.1 sums up some cases in which District Officers walked out of the DC meetings. Some pro-democracy DC members raised the issue of the PRC's June Fourth Incident; some set up a new panel on security and constitutional affairs; and some initiated motions to criticize the local police for their handling of the 2019 protests. In response, the District Officers concerned left the meeting. Nevertheless, some pro-democracy DC members criticized the District Officers for "violating"

Table 8.1: District Officers Walked Out from District Councils Meetings, January–May 2020

Date	Event
January 15, 2020	Some of the terms of reference proposed by the Tai Po DC's Panel on Security and Constitutional Affairs, including the study of immigration in the district and the discussion of constitutional matters, were "in conflict with the District Councils Ordinance," and it was recommended by District Officer Chan Hau-man that district board members should amend the relevant terms of reference before electing the Chairperson, and that elections "might not be secure if they violated the Ordinance." The democrats questioned whether the authorities deliberately blocked the establishment of the relevant committees. DC members in Tai Po insisted on continuing to elect the vice-chair. As such, the District Officer and the staff of the District Council Secretariat left the meeting.
January 16, 2020	The Police Commissioner, Chris Tang, went to the Central and Western District Council and he was questioned by DC members. Towards the end of the meeting, District Councilor Yip Kam-lung moved an interim motion condemning Mr. Tang for harboring "police violence" and demanding that he should step down. Chris Tang and the District Officer walked out of the meeting.
February 26, 2020	The Kowloon City DC held a special meeting to elect chairs and vice-chairpersons of the DC sub-committees, but the district's proposal to set up a police law enforcement monitoring committee was challenged as inconsistent with the terms of reference of the DC. The Kowloon City District Officer suggested that the name of the Committee should be reviewed. When the DC chair, Siu Leung-sing, insisted on holding the election of the vice-chairman, the District Officer and the staff of the DC secretariat walked out before the election of the vice-chairman.
April 16, 2020	The Yau Tsim Mong DC passed a motion by 17 pro-democracy members to "stop the indiscriminate rioting of the police force" and to "reorganize the police," but during the discussion the police representatives and District Officer Yu Kin-keung left the scene. Obviously, the government believed that DC members acted in a way that violated the DC's terms of reference.
May 12, 2020	The Chairman of Kwai Tsing DC at the DC meeting decided that the 1989 June 4 motion about China was directly or indirectly in line with the welfare of the residents and he ruled that it could be discussed. The Kwai Tsing District Officer said that the motion was "contrary" to the functions of the District Councils and that if discussions continued, the HAD staff would not provide Secretariat services and then leave the scene. When the staff left the meeting, a group of pro-democracy DC members shouted slogans in protest.
May 11, 2020	The Yuen Long DC held a general meeting to discuss the June 4 incident in the PRC, but the Secretariat had earlier refused to put the discussion on the agenda. However, the Chairman of the Yuen long DC insisted on the discussion. Eventually, the District Officer left the meeting.
May 18, 2020	The Wan Chai DC discussed the June 4th incident, July 1 rally and the arrangements for public events in the Wan Chai District. The District Officer said in the meeting that such actions "violated" the terms of reference of the DC. He then left the meeting together with other government representatives.

Date	Event
May 26, 2020	The Yau Tsim Mong DC held a general meeting and recommended that the police should send staff to maintain the smooth passage near the 64 Memorial Hall on Mong Kok Road on 4 June 2020. The initiator of the motion, Li Wai-fung, delivered a speech in which he mentioned that there were "dead people" on June 4, and the District Officer immediately criticized the motion as inconsistent with the scope of the DC. The officer led other officials to leave the meeting.
May 29, 2020	The Kwun Tong DC held a meeting of the Panel on Security and Constitutional Affairs to discuss a provisional motion on "the opposition to the implementation of the National Security Law in Hong Kong." The District Officer pointed out at the meeting that the motion was unrelated to district affairs and officials left the meeting. But this did not prevent the 28 DC members from approving the provisional motion.

Sources: Various Hong Kong Chinese newspapers from January to May 2020, such as *Ming Pao*, January 16, 2020, p. A8; *Wen Wei Po*, January 19, 2020, p. A5; *Apple Daily*, January 20, 2020, p. A8; *Hong Kong Economic Journal*, January 21, 2020, p. A14; *Oriental Daily*, February 26, 2020, p. A11; *Apple Daily*, February 26, 2020, p. A10;

the principle of political neutrality and they defended that their actions were in the interest of the members of the public. From the government's perspective, however, these panels, motions, and actions on the part of DC members exceeded the scope of the DC's terms of reference by touching on the existing law, system, and policy review. Both sides had their arguments, but the November 2019 DC elections brought about unprecedented tense relations between the government and directly elected DC members, especially as most councilors are pro-democracy and supportive of the 2019 protests.

Even after the inception of the meetings of 18 DCs in December 2019, there were 15 DC members arrested by the police, including three chairpersons and one vice-chairperson.[1] From the perspective of pro-democracy DC members, the 18 District Offices led by District Officers were "uncooperative," boycotting meetings, failing to provide conference rooms and secretariat services, and selectively implemented those motions passed by DCs.[2] They argued that District Offices and Officers exceeded their powers and duties, especially District Officers who withdrew from meetings and did not incorporate the discussions among DC members into formal minutes of the meetings. In other words, some DC members believed that the government did not respect the 18 DCs. They pointed to the fact that as early as 2015, DCs discussed various territory-wide issues like (1) the legislation on Article 23 of the Basic Law, which was supported by some DCs in late 2002 and early 2003; (2) the government's political reform plan, which was supported by many DCs in 2015; and (3) the 2017 policy of co-location checkpoints in West Kowloon, which was also backed up by DCs.[3] In other words, in the past, the government put forward those territory-wide policies to DCs and solicited their support due to the fact that most DCs were dominated by pro-establishment and pro-Beijing members. But when the political landscape changed and 17 of the 18 DCs were captured by the pro-democracy forces, the government refrained from cooperating with them. In fact, the government refrained from putting forward some issues to the agendas of DC meetings.[4] If political neutrality refers to a position without siding with any political forces, the District Offices led by District Officers were naturally and politically in favor of the government in the first place. The political neutrality of District Offices and District Officers was perhaps a myth.

The HKSAR government in August 2020 issued a guideline to all District Officers and officials who attended DC meetings.[5] The guideline aimed at standardizing the responses of District Officers and officials to the ways in which DC members handled their district meetings and matters.[6] It was criticized by pro-democracy DC members for "curbing the space of DC representatives to reflect the views of ordinary citizens."[7] For example, some DC members wanted to raise the issue of how the government coped with COVID-19, but the government did not allow them to do so. The most controversial part of the guideline is that if DCs discuss territory-wide issues, officials can refrain from attending DC meetings.[8] The pro-democracy DC members agreed that DCs should not discuss cases that were undergoing legal proceedings. But they disagreed with the guideline saying that government officials can avoid attending DC meetings if "there are other platforms, statutory bodies and consultative agencies" to discuss those issues raised by DCs.[9] Pro-democracy DC members complained that 99.9% of those elites appointed to the government's advisory committees and consultative bodies were pro-establishment, and that liberal-minded critics were consistently excluded from participation in these institutions. Hence, selective appointment of pro-government elites into consultative bodies was exacerbated by the government's hostility toward the DCs in early 2020. Some Sha Tin DC members wanted to discuss the Hong Kong National Security Law, which was promulgated by the PRC National People's

Congress on June 30, 2020, but again the government disallowed them to do so.[10] Objectively speaking, some DC members exceeded the powers of DCs, which was to play an advisory role rather than be an organ of political power. As such, the tense and confrontational relations between the government and some elected DC members stemmed from the problematic or *ultra vires* way in which DCs operated.

Moreover, the new government guideline said that if there were any slogans and banners violating the "one country, two systems" and the National Security Law, government officials could leave DC meetings.[11] According to the guideline, officials could leave the DC meetings if they felt "offended and humiliated."[12] The poor relations between the elected DC members and the government after late 2019 were unprecedented, mainly because the democrats were occupying most directly elected seats in DCs and attempting to expand the DC powers beyond the terms of reference as stipulated by the DC Ordinance, and partly because of the impacts of the enactment of the Hong Kong National Security Law. Both sides demonstrated profound distrust toward each other, perpetuating a vicious cycle in which there was no real breakthrough and improvement in their sour relationships.

A pro-Beijing newspaper, *Ta Kung Pao*, revealed other aspects of the guideline adopted by the government to deal with DCs (Table 8.2). One was to allow District Officer and government officials to consult the legal advice from the Secretary for Justice on controversial legal matters, including the possibility of DC members and actions that might exceed their terms of reference.[13] District Officers could also set up cross-departmental ad-hoc groups to deal with issues that necessitated coordination straddling different departments. Departmental secretaries, who originally were planned to go down to attend DC meetings — a proposal under the Donald Tsang's district administrative reform blueprint — no longer needed to do so after August 2020.[14] However, government heads and permanent secretaries could temporarily attend the meeting of each DC once. As such, the HKSAR government rolled back some reforms planned by the Tsang administration, a setback in district administrative reform due to the heavy politicization of DCs after the November 2019 elections.

Furthermore, to balance the influence of the pro-democracy DC members in different districts, the HKSAR government appointed 99 pro-establishment elites, who participated in the 2019 DC elections and

Table 8.2: New Guideline for Government Officials to attend District Council Meetings

Government officials must leave the meetings if district councilors display any banners or slogans that violate "one country, two systems" and the Hong Kong National Security Law during the DC meeting.

If DC members continues the related behavior, government officials can refuse to continue participating in the meeting of the day. If a member uses "offensive and insulting words" in his or her speech, the official concerned can ask the chairperson to deal with it. If the chairperson fails to deal with it properly, or if the official is dissatisfied with the handling method, he or she can leave the scene.

The government also regulates the content of the topics discussed. If the topics involve territory-wide and criminal ones, or if members have other more suitable platforms for discussion, officials can avoid attending the meetings.

Government bureau and departments should give advice to the District Officers, who can seek the advice of the Secretary for Justice if DC agenda has controversies or issues that may be *ultra vires*.

All government bureau and departments need to notify District Officers of the potentially controversial issues. The District Officers can convene cross-departmental group meetings to deal with controversial issues. Related departments should also cooperate and their exercise statutory and administrative powers within their respective jurisdictions.

Sources: *Ta Kung Pao*, August 14, 2020, p.A2

Table 8.3 Number of Pro-Establishment Elites Who Participated in the 2019 District Council Election and who were appointed as Members of Area Committees

District	No. of Pro-Establishment Elites who participated in 2019 DC Election
Eastern	15
Yuen Long	13
Sha Tin	12
Tuen Mun	12
Yau Tsim Mong	11
Sham Shui Po	9
Kwun Tong	8
Sai Kung	6
Wan Chai	4
Kwai Tsing	4
Tsuen Wan	2
Central and Western	1
Wong Tai Sin	1
Islands	1
Southern	0
Tai Po	0
North	0
Kowloon City	0

Sources: http://www.inmediahk.net/node/1075895 (access date: October 5, 2020).

were defeated, into the Area Committees (ACs) (Table 8.3). The ACs were traditionally established by DCs to deal with district affairs on the basis of different areas. In Table 8.3, the Eastern district witnessed 15 pro-government elites being appointed as members of the ACs, followed by Yuen Long with 13, and Sha Tin and Tuen Mun with 12, as well as Yau Tsim Mong with 11. By appointing pro-government elites into 67 ACs in 18 districts, the government re-politicized these bodies, which were simultaneously excluding the democrats. The implication was that ACs, which are responsible for helping DCs to deal with district issues, can check the influence of all pro-democracy dominated DCs.

The appointment of defeated pro-government candidates in the 2019 DC elections into various ACs in 2020 was a move in conformity of how the HKSAR government excluded the directly-elected and pro-democracy DC members from the Fight Crime Committees (FCCs) and Fire Safety Committees (FSCs) in the eighteen districts in 2020. Some directly elected and pro-democracy DC members confirmed to the authors that they were excluded from participation in the FCCs and FSCs.[15] The FCCs are chaired by the police commanders in various districts, and due to the poor relations between the pro-democracy DC members and the police force, the exclusion of pro-democracy DC members from FCCs is understandable. Two former DC chairs told the authors that the HKSAR government decided not to raise issues in the newly elected DCs after November 2019, leading to a scenario of non-cooperation.[16] The non-cooperative approach adopted by the HKSAR government and the appointment of formerly defeated candidates into the ACs, together with the exclusion of pro-democracy DC members from the FCCs and FSCs, illustrate the politicization of DCs after the November 2019 elections.

The politicization of DCs and DC members could be seen in the active participation of many directly elected and pro-democracy DC members in the election "primaries" held by the pan-democracy camp that prepared for the originally scheduled September 2020 Legislative Council (LegCo) elections. The democrats held the "primaries" on July 11 and 12, attracting a voter turnout of 600,000 supporters. Many pro-democracy DC members participated (Table 8.4), but the government in late July announced that the LegCo elections scheduled on September 6 would be postponed due to the continuous outbreak of COVID-19. Yet, as Table 8.4 shows, many localist DC members were elected as the LegCo candidates in the

Table 8.4: Pro-Democracy District Council Members Participating in the Primaries of 2020 Legislative Council Elections that were Postponed by the Government Later

Name (Faction)	Constituency	Number of Votes Gained (%)
Hong Kong Island		
Ted Hui Chi-fung (Moderate Democrat)	Central and Western	28,189 (31.17%)#
Tiffany Yuen Ka-wai (Localist)	Southern	19,844 (21.94%)#
Fergus Leung Fong-wai (Localist)	Central and Western	14,743 (16.30%)#
Tat Cheng (Moderate Democrat)	Eastern	11,090 (12.26%)#
Chui Chi-kin (Progressive Democrat)	Eastern	7,974 (8.82%)
Clarisse Yeung Suet-ying (Progressive Democrat)	Wan Chai	5,707 (6.31%)
Pang Cheuk-kei (Localist)	Southern	2,880 (3.18%)
Kowloon West		
Jimmy Sham Tsz-kit (Progressive Democrat)	Sha Tin	25,650 (31.68%)#
Kalvin Ho Kai-ming (Moderate Democrat)	Sham Shui Po	7,791 (9.62%)#
Lau Wai-chung (Progressive Democrat)	Sham Shui Po	6,295 (7.77%)
Kowloon East		
Li Ka-tat (Localist)	Kwun Tong	15,194 (16.48%)#
Sze Tak-loy (Moderate Democrat)	Wong Tai Sin	985 (1.07%)
New Territories West		
Sam Cheung Ho-sum (Localist)	Tuen Mun	35,513 (20.15%)#
Ng Kin-wai (Localist)	Yuen Long	20,525 (11.63%)#
Andrew Wan Siu-kin (Moderate Democrat)	Kwai Tsing	18,608 (10.54%)#
Tam Hoi-pong (Progressive Democrat)	Tsuen Wan	4,865 (2.76%)
New Territories East		
Lam Cheuk-ting (Moderate Democrat)	North	15,315 (9.35%)#
Gary Fan Kwok-wai (Progressive Democrat)	Sai Kung	10,156 (6.18%)
Ricky Or Yiu-lam	Sai Kung	1,489 (0.91%)
District Council (Second)		
Roy Kwong Chun-yu (Moderate Democrat)	Yuen Long	268,630 (50.69%)#
Lester Shum (Localist)	Tsuen Wan	129,074 (24.35%)#
Wong Pak-yu (Localist)	Yuen Long	71,706 (13.53%)#
James To Kun-sun (Moderate Democrat)	Yau Tsim Mong	49,991 (9.43%)#
Lee Yue-shun (Moderate Democrat)	Eastern	10,079 (2.00%)

#=Nominated

Source: "Candidates for Democratic Primaries," available in https://legco2020.vote4.hk/en/primaries/, access date: November 2, 2020.

"primaries" held on July 11 and 12. These included Tiffany Yuen, Fergus Leung, Pang Cheuk-kei, Li Ka-tat, Sam Cheung, Ng Kin-wai, Lester Shum, and Wong Pak-yu. Other factions included the moderate and progressive democrats. Those who were eventually elected by 600,000 pro-democracy voters and nominated as LegCo candidates were composed of the three factions: localists, moderate democrats, and progressive democrats. After the promulgation of the Hong Kong National Security Law by the Standing Committee of the PRC National People's Congress on June 30, 2020, the pro-Beijing mass media criticized the "primaries" in July as "violating" the National Security Law.[17] Eventually, the LegCo elections in September 2020 were postponed.

From the LegCo's "Primary" Elections to the Disqualifications of District Councilors

In January 2020, 17 of the 18 DCs which were controlled by the pan-democrats began to engage in a power struggle with the HKSAR government. Due to the initiative made by the pan-democrats to set up DC sub-committees that would investigate the police performance in the 2019 protests, the government reacted to this attempt at seizing political power at the district level quickly. The internal guideline issued by Chief Secretary Matthew Cheung Kin-chung to all the district-based officials in the 18 districts laid out the duties of DCs, including several points.[18] First, if any DC members showed problematic slogans and songs that were suspected of violating the National Security Law and the "one country, two systems," then the officials concerned who felt "humiliated" or "attacked" can leave the scene. If the officials identified problematic agenda items, the government will set up a cross-departmental group to tackle the issues concerned. Moreover, the previous practice of sending principal officials down to DCs to attend district activities was cancelled in the current term of office of the DCs. In January 2020, during a meeting of the Central and Western DC, Police Commissioner Chris Tang and District Officer Wong Ho Wing-sze left the meeting in which some members initiated a motion to "reprimand" the Police Commissioner for "not supervising the police force sufficiently." The government replied to the media later that such a motion carried "unfound accusation" and that it did not agree with its content. The guideline included detailed advice on how the government officials who attended DC meetings could respond if any DC member made remarks and performed actions that were suspected of violating the "one country, two systems." It also made suggestions on how the officials concerned could respond verbally to the DC chairperson who might take no action on the "offensive" remarks and action of a DC member. In response to the "offensive" remarks and actions from any DC member, the guideline said that the District Officer concerned could consult the opinion of the Legal Department. In fact, in January 2020, the Tai Po DC made an unprecedented move by setting up "a security and political reform affairs committee," a move that did not really belong to the jurisdictions of DCs and an initiative that, according to Matthew Cheung, "exceeded the council's powers" by discussing immigration-related affairs.[19] A report in *HK01* also reported in August 2020 that the government's guideline on DCs was already changed in such a way as to allow officials to leave the meetings in which any DC members might utter remarks or perform actions that were deemed as "violating the National Security Law."[20]

In fact, in September 2020, the Kwai Tsing and Sham Shui Po DCs acted in an *ultra vires* manner, leading to the departure and boycott of government officials who initially attended the meetings.[21] At the end of the Kwai Tsing DC meeting, some members initiated a joint motion to request a discussion of 12 young people who tried to escape from Hong Kong to Taiwan and were arrested by mainland marine police. They requested that the government should raise the issue of "transferring the 12 suspects" back to the HKSAR.[22] District Officer Cheng Kin opposed the motion and said the motion exceeded the power and jurisdictions of DCs. But DC chairman Sin Chung-kai allowed members to discuss, leading to the departure of the secretaries of the DC and the Kwai Tsing district police commander. Similarly, in the Sham Shui Po DC meeting, its agenda items—"strongly opposing Education Department to force book publishers to revise and delete the historical facts" and "Secretary of Justice should prosecute a taxi driver"—were seen by district officials as an act of *ultra vires*.[23] District officials also left the Sham Shui Po DC meeting.

Other DCs also demonstrated the problem of exceeding their power and jurisdictions. In late August, the Central and Western DC attempted to discuss the issue of mobilizing the masses to have the testing of COVID-19, while the Wan Chai DC tried to discuss the issue of the dormitories where foreign domestic helpers resided.[24] Several pan-democratic members of the

Central and Western DC questioned why the government did not allow them to raise the issue of mass testing of COVID-19. One of them, Kam Nai-wai, questioned whether the government was afraid of antagonizing the central government by discussing the matter of mass testing of COVID-19. In response, District Officer David Leung said that this was a territory-wide issue and that it did not fall into the council's duties and responsibilities. After Leung left the meeting, a pan-democratic council member Yam Kar-yee said that mass testing of COVID-19 would be "useless," while Kam Nai-wai remarked that the Hong Kong style of public health code would be similar to the mainland's social credit system in which personal freedom would be restricted.[25] Kam called for the government to stop the measure of introducing the public health code—a motion "approved" by only 12 council members who were present in the meeting.[26] On the other hand, the District Office in Wan Chai reportedly deleted some agenda items of the Wan Chai DC—a phenomenon showing the power struggle between the pan-democrats in DCs and the HKSAR government.

In September 2020, when the Central and Western DC convened its meeting, the police representatives were asked to leave.[27] The police commander in the Western district, Wong Siu-hing, remarked that she hoped the DC could respect government departments in mutual communication, and that the police wanted to discuss issues rationally together with other government departments for the sake of the community welfare. Yet, one of the agenda items of the Central and Western DC was to "reprimand the police for negligence" and for "being absent" in council meetings—an accusation that could be traced back to May 2020 when the Council had passed a motion "banning" the police commander and her representative to attend its meetings.[28] The worsening relationship between the Council and the police could be attributed to the fact that the Council exceeded its power and jurisdiction first. From an objective standpoint, the Central and Western DC did not have the power and jurisdiction to "ban" any government officials from attending its meetings. During the first eight months of 2020, there were over 30 times in which government officials left the meetings of DCs, which raised all kinds of issues beyond their scope of duties and responsibilities, including the motion of discussing police power and the commemoration of the June Fourth incident in China in 1989.[29]

Another confrontation between DC members and District Office officials took place in the Tuen Mun DC in October 2020, when some council members initiated a discussion of a detention center in which the detainees complained about the immigration authorities.[30] However, District Officer Aubrey Fung said that the issue did not belong to the jurisdiction of the council concerned. District officials left the meeting and switched off the audio system, leading to the anger of a few council members who accused them of being "cold-blooded." After the departure of government officials, the remaining council members continued the meeting presided over by chairwoman Chan Shu-ying. A few pro-government council members, like Lau Yip-keung and So Kar-man, remained seated in the meeting, while a number of government officials including a police representative could not leave the meeting room where the exit was blocked by four pan-democratic council members.

From an objective perspective, the main reason why some DC members targeted at the police power after they were directly elected in November 2019 was the controversial way in which the police dealt with protesters in the anti-extradition movement. In October 2020, a member of the Tsim Sha Tsui and Mong Kok DC, Lam Siu-bun and 76 residents complained to the Municipal Services Appeals Board against the renewal of the liquor license of a restaurant of police officers inside the Mong Kok Police Station.[31] Lam argued that over a thousand citizens had opposed the renewal of the liquor license, but the Appeals Board chairman said that there was no evidence to show police officers who drank alcohol in their restaurant "harassed" any citizen.[32] Members of the Appeals Board were appointed by the Chief Executive and they included one chairperson, six deputy chairpersons, and 53 members. In February 2021, the Appeals Board reached a decision saying that the liquor license's renewal made by the Liquor Licensing Board was "legal and justifiable."[33]

The government's guideline of advising how its district officials dealt with DCs led to the deterioration of its relations with the pan-democratic council members. Kam Nai-wai, a directly elected member from the DP, complained in September 2020 that the government did not provide meeting venues for the members of Central and Western DC, that its officials did not attend meetings, that it did not reimburse the subsidies for DC members to operate their offices, and that the term "supervisory department" could not be used in the DC's scope of duties and responsibilities.[34] He also criticized the Carrie Lam administration for "marginalizing DCs."[35] However, if

DCs firstly exceeded their powers and jurisdictions, it was natural that government officials boycotted their meetings that operated in an *ultra vires* way. A vicious circle persisted in the operation of the democrats-dominated DCs, the boycott of meetings by officials, and the council members' profound distrust of the government.

According to the statistics of the first year of operation of DCs after the 2019 elections, District Officers left the meetings of DCs 73 times — a figure showing the deteriorating relations between the HKSAR government and the directly elected pan-democratic members of DCs.[36] Of the 73 times during which District Officers led other officials to leave the meetings, 12 times occurred in the Central and Western DC where pan-democratic members were relatively assertive and aggressive. Tsuen Wan witnessed seven times in which government officials boycotted its meetings, while DCs in Wan Chai, Kowloon City, and Sai Kung saw five times. In Kowloon City and Sham Shui Po DCs, each council had 12 occasions in which the motions and papers initiated by council members were rejected by the secretariat to be included in the agenda discussion. Only the Islands DC witnessed a relatively harmonious relationship between government officials and members, for there was no incident in which District Officers boycotted its meetings. The poor relationship between the HKSAR government and DCs from the November 2019 elections to November 2020 could be seen as unprecedented. This "new normal" situation could be attributable mainly to the attempts by some DC members to exceed the power of their councils to discuss territory-wide matters, and partly to the non-cooperative approach adopted by government officials who had to follow their internal guideline issued by the HAD, and who could not provide logistical support for DCs that exceeded their scope of duties and responsibilities.

Termination of the Term of Office of Some District Council Members after the Implementation of the National Security Law in Late June 2020

The enactment of the National Security Law for the HKSAR in late June 2020 had a far-reaching repercussion on many pan-democratic and directly elected DC members. Article 6 of the National Security Law says:

> It is the common responsibility of all the people of China, including
> the people of Hong Kong, to safeguard the sovereignty, unification and
> territorial integrity of the People's Republic of China. Any institution,
> organization or individual in the Hong Kong Special Administrative
> Region shall abide by this Law and the laws of the Region in relation to
> the safeguarding of national security, and shall not engage in any act or
> activity which endangers national security. A resident of the Region who
> stands for election or assumes public office shall confirm in writing or take
> an oath to uphold the Basic Law of the Hong Kong Special Administrative
> Region of the People's Republic of China and swear allegiance to the
> Hong Kong Special Administrative Region of the People's Republic of
> China in accordance with the law.[37]

In July 2020, it was reported that all DC members would be invited to take the oath under the supervision of the Secretary for Home Affairs, Caspar Tsui Ying-wai.[38] There were speculations saying that approximately 300 pro-democracy DC members would not be considered qualified to take the oath as they might violate the Public Offices (Candidacy and Taking Up Offices) Ordinance which was passed and enacted by the LegCo in May. From the promulgation of the National Security Law in late June 2020 to mid-July, about 230 DC members resigned partly due to personal reasons and partly because some members were unseated after their prolonged absence from meetings. The criteria of disqualifying DC members included the following: (1) those members who allowed their offices to be used as the polling stations during the unofficial pro-democracy camp's primary elections held for the LegCo in July 2020; (2) those members who signed a declaration supporting the 2019 anti-extradition movement and promised to vote against the government's appropriation bill to pressure the Chief Executive; (3) those whose office displayed the banner of "Liberating Hong Kong, revolution of the times"; and (4) those who called for foreign sanctions (an act that violated the National Security Law) against Hong Kong, like calling for foreign states to end Hong Kong's special customs status in 2020.[39] However, the HKSAR government had not yet reached a decision on the amount of money that it would ask each disqualified DC member to repay his or her salaries and paid expenses. Rumors were circulated in the political circle that if the pan-democratic DC members resigned prior to the new oath-taking ceremony, the HKSAR government would not pursue their repayment of salaries and office expenses. There were claims saying that each disqualified council member might be asked to repay more than HK$1 million in wages and paid expenses, and that the HKSAR government authorities would not pursue those members who opted for early resignation.[40] Due to the fear of many DC members that they would be disqualified and might be asked to repay their salaries and expenses, they decided to simply resign before the new oath-taking ceremonies would be held from August to October 2020. In late July, the Central and Western DC and the Wong Tai Sin DC saw only three members remaining in each council from an original number of 15 and 25 members respectively. Even if DC members took the oath, the HKSAR government also checked their past behavior to see whether they had previously performed acts that might violate the National Security Law. The government could ask some DC members on their past actions and political stance. In September 2020, a batch of seven pan-democratic DC members lost their seats after the government declared that their oaths were "invalid" and that they needed to provide further information. Since a number of core leaders of the pan-democratic camp including the moderate and the radical factions fled the HKSAR for other countries immediately after the promulgation of the National Security Law, some DC members also opted for the path of leaving Hong Kong. Some took the oath but were disqualified as they failed to pass the allegiance test after the government's screening and investigatory process. The National Security Law turned out to be a very effective legal instrument for the HKSAR government to eliminate and disqualify all those DC members whose previous actions were seen as violating the National Security Law.

In Table 8.5, a large number of DC members had their office officially terminated before and after the formal promulgation of the National Security Law on June 30, 2020. A total of 332 DC members had their term of office formally terminated for several reasons, including the voluntary resignation of DC members (some of whom used personal or health reasons), the disappearance of some council members from meetings, the escape of some DC members from Hong Kong to other places like United Kingdom and elsewhere, the detention of a few council members who were involved in the organization of the illegal "primaries" held by the democrats in July 2020, and the imprisonment of a few council members who violated the National Security Law. When news reports in April 2020 revealed that the PRC would formulate and enact a National Security Law for the

Table 8.5: The Time of which the Term of Office of District Council Members was Terminated due to Various Reasons

Date	A	B	C	D	E	F	G	H	J	K	L	M	N	P	Q	R	S	T	Total
Original	15	13	35	17	20	25	25	25	40	21	32	45	22	21	31	42	32	18	479
26 February																	1		1
15 March															1				1
24 March							1												1
30 March													1						1
31 March			1											1					2
18 April								1											1
19 April										1									1
30 April	2											1			1				4
3 May								1		1				2	1				5
4 May												1							1
9 May			1									1							2
10 May			1														1		2
11 May														1					1
16 May														1					1
20 May				1						1									2
26 May	1																		1
27 May																	1		1
28 May	1																		1
31 May			4			1		1	2		1	1	2		1	1	1		13
3 June	1														1				2
8 June						1		1											2
6 July												2				2			4
7 July	3	1	5		2	7	2	4		1	6	5	5	2	1	7	2		53
8 July	3	5	6	9	3	5	4	7	4	3	5	2	1		2	5	6	1	71
9 July			2	1	1			4	4		1				1	1	4	1	20
10 July	1		2	2	1		2	4	2	2		1	1		1	1		1	21
11 July	1				1	2	1		3	1		2	1	1	3	2	2		20
12 July								1		1		4		1	6				13
13 July												2							2
14 July			2									1				2			5

Table 8.5 Continued

District Councils																			
Date	**A**	**B**	**C**	**D**	**E**	**F**	**G**	**H**	**J**	**K**	**L**	**M**	**N**	**P**	**Q**	**R**	**S**	**T**	**Total**
15 July					1														1
16 July										1									1
17 July								2	1										3
18 July								1									1		2
19 July								3									1		4
20 July														1					1
31 August			1											1					2
2 September												1		1					2
9 September			1																1
14 September		2	4	1															7
21 September												1							1
23 September					1														1
28 September					3	1	3	1	1										9
30 September															1	1			2
2 October																1			1
7 October										2	1			2	4	9	1		19
10 October												1							1
20 October								2	2	8							2	2	16
21 October												1							1
11 November																	1		1
31 December												1							1
Total	**13**	**8**	**29**	**14**	**13**	**17**	**13**	**23**	**24**	**13**	**21**	**34**	**12**	**14**	**23**	**33**	**24**	**5**	**332**

Note (1): District Codes are: A—Central and Western, B—Wan Chai, C—Eastern, D—Southern, E—Yau Tsim Mong, F—Sham Shui Po, G—Kowloon City, H—Wong Tai Sin, J—Kwun Tong, K—Tsuen Wan, L—Tuen Mun, M—Yuen Long, N—North, P—Tai Po, Q—Sai Kung, R—Sha Tin, S—Kwai Tsing and T—Islands; the days on 14 September, 28 September, 7 October and 20 October are councilors disqualified by oath taking.

Note (2): The term of office of council members was terminated because of various reasons, including (a) council members who voluntarily resigned immediately after the promulgation of the National Security Law; (2) council members who took the oath of swearing allegiance to the National Security Law but who were still disqualified by the government for their previously problematic action and behavior; (3) council members who fled Hong Kong after the National Security Law; (4) council members who violated the National Security Law and who were detained immediately by the government; and (5) council members who simply disappeared in meetings after the National Security Law.

Source: District Council website, https://www.districtcouncils.gov.hk/index.html, access date: March 15, 2022.

HKSAR, some council members were concerned and began to leave their office for personal or health reasons. In July alone, as shown in Table 8.5, 219 DC members had their office terminated formally—a figure showing a large number of elected council members who abandoned their office for various reasons.

The Decline of the Civic Party after the National Security Law

The impact of the National Security Law was felt on some members of the Civic Party, which could be seen as the second largest pro-democracy party occupying directly elected seats in DCs. Established in March 2006, the Civic Party had four members—legislators Alvin Yeung, Kwok Ka-ki, and Dennis Kwok, as well as Eastern DC member Cheng Tat-hung—who received the notification from the election director on July 30, 2020 that they would not be qualified to run for the LegCo elections.[41] On the next day, the vice-chairlady of the Sham Shui Po DC, Janet Ng Yuet-lan, announced that she withdrew from the Civic Party. On September 29, Tanya Chan Suk-chong, a founding member of the party and a legislator, announced that she withdrew from the party due to personal reasons. On October 19, a member of the Sha Tin DC, Chandler Chan Nok-hang, said he was unhappy with the party's performance in LegCo and withdrew from the party. On November 11, the PRC's NPC empowered the HKSAR government to handle the qualifications of Hong Kong's elected politicians, including legislators and DC members. Then the HKSAR government announced that three Civic Party legislators—Dennis Kwok, Alvin Yeung, and Kwok Ka-ki—lost their seats at once. The only Civic Party legislator who was not disqualified, namely Jeremy Tam Man-ho, expressed his gratitude to the voters who had supported him. Tam resigned with other 14 pan-democratic legislators from the LegCo. From December 12 to 15, three Civic Party members withdrew from the party, including Sin Ho-fai, Tam Ka-chun, and Cheng Tat-hung. From March to October 2021, 27 Civic Party members who were also DC members withdrew from the party for personal and health reasons. In July 2021, Lai Chi-keung, a Civic Party member, Eastern DC chairman, and a District Councilor for 33 years, announced that he withdrew from the party due to the "rapid and drastic deterioration of the political circumstances."[42] Another Civic Party member Yu Tak-po also resigned from Yau Tsim Mong DC, adding that although democracy in Hong Kong "reaches its sunset,"

Table 8.6: The Decline of Civic Party: Withdrawal and Resignation of Members after the National Security Law Withdrawal

Date	Issues
30 July 2020	Four candidates of the Civic Party, including legislators Alvin Yeung, Kwok Ka-ki, Dennis Kwok and Eastern DC member Cheng Tat-hung received the notification from the election officer that their electoral nominations of running in the originally scheduled September elections held for the LegCo were "invalid."
31 July 2020	Vice-chairlady of the Sham Shui Po DC, Janet Ng Yuet-lan, announced that she withdrew from the Civic Party.
29 September 2020	Tanya Chan, who was a legislator, a founding member of the Civic Party and the vice-chairlady (external affairs) of the party, announced that she withdrew from the Civic Party due to personal reasons. In January 2022, it was reported that she went to reside in Taiwan.
19 October 2020	Chandler Chan Nok-hang, a Sha Tin DC member, expressed his dissatisfaction with the Civic Party's performance in LegCo and announced his withdrawal from the party.
11 November 2020	The National People's Congress made a decision to empower the HKSAR government to deal with the eligibility of elected officers, including LegCo members and DC members. Immediately, the HKSAR government announced that three Civic Party legislators—Dennis Kwok, Alvin Yeung and Kwok Ka-ki—lost their status as legislators. The only Civic Party member left in the LegCo, Jeremy Tam Man-ho, expressed his gratitude to the voters who supported him in the 2016 LegCo elections. He announced his resignation from the LegCo together with 14 other pan-democratic legislators on November 12 and the effective date of his resignation would be December 1, 2020.
12 December 2020	Kwai Tsing DC members, Henry Sin Ho-fai and Warren Tam Ka-chun, and Southern DC member James Yu Chun-hei announced that they withdrew from the Civic Party.
15 December 2020	Eastern DC member Cheng Tat-hung announced that he withdrew from the Civic Party. Later, in May 2021, it was reported that he resigned from the position of DC member.
3 March 2021	Alvin Yeung, Kwok Ka-ki, Jeremy Tam and Eastern DC member Lee Yue-shun announced that they withdrew from the Civic Party.
12 March 2021	The Civic Party informed the Civil Human Rights Front (CHRF) that it terminated the Front's work and meetings. The CHRF announced in August 2021 that it was disbanded after its activities were criticized for violating the National Security Law.
16 March 2021	Wong Tai Sin DC member, Jay Cheng Man-kit, announced that he withdrew from the Civic Party.
5 April 2021	Tsuen Wan DC member Wong Ka-wah revealed that he had resigned from the Civic Party in March 2021.
12 April 2021	Kwun Tong DC member Antony Bux resigned from the position of council member on health reasons and the effective date of resignation would be June 1, 2021.
13 April 2021	Kwun Tong DC member Steven Lee Kwan-chak announced that he withdrew from the Civic Party,
19 April 2021	Kwun Tong DC member Li Wai-lam announced that he withdrew from the Civic Party.
30 April 2021	Sha Tin DC member Leticia Wong Man-huen announced that she withdrew from the Civic Party and would not participate in the oath-taking ceremony.
6 May 2021	Sha Tin DC member Stanley Lui Kai-wing announced that he withdrew from the Civic Party and that he would focus on district work.

Table 8.6 Continued

Date	Issues
7 May 2021	Sham Shui Po DC member Eunice Chau Yuen-man submitted her resignation letter to the Council Chair on personal reason. Her resignation would be effective from June 1 onwards.
11 May 2021	Wong Tai Sin DC member Carmen Lau Ka-man announced that she withdrew from the Civic Party and that she would not participate in the oath-taking ceremony.
21 May 2021	Central and Western DC member Cherry Wong Kin-ching resigned from the Council for health reasons and her resignation would be effective from June 1 onwards.
Late June–early July 2021	Sixteen members of the Civic Party resigned from DCs or the party. They included Derek Ngai, Patrick Leung and Joseph Lai Chi-keung from the Eastern DC; Mike Chan Pui-ming and Michael Yung Ming-chau from the Sha Tin DC; Sarah Wong Ka-ying from the Kwun Tong DC; Andy Yu Tak-po from Yau Tsim Mong DC; Andy Lao Ka-hang and Joshua Li Chun-hei from Sham Shui Po DC; Sumly Chan Yuen-sum and Antonio Luk Ling-chung from Tsuen Wan DC; Steven Cheung Kwan-kiu from Kwai Tsing DC; Ken Mak Tse-kin and Vienna Luk Tze-tung from Sha Tin DC; and Lee Ka-ho from Islands DC. Amy Yung from the Islands DC withdrew from the Civic Party in June 2021.
8 July 2021	Sha Tin DC member Michael Yung resigned from the Council.
3 October 2021	Sha Tin DC member Mike Chan Pui-ming announced that he resigned from the Council. His resignation meant that the Civic Party no longer had any member in the DCs.

Sources: For the development of the Civic Party, see 公民黨 (香港)—維基百科，自由嘅百科全書 (wikipedia.org), access date: March 21, 2022. Also see "Civic Party has a tide of mass resignation with 11 members' withdrawal," HK01, June 20, 2021, in 公民黨爆退黨潮　至少11區議員先後退出　余德寶：繼續服務街坊 (hk01.com), access date: March 21, 2022.

citizens should maintain their "temperature" and work hard in different aspects.[43] The vice-chairman of the Association for Democracy and People's Livelihood (ADPL), Yeung Yuk, also resigned from his position in the Sham Shui Po DC, revealing that because the government spread the news pointing to its pursuit of councilors' salaries and expenses if they did not resign, he and his ADPL members conducted risks assessment and decided to resign. By October 2021, the Civic Party lost all the directly elected seats it won from the November 2019 elections (see Table 8.6). The decline of the Civic Party in DCs was prominent after the promulgation of the National Security Law.

Table 8.7 shows that there were five types of DC members who lost their directly elected seats; 233 council members resigned shortly before and after the implementation of the National Security Law in late June 2020; 50 decided to take the oath but they were then disqualified by the HKSAR government based on their previous remarks and action; 24 of them lost their seats due to their involvement in national security-related

Table 8.7: Five Types of District Council Members Who Lost their Seats after the Implementation of the National Security Law

District Code	District Council members who were disqualified by the court after being judged violating the law	District Council member who resigned	District Council members who were involved in national security-related cases	District Council members who took the oath but who were disqualified by the HKSAR government	District Council member who refused to take the oath
A	0	10	2	0	0
B	0	5	1	2	0
C	0	20	4	4	1
D	0	11	2	1	0
E	0	8	1	4	0
F	0	13	2	1	1
G	1	9	0	3	0
H	0	22	0	1	0
J	1	20	1	1	0
K	0	10	1	2	0
L	1	15	1	2	2
M	1	20	3	9	1
N	1	10	1	0	0
P	0	11	0	3	0
Q	0	16	3	4	0
R	0	23	1	9	0
S	3	17	1	2	1
T	0	3	0	2	0
Total	**8**	**233**	**24**	**50**	**6**

Note: District codes are the same as the previous table.

Sources: HK01, July 9, 2021, available in: https://www.hk01.com/政情/648306/持續更新-387名民主派區議員逾半已辭職-三區建制重奪多數, access date: February 24, 2022; and VOA News, October 25, 2021, in https://www.voacantonese.com/a/cantonese-it-hong-kong-reactions-to-16-more-district-councilors-ousted-over-loyalty-oaths-20211025-ry/6284334.html, access date: February 24, 2022.

cases; eight of them were disqualified by the court after they were found guilty of violating the law in the 2019 protests; and six of them refused to take the oath and thereby lost their seats. For the 233 DC members who resigned, they did not want to repay their salaries and expenditures to the government, which had spread the news that council members who did not resign would have to repay their salaries and expenditures—a strategy that worked well in favor of the government as a large number of directly elected council members simply resigned before the oath-taking ceremony for them to swear allegiance to the National Security Law. Some of them claimed that they did not want to become bankrupt, and so they opted for resignation. Some opted for resignation and left the HKSAR for other countries and places, including the United Kingdom, in a low-profile manner. Some who resigned decided to re-start their new careers, understanding that their pro-democracy movement was politically lost.

The Political Impacts of Mass Resignation and Member Disqualification on District Councils

Table 8.8 shows the situation before and after the disqualification and mass resignation of DC members. Originally, there were a total of 479 members of DCs elected after November 2019, including 27 ex-officio members from the rural district organization HYK. While there were only 63 pro-establishment members, the pro-democracy members amounted to 389—a majority domination unprecedented in the political history of Hong Kong's district elections. However, after mass resignation and disqualification of council members in the latter half of 2021, the political profile of all 18 councils changed significantly. From July 6 to 20, 2021, 219 members resigned from DCs within 15 days. Eventually, 147 members took the oath effectively and 58 of them were pro-democracy in political orientation. One of the 63 pro-establishment members did not take the oath for unknown reasons, while 27 ex-officio members also took the oath. Together with 58 democrats who took the oath and who passed the allegiance test, there were a total of 147 DC members in the DCs after the National Security Law's implementation, mass resignations, and disqualification of councillors.

Table 8.9 shows the political profile of DCs after the mass resignation and disqualification of members in late 2021. It illustrates that the democrats remain the majority faction in five DCs: Central and Western, Yau Tsim Mong, Sham Shui Po, Wong Tai Sin, and Sha Tin. Nevertheless, the factional rivalries between the democrats and pro-establishment forces became a thing of the past; due to the National Security Law and the rapid change in political atmosphere, the operation of these democrats-dominated councils tend to be far more harmonious than the situation shortly after the November 2019 elections. DCs which have no dominant political force include Eastern

Table 8.8: The Political Situation of District Councils before and after Mass Resignation and Disqualification of Members from July to December 2021

Date	A	B	C	D	E	F	G	H	J	K	L	M	N	P	Q	R	S	T	Total
Total Seats	15	13	35	17	20	25	25	25	40	21	32	45	22	21	31	42	32	18	479
Ex-official members										2	1	6	4	2	2	1	1	8	27
Pro-Establishment members	1	4	3	2	3	3	10	0	12	3	3	6	3	0	3	1	3	3	63
Pro-Democracy Members	14	9	32	15	17	22	15	25	28	16	28	33	15	19	26	40	28	7	389
Council Members Who Resigned in July 2021	7	6	17	12	9	14	9	20	19	9	14	17	8	5	14	20	16	3	219
Number of members who took the oath effectively	3	5	6	3	7	8	12	2	16	8	11	11	10	7	8	9	8	13	147
Number of Pro-democracy Members who remained in District Councils	2	1	3	1	4	5	2	2	4	3	7	0	3	5	3	7	4	2	58

Source: Authors' tabulation from District Councils' website, March 20, 2022.

Note: One out of 63 pro-establishment members did not take the oath. As a result, while 62 pro-establishment members successfully took the oath of swearing allegiance to the National Security Law, 23 other ex-officio members did so together with 58 democrats who took the oath and who passed the allegiance test.

district, Sai Kung district, Tai Po district, and Tsuen Wan district. All other DCs are dominated by the pro-establishment forces. Having said that, because of the onset of Omicron variant of COVID-19 in the HKSAR in early 2022, the operation of DCs were affected. Many civil servants in the secretariat of DCs were redeployed to deal with the lockdown of buildings where some residents were infected with Omicron.[44] As such, the priority of the HKSAR government was to tackle the spreading Omicron in the early months of 2022, leading to the relative lack of activities of DCs.

In fact, some DCs operated in a partial and paralysed manner after the mass resignation and disqualification of council members. Some DCs had vacant positions in their chairpersons and deputy chairpersons, including Eastern district, Wong Tai Sin, and Sha Tin.[45] In late October 2021, eight DCs lacked 11 chairpersons and deputy chairs. A difficult scenario of lacking

Table 8.9: The Political Profile of District Councils after Resignation and Disqualification of Members in late 2021

District	Number of Democrats	Number of Pro-Government	Number of Moderate Force	Dominant Faction
Central and Western	2	1	0	D
Wan Chai	1	4	0	P
Eastern	3	3	0	No dominant faction
Southern	1	2	0	P
Yau Tsim Mong	4	3	0	D
Sham Shui Po	5	3	0	D
Kowloon City	2	10	0	P
Wong Tai Sin	2	0	0	D
Kwun Tong	2	14	0	P
Kwai Tsing	3	5	0	P
Island	2	11	0	P
Sai Kung	3	3	2	No dominant faction
Taipo	6	2	0	D
Sha Tin	7	2	0	D
Yuen Long	0	11	0	P
Northern	3	7	0	P
Tuen Mun	5	6	0	P
Tsuen Wan	4	4	0	No dominant faction
Total	54	89	2	

Sources: VOA News, October 25, 2021 https://www.voacantonese.com/a/cantonese-it-hong-kong-reactions-to-16-more-district-councilors-ousted-over-loyalty-oaths-20211025-ry/6284334.html (access date: Feb 24, 2022).

chairs or deputy chairs emerged because, according to the DC Ordinance, if there is any vacant position of chairperson or deputy chairperson, then a by-election would need to have the nomination of three council members, who cannot nominate himself or herself. As such, there has to be at least four council members in the process of nominating a candidate to be a chairperson or deputy chairperson. The Central and Western DC had only three remaining members, meaning that they could not select a chairperson or deputy chairperson. Similarly, there were only two members in the Wong Tai Sin DC, meaning that it could not select a chairperson or a deputy chairperson. In the Southern DC, there were four members and in theory it could select a chairperson; nevertheless, a member was involved in the court case on the pan-democratic "primary election." Although this member, namely Pang Cheuk-kay, was granted bail by the court, one of the conditions of such bail was that he could not participate in any election. Later, Pang was disqualified from becoming a council member again. As a result, the Southern DC could not elect any chairperson. Similarly, in the Eastern DC, there were three members from the pan-democratic camp and three from the pro-establishment camp; it was very difficult to elect a chairperson.

In November 2021, the Tsuen Wan DC witnessed the election of pro-establishment Yau Kam-ping to be its deputy chairperson after two democrats failed to reach a consensus on who should compete for the position.[46] The original deputy chairperson, Lee Hung-po, was disqualified although he took the oath. As a result, two democrats — Luk Ling-chung and Wong Ka-wah — wanted to run for the deputy position, but they did not reach a consensus. Only Yau ran in the election and was elected as the deputy chair, perhaps showing the loosely organized nature of some democrats even after they passed the national security test through the oath-taking ceremony.

Table 8.10 shows the changes of chairpersons and deputy chairpersons after the mass resignation and disqualification of many DC members in the latter half of 2020. In total, 11 chairpersons and eight deputy chairpersons resigned from DCs. Moreover, three chairpersons and two deputy chairpersons were disqualified. Of the 18 DCs, only Sha Tin and Islands DCs had no change in their chairpersons and deputy chairpersons, who were elected among the members of the DCs concerned. As of March 2022, three DCs still lacked chairpersons, including Southern, Eastern, and Wong Tai Sin DCs where the number of members was reduced to very few, and where a minimum number of three nominations could not be acquired to nominate the chairperson. Some DCs still lack deputy chairpersons, including Central and Western, Eastern, Wong Tai Sin, and Tai Po districts. Two DCs — Eastern and Wong Tai Sin — do not have chairpersons and deputy chairs as of March 2022.

The Reduced Role of District Councils

Most importantly, the role of DCs has been curbed significantly. First and foremost, with regard to DCs whose members were reduced, the

Table 8.10: The Chairpersons and Deputy Chairpersons of District Councils as of March 2022

District	Democrats versus pro-government members	Dominant force	Chairperson	Deputy Chairperson	Situation after mass resignation and disqualification
Central/Western	2 versus 1	democrats	Victor Yeung Sui-yin (originally deputy chair)	Vacant	Change: The original chair, Cheng Lai-king, resigned in July 2021
Wan Chai	1 versus 4	pro-government	Ivan Wong Wang-tai	Anson Lam Wai-man	Change: The original chair, Clarisse Yeung Suet-ying, was disqualified in 2021. The deputy chair, Mak King-sing, resigned in July 2021.
Southern	1 versus 2	pro-government	Vacant	Paul Zimmerman	Change: The original chair, Lo Kin-hei, resigned in July 2021.
Eastern	3 versus 3	Tie	Vacant	Vacant	Change: The original chair, Joseph Lai Chi-keung, resigned in July 2021. The deputy chair, Andrew Chiu Ka-yin, also resigned in July 2021.
Yau Tsim Mong	4 versus 3	democrats	Lam Kin-man	Leo Chu Tsz-lok	Change: The original deputy chair, Yu Tak-po, resigned in July 2021.
Sham Shui Po	6 versus 2	democrats	Chum Tak-shing (ADPL)	Janet Ng Yuet-lan	Change: The original chair, Yeung Yuk of ADPL, resigned in July 2021.
Kowloon City	1 versus 11	pro-government	Yang Wing-kit	Ho Hin-ming (Liberal Party)	Change: The original chair Siu Leong-sing of DP resigned in July 2021. The deputy chair, Kwong Po-yin, resigned in July 2021.
Wong Tai Sin	2 versus 0	democrats	Vacant	Vacant	Change: The chair, Hui Kam-shing of ADPL, resigned in July 2021. The deputy chair, Wong Yat-yuk, resigned also in 2021.
Kwun Tong	2 versus 14	pro-government	Wilson Or Chong-shing (DAB)	Lui Tung-hai	Change: The original chair, Choi Chak-hung, resigned in July 2021. The deputy chair, Mak Kin-shing, resigned in July 2021.

Table 8.10 Continued

District	Democrats versus pro-government members	Dominant force	Chairperson	Deputy Chairperson	Situation after mass resignation and disqualification
Tai Po	6 versus 2	democrats	Mo Ka-chun	Vacant	Change: The original chair, Kwan Wing-yip, resigned in uly 2021. The deputy chair, Lau Yong-wai, was disqualified.
Sai Kung	3 versus 5	pro-government	Chau Yin-ming	Choi Ming-hei	Change: The original chair, Ben Chung Kam-lun, resigned in 2021.
Sha Tin	7 versus 2	democrats	Mak Yun-pui	Sin Cheuk-nam (DP)	No change
Northern	4 versus 7	pro-government	Law Ting-tak	Lee Koon-hung	Change: The original deputy chair, Chan Yuk-ming, resigned in July 2021.
Tsuen Wan	4 versus 4	Tie	Sumly Chan Yuen-sum	Yau Kam-ping	Change: The deputy chair Li Hung-por was disqualified in October 2021.
Tuen Mun	7 versus 4	democrats	Chan Yau-hon (FYU)	Wong Tan-ching	Change: The original chair, Chan Shu-ying, resigned in July 2021.
Yuen Long	0 versus 12	pro-government	Shum Hon-kit	Tang Ho-nin	Change: The original chair, Wong Wai-yin, was disqualified in 2021. The deputy chair, Mak Ip-shing, resigned in 2021.
Kwai Tsing	4 versus 5	pro-government	Lo Yuen-ting	Chan Chi-wing	Change: The original chair, Sin Chung-kai, resigned in May 2021 and he was replaced by Leung Lam-wai, who however was also disqualified in November 2021. The original deputy chair, Cheung Man-lung, resigned in July 2021.
Islands	2 versus 11	pro-government	Yu Hon-kwan	Wong Man-hon	No change

Sources: Websites of 18 District Councils, District Council (districtcouncils.gov.hk), access date: March 22, 2022. Also see "Three District Councils are like ending their operation, Eight district lacks chairs and deputy chairs," *Oriental Daily*, October 21, 2021, in 3區議會形同停擺　8區欠11正副主席 | 即時新聞 | 港澳 | on.cc東網, access date: March 22, 2022.

financial responsibilities of dealing with expenditure have been returned to District Officers.[47] The minor projects that were previously approved in their funding continued, but new projects have been stalled. Perhaps the operation of the DCs that is the least affected is in the Islands district, which has already been dominated by the pro-establishment camp after the November 2019 DC elections. Second, after the November 2019 DC elections, the pan-democratic DC members were no longer appointed to be the members of ACs, where some members were the formerly defeated pro-establishment candidates in DC elections. This kind of patron-clientelist tactic of appointment made by the government was understandable, for it did not want to witness the politicization of ACs by appointing the more vocal, critical, and pro-democracy members. Third, DMCs have not been active in some districts, particularly where chairpersons and deputy chairs are even vacant.[48] The members of the secretariat of some DCs were redeployed to deal with the lockdown of buildings where residents were found infected with COVID-19 and its variants, such as Omicron, in early 2022. With the much-reduced role and work of DCs, it was natural that the secretariat staff of DCs could be better redeployed and mobilized in the territory-wide combat against the spread of Omicron.

The decline in the role and operation of DCs since the mass resignation and disqualification of their members in the latter half of 2021 was accompanied by a corresponding increase in the influence of the appointed members of the ACs, District FCCs, and District FSCs. Most of these appointed elites came from *kaifong* or neighborhood associations, while some of them failed to be elected or re-elected in the 2019 DC elections. Only 24 out of 156 Election Committee members, who were entitled to vote for members of the LegCo in November 2021 and the Chief Executive in May 2022, came from those who were successfully elected or re-elected in the 2019 DC elections. As such, the patronage color of Hong Kong politics has become very prominent after the mass resignation and disqualification of many DC members in the latter half of 2021.

Area Committees (ACs), which were set up in 1972 to help the Clean Hong Kong Campaign and Fight Crime Campaign in the British colonial era, have been traditionally under the administrative jurisdiction of District Offices. After the establishment of the former District Boards (DBs) in 1982, ACs played an auxiliary role in the promotion of public

Table 8.11: The Composition of the Election Committee Members who came from Area Committees, District Fight Crime Committees and District Fire Safety Committees

Organization	No.	%
Members from different *kaifong* or neighborhood associations	72	46.15%
Members who failed to re-elected or elected in the 2019 District Council Elections	57	36.54%
Members who were successfully re-elected or elected in the 2019 District Council Elections	24	15.38%
Former District Council members	3	1.92%
Total	156	100%

Source: Calculated from the database of the members of Election Committee in HK01, https://ele-committee.hk01.com/2021, access date: February 24, 2022.

Note: (1) The Election Committee had 1,200 members who could select the 40 of the 90 LegCo members in November 2021 and who could also elect the Chief Executive in May 2022. There were 156 out of 1,200 Election Committee members coming from the Area Committees, District Fight Crime Committees and District Fire Safety Committees.

participation in social affairs. As of July 2020, there were 67 ACs in 16 of the 18 districts and they appointed some 1,600 members, except for Tai Po and North districts which have traditionally been regarded as having "rural characteristics" and do not need ACs.[49] In July 2020, it was reported that 96 defeated candidates in the 2019 DC elections were appointed to ACs, leading to questions on whether such a move would curb and "hijack" DCs. The elected DC members were no longer appointed by the government to ACs.[50] In April 2021, the government suddenly set up four ACs in Tai Po and North districts, appointing a total of 80 members of which 17 were defeated candidates in the 2019 DC elections.[51] With the benefit of hindsight, the HKSAR government after the promulgation of the National Security Law in late June 2020 had a series of steps to elevate the role of ACs, to clarify the criteria of elected council members of passing the political allegiance test, and to require the elected councilors to undergo a new oath-taking ceremony to swear allegiance to the National Security Law. As such, ACs suddenly became a vehicle which the government used for the sake of filling the void of the "hyper-politicized" DCs. Objectively speaking, such hyper-politicization was partly due to the assertive and *ultra vires* behavior of some elected councilors after November 2019, and partly due to the government's determination to reverse democratization of DCs in the HKSAR. In other words, DCs had to be politically curbed by the prospects of disqualification. On the other hand, ACs, whose rationale and existence were discussed once in LegCo's panel on home affairs in 1998, had to be politically elevated in the summer of 2020 to a status unparalleled in the history of district administration in Hong Kong. The fact that some members of ACs, together with those from District FCCs and District FSCs, were later coopted as members of the Election Committee which select 40 LegCo members and the Chief Executive was a testimony to the blueprint of utilizing these committees to replace the DCs. As the most powerful patron in Hong Kong's district politics, the government naturally appointed the pro-establishment elites and previously defeated candidates in the 2019 elections back to the ACs, District FCCs, and District FSCs.

An interesting political phenomenon in the 18 DCs after the November 2019 DC elections was that the democrats reached a consensus of not appointing ad-hoc members — persons appointed from the community to help district council's work — into DCs. Traditionally, each DC decided whether it should have ad hoc members, their number, and whether they should have voting power. The idea of having ad-hoc members in DCs originated from the democrats and the pro-government members, who sensed the need to groom their supporters in DCs. In case councillors were absent, they could rely on their political followers to participate in meetings and sub-committee work. Ad-hoc members stemmed from two main sources: political followers and clients who could be groomed as potential candidates in elections and chairpersons and executive members of the Mutual Aid Committees and Owners' Corporations.[52] The democrats were very eager to control a DC. For instance, in the 1988 Kwai Tsing DB elections, the democrats grasped 15 of the 16 directly elected seats; and there were eight appointed seats and one ex-officio member.[53] As such, the democrats occupied the majority of the Kwai Tsing DB. Appointing their supporters as ad-hoc members could even strengthen the pan-democratic control of the DB or DC, including the utilization of funding and resources. In 1994, the Hong Kong government abolished all appointed seats in DCs and the democrats captured four of the councils. Ad hoc members could play the role of assisting the democrats to consolidate their political grip of the councils concerned. After the establishment of the HKSAR, the government reintroduced some appointed seats to DCs, making it difficult for the democrats to capture the majority of the councils until 2016, when the Donald Tsang administration abolished all appointed seats. Such a move facilitated the democrats to capture 17 of the 18 DCs in the 2019 elections after which they believed that it was politically unnecessary and contradictory to appoint their followers to the councils as ad-hoc members. As a result, ad-hoc members became a thing of the past after the 2019 DC elections. From the perspective of patron-client politics, it has traditionally been serious in DBs and DCs. While the British colonial administration favoured the appointment of pro-government elites to balance the directly elected and pro-democracy DB members, the same can be said of the HKSAR government. On the other hand, while pro-government elites were keen to influence district affairs through the patronage of the HKSAR administration, the democrats were eager to groom their followers as ad-hoc members in DCs until their massive victory in the 2019 DC elections.

The Idea of Abolishing Mutual Aid Committees

In January 2022, the government planned to disband all the Mutual Aid Committees (MACs) starting from July onwards. The MACs, which were established in the 1970s in private and public housing estates to promote a stronger sense of community among residents, have been politicized since the penetration by political parties in the 1990s. Still, the 1,663 MACs had their functions, such as conducting better liaison work among residents in the buildings and districts and forging a strong sense of community identity among residents. Unfortunately, the HKSAR government claimed that it has lots of channels of communication with residents, and that "there are opinions within the community" pointing to the diminishing role of MACs.[54] Critics pointed to the phenomenon that the government might be afraid of the domination of democrats in many MACs, which were in the past controlled by pro-establishment community elites. Tsuen Wan DC chairman Sumly Chan remarked that MACs only dealt with estate management and the organization of fund-raising activities for charity purpose, and that he did not understand why the government had to dissolve them. Nevertheless, a pro-government Kwun Tong district councilor Frankie Ngan Man-yu pointed to the overlapping functions of MACs and ACs. Financially speaking, the government could also save the quarterly subsidy of HK$1,000 to each MAC, but the amount that could be saved was relatively minimal. When a moderate pro-democracy legislator, Tik Chi-yuen, in January 2022 asked the government whether it could consult public opinion before it decided to terminate the operation of MACs, the administration's written reply was as follows:

> Neighborhood network and modes of building management have evolved in tandem with societal development and changes over the past few decades. For instance, many buildings have already engaged property management companies to take charge of their management or have formed other residents' organizations. In addition, with the development of information technology, there have been more direct communication channels between the government and the residents. In fact, the number of MACs was on a continuous decline, down by nearly half to around 1,600 over the past 15 years or so. On the other hand, MAC formation remained at a low level, with an average of less than 30 MACs formed annually in recent years. Some in the community consider that MACs are playing a diminishing role in the relevant areas. After careful consideration, the Home Affairs Bureau has decided to terminate the MAC scheme by phases. That said, the government will continue to enhance communication at the local level by, for example, strengthening ties with the community through different district committees, including Area Committees, District Fight Crime Committees and District Fire Safety Committees. For private buildings that have not engaged property management companies or formed any residents' organizations, the District Building Management Liaison Teams of the District Offices will assist relevant owners in forming residents' organizations such as owners' corporations.[55]

From a critical perspective, the HKSAR government failed to critically assess its weaknesses in conducting united front work at the 18 districts. Traditionally, district organizations such as DBs, ACs, MACs, District FCCs, and District FSCs were used by the British colonial administration skilfully to tap the views of residents and to narrow the communication gap between the rulers and the ruled. The PRC government's united front work in the HKSAR was also relatively weak until the outbreak of the 2019 anti-extradition movement, which exposed the limited inroads made by the PRC authorities in winning the hearts and minds of many Hong Kong people, especially the youth and the educated intellectuals.[56] However, if the Secretary for Home Affairs has been responsible for conducting united front work at the district level, trying to win the hearts and minds of the residents in 18 districts, the decision of abolishing MACs was arguably an ill-advised one. In particular, in March 2022, when the outbreak of Omicron cost the lives of many elderly people, Chief Executive Carrie Lam revealed in a press conference that the mainland's public health experts pointed to the "weak" mobilization ability at the district level.[57] Although the pro-establishment Anti-COVID Joint Alliance was set up by pro-Beijing elites and community groups to mobilize residents as volunteers, its mobilization remained relatively weak and limited. MACs could have played crucial role in mobilizing residents in private and public housing estates to combat the spread of COVID-19 and its variants, like Omicron. Sadly, neither the former Secretary for Home Affairs, Caspar Tsui, nor his acting successor, Jack Chan, realized the utility of mobilizing residents' participation through the organization and leadership of MACs.

In fact, politicization was even more serious in Owners Corporations or Committees (OCs) than MACs. In October 2018, Joshua Wong Chi-fung, who was the leader of a student group named Scholarism which mobilized students and parents to oppose the government's national education policy in the summer of 2012, got 840 votes and was defeated by a pro-establishment candidate with 1,256 votes in an election held for the OC representative in South Horizon's Block 18 at Aberdeen.[58] Many other OCs were involved in bitter disputes and political struggles, ranging from the political struggle between pro-democracy camp and pro-establishment forces to the managerial controversy over repair work, and from voting irregularities to the controversies over auditing and budgetary affairs.[59] If the abolition of MACs aimed at depoliticizing district housing politics, such a move could not tackle the equally politicized circumstances in the existing OCs. If the government uses OCs to replace MACs, the inevitability of politicization cannot be avoided so long as ideology seeps into the electoral politics of district-based residents' associations.

Objectively speaking, DCs operated in a paralyzed way after the mass resignations and disqualification of many council members. Table 8.12 shows that 131 working groups and 38 committees were discontinued in 13 DCs, while the working groups and committee remained unchanged in five DCs. The working groups were formed under the committees. If the committees did not operate, their working groups naturally ceased to function. The paralysis of DCs was unfortunate. In the first place, the victory of the pan-democratic camp in the November 2019 DC elections

Table 8.12: The Number of Discontinued Committees and Working Groups in 13 District Councils in March 2022

District Council	Number of Discontinued Committees	Number of Discontinued Working Groups
Wan Chai	0	2
Eastern	0	9
Kwun Tong	8	0
Sham Shui Po	0	18
Yau Tsim Mong	3	4
Kowloon City	1	3
Tseun Wan	0	14
Yuen Long	7	12
North	6	5
Sai Kung	4	19
Kwai Tsing	3	21
Tai Po	0	5
Tuen Mun	6	19
Total	**38**	**131**

Source: The authors' tabulation from the websites of 18 District Councils, March 2022.

Note: The other five District Councils did not show any change in their committees and working groups.

was arguably an outcome of democratic operation. Yet, the assertive and aggressive behaviour of some democrats was seen as an attempt at exceeding the powers of DCs, whose operation has been deeply undermined by the mass resignation and governmental disqualification of many members shortly after the promulgation of the National Security Law in late June 2020.

The Politics of Resignation of Caspar Tsui in February 2022

The Secretary for Home Affairs, Caspar Tsui Ying-wai, resigned in February 2022 after he attended a birthday party hosted by NPC member Witman Hung Wai-man. Tsui was heavily criticized by the media and commentators for not wearing a mask and socializing without the political sensitivity that mass gatherings were prohibited during the outbreak of the fifth wave of COVID-19 in the HKSAR. Chief Executive Carrie Lam said that Tsui's behaviour was "especially disappointing" because he did not utilize the LeaveHomeSafe app, although he was one of the principal officials responsible for fighting the spread of COVID-19 and its variants, such as Omicron.[60] The PRC State Council decided to dismiss Tsui on Carrie Lam's recommendation. Fifteen other officials attended Witman Hung's birthday party—an indication showing the seriousness of *guanxi* relations at the top level of the political elites in the HKSAR government. Although Ip Kwok-him, Tsui's DAB colleague and Executive Council (ExCo) member, thought that Tsui should not be "punished,"[61] the scandal that involved 15 officials suddenly plunged the Carrie Lam administration to a crisis of legitimacy at a time when Omicron started to break out. Two other officials were verbally warned, including Allen Fung Ying-lun, a political assistant to the Secretary for Development, and Vincent Fung Hao-yin, the deputy director of the Policy Innovation and Coordination Office.[62] Fung was warned as he had stayed in the birthday party for more than four hours, while Lam continued to return to work in his office the next day after he received the health notification for him to get tested for COVID-19. The partygate scandal involving Caspar Tsui failed to win the hearts and minds of many Hong Kong people, who expected top government officials to adhere to the strict quarantine rules established by the HKSAR administration. As a secretary responsible for united front work, Caspar Tsui's resignation was understandable and reasonable.

Table 8.13 sums up the contributions and controversies of the various Secretaries for Home Affairs in the HKSAR after July 1, 1997. David Lan contributed to the organization of various district activities that celebrated the smooth transfer of sovereignty from Britain to China on July 1, 1997, but the dissolution of UrbCo and RegCo was highly controversial. Lam Woon-kwong reviewed the role of DCs without much controversies. Patrick Ho was the Secretary for Home Affairs when the double village heads elections were introduced—a proposal that remained controversial although it was eventually adopted. The idea of legalizing soccer betting was also controversial in the community and eventually shelved, but it did stimulate the community to ponder the issue of how to deal with the modernization of soccer in the HKSAR. Tsang Tak-sing contributed to the implementation of the DC Pilot Scheme, but his record was perhaps marred by the controversy over the expenditure in the organization of the East Asian

Table 8.13: Contributions and Controversies of the Secretary for Home Affairs, 1997–2022

Name	Contribution	Controversy
David Lan (1997–2000)	Organized various activities to celebrate the smooth return of sovereignty from Britain to the PRC	The dissolution of Urban Council and Regional Council
Lam Woon-kwong (2000–2002)	Review the role of District Councils	No controversy in his handling of district affairs
Patrick Ho Chi-ping (2002–2007)	He introduced the double village heads elections and helped organize the equestrian events of Beijing Olympics in Hong Kong	The double village heads elections divided the rural elites, some of whom supported but some opposed it. The proposal of legalizing soccer betting was also controversial in the community, but it did stimulate the members of the public to ponder deeper issues such as the modernization of soccer in Hong Kong.
Tsang Tak-sing (2007–2015)	He helped organize the East Asian Games in Hong Kong and also contributed to the implementation of District Councils Pilot Scheme. In March 2009, he made a historical visit to Taipei—the first visit by a senior government official of the HKSAR to Taiwan.	The East Asian Games event was criticized by the Audit Commission in April 20111 for using a lot of government expenditure. Some members of the LegCo's Public Accounts Committee criticized the government for not conducting a review after the East Asian Games.
Ray Lau Kong-wah (2015–2020)	He promoted the development of the Kai Tak sports park and proposed to build another sports park in Pak Shek. He also communicated with the directly elected DC members—a kind of communication channel between the government and the directly elected councilors at the district level.	The ideas of rebuilding the Wan Chai Sports Ground and the Hong Kong Stadium were controversial in the community.
Caspar Tsui (2020–early 2022)	He successfully implemented the oath-taking ceremony of District Council members who had to swear allegiance to the National Security Law.	He was criticized for his participation in the birthday party that involved 15 government officials.

Source: Analyzed from reports of various newspapers from January 1997 to March 2022.

Games. Lau Kong-wah's performance did not show much contributions to district affairs from a critical perspective although he established a communication channel with the directly elected DC members. Finally, Caspar Tsui contributed to the organization and implementation of the oath-taking ceremony for all DCs, but the scandal involving his participation in the birthday party of Witman Hung amid the outbreak of COVID-19 cost him the ministerial position.

Administrative Recentralization: Suspension of the Role of District Councils in Managing Minor Works Projects

The political impacts of mass resignations and disqualifications of many DC members were detrimental on the council operation, which was disrupted and paralyzed and led to the government's decision of recentralizing the power of district administration. In October 2021, the HKSAR government submitted an item on the District Minor Works Program (DMWP) to the Finance Committee for discussion.[63] The item argued that the DMWP, which was created in 2007 in four pilot districts and to all 18 districts in 2008 to implement district-based projects up to HK$50 million each for improving local facilities, living environment, and hygienic conditions, should be revised operationally so that HAD, District Offices, and the Leisure and Cultural Services Department (LCSD) would be responsible for proposing district minor works projects (building and fitting out works, rain shelters, benches, walkaway cover, horticultural maintenance, furniture and equipment replacement, improvement work on slope and community halls, consultants' fees, feasibility studies, and site investigations). The annual provisions under these minor projects were HK$340 million from 2013–14 to 2019–20 and HK$346.19 million in 2020–21 and 2021–22. The justification for the recentralization in the use of DMWP into the hands of the government was as follows:

> With the latest development in the DC landscape, the total number of serving DC members has reduced to 189, and 14 DCs have their membership size more than halved as of October 4, 2021. With a significant proportion of DC seats remaining vacant, the current arrangement of having to seek DCs' endorsement for all such projects has become untenable. In addition, there are DCs which do not have sufficient members to proceed with the election of Council Chairman and for that matter unable to convene DC meetings. The public may also consider it unfair and unreasonable to leave the interest of their community to a very small minority of DC members … To ensure the proper use of public money, we will suspend the role of DCs in endorsing District Minor Works project during the Sixth Term. Instead, HAD, District Offices and LCSD will be tasked to propose worthwhile District Minor Works projects having regards to the community's views. Under the revised arrangement, District Offices will proactively collect views from the community through different

channels such as consultations with local organizations, area committees and DC members, with a view to identifying minor works projects for the benefit of the local community. Worthwhile projects will be put forth for feasibility studies and local consultation as appropriate. Following the established mechanism, funding approval will be sought for feasible and worthy projects from Director of Home Affairs or officers under delegated authorities.[64]

Some DC members felt powerless in how the HKSAR government suddenly revised the operation of DMWP. The Southern DC's vice-chairman Paul Zimmerman wrote a submission to LegCo's Finance Committee, saying that his Council "has not been consulted nor informed."[65] He also asked whether by-elections would be held and expedited for DCs rather than suspending their roles.

In the discussions of LegCo's panel on home affairs, the HKSAR government simply reiterated the need to recentralize the utilization of the funding for the minor works program back to the HAD, District Offices, and LCSD.[66] It added that for the list of new projects that "will be subject to the DCs' initiation and endorsement," it would be submitted to the LegCo's Finance Committee for "transparency" and "accountability."[67]

Although members of the LegCo's panel on home affairs supported the government's proposals of suspending the role of DCs in dealing with minor works projects and recentralizing the use of funding back to the HAD, District Offices, and LCSD, some members did have reservations about the government's move. LegCo member Yiu Si-wing asked whether the government's initiatives for funding under the community involvement programs and DMWPs "might lead to a loss in flexibility in operation."[68] Chairman Chan Kin-por asked whether the projects which were approved by DCs would still be pursued. In response, the Secretary for Home Affairs Caspar Tsui said that approved projects would continue. Another LegCo member Yung Ho-yan asked whether members of the ACs, District FCCs, and District FSCs would be consulted in district matters. In response, Tsui promised that the government would reach out to the community to listen to their views. When asked by some members whether the proposed revised arrangements were only applicable to the sixth term of DCs, Caspar Tsui remarked that the operational arrangements after the sixth term would be "decided after the administration had conducted a review of district administration."[69]

During the LegCo's Finance Committee meeting that was held on the afternoon of October 22, 2021, some members continued to express their reservations about the proposal although the committee supported the proposed arrangement.[70] Twelve members expressed their support of the government's proposal, saying that it was "reasonable" in view of the fact that some councils could neither elect their chairpersons "nor effectively reflect the views of the local communities."[71] Other LegCo members, such as Regina Ip, Priscilla Leung, and Christopher Cheung called for the government to proactively reach out to listen to the views of the community and residents. Three LegCo members — Kwok Wai-keung, Lo Wai-kwok, and Holden Chow — said that, in view of "the failure of officers in some District Offices to consult the respective ACs on district affairs regularly," the government should "include consultation with incumbent DC members in the district consultation mechanism, visit districts to understand residents' demands, and provide more channels for collecting public opinion (such as creating electronic mailboxes)."[72]

Some LegCo members expressed their concern about the accountability of the new arrangement. Elizabeth Quat was concerned about the "high" consultants' fees and the "slow" implementation as well as the "impractical design" of some projects.[73] She called for the government to improve planning, supervise the projects, streamline the workflow, humanize the design, and reduce expenses. Similarly, Tony Tse was worried about whether the government could smoothly undertake minor work projects to meet the needs of districts. Martin Liao enquired whether the government would release progress reports on various projects to ensure that there would not be delay and cost overruns. Kwok Wai-keung added that the government should monitor the standard of the work projects. Overall, some LegCo members were concerned about the accountability, efficiency and effectiveness of the minor works projects that would be recentralized by the government.

Summary and Future Development of District Councils

It is unfortunate that the operation of DCs was heavily politicized after the victory of the pan-democrats in the 2019 DC elections. Mainly because of the determination of the PRC authorities and the HKSAR government to reverse the progress of democratization in Hong Kong, and partly because of the over-aggressive behavior of some pro-democracy council members,

DCs and some of their members were regarded as operating *ultra vires*. The legal requirement for all DC members to take the oath that pledged their allegiance to the national security law brought about mass resignations and disqualifications. As a result, the operation of DCs became paralyzed. It can be said that DCs and their directly elected and pro-democracy council members became a victim of their own "success."

The HKSAR government plans to review the direction and development of DCs in the next term of the Chief Executive from July 2022 to June 2027. Some political elites have already discussed at least several possibilities: (1) retaining the directly elected elements in DCs; (2) reappointing some elites into DCs, especially those appointed members from ACs, District FCCs, and District FSCs; and (3) merging the 18 DCs into larger ones but with larger constituencies and fewer number of elected members. No matter which option that the government decides to take to reform DCs, it is hoped that the democratization of district administration will not be significantly reversed or rolled back. Although the DC Ordinance states that DCs are of advisory nature, the room for reforming DCs in a more democratic and transparent manner was maximized from the Donald Tsang administration to the November 2019 DC elections. The recent recentralization of district administration to the government, including the HAD, District Officers, and the LCSD, did not bode well for the future development and directions of DCs. However, it is hoped that both the central authorities in Beijing and the HKSAR leadership can and will appreciate the tremendous contributions that DCs and their directly elected members played in not only bridging the communication gap between the rulers and the rules, but also democratizing district governance to an extent of being accountable and acceptable to most Hong Kong people. Yet, politics and district administration in the HKSAR are clearly intertwined. The reduced role and functions of DCs after the November 2019 DC elections were attributable to long-standing political disputes, confrontations, distrusts, and struggles. The hyperpoliticization of the HKSAR did unfortunately undermine the operation of DCs, whose paralysis after mass resignations and disqualification of many members in the latter half of 2020 left an indelible imprint on the history of district elections, politics, and administration in Hong Kong.

Notes

1 *Apple Daily*, April 24, 2020, p. A16.

2 *Ibid.*

3 *Ibid.*

4 Two former DC members, who were pro-establishment, in two districts told one of the authors, February 2020.

5 *Sing Pao*, August 15, 2020, p. A2.

6 *Ibid.*

7 *Ibid.*

8 *Ibid.*

9 *Ibid.*

10 *Ibid.*

11 *Hong Kong Economic Journal*, August 15, 2020, p. A8.

12 *Ibid.*

13 *Ta Kung Pao*, August 14, 2020, p. A2.

14 *Ibid.*

15 The authors' discussions with several DC members, November 2020.

16 The authors' discussions with two former DC chairs, who were pro-government. One did not run in the election in 2019 and one was defeated. Discussions with them in February 2020.

17 Yang Sheng, "Hong Kong opposition 'primaries' challenge National Security Law, illegal acts may become first major case on security in Hong Kong: analysts," *Global Times*, July 14, 2020, in https://www.globaltimes.cn/content/1194549. shtml, access date: November 15, 2020.

18 "District Officers leave the scene and boycott the meetings: Matthew Cheung says setting up a security and political reform committee is ultra vires, and therefore civil servants cannot support and officials cannot attend the meetings," *The Standnews*, January 18, 2020.

19 "District Council's security and political reform committee exceeds its power and violates the law," *Wen Wei Po*, January 19, 2020, in 區會「保安政制委會」越權犯法—香港文匯報 (wenweipo.com), access date: March 13, 2022.

20 For details, see "Government change the guideline on District Councils and officials can leave the meeting and report the incident if slogans and banners violating the National Security Law were shown," HK01, August 13, 2021, in 政府改區議會指引　官員遇違國安標語可離場　須通報爭議事件 (hk01.com), access date: March 13, 2022. Also see "Officials who face slogans and banners violating the National Security Law must leave the meetings," *Hong Kong Economic Journal*, August 15, 2020, in 官員區議會遇違國安標語須離場 - 信報網站 hkej.com, access date: March 13, 2022.

21 "District Council members who tolerate violence exceeded their power and initiated motions, but the chairs protected them and confused the decision,"

Speakout, September 8, 2020, in 【離場正確】縱暴派區議員越權動議、議會主席包庇亂裁決 葵青、深水埗區議會上政府人員被迫離場 - 焦點新聞 - 港人講地 (speakout.hk), access date: March 13, 2022.

22 *Ibid.*

23 *Ibid.*

24 "New Guideline of District Officers leaving District Councils: Go away with the Central District discussing mass testing. Go Away with Wanchai District discussing foreign helpers' dormitories," August 27, 20202, in民政區議會「離場」新指引 中西區傾全民檢測，走！灣仔傾外傭宿舍，走！｜獨媒報導｜獨立媒體 (inmediahk.net), access date: March 13, 2022.

25 *Ibid.*

26 *Ibid.*

27 See "Police criticized District Council members for causing trouble and humiliating them. They were asked by Central and Western District Council to leave," Radio Television Hong Kong, October 2, 2020, in 被中西區區議會要求離場 警斥區議員刁難侮辱 | 香港電台 | LINE TODAY, access date: March 13, 2022.

28 *Ibid.*

29 "Showing the Swords and Pulling the Arrow: District Councils expel officials from meetings and Government uses new guidelines and refuses to talk about issues that are ultra vires," October 4, 2020, in 劍拔弩張：區議會趕官員離場 港府立新指引拒談超越職權事務 (rfi.fr), access date: March 13, 2022.

30 "Tuen Mun District Council discusses hunger strike of people at Tsing Shan Wan detention center, and District Officer leaves the scene," *Sing Tao Daily*, October 5, 2020, in 屯門區會討論青山灣羈留人士絕食 民政專員離場 | 星島日報 (stheadline.com), access date: March 13, 2022.

31 "P   olice Station's liquor license renewed but it is opposed by district council member, and the Appeals Board chair says the right of having liquor license renewed cannot be revoked by public opinion," October 7, 2020, in 警署續酒牌遭區議員反對 上訴委員會主席：唔可以用民意剝奪 ｜ 獨媒報導 ｜ 獨立媒體 (inmediahk.net), access date: March 13 2022.

32 *Ibid.*

33 See the Appeals Board's decision on February 19, 2021, Appeal Case No. 16/2020, in MSA-16_2020 (Decision)-Chi.pdf, access date: March 13, 2022.

34 Kam Nai-wai, "More suppression, more fight from the District Council (越打壓議會越奮戰到底)," *The Standnews*, September 28, 2020.

35 *Ibid.*

36 "73 times that District Officers left District Councils in various districts, showing the new normal and the cases of Central and Western District Council occupied one-sixth," *Citizen News*, November 22, 2022,, in 眾新聞 - 【區選一年】各區民政離場73次成「新常態」 中西區佔六分一 (hkcnews.com), access date: March 16, 2022.

37 *The Law of the People's Republic of China on Safeguarding National Security in the Hong Kong Special Administrative Region* (2020), in https://www.elegislation.gov.hk/fwddoc/hk/a406/eng_translation_(a406)_en.pdf, access date: March 17, 2022.

38 "60 District Councilors would be disqualified," *The Standard*, July 22, 2021, in 60 District Councilors would be disqualified | The Standard, access date: March 17, 2022.

39 *Ibid.* Also see "District Council members who would be disqualified would have to return to the government their salaries and expenditure and this would make them bankrupt. Those who put up the banner of "liberating Hong Kong" would also be disqualified," HK01, July 6, 2021, in 01消息｜區議員宣誓遭DQ須償還薪津恐破產　貼「光時」標語亦中招 (hk01.com), access date: March 20, 2022.

40 " See 60 District Councilors would be disqualified," *The Standard*, July 22, 2021.

41 For the details, see the evolution of the Civic Party, in 公民黨 (香港) - 維基百科，自由嘅百科全書 (wikipedia.org), access date: March 17, 2022.

42 "District Council members continue to resign. Lai Chi-keung painfully ended his political career, while Yu Tak-po appeals to citizens to maintain their temperature

43 *Ibid.*

44 TVB's Sunday File, March 20, 2022 at 7 pm, reporting that 50 to 60 civil servants in the Tuen Mun District Council were redeployed to deal with building lockdown in Tsuen Wan district.

45 "Three District Councils stop and fluctuate in their operations, and 8 districts lack 11 chairs and deputy chairs," *Oriental Daily*, October 21, 2021, in https://hk.on.cc/hk/bkn/cnt/news/20211021/bkn-20211021153653414-1021_00822_001.html, access date: March 20, 2022.

46 "Two Pro-democracy District Council members fail to coordinate among themselves and pro-establishment Yau Kam-ping is elected as Tsuen Wan District Council's deputy chairperson," *Sing Tao Daily*, November 23, 2021, in 兩民主派區議員未能協調 建制派邱錦平當選荃灣區會副主席 | 星島日報 (stheadline.com), access date: March 21, 2022.

47 Informal discussion with a District Council member, March 22, 2022.

48 This was even so in the case of the Southern district.

49 "Almost 100 defeated candidates are appointed to Area Committees. Is this move hijacking District Councils?" HK01, July 31, 2020, in 深度｜近百建制落選人獲委任分區委員會席位　會否架空區議會？ (hk01.com), access date: March 25, 2022.

50 "New Term of Area Committees does not have elected District Council members. Critics says politics hijack livelihood," HK01, July 27, 2020, in 新一屆分區委員會罕見無現任區議員　民主派：政治綁架民生 (hk01.com), access date: March 25, 2022. For example, from 2018 to mid-2020, Tuen Mun had 126 members of Area Committees. Of 126 members, 28 were the elected council members, including 8 democrats. Seven of the eight democrats were elected in the 2019 elections, but all of them were excluded from the Area Committees.

51 "District Offices suddenly set up Area Committees in Tai Po and Northern districts and 17 appointees were defeated candidates," April 7, 2021, in 民政突設大埔、北

區分區會 17人為前年區選敗部 | 獨媒報導 | 獨立媒體 (inmediahk.net), access date: March 25, 2022.

52 One of the authors, Steven Hung, was an experienced District Council members in Kwun Tong and he offered these insights, March 2022.

53

54 Michael Sham, "Mutual aid committees on chopping block," *Hong Kong Standard*, January 7, 2022, in Mutual aid committees 'on chopping block' | The Standard, access date: March 26, 2022.

55 "LC10: District administration: A written reply by the Acting Secretary of Home Affairs, Jack Chan, to a question raised by the Honorable Tik Chi-yuen in the LegCo, January 26, 2022," January 26, 2022, in LCQ10: District administration (info.gov.hk), access date: March 26, 2022.

56 Sonny Shiu-Hing Lo, Steven Chung-fun Hung and Jeff Hai-chi Loo, *China's New United Front Work in Hong Kong: Penetrative Politics and Implications* (London: Palgrave Macmillan, July 2019).

57 See Chief Executive Carrie Lam's remarks in her press conference on March 21, 2022, TVB News.

58 "Trying to penetrate the community, Joshua Wong and his father participated in OC elections but were defeated," *Ta Kung Pao*, October 19, 2018, in "港獨"圖滲社區 黃之鋒父子檔參選業委會敗陣_大公網 (takungpao.com), access date: March 26, 2022.

59 For examples, see 杏花邨業委會明改選 爭連任「開明派」稱遭抹黑 對手否認：清者自清 | 獨媒報導 | 獨立媒體 (inmediahk.net), March 26, 2021 (access date: March 26, 2022); 全港業主反貪腐反圍標大聯盟 - Posts | Facebook, March 22, 2021 (access date: March 26, 2022); "Kwun Tong Hiu Lai re-elects OC and former pro-establishment chair steps down," *Epoch Times*, February 1, 2021, in 觀塘曉麗苑重選立案法團 前任建制派主席黯然下台 | 大紀元時報 香港 | 獨立敢言的良心媒體 (epochtimes.com), access date: March 26, 2022.

60 Michael Shum, "Lam gets Beijing's blessings at long last for Tsui's exit," *The Standard*, March 1, 2022, in Lam gets Beijing's blessings at long last for Tsui exit | The Standard, access date: March 26, 2022.

61 Tony Cheung, "Hong Kong top official Caspar Tsui got the boot for 'partygate' but critics ask, should others, like Witman Hung, also be held responsible?" *South China Morning Post*, February 4, 2022, in Hong Kong top official Caspar Tsui got the boot for 'partygate' but critics ask, should others, like host Witman Hung, also be held responsible? | *South China Morning Post* (scmp.com), access date: March 26, 2022.

62 *Ibid.*

63 "For discussion FCR(2021–22)81 on October 2021, Items for Finance Committee: Capital Works Reserve Fund. Head 707: New Towns and Urban Area Development. Subhead 7016CX District Minor Works Program," in f21-81e.pdf (legco.gov.hk), access date: March 25, 2022.

64 *Ibid.*, p. 3.

65 Letter from Paul Zimmerman to Honorable Chan Kin-por, the Chairman of LegCo's Finance Committee, on October 21, 2021, in fc-let20211021-ec.pdf (legco.gov.hk), access date: March 25, 2022.

66 See "LC Paper No. CB(4)1655/20-21(01), for discussion on October 20, 2021, LegCo Panel on Home Affairs: Revising the Arrangements for Implementing Community Involvement Program and District Minor Works Program," in ha20211020cb4-1655-1-e.pdf (legco.gov.hk), access date: March 25, 2022.

67 *Ibid.*, p. 6.

68 "LC Paper No. CB(4)1734/20-21: Panel on Home Affairs — Minutes of special meeting held on 20 October 2021 at 10:00 am," in ha20211020.pdf (legco.gov. hk), access date: March 25, p. 3.

69 *Ibid.*, p. 4.

70 "LC Paper No. FC274/20-21. Finance Committee of the LegCo: Minutes of the 38th meeting held in conference room 1 of the LegCo Complex on Friday, 22 October 2021, from 2:30 pm to 3:39 pm," in fc20211022.pdf (legco.gov.hk), access date: March 25, 2022.

71 *Ibid.*, p. 4.

72 *Ibid.*, p. 5.

73 *Ibid.*, p. 6.

Conclusion

District elections and administration in Hong Kong have been closely intertwined. In 1982, when District Boards (DBs) were introduced by the British colonial administration, they aimed at achieving deconcentration, which according to John Loughlin refer to the process of transferring some administrative functions of the central government to the sub-levels of the administration.[1] Nevertheless, deconcentration occurred in British Hong Kong without substantial political decentralization, meaning that the decision-making powers over policies were retained by the British expatriates together with the senior Chinese civil servants at the top level of the political system. Yet, once DBs were formally set up, the colonial government delegated the administrative powers of dealing with environmental affairs, district transport, and recreational and cultural activities downward to the local level. Most importantly, deconcentration in British Hong Kong provided an impetus to stimulate elite and mass participation in DBs elections. New political groups sprung up and evolved with the passage of time. Some limited degree of democratization took place at the district level because elected Board members could question government officials and hold them to be more accountable than ever before. This phenomenon conformed with the original intent of Governor MacLehose, who hoped that DBs would be able to improve the delivery of public services and inject an ingredient of accountability to district administration. As such, administrative deconcentration could bring about limited democratization and government accountability at the district level. It also stimulated the political participation of some Hong Kong people and the emergence of new political groups.

DB elections were politically and administratively significant, also because the colonial government had to set up the Electoral Affairs Commission to handle a multiplicity of issues, ranging from voters' registration to the handling of voters and votes on the election day. Electoral administration became increasingly important, laying the foundation of a smooth process of handling Legislative Council (LegCo) direct elections that were introduced in 1991.

Most importantly, political groups and local politicians emerged from their contests for the directly elected seats in DBs. Even the appointed members of DBs learnt how to govern their community in partnership with government officials. District elections triggered political participation, electoral administration, and partnerships between the elected politicians and government officials. These district politicians could gradually climb up the political ladder, learning how to compete in elections and nurturing the ambitions to become higher-level politicians at the LegCo and territorial level.

If the concepts of direct and indirect rule are used to study Hong Kong under the British rule, both aspects were also intertwined. The Executive Council (ExCo) and LegCo witnessed the direct rule by the British expatriates. As with other former British colonies, Hong Kong in the 1970s and 1980s witnessed gradual decolonization without independence; more local Chinese community leaders were appointed into LegCo and ExCo. At the district level, indirect rule was adopted by the British colonial administration, which relied on the Cantonese-speaking British expatriates, like Dennis Bray and David Akers-Jones, as District Officers, who acted as the eyes and ears of the colonial rulers and bridged their communication gap. These British District Officers played a critical role in overseeing the transformations of District Watch Force to District Watch Committee, the alteration from District Advisory Boards to DBs, the evolution from Urban Council (UrbCo) to Regional Council (RegCo), and the proliferation of many district-level bodies, such as District Management Committees, Area Committees, Owners' Corporations, and Mutual Aid Committees. If "administrative absorption of politics," as Ambrose King observed, was a hallmark of British colonial rule, the political elites coopted into all the political institutions and grassroots-level organizations became the safety valve of the colonial regime. Their participation in the colonial institutions strengthened the legitimacy of the British colonial administration.

The timing of the introduction of DB elections in 1982 coincided with the inception of the Sino-British negotiations over Hong Kong's future. Although some people speculated that the establishment of DBs aimed at achieving a "glorious" British withdrawal from Hong Kong in July

1997, Governor MacLehose and Jack Cater maintained there was in fact no connection between the two issues. The introduction of DBs signaled merely an attempt of the British colonial authorities to experiment with some degree of administrative deconcentration and decentralization.

District politics became increasingly intense, fragmented, factional, and competitive when Hong Kong approached July 1, 1997, when the transfer of sovereignty from Britain to China took place. New political groups emerged from district elections and they replaced the old political groups like Reform Club and Civic Association—a generational change in group and party politics could be gradually seen. District-level elites, including those in the rural areas, increasingly became the target of political cooptation by the PRC authorities. On the other hand, the rise of the local democracy movement gave rise to a diversity of democrats, who advocated the need for democratizing Hong Kong further well before 1997. Their demands indeed raised the eyebrows of the PRC officials, who saw political stability in Hong Kong as maintaining the status quo and having minimal change in the local political institutions. Gradually, DBs and later District Councils (DCs) became the arena of political bickering, contests, struggles, and control. The fragmentation of political elites in Hong Kong took place at the district and LegCo levels. At the district levels, directly elected seats for the DBs, UrbCo, and RegCo became the target of capture between the pro-democracy camp on the one hand and the pro-establishment and pro-Beijing front on the other.

Interestingly, the fragmentation of political elites in Hong Kong also took place at the rural areas, where the pro-democracy and pro-establishment forces were competing fiercely from the late 1980s onwards. The China factor came into the picture of rural politics as PRC officials identified the rural elites as the target of political absorption. Yet, PRC authorities could not coopt all the rural elites, some of whom joined the pro-Beijing DAB and some remained loyal to the Heung Yee Kuk (HYK). In the colonial era, the rise of the HYK leaders could be facilitated by the support of the British colonial authorities, who could tip the political balance in favor of those rural elites they groomed. Traditionally, the leaders of the HYK have adopted a pro-Beijing or politically patriotic stance, but they sometimes distanced themselves from the local government, especially when government policies were deemed as detrimental to the rural interests. Some government policies, such as the double village elections, divided the rural elites into pro-government and anti-government factions. Yet, the pro-government faction remained unstable later, especially as the issue of transferring the concessionary rights of small houses became legally controversial. Hence, it can be said that the HYK has a curious relationship with the Hong Kong government. Apparently, it is decidedly pro-Beijing, but the HYK members may oppose unpopular government policies that can endanger their interests. The politics of district administration in the HKSAR remains intense because local interests are deeply fragmented and diversified.

Most significantly, rural leaders of the HYK have traditionally acted for the government to facilitate the process of policy implementation in the New Territories, but they sometimes bargained with the government for the sake of achieving the interests of the rural residents. As such, the rural leaders remain the indispensable intermediary between the rulers and the ruled in Hong Kong from the British colonial era to the post-1997 period.

District politics in Hong Kong have been characterized by the intense competition among political parties and groups. The pre-2019 period in the HKSAR witnessed the persistence and proliferation of small pro-democracy, pro-government, and pro-Beijing groups. However, the business groups tended to be traditionally weak, a phenomenon ascribable to the fact that the business elites were politically spoiled by the colonial and post-1997 authorities, who must appoint them into the influential political institutions and bodies. Without the need to participate in politics through competitive elections, the business elites remain relatively inactive and fail to appeal to most voters in district elections. The weakness of the Liberal Party, and its recent decline, in electoral performance at the district level is a case in point.

The 2019 DC elections were the most important turning point in the political development and history of the HKSAR in many aspects. The number of competitors was unprecedented without any seat or incumbent returned automatically. New pro-democracy groups flourished and benefited tremendously from the 2019 anti-extradition protests. Better coordination work among the pan-democrats could be seen, resulting in a strong showing in their electoral performance. The pro-government and pro-Beijing forces suffered from a sounding defeat. Voters, as Chapter Six discussed, cast their ballots for the democrats due to a variety of reasons, seeing them as "the lesser of the two evils," resisting the pro-government camp, opposing the pro-Beijing forces, and expressing their sadness toward the performance of the police during the protests from June to November 2019. In short, the 2019 DC elections constituted a referendum for the voters to express their grievances against the government, whose unpopularity became a huge political liability and burden to the candidates of the pro-establishment and pro-Beijing forces.

Unfortunately, the massive victory of the pan-democrats in the 2019 elections was a key factor contributing to the politicization of district administration. Because some DCs operated in an *ultra vires* manner, the HKSAR government required all council members to take the oath pledging their allegiance to the National Security Law, which was promulgated by the National People's Congress in late June 2020. In the summer of 2020, administrative re-concentration and recentralization of district affairs began. There was a tendency for the HKSAR government to recentralize its decision-making and curb the powers of DCs, where many directly elected democrats were seen as the "political troublemakers" under the newly enacted National Security Law. The directly elected DC members were excluded from participation in the Fight Crime Committees (FCCs) in the 18 districts, reflecting a poor relationship between the directly elected politicians and the police on the one hand and a tense relationship between them and the HKSAR government on the other. District Officers and other departmental officials representing the government had to observe new guidelines, including the action of boycotting the meetings of the Councils if the directly elected council members did anything beyond the scope of the terms of reference of DCs.

The tense relationships between the directly elected council members and the HKSAR government were exacerbated by the enactment of the National Security Law for Hong Kong by the SCNPC on June 30, 2020. As such, administrative recentralization returned in the HKSAR, a phenomenon contrary to the determination of the Donald Tsang administration to keep the momentum of administrative decentralization by putting forward a pilot plan of district reforms. Unfortunately but perhaps naturally, Tsang's blueprint, as discussed in Chapter Seven, was not carried out fully by the Secretaries for Home Affairs, including Tsang Tak-shing and Lau Kong-wah. The 2019 elections became a turning point that rolled back the district administrative reforms partially undertaken by the administration of Chief Executives Donald Tsang and CY Leung. Hence, it can be argued that, by having an overwhelmingly pro-democracy victory in the November 2019 elections, drastic electoral and political transformations at the district level stimulated the HKSAR government to adopt a more politically conservative approach to dealing with the electoral outcomes. By early 2020, the minor projects work of all DCs returned to the remit of the Home Affairs Department and District Offices—a clear direction toward administrative recentralization. In short, electoral politics in November 2019 led to the politicization of DCs and administration, which in turn triggered administrative recentralization by the government.

Arguably, even before the 2019 elections, the HKSAR government adopted a politically conservative approach to dealing with district administrative reforms. The abolitions of the UrbCo and RegCo were a testimony to such political conservatism of the HKSAR government, which used the better control of environment and hygiene after the outbreak of bird flu in late 1997 and early 1998 as a justification to apply its brake on district-level decentralization and democratization. The abolition of the two directly elected bodies could be seen as a retrogressive move made by the HKSAR government to recentralize district administration into the hands of government departments, believing that the government could do a much better job in managing environmental issues, hygiene, and crises. Most importantly, the dismantling of the two councils had financial and political grounds, centralizing the financial resources to the government headquarters while depriving the chances of more democrats to grasp directly elected seats and to enjoy receiving their regular stipends from the administration. Yet, the abolition of the two elected bodies was a short-sighted step that cannot really bring about the better delivery of public services. Even before outbreak of COVID-19 in early 2020, the mass media had already severely criticized and exposed the HKSAR government for failing to deal with environmental hygiene, ranging from the failure to control the rapidly growing number of rats on the streets to the absence of any effective measures to maintain the hygiene district-based markets. The role of District Officers was curbed in their status after July 1, 1997, because they are only one of the players coordinating with other central-level government departments. Chief Executive Donald Tsang's plan of administrative reforms tried to empower District Officers, but unfortunately his reform blueprint was implemented in a slow, half-hearted, and limited way and has been virtually abandoned after the November 2019 DCs elections.

If DB elections were first introduced by the British colonial administration to improve the public delivery of services, this rationale of tolerating elections remained valid shortly after July 1, 1997 until the outbreak of the anti-extradition bill in the latter half of 2019. The riots that stemmed from the opposition of many interest groups and citizens who resisted the extradition bill, including some pro-democracy DC members, proved to be politically costly. Shortly after the promulgation of the National Security Law in late June 2020, both the central authorities in Beijing and the HKSAR government no longer saw DCs as the vehicles of improving the delivery of public services. Due to the fact that DCs exceeded their power in their operation, the HKSAR government decided to boycott those council meetings that were deemed as *ultra vires*. In the face of the legal requirement that all council members would be required to take the new oath swearing their allegiance to the National Security Law, a large batch of directly elected council members resigned. Some took the oath, but a minority of them was disqualified. As a result of the combined effects of mass resignation and disqualifications, DCs since the latter half of 2021 have been operating partially. Witnessing the administrative paralysis of many councils, the HKSAR government has decided to recentralize the funding of district minor work projects. At this juncture, the improvement of public delivery of services is no longer the responsibility of DCs, unlike the British colonial era. Government departments have been seen as the most effective tools of delivering public services to the community far more effectively than DCs.

This changing political logic of district administration, however, has its weaknesses. First and foremost, government departments cannot be expected to be held accountable among themselves and they should ideally be accountable to the members of the public. If democracy can be defined broadly as governmental responsiveness to citizen demands, then DCs can be seen as the intermediary that can bridge the communication gap between the rulers and the ruled and improve governmental responsiveness. Second, the outbreak and rapid spread of Omicron in the first three months of 2022 proved that government departments responsible for health, food, and environmental hygiene performed unsatisfactorily. If so, the existence of DCs has their political value and administrative functions. Politically, DCs are composed of directly elected members who represent the wishes of voters and who can articulate the interests of ordinary citizens. They can act as a safety valve between the rulers and the ruled, sending any alarming signals to the government on areas of maladministration that should be remedied. Administratively, they can hold the government departments and officials accountable and improve the public delivery of services. The political and administrative functions of DBs were long recognized by the British colonial administration from the early 1980s to 1997.

It remains to be seen how the HKSAR government will review the role and functions of DCs in the coming years. No matter whether some appointed seats would be reintroduced to DCs, it is hoped that their political and administrative functions will not be swept under the carpet. Otherwise, reverse democratization, administrative reconcentration, and political centralization are by no means the solutions for the improvement of public delivery of services at the district and grassroots level in the HKSAR.

In a nutshell, the metamorphosis of district administration in Hong Kong has been characterized by political oscillations, fluctuating from decentralization in the early 1980s to recentralization in December 1999, and then moving from Donald Tsang's attempts at district-level empowerment to administrative recentralization immediately after the November 2019 DCs elections. The intertwined relationships between district elections and district administration can be easily seen. While the introduction of district administration during the early 1980s stimulated political development in Hong Kong under the British rule, the rapid development of electoral politics, factional fragmentation, political polarization, and hyper-politicization after July 1, 1997 has brought about a fluctuating pattern between administrative recentralization, the Tsang administration's attempts at decentralization, and the post-2019 administrative recentralization. Clearly, while administrative reforms propelled political development of the DBs and Councils shortly before and after 1997, political development and bitter struggles after July 1, 1997 have also contributed to administrative re-concentration and recentralization without political democratization. The future development of DCs and district administration deserve our close attention, because the intertwined relations between electoral politics and district administration have become the defining characteristic of district politics and public administration in the HKSAR.

In the final analysis, patronage politics have been traditionally serious in the operation of DBs and DCs. While the British colonial administration appointed its friends and followers to DBs to curb the influence of the directly elected board members, the HKSAR government has since late 2019 attached far more importance to the Area Committees, District Fire Crime Committees, and District Fire Safety Committees (FSCs) as the arenas of political patronage than ever before. Similarly, when the pan-democrats seized control of some DBs and DCs, they favored the appointment of their supporters as ad-hoc members until the massive victory in the 2019 DC elections. If patron-client politics have cut through district politics and administration through the British colonial era and the post-1997 period, the future operation of DCs is perhaps destined to be political. As such, district administration will continue to be shaped by the politics of patron-clientelism, whose existence is merely a matter of degree. The challenge is perhaps how to strike a delicate balance between politicization and patronage on the one hand and the effective delivery of public services on the other hand, and between centralization and recentralization on the one hand and deconcentration and decentralization on the other. Most importantly, if the establishment of DBs signaled a positive and small step toward democratization, and if the abolition of all appointed seats in the DCs was also a move toward further democratization, it is hoped that the review of DCs in the future will take into consideration the question of democratization and accountability. If not, any reverse democratization of DCs in the HKSAR would dilute the uniqueness of the district-level advisory bodies that have been attracting so much public attention and stimulating progressive elite and mass participation in politics.

Notes

1 John Loughlin, "Federal and local government institutions," in Daniele Caramani, ed., *Comparative Politics* (New York: Oxford University Press, 2008), p. 280.

Bibliography

1.   Newspapers, Magazines, Website Commentaries, and Government Reports (Chinese and English)

"60 District Councilors would be disqualified," *The Standard*, July 22, 2021, in 60 District Councilors would be disqualified | The Standard, access date: March 17, 2022.

"73 times that District Officers left District Councils in various districts, showing the new normal and the cases of Central and Western District Council occupied one-sixth," *Citizen News*, November 22, 2022,, in 眾新聞 - 【區選一年】各區民政離場73次成「新常態」 中西區佔六分一 (hkcnews.com), access date: March 16, 2022.

"A summary of views of various stakeholder groups on the Pilot Scheme," available in: https://www.td.gov.hk/filemanager/en/content_4838/eng_td_pe1report_annex_2.pdf (access date: October 12, 2020).

"Almost 100 defeated candidates are appointed to Area Committees. Is this move hijacking District Councils?" HK01, July 31, 2020, in 深度 | 近百建制落選人獲委任分區委員會席位 會否架空區議會？(hk01.com), access date: March 25, 2022.

"Background brief on processing of small house applications and review of small house policy," Legislative Council, LC Paper No. CB (1)986/05–06(01). Also see "Small House Matters," Lands Department, https://www.landsd.gov.hk/en/small%20house/small%20hse.htm, access date: August 3, 2020.

"Candidates for Democratic Primaries," available in https://legco2020.vote4.hk/en/primaries/, access date: November 2, 2020.

"Chief Executive Policy Address, 2005–2006," in https://www.policyaddress.gov.hk/2005/eng/index.htm, access date: August 17, 2020.

"Civic Party has a tide of mass resignation with 11 members' withdrawal," HK01, June 20, 2021, in 公民黨爆退黨潮 至少11區議員先後退出 余德寶：繼續服務街坊 (hk01.com), access date: March 21, 2022.

"Democratic dilemma: Government caught at the cross-roads*," South China Morning Post*, June 15, 1985.

"Direct and Indirect Rule," in https://nigerianscholars.com/tutorials/west-african-colonial-administration/direct-and-indirect-rule/, access date: August 3, 2020.

"District Administration," Factsheet provided by the Hong Kong government, July 2020, in https://www.gov.hk/en/about/abouthk/factsheets/docs/district_admin.pdf, access date: August 2, 2020.

"District Council Election 2019," Registration and Electoral Office, in website https://www.elections.gov.hk/dc2019/eng/intro_to_can.html, access date: October 1, 2020.

"District Council members who tolerate violence exceeded their power and initiated motions, but the chairs protected them and confused the decision," *Speakout*, September 8, 2020, in 【離場正確】縱暴派區議員越權動議、議會主席包庇亂裁決 葵青、深水埗區議會上政府人員被迫離場 - 焦點新聞 - 港人講地 (speakout.hk), access date: March 13, 2022.

"District Council members who would be disqualified would have to return to the government their salaries and expenditure and this would make them bankrupt. Those who put up the banner of "liberating Hong Kong" would also be disqualified," HK01, July 6, 2021, in 01消息｜區議員宣誓遭DQ須償還薪津恐破產 貼「光時」標語亦中招 (hk01.com), access date: March 20, 2022.

"District Council Paper Implementation of Signature Project Scheme," available in: https://www.had.gov.hk/file_manager/en/documents/home/DC_paper_on_SPS_20130225_BIND_eng.pdf (access date: August 30, 2020).

"District Council's security and political reform committee exceeds its power and violates the law," *Wen Wei Po*, January 19, 2020, in 區會「保安政制委會」越權犯法 - 香港文匯報 (wenweipo.com), access date: March 13, 2022.

"District Officers leave the scene and boycott the meetings: Matthew Cheung says setting up a security and political reform committee is ultra vires, and therefore civil servants cannot support and officials cannot attend the meetings," *The Standnews*, January 18, 2020.

"District Offices suddenly set up Area Committees in Tai Po and Northern districts and 17 appointees were defeated candidates," April 7, 2021, in 民政突設大埔、北區分區會 17人為前年區選敗部｜獨媒報導｜獨立媒體 (inmediahk.net), access date: March 25, 2022.

"Election Results of 2019 District Council Elections," Registration and Electoral Office, in https://www.elections.gov.hk/dc2019/eng/results_hk.html, access date: November 15, 2020.

"ERP in Hong Kong," available in: https://www.td.gov.hk/mini_site/erpgovhk/erp_in_hk.html (access date: October 12, 2020).

"For discussion FCR(2021–22)81 on October 2021, Items for Finance Committee: Capital Works Reserve Fund. Head 707: New Towns and Urban Area Development. Subhead 7016CX District Minor Works Program," in f21-81e.pdf (legco.gov.hk), access date: March 25, 2022.

"Government change the guideline on District Councils and officials can leave the meeting and report the incident if slogans and banners violating the National Security Law were shown," HK01, August 13, 2021, in 政府改區議會指引 官員遇違國安標語可離場 須通報爭議事件 (hk01.com), access date: March 13, 2022.

"HKMAO chief Zhang Xiaoming demoted," February 23, 2020, in https://news.rthk.hk/rthk/en/component/k2/1508301-20200213.htm, access date: October 25, 2020.

"Hong Kong reform package rejected as pro-Beijing camp walk out in 'miscommunication,'" *South China Morning Post*, June 18, 2015, in https://www.scmp.com/news/hong-kong/politics/article/1823398/hong-kong-political-reform-package-voted-down-legco-leaving, access date: September 4, 2020.

"How to apply for a small house grant," in http://www.landsd.gov.hk/en/images/doc/NTSHP_E_text.pdf, access date: July 28, 2020.

"Issues relating to New Territories small house policy and small house concessionary rights," The Hong Kong government's press release, December 14, 2016, in https://www.info.gov.hk/gia/general/201612/14/P2016121400461.htm, access date: September 17, 2020.

"Jasper Tsang says Carrie Lam wanted to fire two DAB secretaries," in https://www.singtao.ca, October 10, 2020.

"Kwun Tong Hiu Lai re-elects OC and former pro-establishment chair steps down," *Epoch Times*, February 1, 2021, in 觀塘曉麗苑重選立案法團 前任建制派主席黯然下台 | 大紀元時報 香港 | 獨立敢言的良心媒體 (epochtimes.com), access date: March 26, 2022.

"Lau Wong-fat and the Traditional Political Force in New Territories," HK01, July 28, 2017, in https://www.hk01.com, access date: August 9, 2020.

"LC10: District administration: A written reply by the Acting Secretary of Home Affairs, Jack Chan, to a question raised by the Honorable Tik Chi-yuen in the LegCo, January 26, 2022," January 26, 2022, in LCQ10: District administration (info.gov.hk), access date: March 26, 2022.

"LC Paper No. CB(4)1655/20-21(01), for discussion on October 20, 2021, LegCo Panel on Home Affairs: Revising the Arrangements for Implementing Community Involvement Program and District Minor Works Program," in ha20211020cb4-1655-1-e.pdf (legco.gov.hk), access date: March 25, 2022.

"LC Paper No. CB(4)1734/20-21: Panel on Home Affairs — Minutes of special meeting held on 20 October 2021 at 10:00 am," in ha20211020.pdf (legco.gov.hk), access date: March 25, 2022.

"LC Paper No. FC274/20-21. Finance Committee of the LegCo: Minutes of the 38th meeting held in conference room 1 of the LegCo Complex on Friday, 22 October 2021, from 2:30 pm to 3:39 pm," in fc20211022.pdf (legco.gov.hk), access date: March 25, 2022.

"LegCo's Home Affairs Committee, "Village Elections," CB(2)928/00-01(01), February 26, 2001, in https://www.legco.gov.hk/yr00-01/chinese/panels/ha/papers/928c01.pdf, access date: September 4, 2020.

"LegCo: The Secretary for Home Affairs made remarks on how to strengthen the role of DCs and their functions," Hong Kong Government News, November 24, 2016.

"Legislative Council Brief: Provision of Municipal Services (Reorganization) Bill," available in: https://www.legco.gov.hk/yr98-99/english/bc/bc73/general/73_brf.pdf (access date: August 16, 2020).

"Legislative Council Panel on Home Affairs District-led Actions Scheme: Progress Report," available in: https://www.legco.gov.hk/yr16-17/english/panels/ha/papers/ha20161221cb2-401-6-e.pdf (access date: August 30, 2020).

"List of Projects from 18 Districts Under Signature Project Scheme," in https://www.had.gov.hk/file_manager/en/documents/home/SPS_Project_list_en.pdf, access date: August 30, 2020.

"Minutes of the 18th Meeting of Yau Tsim Mong District Council (2016–2019)," in https://www.districtcouncils.gov.hk/ytm/doc/2016_2019/en/dc_meetings_minutes/YTM_DC_18th_Minutes_EN.pdf, access date: October 13, 2020.

"New Guideline of District Officers leaving District Councils: Go away with the Central District discussing mass testing. Go Away with Wanchai District discussing foreign helpers' dormitories," August 27, 20202, in民政區議會「離場」新指引 中西區傾全民檢測，走！灣仔傾外傭宿舍，走！ ｜ 獨媒報導 ｜ 獨立媒體 (inmediahk.net), access date: March 13, 2022.

"New Term of Area Committees does not have elected District Council members. Critics says politics hijack livelihood," HK01, July 27, 2020, in 新一屆分區委員會罕見無現任區議員　民主派：政治綁架民生 (hk01.com), access date: March 25, 2022.

"Official Record of Legislative Council Proceedings, December 2, 1999," available in:

https://www.legco.gov.hk/yr99-00/chinese/counmtg/floor/991202ca.pdf (access date: August 16, 2020).

"Official Record of Legislative Council Proceedings, December 2, 1999," in https://www.legco.gov.hk/yr99-00/chinese/counmtg/floor/991202ca.pdf, access date: August 16, 2020.

"Official Report of Proceedings, January 21, 1981," Hong Kong Legislative Council, in https://www.legco.gov.hk/yr80-81/english/lc_sitg/hansard/h810121.pdf, access date: August 2, 2020.

"Officials who face slogans and banners violating the national security law must leave the meetings," *Hong Kong Economic Journal*, August 15, 2020, in 官員區議會遇違國安標語須離場 - 信報網站 hkej.com, access date: March 13, 2022.

"Paper for the Bills Committee of the LegCo on Village Representative Election Bill," LC Paper No. LS 15/02-03, in https://www.legco.gov.hk/yr02-03/english/bc/bc51/papers/bc511122cb2-ls15-e.pdf, access date: September 13, 2020.

"Police criticized District Council members for causing trouble and humiliating them. They were asked by Central and Western District Council to leave," Radio Television Hong Kong, October 2, 2020, in 被中西區區議會要求離場　警斥區議員刁難侮辱 | 香港電台 | LINE TODAY, access date: March 13, 2022.

"Police Station's liquor license renewed but it is opposed by district council member, and the Appeals Board chair says the right of having liquor license renewed cannot be revoked by public opinion," October 7, 2020, in 警署續酒牌遭區議員反對 上訴委員會主席：唔可以用民意剝奪 | 獨媒報導 | 獨立媒體 (inmediahk.net), access date: March 13 2022.

"Progress Report of Pilot Scheme on Enhancement of District Administration Through District Management Committees in Sham Shui Po and Yuen Long," in https://www.legco.gov.hk/yr14-15/english/panels/ha/papers/ha20141212cb2-407-6-e.pdf, access date: August 30, 2020

"Public Housing Development," in https://www.housingauthority.gov.hk/en/about-us/public-housing-heritage/public-housing-development/index.html, access date: August 9, 2020.

"Real and Fake District Councils," in https://www.thestandnews.com/politics, access date: July 29,2020.

"Request for the Government to Enact Legislation for the Effective Management of Street Performances," in https://www.districtcouncils.gov.hk/ytm/doc/2016_2019/en/dc_meetings_doc/14748/YTM_DC_103_2018_TC.pdf, access date: October 13,2020.

"Review of CY Leung Policy Address," in https://www.hk01.com/, access date, August 30, 2020.

"Review the Role, Functions and Composition of District Councils," in https://www.legco.gov.hk/yr05-06/english/panels/ca/papers/ca0427cb2-consultation-e.pdf, access date: August 17, 2020.

"Sai Kung District Council Pilot Scheme," in https://www.had.gov.hk/file_manager/tc/documents/home/sai_kung_district.pdf, access date: August 30, 2020.

"Showing the Swords and Pulling the Arrow: District Councils expel officials from meetings and Government uses new guidelines and refuses to talk about issues that are ultra vires," October 4, 2020, in 劍拔弩張：區議會趕官員離場 港府立新指引拒談超越職權事務 (rfi.fr), access date: March 13, 2022.

"Simon Cheng: Former UK Consulate Worker Says He Was Tortured in China." *BBC News*, November 20, 2019, in https://www.bbc.com/news/world-asia-china-50457262, access date: August 25, 2020.

"Small house grants in the New Territories," Audit Commission, 15 October 2002. http://www.aud.gov.hk/pdf_e/e39ch08.pdf, access date: July 28, 2020.

"Suggestions of Introducing Regulatory System for the Promotion of Street Performance Culture," in https://www.districtcouncils.gov.hk/ytm/english/records/dc_meetings_doc.php?year=2018&meeting_id=14748, access date: October 13,2020.

"Survey conducted by the Social Sciences Research Centre of the University of Hong Kong [CB(2)343/98-99(01)]," in https://www.legco.gov.hk/yr98-99/chinese/panels/ca/papers/p343c01.pdf, access date: August 16, 2020.

"Tear Gas Sparks Public Health Anxiety in Hong Kong," December 4, 2019, in https://time.com/5743663/tear-gas-hong-kong/, access date: August 19, 2020.

"The Basic Law of the Hong Kong Special Administrative Region of the People's Republic of China," promulgated in April 1990, in https://www.basiclaw.gov.hk/en/basiclawtext/chapter_3.html, access date: August 12, 2020.

"The History of Heung Yee Kuk," *Wen Wei Po*, October 24, 2006.

"The HKSAR Government, "Prohibition on Face Covering Regulation Gazetted." *HKSAR Press Release*, October 1, 2019, in https://www.info.gov.hk/gia/general/201910/04/P2019100400613.htm, access date: August 5, 2020.

"The Issue of Street Performance Needs to be Addressed, Calling for Improved Cultural Policy and Re-consideration of Establishment of a Culture Bureau," in https://www.districtcouncils.gov.hk/ytm/doc/2016_2019/en/dc_meetings_doc/14748/YTM_DC_102_2018_TC.pdf, access date: October 20, 2020.

"The LegCo Debates: Official Report, October 1, 1980," in https://www.legco.gov.hk/yr80-81/english/lc_sitg/hansard/h801001.pdf, access date: August 2, 2020.

"The New Territories Small House Policy," in https://www.landsd.gov.hk/en/images/doc/NTSHP_E_text.pdf, access date: September 17, 2020.

"The Negotiation Process of Hong Kong's Future in the 1980s," September 30, 2017, in https://medium.com/recall-hk/t-d679f9564ed1, access date: August 2, 2020.

"Three District Councils stop and fluctuate in their operations, and 8 districts lack 11 chairs and deputy chairs," *Oriental Daily*, October 21, 2021, in https://hk.on.cc/hk/bkn/cnt/news/20211021/bkn-20211021153653414-1021_00822_001.html, access date: March 20, 2022.

"Time has passed for officials not to tell lies," *Citizen News*, February 9, 2017, in https:///www.hkcnews.com/article/1622/, access date: July 28, 2020.

"Trying to penetrate the community, Joshua Wong and his father participated in OC elections but were defeated," *Ta Kung Pao*, October 19, 2018, in "港獨"圖滲社區黃之鋒父子檔參選業委會敗陣 _大公網 (takungpao.com), access date: March 26, 2022.

"Tsang Tak-shing's departure raises rumours and C. Y. Leung and traditional pro-Beijing force were at loggerheads," in https://www.thestandnews.com, July 21, 2015.

"Tuen Mun District Council discusses hunger strike of people at Tsing Shan Wan detention center, and District Officer leaves the scene," *Sing Tao Daily*, October 5, 2020, in 屯門區會討論青山灣羈留人士絕食 民政專員離場 | 星島日報 (stheadline.com), access date: March 13, 2022.

"Tuen Mun District Council Pilot Scheme," in https://www.had.gov.hk/file_manager/tc/documents/home/tuen_mun_district.pdf, access date: August 30, 2020.

"Two Pro-democracy District Council members fail to coordinate among themselves and pro-establishment Yau Kam-ping is elected as Tsuen Wan District Council's deputy chairperson," *Sing Tao Daily*, November 23, 2021, in 兩民主派區議員未能協調 建制派邱錦平當選荃灣區會副主席 | 星島日報 (stheadline.com), access date: March 21, 2022.

"Voter Turnout Rate," in https://www.elections.gov.hk/dc2019/eng/turnout.html, access date: October 11, 2020.

"Wan Chai District Council Pilot Scheme," in https://www.had.gov.hk/file_manager/tc/documents/home/wan_chai_district.pdf, access date: August 30, 2020.

"Wong Tai Sin District Council Pilot Scheme," in https://www.had.gov.hk/file_manager/tc/documents/home/wong_tai_sin_district.pdf, access date: August 30, 2020.

Appeals Board's decision on February 19, 2021, Appeal Case No. 16/2020, in MSA-16_2020 (Decision)-Chi.pdf, access date: March 13, 2022.

Apple Daily, various years.

Asiaweek, No. 3, 2016.

Campbell, Duncan, "A Secret Plan for Dictatorship," *New Statesman*, December 12, 1980, p. 8.

Chan, Kabon "Rural leaders vow to defend sale of small house right," *China Daily*, December 25, 2015.

Cheung, Tony ,"Hong Kong top official Caspar Tsui got the boot for 'partygate' but critics ask, should others, like Witman Hung, also be held responsible?" *South China Morning Post*, February 4, 2022, in Hong Kong top official Caspar Tsui got the boot for 'partygate' but critics ask, should others, like host Witman Hung, also be held responsible? | South China Morning Post (scmp.com), access date: March 26, 2022.

Chiu Kwan-sok, "The Meaning of District Council Elections," Voice of Tang, November 25, 2019, in https://www.voicettank.org/single-post/2019/11/25/112501, access date: October 25, 2020.

Choi Chi-keung, "the DC election was converted to be a referendum—why the pan-democracy faction got a landslide victory" *Apple Daily*, November 27, 2019, in https://tw.appledaily.com, access date: August 1, 2020.

Choi Chi-keung and Chan Chun-man, "Which districts were defended by the pro-establishment forces?," *Ming Pao*, December 6, 2019, in https://news.mingpao.com/, access date: November 1, 2020.

Choy, Murphy ,Michelle L. F. Cheong, Ma Nang Laik and Koo Ping Shung, "A Sentiment Analysis of Singapore Presidential Election 2011 Using Twitter Data with Census Correction," 2011, in http://arxiv.org/abs/1108.5520, access date: August 5, 2020.

Civic Association's newsletter, February 1990.

Civic Party, in 公民黨 (香港) - 維基百科，自由嘅百科全書 (wikipedia.org), access date: March 17, 2022.

David Mills, "Durham Report," November 6, 2019, in https://www.thecanadianencyclopedia.ca/en/article/durham-report, access date: August 3, 2020.

DeGolyer, Michael ,in "Submissions to LegCo Panel on Constitutional Affairs," November 2, 1998, LC Paper No. CB(2)570/98-99/01, in https://www.legco.gov.hk/yr98-99/english/panels/ca/papers/p_submis.pdf, access date: October 4, 2020.

Despatch of Governor Grantham to the Secretary of State, September 1, 1949, Colonial Office file 54145/4/49, no. 58.

District Council Elections 2015, https://www.elections.gov.hk/dc2015/chi/intro_to_can.html, and https://www.elections.gov.hk/dc2015/chi/results_hk.html?1527837316296 access date: October 1, 2020.

District Council Elections 2019, https://www.elections.gov.hk/dc2019/eng/intro_to_can.html, and https://www.elections.gov.hk/dc2019/eng/results.html, access date: October 1, 2020.

Eastweek, August 8, 2012, pp. 26–30.

Fong Foon-li, "Tak Ming Secondary School and Chan Shu-woon," *Ming Pao Monthly* (April 2006).

Fung Chia-chi, "November 2 Rally: Three candidates running for the DC elections arrested in the rally of Victoria Park are go to the court with the charge of holding illegal assembly," November 4, 2019, in https://www.hk01.com/, access date: August 1, 2020.

Green Paper: The Further Development of Representative Government in Hong Kong (Hong Kong: Government Printer, July 1984).

Headline News, 2013 and 2015.

Home Affairs Department, *A Guide on Building Management Ordinance (Cap. 344)* (Hong Kong: Logistics Department, Hong Kong Government, January 2017), in https://www.buildingmgt.gov.hk/file_manager/en/documents/bmo_guide/a_

guide_on_building_management_ordinance_cap344_en.pdf, access date: August 2, 2020.

Hong Kong Chinese Reform Association, in http://www.hkcra.com/web/subpage. php?mid=15, access date: August 9, 2020.

Hong Kong Commercial Daily, March 2009.

Hong Kong Daily News, 2006, 2008 and 2014.

Hong Kong Economic Journal, 2005, 2014, 2017, 2020.

Hong Kong Economic Times, 2004 and 2005.

Kam Nai-wai, "More suppression, more fight from the District Council (越打壓議會越奮戰到底)," *The Standnews*, September 28, 2020.

Kemp, Simon ,"Digital 2020: Hong Kong. DataReportal—Global Digital Insights," February 13, 2020, in https://datareportal.com/reports/digital-2-2--hong-kong, access date: August 15, 2020.

Kung Sheung Yat Pao, October 31, 1967, https://1967riot.wordpress.com/2012/10/31/ksyp-19671031/, access date: May 3, 2020.

Lai Ying-kit, "Rural leaders slammed over illegal structures U-turn," *South China Morning Post*, November 20, 2012, in https://www.scmp.com/news/hong-kong/article/1086807/rural-leaders-slammed-over-illegal-structures-u-turn, access date: September 13, 2020.

Lee, Francis Lap-fung, "The figures of the ballot and the survey in the District Council election, and the current state of the public opinion." *Ming Pao*, December 5, 2019, in https://news.mingpao.com, access date: August 19, 2020.

Lee Hong-yan, "Unveiling the big data for the District Council election; the police to 'assist' the pro-democracy faction at the last moment," *CitizenNews*, December 16, 2019, in https://www.hkcnews.com/, access date: August 25, 2020.

Letter from Paul Zimmerman to Honorable Chan Kin-por, the Chairman of LegCo's Finance Committee, on October 21, 2021, in fc-let20211021-ec.pdf (legco.gov. hk), access date: March 25, 2022.

Liu, Daosheng, "Local Constables in the Basic Level of the Society of the Qing Dynasty," (清代基層社會的地保), in https://www.1xuezhe.exuezhe.com/Qk/art/405096? dbcode=1&flag=2 access date: July 16, 2020.

Lo Chi-kin, "'Making violence' failed to drum up votes, the regime [should be] tuned to couple hardness with softness," *CitizenNews*, December 18, 2019, in https://www.hkcnews.com/, access date: August 19, 2020

Meeting Point's archival documents, in https://web.archive.org/web/20120425045705/http://meetingpoint.hk/PDF/doc02.pdf, access date: August 12, 2020.

Ming Pao, various years.

Next Magazine, 2002 and 2013.

Oriental Daily, 2004, 2013, 2014, 2015, 2016.

Pui Ka-yee, "China calls me: Percy Chen's revolutionary path," in https://sparkpost. wordpress.com/2014/02/06/percy-chen/, access date: August 9, 2020.

Pui Ka-yee, "The Abortive Democratic Promises: The Young Plan," in https:// sparkpost.wordpress.com/2014/07/16/young-plan/, access date: August 9, 2020.

Pui Ka-yee, "The Father of 'Hong Kong independence:' The Democratic Movement in the 1960s," in https://sparkpost.wordpress.com/2012/ 12/04/ma-man-fai-1/, access date: August 9, 2020.

RTHK, "Trump 'HK Obliterated in 14 Minutes without Me,'" November 22, 2019, in https://news.rthk.hk/rthk/en/component/k2/1493927-20191122.html, access date: August 19, 2020.

Sham, Michael, "Mutual aid committees on chopping block," *Hong Kong Standard*, January 7, 2022, in Mutual aid committees 'on chopping block' | The Standard, access date: March 26, 2022.

Sham, Michael, "Lam gets Beijing's blessings at long last for Tsui's exit," *The Standard*, March 1, 2022, in Lam gets Beijing's blessings at long last for Tsui exit | The Standard, access date: March 26, 2022.

Sing Pao, various years.

Sing Tao Daily, various years.

Ta Kung Pao, various years.

The City District Officer Scheme: A Report by the Secretariat of Chinese Affairs (Hong Kong: Government Printer, 1969).

The Heung Yee Kuk Ordinance, in https://www.elegislation.gov.hk/hk/cap1097!en-zh-Hant-HK?INDEX_CS=N, assess date, July 27, 2020.

The Law of the People's Republic of China on Safeguarding National Security in the Hong Kong Special Administrative Region (2020), in https://www.elegislation.gov.hk/ fwddoc/hk/a406/eng_translation_(a406)_en.pdf, access date: March 17, 2022.

The Nineties, no. 182 (March 1985), p. 54.

The News Lens, "Joshua Wong is disqualified for the District Council Elections: Is there a plan of depriving my right to be elected for life?," *The News Lens*, October 29, 2019, in https://www.thenewslens.com/article/126680, access date: August 25, 2020.

The Sun, 2004 and 2006.

Tsang Tse-yeung, Chung Wai-tak and Lee Chak-tong, "A History of District Administration: The worry of the Colonial Government that it could become grassroots representatives, March 2, 2017, in http://www.hk01.com, access date: August 1, 2020.

VOA News, October 25, 2021 https://www.voacantonese.com/a/cantonese-it-hong-kong-reactions-to-16-more-district-councilors-ousted-over-loyalty-oaths-20211025-ry/6284334.html (access date: Feb 24, 2022).

Wen Wei Po, various years.

White Paper: District Administration in Hong Kong, January 1981 (Hong Kong: Government Printer, 1981).

White Paper: The Further Development of Representative Government in Hong Kong, November 1984 (Hong Kong: Government Printer, 1984).

White Paper: The Development of Representative Government: The Way Forward, February 1988 (Hong Kong: Government Printer, 1988).

Wide Angle, no. 118, (April 16, 1982), pp. 18–20; and no. 118, (July 16, 1982), p. 31.

Yang Sheng, "Hong Kong opposition 'primaries' challenge national security law, illegal acts may become first major case on security in Hong Kong: analysts," *Global Times,* July 14, 2020, in https://www.globaltimes.cn/content/1194549.shtml, access date: November 15, 2020.

2. Academic Literature (in Chinese and English)

Bae, Jung-Hwan, Ji-Eun Son and Min Song, "Analysis of Twitter for 2012 South Korea Presidential Election by Text Mining Techniques," *Journal of Intelligence and Information Systems,* vol. 19, no. 3 (2013), pp. 141–56.

Barkan, Joel D. "Legislators, Elections and Political Linkage," in Joel D. Barkan and John J. Okumu, eds., *Politics and Public Policy in Kenya and Tanzania* (New York: Praeger, 1979).

Borins, Sandford F.,"Electronic road pricing: An idea whose time may never come," *Transportation Research Part A: General,* Volume 22, Issue 1, (January 1988), pp. 37–44.

Bray, Dennis, *Hong Kong Metamorphosis* (Hong Kong: Hong Kong University Press, 2001).

Budiharto, Widodo and Meiliana Meiliana, "Prediction and Analysis of Indonesia Presidential Election from Twitter Using Sentiment Analysis," *Journal of Big Data,* vol. 5, no. 1 (2018), pp. 1–10.

Bustin, Edouard *Lunda Under Belgian Rule: The Politics of Ethnicity* (Cambridge: Harvard University Press, 1975).

Chan, Chak-kwan, *Social Security Policy in Hong Kong: From British Colony to China's Special Administrative Region* (Maryland: Lexington Books, 2011).

Chan, Kwok-Shing, "The regulation of customary practices under colonial administration: Kinship and mortgages in a Hong Kong village," *China Information,* Vol. 29, Issue: 3(2015), pp. 377–396.

Chan, Kwok-shing, *Fanling* (in Chinese) (Hong Kong: Hong Kong Joint Publishing, 2019).

Cheung, Yat-fung, "Modernization and Rural Politics in Hong Kong." Unpublished MPhil Thesis, University of Hong Kong, 2004.

Chiu, Stephen W. K. and Ho-fung Hung, "The Colonial State and Rural Protests in Hong Kong," occasional paper no. 59 (Hong Kong: Hong Kong Institute of Asia-Pacific Studies, The Chinese University of Hong Kong, April 1997).

Chong, Xu, "Imperialism in the city: war and the making of the municipal administration in the French Concession of Shanghai in the Taiping period, 1853–1862," *Urban History*, vol. 47 (2020), pp. 126–151.

Chow, Chin-wah, *The Development of Hong Kong Political Parties and Elections, 1949–1997* (in Chinese) (Hong Kong: Misi Dalei Technology and Art, 2003), pp. 82–192.

Chow, Kin-wah, "An Analysis of Political Party Development in Hong Kong before and after 1997," *Journal of Guangdong Institute of Public Administration*, vol. 17, no. 2 (April 2005).

Constantine, Stephen, "Governor Sir John Field in St Helena: Democratic Reform in a Small British Colony, 1962–68," *Journal of Imperial and Commonwealth History*, vol. 44, no. 4 (2016), pp. 672–696.

Democratic Alliance for the Betterment and Progress of Hong Kong, *The 25th Anniversary Commemoration of the Democratic Alliance for the Betterment and Progress of Hong Kong: Choices and Promises* (Hong Kong: Democratic Alliance for the Betterment and Progress of Hong Kong, 2017).

Duffy, James, *Portuguese Africa* (Cambridge, Massachusetts: Harvard University Press, 1959).

Endacott, G. B. *A History of Hong Kong* (Hong Kong: Oxford University Press, 1973).

Fieldhouse, D. K. *The Colonial Empires: A Comparative Survey from the Eighteen Century* (London: Macmillan, 1966).

Fok, K. C. *Lectures on Hong Kong History : Hong Kong's Role in Modern Chinese History* (in Chinese) (Hong Kong: Commercial Press, 1990).

Fok, K. C. *Hong Kong and Modern China* (in Chinese) (Hong Kong: Commercial Press, 1992).

Fratkin, Elliot, "The Samburu laibon's sorcery and the death of Theodore Powys in colonial Kenya," *Journal of Eastern African Studies*, vol. 9, no. 1 (2015), pp. 35–54.

Frankema, Ewout and Marlous van Waijenburg, "Metropolitan blueprints of colonial taxation? Lessons from fiscal capacity building in British and French Africa," *Journal of African History*, vol. 55 (2014), pp. 371–400.

Fung, Wai-chung, "The Influence of Land Policy on the New Territories Heung Yee Kuk under the British Hong Kong Government from 1968 to 1984," MPhil Thesis (in Chinese), National Cheng Kung University, Taiwan, 2019.

Gallagher, Michael, "Elections and Referendums," in Daniele Caramani, ed., *Comparative Politics* (New York: Oxford University Press, 2008).

Gerring, John Daniel Ziblatt, Johan VanGorp and Julian Arevalo, "An Institutional Theory of Direct and Indirect Rule," *World Politics*, vol. 63, no. 2 (July 2011), pp. 377–433.

Grantham, Alexander, *Via Ports: From Hong Kong to Hong Kong* (Hong Kong: Hong Kong University Press, 1965).

Green, Erik, "Indirect Rule and Colonial Intervention: Chiefs and Agrarian Change in Nyasaland, ca. 1933 to the Early 1950s," *International Journal of African Historical Studies*, vol. 44, no. 2 (2011), pp. 249–274.

Hamilton, Sheliah E., *Watching Over Hong Kong: Private Policing 1841–1941* (Hong Kong: Hong Kong University Press).

Havik, Philip "'Direct' or 'Indirect' Rule? Reconsidering the roles of appointed chiefs and native employees in Portuguese West Africa," *Africana Studia*, vol. 15 (2010), pp. 29–36.

Home, Robert, "From cantonments to townships: Lugard's influence upon British colonial governance in Africa," *Planning Perspectives*, vol. 34, no. 1 (2019), pp. 43–64.

Hong Kong Institute of Land Administration, "A Review of the Approach in Land Acquisition of Choi Yuen Tsuen for the Guangzhou-Shenzhen-Hong Kong Express Rail Link Project, and Recommendations for a Possible and Reasonable Approach in Land Acquisition in Future Government Projects," 2012, in https://www.fig.net/resources/proceedings/2012/Hungary_2012_comm7/6.5_paper_fung.pdf, access date: September 8, 2020.

Hung, Steven Chung-fun, "A historical comparative analysis of the community transformation of Tin Hau temples in Sai Kung and Shaukiwan," *Asian Education and Development Studies*, vol. 10, no. 3 (2021), pp. 481–491.

Hung, Steven Chung-fun, "Historical Comparative Analysis of the Development and Transformation of Lei Yue Mun and Cha Kwo Ling with their Tin Hau Temples," *Social Evolution & History*, Vol. 19, No. 1 (March 2020), pp. 147–169.

Huntington, Samuel P. ,*Political Order in Changing Societies* (New Haven: Yale University Press, 1966).

Johnson, Graham E, "Leaders and Leadership in an Expanding New Territories Town," *The China Quarterly*, Number 69, (1977), pp. 109–125.

Jones, Carol and Jon Vagg, *Criminal Justice in Hong Kong* (London: Routledge, 2016).

Kiani, Azeen, and Hossein Sartipi, "Functions of Election in a Democratic System," *international Research Journal of Interdisciplinary & Multidisciplinary Studies*, vol. 2, no. 9 (October 2016).

King, Ambrose Yeo-Chi, "Administrative Absorption of Politics in Hong Kong: Emphasis on the Grassroots Level." *Asian Survey,* vol. 15, no. 5 (May 1975), pp. 422–439.

Kishore, Raghav, "Urban Failures: 'Municipal Governance, Planning and Power in Colonial Delhi, 1863–1910," *The Indian Economic and Social History Review*, vol. 54, no. 2 (2015), pp. 439–461.

Ngozi Caleb Kamalu, Ngozi Caleb ,"British, French, Belgian and Portuguese Models of Colonial Rule and Economic Development in Africa," *Annals of Global History*, vol. 1, no. 1 (2019), pp. 37–47.

Kuhne, Winrich "The Role of Elections in Emerging Democracies and Post-Conflict Countries: Key Issues, Lessons Learnt and Dilemmas," August 2010, in http://library.fes.de/pdf-files/iez/07416.pdf, access date: August 5, 2020.

Kwong, Chi-man, "From the "New Territories People" to 'Indigenous Inhabitants' Identity Construction of the Rural Population in Colonial Hong Kong," *Hong Kong Journal of Social Science*, vol. 52 (2018), pp. 39–72.

Lau, Siu-kai, "Local Administrative Reform in Hong Kong: Promises and Limitations," *Asian Survey*, vol. 22, no. 9 (September 1982), pp. 863–868.

Lau, Siu-kai, "Decolonization without Independence: The Unfinished Political Reforms of the Hong Kong Government," Occasional paper no. 19, Centre for Hong Kong Studies, Institute of Social Studies, the Chinese University of Hong Kong, May 1987.

Lau, Yun-wo, *A History of the Municipal Councils of Hong Kong: 1883–1999: From the Sanitary Board to the Urban Council and the Regional Council* (Hong Kong: Leisure and Cultural Service Department, Hong Kong Government, 2002).

Lazar, Harvey and Aron Seal, "Local government: Still a junior government? The place of municipalities within the Canadian federation," in Nico Steytler, ed., *The Place and Role of Local Government in Federal Systems* (Johannesburg: Konrad-Adenauer-Stiftung, 2005).

Lethbridge, Henry J. "The District Watch Committee: 'The Chinese Executive Council of Hong Kong,'" *Journal of the Hong Kong Branch of the Royal Asiatic Society*, vol. 11 (1971), pp. 116–141.

Leung, Benjamin K. P. *Perspectives on Hong Kong Society* (London: Oxford University Press, 1992).

Lipset, Seymour Martin ,*Political Man: The Social Bases of Politics* (London: Heinemann, 1960).

Lo, Shiu-Hing, "Colonial Policy-Makers, Capitalist Class and China: Determinants of Electoral Reform in Hong Kong's and Macau's Legislatures," *Pacific Affairs*, vol. 62, no. 2 (Summer 1989), pp. 204–218.

Lo, Shiu-hing, "An Analysis of Sino-British Negotiations Over Hong Kong's Political Reform," *Contemporary Southeast Asia*, vol. 16, no. 2 (September 1994), pp. 178–209.

Lo, Sonny Shiu-hing "Legislative Cliques, Political Parties, Political Groupings and Electoral System," in Joseph Cheng and Sonny Lo, eds., *From Colony to SAR: Hong Kong's Challenges Ahead* (Hong Kong: The Chinese University Press, 1995).

Lo, Shiu-Hing, *Political Development in Macau* (Hong Kong: The Chinese University Press, 1996).

Lo, Shiu-Hing, *The Politics of Democratization in Hong Kong* (London: Macmillan, 1997).

Lo, Shiu-Hing, "Political Parties, Elite-Mass Gap and Political Instability in Hong Kong," *Contemporary Southeast Asia*, vol. 20, no. 1 (April 1998), pp. 67–87.

Lo, Shiu-Hing, "Democratization Without Decentralization: Local Government in Hong Kong," *Journal of Contemporary China* (USA), vol. 8, no. 21 (July 1999), pp. 297–318.

Lo, Sonny Shiu-Hing , "Party Penetration of Society: Political Parties and Mutual Aid Committees in Hong Kong," *Asian Journal of Political Science*, vol. 12, no. 1 (June 2004), pp. 31–64.

Lo, Sonny Shiu-Hing , "Ideologies and Factionalism in Beijing–Hong Kong Relations," *Asian Survey*, vol. 58, no. 3 (2019), pp. 395–415.

Lo, Sonny Shiu-hing and Cheung Yat-fung, "The Political Attitude of Village Representatives in the New Territories," paper presented at the Foreign Correspondents Club, December 12, 2001.

Lo Sonny Shiu-Hing and Eilo Wing-Yat Yu, "The Politics of Electoral Reform in Hong Kong," *Journal of Commonwealth & Comparative Politics*, vol. 39, no. 1 (July 2001), pp. 98–123.

Lo, Sonny Shiu-Hing; Steven Chung-Fun Hung; and Jeff Hai-Chi Loo, *China's New United Work in Hong Kong: Penetrative Politics and Its Implications* (London: Palgrave Macmillan, 2019).

Lo, Sonny Shiu-Hing, Steven Chung-Fun Hung and Jeff Hai-Chi Loo, *The Dynamics of Peaceful and Violent Protests in Hong Kong: The Anti-Extradition Movement* (London: Palgrave, 2020).

Loughlin, John, "Federal and local government institutions," in Daniele Caramani, ed., *Comparative Politics* (New York: Oxford University Press, 2008).

Louie, Kin-shuen and Shum Kwok-cheung, eds., *A Compilation of Election Materials in Hong Kong, 1982–1994* (Hong Kong: The Hong Kong Institute of Asia-Pacific Studies, The Chinese University of Hong Kong, 1996);

Mainland Affairs Council (Taiwan), *A Comparative Study of Hong Kong Political Parties* (Taipei: Mainland Affairs Council, 1995).

Markides, Diana, "Nicosia and its municipal administration during the very early years of British rule in Cyprus," *Byzantine and Modern Greek Studies* Vol. 37 No. 1 (2013), pp. 92–110.

Miners, Norman, *The Government and Politics of Hong Kong* (Hong Kong: Oxford University Press, 1981).

Miners, Norman, "Constitutional Reform in Hong Kong, 1945–1952," *Asian Journal of Public Administration*, vol. 11, no. 1 (June 1989), p. 96.

Mizuno, Nobuhiro and Ryosuke Okazawa, "Colonial experience and post-colonial underdevelopment in Africa," vol. 141 (2009).

Morissette, Benoit,"The Foundations of Freedom and Civilization: The Durham Report, Municipal Institutions and Liberalism," *World Political Science*, vol. 15, no. 1 (July 2019), pp. 99–124.

Naseemullah Adnan and Paul Staniland, "Indirect Rule and Varieties of Governance," *Governance*, vol. 29, no. 1 (January 2016), pp. 13–30.

Nickson, Andrew, Alex Brillantes; Wilhelmina Cabo; Alice Calestino; and Nick Devas, "Asia-Pacific," in Elisabeth Gateau, ed., *Decentralization and Local Democracy in the World: First Global Report by United Cities and Local Governments* (Spain, Barcelona: United Cities and Local Government, 2008).

Norton-Kyshe, J. W., *History of the Laws and Courts of Hong Kong* (Hong Kong, Noronha and Co., 1898), vol. 2.

O'Donnell, Guillermo, and Philippe C. Schmitter, *Transitions from Authoritarian Rule: Tentative Conclusions about Uncertain Democracies* (Baltimore, Maryland: Johns Hopkins University Press, 1986).

Ochonu, Moses,"Colonialism within Colonialism: The Hausa-Caliphate Imaginary and the British Colonial Administration of the Nigerian Middle Belt," *African Studies Quarterly*, vol. 10, numbers 2 & 3, (2008), pp. 95–127.

Ogot, Bethwell A. "British Administration in the Central Nyanza District of Kenya, 1900–60," *Journal of African History*, vol. 4, no. 2 (1963), pp. 249–273.

Or, Nick H. K. "How policy agendas change when autocracies liberalize: The case of Hong Kong, 1975–2016," *Public Administration*, vol. 97 (2019), pp. 926–941.

Pablo, Barberá and Rivero Gonzalo, "Understanding the political representativeness of Twitter users," *Social Science Computer Review*, vol. 33, no. 6 (2015), pp. 712–729.

Palmberg, Mai ed., *The Struggle for Africa* (London: Zed Press, 1983).

Paine, Jack "Democratic Contradictions in European Settler Colonies," *World Politics*, vol. 71, no. 3 (July 2019), pp. 542–585.

Patten, Chris, "Policy Address (1992 Excerpt)," in Jiang Shigong, ed., *A Compilation of Information on Hong Kong's Political Development (1): From Colonial Period to the Drafting of Basic Law* (Hong Kong: Joint Publishing, 2015),

Roberts, Margaret E. ,Brandon M. Stewart and Dustin Tingley, "Stm: R Package for Structural Topic Models." *Journal of Statistical Software*, vol. 20, no. 2 (2016), pp. 1–40.

Robinson, Kenneth, *The Dilemmas of Trusteeship: Aspects of British Colonial Policy Between the Wars* (London: Oxford University Press, 1965).

Rodney, Walter, *How Europe Underdeveloped Africa* (London: Bogle-L'Ouverture Publications, 1972).

Sandbrook, Richard, *The Politics of Basic Needs: Urban Aspects of Assaulting Poverty* (Toronto: University of Toronto Press, 1982).

Sandbrook, Richard, *The Politics of Africa's Economic Stagnation* (London: Cambridge University Press, 1985).

Scott, Ian, *Political Change and the Crisis of Legitimacy in Hong Kong* (Honolulu: University of Hawaii Press, 1989).

Sheel, Alok "Agricultural Trade and Markets in British India: Shahabad and Gaya Districts, 1800–1920," *Indian Historical Review*, vol. 42, no. 1 (2015), pp. 90–112.

Sit, Victor Fung-suen and Chi-man Kwong, *The New Territories Heung Yee Kuk* (in Chinese) (Hong Kong: Hong Kong Joint Publishing, 2011).

Sit, Victor Fung-suen and Kwong Chi-man, *A History of Heung Yee Kuk in the New Territories* (in Chinese) (Hong Kong: Hong Kong Joint Publishing, 2011).

Siu, Kwok-kin, *Baoan History: Study and Collections* (Hong Kong: Hin Chiu Books, 1988).

Sutton, Deborah,"Devotion, Antiquity, and Colonial Custody of the Hindu Temple in British India," *Modern Asian Studies*, vol: 47, no:1 (2013) pp. 135–166.

Thomas, Nicholas, *Democracy Denied: Identity, Civil Society and Illiberal Democracy in Hong Kong* (London: Routledge, 2018).

Tsang, Edmond Yik-man *The Earliest Political Parties and Fighter for Democracies: Reform Club and the Hong Kong Civic Association* (in Chinese) (Hong Kong: Chung Hwa, 2019).

Tsang, Steve, *Governing Hong Kong Administrative Officers from the Nineteenth Century to the Handover to China, 1862–1997* (Hong Kong: Hong Kong University Press, 2007).

Tsang, Steve, ed., *Government and Politics*, pp. 122–127; and Suzanne Pepper, *Keeping Democracy at Bay: Hong Kong and the Challenge of Chinese Political Reform* (Lanham: Rowman & Littlefield, 2008), pp. 95–97.

Ure, Gavin ,*Governors, Politics and the Colonial Office: Public Policy in Hong Kong, 1918–58* (Hong Kong: Hong Kong University Press, 2012),

Verghese, Ajay, "British Rule and Tribal Revolts in India: The curious case of Bastar," *Modern Asian Studies*, vol. 50, no. 5 (2016), pp. 1619–1644.

Vojnovic, Igor, "Municipal consolidation in the 1990s: an analysis of British Columbia, New Brunswick, and Nova Scotia," *Canadian Public Administration*, vol. 40, no. 2 (1998), pp. 239–283.

Wamagatta, Evanson N.,"British Administration and the Chiefs' Tyranny in Early Colonial Kenya A Case Study of the First Generation of Chiefs from Kiambu District, 1895–1920," *Journal of Asian and African Studies*, vol. 44, no. 4 (2009), pp. 371–388.

Wesley-Smith, Peter, *Unequal Treaty, 1898–1997: China, Great Britain and Hong Kong's New Territories* (Revised Edition), (Hong Kong: Oxford University Press, 1998).

Wong, Aline K., "Chinese voluntary associations in Southeast Asian cities and the *Kaifongs* in Hong Kong," *Journal of the Hong Kong Branch of the Royal Asiatic Society*, vol. 11 (1971), pp. 62–73.

Wong, Aline K. , *The Kaifong Associations and the Society of Hong Kong* (Taipei: The Oriental Cultural Service, 1972).

Yip, Tin-sang, ed., *A Compilation of Election Materials in Hong Kong, 1996–2000* (Hong Kong: The Hong Kong Institute of Asia-Pacific Studies, The Chinese University of Hong Kong, 2001).

Yip, Tin-sang, ed., *A Compilation of Election Materials in Hong Kong, 2001–2004* (Hong Kong: The Hong Kong Institute of Asia-Pacific Studies, The Chinese University of Hong Kong, 2005).

Yip, Tin-sang, ed., *A Compilation of Election Materials in Hong Kong, 2005–2012* (Hong Kong: The Hong Kong Institute of Asia-Pacific Studies, The Chinese University of Hong Kong, 2015).

Yuen, Bong-kin, *A Brief History of Hong Kong* (in Chinese) (Hong Kong: Chung Liu Publisher, 1997).

INDEX